BARACK OBAMA

The Making of the Man

'What Maraniss skilfully dissects is the voyage of self-discovery
– and quest for racial self-identity – that launched Obama on his
historic march to the White House'
Daily Telegraph Books of 2012

'A blistering new biography'
Daily Mail

'Offers revelations extending far into Obama's disparate
family past . . . helping us to understand how it was that a sense
of destiny awoke in a young man'
New Statesman

'Full of riveting stories, shrewd observations and fascinating details'
New Yorker

'The best biography ever written about a president in office'
New York Post

'Biography at its best. A prodigiously well researched and
exquisitely written multigenerational account'
San Francisco Chronicle

'Remarkable . . . Maraniss captures Obama's search for
purpose and kindling of his ambition with an intimacy unlike
that of other biographers . . . including Ob———'

BARACK OBAMA

*The Making of
the Man*

DAVID
MARANISS

Atlantic Books
London

First published in the United States of America in 2012 by Simon and Schuster.

First published in Great Britain in 2012 by Atlantic Books,
an imprint of Atlantic Books Ltd.

This paperback edition published in Great Britain in 2013 by Atlantic Books.

10 9 8 7 6 5 4 3 2 1

A CIP catalogue record for this book is available from the British Library.

Paperback ISBN: 978-1-84887-281-3
E-book ISBN: 978-0-85789-856-2

Atlantic Books
An imprint of Atlantic Books Ltd
Ormond House
26–27 Boswell Street
London
WC1N 3JZ

www.atlantic-books.co.uk

Printed in Italy by 🦓 Grafica Veneta S.p.A.

To the wondrous girls of my life –
Linda, Sarah, Ali, Heidi, Ava, and Eliza –
and to Alice

The mind that has conceived a plan of living
must never lose sight of the chaos against which
that pattern was conceived.

RALPH ELLISON, Invisible Man

CONTENTS

BARACK OBAMA

INTRODUCTION

It's Not Even Past

This volume is not a traditional biography. It begins long before Obama was born and ends before he entered politics. He is inevitably the principal subject, and I would not have undertaken the book if not for his history-making rise, but he does not appear until the seventh chapter and even after that at times gives way to other relatives. He came out of an uncommon family, brilliantly scattered and broken, and although the parts could never be fitted neatly together again, my goal was to examine them as a whole and see the story in all its jagged and kaleidoscopic fullness. We are all random creatures, in one sense, our existence resulting from a particular series of random events, but Barack Obama's life seems more improbable than most, and I saw in the story of his family a chance to write about many of the themes of the modern world. And then, given the circumstances into which he was born, how did he figure it out? How did he create a life that made it possible for his political rise? Those are the twin obsessions that drove me as I researched this book—the world that created him and how he created himself. Four years ago, I set off in search of answers.

On a whitewashed ledge at Punahou School bathed in Honolulu sunshine, Alan Lum and I sat and talked about the past, revisiting the days when Lum and his friend Barry were teammates on Hawaii's state championship basketball team. Then we got up and took a short walk. We left the athletic center and strolled past the prep school's outdoor pool, constructed since their days there in the late 1970s, and along the edge of a vast green playing field, before climbing the broad steps leading up to the Dole Center, the student cafeteria. Lum turned left on the lanai and cast his eyes downward, examining the concrete sidewalk. Where was it, again? He walked farther toward a set of outdoor benches, then stopped and brushed the pavement with his shoe, cleaning away the daily soot. There it was, etched in block letters decades ago by a stick or index finger before the concrete had set. OBAMA.

No historical marker designated the site. Generations of students had walked over and around it without taking notice of the name below their feet. For the first twenty-five years or so after it was written, the name would have provoked little interest in any case. Just one name among multitudes, and locals might have assumed Obama was Asian American; the syllables had a familiar Japanese cadence. The testament of a teenage boy, and he didn't even write it himself. The story goes that one of his buddies scratched his name there to get him in trouble. But it had the same meaning nonetheless. A name etched in concrete, like *Kilroy was here* carved into rock, is an expression of time and history and fleeting existence. Looking down, I could only think: That could have been the lone mark he left.

One April morning in Topeka, the capital of Kansas, my wife and I went searching for an address in the eleven-hundred block of Sixth Avenue. Long ago there had been an auto garage there—the Palace, it was called—and a drugstore next door. In the intervening decades, as often happens, addresses had changed and seemed two or four off from what they had been in the 1920s. The drugstore had vanished. A wide driveway now opened from the avenue into a few parking spaces in front of a nondescript building. A sign said it was an auto repair shop, an unwitting reiteration of what once had been. In front, a single-room office had gone up in recent decades, sparsely furnished with desk, telephone, and shelves of manuals, but farther into the interior was the old garage, with a high-ceilinged work area where one could envision the scene from more than eighty years earlier: a mechanic in overalls sweating under the hood of a Studebaker Big Six. Windows had been bricked up, and most of the old tin ceiling had been covered, but the place seemed to trap the dust and suffocating air of the past.

The shop manager was obliging, and let us look around. As we stood in the dingy garage, staring up at the ceiling, I asked whether he knew the building's history. It had undergone many transformations over the years, he said. There had been a pharmacy attached to it once, and next to the pharmacy was an apartment building. According to legend, the landlord had built a secret passageway from the shop to the back door of one of the apartments, where his mistress awaited for illicit trysts. Quite a story, but there was another bit of history about which the present-day tenants knew nothing. It was in that very garage that Obama's great-grandmother Ruth Armour Dunham took her own life on a chilly Thanksgiving night, setting off a chain of events that changed the course of American history.

Out in the western reaches of Kenya, a harrowing seven-hour drive from the capital city of Nairobi, in the region hugging the uppermost gulf of Lake Victoria, I encountered a tale of two villages. The first village was Nyang'oma Kogelo, up in the brushland northwest of the major city out there, Kisumu. That is where a woman known as Mama Sarah lived. She had become a celebrity in Kenya as the step-grandmother of Obama and a figure in his best-selling memoir. A trip to her compound now was like visiting royalty. The entrance was gated. Vendors sold tourist trinkets at tables just inside the grounds. She was connected to the outside world by giant satellite dishes, and protected by armed guards. There were lists to be checked, names to be vetted, rules to be imposed, factotums to accommodate. "Mr. David . . . [*pause*] . . . David," said one young relative during his inquisition in the shade of a mango tree, stopping to assess my name and worthiness. "Is that Christian or Jew?" "Both," I responded. All to see a woman who had no blood relationship to the famous American, and was, as one Kenyan put it, nothing more than a historical accident.

The second village was Oyugis. It was around the gulf, down and to the east, a bumpy journey into the hills of south Nyanza. An old toothless woman named Auma Magak lived there with several relatives, including her son, Razik. In her seventies, Auma was a recovering alcoholic who scratched out a living by selling charcoal from a shack by the side of the road. It was Auma, in her isolation and anonymity, who had the strongest link to the Kenya side of the Obama story. She was the younger sister of Barack Hussein Obama Sr.— the president's father — and in a tribal culture where polygamy was routine, her bloodlines were the most direct in that she and Obama Sr. had both the same mother and father. Her compound was not on the tourist maps. It was surrounded by high euphorbia bushes, but no guards checked visitor lists and there were no vendors selling trinkets. Yet step inside her hut, into the darkened stillness, and there were the testaments on her mud walls: four framed photographs of President Obama with his wife and two daughters, along with two posters and a calendar from his most recent visit as a U.S. senator. And she and Razik had stories. She talked about how her mother ran away from a brutal husband and how the little children, including Obama Sr., ran after her. Razik recalled the time in the late 1980s when his American cousin came to visit and they went fishing for Nile perch in the great lake and drank *chang'aa*, a potent gin distilled from fermented corn, and smoked weed together.

In Jakarta, in the midmorning humidity of early September, our *taksi* driver wended through the traffic-clogged roadways of Indonesia's booming capital city until we came to the corner of Dr. Supomo and Haji Ramli streets, where he turned left and let us out at the entrance to the Menteng Dalam neighborhood, or *kampung*. To the right, we looked down at a swampy urban culvert strewn with trash. Straight ahead, up a gentle slope, ran the opening stretch of Haji Ramli, a row of storefronts at first, then zigging and zagging left-right-left up to the small whitewashed house on a corner where Obama lived forty-plus years earlier when he was six, seven, and eight years old. He was Barry Soetoro then, taking the family name of his stepfather, Lolo Soetoro, his mother's second husband. Some things had changed in the ensuing decades. Then the neighborhood was on the edge of a city of about three million residents; now it is surrounded by an urban sprawl that goes on for several more miles, skyscrapers sprouting in every direction as Jakarta's metropolitan population has swelled to nearly twenty million. Then Haji Ramli was unpaved, nothing but dirt that turned to mud in the rainy season, and a small playing field and forest were within an easy walk of the Soetoro house. The street is paved now and the green space long gone; houses and people are everywhere. But the sensibility of the neighborhood remains much the same: the narrow pathways and alleyways; the street carts with pungent offerings of *nasi goreng* and *rendang*; fried rice and spicy beef; the symphony of neighborhood rhythms and sounds and a daily song of the *kampung*—the low undulating buzz of a call to prayer at the nearby mosque; the beseeching voice of the bread seller; the hollow bock-bock-bock-click of a meatball vendor knocking his bamboo *kentongan*; and the shrieks and laughs of children down on the playground at the neighborhood school, SD Asisi.

There are no markings outside the gate at No. 16 Haji Ramli to designate that Barack Obama once lived there, nor are there any official designations of his presence at the nearby school. The first section of SD Asisi was built in 1966, one year before Barry arrived. It was long and narrow, one story, with the look of an army barracks. That structure still stands, but is enfolded into a handsome complex of buildings that now hold classes for more than five hundred students in kindergarten through grade 12. Then and now, the fact that the school happened to be Catholic in a predominantly Muslim community seemed to make little difference to the residents, reflecting both the moderate form of Islam that prevails in Jakarta and the common appreciation of a good school no matter its denomination. Barry was just another neighborhood kid here. He learned Bahasa Indonesia, the national language, so well that by the end of his first year his classmates assumed he was Indonesian, a little darker than the rest, probably from one of the easternmost islands. Just another kid playing *kasti,* a form of softball, under the shade of the commodious mangosteen tree. No one special. But now there is one telltale sign, something inside Kelas III, the third-grade classroom, on the wall above one of the tiny wood-on-metal chairs where he once sat. It is a color poster showing the president and First Lady smiling on the night he accepted the Democratic nomination for president in 2008. Seeing that classroom and strolling up and down Haji Ramli street in the morning and at sundown, I could not help but be overwhelmed by how utterly improbable it was that Barry Soetoro, the boy from Menteng Dalam, had made his way to the scene depicted in that poster.

One glistening afternoon in Chicago, I sat across from the Reverend Alvin Love as he peered out the window of his second-floor office in the rectory of Lilydale First Baptist Church on 113th Street on the city's sprawling South Side. A young man stood down below on the sidewalk, gesturing up, trying to catch the minister's attention, a pantomime plea for some kind of handout. It was through that same window, a quarter century earlier, that Love watched a tall and slender stranger wearing khaki pants and a short-sleeve shirt stroll down the sidewalk, stop at the front entrance, and ring the doorbell. He thought it was another unexpected visitor needing some kind of help. It was, in fact, Barack Obama, community organizer, who was asking not for assistance, but for fifteen minutes of the pastor's time. This happened in 1985, not long after Obama had left New York to start a new life in Chicago. He and "Rev," as he would come to call Love, ended up talking much longer than fifteen minutes. From that initial meeting they developed a relationship that carried through the years. Love was Obama's first guide through the subculture of African American churches in Chicago, and later helped connect him to a larger network of Baptist ministers throughout the state of Illinois. He came to his aid when Obama's relationship with another Chicago preacher, the Reverend Jeremiah Wright, jeopardized his political career just as it reached sight of the promised land of the White House. Love had watched Obama rise from an unseasoned young man trying to organize a troubled neighborhood to president of the United States trying to organize a divided country.

Now, as we sat in the same office where they first talked, Love took me back into the past, recalling that visit and their subsequent struggles to force political change in places where people were poor and powerless. He spoke of preachers who were supportive and preachers who were not, of how young Barack helped him and his church as much as he helped Barack, and he closed with the story of how President Obama, hours after taking the oath of office, paid a private visit to a gathering of old friends who had traveled to Washington for the inauguration, shaking hands with fifty of them one by one in a hotel conference room, until he came to Love and said, "Rev, you gotta keep me in prayer. This is something else," and minutes later, as he left the room, turned back one more time, his eyes fixing on Love in the crowd, and said, "Rev, I wasn't playing. Don't forget me."

"The past is never dead. It's not even past," William Faulkner wrote in *Requiem for a Nun*. They are words that Barack Obama himself has paraphrased more than once in his writings and speeches, and for a biographer and historian, their meaning seems self-evident. That is why I went looking for that name in the concrete in Hawaii, and stepped inside the auto garage in Kansas, and visited those villages in western Kenya, and walked the alleyways of Menteng Dalam in south Jakarta, and roamed the South Side of Chicago, and made many other ventures from the present into the past during four years of travel researching the world that created Obama. The past is where many of the most revealing clues to the present and future are found, clues to the shaping of individuals and of cultures and societies.

To write a book that leaves its protagonist before his days of notable accomplishment requires an implicit belief that the past is never dead. But when it comes to this book, to the particulars of the Obama story, there are some crosscurrents and countervailing notions to consider.

Obama grew up without his father, with his mother often gone, and in a sense raised himself, working his way alone through many confounding issues life threw his way. If he emerged in adulthood as a self-creation, one argument goes, how relevant are the genealogy and geography of his family, and his own early life, in decoding what he later made of himself? Valid question. My answer: they are certainly not everything, but they are crucial. The supposition of Obama being a self-creation is inadequate. One can see the imprint of his mother and maternal grandmother in almost every aspect of his character. That is nurture. The effects of his childhood in Hawaii and Indonesia are also readily evident in the adult Obama, his uncommon combination of cool remove and adaptability. That is environment. As for nature, there are parts of his appearance and personality—his voice and self-confidence, for starters, each of which should not be underestimated as factors in his political ascent—that can be traced clearly to his absent father. He has his white grandfather's long face and his motions and gestures. And, all in all, the past might be even more essential in figuring out someone who has re-created himself. People are shaped equally by action and reaction, by what they accept and what they reject from their own inheritance. Obama is best understood with that in mind, not only by how his family and environment molded him but how he reshaped himself in reaction to them.

Then there is the aspect of his past that tends to overwhelm everything else, the fact that he was the product of different continents and different races, an American made from the multifarious world of color and culture. He was reared by white relatives and grew up mostly in a place, Hawaii, where being *hapa*—half and half—was almost the norm, though the multihued combinations involved mostly Asians and very few blacks. He came from all sides and no sides, a fact equally relevant to his past, present, and future. When he first arose to political prominence, there was a familiar lament when white people talked about Obama. He is black *and* white, some would say, so why is he called only black? Most of the answer comes from the history of this country. That is how society categorized him before he could choose. But he also did make that subjective choice. The arc of his life, emotionally and geographically, traced a route toward blackness and home, which he found in Chicago. From the other side, less frequent but still noticeable, came the question of whether he was black enough. He had no slaves in his heritage and had never fully experienced the African American condition until well into adulthood, some blacks argued, so what did he know?

His memoir, *Dreams from My Father*, confronts those and other questions about race. It is much more about race than about his father, a man he barely knew. I consider it an unusually insightful work in many respects, especially as an examination of his internal struggle. In that sense it is quite unlike the average book by a politician, or future politician, which is more likely to avoid self-analysis. But it is important to say that it falls into the realm of literature and memoir, not history and autobiography, and should not be read as a rigorously factual account. In his introduction, Obama states that "for the sake of compression, some of the characters that appear are composites of people I've known, and some events appear out of precise chronology." There is more to it than that. The character creations and rearrangements of the book are not merely a matter of style; they are devices of compression but also of substance. The themes of the book control character and chronology. Time and again, the narrative accentuates characters drawn from black acquaintances who played lesser roles in his real life but could be used to advance a line of thought, while leaving out or distorting the actions of friends who happened to be white. Sometimes the composites are even more complex; there are a few instances where black figures in the book have characteristics and histories that Obama took from white friends. The racial scene in his family history that is most familiar to the public, the time when he overheard his grandparents in Hawaii argue because his grandmother was afraid of a black man down at the bus stop, also happens to be among those he pulled out of its real chronology and fitted into a place where it might have more literary resonance. Like many other riffs in the book, it explored the parameters and frustrations of his blackness.

Without dismissing the anger and confusion that he surely felt as he tried to sort out his identity, I would argue that to view him primarily through a racial lens can lead to a misinterpretation of the root causes of his feelings of outsiderness and a misunderstanding of his responses to it. In any case, the point of my book is not to keep a scorecard recording the differences between the memoir and the way things were remembered by others; that would distort the meaning and intent of his book, and of mine. But I do not hesitate to explain those discrepancies when they occur.

Throughout the first four years of his presidency, and as he prepared to be sworn in for a second term, some people considered Obama as much of a mystery as when he first took office. This seemed especially true for those who supported him and wanted him to succeed but were frustrated by his performance at various points. It is always dangerous for a biographer to deal in the present. The present is transitory and mutable. What could seem relevant today fades into irrelevance tomorrow. But there are certain tendencies and recurring themes from Obama's history that help explain his presidency. When I wrote a biography of Bill Clinton, one central theme that emerged from my study of his past was a repetitive cycle of loss and recovery. Whenever Clinton was on top, one could see the seeds of his own undoing, and whenever he was down, one could see that he would find a way to recover. Again and again, here was a pattern in his life that played out in his presidency.

With Obama, a comparable recurring theme has to do with his determination to avoid life's traps. First he escaped the trap of his unusual family biography, with the challenges it presented in terms of stability and psychology. Then the trap of geography, being born and spending most of his childhood in Hawaii, farther from any continental landmass than anywhere in the world except Easter Island, along with four formative years on the other side of the world, in Indonesia. And finally the trap of race in America, with its likelihood of rejection and cynicism.

The totality of the effort it took to get around these traps shaped his personality. It helped explain his caution, his tendency to hold back and survey life like a chessboard, looking for where he could get checkmated, analyzing the moves two and three steps ahead. There were times when this approach made him appear distant, slow, reluctant to decide, and out of the zeitgeist. Sometimes that perception was accurate, sometimes not. He could be behind the curve, or ahead of the curve, but with the notable exception of his two presidential campaigns, rarely right at the curve. But wherever he was, it helps to keep in mind the patterns of his caution and the reasons for it. As he worked his way through the traumas and troubles of his young life, he developed what one close friend called "a perfectionist's drive for unity"—within self and within community. It burned inside, underneath his cool exterior, and was another reason why he would have so much trouble with confrontation. To confront was to acknowledge division, rupturing, imperfection, the traps of life he so wanted to transcend. One of the ideas he became obsessed with as he reached adulthood was the notion of choice—how much choice he really had in determining his own future and how much was already shaped for him by his history and family. He worried about the narrow choices being made all around him, and concluded that the only path he could follow, the only choice he had, was to "embrace it all"—meaning a philosophy that was large enough to take in life in all of its colors and contradictions. That is not to say that he disparaged the role and meaning of struggle—his entire early life was a struggle, inside and out—but that he was always trying to look past that, to resolution.

It is instructive here to compare his rise with the ascent of Bill Clinton, another president I have studied. They both came out of remote places far from the centers of power (Hawaii and southwest Arkansas); they both grew up without fathers and with alcoholism and other dysfunction in their family; and they dealt with these factors in diametrically different ways.

Clinton's method was to plow forward no matter what, to wake up every morning and forgive himself and the world. He did not address and resolve the broken parts of his life, but rushed past them. He reinvented himself when he needed to and developed a preternatural ability to survive. These skills got him to the White House and got him in trouble in the White House—and out of trouble in the White House. Obama, on the other hand, spent nine years of his early adulthood, from the time he left Honolulu for college to the time he left Chicago for the first time to attend Harvard Law School, intensely trying to resolve the contradictions life threw his way—racially, culturally, sociologically, professionally—and came out of that introspective process with what could be called an "integrated" personality. That quality helped direct him to the White House, then in its own way caused him trouble in the White House. He was not naive so much as overconfident and not fully prepared for the level of polarization he would confront. If he could resolve the contradictions of his own life, why couldn't the rest of the world? Why couldn't Congress?

There is a chapter in this book about his college years that I titled "The Moviegoer," a notion drawn from the Walker Percy novel of that name in which the main character is one step removed from his life and unable to live in the moment. That was young Obama, through and through. He was the son of an anthropologist, with an anthropologist's mind-set as a participant observer, sitting on the edge of a culture and learning it well enough to understand it from the inside, yet never feeling fully part of it. He was at the same time a double outsider, both as a biracial kid and a cross-cultural kid, living in a foreign country, often on the move, tending toward contradictory feelings of inclusiveness and rootlessness. If he had not gone into politics, he would have been a writer, and he still holds onto much of that sensibility. He stands not alone but apart, with the self-awareness of a skeptical witness to everything around him, including his own career. These are unlikely characteristics for a successful politician, the seeming antithesis of what it takes to rise in a world of emotion and visceral power, yet Obama holds that contradiction in subtle balance with his uncommon will and overriding sense of purpose.

When examining a subject's ancestry and early life it is important to draw a distinction between revelation and responsibility. No one wants to be judged or held responsible as an adult for how they behaved in their youth, or for how their relatives behaved. That should be neither the function nor the intention of a biographer. But there is an important difference between laying blame and searching for clues to a life, and many important clues come in the early years. The point in any case is to explore that territory in search of understanding, not retroactive condemnation. It seems obvious, but it demands explanation in the modern American political culture, where facts are so easily twisted for political purposes and where strange armies of ideological pseudo-historians—predominantly, these days, on the irrational flank of the political right—roam the biographical fields in search of stray ammunition.

My perspective in researching and writing this book, and my broader philosophy, is shaped by a contradiction that I cannot resolve and never intend to resolve. I believe that life is chaotic, a jumble of accidents, ambitions, social forces, geography, misconceptions, bold intentions, lazy happenstances, and unintended consequences, yet I also believe that there are connections that illuminate our world, revealing its endless mystery and wonder. I find these connections in story, in history, threading together individual lives as well as disparate societies—and they were everywhere I looked in the story of Barack Obama. In that sense, I reject the idea that every detail in a book must provide a direct and obvious lesson or revelation to be praised or damned. The human condition is more ineffable than that, and it is by following the connections wherever they lead, I believe, that the story of a life takes shape and meaning.

As the paperback edition of this book went to press, Barack Obama was preparing for his second term, a period historically fraught with dangers and possibilities. Second terms often bring a new set of unexpected frustrations, and the job only becomes more difficult as the end of power draws closer and the laws of diminishing returns take hold. But history also reinforces the notion that it requires a second term to create presidential greatness, or to ratify it—and Barack Obama in that sense is not ambivalent about his ambitions. Since he first thought about being president—a notion that came relatively late to him compared with most politicians—he has wanted to be a great one.

His reelection solidified his past and opened his future. A defeat after one term would have forever changed the meaning of his being the first African American president. Regarding the integration of major league baseball, the argument used to go that Frank Robinson's *firing* as the first black manager was a step toward equality as important as his *hiring* as the first black manager. An interesting notion, but not easily applied to the presidency, where the stakes are so much higher and the historical resonance so much deeper. Obama's defeat would have brought more comparisons, fair or not, to the racial backsliding of Reconstruction than to professional sports. But that is separate from the way Obama himself viewed his situation. The fact that his reelection affirmed his first-term accomplishments, and especially assured the survival of his health care initiative, seemed more important to him than any racial ramifications of victory or defeat.

On November 6, 2012, election night in Chicago, a colleague came up to me in the press workspace at McCormick Place, where Obama's supporters were gathering for the victory celebration, and asked if he could pose a sensitive question: Was I at some deep level feeling a sense of pride in what the subject of my biography had accomplished? I said that it was not a personal matter. I have no personal relationship with the president. I did not fly around with him on Air Force One and play basketball with him and ask him what the tricks were to being president. I just studied his life and tried to figure him out, for better or worse. And in that sense, I felt a sense of pride *for* him. I could see the uncommon arc of his life, the distance he had traveled, all the contradictions he had tried to resolve, what had burned inside him, and how far he had come.

CHAPTER 1

IN SEARCH OF
EL DORADO

On Thanksgiving morning in 1926, the Dunhams set out from their home in Topeka, traveling south down U.S. Route 75 on a forty-five-mile ride through the autumn countryside. Five people were in the car: the parents, Ralph and Ruth Armour Dunham; their two young sons, Ralph Jr. and Stanley; and Ralph Sr.'s brother, Earl, who worked with him at an auto garage. They were on their way to the town of Melvern to spend the holiday with the Whitneys. Mabel Whitney was Ralph and Earl's sister. The Dunham brothers and their brother-in-law, Hugh Whitney, had made plans to go hunting while the women prepared a holiday meal and the children played. The morning broke clean and bright, an Indian summer reprieve with temperatures climbing to sixty-eight degrees, the warmest in three weeks. Most

1

Kansans had the day off and were outside enjoying the balmy weather. Ruth's younger sister, Doris Armour, who lived in El Dorado with their parents, rode up to Emporia with two friends to attend a football game between the College of Emporia and her old school, Kansas State Teachers College, one of dozens of college and high school football rivalries scheduled around the state that afternoon.

Ruth might have preferred going to Emporia with her sister. She and Ralph were quarreling again, a common occurrence. Only twenty-six, she had been married for eleven years already, since she was fifteen, when she had dropped out of high school in the second month of her junior year. The wedding, held at nine at night at her sister-in-law's house in Wichita, had been a tightly held secret, with friends and parents "kept in the dark" until a week later, according to a belated announcement in the *Wichita Eagle*. Married life had been difficult from the start, as Ruth endured the serial philandering of her husband, who was seven years older. Their latest argument ended that afternoon, when Ralph departed with his hunting party. Ruth, distraught, waited until he was gone, then left for home, leaving her boys with Mabel and the other children.

Sometime that evening, back in Topeka, she emerged from their house at 703 Buchanan and walked in the darkness two blocks toward Sixth Avenue. Seasons had changed at sundown, from summery day to wintry night. There was a lashing wind and the temperature was in free fall, plummeting to an overnight low of twenty-four. Most of the shops along the avenue – Fritton Grocery, Golden Gate Coffee Shop, Home Bakery and Lunch – were closed, but lights were on at the Lawrence Drug Store next to the Palace Garage, Ralph's place. The pharmacist, George W. Lawrence, was working inside. Ruth entered and told Lawrence that a dog had been hit by a car and she needed something to put the poor critter out of its misery. Lawrence, amenable to the idea, suggested chloroform. Ruth said that would not do; the smell of chloroform made her sick. She asked for strychnine, and Lawrence relented, selling her ten grams. For whatever pain the dog was in, Ruth seemed in no hurry. Lawrence later recalled that she lingered in the pharmacy and talked to him for several minutes "seemingly in the best of spirits, joking and visiting."

After leaving, Ruth went next door to her husband's office and sat at his desk. One call from the Palace Garage, telephone exchange 2-7312, was placed that night, a twenty-five-cent evening call to El Dorado. Ruth had phoned her parents, Harry and Gabriella Armour, who had not seen her since late October, when she came home for the weekend of the Kafir Corn Carnival. Harry Armour had been laid up at St. Luke's Hospital; he had fallen off a tank ladder in the oil field and broken a shoulder bone. But the accident did not stop the family from luxuriating in the news that Doris, a former Pi Kappa Sigma sweetheart described as "a genuinely beautiful girl with dark brown bobbed hair, brown eyes, and a delicate coloring that is entirely natural," had been elected Miss El Dorado for the carnival. Six years younger than her sister, Doris was the jewel of the family: a popular beauty queen, smart and fun-loving, with a year of college education and a secure job in town. Ruth, by contrast, though equally attractive and intelligent, was a high school dropout in a difficult marriage. In the call to her parents that night from the Palace Garage she apparently did not discuss her troubles, but presented herself as being "in the best of health."

Two people saw her after that phone call. The first was W. E. Briggs, who owned an auto paint shop in the same building as the garage and lived nearby. Briggs later remembered that at ten-thirty, as he put away his car, he caught sight of Mrs. Dunham sitting at Ralph's desk, writing something. He presumed that she was waiting for her husband. About half an hour later, George Lawrence, the pharmacist, who also kept his car in the tin-ceilinged garage, noticed the same sight: Ruth sitting at her husband's desk.

In Melvern the men returned from their hunt after dark. When Mabel told Ralph that his wife was long gone, he and Earl left for Topeka to find her. No one was home when they reached 703 Buchanan. Ralph started a search with Earl. Eventually, shortly before two in the morning, Ralph stopped at his garage, where he intended to make another call back to Melvern. As he entered his office, he saw Ruth lying on the floor behind the desk.

"Here she is!" he called out to his brother. "She's asleep."

As they moved closer, they could see that she was not breathing. She was taken by ambulance to nearby St. Francis Hospital, but was already dead. The county coroner, Dr. Herbert L. Clark, began an investigation, interviewing the Dunham brothers along with the pharmacist and the auto paint shop owner, and determined that she had killed herself, dying of strychnine poisoning. By the time her husband found her she had been dead no more than two hours. The letter that Briggs saw her writing at the desk hours earlier was a suicide note. In it, according to the coroner, "Mrs. Dunham declared that the reason for her act was that her husband no longer loved her."

The staggering news of Ruth's death reached El Dorado a few hours later. Doris was home from the football outing to Emporia, and she and her parents drove up to Topeka in the early morning of Friday, November 26. Whether they were told the circumstances of the death when they reached the capital is unclear. Most likely they knew. An enterprising reporter at the *Topeka State Journal*, with nothing juicier to pursue during a placid holiday stretch – only one arrest in the police logs since Tuesday night – had already found the coroner and pieced together parts of the story, which would appear in the newspaper that afternoon. It was not as though suicides were unmentionable in the Kansas culture of that era. That same week, C. J. (Pat) Kroh of Oil Hill, a druggist who had talked about opening a cigar and confectionery store at the Philips Petroleum camp in Borger, Texas, chose instead to die "by his own hand," according to an obituary in the *El Dorado Times,* poisoning himself with carbolic acid: "Each heart knoweth its own sorrow, so poor Pat took a shortcut out of it all."

But in dealing with newspapers in their home turf, 140 miles from Ruth's death scene in Topeka, the Armours and family friends felt compelled to conceal the suicide and concoct a more benign version of the tragedy. Doris sent a telegram to the *El Dorado Times* claiming the cause of death was food poisoning. A similar account was presented to the *Wichita Eagle* by Ruth's close friend there, Mrs. Roy Reeves. Under the headline "Former Wichita Woman Ptomaine Poison Victim," the account noted that "Mrs. Dunham had been feeling well up to a late hour Thursday night, and it is believed that food eaten at Thanksgiving dinner was responsible for her death."

The mythology surrounding Ruth's passing began then and there. It would take on another variation later, when retold by her younger son, Stanley, the grandfather of a future president. He would get the essence of the story correct, calling it a suicide, but then place himself at the dramatic center, claiming he had discovered her body. He told this story later to his wife and daughter and then to his grandchildren and anyone else who would listen, and though most knew he was a teller of tales, this particular tale was accepted, often as a psychological explanation for his later rebellions and peculiarities. But the boy was not at the Palace Garage at two in the morning when Ruth's body was discovered. "Stanley," said Ralph Dunham Jr., his older brother, "did *not* find my mother dead."

From the distance of eight decades, Ralph Jr., who was ten at the time of the suicide, remembered an unseasonably warm day, a picnic (in Melvern), the boys playing with other kids. He recalled the sudden, surprise arrival of his grandparents from El Dorado. And there was one other shard of memory, the sort that can be trusted because of its odd specificity. Ralph Jr. and his eight-year-old brother, Stanley, had read books about Uncle Wiggily, the lame old rabbit with the striped barber-pole cane, and his cast of creature friends and enemies, the Skeezicks, Bushy Bear, Woozy Wolf, Jimmie Wibblewobble, and Nurse Jane Fuzzy Wuzzy. Milton Bradley had issued a board game based on the Uncle Wiggily stories, and the Dunham sons coveted it. Soon after the grandparents arrived from El Dorado, they gave the boys some money and sent them to the drugstore to buy the game. It was while playing Uncle Wiggily, as Ralph Jr. remembered it, that he and Stanley were told their mother was dead.

The house where the boys learned of their mother's death was in the oldest section of Topeka, where numbered streets were intersected by side streets named for presidents of the United States. The next block over was Lincoln. One block up Buchanan stood the governor's mansion, a twenty-room brick bulwark with striped awnings, gingerbread trim, and fanciful turrets that accommodated Governor Benjamin Paulen and his wife, along with a cook, chauffeur, and private secretary. Despite their proximity to power, the Dunhams dwelled at the other end of the social order. Ralph Waldo Emerson Dunham was the full name of the father, a literary appellation passed down from his father, a Wichita pharmacist and graduate of the University of Kansas who considered himself a Middle American disciple of the New England transcendentalist poet. This latest Ralph Waldo never thought much of his name, never went to college, never read Emerson, and pursued less elegiac lines of work. He had managed the Little Traveler Café next to the central fire station in Wichita, then was a mechanic for several years at the Oakland auto dealership in El Dorado before relocating again to Topeka, where he repaired cars at the garage on Sixth Avenue. Their house on Buchanan was plain and wooden, dirty white slats on a narrow slab, ten yards wide as it faced the street. The most recent census noted that the coal furnace needed repair. The neighbors to one side were the Wilkersons, a truck driver and his wife, and to the other side the widowed sisters Mrs. Waters and Mrs. Embry. The landlord was a local plumber. This was eighty-two years before a great-grandson of Ruth and Ralph joined Buchanan and Lincoln in the line of presidents. This was how it began, with an ending.

The funeral was held that Sunday at the First Baptist Church on Central Avenue in downtown El Dorado. Services were conducted by the minister from West Side Baptist in Wichita who had married Ruth and Ralph eleven years earlier.

Twenty-six years – a life cut short in every respect. When she was a child Ruth thought she would grow up to be a schoolteacher, as her parents had been when they were young adults. She played the role of teacher even before she went off to first grade. Classroom discipline in that era began with the barked order "Position!" At the command the students were to sit upright at their desks, mouths shut, hands folded in front of them. As a toddler, Ruth would call for order with the shout "Pa-dish-shun!" She was smart enough to skip a grade, but an early marriage and teenage motherhood ended her education before high school. Her boys remembered running into the house, where their mother held out a clenched fist to the first one to reach her. When he tapped it she would open it to reveal the gift of a Life Saver candy. She would then hide her other fist behind her back until the second boy circled around her waist and tapped the fist, which opened to another candy prize.

Four churchwomen, members of the Sunday school class Ruth had attended when she lived in El Dorado with her young family, sang "Abide with Me" and "Beautiful Isle of Somewhere." "Somewhere the heart is stronger; somewhere the prize is won."

The boys never went back to the small white house on Buchanan Street in

Topeka. Their father lost his garage, moved to Wichita, tried the drugstore business, and lived with one woman, then married another (Martha Mae Stonehouse in 1932, when she was twenty-two and he was thirty-five). The end of the first of those later relationships also came during a hunting trip, though the disintegration this time seemed more farce than tragedy, as his son Ralph Jr. later recalled: "He went away on a hunting trip one weekend, and when he came back, the woman had taken up with some other fella and they had backed up to the drugstore while everyone was away and packed up everything into the truck and moved off, and that was the end of the drugstore." By then Stanley and Ralph Jr. were out of their father's life, mostly. From the time of their mother's death through the rest of their school days, they lived with their maternal grandparents in El Dorado, setting a generational pattern that would be repeated a half century later.

In Section 5 of the Sunset Lawns South Cemetery, on the edge of El Dorado, across the street from an old oil refinery, stands a simple red granite gravestone that reads:

RUTH ARMOUR

DUNHAM

1900–1926

It is a lonesome plot surrounded by parched grass, with no other markers within fifteen yards. Her relatives are buried elsewhere, and her descendants live far away.

El dorado is Spanish for "the golden one," or "the gilded one." By most accounts, the long version was *El Hombre Dorado,* and the original myth was of a tribe so opulent that the chief hombre was painted in gold. The phrase grew shorter, the myth longer. The legend of *el dorado* began in South America, but the yearning for it is universal: to find that magical place of gold. *El dorado* is out there, somewhere. John Milton depicted El Dorado in book 9 of *Paradise Lost* as the mythical land of fabulous wealth. In Voltaire's *Candide,* El Dorado is the paradise of happiness. Edgar Allan Poe wrote "Gaily bedight a Gallant knight, / In sunshine and in shadow / Had journeyed long, singing a song / In search of El Dorado." Poe's gallant knight never could find that elusive place that lay "o'er the mountains of the moon." Nor could the conquistadors who went searching throughout the Americas. Francisco Vásquez de Coronado ventured out from Mexico in search of the Seven Cities of Gold in 1540, following one false lead after another as native peoples toyed with his grandiose imaginings. He pushed his expedition of Spaniards, Mexicans, and African slaves through what would become Arizona, New Mexico, Texas, and Oklahoma before ending up in the middle of Kansas, where, instead of a golden city high on a hill, he found some naked Indians.

More than three centuries later, in 1857, a party of Scots-Irish settlers traveled from Lawrence south and west across the Flint Hills of Kansas, moving through a sea of big bluestem and Indian grass. When they reached the crest of a hill above the Walnut River, the soft valley below seemed gilded in a sunset glow. The captain of the party gazed down at the sweetly winding river, with stone bluffs shimmering in gold and scarlet, and was moved to shout "El Dorado!" So goes the founding story of the town where Ruth Armour Dunham was buried, the town to which her young sons, Stanley and Ralph Jr., moved at the end of 1926.

El Dorado, Kansas. The locals pronounce it to rhyme with Laredo, *el da-RAY-dough*. Thirty miles east-northeast of Wichita, El Dorado is the county seat of Butler County, a rectangular jurisdiction that at 1,440 square miles is the largest county in Kansas. When the Dunham boys arrived, the county was booming again, which meant that oil was booming, with the longest unbroken stretch of rising petroleum prices in the 1920s. The Flint Hills had been the domain of cattle ranches and kafir corn farms until oil was discovered in 1915. On October 16 of that year, the season when young Ruth Armour Dunham married and dropped out of school, drillers for Wichita Natural Gas Co. hit pay dirt in an anticline 549 feet belowground on the property of John Stapleton. It was one of the first times the company had employed precise geology rather than scents, hunches, and luck to divine their spot. And here it was, a few miles outside the El Dorado town limits – black gold, the real *el dorado*.

Along with the gusher at Stapleton No. 1 came the sudden spasms of an oil frenzy. Roustabouts, wildcatters, pipe fitters, lumbermen, teamsters, preachers, prostitutes, surveyors, carpenters, organizers, political rabble-rousers, gamblers, restaurateurs, scofflaws, hired guns – the full traveling cast of American searchers came clamoring down to Butler County looking for action. The population of El Dorado grew by half to more than five thousand in that first year, on its way to more than ten thousand, and smaller company oil towns littered the surrounding countryside: Midian, Oil Hill, Browntown, Millerville, Haskin's Camp, Haverhill. Refineries were constructed in El Dorado and Augusta, the county's second-largest town, twelve miles south, to process the petroleum into gasoline. Pipelines were laid to carry the gas away, and more wells went into operation every week in every direction, more than six hundred in all, producing twenty-three million barrels of oil a year.

The backstreets of El Dorado and Augusta erupted with boardinghouses where men slept in shifts, one bed serving two or three men consecutively during a twenty-four-hour cycle. A single boardinghouse prepared dinners for two hundred men a day: white bread, boiled beef, potatoes, canned corn, sliced tomatoes, celery, boiled cabbage, ice tea, rice pudding – all for forty cents. The few boarders who found space in the rooming house of Mrs. Vincent Brown were perhaps the luckiest; she baked nine pies a day, her crust considered the flakiest in Butler County. Some stores stayed open around the clock seven days a week. It was said, with a touch of hyperbole, that crowds were so dense at midnight it was difficult to make one's way down the sidewalks of Central Avenue in El Dorado or State Street in Augusta. Oil Hill and Midian, the two largest made-from-scratch boomtowns, morphed into full-blown communities replete with schools, golf courses, churches, general stores, swimming pools, and row after row of shotgun houses (three rooms and an outhouse). The towns and oil companies sponsored semi-pro baseball teams, attracting players from all over, including an outfielder named Charles D. (Casey) Stengel, a Kansas City native who hired himself out after one major-league season to play in a series between rivals Oil Hill and Midian. (In the seventh game, mighty Casey struck out, according to one report, getting "nothing more than a loud foul ball.") During the heat of the First World War, the El Dorado oil field was the most productive in the nation, considered essential to the war effort by military planners in Washington.

Harry Ellington Armour and Gabriella Clark Armour had been among

9

the searchers who found their way to El Dorado during the oil boom. Harry was born in Illinois, but he and Gabriella had both grown up in the towns of La Grange and Canton in northeastern Missouri and had acquired enough education – short of college degrees, but sufficient – to teach elementary grades in rural schoolhouses where classrooms were lit by oil lamps and teachers were also janitors. Gabriella, who disliked her nickname (*GAY-be*), was a tall woman, about five-eight, and came from a line of taller men. Harry, who was about the same height as his wife, with black hair and blue eyes, was known to his grandsons as Streetcar Papa. He loved to talk about streetcars and show the boys photographs of the few years he had lived up north and worked on the streetcars in Rock Island and Moline, Illinois. He was also proud to have been a member of a literary society, and was especially proficient in math, an attribute that served him well when he found employment in the oil fields for the Magnolia Petroleum Company, a Texas-based outfit eventually swallowed up by Standard Oil. Though census documents listed Armour as a roustabout and pumper, he was more valuable for his brains than his brawn. If the bosses needed to know how many gallons of oil were in a storage tank, they turned to Harry. He developed a chart for each cylindrical tank (they were of various depths and widths) that listed how many gallons the tank held and how to calculate the volume on hand and the amount that could be added to top it off. In his off-duty hours, he found relaxation by working out mathematical puzzles published in the back pages of magazines and newspapers.

When the Dunham sons were taken in, Streetcar Papa and Mama Armour lived at 402 North Washington Street near the corner with Third, only a few blocks from the center of El Dorado. Money was tight, and to help the grandparents take care of the boys, their father, Ralph Dunham Sr., who was still their official guardian, took out a $2,500 loan from the Railroad Building Loan and Savings Association in nearby Newton. As collateral he used the mortgage on a parcel of land in El Dorado's Cooper Park that had been owned by his late wife and had been passed along to Stanley and Ralph Jr. when her will was probated. The town was not alien to the boys. They had been born in Wichita but lived with their parents in El Dorado for about four years at the start of the 1920s, first at the Opperman apartments next to the railroad station and later at an old house at 321 North Emporia that was owned by their grandfather. They had friends in El Dorado and knew the characters on Main Street and Central Avenue and the shortcuts through neighborhoods.

The boys were motherless, but lived in a home with two women: their grandmother, then forty-nine, and Aunt Doris, twenty. The twelve-year and ten-year age difference between Doris and the boys was close enough for them to be treated as siblings in many large midwestern families, but though Doris was close to them her whirlwind life allowed her little time to assume the watchful duties of an older sister. Like her father, Doris brought home a paycheck from the oil industry, working full-time as personal secretary to Dow Williams, an executive at the local offices of Skelly Oil. And she was among the most promising young women in town. As much as Ruth's death cast a sorrowful shadow over the family, a gleam of light still shone from Doris's stature as Miss El Dorado, one of the reigning elite of the 1926 Kafir Corn Carnival.

Oil ruled the economy, but kafir corn, and the carnival celebrating it, delineated the local culture. Far more than a county fair, more than a rite of autumn harvest, the Kafir Corn Carnival was the paramount event on the social calendar in El Dorado and all of Butler County. Observed for three days in October, the carnival engaged the entire populace, from farmers and ranchers to bankers and shopkeepers to teachers and schoolchildren, all of whom willingly suspended disbelief to partake in an elaborate fantasia with its own peculiar customs and lexicon, entering a faraway land in which kafir was king and a brotherhood of businessmen wearing orange fezzes with black tassels walked around saying they were symbolic travelers to the exotic city of Bulawayo.

The inspiration for all this, kafir corn, technically was not corn at all, though close enough. It was a member of the sorghum family that served the same function as feed corn for cattle but was even hardier, able to survive the driest summer. Unlike maize, it was not an indigenous plant but an immigrant to America, first arriving at the Philadelphia Centennial Exposition in 1876 and brought down a decade later to Butler County, where it became a staple for cattle ranchers. The crop came from what was then known as Southern Rhodesia, a product of Africa joining a bit of Kansas for the first time in this chronicle, though not the last. The very name *kafir*, also spelled *kaffir*, reflected the racial insensitivity of that era. A kafir is what some white

11

colonialists called a black African. It had a derisive connotation, equivalent to *nigger* in America. Kafir corn, cheap and tough, was at the bottom of the agricultural chain, a crop that black African subsistence farmers were allowed to grow on their little plots.

To the citizens of Butler County, kafir corn was a cash crop, a boon to the economy. The lone human connection they had to the African prologue was a black orphan who had been brought from Southern Rhodesia by a kafir corn farmer after a visit there. They called him Kafir Boy, and for several years he was the carnival's mascot, an exotic creature put out in front of the parade dressed in a loincloth and carrying a spear. The stereotype of Kafir Boy meshed with the carnival's pseudo-African mythology. Civic organizers had formed a fraternity known as the Knights of Mapira in which initiates, referred to as Wakupolata, were to carry stalks of Mapira (another name for kafir corn) that would "light the way and warn the Great Lomagundi of their approach." Like members of most fraternal organizations, they had secrets to keep, odd hats to wear, and oaths of loyalty to swear for the cause. Approaching under a lighted Triumphal Arch at the main intersection downtown, carnival-goers entered the mythical world of Kafirville, where booths, floats, storefronts, and entire houses along Central Avenue were intricately decorated in the reds, browns, yellows, and whites of kafir corn.

In the royalty of Kafirville, there were two leading ladies. One, the queen of the Kafir Corn Carnival, was chosen from among young women in Butler County's twenty-eight communities outside El Dorado. For residents of the host city itself, there was Miss El Dorado. To be elected Kafir Corn Carnival queen offered the promise of something more alluring than local fame; it was a possible ticket out of rural Kansas. Thelma Marsh, the queen in 1924, made her way to the Broadway stage (playing the daughter of a Kansas ink manufacturer in *That's Gratitude*), and Lorene Ferrier, queen in 1926, was eager to follow Marsh to New York.

Miss El Dorado held only slightly less prestige. Doris Armour was the daughter of an oil field worker, not a banker or oil executive, and for her even to be nominated for the title had been a high honor for her family. The fact that she was secretary to an oil officer certainly eased the way, as did the support of several society figures in town, including her campaign manager, Miss

Nelle Johnson, who was "noted for succeeding in any worthwhile project she undertakes – and she doesn't undertake anything that isn't worthwhile." The election had been waged with the seriousness of a mayor's race as campaign troops persevered through a long spell of rain and mud to collect the winning votes. "Miss Doris is immensely well liked by office associates and they stood by her until she went smilin' through," the local newspaper reported. Ruth and her boys traveled down from Topeka for the carnival – it was never to be missed – and watched as Doris waved from a kafir corn float in all her slinky splendor, wearing a bejeweled and fringed flapper dress that shimmered above her knees.

Harry, the proud father, received the news while still recuperating at the hospital from his injury. Not long after he was released and returned to his home on Washington Street, word came of Ruth's sudden death, followed by the arrival of two lost boys.

Around the time the Dunham sons landed in El Dorado, the local newspaper ran a brief preview of a movie that was coming to town. The movie was based on the wildly popular book *Laddie: A True Blue Story* by Gene Stratton-Porter, a well-known naturalist and writer of her time, and the plot was a loosely autobiographical account of a tomboy little sister's relationship with Laddie, a big brother of impeccable character. Whoever wrote the preview (there was no byline) apparently thought a good deal of the movie. The "combination of well-known novelist, sterling cast, and clever direction by J. Leo Meehan," the reviewer remarked, "makes the story stand out like a nigger in a white fog."

To employ such a phrase in an article about a movie that evokes gentle romance and nostalgia, and to use the simile with the intent of praise, reveals the racial mores of that time and place. The intent of the sentence had nothing to do with race. The racial slur had no larger purpose than to complete the metaphor. It was all matter-of-fact, a small-town-Kansas variation of the banality of prejudice.

There was no Jim Crow segregation in El Dorado, no whites-only drinking fountains or restrooms. Ralph Jr. and Stanley went to school with black classmates. For the most part, the handful of black families in town were not treated as subhuman, nor as exotics like Kafir Boy, but often with a paternalistic sensibility. This attitude was set by the cultural arbiter of the community, Rolla A. Clymer, longtime editor of the *El Dorado Times*. Clymer was a man of moderate temperament and platitudinous prose. In one of his patented "Farewell" obituaries, he wrote after the death of a black citizen, "The town paid its tribute of respect to John Wesley Law, colored, at the unusually large funeral gathering yesterday. Both whites and blacks joined in the tribute for despite his color 'Wes' Law had earned a high place in the town's regard. For forty-one years he had lived a decent, respectable life in this town. He was hard-working and thrifty, he paid his bills and he reared a useful family. He was no whiner and no agitator, he was scrupulously polite and he tended to his business. His life is the best possible example to his race. A man's color makes no difference in his success if he observes the fundamental rules of good conduct."

In the context of the surrounding political climate, Clymer's obituary of John Wesley Law was a statement of tolerance. It came against the 1920s backdrop of a resurgent Ku Klux Klan, a time when KKK organizers moved through Kansas recruiting ministers and business leaders, luring them with free memberships and promises of official positions as chaplains and Kleagles. The Klan's hatred of outsiders – Catholics, immigrants, northerners, social-ists, communists, but especially blacks – was central to the cause, though it tried to maintain the veneer of a benevolent men's club, placing itself among the Freemasons and the Knights of Mapira. Its insinuation into the fabric of Butler County was particularly noticeable for a few years. A 1923 edition of the *Jayhawker American*, a Klan newspaper published in Wichita, carried ads from a who's who of Augusta and El Dorado merchants ranging from Peoples Meat Market to Kepler's Bakery, Pierce's Shoe Shop, and the Kansas State Bank. In 1924 the carnival in El Dorado went by a different spelling, Kafir Korn Karnival, that intentionally reiterated the triple-*K* of the Klan. There was a Klan rally in El Dorado that August that drew a crowd of more than three thousand people to a field at the west end of town. A minister, Reverend W. I. Palmer of Wichita, spoke about the "dangers confronting the republic" – the main one, in his opinion, being the influx of new immigrants.

The Klan's statewide Konclave the following year was held in nearby Augusta, hometown of a prominent businessman who had been elevated to statewide Klan leader. Burl Allison, a Butler County historian, was twelve at the time, and later recalled the early September evening when he witnessed the passing Klan parade: "These were strangers to us. We took our stand at the corner of Main and State and looked south. . . . We could see the first line crossing Seventh. From there State Street was a solid sea of white . . . from shoe tops to crowns of heads, the marchers were all in white. High conical headgear was much in evidence. Flowing robes. Quite an impressive sight. Several lines of men went by, then came mounted Klansmen. The parade continued all the way out to Moyle's pasture, where there was a ceremony with a flaming cross."

Various threads of nativist intolerance weave through the history of Kansas, but so too do countervailing threads of bold opposition to slavery and prejudice. The most outspoken critic of the Klan during the 1920s was William Allen White, who grew up in El Dorado before becoming editor of the *Emporia Gazette*, halfway up the road northeast to Topeka, where he gained a national reputation as a progressive proponent of Middle American common sense. White wrote a series of blunt editorials against the Klan in 1921. Three years later he became so concerned about the secret society's growing influence in Kansas that he felt compelled to run for governor. White realized that he would not win the 1924 Republican nomination, but used the campaign to challenge the timidity or acquiescence of other state politicians. The prospect that Kansas could have "a government beholden to this hooded gang of masked fanatics, ignorant and tyrannical in their ruthless oppression, is what calls me out of the pleasant ways of my life into this distasteful but necessary task," White declared. "It is a nationwide menace, this Klan. . . . Our national government is founded on reason and the golden rule. This Klan is preaching and practicing terror and force."

White was a giant figure of the Kansas prairie, cherubic in appearance, fierce in intellect, apart from the rest and yet one of the people. The Dunhams and Armours shared his moderate Republican politics and could even claim to know him personally. Around the time he was running for governor he needed repairs on his Pierce-Arrow luxury car, and it was taken down to the auto shop in El Dorado where Ralph Dunham was then working as a mechanic. After fixing the car, Dunham was assigned to drive it back to

Emporia. He made a family outing of it, bringing along Ruth, Ralph Jr., and Stanley. There was a ferocious summer rain that morning, and the roads, some unpaved, grew muddy and nearly impassable. What should have been a two-hour journey took all day, with the Dunhams showing up at White's home after sundown. The great editor invited them to stay the night. Ralph and Stanley would never forget the outing because of one little detail: the commodious bed they slept in was so high off the ground they couldn't get into it without a stepstool.

The founding stories of El Dorado and Butler County reveal the same sharp duality on the issue of race as Kansas at large. That first caravan of settlers who arrived at the bend in the Walnut River in 1857 and gave El Dorado its name was traveling with a political purpose in mind: to populate the area with people who opposed slavery. They were Free Staters, some of whom had been jailed in Lawrence for antislavery activism. Their passage down to El Dorado was one small act in the passion play of "Bleeding Kansas," in which abolitionist and proslavery forces battled for control of the territory. In Lawrence only a year earlier, a posse of eight hundred southern agitators known as Border Ruffians had sacked two antislavery newspaper offices and burned down the Free State Hotel in what amounted to a terrorist attack on the capital of the territory's Free Soil movement. In response to the sacking of Lawrence, the radical abolitionist John Brown and his sons had raided a proslavery stronghold near Pottawatomie Creek and slaughtered five settlers with broadswords.

The question of whether Kansas would be free or slave had been contended violently since passage of the Kansas-Nebraska Act in 1854, legislation that opened the territories to white settlement and eventual statehood with a proviso, insisted upon by southern senators, that repealed the Missouri Compromise and allowed voters in Kansas and Nebraska to choose their own course on slavery before entering the Union. Senator Stephen A. Douglas, Democrat of Illinois, the act's principal northern sponsor, viewed it as a means of soothing relations between North and South while also serving business interests. Opening the territories was a priority of the railroad barons, who richly profited from westward expansion. It was in debates with Douglas in the fall of 1854, just after the act's passage, that Abraham Lincoln, challenging

Douglas for the Senate seat as a Republican, refined his arguments against slavery. Lincoln asserted that the Kansas-Nebraska Act was not indifferent to slavery but in fact inspired its spread. "I cannot but hate it," he said during a debate in Peoria. "I hate it because of the monstrous injustice of slavery itself. I hate it because it deprives our republican example of its just influence in the world."

A final irony closes the circle. El Dorado was founded by Free State settlers who traveled there in the bloody wake of the Kansas-Nebraska Act, yet the jurisdiction in which El Dorado is the county seat was named for an ardent pro-slavery senator from South Carolina, Andrew Pickens Butler, who served as Douglas's ally in pushing the Kansas-Nebraska Act through Congress. It was Butler's fervent hope, and a common expectation when the act was debated, that Kansas would emerge as a slave state. Northern abolitionists in the Senate detested him. Charles Sumner of Massachusetts took to the Senate floor before the vote and, alluding to Don Quixote's devotion to Dulcinea, said of Butler, "He has chosen a mistress to whom he has made his vows and who, though ugly to others, is always lovely to him, [and] though polluted in the sight of the world, is chaste in his sight. I mean the harlot, slavery." Sumner's speech was entitled "The Crime against Kansas," but his words incited an act of thuggery against Sumner himself. Butler's nephew, Congressman Preston S. Brooks, was so enraged that he stormed at Sumner in the Senate chamber and beat his head severely with a cane.

When Kansas finally joined the Union in 1861, it did so as a free state, foiling Butler and all those with other designs. The new state took as its motto *Ad Astra per Aspera,* a Latin phrase that translates as "To the Stars, through Difficulties," reflecting the bloody battle to join the Union. "The origin of Kansas must ever be associated with the struggle against slavery," wrote the noted Kansas historian Carl L. Becker. "The belief that Kansas was founded for a cause distinguishes it in the eyes of its inhabitants as preeminently the home of freedom."

By the time the Dunham boys reached high school age, their aunt Doris had married and gone to live with her husband, Edgar Hamaker, who ran the filling station on North Main at the edge of town. Another relative had replaced Doris in the Armour home. He was Gabriella's father, a great-grandfather of

Ralph Jr. and Stanley, Christopher Columbus Clark. It is remarkable to consider the long river of American racial history that flows through the story of Stanley Armour Dunham. This white Kansan would help rear a grandson who would go on to be president of the United States and to make history as the first president whose skin was black. As a teenager, Stanley was growing up in a town founded by Free State settlers and with a great-grandfather who fought for the North during the Civil War. From the Kansas-Nebraska Act and the struggle to end slavery on one end to Barack Obama on the other – 150 years and six generations running through a single unlikely life.

The family had moved to the outskirts of El Dorado by then, living in a circle of company houses on what was called the Magnolia Koogler lease. When oil reserves were discovered there, the land had been owned by the Koogler family, whose daughter Marion Koogler McNay became a high-society matron and patron of the arts in San Antonio and New York. Her path to wealth led from the subterranean grit of this property, now dotted with petroleum tanks and surrounded by a matrix of derricks and pumps phut-phutting day and night. Harry Armour walked to work. Stanley and Ralph Jr. drove an old Pontiac, and later a new Chevy, into town to attend El Dorado High. The house had two bedrooms, which meant the brothers spent much of the year sleeping next to a washing machine on the back porch, which was screened for the summer months; in the winter only sideboards protected them from the Flint Hills frost.

Their great-grandfather was now in his late eighties. Columbus Clark, as he called himself, had been fourteen when the Civil War began. He came from northeastern Missouri near the Illinois line. Young men in Missouri were up for grabs in the War between the States; about 100,000 fought for the North, perhaps half that many for the South. In April 1864, when he was eighteen, Clark enlisted in Company M, 69th Regiment of the Missouri Militia, which was affiliated with Union forces though not an official unit of the federal army. He was in active service for seven months, until early December, and told stories about it for the rest of his life, finding a new audience in the boys out on

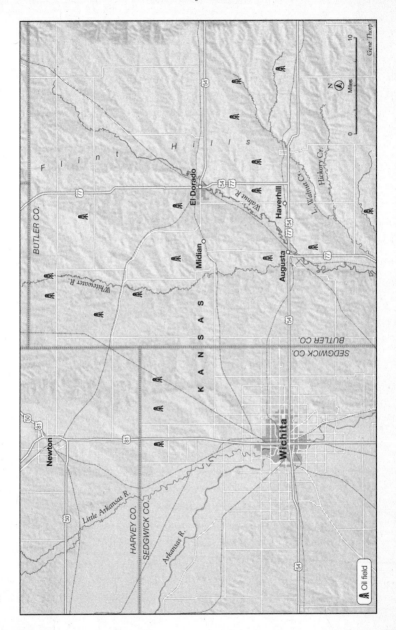

the porch. His favorite story was about the time his unit surrounded a house that had a Confederate bushwhacker captain inside. The captain shouted, "Come in and get me if you want," and young Columbus Clark himself kicked in the door and brought him out without a shot. They hanged the bushwhacker the next morning.

There were precious few Civil War veterans left in El Dorado to challenge the veracity of the story or, more likely, to follow it with derring-do tales of their own. The last publicly identified local man who had fought with the Army of the Potomac was C. B. Dillenbeck, who followed General Philip Sheridan through the Shenandoah Valley in 1864 before settling in El Dorado to make his fortune in beef and real estate. Dillenbeck died a year before the Dunham boys moved back to town. Jimmy Dodwell was still around and had his own story to tell, about how he had run away to enlist in the Union army but was too young to carry a rifle, so served as a drummer boy at the horrific Battle of Shiloh in southwestern Tennessee.

The war was long gone from Kansas, but it still shaped everything about old Columbus Clark. With his fellow Missouri Militia veterans he had taken a vow never to vote for a Democrat in his life, and he had kept that vow through the decades. To him, Democrats were associated with slavery. He had not been an abolitionist (and his late wife, Susan Overall Clark, from Kentucky, had grown up in a family that owned a slave), but Clark tried to treat everyone alike. The boys noticed that when the horse-drawn ice-cream cart came clopping by, driven by one of El Dorado's black peddlers, their great-grandfather made a point of going out to talk with him. When Clark regaled the boys with the bushwhacker story and taught them how to play checkers and the card games euchre and pitch, he often leaned on a weathered cane. It was made of slippery elm taken from the banks of the Wyaconda River in Missouri and had a snake's head with eyes fashioned into its crook. A friend had carved the cane and given it to Clark right after the war, when he sprained his foot. Now he needed it even more; cataracts had rendered him nearly blind. The world hazy to him, his past foremost in his mind, he wielded the cane like a rifle, ordering Stanley and Ralph Jr. outside to march them through the paces, instructing them on right shoulder arms and left shoulder arms and different military maneuvers.

The neighborhood configuration on the Magnolia Koogler lease was suitably safe for a nearly sightless octogenarian. The compound of twenty or so houses was encircled by a sweeping outer road, with all the houses situated inside the giant oval and only a sidewalk cutting across the radius, making it possible for Clark to take daily constitutionals inside the perimeter without being flattened by an unseen automobile. He was a proud six-footer who stood erect even in his dotage, his waist wrapped in a truss because of an unrepaired hernia, as he tap-tapped his way down the sidewalk. There was also ample room between the houses and in the common grounds for the Dunham boys to play pickup football and baseball games, tennis, croquet, and, with a pair of five irons (then called mashies) they bought in town, ad hoc rounds of golf with trees serving as pins. Both boys were lean and tall like their grandmother and great-grandfather, each about six-one-and-a-half, and fairly good athletes, though they never made the high school teams. They brought in money for the family by mowing lawns (not an easy task; the buffalo grass was "like cutting wire") and working part-time at the oil wells. Using what was called a gas gooser, they cleared an area circling out forty feet from the wells of grass and shrubs, roots and all, down to the bare soil, so that the occasional prairie fire could not start a conflagration. Clearing one well took all day and earned the boys seventy-five cents.

Of the two brothers, Ralph was the scholar, Stanley the dreamer, schemer, and misfit. Ralph took after his grandfathers on both sides. He loved literature and philosophy like the original Emersonian Dunham and had a talent for math like Harry Armour. School was always easy for Ralph. Stanley had a fertile imagination, a gift for talking and telling stories, and a desire to be a writer, but he lacked the attention span or discipline to perform well in class. He was always more interested in having fun. Out on the porch, late at night, he heard Ralph speaking Spanish in his sleep but could never learn the language himself. One of his proudest achievements at school was a batik work in art class that featured a vivid splash of colors and a futuristic outer-space design, a prized possession he kept with him for years thereafter.

It is tempting to say the absence of parents shaped his personality, but it is not clear that Stanley would have turned out differently had Ralph Waldo Emerson Dunham remained close to his sons. Stanley was willful and footloose, a combination that made him hard to control. His mother, an avid reader, named him in honor of one of her favorite historical characters, Sir Henry Morton Stanley, the British newspaperman and adventurer who became famous probing the nether regions of interior Africa. This Kansan Stanley's urge to escape his confines and explore began at age four, when the family was living in El Dorado, and he and a neighbor boy decided to run away from home, a lark that lasted until after dark. In his early teens he began smoking Philip Morris cigarettes and hopping freight trains to Augusta or Wichita and back. He once broke an elbow as he tumbled from a moving railcar, an injury that was reset badly and left him with stiffness in that arm the rest of his life. His grandparents were not strict. Grandmother Armour would never forgive the boys' father for the events leading to Ruth's death, and she did not want them to suffer because of his irresponsibility. "Just don't do anything to disgrace the family," she would say to Stanley.

On at least one occasion she reined him in, and perhaps saved his life. Stanley and an older boy named Beach Powers, along with another El Dorado pal, Claude Forshee, were planning to go out with two girls from Eureka, the fifteen-year-old twins Evelyn and Dorothy Coalscott. Powers, though already twenty-three, was dating Evelyn. He was a dashing figure, cool and handsome, a playwright, actor, and amateur theater director with a voice so smooth that he sang with local swing bands. Stanley would have followed him anywhere, but Gabriella told her grandson that he had to stay home. Here was a rare instance when he was talked out of something. At eight-thirty that Monday night, November 4, 1935, as Powers and Forshee were driving with the Coalscott girls from Eureka to El Dorado to go to a movie, speeding down Highway 54 about ten miles from town, a stray cow stepped onto the road in front of them, forcing Powers to swerve left into the oncoming lane, where his car was met head-on by an oil transport truck coming the other way. The four young people and the truck driver were all killed in a fireball that burned their bodies into unrecognizable charred torsos. The genealogy of any family involves countless what-if moments; here was one in the line of generations leading out from Stanley Dunham, the what-if of a less insistent grandmother, a disoriented cow, and the teenage Stanley immolated on a roadway in Kansas.

If Stanley had been the only one to tell that story, there might have been justifiable reason to question it, but there are newspaper accounts of the incident itself, and his brother vouched for the family's side of the story. Stanley had a constant need to present himself as more than he was, good or bad. He would unfold tales that had to be apocryphal but were so outrageous or imaginative that people liked hearing them nonetheless. Many involved the supposed escapades of him and his buddy Keith Allen, an equally bold storyteller. Allen wanted to be a writer, like Beach Powers, and was one of the pallbearers at Powers's funeral. The Allens were close to the Armour family in El Dorado; they rented a house that Harry Armour owned as a real estate investment. Keith's father lost his job during the earliest days of the Depression and remained out of work for years, a fact that lends context to one of their favorite stories.

Late in the winter of 1935, two years after he had left office, former president Herbert Hoover undertook a touring car trip from Chicago back to California, accompanied by his twenty-five-year-old son, Allan. They stopped in Hannibal, Missouri, to visit the house of Mark Twain, then made their way to Emporia to spend time with Hoover's old friend William Allen White. On the morning of February 18, with Henry J. Allen, a former Republican senator from Kansas, now also along for the ride, they drove through El Dorado on the way to Wichita. Hoover was still popular in Kansas, and with advance word of his schedule, schools were let out so students could greet the former president as his car rolled through the Flint Hills. All the students except Stanley Dunham and Keith Allen, that is, who slipped away and failed to reappear until that night, armed with their story. They were walking south of town, they said, when a car carrying none other than Herbert Hoover himself pulled over and picked them up. One of the young men – if you're going to concoct a story, why not make it brazen? – then lit a cigarette in the backseat, which prompted Hoover to call out, "Butts on that!" The phrase meant he wanted the last drag on the cigarette. It is a deliciously preposterous scene to re-create in the mind's eye: the conservative, white-haired former president jostling for position in his suddenly overcrowded sedan, using the latest slang with an obstreperous young hitchhiker. Perhaps this fabrication served as inspiration for Keith Allen, who eventually wrote screenplays in Hollywood.

When he recalled his early years to his family in later decades, Stanley's two defining stories were that he found his mother after her suicide and that he punched his principal and got expelled from El Dorado High. That second story seems to be in the same fictitious realm as the first. It is true that Stanley did not graduate with his class, the class of 1935, at El Dorado High School. But neither his brother nor any classmates could remember the principal-punching incident. "I think that is an apocryphal story," Ralph Dunham Jr. said. "We had known the principal [E. L. Harms] for years. My family was very good friends with the principal. His son was in my brother's class. I don't think he punched the principal. I think he may have been goofing off and skipped a few more times than he should have and wasn't passing courses, and had a discussion in [the principal's] office about this."

Stanley graduated one year late, with the class of 1936, with Betty Lu Steere and Betty Lou Smart, with Flossie Bassett and Thelma Crommett, with Bryon Lee McCall and Maeabelle Hudson. He was not the only young wise-acre in his crowd. Of classmate Donald Dawson the yearbook editors wrote, "Study is a weariness of the flesh, and he thinks much of his health." Of Jack Jenkins, a pallbearer at the funeral of Beach Powers, it was said, "Teachers wish he'd cut class so order might be maintained." And of Roy Hanney, a pall-bearer for Claude Forshee, "We never know what to expect from Roy."

Any of those descriptions might have been apt for Stanley Dunham, though his own line was more prosaic: "A loyal member of the class of '36."

The name of the El Dorado High yearbook, appropriately, was *The Gusher*. Symbols of an oil derrick, an oil drum, and oil cars defined the cover. In his message to seniors, Principal Harms communicated in the metaphor of the oil field. "We have enjoyed the opportunity of observing your drilling operations. You have struck pay-sand where the samples were of good grade," he wrote. But that was only the first step. "We know that the oil industry does not stop with the drilling and bringing in of the oil, after that comes the important process of refining the product."

The effusive graduation rhetoric contradicted the economic realities of that time and place. Butler County's headiest days of oil were long gone. Drilling and refining were still the region's major industries, but the gusher era was over. Rural boomtowns had lapsed into ghost towns. Great Depression scenes of struggle and despair were all around: home foreclosures, boarded-up stores, dusty fields and abandoned farms, hobo camps spreading over the ridges of railroad beds. Only days after Stanley Dunham left high school, the Railroad Building Loan and Savings Association won a court order forcing the family to lose the property that had been used as collateral for the $2,500 loan that helped the grandparents take care of the orphaned boys eight years earlier. Harry Armour had been unable to keep up with taxes and insurance on the property. Two months after the court order, the land was put out for bid in a sheriff's sale.

Augusta, Kansas, in 1936 was caught between old and new. In a summer stretch that had been the hottest ever, with a record 121 degrees in mid-July and recordings of 114, 112, and 116 that same week, the populace found relief in a new architectural wonder. The Augusta Theatre was reputed to be the lone theater west of the Mississippi lit entirely in neon, and an elegant work of Art Deco, with its jade and black tiles of carerra structural glass; it was also the only building in town cooled by air-conditioning. As the rivalrous little sister to the bigger El Dorado, Augusta took great pride in having a more modern theater. The local Bisagno family built it from oil money, which had slowed noticeably but still trickled during the tight years of the Depression. Townspeople hungered for the newest thing. First came miniature golf; four courses popped up within a few blocks in the center of town, long lines forming every night. But soon that became passé, to be replaced by the yo-yo.

Madelyn Payne, born in a farmhouse in 1922 in Peru, Kansas, a small dot on the map near the Oklahoma border, was now in her teenage years in Augusta. She necessarily lived by the rhythms of her family, shaped by the farm, with lunch called dinner and considered the big meal of the day – meat, potatoes, and gravy – followed in early evening by a light supper. But she longed for a modern life beyond the dimensions of rural Kansas. On the big screen at the Augusta Theatre she became enraptured by the actress Bette Davis, who exuded an urban sophistication and manipulative coldness that shattered the mythology of small-town sentimentality. Madelyn was not devious like the characters played by her Hollywood idol, but she practiced a studied aloofness on her younger siblings, Charles and Arlene, making it clear that she did not want to be considered one of a brood of children. She was forced to share a bedroom with her sister, but wanted little else to do with her. "There was an interesting gap, even though it wasn't so pronounced in years," recalled Charles Payne, who was two years younger than Madelyn. "There was Madelyn – and then there was me and then there was Arlene, a year and a half younger than I was. And from early on Madelyn sort of disdained us as the kids. We played together and she was off with Francine."

Francine was Madelyn's best friend, Francine Elizabeth Pummill, the most popular girl in school. Most of the young women went by first and middle names. Francine Elizabeth and Madelyn Lee, they called themselves, until at some point in high school they mutually decided that the two-name phenomenon was decidedly small-town corny. They were in a class with Mary Margaret and Billy Jane, Alma Lorene and Betty Darlene, Helen Lucille and Mary Frances, Mildred Faye and Byra Lee.

Like many of their classmates, Madelyn and Francine moved to Augusta when their fathers landed jobs in oil. E. J. Pummill, a chemical engineer, had the more prestigious position, as assistant superintendent at the White Eagle refinery, owned by Mobil. Rolla Payne, who hated his first name and insisted that everyone, including his wife, call him Payne, was the warehouseman and ledger man for Prairie Oil and Gas Company, owned by Sinclair. The Pummills were from Fort Worth and had to adjust to life in a small town, but to the Paynes, or at least the parents, Augusta itself, with four thousand residents, was the big city. Payne and his wife, Leona, who went by Lee, both had grown up in farmhomes without electricity or indoor plumbing. In Lee's poetic words, her father "planted potatoes by the dark of the moon." Like the Armours and Old Man Columbus Clark, her family had migrated to Kansas from Missouri. Family legend, passed down to future generations by Lee's sister, Ruth, claimed the McCurrys were abolitionists who left Missouri after being harassed by proslavery bushwhackers.

Together Madelyn Payne and Francine Pummill walked to school in the morning and back home for lunch, then back to school after lunch and home again, or over to Peterson's Drug Store (known as Pete's). All within seven blocks – the Paynes lived at 12th and State; the high school was three blocks down, at the corner of Clark and State; and the drugstore was downtown, at 5th and State. Together, as the only two representing their school, they attended the YWCA-sponsored Girls Reserve conference in Arkansas City during their sophomore year, and together they sang in front of a school assembly. Francine, with her blonde locks and big blue eyes, had been comfortable performing since she was seven years old, when she had been chosen the 1929 princess of the baby parade at the Kafir Corn Carnival in El Dorado. Madelyn took to the stage for the school's rendition of *Spring Fever*. She had the role of the mother, Mrs. Phoebe Purcell, in a story in which her daughter, Ann, was in love with a guy who did not meet the family's expectations – art prefiguring life in a way that would play out more than once in her own future.

Madelyn was also a first-rate student, on the honor roll semester after semester, in the top tier of classes in a tracked system that essentially categorized classrooms as smart, average, and unruly. Sidney DeVere Brown, a school brain who would go on to become a professor of Japanese history at the University of Oklahoma, was in first-year Latin with Francine and Madelyn, who sat one behind the other. Latin I met on the second floor in the southeast corner of the high school, Brown remembered: "When a south wind blew from the Socony refinery one mile to the south, the characteristic stench was carried into our classroom." The Latin teacher was Miss Ella Larner, "a thin red-haired spinster of about forty . . . polite to a fault, but demanding." Madelyn was one of the better students in the class, facile with declensions and conjunctions, but what stood out in Brown's memory more than Madelyn was her mother, Lee, who came to Parents Night and recited several lines of Caesar in Latin. "Miss Larner," he recalled, "was mightily impressed."

Most everyone who met Lee Payne came away impressed by her intellect. She never worked after having children (she was twenty-five when Madelyn was born), but before that had been a schoolteacher in Peru, along with her sister, Ruth, who did not marry and continued teaching. Both sisters had received teaching certificates from Pittsburg State Teachers College to the east of Peru, near the Missouri line. Charles Payne, who eventually became a librarian at the University of Chicago, said Lee encouraged her children to excel at their studies. "She was smart," he said. So smart, in fact, that Charles's wife many decades later would suggest that one of Lee Payne's great-grandsons, the one who became president of the United States, got his brains from her. There was no shortage of intellect in any branch of the family tree, as it would turn out, but

Lee was certainly one sharp root. An avid reader, she was an early subscriber to a monthly series of paperbacks published by Pocket Books in 1939, the first of its kind in the country, and proudly displayed the classics in a bookcase in the living room: *Wuthering Heights, Lost Horizon, Five Great Tragedies of William Shakespeare, The Bridge of San Luis Rey, The Way of All Flesh.*

Lee was open to change. She had been reared a Republican and married a Republican, but now was in the process of turning into a Roosevelt Democrat, a political inclination that she would pass down to her older children. The first step in the process occurred on October 16, 1936, when she and Mrs. Pummill packed five of their children into the backseat and drove to Wichita to meet a train carrying FDR, who was making a whistle-stop tour through Kansas in his bid for reelection. It might seem the president was roaming deep into alien territory that year – Republican Kansas with its favorite-son Republican nominee, Governor Alf Landon. But Landon had not made a race of it. For much of the campaign he had stayed in Topeka, in that turreted governor's mansion on Buchanan Street one block from the tiny lease house where the Dunhams once lived, on his way to a landslide loss in which he could neither carry Kansas nor win the vote of Lee Payne.

Lee's husband, the man who answered to Payne, or sometimes R. C. (only an older sister could call him Rolla), showed less intellectual curiosity, though he was precise at his work. As the warehouseman for Sinclair's Prairie Oil, which was in the drilling and production part of the industry, Payne lived and worked on the same property at the corner of State and 12th. Their first house faced State, but by Madelyn's high school years they were in another house, on the 12th Street side. There was a large common yard leading back to Osage Street that held stacked rows of pipes and other oil field supplies and a small warehouse that served as Payne's office. He kept track of supplies, noting the day's comings and goings in large ledger books. Brown hair, gray eyes, medium build – Payne was a shy and retiring man whose wildest trait was occasionally smoking a cigar. He let his wife run the house and take care of the children, while he focused on his job, which he held on to through the worst years of the Depression. Though his wife and daughters did not work, Payne's income eventually was supplemented by son Charles, who through high school held a job at the Phillips Pantree grocery.

The Paynes were not defined by religion. They happened to be Methodists, as were the Pummills. As teenagers Madelyn and Francine took turns driving to church, but their outings were more social than spiritual, and Francine's lasting memory is not of a sermon but of Madelyn's farcical efforts to drive the family's 1937 Chevy, their Sunday hats flying off as the car buck-buck-bucked pulling away from the curb. The family was only "nominally religious," according to Charles. "My father would go to church maybe twice a year. My mother maybe six times a year. That's not heavily religious. And we didn't have any religious strictures at home. We were allowed to dance, and we did. We weren't allowed to swear, within mother's hearing, not allowed to smoke, with anyone's knowledge, and we were not allowed to drink, with anyone's knowledge – and we did all of those. Probably with their knowledge but without them saying anything."

Dancing was not only allowed, it was encouraged by many mothers. Mrs. Bisagno recruited dance instructors from Wichita to teach her children and their friends in special classes inside her Augusta Theatre. Francine's mother turned the family living room into a veritable dance hall. "I want my children to roll up the carpet and dance," she declared, and Francine and Madelyn and their crowd enjoyed dance parties at the Pummill house after basketball and football games, swinging to the music of Artie Shaw and Glenn Miller. With pressure from determined students who staged a walkout to protest school policy, Augusta High officials eventually relented and let a swing band play at a school party. When the local school board formally liberalized its policy to allow live bands at school dances, the key proponent was board member E. J. Pummill, who was responding to the intense lobbying of his rug-cutting wife.

As in El Dorado, the story of race in Augusta was buffeted by contradictions. The malevolence of Jim Crow segregation was apparent only an hour's ride away, in Oklahoma, and Augusta's own history had its share of racial ugliness, from the Ku Klux Klan parade down State Street in 1925 to whispers that it had once been known as a sundown town, meaning it was not safe for unfamiliar blacks to be seen there at night. But the prevailing sentiment was similar to the paternalistic attitude taken by the editor Rolla Clymer at the *El Dorado Times.* "There were two black families in Augusta," recalled Earl Leon Mercer, a classmate who occasionally dated Madelyn. "One had twin girls and the other twin boys. They were younger than us. Their folks were well thought of. They did their work and stayed in their area. [The fathers] both worked at night to clean banks and during the day they might be in the barbershop shining shoes. And they were real nice people." One of those four black students, in the grade behind Madelyn's, was Herman Reed Jr., whose father worked at the barbershop. An excellent athlete, Reed was chosen captain of the Augusta High Orioles football team in his senior year.

The history Madelyn learned at school was unequivocally northern and progressive. Once a week she and her classmates filed upstairs to the second-floor auditorium for a school assembly. As they faced the stage, they would see a banner on the front wall that displayed Abraham Lincoln's Gettysburg Address. Her history teacher, K. L. Grimes, described by fellow student Sidney DeVere Brown as "balding . . . pudgy . . . bandy-legged, mouth permanently shaped in a puckish smile," was a Lincoln buff who told stories about Old Abe's career in Illinois along with a vivid account of young Lincoln going down the Mississippi all the way to New Orleans, where he witnessed a slave auction and vowed, at least as Grimes recounted the scene, that if he ever had a chance "he would hit the slavery system, and hit it hard."

Grimes pushed his students to explore the intellectual and social forces that shaped modern times. They studied *Babbitt* and *Main Street,* works by Sinclair Lewis that challenged the conventions of Middle America. They listened to "Rhapsody in Blue" by George Gershwin. They examined law and religion from the perspective of the Scopes trial. And as events unfolded in Europe, in faraway countries that Grimes had visited during his yearly forays out of Kansas, the ominous developments became material for his classroom lectures in Madelyn's junior and senior year: the Munich agreement, the German invasion of Poland, the march toward world war.

In the transportation latticework of Butler County, Highways 54 and 77 conjoined from the east and north in El Dorado. Running together for a stretch, they laced a straight line south for twelve miles, then took a ninety-degree right turn into Augusta, before diverging again, with 54 continuing due west sixteen miles into the big city of Wichita. Anyone driving the last section of that well-traveled route in the 1930s was likely at some point to see a character straight out of the Old Testament standing at the side of the road. No one knew his name. They called him Walking William. He leaned on a staff, an ancient visage with long white hair and long white beard. This was no hitchhiker. Walking William never had his thumb out looking for a ride, but people inevitably stopped anyway, and when they invited him in he would accept, though only for a brief spell. Somewhere down the road he would declare, "Stop the car. The Lord has told me to get out and go back!" When traffic cleared, he would amble across to the other side and await an unsolicited return toward Augusta. Until he died near the end of that decade, the aged roadway prophet was part of the landscape, as familiar as the oil derricks, the cattle, and the vast fields of scorched black earth left by controlled prairie fires each spring.

Madelyn Payne and her cohorts traveled the stretch of Highway 54 from Augusta to Wichita many times during the summer before their senior year, and on weekends after school began. They were often heading to one of the dance pavilions where the big swing bands played, the 21 Club, the Forum, and John Dotson's just-opened Blue Moon out by the Boeing aircraft plant. Along with jitterbuggers from Wichita, there were contingents from El Dorado and Augusta at the dance halls. The Butler County towns were rivals, but it was nonetheless common for boys from El Dorado to look for Augusta girls to date. It was a truism that the young women were always prettier the next town over. With dark brown hair parted on the side, alluring brown eyes, and long, shapely legs that were a trademark of the McCurry family, Madelyn was in that category. She was self-conscious about one facial feature, a hook nose, another characteristic of the McCurry side. Some relatives claimed the nose derived from what they called their "scratchy Apache" heritage, but genealogical research by one of Lee McCurry Payne's grandnephews showed no Native American connection.

As she entered her senior year, Madelyn was without her best friend. Francine Pummill had moved far from Augusta, to Caspar, Wyoming, where Mobil Oil had transferred her father. For Madelyn, the claustrophobic expectations of a small town were closing in. Her family lacked the financial wherewithal to send her to a university, despite her excellent grades. She longed for a sophisticated life and felt in danger of being trapped in Butler County. She started to smoke more and study less, uncharacteristically skipping school one fall afternoon. Joining Mary Frances Kennedy and Darlene Scott, she left "the ledge," where kids hung out until classes resumed after lunch, and walked down State Street to puff on cigarettes and while away the rest of the day. The principal got word of the truants, resulting in a one-day suspension. Madelyn's frustration was apparent to her brother Charles, who thought she was flailing against fate. "She wanted to go to college. She was smart and a great reader. She read book after book. What she didn't want to do, which is what she was being pushed toward, was to go to El Dorado Junior College and become a teacher – the route my mother had taken and Aunt Ruth had followed. And she was being pushed toward that and she was determined not to do that."

Along came Stanley Dunham. Four years out of El Dorado High, Stanley had found part-time work on a construction crew renovating the Socony-Vacuum refinery in Augusta and was now a familiar figure in Madelyn's haunts. On late afternoons he could be seen hanging around Pete's or Cooper's on State Street, and on weekend nights there he was again in the crowds at the dance halls over in Wichita. He was tall and tan with slicked-back wavy brown hair, a quick-flash smile, and exotic stories to tell. He would talk about the places he had been and the means by which he had traveled: hitchhiking, riding the rails, driving north to Chicago and cross-country to the West Coast. Among the girls who listened to his tales, Madelyn was especially interested in hearing about life beyond Kansas. Stanley said he had been to California with his friend Keith Allen. He talked about San Francisco, Oakland, Monterey, Hollywood. He said he was friends with John Steinbeck and William Saroyan. He was doing some writing of his own, he said, working on plays and screenplays. So many story ideas swirled around in his head. The trunk of his car, he confided, was full of scripts. He couldn't wait to get back out to the coast. Madelyn fell, hard.

In her final semester at Augusta High, she stayed after school many afternoons to rehearse the spring play, a comedy by Charles Quimby Burdette titled *Foot-Loose* that took place in the Chicago suburbs and dealt with the question of when parents should interfere in the lives of their teenage children. At that time, Madelyn was hoping to avoid a real-life variation on the theme. It was clear that her parents did not think much of her new boyfriend.

Her mother was mortified by Stanley's age and worldliness, and her father, a man of few words, remarked after first meeting Stanley that he looked like a "wop." Friends were no kinder. They thought Stanley was full of himself, cocky, stuck up, jealous, too old, and too vain, and they disliked his being from El Dorado. "Most of us felt those guys should stay in El Dorado," said Earl Leon Mercer. They gossiped about the new couple, some boys saying that Stanley was a stud who had modeled underwear in a Sears Roebuck catalogue. It must have been sex that brought them together, decided Mary Frances Kennedy.

Near the end of the school year, the upperclassmen gathered at Community Hall for the junior-senior banquet, an annual tradition where juniors hosted and honored the seniors. Miniature graduation caps adorned each table for the eighty-four seniors, forty-two boys and forty-two girls. Ten of the seniors, including Madelyn, had gone through school together since kindergarten. The superintendent, J. W. Murphy, delivered the after-dinner speech on the predictable subject, "After graduation, what?" At the end of the evening Madelyn, like the other girls, left the dinner carrying red roses. Instead of going home, she slipped off to Wichita with Stanley and, three weeks before graduation, secretly married him. Twenty-five years earlier, his parents had secretly married in the same city.

Madelyn returned to her bedroom that night without telling her parents what she had done and continued to live at home as though nothing out of the ordinary had happened. She soon confided in her brother Charles, but swore him to secrecy. "She said 'Don't tell anybody!' so I didn't," he remembered. A week later she joined eleven girls at a slumber party at Nina June Swan's downtown apartment above LoVolette's China and Gifts, and as they crowded into the living room, sprawled on the floor, gabbing late into the night, a few sensed that Madelyn was keeping a secret. When one girl kept prodding her, she confessed. Yes, she said, she had secretly married Stanley Dunham the night of the junior-senior banquet. They had to keep quiet about it, she said, because her parents still did not know.

The remaining end-of-school traditions were endured by Madelyn with her secret relatively intact: attending the all-girls picnic at Garvin Park; taking part in the relay races and treasure hunt; participating in the class pageant (a history of Kansas that began with Coronado stumbling his way into Butler County in 1540); dressing up for the class sermon; and finally attending commencement exercises on the Friday night of May 24. Across the ocean that day, the German 1st Panzer division had trapped British expeditionary forces at Dunkirk, and for a fearful moment it appeared that Hitler's troops might defeat the Brits and capture all of Europe. Mr. Grimes, the history teacher, had provided his students the context to understand what was going on overseas, but it still seemed distant, someone else's war. Without money to fund a cloth-bound yearbook, the class of 1940 memorialized itself in a special graduation supplement of the *Augusta Daily Gazette.* The supplement named the honor roll students, a list that for the first time failed to include Madelyn Payne. In a section where seniors willed personal attributes to juniors, Madelyn was said to will "her excitable ways" to Betty Watt. In an article that foretold what they would be doing in twenty years, her prediction read, "Madelyn Payne gives her advice free to all girls in her 'Advice to the love-lorn' column in the *Minneapolis Daily News.*"

One can only wonder what advice that column might have given Madelyn herself. Soon after commencement she revealed to her parents that she had secretly married Stanley. "By good fortune I was off at a two-week Boy Scouts camp when the whole thing broke," Charles recalled. "My father was furious and my mother was heartbroken, and they talked around about it and Madelyn prevailed. She was a strong person." Stanley's family – Ralph Jr. and Streetcar Papa and Mama Armour (old Columbus Clark had died in 1937, age ninety-one) – were told about it then for the first time too, and took the news with equanimity. They did not know Madelyn, but she might be a positive influence on Stanley. As word spread, kids from Augusta High became convinced that Madelyn was pregnant. As soon as she could, she left home – left Augusta, left Butler County, left Kansas. Mr. and Mrs. Stanley Dunham were California-bound.

CHAPTER 2

LUOLAND

At the time of the final insult from the local chief, and the disruptive uprooting that followed, the Obama family lived in the village of Kanyadhiang in western Kenya. Kanyadhiang was not considered significant enough to appear on official maps. It was nothing more than a scattering of family homesteads, each compound bordered by high protective hedges of thorny euphorbia and laid out in a ritually prescribed arrangement of mud huts with thatched roofs, dirt floors, and walls plastered in cow dung. The hub of village life was a stone dance hall situated at the bend of a rutted oxcart path that wended up from Kendu Bay, the nearest town. Kendu Bay was populous enough to merit place-name status, with roadside vegetable and charcoal stands, cattle and fish markets, beer bars and churches. It hugged the weedy, mosquito-infested lower shore of what was then known as the Gulf of Kavirondo atop Lake Victoria, the second-largest freshwater lake in the world. Life and death in equal measure emanated from the great African lake: the bounty of vast schools of perch and tilapia; the menace of sleeping sickness, malaria, and foraging hippopotamuses in the shallows.

During the years spanning the First and Second World Wars, an unconventional man named Hussein Onyango was the patriarch of a subclan of Obamas who lived in Kanyadhiang. In the Dholuo language, the tongue of the Luo (pronounced *Loo-oh*) tribe of that region, the name Obama derived from a word that meant "bent." It could also connote "curved spine," and that likely was the origin of the name of these Obamas. Onyango was a common given name in Luo society. It meant "born in the early morning." The name Hussein was less prevalent. Other local Obamas, several score strong, were native pantheists or Seventh Day Adventists, but Onyango had taken the Arabic name Hussein when he converted to Islam, agreed to be circumcised, and married a Muslim woman while living on the island of Zanzibar. It was the name he preferred and how he was addressed by *wazungu*, white people.

Some Luo in Kanyadhiang had a different name for him. They called him *jadak*. Pronounced *juh-DAK*, it meant "foreigner," "immigrant," "alien," and was delivered and received as an insult. The last time this happened was in 1941, sixty-seven years before Hussein Onyango's grandson was elected president of the United States. *Jadak* was to define the Obama family from generation to generation, from Africa to America, the condition of being disdained by some as an alien. The name Luo itself denotes "people who follow the river," and in the chronicle of Luo migration the outsider sensibility traced back to the fifteenth century, when these travelers – categorized as Nilotic because of their origins in the valley of the White Nile – started their long journey along the waterways from the swampy lowlands of southern Sudan. But the modern story begins in the little village up the oxcart path from Kendu Bay.

The pejorative had little to do with the fact that Hussein Onyango had once lived in Zanzibar and traveled to Ethiopia and Somalia and overseas to faraway Burma with the British military. Nor was he called *jadak* because he spent most of each year several hundred miles from his Lake Victoria homestead, working in Nairobi, the capital of the colony of Kenya, where he was a cook for various missionaries, adventurers, and British colonialists. Luo men from western Kenya undertook the migration to Nairobi or the more distant coastal city of Mombasa as a necessary routine, a matter of supply and demand and custom. They supplied the labor force, the cities had the white people with money who demanded help, and Luo custom accepted the disappearance of men for long stretches of time, with no thought that wives and children would follow.

What made him a *jadak* was the notion that Hussein Onyango's people were relative newcomers to the area, going back only four generations. He was born in Kanyadhiang, probably in 1896, one of eight sons and seven daughters of Obama Opiyo, who had five wives, including two who were sisters. Obama Opiyo was also born in Kanyadhiang, and so was the grandfather, Opiyo. But Hussein Onyango's great-grandfather, Obong'o, was indeed an alien of sorts. He moved to Kendu Bay in the 1820s in search of better fortune, finding there a place where the soil was fertile, the nearby forested hills brought rain year-round, three rivers (Miriu, Oluch, and Kanyadhiang) coursed through the farmlands, and fish from the great lake ensured that few went hungry.

Obong'o came to this land of relative plenty from a very different place, a village called Nyang'oma Kogelo, his ancestral home, in an interior valley more than 120 kilometers to the northwest, around the Gulf of Kavirondo, on the far side of Kisumu, the biggest city in western Kenya. Looping past marshy fishing villages and into a dusty equatorial terrain of spotted hyenas, reddish dirt, green scrub, and subsistence farms of maize and cassava, the road to Nyang'oma Kogelo was rimmed by tawny hills where giant boulders balanced defiantly one atop another in prehistoric formations to which the local inhabitants ascribed mystical meanings. This was far enough away to be the territory of a different branch of Luo, the Alego subtribe, named for a noted ancestor of that name, with different settlement patterns, attitudes, and oral histories. No matter how long they had been gone, the Obamas were still from this *piny,* a word that encompassed physical and cultural territory, above the lake, the Alego people of Nyang'oma Kogelo in the district of Siaya. And no matter how long they lived to the south in Kanyadhiang, they might still hear the insult *jadak.*

To slot these jurisdictions in familiar perspective, consider Kanyadhiang as comparable to the Magnolia Koogler lease on the other side of the world, where Stanley and Ralph Dunham were living during much of that same era. In that parallel universe, Kendu Bay was like El Dorado. The constituency surrounding Kanyadhiang was known as Karachuonyo, the rough equivalent of Butler County. And the province containing all of this, including Kisumu and villages stretching past Kendu Bay to the south and Nyang'oma Kogelo to the north and west to the Ugandan border, was Nyanza, comparable to the state of Kansas. Nyanza took its name from Lake Victoria; it meant "large body of water." The province was mostly rural, like Kansas, but one-eighth the size and more densely populated, with about one and a half million Africans along with ten thousand transplants from India, mostly traders and shopkeepers, and a mere fifteen hundred whites who ran the government and set rules for how and where the indigenous people should live. Because most of the native Africans in Nyanza were Luo, the third-largest tribe in colonial Kenya, the region was also known as Luoland, a designation that reflected an overriding tribal emphasis with no apt parallel in America.

Hussein Onyango could be derided as an alien in Kanyadhiang and the surrounding villages, but by no means was he unknown. Quite the contrary, he was one of the most vivid characters in that part of Luoland, a tall man with a formal, erect bearing, neatly dressed in Western slacks and a long red vest, a white fez atop his head. His mouth, described as large in British documents, was fitted with modern dentures filling a hole where six lower teeth had been pulled as part of an initiation rite inflicted upon young Luo males of his generation, the replacements making it easier for him to chew his favorite meal, *kuku choma*, a grilled chicken. His style of dress and his refusal to take tribal pride in yanked teeth were among many ways that he challenged old customs when he returned in the early 1920s after several years away from home, first with a regiment of the King's African Rifles and then in postwar Zanzibar. He came back with material things that seemed otherworldly to his family: a bicycle upon which he could be seen pedaling to and from the Islamic mosque in Kendu Bay that he helped build; a battery-operated radio that some neighbors feared was a voice of evil; and a canvas army tent that he even slept in at first, flaunting the Luo tradition of taking a specified hut that defined his status by its location within the compound.

He also, more noisily, brought back a rifle. Relatives later recalled the familiar scene of Hussein Onyango toting the rifle over his shoulder as he strutted along the village paths, sometimes firing into the air to make it known he was around. When he received news that his father, Obama Opiyo, had died, he was working in Nairobi and sent word back that he would return, and people should stay in their huts upon his arrival. That night he fired his rifle for a half hour, his version of a twenty-one-gun salute. Though he had often fought with his father, in death he exhibited an emotional soft spot for the old man. In the years after that first rifle salute, he marked the anniversary by instructing people to scream and cry as though Obama Opiyo had just died. According to archival records, only four hundred native Africans in southern Nyanza then had legal firearms, which were restricted by British colonial administrators and "were not to be granted to a person known to be of intemperate habits or unsound mind." At some later point, Hussein Onyango's license was revoked and his rifle repossessed.

In one sense, his mind seemed sound enough. He was a keenly intelligent man who had learned to read and write in English. He was obsessive about cleanliness, though against Muslim dictates he was a drinker, and he had other characteristics that were considered intemperate. The most common descriptions of him were that he was *mkali* (very harsh), *mtu matata sana* (very troublesome), and *juoki* (easily irritable). Friends and family described him as a perfectionist who could be violent, cunning, and cruel. He had a reputation for pummeling enemies with his fists, smacking children who did not show proper manners at the dinner table, and beating women who failed to meet his standards, including five wives (two of whom he essentially divorced; in Luo custom, a man could end a marriage simply by saying so, or leaving) and what some friends and relatives counted as at least ten other brief live-in women partners at various points. A common Luo metaphor depicting his behavior was that he had "ants in his anus."

What is most striking in retrospect about Hussein Onyango is the way he straddled different worlds, black and white, rudimentary and modern, superstitious and rational. He was Eastern in religion, Western in dress and demeanor, African in political sensibility. Here again was a variation of a characteristic passed down from generation to generation and across the world: an Obama who could operate in distinct cultures but was not wholly absorbed by any. There were times, foreshadowing the circumstances of his American grandson, when he was dismissed by some of his own people for acting white, or not seeming black enough, in his case rejecting too many totems of Luo heritage.

In the tradition of his father, Obama Opiyo, a peanut and millet farmer, he was an herbalist who was thought to conjure curing powers with the potions he concocted from plants, yet he roundly rejected traditional Luo superstitions and was not afraid to confront local witch doctors, scoffing at their threatened curses. The word throughout the region of Kendu Bay and Kanyadhiang was that he was a disciplinarian in the mold of the most sadistic British official, that he "behaved like a European," and that *wazungu* especially liked him for that. His table featured an English tea setting. He mentored younger Luo men in how to handle the British. "He used to speak like a white man," said Joshua Odoyo Odongo, a relative by marriage, meaning his accent sounded British. John Ndalo Aguk, another relative who apprenticed as a cook under Hussein Onyango, recalled his instructions: "He would say whites loved people who appeared clean and energetic. He would tell me, 'You have to be smart and look like one who is very healthy.'" With Hussein Onyango this attitude was more a matter of survival – getting and holding a job – than of subordination. He would not genuflect to difficult white employers.

Dealing with whites certainly proved easier for him than interacting with a fellow Luo named Paul Mboya, a contemporary who had become the favorite of British officials in southern Nyanza. A substantial local figure with his own *askari* security force at his compound in Gendia, Paul Mboya had been ordained as a pastor for the Seventh Day Adventist mission and was the colonial administration's designated native chief for the larger district of Karachuonyo from 1935 to 1948. In an annual political report, one British official called him "by far the most intellectual and cultured man in the district . . . an example of what is almost ideal in an African chief." He so impressed colonial authorities with his integrity and mastery of English that they had him perform tasks in the provincial office normally assigned to whites. In the winter of 1942 he received the honor of a silver king's medal, presented personally by the colonial governor of Kenya, Sir Henry Monck-Mason Moore.

Along with instructing his people to brush their teeth and build outdoor latrines, Chief Mboya impressed the British administration with the efficiency with which he and his assistant headmen collected taxes. The main tax imposed on native tribes was a hut tax, a form of property tax based on the number of huts in a family compound. Most Luo viewed the hut tax as hostile to their culture, since Luo men were polygamists who could have several wives, each with her own hut. The hut tax was always controversial, one rallying point for tribal resistance against the British, and a constant struggle to collect. In addition to the chief's salary he received from the British, Paul Mboya was awarded annual bonuses based on his ability to gather hut taxes faster than other chiefs.

Hussein Onyango had known Paul Mboya since childhood. They grew up two miles from each other, attended the same primary school for a few years, and similarly had been introduced to Western ways by missionaries. Each displayed a large ego and a gruff, stubborn personality. Hussein Onyango even worked for Chief Mboya for a time as the head bodyguard at his camp, where Mboya would hold daily meetings under the shade of a giant fig tree. But they differed in religion – one now Muslim, the other Adventist – and in political inclinations. Paul Mboya seemed more aligned with the British establishment. Hussein Onyango, although not overtly political, was more in sympathy with the nascent anticolonial movement, which in Nyanza came to be known as Piny Owacho (meaning "the territory has said," or "the people have said"). The leader of Piny Owacho was Daniel Ojijo Oteko, who had been trained in the United States and used the rhetoric of the American Revolution to promote the cause of Kenyan independence. He and Hussein Onyango had both been born in the same area of Karachuonyo in 1896, both spoke English, and knew each other well. Ojijo pushed the issue of tax fairness through his Kavirondo Taxpayers Association, which he had founded back in 1922 and which in later years pushed up against the chief and his collection of the hut tax.

The relationship between Paul Mboya and Hussein Onyango became increasingly strained and eventually ruptured. Some people thought Hussein Onyango had chiefly aspirations and was angling for Mboya's job, or at the least that his notoriety was seen as a threat to Mboya. According to the later recollections of Daniel Abuya, a member of Mboya's family, Hussein Onyango would tell people that "one day he would be the king of Karachuonyo," the chiefdom's constituency surrounding Kanyadhiang. At a public hearing known as a *kamukunji*, Hussein Onyango debated the chief on several matters about which they disagreed. He accused Mboya of being complicit with the British in using Luo men as forced laborers. Their final confrontation involved a football (soccer) trophy. As district chief, Mboya looked for ways to elicit cooperation from constituents. In his efforts to promote modern agricultural techniques or sanitary waste systems, he came up with the idea of distributing prizes, and often dipped into his hut tax bonuses to fund them: plows, tables, chairs, clocks, a maize-shelling machine. The prize system had an effect beyond encouraging better practices; it solidified the chief's hold on his community, a sort of Luoland version of the patronage system perfected in American cities like Chicago.

Hussein Onyango, looking to get in on the action, announced that prizes would be awarded to clubs in the Kendu Bay area who excelled against outside competition. He was a football fanatic who supported local Luoland teams and also followed the sport in Nairobi, dressing up in his off-duty suit on Sundays to attend games there at City Stadium, a field the British colonialists built for use by native Africans. To promote the game in his home region out west, he proposed a trophy, an engraved bell, that would be called the Obama Cup. Mboya disliked the idea, especially the name.

"What Paul Mboya did not want was someone to feel he was greater than he was, so he told [Hussein Onyango] to stay low, and then came this question of the trophy for football," recalled Dick Opar, a relative by marriage to Hussein Onyango. "He didn't like it for this to be called the Obama Cup. This didn't please Old Man Mboya. These were small and petty things, but Mboya didn't like the idea of bringing prominence to Obama." As Opar and three other relatives recalled, the chief expressed his displeasure with a cascade of insults, all on the same theme, as the two rivals stood under the shade of Mboya's capacious fig tree. Hussein Onyango was nothing more than a *jadak*. He was an Obama. Obamas were aliens, foreigners, settlers in the Kendu Bay area. They came from somewhere else. Kanyadhiang was not their ancestral homeland, not where they should be buried. *Jadak*.

Soon after the confrontation, Hussein Onyango packed up his radio, his bicycle, his Koran, his little red book proving he was registered by the colonial government as a domestic servant, rounded up his substantial herd of cattle and goats, and retraced the route that his great-grandfather Obong'o had taken to Kanyadhiang four generations earlier: down the oxcart path to Kendu Bay, across the waters by dhow and steamship, north and west to Kisumu, beyond the swampy fishing villages, out along the dusty road past the giant boulders, and on to the valley of his ancestral homeland in Nyang'oma Kogelo. Even some of his brothers and other relatives were not sorry to see Hussein Onyango go. They thought he was too disruptive, unpleasant, and bossy, and had made their own complaints about him to Chief Mboya in recent years. And now that he was back in the land of his ancestors, once again he was taken for an outsider. He was approaching fifty. He also had with him his twenty-five-year-old fourth wife, his teenager fifth wife, and three young children, two daughters and a son, all from the fourth wife. Their names were Nyaoke, Auma, and Barack.

Hussein Onyango's son was not yet seven. He had been born inside the euphorbia hedges of the K'obama homestead on June 18, 1934. In Luo tradition, his placenta was buried on the grounds. In Muslim practice, against Luo tradition, he was circumcised. In local oral history, the period of Barack Hussein Obama's coming into the world would be remembered as the time of the hippo disaster in nearby Lake Victoria. A crew of Luo men were clearing brush along the shoreline, part of a government effort to combat sleeping sickness, the parasitic disease transmitted by the tsetse fly. Along came a party of Dutchmen who had traveled to western Kenya for their annual hippopotamus hunt. Whether the Luo volunteered as guides or were ordered to help was a question raised afterward, but not answered. They took the Dutch sportsmen out in their long canoes, and at ten in the morning a hippo surfaced under one of the boats and upended it, splashing ten Africans and one white hunter into the dark waters. Three natives drowned or were eaten by the hippo before other canoes could paddle to the rescue.

By then the Luo had experienced six decades of interaction with Europeans, whose existence previously had been unknown to almost all of them. Henry M. Stanley, the famed British journalist and adventurer, had circumnavigated the great African lake in 1875 and 1876, passing along the shores of Luoland on his way to Uganda. (This was the same Stanley after whom Stanley Armour Dunham was later named by his young mother, Ruth, in faraway Kansas.) As European nations large and small undertook a frenzied scramble for control of the African continent, the British East Africa Protectorate was established, and by 1894 the British were imposing the first semblance of colonial governance in western Kenya, led by an official named Charles William Hobley.

With superior technology and weaponry and a penchant for organization that marked their colonial empire, the British spent the next two decades solidifying their hold in the region, here squelching an uprising with an expeditionary force, there using the enticements of jobs or spiritual salvation. In the larger scheme of Kenyan colonization, most of western Kenya, away from the lake, was a distant afterthought, the people dismissed as poor and primitive, their land only moderately arable and less coveted by white settlers than fertile swaths in the Rift Valley and central highlands. But from the start, the Luo exhibited a keen ability to categorize white officials who tried to oversee them. They gave Hobley the name of a respected elder, Obilo. Their nicknames for other early colonial officials were more discerning: H. R. Tate was Arm Swinger; P. L. Deacon was Long Neck; D. R. Crampton was Hard Hitter; S. H. Fazan was Ladies' Man; W. E. Brock was Bull Neck; H. H. Horne was Tall Hen; C. A. Adams was Keeps to Himself; J. M. Pearson was Stammers; and Major F. C. Jack was Can a Leopard Answer Questions.

Onyango, in the years before he converted to Islam and adopted the name Hussein, was part of the first generation of Luo who grew up with white people constantly within range and taking charge. He was five years old when the area was opened to railroad service in December 1901, following the completion of the six-hundred-mile Uganda Railway from Mombasa on the Indian Ocean inland to a railhead at the top of the Gulf of Kavirondo. The British called this settlement Port Florence, named for the wife of Ronald Preston, the lead railway engineer. It later became the provincial capital, Kisumu. Within a few years Port Florence was a major transportation hub, with the railway connecting to the SS *Winifred* and five other British steamers that plied Lake Victoria to ports in Uganda.

The construction of the Uganda Railway was regarded by many as a dumbfounding exercise, so much so that it was nicknamed the Lunatic Express. It cost the British treasury about 6.5 million pounds, an enormous sum in that day, and in the five-plus years that it was being built hundreds of workers died, many victims of lion attacks along the plains of Tsavo that were so frequent and bloodcurdling they became worldwide news. Workers imported from India seemed especially vulnerable to the lion attacks. But the railway was completed, for all that, and in a precise, British sort of way, an achievement that quickly drew the praise of young Winston Churchill, then undersecretary for the colonies in the Foreign Office. "Short has been the life, many the vicissitudes, of the Uganda Railway," Churchill exclaimed from London in *My African Journey,* a travelogue that included an account of his adventures along the route to Port Florence, during which he disembarked here and there to hunt lions and rhinos. "Nearly ten thousand pounds a mile were expended on construction. And first, what a road it is! Everything is in apple-pie order. The track is smoothed and weeded and ballasted as if it were the London and North-western. Every telegraph has its number, every mile, every hundred yards, has its mark."

Three motives were ascribed to the creators of the Lunatic Express. First was a convoluted military argument that a rail connection to Lake Victoria would be of strategic value to the British in dissuading an enemy – the Germans, in most scenarios – from trying to dam the Nile at its source in the East Africa Protectorate. Second was that the rail would carry settlers to the western reaches of the territory in the effort to make the colony white man's country. And third, a companion to the second, was that it would bring missionaries who could inculcate in the natives Western values through the structured influence of Christianity. That last idea brought the earliest results to Luoland.

Generations later, when the American grandson of Hussein Onyango was running for president of the United States and then serving in that office, some of those opposing him would make much of the notion that he was the descendant of a Muslim and perhaps, they claimed, a closet Muslim himself – a *jadak* in their midst. History tells another story, and a large part of it is this: in the improbable journey that took the Obamas from a mud hut in the village of Kanyadhiang to the White House in Washington, D.C., the Muslims had virtually nothing to do with it. On the other hand, Christian missionaries played pivotal roles at several critical junctures along the way. President Obama never would have existed without them.

The evangelism began in late November 1906, when Onyango was ten, with the arrival of Arthur Asa Carscallen, a pastor in the Seventh Day Adventist Church. Carscallen, a Canadian farm boy who had trained in London to "sell the gospel," rode the Lunatic Express across Kenya from Mombasa to Port Florence, eager to bring religion to the natives. After being put off by an acerbic colonial functionary who said that Kenya had more than enough missionaries of all shapes and sizes, he found a white trader to ferry his small party of missionaries across the water to Kendu Bay. Before the year was out, with the help of some accommodating Luo men, they had built a mission house, an oblong grass hut, in the village of Gendia, high on a hill several hundred feet above the mosquito zone, a perch from which they could look down on scores of homesteads around the perimeter of Kendu Bay. One of those was the Obama compound in Kanyadhiang, not two kilometers away.

In the fashion of other Westerners who made their way to Africa, Carscallen brought with him a peculiar bag of attributes. He traveled through Kendu Bay outfitted like a London merchant, in fine shoes, well-cut suit, and elegant necktie, bumping around on his ubiquitous bicycle, part evangelist, part trader, the gospel one of many goods he was adept at peddling. Though he dropped out of school at age ten in Canada, he was a self-taught scholar, gifted enough to pick up Luo, an unusual Nilotic language (tonal and sing-songy) unlike the Bantu dialects spoken by other tribes in Kenya. "I started preaching in the native language in three months," he later wrote, "but I still wonder whether the natives understood me or not." Luo had an oral tradition, no written history, but Carscallen, using a donated typewriter, compiled a five-thousand-word Luo–English dictionary and began translating the Gospel of Matthew into Luo. "From the beginning the natives were very friendly and seemed glad to have us," he noted. "They asked us if we were married and brought young girls for our wives. We told them that we did not want to get married" – in fact he married an American woman who arrived a year later – "and hired boys to do work in our houses. . . . At first the natives came to church absolutely naked."

Onyango was one of the Luo boys who encountered the Seventh Day Adventists soon after Carscallen's group arrived. Smart and curious, he was intrigued by their dress, language, and precise manner. Another Luo, Paul Mboya, was equally taken by the missionaries, and as a young man left his compound to live and work in the household of Carscallen's colleague, L. E. A. Lane. Mboya learned to read and write English and eventually became ordained in the church. How enthusiastically Onyango took to the religion is not clear, but he did attend the mission's Gendia Primary School for a few years and also achieved English literacy. In the oral history of the Obamas, family members say that Onyango disappeared for a time during his teens and came back wearing Western clothes and acting strangely, more like a white man. He might have been living at a missionary's house, or on the Adventist compound, where there was a large grass hut housing many of the Luo boys, a rough version of a boarding school.

The grip white men held on western Kenya had tightened considerably by then. In October 1911 the British colonial commissioner of what later became Nyanza province announced new rules limiting the freedom of natives, who were defined as "any person whose mother belongs to an aboriginal race or tribe of Africa." Natives were to live only in their tribal villages, now called reserves, and were not to reside in towns or settlements with Europeans unless they worked there and had been issued employment passes. Commissioner John Ainsworth said he was most concerned about natives straying into towns and away from tribal influence. "Practically none of these people are able to understand the responsibilities of individual citizenship, they are in fact just a rabble, uncontrolled and leaderless," he wrote. "They consequently become in a very short time a lazy good-for-nothing part of the population and a common danger to society generally."

Even with such dismissive rhetoric, Ainsworth was among the least reactionary colonial officials. Within the context of that time and place, he was more sympathetic to Africans than were many of his peers. One year after imposing the restrictive regulations, he urged the creation of local councils to address native conditions. "Unless they are understood by the white public there exists the great danger of a rift between black and white which in

equatorial Africa cannot do any good to the white," he wrote. "It therefore behooves us to try and bring native affairs out of the narrow groove which many
have so far followed and to try to give them the importance they deserve."
That modest concession came with a price. It was soon followed by a range
of taxes – the hut and poll tax, liquor licenses, fishing licenses, game licenses,
opium licenses – all with the effect of further controlling native lives.

The reaction to white domination took many forms in western Kenya,
political and religious, but one of the first and most strident anti-European responses arose with the cult of Mumbo, which began in 1913 and took root in
the two disparate locales of the Obamas in Luoland, not far from their old and
new homesteads in Nyang'oma Kogelo and Kanyadhiang. Mumbo was the inspiration of Onyango Dunde, a member of the Alego subtribe near Nyang'oma
Kogelo. As he recounted the story, he was sitting in his hut one evening looking toward Lake Victoria when a giant snake appeared on the watery horizon,
standing on end, so big that its head reached the clouds. The snake swallowed
Onyango, then spit him out back into his hut and spoke to him. "I am the god
Mumbo," the serpent deity announced. "I have chosen you to be my mouth-
piece. Go out and tell all Africans, especially the people of Alego, that from
henceforth I am their god. Those who believe in me will be rich in cattle and
sheep, those who don't their livestock will die out. Let your hair grow, don't
cut it. Don't wear Western clothes. The day is coming when white people will
disappear."

The snake then vanished, and Onyango Dunde started spreading the word.
In his interpretation, Christianity was evil, and white people and those who
cooperated with them would be removed from Luoland or turned into monkeys. Mumbo swiftly spread around Lake Victoria, and from down near Kanyadhiang four Luo elders made a pilgrimage to Onyango Dunde with goats
and oxen and became his adepts. In the annual administrative report for the
province, a British official tried to describe these disciples of Mumbo: "They
would throw some kind of fit of religious ecstasy during which words poured
out in unintelligible torrent. They became priests and witch doctors invested
with supernatural powers."

The cult of Mumbo was intoxicating but extreme. Most Luo in the region
found ways to accommodate old and new, blending the gospel with tribal

rituals, assuming both Western and tribal names. This was the case in the Obama family, as Onyango briefly adopted the name Johnson and his younger brothers were named Solomon, Zak, Joshua, Patrick, and Jonathan. As Mumboism gained followers around Kendu Bay, its renunciation of Christianity put it into direct conflict with the Adventists, whose proselytizing had won more converts from the Luo population, including powerful tribal headmen. When the two clashed in the summer of 1915, the Christian adherents prevailed, and not in a spirit of brotherly love. Using whips, they rounded up long-haired Mumboites and sent them off to work on a road gang.

Onyango missed that melee. At the start of World War I, as German troops based in German East Africa (much of which became Tanganyika and then Tanzania) started to move on Nyanza, one of the men in Carscallen's party left for Nairobi and took Onyango along "because he was so enterprising," recalled John Ndalo Aguk, who decades later was mentored by him and heard his many stories. "They saw him as a very promising boy. They liked him. . . . And when the war broke out he was away, working for the white man in Nairobi. . . . I think the whites he stayed with in Nairobi convinced him to join the army and go to war." The records of Onyango's service with the British in World War I no longer exist. Relatives and friends say he served with the Carrier Corps of the King's African Rifles and that because of his facility with English, Luo, and Swahili he was valuable to British officers as an interpreter for African porters, cooks, and laborers. His service took him throughout Kenya and south into German East Africa, ending on the island of Zanzibar, where after the war he married, converted to Islam, and took the name Hussein.

That first wife and his next two from Nyanza bore no children. For a time after the war he brought in an orphaned nephew named Peter as an adopted son and took him to Nairobi to work with him, calling him by the Muslim name Hassan. When Hassan came of age he moved out, disowned Islam, and reverted to being Peter. His descendants still live in the K'obama compound in Kanyadhiang. It was the fourth wife of Hussein Onyango who became pivotal in the generational progression of the Obamas. She was the one who gave birth to the first Barack Hussein Obama. Her name was Akumu, the daughter of Njoga. She was beautiful and light-skinned, and her relatives say that her American grandson's complexion and bearing remind them of her. If she seemed the most distant and disconnected of the four grandparents of the future president, it was because her relationship with Hussein Onyango was brutish and short.

Akumu, born around 1918, the year of Stanley Dunham's birth in Kansas, grew up not far from Kendu Bay in a family homestead on the edge of Simbi Nyaima, a crater lake, one of the hallowed sites in Luoland. Simbi Nyaima means "the village that sank." In Luo legend, an ugly old woman appeared in the village one day begging for food and shelter. There was a celebration going on at the chief's house when she arrived, but the chief was unsympathetic to the stranger's plight, telling her that he would strike her unless she left. Only one mother in the village looked out for her and gave her something to eat. The old woman thanked the generous villager by warning her to gather her family and flee. As soon as they left, a ferocious storm struck the village, which vanished into what became the crater lake Simbi Nyaima.

By the time of Akumu's childhood, her family had been converted to Christianity by Pastor Carscallen and the local Seventh Day Adventists. She attended primary school for three years, a standard amount of education for Luo girls then, and was active at church and sang in the choir. As the accepted story goes, told by relatives on both sides, she was fifteen when Hussein Onyango caught sight of her in 1933 carrying fish to market in a basket balanced atop her head. He was so taken by Akumu that he grabbed her by force and took her home. Her brother, hearing what had happened, went to the local chief, and together they rounded up a posse of men who found Hussein Onyango, arrested him, and placed him in jail. He got out of the mess by proclaiming that he loved Akumu, that he had not attacked her, and that he intended to marry her. An agreement was reached: he could have her as his wife for a herd of cows. Some say it was thirty-five cows; others say sixteen, and note that Luo were suspicious when too many were offered, assuming that meant some cows were defective. As the fourth wife of Hussein Onyango, Akumu converted to Islam and took the name Habiba.

Life with Hussein Onyango was never easy, at least not during the rare times when he was around. Akumu had three children in short order, in 1933, 1934, and 1938, and two more who died in infancy. Her husband's demands were relentless, and he whipped her when she disappointed him. If she tried to leave, he found her and dragged her back to her hut. He worked as a cook in Nairobi, then in the city of Gulu in the north of Uganda, then back in Nairobi, then went off for a year with his British employer, Major Dickson, to serve as the man's personal chef during the early stages of World War II, then came back to work in Nairobi again as the "head boy" at the house of the district commissioner. Akumu grew distant from him, and when Hussein Onyango revisited Kanyadhiang in late 1940 he started looking for a fifth wife.

An old man in Kendu Bay told him of a granddaughter named Sarah Ogwel, an illiterate teenager who had not attended school but was "smart, clever, and hardworking and who could take care of him." Sarah was born in 1922, marked in western Kenya as the first year an aircraft appeared in the sky. She was the daughter of Omar Oketch, a Kendu Bay butcher, and Apia, who sold *ugali* (a popular gruel that served as a staple for most meals) and *nyoyo* (corn mixed and boiled with beans) to fishermen and sailors at the Kendu pier along the Lake Victoria shoreline. The parents did not want to consent to her marriage. They had heard horrible things about Hussein Onyango, she said later, that he "was cruel and brutal [and] accustomed to caning wives with whips." But the grandfather persuaded them that Sarah was clever enough to survive, and the marriage was consummated in 1941. Hussein Onyango won her hand by providing her family with cattle, the number increased to compensate for his known brutality, a common practice among the Luo. Three goats for Sarah's uncle were also thrown into the deal. "He paid a price because he was a bad person," Sarah said.

Not long after, when Hussein Onyango moved his entire family to Nyang'oma Kogelo after being called *jadak* by Chief Paul Mboya in the quarrel over the football trophy, Akumu's disillusionment grew and her fights with her husband turned more violent. She felt isolated in the dusty village with the Alego people, so far from her Kendu Bay roots. The neighbors were unfriendly, many believing that Hussein Onyango had brought bad luck by moving into an abandoned homestead that had been haunted by sudden deaths two decades earlier. The younger wife, Sarah, was spending more time with Hussein Onyango there and in Nairobi. On a rare trip home, after a disagreement with Akumu, he walked around his property, where they were growing mangos, oranges, and maize, and found a plot to dig a grave. He told Akumu that he would bury her alive.

Fearing for her life, Akumu fled on foot, making it to Kisumu that night. The next day she continued on, taking a dhow across the gulf and down to her family's homestead on the edge of the crater lake Simbi Nyaima. She was welcomed. The village did not vanish. But her life in the Obama subclan was over. Akumu had left Nyang'oma Kogelo without her children, Hussein Onyango did not attempt to retrieve her, and she never went back. She did not take her own life, as Ruth Dunham had done in Topeka after feeling mistreated by her husband, but the story line in Kenya had parallels to the one in Kansas: a mother removing herself from the scene, leaving young children behind.

Not long after Akumu fled, her two oldest children, Nyaoke and Barack, ran away from their new homestead and tried to find her. They planned to take their little sister, Auma, with them, but decided that it would be too hard to carry her. Auma would later say the children wanted to be with their mother and felt shunned by their stepmother, Sarah. Nyaoke and Barack made it down to Lake Victoria before a local chief found them and returned them to Nyang'oma Kogelo.

For all the family melodrama and comings and goings in the outlands of western Kenya, most of Hussein Onyango's time was spent in the big city of Nairobi. In some work years during the 1940s his most extended stay in Nyanza would be for no more than two or three weeks. Sometimes he would walk the entire distance there and back. The rest of the year he was in the colonial capital, where he moved easily between worlds that were sharply separated physically and culturally, black and white, rich and poor. His connections were all over town. He would go to the Kaloleni Estate, one of the main working-class neighborhoods for African migrants from western Kenya, mostly Luo, but also some from the Luhya tribe. The Luo and Luhya, whose home territory was to the north of Luoland, had been on friendly terms historically although their tribal languages derived from different roots and were largely unintelligible to one another, so that they communicated in Swahili or English.

Kaloleni was a densely populated district with its own bars and butcheries, a large all-purpose social hall, and rows of stone houses, low and dark with black tile roofs, that lined the dusty dirt roads. Anyim Nyindha, a bar owner in Kaloleni who came from Siaya district, not far from the Obama homestead in Nyang'oma Kogelo, put Hussein Onyango up for a time between jobs. When not working, Luo men would congregate at the social hall, where they gossiped and looked after one another, seeing who might need help because of a family problem, an accident, a funeral. Hussein Onyango was considered a leader in that group. He also spent time in Majengo, a more impoverished urban sector for native blacks in Nairobi, where, as a less than devout Muslim, he enjoyed drinking *chang'aa*, a traditional gin made from dry corn and sugar. Majengo was known for its sex-for-cash trade (later inspiring a famous local song: "*Majengo siendi tena kuna ndogo ndogo wengu* / I will never ever venture to Majengo again, it is very adulterous, it has so many prostitutes"). He also eventually developed his own urban homestead in Kibera, a district in southwestern Nairobi. Over the decades Kibera had metastasized from its origins as a relatively out-of-the-way reserve set aside for Sudanese Nubian soldiers who had fought for the British in World War I into a chaotic and sprawling slum, one of the largest in all of Africa, lacking water, electricity, and other basic services. Fastidious as he was, Hussein Onyango could find comfort there. Along with the Nubians, with whom he shared being both a war veteran and a Muslim, there were also so many Luo in Kibera that one section was called Little Kisumu.

Most of the time, though, Hussein Onyango was in places that had nothing in common with Kaloleni or Majengo or Kibera. He was working and living in the wealthy white neighborhoods of Milimani and Muthaiga, home of the Muthaiga Country Club, with its high tea, lush hedges, and impressive taxidermy, where the prized lion could startle but not pounce, having been stuffed in a fierce attack position. At different times he worked for a mayor, a district commissioner, an army officer, and various embassy officials, all of whom expected him to be available at all hours. He and other African help slept in small bunks or dorms, usually located at the back of the property. For most of his employers, Hussein Onyango was the main chef and supervisor of the staff, according to John Ndalo Aguk, the Kanyadhiang relative who worked with him for several years. He would wake at five, bathe and put on his house uniform of trousers and shirt (each employer required a different color), then set about directing the kitchen staff making breakfast, ensuring that the proper ingredients had been acquired and prepared, the table was set, and the workplace was kept to his immaculate standards. After serving breakfast he would take orders for lunch, and after lunch he would be free until four-thirty, when he would start preparing supper. (It was often during that break between lunch and dinner preparation that he would walk the four kilometers to Majengo to enjoy his *chang'aa*.) The employers called him Hussein and dealt directly with him. He stood out for his ability to handle budgets, arrange a table, and cook specialty dishes, including potato crisps. His salary was on the higher end of the scale for native "head boys" – as much as a hundred shillings a month.

More than sixty years later, long after he had died, his fifth wife, Sarah Ogwel, would relate a story about how Hussein Onyango had surreptitiously helped anticolonial insurgents in Nairobi and ended up being detained and imprisoned in 1949 by British officials. According to the story she said was told to her, he was taken to Kamiti Prison outside Nairobi, where he was whipped and tortured by African guards acting on the instruction of their British overseers. The most gruesome means of trying to get him to talk, by her account, was to squeeze his testicles with iron pincers. No one was allowed to see him, she said, and he lingered in prison for four to six months before finally being released.

Incidents of that sort certainly happened in that period, the beginning of a decade of increasing rebellion by native Kenyans and brutal and massive retaliation by British authorities. And yet in its specifics the story seems unlikely. There are no remaining records of any detention, imprisonment, or trial of Hussein Onyango Obama. Sarah did not witness any of it, and she is the only person to offer details. While there would be no obvious reason for her to contrive such a tale, her accuracy on other matters that can be documented is uneven. She speaks only in Luo, knowing some Swahili and no English, so her quotes are dependent upon the inclinations of the interpreter. And five people who had close connections to Hussein Onyango said they doubted the story or were certain that it did not happen.

John Ndalo Aguk, who worked with him before the alleged incident and kept in touch with him on a weekly basis in Nairobi thereafter, when he was placed in the homes of several employers at Hussein Onyango's recommendation, said he knew nothing about a detention or imprisonment and would have noticed if his mentor had gone missing for several months. Zablon Okatch, a Luo who worked with Onyango after the supposed incarceration, when they were servants in the house of American embassy personnel, said, "Hussein was never jailed. I know that for a fact. It would have been difficult for him to get a job with a white family, let alone a diplomat, if he once served in jail. . . . All prospective workers had to have details about themselves scrutinized at the Labour Office." Charles Oluoch, whose father, Peter, had been adopted by Hussein Onyango when he was a young boy, said he doubted the story: "He did not take part in politics, nor did he have any trouble with the government in any way." Auma Magak, Hussein Onyango's daughter, disputed the story but offered a different version: "He was not detained. There was an incident where some thugs kidnapped him. He mysteriously disappeared. He was taken to a river where he was tied and left there. Some leopards were around but left him alone. But the detainment never happened. He was working in Nairobi during those years. He never disappeared [for six months]." Perhaps the most authoritative account disputing Sarah's story came from Dick Opar, who went on to become a senior police official in Kenya. "At that time I would have known," Opar said. "It may have been for a day or two. People make up stories. If you get arrested, you say it was the fight for independence, but they are arrested for another thing. No. No. I would have known. I would have known. If he was in Kamiti Prison for only a day, even if for a day, I would have known."

Several pieces of logic contradict the story. First, if Hussein Onyango had been imprisoned, even if one were to further accept that he was eventually cleared of whatever charges were against him, he likely would have had difficulty, as Zablon Okatch noted, securing employment in the homes of security-conscious white officials in the following years, when the country was in turmoil and there were increasing concerns about the motives and loyalties of Kenyan workers. Yet he continued to be hired throughout the next decade, and became especially popular with foreign officers at the American embassy in Nairobi. Second, it is also unlikely that his son would have been accepted into the most prestigious boarding school in western Kenya within a year of his father's imprisonment, or that after many months without a salary the family would have been able to afford the tuition.

He was a stubborn man, a stern man, and could be an intemperate one too, but Hussein Onyango was not hidebound or narrow. As a converted Muslim, he did not let his religion define him, nor did he impose it on his son beyond the name he bestowed upon him, Barack Hussein Obama. They both were registered as members of the Nyanza Luo Muslim Association on the British colonial list of "Mohamedans in South Nyanza" (the son under the name Baraka Onyango), but the old man seemed to live two different lives. He rarely visited the mosque during his long periods in Nairobi, where he lived a less than devout life in his free time. And he did not hesitate to send Barack to schools run by Christian missionaries for his entire education in Kenya, from 1941 to 1953. Before the family left Kanyadhiang, young Obama had attended the Gendia Primary School run by the Seventh Day Adventists on the hill above Kendu Bay. After they moved to Nyang'oma Kogelo in 1942, he was sent to Ng'iya Intermediate School in the Siaya district, run by the Church Missionary Society (CMS), the evangelist arm of the Anglican Church. His stepmother, Sarah, would later tell the story that he was first enrolled at a Presbyterian Church school closer to home but left because Leonora Odima was the teacher and he did not want to be disciplined by a woman. It was just as likely that Hussein Onyango wanted him to go to Ng'iya because it was a better institution. Ng'iya had its own building and classrooms, which most other schools in the area did not. It also offered the opportunity for young Barack to continue to learn in Swahili and English, along with Dholuo, the only language Sarah knew. Hussein Onyango hoped that his son would be even more of an African Englishman than he was, able to compete with *wazungu* at their own game. Though it was never easy to please Hussein Onyango, Barack had always impressed him with his superior intelligence. He had memorized the English alphabet when he was still a toddler, could read by the age of five, and always learned new things faster than his peers.

When he was fourteen, young Obama was among three boys from Ng'iya who tested well enough to be selected for interviews at CMS Maseno, the Anglican secondary school in the town of Maseno, located on a hill a few miles

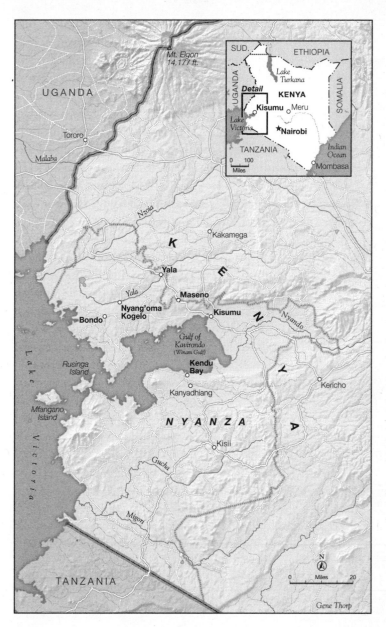

inland from Kisumu. At the time, there were only two high schools for native Africans in all of Nyanza province, both sponsored by Western churches: CMS Maseno and St. Mary's, a Catholic school in the town of Yala in the Gem district farther to the northwest. The government was so sluggish in providing educational opportunities in western Kenya that it was criticized by its own bureaucrats in the district commissioner's office in their 1950 annual report from Kisumu. The colonial administration in Nairobi had failed to send a government education officer to the province for two years, the report noted, adding that it was "a sore point with Luo" that Nyanza lacked a single government-sponsored secondary school. Luo students who could not afford or qualify for Maseno or St. Mary's faced unsatisfactory alternatives. "The demand for educational facilities is insatiable, but it tends to be easily appeased by the provision of very elementary instruction in reading and writing dispensed by poorly qualified and unsupervised teachers in the pathetic belief that that is 'education,'" the report concluded.

Barack found himself among the lucky few when a letter of acceptance to the Anglican school reached his Kogelo homestead. "You will be pleased to learn that you have been admitted to a two-year course at the CMS Maseno School. Entry to Form 3 will depend on character, conduct, and classwork," the school's venerated three C's. In other words, getting in was one achievement; staying there through graduation was another. Satisfying Hussein Onyango was never an easy task, but Barack's being accepted at Maseno pleased him immensely. The old man made the daylong bus ride from his work duties in Nairobi to celebrate and slaughtered a lamb in honor of his son's accomplishment.

The phrase *equatorial Africa* might evoke images of dense and lush jungle in the minds of many Westerners, yet no place could be more equatorial than CMS Maseno: zero degrees latitude, precisely. If one were to draw an equator chalk line around the world, the stripe would run right through the middle of the school property. An Anglican priest named J. J. Willis founded the school in 1906, the same year that A. A. Carscallen began his Seventh Day Adventist mission across the gulf near Kendu Bay. Willis had first traveled through the region in 1900, a year before the Lunatic Express was completed. He was on his way to Uganda then, riding a bicycle, and was struck by the reaction of the local people, friendly and utterly naked, shouting and trying to keep up as they ran behind a wheeled contraption they had not seen before. He returned later with the idea of a church school as a base for spreading the gospel, and built a grass-thatched chapel near an old fig tree with a charred trunk that had been split violently by lightning. The location was chosen with a purpose; the Luo believed the tree was haunted by evil spirits, and Willis wanted it to symbolize the Anglican answer to native superstition. The first four students that year were the sons of local chiefs.

The school grew over the years from one modest building where instruction was only in Dholuo to a sprawling campus modeled on the elite schools of England and featuring several dormitories, an E-shaped brick classroom center, a chapel, farm and work sheds, administrative offices, a hospital, playing fields, debating societies, football clubs, even an outdoor stone squash court. The emphasis throughout the first few decades was on technical skills, but by the time Obama enrolled, although there were still hobby courses in carpentry, printing, construction, tailoring, and clerical work, there was more of an academic focus on the sciences, languages, literature, and the arts.

Two school leaders prior to Obama's time there lifted the standards at Maseno. The first was Edward Carey Francis, an educator revered in Kenya for decades thereafter, who had been a mathematics don at Cambridge University before heeding the call in 1928 to leave England and teach in Africa. Francis wrote many textbooks used at the school, including African geography texts, and was overtly sympathetic to Luo students and their families. If he was an evangelist, it was to spread the word of the glory of education more than the prospect of salvation through the Anglican religion. "Maseno," he said, "is and should be a school for [Nyanza] rather than for adherents of our own or any other missionary society." His successor as headmaster, Arthur William Mayor, built on Francis's efforts to turn Maseno into an African replica of a British school. It was during his tenure that graduates were instructed so they could pass examinations leading to the Cambridge School Certificate.

Mayor was in his final year as headmaster when young Obama arrived at Maseno in the fall of 1950. Here was a student who stood out from the beginning: fiercely intelligent, cheerful, flamboyant, with a pride that bordered on arrogance and a deep, reverberating voice that lent him an authority beyond his teenage years. He was called Barry by classmates, or if they used his full first name they pronounced it *BARE-ick*. In Luo he was also known as Wuod Akumù Nyanjoga, the son of Akumu, who was the daughter of Njoga. His personal identity remained with the biological mother who had left, but in school he would stress that he lived in Siaya district, the larger region surrounding Nyang'oma Kogelo. Siaya was known for its brainpower, producing many of the most brilliant students preceding Obama at Maseno, including Bethwell A. Ogot, who would become a prominent Kenyan historian, and five future cabinet ministers.

These graduates, even those who later fought against colonial rule, took on classic British affectations. They called themselves Old Boys and returned annually for Maseno Old Boy reunions. Their motto was *Sinani e Lweny, Kinda e teko* – If one did not go to Maseno, then where did one go to school? When they were together, as Ogot later recalled, inevitably they would sing the Maseno Old Boys song "with great gusto." "Whenever I may wander / The spirit leads back to her / My cradle home Maseno / I love you so." The melody was borrowed from an American tune of the Jim Crow South, "I'se Going Back to Dixie."

Tuition at Maseno was many times the cost of Ng'iya Intermediate, with additional examination fees adding up to 160 shillings. Even with aid from Hussein Onyango, who chipped in from Nairobi with part of his cook's salary, and from his stepmother, Sarah, who said she harvested beans and sold them to Indian merchants in nearby Ndere to help, Barack also worked in the farm field during breaks from school and, like many of his classmates, performed chores at the boarding school to fulfill his financial obligations. There was little leeway in the collection of fees. When one of Obama's classmates from Kendu Bay was short on payment, the boy had to walk all the way home around the gulf and persuade his father to sell three cows to make up the difference, a process that cost him a week at school.

Obama lived in Willis House, the oldest dorm, named for the school's founder, played midfielder on the house's intramural football team, and was one of the leading members of its debating society. He wore the school uniform: white shirt, khaki shorts, no tie but a badge on the shirt with an image of the Bible and the cross and the saying PERSEVERANCE LEADS TO SUCCESS. Although his father was a Muslim and he and his classmates attended mandatory prayer services in the chapel every morning before class and again in early evening, he showed no religious inclinations. "We prayed too much – that was a summary of it," recalled Gilbert Ogutu, who would later become a professor of religious studies at Nairobi University. "The moment you got to Maseno there is no way you are going to tell anybody that you are a Muslim or you are an atheist. You have to go to church, or you are out. You have to fit into the Maseno way of doing things. . . . And we were going to heaven while the neighboring schools were going to hell."

Midway through Obama's first year, the administration changed. A. W. Mayor was replaced as principal by B. L. Bowers, a hefty Englishman with a wheezy voice who put renewed emphasis on Maseno's religious roots but lacked his predecessor's stature. Bethwell Ogot remembered how he and his classmates in biology, one of the science classes Bowers taught, would challenge him to the point of exhaustion: "I remember one day when he was teaching us evolution we raised so many whys until we got back to the beginning of the universe. He could not explain this. In desperation he threw his hands in the air and shouted 'GOD MADE IT SO!'" Challenges of that sort became increasingly common at Maseno as the 1950s began, delineating a change in attitude of young Luo men toward white authority figures that corresponded with a larger turning point in the relationship between Africans and Englishmen in the colony.

In the Maseno log book for 1951, school officials made note of a rebellion among students in the class ahead of Obama's. No reason for it was stated in the document, but Maseno graduates from that era recalled later that they were protesting harsh treatment and the amount of chores expected of them on top of schoolwork. According to the log, a group of students marched to the principal's office and "refused to disperse when ordered to do so. As a result, the principal delivered an ultimatum." The students responded by collecting their belongings and staging a walkout, and by noon that day they were all on the way back to their various homesteads scattered around Luoland. But the protest did not last long. By one o'clock "the nearest parent had ordered his son to return to school," and gradually all but one came back. When punishments were meted out, ten prefects – the upperclassmen responsible for overseeing their peers – were expelled.

By then the school was hearing distant echoes of an anticolonial insurgency that came to be known as Mau Mau. The name has no literal or symbolic meaning in any tribal language, and was first used, or misused, by British officials in 1948 to depict a secret society within the largest Kenyan tribe, the Kikuyu, who had sworn oaths (holding the bloody meat of a sacrificed goat in the left hand) to rid their land of colonial domination. The Kikuyu had the strongest grievance against the British. For several decades they had been displaced from their farms and homesteads in the territory outside Nairobi, in Central province and the Rift Valley, to make way for European settlers who coveted the land and were determined to make Kenya a "white man's country." Though whites constituted less than 1 percent of the population, they controlled nearly 33 percent of the best farmland in the colony, which was placed off-limits to anyone with dark skin.

In the Western imagination, Mau Mau evoked stereotypes of large gangs of primitive Africans slipping in and out of forest hideaways and randomly inflicting horrific violence on white people with their machete-like *pangas*. The facts, when they eventually emerged, told a different story, but the prevailing narrative at the time had the hyperbolic effect of placing many black Kenyans who opposed colonialism, especially Kikuyu, in the category of ritualistic murderers and terrorists. In October 1952 the new governor of Kenya, Sir Evelyn Baring, intensified the colonial response by declaring a state of emergency and detaining the most outspoken Kikuyu political activists, including Jomo Kenyatta, leader of the Kenya African Union, claiming they were all part of the Mau Mau conspiracy. Obama was in his third year at Maseno when that happened.

For three reasons – because the Luo had not been displaced by white settlers, because Nyanza province was thought to be improving economically, and because there was historic tension between the Kikuyu and Luo tribes – British authorities in western Kenya assumed that Luoland would be relatively free of the troubles bubbling up elsewhere. The annual political report from Kisumu in 1952 expressed some concern that the large number of Luo men who migrated to Nairobi for jobs might return home with more political awareness, and also noted a few pockets in the region that might be "favorable germinating beds for the seeds of sedition," but concluded that "the bulk of Nyanza Africans remain disinterested."

The principal at Maseno reflected this attitude as the 1952 school year got under way. In a letter to alumni, B. L. Bowers seemed preoccupied with prettifying the chapel's interior by fitting new blue curtains behind the altar, finding some way to rid the building of white ants that were "playing havoc" with the walls, and reroofing four dormitories with corrugated iron sheets. "We can count ourselves fortunate that we have not had to contend with subversive propaganda or work in a hostile atmosphere of suspicion and hatred," Bowers wrote, alluding to Mau Mau. "Nevertheless, certain articles in the press, and idle talk, have done much to harm race relations, and it behooves us all to judge ourselves before we start to criticize others. The devil is doing his utmost to tear the world to pieces by turning men against their fellows, and there is only one power that can resist him: the power and love of Jesus Christ and his Church."

Some students questioned the universality of Bowers's version of Christian love. Did it apply to them? Y. F. O. Masakhalia, who decades later would serve as a cabinet minister, fondly remembered Bowers as a "highly religious and disciplined man" who wrote a fine recommendation for him when he graduated and whose wife generously tutored him at their home. But James Mbori, the student who had been suspended from school until his family sold cows to pay his tuition fees, found his treatment at the hands of the principal and his wife less pleasant. "Mrs. Bowers would turn her nose on you and show contempt," Mbori asserted. "She would not look at you, and never smiled. She considered you some belittled wild animal. When you left, she would physically spray the place with an antiseptic used for spraying the latrine . . . treating us as if we were wild animals because we were dark. She was contemptuous."

There was one Kikuyu student in Obama's class, and he disappeared soon after the emergency was declared. The other students knew what was happening beyond their school walls, perhaps far more than Bowers and his white colleagues realized. "When it [the emergency] was declared, it affected us. We were fairly mature students, we had an understanding of current affairs, and it was a shock," James Mbori said. Some of the teachers were fellow Luo who had been educated in England and returned with an anticolonialist political perspective that they hid from their employers. One African staff member, S. G. Anyany, who came from the home village of Jaramogi Oginga Odinga, the prominent Luo political activist (and himself a Maseno Old Boy), ordered his students to close all the windows of the history classroom one day. Then, in a soft voice, Anyany said that the British had dominated native peoples all over the world and Kenya needed nationalists who would resist colonialism.

By the end of that semester, the native uprising seemed to be coming closer to home. Several Luo political leaders affiliated with the Kenya Africa Union were arrested; a transit camp in nearby Kericho bulged with detained Kikuyu; and there were reports of antiwhite gangs squatting in the Kakamega forest some thirty miles north of Kisumu. Principal Bowers was now taking up the rhetorical fight against the rebellion and the racial violence he believed it was perpetrating. "In these days most of us are disturbed by the troubles which have fallen upon this land," Bowers wrote to alumni. "We have seen how easy it is for a few evil men to sow the seeds of hate in the hearts of others until they are capable of committing the most savage atrocities against men, women, and even little children. . . . God is calling us to 'Arise and gird up our loins' in His service. To shake off the apathy that has overtaken us. To fill our lamps with oil that they may burn brightly in the darkness that presses upon us." In a separate address to the Old Boys, Bowers acknowledged that the rebellion had breached the walls of his school, though barely. He noted that there had been an "unsettled atmosphere" at Maseno, but said he believed the tension was passing and that "except for the odd boy" the spirit in the school was good.

It is not documented whether young Obama was one of the "odd boys" to whom Bowers was referring, but the timing makes it possible. This was around the period of his troubles at Maseno. Until then, the records show that he had progressed to the top form with academic ease. A brown index card, No. 3422, notes in the precise handwriting of B. L. Bowers the school administration's assessment: "Very keen, Steady, Trustworthy and Friendly, Concentrates, Reliable and Outgoing." "He did brilliantly, he had very good scores," recalled Masakhalia. Obama was among the most popular students in his class, and was known for bringing many friends home with him to Nyang'oma

Kogelo during school breaks or to his old haunts near Kendu Bay and staying up until three in the morning talking and dancing.

But complaints against the Maseno administration that had first surfaced during the quashed student rebellion of 1951 came around again in the spring semester of 1953. This time the atmosphere had grown far more tense because of the nationwide emergency and the pervasive sense of upheaval. The private missionary schools in Kenya were seen as symbols of British colonialism and thus potential Mau Mau targets. Philip Ochieng, a Luo from Rusinga Island in Nyanza province, attended Alliance High School during that era, a school run by the Alliance of Protestant Churches in the heart of Kikuyu country above Nairobi. At pep talks every Friday, his headmaster described the Kikuyu as a criminal tribe and the insurgents as evil Satanists whose aim was to destroy civilization. That included not only Jomo Kenyatta, the political leader who had been imprisoned, but also Ochieng's hero, Tom Mboya (no relation to Chief Mboya, whom Hussein Onyango tangled with), a Luo whose family homestead was also on Rusinga Island and who was gaining prominence in Nairobi as a brilliant labor leader and orator for the cause of independence. Ochieng listened to the headmaster's denunciations and did not speak out, but began to question what he was being told, even while living with a fear of sudden violence. "We used to sleep with *pangas* under our mattresses. We were afraid of Mau Mau, they attacked anything British," recalled Ochieng, who went on to become an illustrious and iconoclastic journalist in Nairobi. "So we literally slept with *pangas*. And we were well guarded on the periphery of the school. We heard noises, screams, in the villages, but we came through four years with no attacks."

In that atmosphere, even out in Luoland, everything was seen through a distorted lens. Student protests that in other eras might have been thought of as a rite of passage for young men testing authority now tended to be viewed as something more sinister. Along with his intellectual prowess, Obama was also known for being "naughty" and "cheeky," two of the favorite Kenyan ways to describe someone who is impertinent. His classmates said he hated to be told what to do by prefects. At a missionary school, when you were told to march, you marched, but Obama took orders as an insult. There were no maids at the school, and the students were expected to clean up their own dorm rooms, but Obama, the son of a man who could become violent when faced with any-thing unkempt, considered cleaning his room beneath his dignity.

When another protest started, an unsigned letter reached the principal's office that wittily and nastily attacked the school administration and listed a set of grievances. An investigation could not determine for certain who was behind the letter, but the headmaster and his aides pinpointed Barack Obama. "I would say they were petty issues, but why his name came up was because he was a very brilliant boy and naturally the school administration thought that whatever was coming from students had to be from him," said Dick Opar, the relative who became a top police official later and studied the matter. "It was a coincidence that such things were going on during the time of the Mau Mau uprising. He was not quite involved with that, but they thought he was. The students just had some grievances." Whatever the motivation, the result was that Obama was suspended from school and never went back, failing to complete the examinations that led to a Cambridge School Certificate.

Rather than return home to Nyang'oma Kogelo or Kanyadhiang, or face the wrath of his father in Nairobi – there would be no slaughtered goat to cele-brate this news – he was dispatched to Mombasa on the Indian Ocean. A close relative was there, Peter Oluoch, who was like Barack's older brother. Peter was the person who had been adopted by Hussein Onyango as a boy, before one of Onyango's five wives produced a son. At age eighteen, Obama took shelter with Peter and his family. His facility with languages and writing skills helped him find a job as a clerk for a real estate company. Nearly a year later, on leave, he passed through Nairobi and stopped at his father's workplace. Hussein Onyango had great hopes for Barack and was not impressed by his salary on the coast. Look for a job in Nairobi, he said. Barack never returned to Mombasa; he stayed in the capital city for five years, until 1959, a critical period in the struggle to create a new nation and also in the rise of the Obama family. It was in Nairobi that Hussein Onyango's son found two crucial people – one a charismatic Kenyan freedom fighter, the other a Christian woman from Texas – who would help him work his way out of the trap that he found him-self in, out of Luoland and Nairobi, out of Kenya, and on to America.

CHAPTER 3

IN THIS OUR LIFE

U nder her sophomore photograph in the Augusta High yearbook, Madelyn Payne chose to characterize herself with the phrase "Don't judge
me by my name." In terms of the homonym, the Kansas teenager was neither
much of a pain nor feeling much pain at that point in her life. But the quote
took on a new meaning five years later, when Madelyn was a young army wife
giving birth to a daughter at St. Francis Hospital in Wichita.

"Corporal and Mrs. Stanley Dunham of Augusta announce the birth of a
baby daughter Sunday," the local newspaper reported. The delivery occurred
on November 29, 1942. The infant weighed seven pounds, two ounces. The
father, his unit still in training before deployment to the war front overseas,
was due home to visit his wife and newborn daughter later that week. The announcement did not give the baby's name, but the birth certificate did.

First name, Stanley. Middle name, Ann. Stanley Ann Dunham – a name
certain to be judged.

Questions, and assumptions, came along with the name. How could her parents do that to her? Stanley Dunham must have been so determined to have a son that he could not relinquish the idea of a namesake, even of a different gender. How could Madelyn allow it to happen? She must have been so proud of her husband, or so smitten by his flashy appearance in his khaki military uniform, tall and trim, with his hat cocked high, that she relented to his wishes rather than disappoint him. That is the story as it was passed along through the years, the explanation offered by Stanley Ann herself when she came of age, and later by her son, who would have problems enough with his own name. It was all quite believable, fitting the established dynamics of the family. But the full story runs in another direction and is more unlikely. The naming of Stanley Ann had less to do with the dictates of a presumptuous father than with the longing for sophistication of a starstruck mother.

Since her teenage years as a moviegoer at the commodious Augusta Theatre, Madelyn had devotedly followed the film career of Bette Davis, her favorite actress. A new picture starring Davis and Olivia de Havilland reached Kansas during the summer of 1942, while Madelyn was pregnant. In the movie, *In This Our Life,* Davis and de Havilland played the two Timberlake sisters, each with a man's name: Davis was Stanley and de Havilland was Roy. A woman named Stanley: "Madelyn thought that was the height of sophistication!" recalled her brother Charles Payne, and the notion of giving her baby girl that name took hold. The coincidence that her husband was also Stanley only deepened the association.

If Madelyn was drawn to the cosmopolitan essence of Bette Davis, she certainly would not have wanted her daughter to mimic the traits of the character Davis played on-screen. Stanley Timberlake was an irredeemably horrid human being who stole her sister's husband, drove him to suicide, ruined the lives of the rest of her family, then killed a woman and her daughter in an automobile accident and lied about it, trying to place the blame on a black law student, the innocent son of the family maid, before meeting her own end in another crash. Davis was never happy with the film. She said later that the script was inferior to the novel by Ellen Glasgow on which it was based, and further that she had wanted to portray Roy, the good sister, not the evil Stanley (raising the possibility that Madelyn's baby could have been named Roy Ann Dunham). The best part of the movie, she and others thought, was its raw portrayal of racism in American society and the reality that the judicial system then would favor an utterly duplicitous white woman over an honest black man.

Madelyn was back in Augusta and living with her parents on 12th Street after Stanley Ann was born. The earlier hopes that she and Stanley had of creating a new and worldlier existence in California had been cut short by the contingencies of economics and war. When the couple escaped Kansas after her high school graduation and resettled in the Bay Area, the plan was that he would network in the artistic community and develop his creative side, mostly as a writer. This meant that until and unless Stanley connected, Madelyn would support them. She had not worked a day in her life before that, not even as a babysitter, but now had to scrape for whatever she could find for them to survive. This was not the romantic West Coast lifestyle Stanley had told her about when he was wooing her. The best job she could get was as a clerk in a dry-cleaning store. In letters home to her family, Madelyn put the best face on it, telling her landlocked parents and siblings stories about wharves in San Francisco and the waterfront in Sausalito. In retrospect, those difficult first months of marriage might have prepared her for the rest of her life with Stanley Dunham. She learned that she was the tough one of the pair and could keep things going if she put her mind to it.

Soon after the attack on Pearl Harbor, the Dunhams retreated to Kansas. Their personal financial difficulties seemed inconsequential now, overwhelmed by the communal sensibility of a nation at war. Stanley returned with a pocketful of rumors about how the Japanese were going to bomb and strafe cities on the coast. He and Madelyn were lucky to get out of there, he said. The family story was that he signed up to join the war effort immediately upon their return, and many later accounts listed the date as January 18, 1942. Records of the Kansas Selective Service indicate that he enlisted at Butler County Draft Board No. 2 five months later, on June 18. It is possible that the later date is a recording error. According to Ralph Dunham, his brother, who enlisted around the same time, Stanley had talked about trying to be a pilot in the Army Air Forces but flunked the Ishihara color-blindness test. "He wasn't that bad, he could detect bright colors, but those tests are not easy," Ralph said. "If you are color-blind, with all those colored electronic wires, you best not get involved in that field."

For some of Stanley's stateside training, Madelyn kept close, following him to Fort Leavenworth and to a camp in New York State, but she went home for the final months of her pregnancy. The Payne house, already crowded, had more people than beds by the time mother and infant arrived from the hospital after Thanksgiving. There were the parents, R. C. and Lee; Madelyn's sister, Arlene; and her two brothers, Charles, a senior in high school, and Jack, who had become an uncle though he was only five. That made seven, plus Aunt Ruth McCurry, Lee's unmarried sister, who was teaching nearby and took a room to herself. "Boy, it was awful," Charles said of the tight living quarters. "I think they were all happy when I went into the army." But that would not happen until six months later, in June 1943, after he had graduated from Augusta High.

Before he left, Charles experienced a revelation concerning his brother-in-law. Perhaps *revelation* is too strong a word, since he had always suspected something of the sort. It had to do with a trunk that Stanley stored at the Payne house after he left for the service. Like other members of the family – all except Madelyn, apparently – Charles was wary of Stanley. The constant braggadocio, he thought, was to be taken with a healthy dose of skepticism. He had heard Stanley's effusive California tales, how he knew Steinbeck and Saroyan, the famous writers, and was a budding playwright himself with a trunk full of scripts that he had written during his artistic interludes on the coast. Now here was that same trunk. No one around. What was inside?

Charles lifted the lid and poked through the contents. He found books, articles clipped from newspapers and magazines, and a notebook or two, but when it came to the writings of Stanley Armour Dunham, the evidence was slim to none.

Madelyn's role in the workforce, born of necessity in California, continued soon after she and Stanley Ann moved in with her family. She never formally asked her mother to babysit the infant, but because Lee Payne was home caring for Jack, the arrangement was assumed and undertaken without discussion. The home front had changed considerably since Pearl Harbor and the American entry into the war, and most of Madelyn's contemporaries were going off to work. Nina June Swan, Virginia Ewalt, and three other Augusta High classmates became receptionists at the Socony oil refinery in Augusta, which was shipping aviation fuel for warplanes. Frances Kennedy took the second shift at Cessna, which had joined the war production team to build CG-4A gliders and AT-17 trainers. And Hazel Grady, her sister Holice, another young woman, and Nina June's aunt all found jobs at the Boeing plant, a bit farther down Highway 54 on the way into southeastern Wichita. Madelyn Dunham, the young mother, joined them at Boeing. She was hired as an inspector on the new B-29 assembly line.

Wichita, birthplace of both Stanley and Stanley Ann, had transformed into a military-industrial dynamo. As early as September 1941, even before the Pearl Harbor attack, it ranked with San Diego as one of the two hottest defense cities in the nation; employment was up 168 percent in 1941 alone. Most of the new jobs were in the burgeoning aircraft industry, which long had been Wichita's manufacturing specialty, with both Cessna and Beech originating there, joined by the massive and still growing midwestern plant of Seattle-based Boeing. As the demands of World War II lifted Kansas and the country out of the long Depression, the lure of well-paying aircraft work brought hordes of job seekers clamoring to Wichita, much as the oil strikes near El Dorado had filled nearby Butler County with newcomers before and during World War I. The population swelled with 57,580 new residents in the first year of the war alone. Makeshift shacks sprouted on the outskirts of town and stayed up until the government built more than five thousand housing units near the aircraft plants in Hillwood Manor and the aptly named Planeview development.

By the time Madelyn was hired in 1943, Boeing was turning to women to fill its workforce. Two years earlier about 10 percent of employees were female, but in short order after Pearl Harbor, thousands of men from Boeing enlisted in the military, and many of their replacements were women, rising to more than 40 percent of the total. A particular emphasis was placed on women who were diminutive and agile enough to finesse their way into the most hard-to-reach crevices of an airframe. Madelyn was a few inches too tall for that task, but her diploma from Augusta High qualified her for inspection work. Out of need, women were almost everywhere but in the executive offices of the plant by 1944, including a few hundred doing sheet metal work. The extraordinary times allowed them a brief spell of pay equity as well; wartime salaries in the aircraft industry were based on the specific job, not the gender of the worker. There was poetic justice in that circumstance, considering the notable role of Kansas women in aviation history, with a squadron of female flight pioneers soaring from the Sunflower State, among them Betty Browning, Louise Thaden, Mary Haizlip, and the world-famous Amelia Earhart.

The temporary gains for women were not so readily attained by blacks. As the economic historian Peter Fearon noted in a detailed analysis of manufacturing workers in Kansas during World War II, "The race barrier was even more effective than the gender barrier." When war production began, there were no blacks on the aircraft assembly lines in Wichita, and not a single African American recruit among the sixteen hundred Kansans learning semi-skilled trades at the Wichita National Defense Training School, a prime hiring ground for the aircraft companies. Two Kansas politicians, Governor Payne Ratner and Senator Arthur Capper, pushed hard for the integration of black citizens into the state's defense workforce but met resistance from white workers and some employers. Capper's aides were told that Cessna Aircraft, for instance, would hire blacks only as janitors, and their supervisor of janitors had to be white because the pay scale for foremen exceeded the maximum wage for black employees. Boeing had hired a significant number of blacks by 1943, but they complained that they were being confined to the lowest-paying jobs. Not long after Madelyn arrived at the plant, there was a sit-down strike by black workers there protesting their slow rate of advancement.

More than just another cog in the war machine, the Wichita plant became essential to American military air strategy. With the main Boeing plant in Seattle already at capacity churning out B-17 Flying Fortresses, and with early fears that the Japanese might bomb the West Coast, the War Department decided to construct a new and bigger bomber in the Midwest, safe from enemy attack, and gave Wichita the main contract for what would be the B-29 Superfortress. In the largest industrial program ever undertaken in Kansas, a sprawling new facility, Plant II, rose in a former wheat field, and most of 1942 was spent preparing tool-and-die designs, setting jigs in place, and amassing parts from fabrication shops. By the time Madelyn reported for work, she was one of 29,795 workers at the plant, which had become the largest employer in Kansas.

The first B-29s were just coming off the 1943 assembly line then, and the production capacity increased steadily over the next year as the war in the Pacific intensified and the United States prepared for massive bombing raids on Japan. The urgency was so great, and the plane was so complicated to construct, that engineers made major adjustments while the Superfortresses were being built and called for corrections after they were supposedly completed. Each B-29, with a pressurized cabin and remote-controlled turret, was so gargantuan that it contained ten miles of electrical wiring. Only after the intricate maze of wiring was completed did tests reveal that most electrical plugs were improperly fitted, forcing workers to disassemble, rebuild, and resolder more than 586,000 connections in planes that had already left the assembly line, a process that ate up an additional forty thousand man-hours. Another late fix involved the glass in the forward cabin of the Superfortress, which created a slight distortion and had to be replaced.

As an inspector on the B-29 line, Madelyn was a vital member of her assembly team. When someone likened her to the home front female icon of that era, Rosie the Riveter, she took pains to point out that she was an inspector, not a manual laborer. Either way, the grind was the same. Her hours, days, and weeks became consumed by the Superfortress effort. The Boeing facility was so massive – more than three million square feet of productive space – that Hazel Grady, one of Madelyn's Augusta friends, would have troubling dreams about "getting lost in that building" sixty-five years later. Working at Boeing became the dominant routine of their lives. It seemed that they were either on the job, commuting back and forth, or asleep. By 1944, with the mission to rush the Superfortresses into timely action now called "the most important in the nation" by an undersecretary of war, Madelyn and her cohorts began working sixty-hour weeks – six straight days, ten hours a day, Sundays off. In one exhausting spell, they worked twenty-one straight ten-hour days. Nearby restaurants remained open all night, and bowling alleys held league competitions at dawn to accommodate workers coming off shifts. The first shift started at six in the morning and went until quarter to five. The second shift reported for work as the first was leaving and stayed through the night, until three-thirty the next morning.

Madelyn and her Augusta friends rose in early-morning darkness to make the first shift in Wichita. For a brief time they rode a commuter bus back and forth, then joined a carpool run by Nina June Swan's aunt. Driving an old two-door coupe, she made several stops in Augusta to pick up four women, including Madelyn, before heading down Highway 54 to the plant. "We didn't do a lot of talking," recalled Hazel Grady. "We were sleepy-eyed going over and tired coming back. If we had a flat tire, we all had a job to do, and we'd change it ourselves. We would leave Augusta, it must have been five in the morning. It would take thirty-five or forty minutes then." Grady recalled that Madelyn brought a lunch pail to work, sometimes saving a bite for the trip home. One other detail about Madelyn's accoutrements stuck in her memory: "A white linen napkin. That just amazed me. It wasn't paper. So I would say she was a classy woman. I was just fascinated when I saw that white napkin." A touch of Bette Davis sophistication in the backseat darkness on the road to Wichita.

There was not much time for taking care of a baby daughter, only a few weary hours at night, but that is not to imply that Madelyn was chilly about motherhood. In the wartime atmosphere, there was nothing uncommon in her family situation. "That is what people did in that period," said Hazel Grady. The unusual aspect was not who took care of Madelyn's baby but what the baby was called. Rae McCurry, a cousin whose father was Lee Payne's brother, later remembered the last time she saw Madelyn: "Her husband was in the army and she worked in Wichita at the Boeing plant. That was when we went to visit Aunt Lee in Augusta. We were at dinner. [Madelyn] had a baby named Stanley Ann. And I thought that was the strangest name I heard in my life. I just sat there at dinner. I remember my mouth falling sort of open."

On the one day a week that Madelyn usually had free, she spent the morning with Stanley Ann, then often put on a Sunday dress and joined friends for an afternoon of relaxation in their hometown. As Virginia Ewalt remembered, "All of us girls did gather on Sunday afternoons and walk out to the park and take pictures and fool around, have an early sandwich at Lehrs café, and then go to a movie at the Augusta Theatre." Some were married, some not, recalled

Hazel Grady, but they tried to "do things together on Sunday." They all smoked, including Madelyn, mostly Camels and Lucky Strikes, though there were occasional cigarette shortages. In their world the quintessence of suave was the moment in *Now, Voyager,* another Bette Davis film, when the actor Paul Henreid put two cigarettes to his mouth, lit both, and casually handed one to Davis.

When Madelyn reached work on the Thursday morning of June 15, 1944, news of the first significant air power results of the Superfortress was resounding through the plant. From an airfield in China's interior, seventy-five B-29s, all constructed in Wichita, had left the previous night on an unprecedented mission. All but four reached the destination, dropping 107 tons of bombs on the Imperial Iron and Steel Works at Yawata, the main steel-producing plant in Japan. That Nipponese spies warned of the attack beforehand; that Yawata was blacked out in preparation, forcing most of the planes to aim by radar; that most bombs missed their targets and did minimal damage to the steelworks – all this was subordinated in the American telling to the heroics of the moment and the pivotal role played by aircraft workers in Wichita. The Yawata attack in fact began a steady run of B-29 missions over the next fourteen months in which incendiary bombs wrought fiery devastation upon Japanese industrial centers and killed hundreds of thousands of civilians from Nagasaki to Tokyo, all leading to the atomic annihilation of Hiroshima on August 6, 1945, and of Nagasaki three days later – and to the resolution of the war. The planes carrying nuclear weapons, the *Enola Gay* and *Bockscar* (or *Bock's Car*), were also B-29s, but they were specially built in Nebraska, not Kansas.

In the middle of that intense stretch, Madelyn and other Boeing employees luxuriated in a three-day holiday for Christmas 1944, the longest plantwide break in four years. Two months later thousands of aircraft workers congregated outside Plant II to celebrate the 1,000th Superfortress to come off the Wichita assembly line (on the way to a total of 1,644). Henry (Hap) Arnold, commander of the U.S. Army Air Forces, who had personally overseen the B-29 project from his post in Washington, came down to Kansas to lead the festivities. That was also about the time the hundredth former Boeing worker was killed in service overseas.

El Dorado, Augusta, and the other, smaller oil and farm communities of Butler County sent 3,250 young men to the war. Charles Payne enlisted the same month that he graduated from Augusta High, June 1943, freeing up space in the overcrowded house on 12th Street. For all of his senior year, there was no doubt that he would soon be gone. Like Madelyn, he was an excellent student, college material, yet he had made no college plans. He knew the war lay ahead, and he did not think he would survive it. For someone who considered himself "a country bumpkin boy from a little town in Kansas," entry into army life was intimidating, until young Payne realized that he was as smart as or smarter than the other eighteen-year-old boys from Seattle and Berkeley, St. Louis and Newark, and that their cultures were not all that different. "All the boys had heard the same dirty jokes and seen the same pornography, so there was some kind of boys' network that flourished in this country in the thirties and early forties," he recalled.

His brother-in-law, Stanley Dunham, in uniform for a year by then, was in many ways a natural for army life. He loved to smoke, play poker, tell stories, complain about superiors, and act like an authority. Unlike Charles, Stanley did not present himself as a hayseed from the Flint Hills. He was more likely to talk about his California days than his associations with Kansas. Assigned eventually to the 1830th Ordnance Supply and Maintenance Company, a unit that serviced army aviation, he moved to Camp Myles Standish near Boston, where he was promoted to sergeant before embarking for Europe at the beginning of October aboard the troopship RMS *Mauretania,* a converted luxury liner from the Cunard and White Star line. Dunham's unit, which maintenanced not planes but automobiles for air personnel, trucked around England from midfall 1943 through the next spring, alighting near American air squadrons at stations operated by the Royal Air Force. They began at Station Langar, a hundred miles northwest of London, moved to Station Ramsbury far to the west of the city through the Christmas season, then in quick succession caravanned to camps at Welford Berks, Warmwell, and Ibsley before settling near Southampton at Stoney Cross, where they were housed in half-cylindrical Nissen huts made of prefabricated steel.

Stanley's aviation supply company had its share of discipline problems. Fifteen enlisted men were placed in confinement after going AWOL in early

March 1944, and eleven were later tried and convicted under the 61st and 96th Articles of War. Sergeant Dunham kept a clean record. One of his duties as a special-services noncom was to keep the men in his unit informed and entertained, an assignment that played to his strengths. He found legitimate ways to get to London on leave or overnight assignments. One night, on a mission to forage food supplies for his undernourished outfit, he was lounging in the lobby of a military hotel off Russell Square when he encountered his brother, Ralph, who was on leave from his army unit's posting in the Midlands near Litchfield. "I had dinner and I was walking down this big flight of stairs afterwards, and there was my brother sitting on a couch," Ralph Dunham recalled. "And he didn't know I was there, and I didn't know he was there." They spent several hours walking the streets of London, seeing tourist sites, going to the theater, and talking about home and military life and women. Ralph, a bachelor who had entered the service as a twenty-six-year-old with a master's degree, told Stanley about "three good-looking" young British lasses from the auxiliary air force that he had kissed at a New Year's party in Yeovil in southwest England, one of whom would later become Ralph's wife, Betty.

As Stanley Dunham's company prepared for another move – this one for keeps, into the combat zone on the continent – he was assigned to deliver a lecture on "care of the gas mask." Replacement troops refilled the unit to full strength under the command of First Lieutenant Frederick Maloof. Stanley and his compatriots constructed large wooden boxes and stenciled cargo crates for shipment across the English Channel. They fired carbines on the practice range. They undertook a long overnight hike with field packs. They attended lectures on minefields and were given courses on waterproofing armaments. Major Kittering from the medical section paid a visit to instruct them on sexual morality. Another officer warned them about chemical warfare. As the anxiety of his troops intensified, Lieutenant Maloof allowed them a last night of frivolity, and he knew just who could best organize an evening dance party at the gym, his fun-loving noncom, Sergeant Dunham. Stanley collected enough payday money to hire an orchestra and buy liquor. He spread the word in Southampton to fill the hall with local women. The party was "a huge success," the company commander later noted, aside from the fact that the beer supply was exhausted before midnight. "A few of the die-hards were still crooning over the empty beer bottles at an early morning hour."

In the tense days after D-Day, a representative from the Ninth Air Force updated them on "the invasion thus far." They were immunized and reissued dog tags, dug protective foxholes, and watched the first casualty ships return from Normandy with the maimed and dying – and on July 24 they joined the cause. From a marshaling area at the Southampton port, Dunham boarded a Liberty Ship that ferried his unit across the Channel to Omaha Beach. Pounding toward shore in their LSTs six weeks after D-Day, Lieutenant Maloof and his men gazed at the imposing cliffs above them: "We all agreed it was a miracle that the Allies were able to land." The way was clear now. On freed French soil, they aligned with the Ninth Air Force's 367th Fighter Group, which was flying out of a progression of temporary airfields, its P-38 Lightnings and P-47 Thunderbolts providing air support for Allied troops as they rolled forward from the beachheads.

The airstrips, known as ALGs (advanced landing grounds), were laid out in flattened farm fields. Each of more than eighty temporary airfields that dotted France required access roads, supply and ammo dumps, tents for billeting, and makeshift runways constructed from heavy wire or burlap that stretched from thirty-six hundred feet to six thousand feet in length. They were used as briefly as a few days or as long as several months and were abandoned when combat moved forward. Dunham's supply unit followed the 367th fliers to ALGs at Cricqueville-en-Bessin in August, then on to Péray and Clastres in a bitterly cold late October, proceeding to a base near Rheims through the New Year, before finally reaching Saint-Dizier, a vintage air base in northeastern France that had been taken from the retreating Germans.

Charles Payne was also in France by then. Like his brother-in-law, he had wanted to join the Army Air Forces, but Charles was even more color-blind than Stanley, and the army was his only choice. After specialized training stateside, he joined the 89th Division, the Rolling W, in the 355th Infantry Regiment, K Company, which had shipped from Boston six months after D-Day. The plan was for the USAT *Uruguay* to land in England, but U-boat bombardments at sea diverted the ship to Le Havre at the mouth of the Seine. The docks were so crowded when they arrived that they bobbed in the harbor for two days. Finally a space came free, allowing them to disembark and ride in open trucks forty winding miles up to Lucky Strike, one of the staging areas known as cigarette camps. Nothing lucky about this strike. They arrived in the bleakest stretch of January: zero degrees, ice everywhere, bitterly cold water sloshing around in the bottom of the landing crafts on the way in and in their snow-covered tents when they reached camp, long walks through the mud to distant latrines. "Eventually the casualty rate from this was very high," Payne remembered. "The number of people I knew who had amputated toes . . ." His own toenails turned black, and his extremities were hypersensitive to cold for the rest of his life.

The fresh regiment began a long trek across Europe on March 4, lurching toward Germany. Not long into the route, Payne, who stood guard for a four-man mortar squad, saw his first dead body. "We came across a place where there had been a battle, and the first thing I saw was an American soldier who had fallen backwards and an American tank had run over his head. That was my entry into the war, I always felt." In the middle of the night on March 16, they crossed the Moselle, where Payne said he liberated a baby buggy full of wine; ten days later they rode navy landing barges down the castle-lined Rhine and reached the other side near the famed rock of Lorelei. "The last natural barrier had been breached," as the 355th's regimental history put it, and Payne's unit moved onto the plains of Germany, setting up a command post in Geisenheim, then pushing farther to Saasen, where they joined the Fourth Armored Division to take Gotha on April 4, bagging more than a thousand prisoners.

Like most foot soldiers, Payne marched without knowing where he was or where he was going until his company reached a recognizable river or landmark. He was allowed no maps or guidebooks. Extrapolating from occasional road signs, he thought they were bound for Berlin, only to realize later that they were going south. K Company faced scant resistance moving through one small burg after another, mostly teenage boys and grandfathers who were not worth rounding up as POWs. The carnage Payne saw along the route was the gruesome detritus of day-old battles waged by battalions ahead of his: "[A] lot of dead people, a lot of mutilated, blown-up kinds of things, mile after mile of dead horses." Scenes of death became routine, anesthetizing, until one afternoon in early April when he and his unit walked into Ohrdruf, notable as the first major concentration camp American soldiers liberated on their march through Europe.

Ohrdruf had been a slave labor camp run by the Nazi SS. At its peak earlier that spring of 1945, it contained nearly twelve thousand inmates from Hungary, Italy, Russia, France, Belgium, Poland, Yugoslavia, Latvia, and Ukraine, mostly Jews and also homosexuals and political radicals. The prisoners lived in windowless barracks, converted horse stables, with no beds, not even shelves, just sleeping on dirty straw, surrounded by electrified fencing, barbed wire, and watchtowers. Many died from starvation and disease, some from hanging. Lashings from SS guards were routine. From five to dusk they were led out to nearby mountains to carve protective stores in caverns and dig tunnels by pickax and hand. Art looted by the Nazis was stashed in some of the caverns. One tunnel was to connect a railroad line to a new Nazi communications center in the basement of the castle at Mühlberg. The project was abandoned before completion as Allied troops approached.

Charles Payne and his unit arrived several hours after the camp was liberated. The Nazis had fled, taking several thousand able-bodied prisoners with them and leaving behind a scene that haunted the young soldier from Kansas thereafter. In the town of Ohrdruf itself, he saw suddenly free, disoriented inmates "running around, stealing what they could steal. Most of them had rags for clothes, starved, emaciated, looking for food and clothes." From that chaos outside the gates, Payne approached the eerily silent death grounds inside the camp. "In the middle of the gate, which was open, there were no Germans, no camp guards, it was wide open. But there was a body right in the middle that had been crushed with a tire iron or piece of metal. He was one of those who had gone over to the Germans and worked with them against his own people and was well fed in payment, and then when the Americans came he slid back into his old clothes and tried to blend in with the others, and they recognized him and killed him on the spot."

Another hundred feet or so inside the gate Payne saw "a semicircle of dead bodies of inmates in their rags" – thirty of them, according to the 355th operations report – "and they each had their cup and they had been machine-gunned. You could see where the machine gun had been and the shell casings were still there. After the machine-gunning [of prisoners too infirm to take along], the Germans had pulled out and left." As the American soldiers moved farther inside the camp, they found a shed that, according to the operations report, was "piled high with more corpses, stacked like cordwood." Payne saw that too and later remembered, "They had stripped [the bodies] and thrown them in and stacked them in a layer, and sprinkled lime, and then another layer, and lime, and I would say the bodies had not been there very long because there was not yet a real strong death smell." On the far side of the camp wall, they found an open-air crematorium where "the charred bodies of former inmates were still visible."

The day at Ohrdruf was "the worst in a whole lot of pretty awful stuff" that Madelyn Dunham's brother encountered during the war. "I handled it, I guess," he said later. His unit worked its way to the Elbe River in the following climactic weeks and was there when word reached them that the war in Europe was over.

Ralph Dunham, an army personnel officer, was in another part of Germany then, but Stanley Dunham never made it across the border. On April 7, one day after Charles Payne's unit left the Ohrdruf horror, Stanley was still at Saint-Dizier in France and learned that he had been reassigned to a replacement depot in England where more new troops were training. From there he was sent back to the States to await an infantry invasion of Japan. He was kept from that fate by the Japanese surrender in August, brought on in no small part by the devastating bombing raids of B-29 Superfortresses built at the Boeing plant in Wichita where his wife worked as an inspector.

Back in Butler County, where R. A. Clymer was editor of the *El Dorado Times* and writing obituaries at the passing of local citizens, it was said that the eulogies in his "Farewells" columns were so flowery that people were lucky to live in a place "where death hath no sting." Clymer was especially busy anesthetizing the pain of irreplaceable loss near the end of the war. Lieutenant Edward Cole, killed in England. Lieutenant Charles Brumback, lost over Germany. Private James McCollum, missing in France. Dick and Charles Wayne, both gone. And scores more, including some who died only after they had returned to American soil, among them Major Richard Strickland, killed in a plane crash in Texas, and First Lieutenant Bill Davidson, who died in a car accident in El Paso after shooting down five Japanese Zeroes in the Pacific. Tall and handsome, a former high school basketball star, Davidson was a conspicuous member of what Clymer called "the court of Boyville" in El Dorado who had "frolicked through a gay and irresponsible boyhood."

The Dunham brothers, motherless products of that same carefree court of Boyville, both made it back to Butler County safely by the summer of 1945. Along with war souvenirs, Stanley returned with the lingering effects of a bad case of crotch rot. Charles Payne, with his icy toes and fingers, remained on duty in Europe an extra year, spending the winter of 1945–1946 as a guard at a POW camp in Austria. "We guarded Germans all winter," he said, "and they were warmer than we were." Guarding German prisoners was something familiar to people from Kansas. Two of the largest POW camps in the United States were in Salina and Concordia, and a smaller group of German prisoners, all captured during the North Africa campaign, had been housed at the County Farm on the edge of El Dorado, from which they were dispatched to daily work duties at forty-seven ranches in the area. There had been at least one escape attempt, thwarted by Patrolman Vernon Mack near Augusta, but a few of the German soldiers became so fond of Butler County they chose to stay and become Kansas wheat farmers rather than seek repatriation after the war.

For Madelyn Dunham, war's end meant the end of her job as an inspector on the B-29 line. With peacetime came the cancellation of $35 billion in government contracts and massive cuts in defense industry jobs, including many at Boeing. Three million people who had supplemented the home front workforce were suddenly out on the street and overwhelmed by more than ten million returning servicemen in the burgeoning labor pool. After experiencing newfound freedoms and responsibilities during the war years, some women were reluctant to revert to subordinate situations, but Madelyn's Augusta classmates and Boeing cohorts for the most part settled into postwar family life. Francine Pummill, her longtime best friend, who had moved to Wyoming in their senior year of high school, was back in the area, married to another Augusta High classmate, David Gruver. Madelyn had been a bridesmaid in the wedding, but the high school kinship would never be revived. Stanley still had "itchy feet," as Madelyn told Francine, and Kansas once again seemed suffocating. After a brief reunion and respite in Butler County, the Dunhams once more headed west to California. It was Stanley's third escape to the West Coast – yet another search for his El Dorado. This time, with family in tow, he was part of a broader demographic realignment.

Boom was the catchword of the postwar era, and California was the center of the boom. *Life* magazine declared that the growth spurt in California was "on its way to becoming one of the biggest in history." The population had surpassed nine million, the start of a decades-long trend of American migration to the far coast, with an influx of at least a half million residents each year. Rather than suffer through a recession at the close of wartime production, as many economists predicted, California experienced the opposite, an unprecedented explosion of economic expansion. Houses, freeways, offices, schools, churches, swimming pools, shopping centers – construction in the state rose by 167 percent in the first year after the war.

Stanley Dunham was in the vanguard of the California boom. Within months of getting home from the war, he took his family back to the scene of his earlier adventures in the Bay Area around San Francisco. In doing so, he joined another postwar movement that reshaped the United States. In September 1945, with assistance from the Servicemen's Readjustment Act (the GI Bill of Rights), he entered the University of California at Berkeley. Madelyn's high school record in Augusta had been far superior to his in El Dorado; he was an unfocused know-it-all, and in every respect she was the better college prospect, but her qualifications were not part of the family equation. Stanley became one of hundreds of thousands of returning veterans who enrolled in college, while Madelyn once again entered the workforce. She found a job in the school's admissions office.

There were so many ex-GIs with young families flocking to big public universities like Cal in the postwar boom that military-style temporary quarters were needed to house them. The Dunhams found an apartment in a makeshift complex the university leased from the housing authority in nearby Richmond. Their apartment was spacious by student standards, with a kitchen, a dining alcove, two bedrooms, and a large living room, where Stanley proudly hung the colorful rocket-ship batik he had made in art class a decade earlier at

El Dorado High. With his plays and short stories hidden, lost, or nonexistent, the unseen or fantasized products of a fertile imagination, the batik wall hanging served as a solitary physical reminder of his artistic hopes and dreams.

It is not clear what Stanley intended as his major. He took courses in geology, English, math, economics, French, and journalism. After his first year, they were joined by Stanley's brother, the more scholarly Ralph, who had earned an undergraduate degree from Kansas State Teachers College before the war and now was enrolled in Cal's graduate school of education. Madelyn, Stanley, and Stannie Ann took one bedroom, Ralph the other. While Ralph's presence cramped the living quarters, he offered certain creature comforts to the family, prime among them his car, an old Hudson straight 8 with which he ferried a group to campus each morning. Crowded in back were Madelyn and two friends who worked with her and lived nearby, along with Stannie Ann, who was dropped off at preschool. "The others paid me [gas money], but Stanley and Madelyn didn't. I was living with them, after all," Ralph recalled. Stanley usually sat up front, spinning yarns, cracking jokes, pontificating on anything but his studies.

When he rode in for class at all, that is. By all accounts, Stanley's approach to coursework had not changed much since his days of teenage truancy in El Dorado. It was not that he lacked the brainpower, it was more that he preferred extracurricular light reading, or talking and partying, to sitting in class or buckling down at the library. According to Madelyn's brother Charles, "Madelyn said Stanley didn't do a thing the whole time they were at Berkeley except lie on the couch and read murder mysteries. She would write his papers. That's Madelyn's story."

Although they were fourteen hundred miles from home, the Dunhams did not feel isolated in the Bay Area. Keith Allen was still out there pursuing the writing career that eluded Stanley, and there were four other acquaintances from Butler County, including an El Dorado friend of Ralph's who had married an Augusta friend of Madelyn's. They would gather on weekends for drinks and card games, reminisce about Kansas, and imagine their futures in California. Stannie Ann, age four, was often among them, the only child in a crowd of adults, and stood out as a bright, artistic, articulate girl who was somewhat fragile because of asthma. When Stanley and Madelyn went out to a movie or dinner, Ralph usually babysat. "She was good, a self-starter," Ralph said later. "She would sit around and draw and finger-paint and we would play games. All in our family were game players. She was beginning to get into reading. I would always read to her. She loved that sort of thing. We usually managed."

For the third and final time, Stanley struck out in California. As much as Madelyn wanted a new and more sophisticated life away from Kansas, she could not see much point in supporting the family if her husband was not going to approach his studies earnestly, especially since Stannie Ann's breathing problems seemed to worsen in the Bay Area. "I'm leaving. I'm going back to Kansas," Madelyn told him after the second year. As it turned out, Stanley had not even registered for classes that second semester of his second year (school records show him attending from September 1945 to December 1946), though from then on he was not above blaming her for his academic deficiencies, asking plaintively, "What can you do when your wife won't let you get an education?"

In resignation, they hitched a summer ride east in the old Hudson with Ralph, who was on a round-trip transcontinental mission of a much rosier nature, embarking on a four-thousand-mile trip to Nova Scotia to meet his bride-to-be, Betty, and return with her for his second year of graduate school at Berkeley. Ralph had received word that Betty was sailing across the Atlantic from England on the RMS *Aquitania*, the ancient four-funneled sister ship of the famed *Lusitania*, and would not reach Halifax until August, so he had time to take a leisurely tour across the country.

On the first leg out of Berkeley, they stopped at Yosemite National Park, 132 miles southeast. It was a most unusual day and night in many respects. The sun was shining when they arrived. Then came rain, followed by sleet. Then it snowed, followed by hail. Five distinct weather systems in a single twelve-hour period. Inside their park cabin that night, Stannie Ann turned violently ill. Madelyn said later that her daughter had never thrown up as much as she did that night. But when she woke up the next morning, her asthma was gone. The leisurely trip continued eastward with the little girl breathing free and easy.

Ralph eventually deposited the family in Augusta before pointing his

Hudson toward his arriving British bride and the far Canadian coast. For Stanley, dumped unceremoniously back on the Kansas plain, the days of pretending were over. He had an anxious wife and a precocious daughter, and it was time for him to get to work.

One thing Stanley could do was gab, and he had a knack for sounding like he knew what he was talking about. He also liked to joke, and to sit around, so perhaps it was inevitable that he became a salesman, and that what he would sell was furniture. The job he landed was not in El Dorado or Augusta, but in Ponca City, one hundred miles due south across the Oklahoma border. Ponca City had a familiar feel and history for the Dunham newcomers. It was another oil town (Conoco was born there under the name E. W. Marland Oil) surrounded by good farm and cattle land. And the townspeople, much like those in El Dorado and Augusta, took pride in their public school system. Stannie Ann was not quite six when she joined the first-grade class at the old Jefferson Elementary School in 1948.

Stanley spent his weekdays downtown at the Jay G. Paris Furniture Store at 409 E. Grand, one of six or seven salesmen who walked the showroom floors. It was an impressive workplace, designed to the owner's specifications in eclectic Spanish style, with a 140-foot storefront, an interior atrium opening to the second and third floors, and an amber glass skylight filtering daylight through the ceiling. The location was choice, across from the Art Deco post office, and the street was the place to be. "On Grand Avenue," the store's stationery boasted. Jay G. Paris, who owned a large ranch outside town, was a big man in Ponca City. He was a leader of the Lion's Club and a close friend of Oklahoma's governor, Roy J. Turner, with whom he shared a passion for Hereford cattle.

The furniture store provisioned young postwar families with almost everything they might need to decorate their homes: bedroom sets and bedding for adults and children, sofas, recliners, consoles, coffee tables, dining room sets, kitchen nooks, bureaus, desks, rugs, carpets. The merchandise was Middle American prime: Ethan Allen furniture, Bigelow and Sanford carpets. The company policy was "No gimmicks," only quality offerings at fair prices. Jay Paris disdained the concept of a sale and never held one. Most sales were tricks, he said; the original price should be the proper one for both sides. This philosophy was both business-related and personal. His strongest competition in Ponca City came from none other than his younger brother, Glenn, who after learning the trade from Jay split off and formed Glenn Paris & Sons a few blocks down, near the intersection of Grand and Main. The younger Paris established his own identity as the king of markdowns. His store also had an in-house decorator, something the older store lacked, at least officially.

With his California sheen and artistic aspirations, Stanley Dunham took it upon himself to help his boss modernize the Jay G. Paris operation and make it more appealing to the modern consumer. When he heard about a series of evening decorating seminars at a hotel in Wichita, he made the drive from Ponca City and back every night. Bob Casey, who worked at the store part-time while he was attending Oklahoma A&M in Stillwater (and who later married the owner's daughter), was impressed by Dunham's approach. "Most of our salesmen would sell a chair or sofa but didn't have the ability to sell a decorating scheme like in *House Beautiful,* and our competition was eating us up on that," Casey recalled. "Stanley thought we ought to sell more room concepts than item selling. He could sell you a roomful of furniture and then help you decorate it."

Stan excelled at working a customer. He was articulate, smooth, and adept at assessing the compulsions and financial possibilities of people who walked into the store. But he also knew the technology of furniture and was honest, according to Casey. "He just did a real good job of convincing the customer that he was there to help." There are always down periods in a showroom, when the salesmen are just standing around waiting for action, and Stanley was always ready to fill the void. "He and I would have discussions about everything. I was going to college and thinking I was really bright," Casey said later. "He would shoot those ideas down once in a while. He would give you advice about everything." As Casey prepared to marry Patricia Paris, Stanley had advice even about that, and told the young couple a joke about what they should do when picking out furniture. He was anything but a prude, his jokes often imbued with sexual innuendo. This joke, as Casey recalled, "had something to do with a bed."

The Dunhams seemed settled in Ponca City. Stanley had a house, a car, and a job. When Madelyn's brother Charles came through town on a business trip (working as a service engineer for an industrial chemical company that dealt with oil refineries in Oklahoma and west Texas), he listened as Stanley talked about "how wonderful [his life] was." But Payne remained skeptical toward his brother-in-law and concerned about the well-being of his sister. Things always sounded wonderful in Stanley's telling, he thought. Charles remembered the revealing moment when he opened the trunk that Stanley had left behind when he went off to war, what was supposed to be the repository of the much-boasted-about screenplays and short stories that Stanley Armour Dunham wrote during his first venture in California. The reality of his wonderful life too often resembled that myth-busting, virtually empty trunk.

It was around this time that Francine Pummill, now Francine Gruver, received news that her best friend from Augusta High – they were both now approaching thirty – had had a hysterectomy and would be unable to have more children. Other friends were told a different story, that the treatment Stanley received for his wartime crotch rot left him sterile. In either case, Stannie Ann remained an only child.

After three years in Ponca City Stanley's itchy feet took them west again, though not back to California. They moved to northern Texas, to the town of Vernon between Dallas and the Panhandle. What precipitated the move is unclear, but the fact that they moved in March and had to pull Stannie Ann out of third grade (her class had switched from Jefferson to Roosevelt Elementary) near the end of school year suggests the reason was related to Stanley and his employment.

In Vernon, Stanley landed a job at Popular Furniture, across the street from the post office. He moved his family into a small white-frame house on Roberts Street that looked much like his ill-fated childhood house on Buchanan Street in Topeka and the Payne family home on 12th Street in Augusta: two bedrooms, a kitchen, a living room, a bathroom, a small backyard. In a line of numbered streets, Roberts would have been 13th Street, but for superstition. It was out of Vernon that a variety of notable and notorious figures came over the years, ranging from Roy Orbison, the majestic rock-and-roll balladeer, to Donald Ray Dixon, the savings and loan crook, to Kenneth Starr (he actually grew up a few miles outside of town), the righteous prosecutor who pursued with Ahab-like obsession and similar results his great white whale, President Bill Clinton. Vernon was 268 miles southwest of Ponca City, barely within a long day's drive of the Dunham family's Kansas homeland, but still inside the cultural orbit of the vast American plains, with its cattle and oil and small towns populated largely by Scots-Irish Protestants. This was farther south, though, with a larger black population, and Texas was part of the old Confederacy, where Jim Crow segregation was woven into the social fabric.

Stannie Ann became Stanley Ann in Vernon. She attended the end of third grade and virtually all of fourth grade at Hawkins Elementary School, one of four grade schools in town that white students could attend. All black children, by contrast, were crowded into a single school, Booker T. Washington, from first grade though senior high. Separate but unequal: their building had no science labs, and the students read from handed-down books with pages torn out. The black section of Vernon, known as the Flats, was on the north side above the railroad tracks, where the roads were unpaved and the typical house was an unpainted wooden shack. Many men picked cotton or were ranch hands; the women worked as domestics. Thessalonia Favors Willie, who lived in the Flats, recalled a well-defined section of Vernon "where blacks did not go": a six-block rectangle between McKinney and Wanderer Streets west of Main.

The public swimming pool was whites-only, as was the library. Of the town's three movie houses, the Vernon, the Majestic, and the Pictorium, known as the Pic, blacks were confined to segregated balcony sections if they were allowed inside at all. Only one uptown restaurant, the Busy Bee Café on Fannin Street, sold food to blacks, Willie said, but "you had to go in the back alley for them to hand you your hamburger." Blacks were commonly referred to as "coloreds" and "nigras" and "niggers." This was the only life Stanley Ann's classmates knew. Tim Reeves's dad ran a gas station with separate colored and whites-only bathrooms. A black woman from the Flats came to Sharon McNabb's house to clean and bake delicious lemon pies; they called her "Colored Ruth." When Carole Ann McDonald's family visited the Texas State Fair in Dallas, her father unwittingly wandered into the ladies room, thinking it must be the white men's room, because the first restroom he entered was full of black men.

The rituals of life for white people in Vernon in the early 1950s took place at church, school, and social functions celebrating the area's cowboy past. The Dunhams joined the First Methodist Church. Stanley had grown up Baptist, but Madelyn was a Methodist, and that was the predominant church of businessmen in Vernon. He took the vow for changing denominations delineated on page 543 of the 1935 Methodist Hymnal: "Will you be loyal to the Methodist Church, and uphold it by your prayers, your presence, your gifts, and your service?" Stanley said yes. Churchgoing was a civic duty, so vital that churches competed to have the best Sunday school attendance, the numbers dutifully reported each week in the Monday edition of the *Vernon Daily Record*. "It was a matter of pride during that era," said Reverend Bill Ivins, who preached at First Methodist later. "There was huge pressure . . . to increase enrollment and attendance." In the church records, Madelyn was listed as a member and Stanley Ann as a preparatory member.

The cowboy heritage of Wilbarger County was a religion of its own in Vernon and environs. Two annual springtime events defined the scene. One was Doan's May Picnic, held along the Red River near the old C. F. Doan trading post, a major stop for cattle drives on the Western Trail to Dodge City, Kansas. A family's social standing in Vernon was determined not just by money but by pioneer lineage. Although the picnic, the oldest annual picnic in Texas, was open to everyone, only the son or daughter of pioneer families could be crowned king or queen of the event. From Stanley Ann's class, Barbara Berry, daughter of the president of Herring National Bank, was the Doan's May Picnic queen. The other ritual was the Santa Rosa Roundup, sponsored by the Waggoner family, whose ranch on the edge of town was one of the largest in the United States. The roundup was a four-day affair that featured a rodeo and began with a grand parade through Vernon. On the day of the parade, a Wednesday, recalled Carole Ann McDonald, "the girls dressed up in squaw dresses and the boys wore cowboy hats, cowboy boots, and jeans, and [we'd all] go to school in costumes. We'd have a competition for best-dressed, then school would let out and everyone would go to the parade."

Hawkins Elementary was regarded as the best grade school in town. Air-conditioning had not arrived; one classroom wall featured a row of high windows that opened from the top with long poles. Wooden desks with inkwells and pencil grooves were nailed to the ground and attached to runners that connected one to the next, so when an overactive boy wiggled an entire row wiggled with him. But a teacher defines a school, and Stanley Ann and her classmates benefited from their fourth-grade teacher, Elizabeth Grady, tall, slender, and raven-haired, who dressed sharply and taught with sympathy and flair. She created an Audubon Bird Club for her class and often took her students to a nearby park, where they watched for birds, studied their habits and nests, and drew pictures of them in their notebooks: goldfinch, scarlet tanager, mallard, bluebird. Carole Ann McDonald kept her notebook for decades.

Stanley Ann was a newcomer at Hawkins, the furthest thing from a pioneer, but not a loner. She made friends with Frances Shepherd, Betty Phillips, Betha Stinnett, and Sunny Rutledge, became part of the Friendly Bluebirds troop that met at Janice Folmar's house at the corner of Wilbarger and 12th, and took part in the Fourth Grade Rhythm Group, which danced at the opening of the new Memorial Auditorium costumed as Dutch boys and girls. There were not enough boys in the group, so Stanley Ann took one of their roles. An athletic girl – "She could catch a ball and throw a ball," said Betty Phillips – Stanley Ann was tall and big boned. Sunny Rutledge said their shapes were similar. "We were no waist, round tummies, probably heavier than some of the other girls. I thought we looked the same in our Bluebird vests, kind of fat. I don't know if she was teased as much as I was; she probably was. . . . I was always teased and called Fatty. Her nose was pointed and interesting. It had a different shape to it than anyone's I'd seen." It was not her nose or her shape that drew the attention of Tim Reeves, the class clown, but her name. He was mean to her, he said later. "I remember she was the brunt of some teasing because her name was Stanley."

As Stanley and Madelyn recounted the north Texas scene to their grandson decades later, or at least as he related their stories in his memoir, there were at least three race-tinged events during their years there that stuck in the family lore. The first, according to Stanley, came when he reported for work at Popular Furniture and was told by his coworkers that black and Mexican customers could be accommodated only after normal store hours and had to arrange their own deliveries. The second was when Madelyn, who went to work at a bank in Wichita Falls, was chastised for addressing the black janitor as "Mister." And the third was when Stanley Ann herself was ridiculed by her classmates and neighbor kids as a "Nigger lover" and "dirty Yankee" for playing innocently with a black girl; Stanley was advised by a parent, "White girls don't play with coloreds in this town."

There is no doubt that events of that sort happened in Vernon during that era, though the accuracy of these specific accounts is uncertain. Stanley was a teller of tales, and it appears that his grandson got these stories mostly from him. Stanley Ann was teased in Vernon, but none of her friends said they thought of her as a Yankee. Her teacher, Mrs. Grady, had a reputation for being sensible and progressive. The janitor in the bank story is called "Mr. Reed." The name was probably made up, if not the story; the most noted black student at Augusta High School during Madelyn's years there was Herman Reed Jr., the captain of the football team. Sterling Greenwood, who grew up in Vernon and was a year behind Stanley Ann at Hawkins, noted that the Dunhams lived "in a really white area" and that she "would have had to go out of the way to find a black girl to play with." On the other hand, Carole Ann McDonald recalled that when she was three or four she once played at a sand pile with some black girls and her mother ordered her into the house. In any case, if the stories were exaggerated, they arose only from good intentions – grandparents wanting their mixed-race grandson to know they were racially sensitive in a racially insensitive culture.

Stanley's grandson understood the old man's penchant for "rewriting history to conform with the image he wished for himself." In his memoir he noted that although Stanley once told him the family left Texas "in part because of their discomfort with racism," his grandmother took him aside later and explained that their leaving was because "Gramps wasn't doing particularly well at his job." During their final years in north Texas Madelyn was back at work, holding down jobs in Wichita Falls as a teller at a bank and at a low-signal radio station where she announced the local events of the day. Her brother, whose chemical company assignment took him to north Texas just as it had to Ponca City, said that during his weekend visits he came to suspect that Stanley was having troubles on and off the job. At work, Charles Payne said, Stanley started off strong, impressing people with his verbal agility, and "then after some period of time it always fell through. My guess is his mouth was bigger than his performance." Outside work, Payne suspected that Stanley was losing money at cards. "Stanley liked to play poker a lot, and sometimes he was a little too good with cards. He always lost money in the end, but that was the story of his life."

CHAPTER 4

―――◈―――

NAIROBI DAYS

During his first years in Nairobi, as he approached his early twenties, Barack Hussein Obama was employed as a clerk at an Indian law firm in the city center. He landed the job in 1955, a period when low-paying office positions were opening to literate Luo men who had migrated to the capital from their homeland in western Kenya. Only one year earlier, scores of thousands of Kikuyu in the Nairobi region had been rounded up in a citywide military sweep known as Operation Anvil and sent off to detention camps – a punitive action taken by British colonialists in response to the Mau Mau rebellion. The sudden imprisonment of vast numbers of one tribe had the secondary effect of reconfiguring the demographics of the local labor pool. The Luo, considered less threatening to Europeans, were not entirely excluded from the crackdown, but they were not arrested or detained en masse and could fill the gaps left by the removed Kikuyu. For the most part they were permitted to go about as usual, which meant their freedom of movement was still constrained by the dictates of the emergency and the strictures of a largely segregated society.

In his résumé, Obama noted that his qualifications for the clerk's job included the fact that he was an "excellent typist." This was both slightly hyperbolic and characteristic of a young man never lacking in self-regard. Almost anyone who encountered him at the start of his adult life said that he was supremely arrogant. Within the Luo culture, this was neither off-putting nor unusual. Thinking highly of oneself was considered a particular Luo trait. "He was arrogant in a way that does not offend you but makes you laugh," said Philip Ochieng, a fellow Luo from the Lake Victoria region who first met Obama in Nairobi during that period. "He was typical Luo." Aside from his typing skills, Obama was boastful of three other attributes: the way his mind worked, the way he danced, and the way he wore clothes. Back in Kendu Bay his friends sometimes referred to him as *Atuech Wuod Akumu,* "the well-dressed son of Akumu."

Obama first lived in Kaloleni, a largely Luo settlement in Nairobi's Eastlands, the African sector. Hussein Onyango, his father, was staying across town in the Muthaiga Estate area, a comfortable white enclave where he was employed by various diplomats and Foreign Service officers attached to the U.S. embassy. For several years starting in 1956, he worked for the Hagberg family, Gordon and Gloria Hagberg and their children, at their massive two-story house made of dark brown tiles and whitewashed concrete, with bay windows and French doors, at 214 Muthaiga Road, just two houses down from the American ambassador's residence. Gordon Hagberg was an officer for the U.S. Information Service. Hussein Onyango oversaw the help, cooked in the large kitchen, and lived with other African employees in the service quarters at the back of the three-acre property. There were four rooms, including a communal kitchen, and three small rooms for sleeping. The first, without a ceiling, was where Hussein Onyango stayed. The bed was about two and a half feet wide and made of wood. There were no chairs or tables. He read at night by kerosene lamplight. The servants did have their own garden on their compound.

The Hagbergs' daughter, Paula, not yet ten years old, found Hussein Onyango a striking figure in the household: "He was very dignified and quiet, and sort of stern looking. I was slightly intimidated. He was never anything but civil and nice to me, but I really did notice this stern thing. A very strong presence there." She remembered that once they were out on the back porch "and he picked up his foot and pulled out a thumbtack. He was barefoot. I was amazed and asked him, 'Didn't that hurt?' He looked at me with an embarrassed smile. He was a man of few words, but he cracked a smile."

Hagberg was well liked by native Kenyans, who said that he was out of the ordinary for an American in that he was not abrasive or loud. He and his wife were enlightened liberals who encouraged the integration of Kenyan society. They joined the United Kenya Club, whose purpose was to provide a setting where European, African, and Asian professionals could socialize freely, and sent Paula to the Hospital Hill School, one of the few racially integrated primary schools in Kenya. Gloria treated the Africans like fellow human beings and made sure they always secured the proper passes and licenses to work and travel. Visitors to their home and the nearby embassy included many African nationalists, including Tom Mboya, the Luo labor leader who was emerging as the strongest voice for independence since the 1952 imprisonment of Jomo Kenyatta. Mboya was a friend of Hussein Onyango and would find time to chat in Dholuo with the Hagbergs' cook in the kitchen or out back during his outings to Muthaiga Road. It was in this same manner that Hussein Onyango became acquainted with Milton Obote, a Luo-related Lango tribesman from neighboring Uganda who lived in Nairobi briefly during the mid-1950s while working at an engineering firm and learning the mechanics of independence politics. (Obote soon returned to Uganda, where, after leading his nation to freedom, he transmogrified into a ruthless "Big Man" autocrat in a troubled postcolonial Africa.)

The father's connections, especially to Tom Mboya, became essential to Barack Obama as he made his way in Nairobi. "Onyango admired people like Mboya who were fighting for independence," said John Ndalo Aguk. "He used to speak highly of Mboya. When Mboya realized that Barack was Onyango's son, he became close to him." Twice a month, usually around five in the afternoon, when his own workday was done, Barack in coat and tie walked to Muthaiga Road to visit with his father and talk over political developments. He started attending political rallies in the African sector, where Mboya enthralled crowds with his electrifying orations, speaking variously in his tribal tongue as well as Swahili and English. And he became a familiar face in the growing entourage of favor seekers and acolytes crowding the narrow corridors outside Mboya's second-floor private offices on Victoria Street above an Indian tailor shop and a dry-goods store in city center, not far from the Indian law firm where the young clerk spent his days typing legal correspondence. Mboya, receiving visitors for hours as he sat behind his green metal desk, did not have a paid staff or secretary, so various volunteers, Obama among them, would help out when they could. Friends recalled that Obama would persuade them to join him for a snack of fermented milk and scones and a walk around the block near Mboya's office to chew over African current events.

During his years in Nairobi, Obama several times made the long trip back to Luoland for weekend and holiday visits by train or occasionally bus. His final journey home in the calendar year 1956 came during the Christmas season. Buses heading west were designed to hold forty passengers, though often many more were wedged inside the old coaches. It took a full day to get from Nairobi to Kisumu, the provincial capital, departure and arrival both accomplished in the darkness that bracketed twelve hours of equatorial sunlight. Obama's route led out from Central province and followed a ridgeline above the historic Rift Valley, with its breathtaking morning vista of villages and pastures that seemed to be floating on the plains below, toward hills on the western horizon. The highway eventually wended down into the valley, its two lanes clogged with pedestrians, carts, goats, cows, traffic police holding things up, lurking for bribes, old trucks breaking down, vendors selling neatly stacked little pyramids of potatoes along with carrots, roast maize, and peas. Baboons scampered along the shoulder of the road, extorting food with menacing smiles, while zeals of zebras galloped and grazed in the middle distance as the highway sliced through a national game preserve. Past the midway point the bus rounded the Mau Forest, dense and deep, temperatures dropping through the hills and curves, then rumbled on past tea plantations on either side of the road, luscious seas of deep green, dotted with laborers waist high in hillside fields, donkeys hauling burlap saddlebags of freshly picked tea leaves. Next came sugar and rice fields that signaled the low-lying entryway into Luoland, suddenly hotter and flatter, the dusty road worsening by the

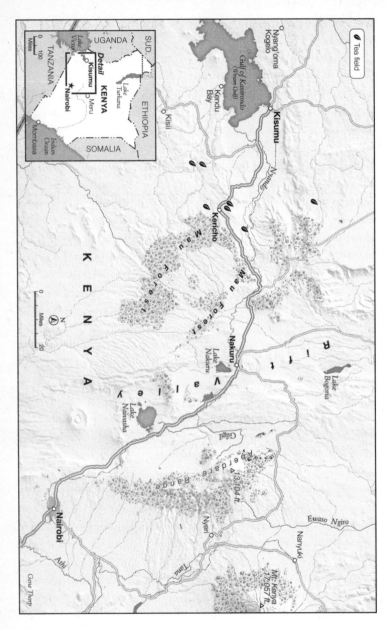

kilometer, humidity spiking in the enveloping blackness on the way toward the great lake.

Obama had his stepmother, Sarah, in Nyang'oma Kogelo, and his natural mother, Akumu, and sister Auma among other relatives to the south in his birth region of Kendu Bay. Though he often visited both places, his preference was to linger in Kisumu, downing bottled beer at a friend's father's bar (an activity made legally available to black Africans only in the late 1940s), before taking the ferry across the gulf to Kendu Bay.

On Christmas night in 1956, soon after reaching his early-childhood home, he visited one of his favorite haunts, the Rachuonyo Social Hall, at the curve in the road on the way to Kanyadhiang. The dance floor was crowded, its cut-stone walls and corrugated tin roof reverberating with the syncopated rhythms of a local Kendu jazz band, with Luo drums, acoustic guitars, and eight-string *nyatiti*. Little children from the neighborhood peeped through the side windows as couples took turns outdoing one another on the dance floor. Several young women wanted to dance with the well-dressed son of Akumu, who was known for the sensuous way he swayed his hips to the hypnotic *benga* music. At some point during the night, two sixteen-year-old schoolmates from Gendia started fighting over him. Gendia was the nearby town where Obama had attended early primary school and where the Seventh Day Adventists had based their Luoland missionary work since the turn of the century. According to a relative, Andrew Ochung, and one of the musicians, Obama had begun the night dancing with one of the Gendia girls, Mikal, but at some point he pulled her classmate Kezia (*KAY-zia*) onto the floor.

Kezia had arrived at the social hall with her cousin William. Taking a first look at Obama, she later recalled, she thought, "Ooh, wow! He was so lovely with his dancing." After a brief commotion Mikal lost out and departed. "Barack was a great dancer. Kezia was also a good dancer. So the crowd gave them a standing ovation, and from there it was love," explained another of Obama's Kanyadhiang relatives, Charles Oluoch.

This was not a precise reenactment of Hussein Onyango's courtship a generation earlier, kidnapping Akumu and bullying his way into marriage with the young girl, but Barack's pursuit of Kezia was a furious courtship in its own way, and followed the Luo tradition of capturing the bride. Every day for the next week after that first dance floor encounter, he showed up at Kezia's compound, her cousin William at his side, trying to make his case that she should quit school, leave her family, and escape to Nairobi with him. Kezia came from a well-respected Gendia family and was reared in the Adventist Church. Obama was the nonbelieving son of a converted Muslim. She was still in school; Obama, four years older, was working far away. None of this warmed the heart of her father. On his final day in Luoland, Obama persuaded Kezia and her cousin to see him off at the railroad station in Kisumu. But after taking the ferry across the gulf and arriving at the depot, instead of returning home Kezia jumped on the train with Barack. They eloped on the eastbound line of the old Lunatic Express. It cost sixteen shillings. Her father, outraged, led a family posse to Nairobi to track them down but could not persuade Kezia to come home. Hussein Onyango mollified Kezia's clan by presenting them with a suitable number of cows – sixteen. By early 1957 Barack and Kezia were married, living in a small house in the Jericho neighborhood, and winning dance trophies as the couple to watch at the Kaloleni Social Hall. They would have two children by the start of a new decade.

Two people, more than any others, changed the life of Barack Hussein Obama during the 1950s in Nairobi and in so doing altered the course of history thousands of miles away and into the following century. One has been introduced. This was Tom Mboya, who came into Obama's orbit in a logical fashion as a fellow Luo, a rising political star who took on a vast cadre of acolytes, and an outspoken nationalist who believed that education was the key to African freedom. Tom Mboya (pronounced by Kenyans as one run-on word, *tomBOYuh*) was not quite six years older than Obama, and they shared much in common. They were of the same tribe, spoke the same languages, and knew many of the same people. They both loved to dance, to party, and to talk, and they radiated a confidence that lapsed into arrogance. Mboya intersected the Obama story many times, as one would learn later, but first to the other person who redirected Obama's path.

This was an American named Sara Elizabeth Mooney, and her connection to Obama was as unlikely as Mboya's was predictable. If the Westernization of the Obamas began a generation earlier, when Seventh Day Adventist missionaries encountered Onyango in Kendu Bay, taught him English, and introduced him to European clothing and culture, the family's rise was furthered in the next generation when his son, Barack, happened upon a woman from the United States who was sent to Kenya to spread the twin gospels of literacy and the Lord. That is how history works, the history of families as well as the history of nations and movements. Along with the rational processes of biology and geography, of politics and economics, there come seemingly random connections that spin out profound and unintended consequences.

Betty Mooney was forty-three years old when she arrived in Nairobi in early May 1957. This was the first time she had been to Africa. An eternal optimist with a toothy smile, thin face, dark wavy hair, and deep-set eyes, Mooney would marry a widower named Elmer Kirk, but not for another three years, after her stint in Kenya was over. For now she was devoted to her job, which was also her cause and was inseparable from her religion. Her job was to teach adults to read and write; her cause was to eliminate illiteracy in the poorest corners of the world, and in so doing she believed that she was following the plan that God had set for her. The granddaughter of Addison Clark, cofounder of Texas Christian University in Fort Worth, Mooney had grown up in Rockville, Maryland, and had been involved in literacy work since she began teaching night classes in Harlem in 1945. Her mentor was Dr. Frank Laubach, an evangelical Christian missionary she had first heard at a spiritual retreat and who was now developing a worldwide literacy program that he called "Each One Teach One." The cause of literacy evangelism had taken her from India to the inner city of Memphis, Tennessee, before she found her way to Nairobi.

Mooney felt ill-prepared when she got there. "When I landed here three weeks ago I felt sure it was all a mistake," she wrote in a letter to friends at the start of her African adventure. "I felt more illiterate than any of the illiterates I had come to help. I thought that I would never understand the official organizations – who's who and what's what. It seemed that there were more people to do things than people to do them for. Everyone was pleasant but everyone was busy with his own job. People all around, but loneliness underneath. And just enough of India to make me homesick for it. I felt like a displaced person." Her first modestly successful session with a group of African women thirsting for knowledge in a settlement outside Nairobi gave her a jolt of confidence, and reassured her, she said, that she was on "God's time table" and that there was "some reason for my being here at this particular time."

There were, as it turned out, more reasons for Mooney to be there than whatever the Almighty had in mind for her. To those who paid her way, the mission had more to do with racial politics than beneficent missionary work. Her assignment in Kenya was arranged by the Kenyan colonial government in concert with the International Cooperation Administration, a foreign aid arm of the U.S. State Department, which paid half her salary. Literacy, it seems, was viewed by both sides in the struggle between Kenyan colonialists and Kenyan nationalists as an important tool that could be used to their advantage.

The British overseers of the Crown Colony of Kenya became more interested in teaching the African masses to read and write after experimenting with literacy programs in the Kikuyu detention camps, according to documents outlining the relationship between Frank Laubach's literacy organization and the Kenyan effort. In the months following Operation Anvil in 1954, one document noted, many of the detainees "remained irreconcilable until they were offered literacy training. By diverting their minds from real or imagined wrongs to the acquisition of a desirable and useful skill, the camp atmosphere changed from sullen obstruction to a spirit of cooperation, which in its turn resulted in a repudiation of Mau Mau leadership. In nearly all the camps, 'confessed' Mau Mau leaders started teaching the illiterate ones under the supervision of rehabilitation officers. This was an eye-opener to authorities. It proved that education was what the underprivileged masses wanted."

Whether or not this was an accurate interpretation of how and why Kikuyu attitudes changed inside the detention camps, government authorities believed it. In the wake of that experiment, Kenyan Ministry of Education officials decided to expand literacy programs in the country as part of a broader effort to tamp down the anticolonial rebellion. Along with the teaching of literacy, the distribution of "cheap, easy-to-read, useful and informative literature for new literates," they argued, could "prevent subversive agencies from utilizing this newly acquired skill for disruptive purposes." When they requested American assistance, the State Department arranged for Laubach to send one of his trained literacy experts to run the campaign. That is how Betty Mooney wound up in Nairobi. They paid her $3,500 a year to direct the Kenya Adult Literacy Program in a country where eight of every ten adults could not read or write.

The adjustment process went both ways: not only did she have to adjust to her new environment, but the people she wanted to help had to adjust to her. Mooney discovered that her connections to the colonial administration made her job more difficult because of "the suspicion of government activities which still lingered from Mau Mau days." Government vans were sent through the city streets with loudspeakers to publicize the literacy program, she recalled, but "the illiterate turned a deaf ear." She was told that people feared the program was another ruse to raise taxes or relocate them. She had brought all of the Laubach method's colorful literacy charts with her, but could not attract people to meetings to look at them. The government ran announcements on the radio. She passed out leaflets, sometimes driving herself around town in a little Volkswagen Beetle. She and volunteers put up posters at social clubs. But they did not have much luck.

"As the weeks rolled by I still had no students, no teachers, and no staff," she noted later. "If I could only get a few of these educated Africans to help me, a few whom the illiterate would trust. But where were they? I began to pray that God would send a few my way. And He did. He sent them one by one." First, at a church mission, she found a young Kenyan who had studied in India and was looking for a job. George Wanyee, a Kikuyu, became her chief assistant. Then she was introduced to Dr. Gikonyo Kiano, another Kikuyu, who had earned a PhD at Stanford and had heard Laubach speak during his student days in America. Kiano, a respected professor, helped her recruit her first batch of teachers.

But it was not until Mooney encountered Tom Mboya that her campaign took hold on a larger scale. Was this the work of a higher power or practical politics? Just as colonial authorities hoped that literacy would satisfy the African masses and quell their rebellious impulses, Mboya was convinced that literacy was a necessary first step in the march to independence. He heard about Mooney and invited her to appear at one of his political rallies. The promise of a mass audience thrilled her. "I knew there were two events in

Nairobi which always drew a large crowd of Africans – a political rally and a football game."

With Mboya himself translating for her, Mooney spoke for ten minutes about her literacy campaign to a crowd filling the sprawling dirt field where rallies were traditionally held, not far from the chaotic clutter of the Majengo market in east Nairobi. Mboya's endorsement changed everything. While it drew a visit from an officer for Kenya's Criminal Investigations Department, who rebuked her and warned her that by appearing at a political event she had violated the British Government Code, it nonetheless proved well worth it. "Thenceforth we did not have to seek out Kenya's elusive illiterates. They sought us," Mooney reported later. "Requests began to come to start new classes. They came from all over. And so did my volunteer teachers."

As an Mboya disciple, Barack Obama was probably a face in the crowd listening to Betty Mooney that day. That point is uncertain, lost to history. What is certain is that Obama befriended Mooney and one of her American volunteers, Helen Roberts of California, shortly afterward and started spending time at the literacy program office in Nairobi. At first he performed clerical duties there, much like those at the law firm. A photograph taken for their literacy bulletin, *The Key,* showed him on the job, wearing a checkered blue sports coat and red tie, his glasses and a pen resting on the desk beside him, as he maneuvered the carriage return of a manual typewriter to start a new paragraph. Soon enough he became part of what Mooney called the "committee for primer." When her office decided to publish reading primers in five tribal languages – Kikuyu, Kamba, Kalenjin, Masai, and Luo – she chose Obama to write the Luo version. The first author named Barack Obama was not the one who penned the twenty-first-century best-seller *Dreams from My Father,* but rather that very father, who a generation earlier wrote an obscure primer entitled *Otieno Jarieko* (Otieno, the Wise Man).

It was a set of three Luo adult literacy primers, to be precise, a series on Wise Ways of Maintaining Life – one on health, another on farming, a third on citizenship, each selling for a single shilling. Copies of the farming primer can be found at the Melville J. Herskovits Library of African Studies at Northwestern University. The title page is in English, the text in Luo. The title page notes, "Written by BARACK H. OBAMA for the Education Department of Kenya under the direction of ELIZABETH MOONEY, Literacy Specialist. Checked by Kenya Agriculture Department. Illustrated by WILLIAM AGUTU. The Luo in which this book is written has been approved by the Luo Language Committee."

Barack Obama was no expert farmer. Much has been made of the fact that he was a goat herder as a youth, but in western Kenya during those days herding goats or cows was no different from walking a dog in suburban America; it was a routine part of life in the villages of Luoland. The Obamas were not wealthy, but the cultural shift toward cosmopolitan habits that began with Hussein Onyango and his English tea set was carried several steps further by his son, who was attuned to the faster pace of urban life. While supporting political change and African independence, he did not romanticize the rural traditions of the tribal past. Still, Obama shared Mboya's belief that literacy was an important weapon in the nationalist struggle; he was confident that he could master any subject, he was interested in bringing modern techniques to his homeland, and he realized he could make a bit of money through writing. So for a time he willingly put himself into the mind of his wise fictional protagonist, Otieno.

The book on farming had ten chapters. Otieno learned how to maintain a farm and fertilize the land, bought an ox plow, acquired seeds, learned proper ways to plant, grew fruits and vegetables, read about soil erosion, studied the best ways to keep healthy livestock, and grew timber. Along with providing simple words and declarative sentences for beginning readers, the primer had a subtle political message: Otieno was wise not only because he could read books on farming, but because he trusted the government. Specialists from the Department of Agriculture helped him every step along the way, and by taking their advice he enjoyed successful harvests and the respect of his neighbors. There was nothing misleading or controversial in the message, yet the propaganda value for the British administration was obvious – and from this book on farming one can safely theorize that a companion primer on citizenship would have had even more to say about the good intentions of the colonial rulers.

It was not necessary for Obama to be a devout follower of everything said and done in the Kenyan literacy campaign. The larger purpose of bringing the tools of education to the masses outweighed whatever side messages of politics or religion came with the task. When Dr. Laubach himself visited the Nairobi office, he attended a session where Obama and other native instructors were reviewing a reading plan that was an account of Jesus' birth. The story used the thousand most common words in the English language and repeated each of them at least five times. A photograph of the session showed Obama – who had been educated by Anglicans, reared by a converted Muslim father, and himself betrayed no religious inclinations whatsoever – standing at the blackboard, a piece of chalk in hand, talking to Mooney at one side of the table and Laubach across from her. In neat cursive writing, the chalkboard plan began, "This is the story of Joseph / This is the story of Mary / This is the story of the baby Jesus / The angel said to Joseph . . ."

In later detailing her mission to Africa, Mooney mentioned that she had taken a trip to western Kenya to conduct a teacher training course. Her American compatriot Helen Roberts accompanied her to "an out of the way place near Lake Victoria where no white woman had been before," she wrote. She did not say whether Obama was there too, leading the way, but the likelihood is strong. Relatives in Luoland remembered decades later the time when two American women who had befriended Barack in Nairobi accompanied him back home. This was during the second year of Mooney's African mission, when her staff was changing and growing. Kariuki Njiiri, the son of a powerful Kikuyu tribal chief, became her top African assistant, replacing George Wanyee, who went off to study in the United States. Njiiri himself had just returned from the United States with a master's degree from Lincoln University and a wife he had met there as well. It was not coincidental that Obama at that very time started to think seriously about furthering his education, and about going to America to do so. Among his friends at the literacy center alone, Dr. Kiano had taken that route, and then Njiiri, and now Wanyee. It made sense for Obama to follow them.

With her optimistic missionary spirit, Betty Mooney was always looking to help the people around her, and she became personal friends with most of them, including Obama. She invited him to her home many times. Among her photographs was one of Obama in her living room, his foot resting on a stool made from an old African drum. Another photo depicted her at a picnic outing on a country hillside with Obama, his young wife, Kezia, and their infant son, known then as Bobby and later as Roy and Malik. The social barriers between whites and blacks in 1950s Kenya, and between bosses and employees, were inconsequential to her.

When Obama decided that he wanted to continue his education by attending college in America, Mooney offered to help. Obama had left Maseno without a Cambridge School Certificate and needed to pass qualifying tests before any college would consider admitting him. On January 28, 1959, Mooney wrote a letter to her brother, Mark Mooney, who lived in Pomona, California, asking him to round up a batch of books on various subjects. "An African here is preparing to take an entrance exam for admission in an American college," she wrote. "He has been out of school for some years so he needs to do some reviewing." She asked her brother to send books and outline review pamphlets on several subjects: biology, European history, English literature, chemistry, grammar and rhetoric, and math. The materials available to them in Nairobi, she said, were not "slanted to American schools." The books had to be sent airmail, she told her brother, so they would arrive in time. "Really the eagerness of Africans for education is heartbreaking," she concluded. The opportunities within Kenya were so limited that "many are going to USA but it is rather expensive."

Nineteen-fifty-nine was a year Americans began to take deeper notice of Kenya, both its past and future, looking far beyond the frightful misconceptions of Mau Mau. The year began with a celebrated tour of East Coast literary salons by Karen Blixen, the grand dame of Kenyan colonial literature who wrote under the pen name Isak Dinesen. She was seventy-four now, and according to Judith Thurman's elegant biography, her struggles with anorexia and addiction to amphetamines made her seem "incalculably old." *Out of Africa,* her defining book about her life as a Danish settler running a coffee plantation in the Ngong Hills near Nairobi, had been published in 1937, three years after Barack Obama was born. Its poetic, haunting, melancholy evocation of a faraway paradise lost had given her an international reputation that remained fervent in the United States more than two decades later (still long before the African story would be romanticized anew in a Hollywood movie starring Meryl Streep and Robert Redford).

Only audiences and adulation could lift her aging spirit, and in New York she got much of both. Richard Avedon and Cecil Beaton came to photograph her. Maria Callas sang for her. John Steinbeck hosted a cocktail party, Babe Paley a lunch, Gloria Vanderbilt a dinner. She presented three trancelike readings to overflow audiences on the Upper East Side. But for all that, her greatest wish was to meet Marilyn Monroe, so Carson McCullers arranged it. As Thurman recalled the scene, at a table with the writers McCullers and Arthur Miller, then Monroe's husband, Blixen seemed most attentive to McCullers's black housekeeper, who reminded her of her African friends, and to Monroe, who wore a tight black dress and who Blixen said "radiates . . . unbounded vitality and a kind of unbelievable innocence. I have met the same in a lion cub that my native servants in Africa brought me."

Blixen's African days were long past; within three years she would be dead. By the spring of 1959 another Kenyan was touring the country with a far different message. It was Tom Mboya, sponsored by the American Committee on Africa, a liberal organization that supported the nationalist cause and whose board included Eleanor Roosevelt, Arthur M. Schlesinger Jr., A. Philip Randolph, Martin Luther King Jr., Reinhold Niebuhr, Harry Belafonte, Sidney Poitier, and Jackie Robinson. Mboya undertook his five-week tour in April and May 1959 with two goals. The first was to connect the struggle of black Africa to the civil rights movement in the United States. The second was to raise money for and spread the word about the African-American Students Foundation, an organization he and some ardent American supporters had created to transport a rising generation of native Kenyans out of Africa for training at American universities.

Independence was inevitable, Mboya argued, but the British had not done enough to help native Kenyans prepare for it. By his count, in the final year of the 1950s only seventy-four black Kenyans were enrolled in British universities and seventy-five in Indian and Pakistani. Within Kenya itself a technical college was open to Africans, but no accredited university; the closest was Makerere in neighboring Uganda. If a new, postcolonial Kenya was to arise and succeed in the way Mboya and others envisioned, he believed the United States and its academies of higher education would have to play a vital role.

With Jomo Kenyatta locked up for a sixth year at the isolated Lokitaung prison camp in northern Kenya, the British secretary of state for the colonies described Tom Mboya as the African leader whom colonial authorities feared most. From the Crown's point of view, the secretary wrote in a confidential memorandum, Mboya had "engaged himself in a definite war of nerves . . . designed to force the government to meet unreasonable demands" – release Kenyatta and grant independence soon thereafter – "take retaliatory action, or give up." Mboya had tried and failed to organize a boycott of the queen mother's visit to Kenya in January, the memorandum said, and was now "using a newspaper he calls *Uhuru* to spread racial hatred, incite fears and promote the Kenyatta cult."

Uhuru means "freedom" in Swahili, and full freedom was something Mboya decidedly did not have in 1959, even though he had headed the Kenya Federation of Labor since 1953, had gained acclaim from all sides for settling a bitter dock strike in Mombasa in 1955, and had been one of the first blacks elected to the colonial government's white-dominated Legislative Council in 1957. Still, he was under constant police surveillance, and before he could deliver a speech in Kenya he had to provide authorities with the time and place of the rally, the agenda, a list of speakers, and the wording of any resolutions that would be presented. Determined to find ways around the restrictions, he would sponsor dances and other festive events, then find time during the evening to promote the concept of *uhuru* to the large crowds. In February he had staged a mass meeting of a new political party he had founded by ostensibly making the occasion a celebration of a British member of Parliament. "You know we're allowed to make no speeches," Mboya said at the event, whose theme was freedom. "I am not going to say anything except that this country – to whom does it belong? And the answer is: Even God knows it belongs to us."

Days after that speech, government agents paid an unannounced visit to the yellow stucco duplex in Nairobi that Mboya shared with a younger brother. He described the raid in a March 12 letter to a Kenyan friend in Ohio: "Last Friday my house was searched for subversive, proscribed, and terrorist documents. Nothing was found."

As soon as Mboya arrived in New York City on April 8, he appeared at a press conference at the Carnegie International Center. Journalists covering the event noticed a sizable ring that he twisted conspicuously on one finger as he spoke. This was not just any ring. With its silhouette of the African continent, it signified the stature he had attained at the first All-Africa People's Conference held in Accra, Ghana, in December 1958, where to the surprise of many and the private jealousy of Ghana's own president, Kwame Nkrumah, Mboya had been elected conference president. With that election, and with *Time* magazine anointing him "the most powerful political personality" in Kenya, Mboya came to America riding a wave of international publicity. At age twenty-eight, he was being called the new face of an emerging continent – an extraordinary rise for the son of an illiterate farmer who had come from the same minority tribe that claimed the Obama family.

Much like Barack Obama, Tom Mboya had been sent to a prestigious high school, in his case Holy Ghost, a Catholic prep school near Thika, but had dropped out before attaining his Cambridge School Certificate. While Obama's early departure from Maseno was ascribed to his supposed rabble-rousing against the Anglican administration at the high school, Mboya was said to have run out of money to pay for the examinations at Holy Ghost. Years after that, in 1955, as he was rising in the labor movement, Mboya was sent to Oxford for two semesters and more than held his own with the brash young British debaters. Both Mboya and Obama displayed quick and brilliant minds, a characteristic that seemed inordinately prevalent among the Luo. In later decades, after independence, Luo professors would hold 40 percent of the chairs at two Nairobi universities even though they made up only 13 percent of the Kenyan population. (Theories abounded to explain their mental acuity, including one that attributed it to a diet of fish from Lake Victoria over the centuries.) But while both men radiated self-confidence and spoke with deep, entrancing voices, Mboya was more charismatic and ambitious, a strategic genius who was far better than his young follower at making friends, influencing people, moving large crowds, and maneuvering his way through the labyrinths of colonial and tribal politics.

During his American lecture tour, Mboya delivered more than a hundred speeches, sometimes as many as six a day, crossing the continent from New York to San Francisco and from Boston to Miami Beach. At event after event, in city after city, the audiences were large, young, and diverse. In Washington he appeared at a rally with Martin Luther King Jr.; a grainy black-and-white film of the rally showed these two stirring orators, each finely dressed in trademark dark suit and tie, looking like brothers, if not twins, about the same age (King a year older), standing onstage together and evoking the commonality of their missions as they looked out on a gathering of thousands of blacks and whites that King said represented "the generation of integration." At Carnegie Hall in New York there was an overflow audience, with hundreds turned away at the door. People seemed restless as Mboya finally took the stage, the last in a long line of speakers, but he silenced the room by enunciating one word, *uhuru*, and asking everyone to stand and think about the meaning of freedom.

Near the end of his tour, he returned to Washington and visited the White House at the invitation of Vice President Richard Nixon. At almost every stop along the way, whether he was meeting privately with Jackie Robinson, the iconic athlete who had integrated Major League Baseball, or his old friend at Northwestern, Professor Melville Herskovits, leader of Africanists in the American academy, Mboya had successfully lobbied for financial support for the proposed airlift of Kenyan students and their acceptance into American universities. But he had made no headway with the Eisenhower administration. He and officials at the African-American Students Foundation, assisted by Congressman Charles Diggs of Detroit, had been trying to persuade the State Department to support the airlift, either through foreign aid or by supplying an aircraft from the Air Force Military Air Transport Service. Each request was roundly rejected. Officials in Washington argued that they could not single out Kenya for assistance at the expense of other African nations. The diplomatic politics were more complicated. Mboya was affiliated with the anticommunist labor movement, and an important ally in the cold war in Africa, someone the U.S. foreign establishment wanted to court and cultivate, but they could only go so far without alienating officials in Great Britain, who were furious at Mboya for his denunciation of their education efforts.

Vice President Nixon, intrigued by the intricacies of cold war foreign policy, and keeping one eye on the presidential campaign only one year away, became so absorbed in his White House discussion with Mboya on May 8 that he canceled several other appointments as they talked on for more than an hour, until Mboya noted that he was late for a speech at Howard University.

Nixon offered to have him driven to the historically black campus, and the two continued their conversation in the back of the sedan. But although Mboya said afterward that Nixon agreed "generally" to examine technical exchange programs, the government's attitude toward the airlift did not shift. That would not change until a year later, when the airlift program was embraced by the Democratic candidate John F. Kennedy and his family's foundation and became a political issue in the 1960 presidential campaign.

When Mboya's plane landed at the airport in Nairobi on May 17, more than three thousand raucous political supporters were there to greet him, Barack Obama among them. Ten men wearing the red shirts of Mboya's banned political party were arrested on the spot and charged with "wearing uniforms illegally." Mboya stepped onto the tarmac wearing a business suit with a colorfully beaded tribal cap atop his head. He was summarily detained and spent several hours in police custody as they searched his belongings. In a letter to Ralph Helstein of Chicago, who had assisted him when his lecture tour reached that midwestern city, Mboya recounted the travail: "You no doubt heard of the rough reception that I had at the Nairobi airport on my return. The police held me for two and a half hours and searched all my luggage and my person for alleged seditious and prohibited documents and publications. They found nothing of the sort. . . . I have never been so treated and humiliated in my life but I guess under colonial rule we have learned to take this sort of thing without any hard feelings. This is what keeps us going."

To call that incident the most humiliating in his life was saying something, but if it was hyperbolic it reflected the scars of Mboya's still young life. His father had worked on a sisal farm for a white manager whose sadistic nickname was Bwana Kiboko because he ruled his African workers with a whip made from hippo (*kiboko*) skin. After high school and training as a sanitation inspector, Mboya was working in a health office lab when a white woman walked in and, looking directly at him, asked, "Is anybody here?" As a black African he was an invisible man. "Do not set yourself against the white man," his father had told him. "He is too powerful and you cannot change him." But Mboya did not take the advice, and now everyone knew when he was around, even those who wished he were not. The correspondence with Helstein itself

reflected the way Mboya was treated by officials upon his return. He had dic-
tated the letter into a Dictaphone that Helstein had given him in Chicago. At
the airport, colonial Customs officials raised questions about the machine and
kept it from Mboya until he paid them "some 30 pounds."

The generational progression of every family is the product of chaos, of countless chance encounters and unlikely occurrences, some more apparent than
others. It is easy to see the direct role that Tom Mboya and Betty Mooney
played in turning Barack Obama toward higher education and America, but
who would expect that a magazine writer from California named Frank J. Taylor, someone Obama never met, would be the one to direct his journey toward
a specific location and school?

After covering World War I as a war correspondent for United Press and
then leaving the news agency a decade later, Taylor spent the rest of his career
pitching stories to magazines and traveling around the world to report them. A
graduate of Stanford, he had made the northern California community of Los
Altos his home base and was deeply immersed in Bay Area society as a member of the Bohemian Club and San Francisco Press Club. Among the many
magazines that kept him solvent over the years as a freelance writer, his cash
cow was the *Saturday Evening Post,* which paid him the then generous sum of
$1,750 per story. Taylor was always looking for topics that would take him to
exotic places and often proposed story ideas that required trips to his favorite
vacation destination, Hawaii. He became such an islander over the years, starting in 1947, when he wrote his first piece there, about the newfound muscle of
Asian American workers in the postwar labor movement, that he took to using
native Hawaiian phrases in his letters, calling his wife *wahine* and thanking
people with *mahalo.*

Taylor was sixty-three when he returned to Honolulu in the last week of
October 1957 for what he dryly called a "grueling assignment": to report on
a feature spread for the *Post* on the University of Hawaii, which was celebrating its fiftieth anniversary. "I think it will make a rather unusual education
piece for us," Ben Hibbs, the editor, wrote in a go-ahead letter to Taylor. The
magazine was shaped to the tastes of its readers – middle brow, middle class,
many from Middle America; this was, after all, the publication that printed

hundreds of cover illustrations by Norman Rockwell – and Hibbs and his colleagues knew that word-and-picture portraits of the sunny, faraway U.S. territory of Hawaii were always well received. Taylor got a raise before taking the assignment, to two thousand dollars, though he swallowed most of his own expenses. "Since we were going to the Islands for a holiday, I am submitting no expense account for transportation, but am enclosing a small one for one-half of the hotel bill for the extra fortnight spent covering the story and for the rent-car needed to get to the various sources of information," he wrote to Hibbs in a letter that accompanied his final draft, which he submitted in early January 1958.

Taylor had reworked the article several times through December and the Christmas holidays before turning in his version, which was then tightened and rewritten again by Hibbs and other *Post* editors at the main office in Philadelphia to fit the magazine's pronounced style. It was published on May 24, 1958, and provoked such a strong response that Willard Wilson, the university's provost, wrote Taylor a long letter of thanks: "I am constantly amazed at the influence of the written word in a country that we deplore frequently as non-reading, but it was pretty obvious from our experience here after that article came out that there are a lot of people in the United States who at least read Frank Taylor's articles in the Post!"

Not only in the United States, as it turned out. Across the world in Nairobi, at the offices of the Kenya Adult Literacy Program, Betty Mooney's library materials included a stack of copies of the *Saturday Evening Post*. One day many months later, Mooney was leafing through a back edition and came across an article on page 38 titled "Colorful Campus of the Islands" by Frank J. Taylor. She passed the story along to her young friend and assistant, Barack Obama, and urged him to read it as well. Taylor's first paragraph set the tone of a story suggesting that the University of Hawaii was a place apart not only in terms of geography but also cultural diversity. Obama had read about Jim Crow segregation in America, but Taylor's words suggested that perhaps Hawaii would be more accepting. "Nestling against the mountains that rise behind Honolulu, at the mouth of the lush Manoa Valley and a mere two miles inland from Waikiki Beach, is one of the most unusual and colorful campuses on American soil," the story began. "The physical setting itself is picturesque enough, but what really sets the University of Hawaii apart is the multiracial make-up of its student body."

As anecdotal evidence to support his theme, Taylor accentuated a story line that, along with accompanying photographs, would be of obvious interest to Obama and most young males: the beauty queens on campus. Every spring, the article noted, editors of the student yearbook *Ka Palapala* held not one but seven beauty contests that reflected "how the East and West have intermingled in this melting-pot university," admitting native Hawaiians, Caucasians, Japanese, Chinese, Filipinos, and Koreans, and cosmopolitans. That last category was established by the university administration to account for students who were "a blend of several races." Of more practical interest to Obama, Taylor's story also quoted a university official saying that out-of-state and foreign students paid the same tuition as in-state students, $170 a year, because leaders of the institution thought it was "a good investment to have youngsters from many states and many countries in our student body."

After reading that article, Obama started to focus on the "colorful campus of the islands." The books and study outlines on history, literature, science, and math that Betty Mooney had requested from her brother had arrived from California only three weeks after she had mailed her letter, and Obama, though five years out of school, aced the examinations and put the University of Hawaii near the top of a list of almost thirty colleges and junior colleges to which he applied, often using Mooney and her colleague Helen Roberts as references. According to a letter that Mooney sent to her brother Mark's wife, Margie, two institutions responded swiftly to the Kenyan's application. Mooney was writing from a safari she had taken with Roberts to Murchison Falls on the Nile in Uganda. After describing the thrill of having "crocodiles and hippos practically at our door step and elephants in the back yard," she closed with a progress report on Obama, the African assistant who wanted to study in America. "You will be glad to know that the boy you sent the books for has received admission both to San Francisco State and Hawaii University. He'll probably go to Hawaii as there is an engineering college there. We both got interested in Hawaii from reading an article about the University in a *Saturday Evening Post*."

Through that late spring and summer of 1959 Obama spent more time at

Mboya's office on Victoria Street. The lecture tour across the United States had created a stir in Kenya. While the colonial government rebuked Mboya for speaking ill of their education efforts, smart young native Kenyans now viewed him, and the airlift to America, as their way up and out – not out of Africa forever, but out from the shackles of their past toward an independent future.

The United States had become the place to go, and scores of students started reading about colleges and cities and towns that they had never heard of before. After checking in with Mboya, prospective airlift students often lined up in the hallway of the U.S. Information Service offices to see Robert F. Stephens, the cultural affairs officer (and a close friend and associate of the Hagbergs, for whom Obama's father worked). Stephens was a font of information on American higher education, his office library stocked with more than eight hundred college catalogues and a blue book of universities and colleges that noted how many foreign students were enrolled at each institution. He was also fluent in Swahili and sympathetic to the airlift even though his bosses at the State Department in Washington would not support it.

More than sympathetic – Stephens became part of a four-man committee in Nairobi that decided which students would qualify for the airlift. The other three were Tom Mboya, Gikonyo Kiano, and Kariuki Njiiri. It was a multitribal group – Mboya was Luo, Kiano and Njiiri both Kikuyu – but all three had strong connections to Betty Mooney, and to Barack Obama. Njiiri connected all the dots for Obama. During his studies in the United States, he had become friends with William X. Scheinman, an iconoclastic young aircraft parts manufacturer who was also Tom Mboya's closest associate in the United States and the founder of the African-American Students Foundation, the New York–based group that was the driving financial and organizing force behind the airlift. Back in Nairobi, Njiiri was working as Mooney's assistant at the Kenya Adult Literacy Program, where Obama was his colleague on the primer committee.

The concept of the airlift was that transporting a planeload of students to the United States would eliminate the prohibitive initial expense of overseas travel for young people who might not make as much money in a year as it cost for a single overseas flight. The African-American Students Foundation would raise the money from donors in the States to pay for a chartered plane that would take the Kenyans from Nairobi to New York, from where they would disperse to colleges around the country. The foundation and other individual supporters would also provide scholarship funds to help the Kenyans pay tuition fees.

One of the best-known Americans aiding the project was Jackie Robinson, who had retired from baseball two years earlier and taken an executive position at Chock full o'Nuts. During his spring lecture tour, Tom Mboya had met privately with Robinson in New York and came away with a promise that Robinson would publicize the airlift and fund a few scholarships himself. In a letter to Mboya after their visit, Robinson said that he was looking forward to working on the airlift and was rounding up allies for the cause. "The most important thing we must do is provide a pride in the colored people of the world," he wrote. "Your trip here was a big step in that direction. I do hope you have continued success in your great work. One of my greatest pleasures was meeting you. It's your kind of leadership that will win the rights we seek."

Jackie Robinson the civil rights activist was much like Jackie Robinson the ballplayer: impassioned and fearless. Not long after his letter to Mboya, he and two of his celebrated friends, the singer Harry Belafonte and the actor Sidney Poitier, sent out a letter supporting the airlift in which they argued that educational opportunities for black Kenyans were "nonexistent under the repressive colonial regime." This further enraged British authorities, sparking a strong exchange of letters in the *New York Times* and elsewhere. Douglas Williams, a colonial attaché in Nairobi, called the letter misleading, noting that in 1958 the government of Kenya was offering a total of one million dollars in aid for 449 native Africans pursuing higher education – 325 at Makerere in Uganda, forty-five in the United Kingdom, two in Canada, and seventy-nine at Royal Technical College in Nairobi.

"I am proud to be part of the airlift," Robinson wrote in reply. "And if the British government is upset because it has been caught with its colonial pants down, I'm sorry." Scheinman also responded, noting in a letter to the editors that the only Kenya-based institution mentioned by Williams, the Royal Technical College, "is not a general college with possibilities for a liberal arts education. Furthermore, it is clear that a total of 79 out of 6 million Africans . . . is not precisely a shining example of generally available higher education in

Kenya."

Meeting throughout the summer, the airlift committee in Nairobi sorted through applications and interviewed students who wanted seats on the plane and sought financial support. The students had to meet four basic requirements: clearance by the Kenya Department of Education; visa issuance by the U.S. consulate; proof of admission to an American college; and at least three hundred dollars to cover incidental expenses. Mboya added another requirement for the young men; he wanted each of them to have at least two neckties.

Obama was already admitted to Hawaii and San Francisco State. He also had acquired a visa and was raising the spending money with help from his father and friends from Luoland, who held a fund-raising party for him at the Kaloleni Social Hall. Money was also raised in Kanyadhiang. Hussein Onyango, who first questioned both whether his son could afford America and whether he should leave his pregnant wife and young son behind, had finally given his blessings. "*Winyo piny kiborne,*" he said, citing an old proverb: "No place is too far for a bird." Betty Mooney and Frank Laubach's foundation were discussing how to provide him with tuition funds. Although he had never attained the Cambridge School Certificate, he had received high scores on college entrance tests. He had Mboya on his side, and Njiiri was a colleague. Only Robert Stephens was not impressed. "I interviewed him in my office [at the American consulate]," Stephens said a half century later, acknowledging he only had a "hazy memory" of the episode. "There were some more than others who stuck in my mind, and he was one of them. I can't tell you why. I think because I had kind of a negative impression. Most were just so easy to like, so eager and so likeable, and he wasn't. He kind of stood out in that way."

The late summer of 1959 marked the final days in the tenure of Sir Evelyn Baring, Kenya's governor and commander in chief. He had arrived seven years earlier, at a time when white settlers were demanding action to stanch the influence of Mau Mau. During his seven years in Nairobi, Baring had imposed a state of emergency, oversaw the arrest and imprisonment of the nationalist leader Jomo Kenyatta, ordered the massive roundup and imprisonment of Kikuyu tribesmen that led to thousands of deaths, and tried to repress the

African nationalist movement by banning political parties, speeches, and rallies. None of that could stop the inevitable, which was becoming obvious to Baring's superiors in London. Independence was in Kenya's future, and the questions now were *how* and *how soon*. The retirement of Sir Evelyn at age fifty-five – sending him back to England, where he could live out his years as Baron Howick of Glendale – was a necessary step toward that future.

Before leaving for home, Baring decided to enjoy Kenya one last time with what he called a farewell tour. His intent was to travel the length and breadth of the colony, and his itinerary included a number of festivities in Luoland, but he never got to the western reaches. The tour began the first week of September in the other direction, with a visit to a resort on the Indian Ocean near Malindi. As the governor was lounging on a nearly deserted beach at Casuarina Point, a young girl approached, screaming for help. Two friends, she said, were struggling in the water, caught by a riptide. Sir Evelyn did not flinch. He ran toward the surf and swam out nearly one hundred yards to the scene of peril.

This unexpected exertion apparently was too much. Baring was about to go under himself when a trusty companion, Captain Ritchie, a former chief Kenyan game warden, ran in to help, pulling his boss and one of the girls to safety. The other girl drowned. Ritchie, who was seventy, and who had survived a recent heart attack, was fine after the episode, but the governor was sent to bed with what was described as inflammation of the lung and strained heart muscles. Duty called him from sick bay a few days later, when he was driven down to Mombasa to announce the development of a new BP Shell refinery. In the stiff-upper-lip fashion of the British peerage, he attended the ceremony in pajamas, dressing gown, and slippers.

The line of colonial service to the Crown had begun with his namesake and father, the first Earl of Cromer, heir to the Barings Bank fortune. The earlier Sir Evelyn had once served as private secretary to the viceroy of India, where he had earned the nickname "Over-Baring," a reputation hardened during a long career in Egypt as controller general and then consul general. The son had followed in those imperial footsteps, working India's Punjab frontier as a district officer, then moving on to assignments in Southern Rhodesia and South Africa before his posting to Nairobi. And here, on the Kenyan coast, with swollen lungs and overworked heart, with the governor parading, brave and clueless, in his sleepwear – here was empire's end for the Baring family.

Sir Evelyn's farewell tour had just begun when several score of native Kenyans prepared to depart Nairobi for schooling in America. They would leave with a common hope and belief: that in a few years they would return to help lead a new nation. One among them had left earlier, carrying British Passport No. 84764, arriving in New York on August 9 on a British Overseas Airways flight from London, on his way to the Hawaiian Islands.

CHAPTER 5

AFRAID OF
SMALLNESS

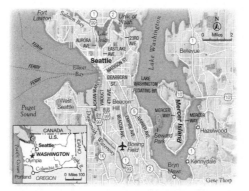

Gene Thorp

Stanley Ann once told her uncle that she was the daughter of the wrong Dunham. She and her father had precious little in common. He was a glad-hander, a boaster, a storyteller and joker who struggled through high school, flunked out of college, lacked the concentrative powers to be an academic, and yet presented himself to the world as a know-it-all. She was sensitive and precocious, an only child who started reading when she was four, loved nothing more than sitting in a tree and leafing through the shiny color pages of *National Geographic* when she was ten, was proficient in math, and by age fourteen had become a budding intellectual, quiet if not shy, with a keen and sardonic sense of humor. "School was easy for her, just as it was always easy for me," said her uncle Ralph Dunham, who had remained at Berkeley in the postwar years, attained a doctoral degree, and held academic posts in education thereafter. "She felt it would have been easier if I had been her father."

As the daughter not of Ralph but of Stanley, she found herself constantly readjusting, mentally and physically, looking for ways to survive in an unsettled world as her father bounced from job to job and the family moved from town to town. Already in her young life she had lived in nine different houses in Kansas, California, Oklahoma, Texas, Kansas again, and finally Washington State. Her parents never owned their own place. While her mother had gone through school with the same Augusta classmates from kindergarten to high school graduation, Stanley Ann had never attended the same school for more than two years in a row until ninth grade, making it impossible during those formative years to maintain a steady group of friends.

Sixth grade in Texas, seventh grade back in El Dorado (her father was selling furniture on the second-floor showroom of the Farm n' Home on Central Avenue), eighth grade at Nathan Eckstein Middle School in Seattle, and ninth grade at a bright new building in the Seattle suburbs, Mercer Island High. By then she could not abide being called Stanley Ann. It sounded childish, but more than that, it evoked the old Middle American affection for double names that seemed as unsophisticated to her in this new milieu in the great Northwest as it had a generation earlier in Augusta, when her mother stopped going by Madelyn Lee. "Just call me Stanley," she told her freshman classmates. She blamed it on her old man, saying that he wanted a boy so badly he named his daughter after him. Either she did not know or did not want to bring up the real story, that her name derived not so much from her father as from her mother's obsession with Bette Davis. In any case, in high school she was Stanley, which is the name this chronicle will use for her during this period as well, with her father now distinguished from her as Stan.

Mercer Island sits in the middle of Lake Washington to the east of Seattle on the way to Bellevue. It looks like a miniature replica of the continent of Africa squished and elongated by a vise. The island runs five miles from north to south and three miles east to west at the widest point, only a half mile across at the narrowest. The only way to get there directly from Seattle was by ferry until the start of World War II, when the north end was connected to the city by what was then the world's largest floating bridge: twenty-five floating concrete sections, most of them 325 feet long. The floating bridge became a symbol of the island and a harbinger of its transformation. Many old Mercer Island families who did not like what was happening to their paradise in the postwar years identified themselves as BBs, meaning "before the bridge."

When the Dunhams reached Mercer Island in 1956 they were part of two larger migration patterns, one from the middle of the country to the coast, another from city to suburb. They had arrived in Seattle the previous summer after a several-months-long hiatus in El Dorado, where they renewed old acquaintances long enough to want to flee again. Stan had taken Madelyn to the El Dorado Country Club one night that June to celebrate the twentieth reunion of his class at El Dorado High, or what should have been his class; he graduated a year late. Not long after that evening, after sitting at a long table and eating baked steak, scalloped potatoes, and buttered corn with the Burnhams and Biggses, Shirks and Straits, Pressons and Pratts, Morrisons and Mosiers, Stan Dunham was out of there, on the way to Seattle, where a friend had told him about a sales job in a big furniture store. His wife and daughter soon joined him, and they rented a house on 7th Avenue N.E. for that first year before moving out to the island. "Another experience at the end of the rainbow where Stan was going to do wonderful things and make his fortune," his brother-in-law Charles Payne said dryly, recounting the move west.

Mercer Island, still unincorporated, was transforming into a booming suburb when the Dunhams moved out from the city. At the start of the 1950s, the island had four thousand residents and no high school. By the time the Dunhams arrived in 1956, Mercer Island High was enrolling students and the population had doubled, on its way to twelve thousand by the end of the decade. The island culture was caught between old and new. There was still only one restaurant, the Floating Bridge Inn, one supermarket, one barbershop, one dry cleaner, two used car lots, no theater. Most of the houses used septic tanks for waste disposal (even a few cesspools remained), and the water system was haphazard and archaic, with some wooden pipes. The perimeter roads on the less developed south end of the island were unpaved on the way into "the Bush," the forested area where high school kids would go to make out. But middle-income single-family homes and developments were popping up month by month. "It was growing fast and a bit topsy-turvy," recalled Susan Botkin Blake, whose family moved to the island the same year as the Dunhams.

For many newcomers, the Mercer Island experience began with a temporary stay at the Shorewood Apartments while their home was being finished. This was not slapdash low-rent lodging; some islanders thought of Shorewood as a touch of Eastern sophistication in the Wild West, with its sturdy brick and wood exteriors, high ceilings, hardwood floors, and sash windows, many offering splendid views of the Cascade Mountains. The complex went up in 1949, at the start of the suburban boom, a large CHILDREN WELCOME sign out front. There were forty buildings in all, starting on the waterfront and sprawling back several acres, a road separating the lower and upper sections, accommodations for seven hundred families, and its own water system with water filtered and chlorinated from Lake Washington. The Dunhams rented unit 219, a quiet corner two-bedroom apartment, and stayed put. There was no new home going up for Stan and Madelyn and their daughter, Stanley.

Madelyn and Stan became suburban commuters for the first time. Madelyn found a ride east to Bellevue, where she worked at a bank, and Stan went the other way, making the 7.2-mile drive west across the floating bridge and into downtown Seattle to the Standard-Grunbaum Furniture store at the corner of 2nd and Pine. It took about twenty minutes, depending on traffic. In landing a sales job at Standard-Grunbaum, Stan had moved up to the big time in the furniture business: giant store, major city, growth market. *First in Furniture, Second at Pine* was the slogan.

The ten-story Standard Furniture building dated to 1907 and the Seattle boom that accompanied the Klondike Gold Rush. Standard merged with Grunbaum Furniture a few years before Stan got there and dominated the region, with the massive downtown store and satellite outlets in the suburbs and Tacoma. The Schoenfelds who ran Standard as well as the Grunbaums and many employees in the merged company were Jewish, and by all accounts

Stan felt an affinity with them. His grandson would later mention as one of the ways the old man expressed his individuality a personality that was starting to take shape in Washington State: "In the back of his mind he had come to consider himself as something of a freethinker – bohemian even. He wrote poetry on occasion, listened to jazz, counted a number of Jews he'd met in the furniture business as his closest friends." This was not the norm in the Seattle area, nor on Mercer Island. In fact a report by the Washington State Advisory Board to the U.S. Commission on Civil Rights found that four sections of Seattle traditionally barred Jews, and sections of Mercer Island "offered evidence of this same kind of religious discrimination."

The year Stan moved to Mercer Island also marked the publication of *The Organization Man*, the defining sociological work by William H. Whyte detailing how corporations and governmental and educational bureaucracies suffocated individuality in the postwar era. It was a book that Stanley would discuss at Mercer Island High a few years later. Her father, for all of his flaws, or perhaps because of them, stood outside the organization-man culture. His allegiances were fleeting; he could never hold a job for long. While Madelyn tried over the years to turn him into a bridge player, a game that required discipline and cooperation, he preferred checkers and the lone-wolf aspects of poker. He was more the disorganization man, a peculiar combination of pride, neediness, eccentricity, frustration, and bonhomie that could seem lovable from a distance and in retrospect but was maddening for those close to him, especially his daughter.

His frustration fueled an anger – what his grandson later called a "violent temper" – that was largely hidden from the outside world but erupted all too often inside the walls of Shorewood's unit 219. "I think it was when he felt he wasn't being given his due as master of the house by both Madelyn and Stanley Ann that he would get upset and start hollering," said Madelyn's brother Charles. In a variation of the assessment of Ralph Dunham, the uncle from the other side of the family, Charles said the father-daughter clash had to do with their different intellects: "I probably shouldn't say this, but it was my observation that Stanley Ann was smarter than her father and she knew it, and that led to a lot of shouting. He shouted at her just like he did at Madelyn on things. And she outwitted him frequently."

Stanley's friends mostly enjoyed being around her father, but they could feel the tension. Maxine Hanson said he was outgoing and "nice to all the friends that Stanley brought home," and that they were happy to hitch rides in his new white convertible, yet she had the impression that Stanley "would just as soon he go away. They locked horns a lot, I think." Susan Botkin Blake remembered trips back from the library in downtown Seattle with Stanley and her parents. "We would climb into the car and immediately Stan would start into his routine. Madelyn was a porcelain doll kind of woman. She had pale wonderful skin, reddish hair, carefully coiffed, and lacquered nails. She was feminine and diminutive. She would temper him all the way home – 'Now, Stan!' Stanley would roll her eyes a lot when she was with her father. If she was irked with something she would roll her eyes. It was a very expressive thing of hers. Stanley dreaded her father's ire. She was respectful of him, but suffered him. And the mother went along with it because that is what mothers did then."

John W. Hunt, another friend from school, often borrowed his parents' car and came by the Shorewood apartment to give Stanley a ride to wherever their crowd was going that night. She did not drive. "Whenever I was there she was desperate to get out of the house," Hunt recalled.

> Her dad was very, very friendly, but she often wanted to get out of the house. I had a car, she didn't. The pretext was I was her date, but we didn't really date. Just got together. [Stan] was definitely a salesman. He had that outgoing personality. Shake your hand. Bring you in. See what was happening. He loved to talk. She found it a little embarrassing. The impression was that he would have liked to have talked more. He would love to pump us. He was a nice guy and very outgoing. The big grin was there. . . . She was, get her out of there. I got the feeling she debated a lot with her folks. I think her dad liked that, liked the repartee, and her mother was like, "Don't argue."

That was the impression of outsiders, but Madelyn was not as docile as some imagined; she simply disdained public demonstrations. In private, within the family, Madelyn was not reluctant to have it out with her husband. Her brother Charles said of their relationship, "Madelyn and Stan as a couple were the opposite of [our] parents, who never said a cross word to each other in the presence of their children. Madelyn and Stan would just yammer and yak all the time about everything. And yet they were a devoted couple and remained that way."

Stanley and her classmates were born during the war, a few years too early to count as official baby boomers, but their high school experience in the late 1950s was much the same as that of the first wave of boomers who followed them in the early 1960s. The teenagers of Mercer Island came to believe they were different, better, the chosen ones, a sensibility fed by postwar prosperity and the attention and money that middle-class and upper-middle-class suburbs were then devoting to their schools. This was before the phrase *generation gap* was coined, before the popular spread of a counterculture, before the war in Vietnam and the antiwar protests at home, but Stanley and her friends were no less curious and challenging than the young people of the next decade. "We thought we were aware, looking for fakes and phonies and for real stuff in the world," said Chip Wall, one of the intellectual boys in Stanley's class. "In search of the truth. We were looking at the world and all the stuff that was going on." It was not yet clear what was coming, but as Susan Botkin Blake put it, they felt they were "on the cusp of change."

If anyone was ready for change, it was Stanley Ann Dunham. Decades later her own daughter would look back on the coming-of-age of her mother during those Washington State years and say, "She just became really, really interested in the world. Not afraid of newness or difference. She was afraid of smallness." It was a variation of the fear that propelled Stan out of Kansas in search of some other *el dorado* and that raced through the mind of Madelyn when she compared her small-town upbringing with the Hollywood sophistication of Bette Davis. Family threads often unspool this way: the daughter was learning a lesson from the frustrations of her parents. In her mind, they came to represent what they had tried so hard to run away from, lives of defined limits, if not smallness, and she was determined not to let the same happen to her.

Here is Stanley as she matured at Mercer Island High. She *owned* her first name, her friends said. No effort to avoid it or pretty it up; just call her Stanley. A young woman named Stanley in other circumstances might be seen as pretentious, but with her it was the opposite; she was without pretension in every way. During her elementary school years in Oklahoma and Texas, according to family lore, she was often teased, called "Stan the Man" (the nickname of baseball's brilliant Stan Musial), but anyone with a first or last name open to verbal manipulation could get ridiculed in childhood. By the time she reached Mercer Island, Stanley was protected by the surest weapon: a penetrating wit that she let loose not only in her own defense but on behalf of anyone else who might appear vulnerable. Kathy Sullivan, a close friend, said she and Stanley shared a sensibility that could be "outlandish . . . devilish." Susan Botkin Blake was nicknamed "Botkie" by Stanley, whom she met on the first day of ninth grade, when their lockers adjoined. From the start, she said, Stanley had a sharp tongue that "could kill. Things would pop out of her that were just so witty. She could have been cruel if she was not such a nice person. . . . She could cut someone down so fast if they were being pompous or thoughtless or unkind. I was always in awe of that wit of hers. I would always look at her if she was receiving information. She could just melt them. Her comments were always very original, nothing hackneyed or trite about her language."

In a high school culture celebrating brawn and beauty, Stanley was one of the brains, on the honor roll all four years, but she was not a loner or outcast. She belonged to the high school service club, the Mercer Girls, was program director of the French Club, worked on the yearbook, *Isla,* and went to slumber parties. Her friends said she had a talent for inventing voices for fun and occasionally slipped into an exaggerated Kansas accent when portraying a hick. There was a gas station manager on the island named Yirka who was constantly telling the kids exotic stories about his travels and adventures, and it was Stanley who jokingly formed the Yirka Movement in his honor. In that spirit, she undertook at least one exotic adventure of her own. As the author Janny Scott recounted in her illuminating biography, *A Singular Woman,* Stanley and a male friend, Bill Byers, in a moment of wanderlust after a night at a Seattle coffeehouse, started driving south in his 1949 Cadillac and rode day and night all the way to San Francisco and Berkeley, picking up a few oddball and potentially dangerous hitchhikers along the way. The police tracked them down and a frantic Stan Dunham, who had been calling around all night, flew down and drove them back home.

Stanley attended all the athletic events and was a particularly avid basketball fan. Maxine Hanson's older brother, Bill, who stood six-eight, was the team's star when she was a sophomore, and she and her pals religiously kept track of his buckets. To one of her pals, who confessed to a crush on the coach, she wrote in the yearbook, "Hope you and Cipriano live happily ever after. I know you love him so much. I love you, too – Stanley." It is worth noting that these minor traits – the sarcastic wit, the facility with voices – were characteristics that Stanley Ann Dunham passed along to her son.

As an only child who lived in an apartment arranged for adults, always neat, with modern Scandinavian furniture, she was thrown by the noise and chaos of her friends' larger families. Her pal Botkie had two little brothers she had to babysit, and she recalled, "Stanley never babysat. She would come over to the house and just stand back. Her eyes would blink and her head would spin. 'Oh my God, what's going on here?'" She was not the sort to primp or pay much attention to appearances, but nor would she make a fashion statement by looking different; she wore plaid skirts (pants were not allowed) and saddle shoes and Peter Pan collars. At five-foot-six she was slightly taller than average. She had a long chin and narrow face, much like her father (and later her son), with a bright smile that flashed less often in her junior year, when she was stuck with braces. Her friends said that her eyes twinkled when she talked and that she had a wonderful laugh that started deep in her throat. John W. Hunt described her as "a little bit heavy. Not fat, but a little heavy." According to Maxine Hanson, Stanley "didn't feel that she was attractive." She spent countless late afternoons at the Hanson residence after school, since no one was home at Shorewood's unit 219 a half mile away – her parents were still at work in Seattle and Bellevue – while Maxine lived only a block and a half from school and had a stay-at-home mother.

Most of her classmates could not remember Stanley dating boys from Mercer Island High. John W. Hunt would drive her around and hang out, but as a friend, not a date. He heard rumors that she might have been dating someone off the island. Susan Botkin Blake said it was a fact, not rumor. "She dated a couple of guys from off the island. She looked beyond the white boys with crew cuts who were prevalent in our class. I remember the Italian she dated. He taught her to ride a horse. He lived in Bellevue. Long wavy hair, gorgeous, the Fonz." Stanley's Fonz seems lost in the mists of time, but there is no reason to doubt the story. It is typical that she would look outside her set for romance. In fact, her entire life thereafter was shaped by that tendency. Going out with an Italian might have been a bit daring in the context of that time and place. Dating someone of an even darker skin was implausible if not unthinkable. "You were never unkind and would not slight someone not of your race, but we didn't mix," Maxine Hanson said. "It was subtle racism. There were no blacks that I remember in our class at Mercer Island High. We had a very sheltered life."

Just getting off the island was an adventure. Trips east to Bellevue, the next suburb, were fairly common, but parents were not so willing to let the teenagers go the other way, into the city. Stanley, regarded by other parents as a responsible young woman, was often able to bring a girlfriend or two along when she would take the bus into town and get off at 45th Street on the edge of the University of Washington campus. John W. Hunt, Chip Wall, and some of the other Mercer Island boys would join them. "We would go to the espresso café, the Café Encore" – jazz-loving owner, thirteen small tables, coffee and pastry for fifty cents – "and order a drink and nurse it at a back table and talk for hours and hours . . . sit and talk and talk and talk," recalled Hunt. "World events, politics, stuff at school . . . sometimes the subject would reflect or interface with what our parents thought about things. 'What did your parents think? What did they say?' Trying to figure out the adult population when we were sixteen or seventeen. You don't have a whole lot of equipment for figuring that out."

"She thought and argued just like a boy," Chip Wall said of Stanley. Stripped of sexist interpretations, he meant it as a sociological statement of that era, and as a compliment. "There were a bunch of very bright and articulate women, no question about it," Wall said, but he and his male friends thought many of them were "shy of argument." Stanley seemed unafraid to formulate arguments and express them. She was, said John W. Hunt, "sometimes rather quiet but measured and forceful when she put forward her ideas. She wasn't a shouter, but sat and thought quite a while before she spoke. She was one of the most intelligent girls in our class, but unusual in that she thought things through more than anyone else and was very cogent in her discussion." It was her ability to argue, Hunt said, that eventually brought Stanley into their intellectual circle, a group that included Chip Wall, Raleigh Roarke, Dennis Hollenberg, and several others.

The other requirement, along with loving to talk and argue, or perhaps a prerequisite for it, was having a keen social awareness – and Stanley had that too. "We socialized with what we considered to be the more intelligent people. Grades could classify that, but also the more liberal thinking," said John W. Hunt. "Some of us came from liberal families, but not all of us. My mother was middle of the road, my father was very conservative." Stanley's parents were not yet overtly political, but they were open to new ways of thinking. They often attended the University Unitarian Church in Seattle and sometimes the East Shore Unitarian Church in Bellevue, spiritual havens for liberals who were uncomfortable with religious dogma. In his memoir their grandson described a discussion about religion between Stan and Madelyn that captured their differing personalities. Stan said he liked the diversity of thinking in the Unitarian Church, that it was "like you get five religions in one," and Madelyn rebuked him with the pragmatic put-down, "For Christ's sake [Stan], religion's not supposed to be like buying breakfast cereal!" But Stan deserves a break here. It was apparent that he was searching for meaning during his Washington State years, and the Unitarians provided a forum and respite for him. At one point, in fact, he was on the speaking circuit himself. On a Sunday morning in May 1957 he traveled to the Port Angeles area above Olympia National Park to deliver a lecture to the local Unitarian fellowship with the provocative title "Why Bother." There was no question mark in the title, but a question lingers as to what Stan meant and what he said. Beneath the bluster and glad-handing, after years of constantly moving around and starting over, it appears he was longing for something beyond just another paycheck.

Any accounting of Stanley during her Mercer Island days inevitably comes around to the story of John Stenhouse. It is worth mentioning primarily as another bit of context for that time and place, though it had no direct effect on what or how Stanley thought. The Dunhams knew the Stenhouses during that period, as did virtually everyone on the island. John Stenhouse was an insurance salesman and chairman of the Mercer Island school board. He lived with his wife and two daughters in what *Time* magazine later described as "a cedar-sided house among the madrona trees." In the spring of 1955, a few months before the Dunhams reached Seattle from El Dorado, and more than a year before they moved across to Mercer Island, Stenhouse testified at a hearing of the House Un-American Activities Committee that he had once belonged to the Communist Party. He said it was before the war, when he was lonely and working for the United Auto Workers union at a plant in Los Angeles. He quit the Party after the war, realizing that he had made a mistake, he testified, and now believed "we have the power to show people throughout the world that we have a better way than the Communists."

The Stenhouse revelation caused a brief firestorm. Three members of the school board demanded his resignation and more than two hundred citizens gathered at the Mercer Crest Elementary School for a discussion on his past and future. "Let's rise on our hind legs and throw him out!" one resident bellowed. The prevailing sentiment was more tolerant. A leader of the local Young Republicans Club reflected the temperate mood by saying, "We urge that individuals who have made candid and complete disclosures be given every fair consideration." Stenhouse kept his position on the school board, and the issue was fading as the Dunhams settled into their Shorewood place. It was part of local lore, perhaps in the same way, though less pervasively and insidiously, as the presence of the Klan in El Dorado when Stan and Ralph Dunham were boys.

Mercer Island High itself, and the challenging curriculum offered to its brightest students, had a far more profound effect on Stanley and her friends. The school was still new; hers was the third class to enter. The emphasis was on preparing students for college, but this was before the era when classroom excellence was judged so much by standardized tests, and also before there was an effort to equalize school districts in a state. Mercer Island was dominated by families with school-age children; although residents might have been stingy in other areas, they were eager to spend money on education. The school quickly established a faculty who encouraged students to argue intelligently, write cogently, and think freely. Val Foubert and James Wichterman stood out from the rest during the late 1950s. They taught the humanities block for distinguished upperclassmen, using college-style lectures and seminar discussions to take their charges through a regimen of literature, philosophy, politics, and the arts. It was in recognition of their willingness to challenge prevailing assumptions and prejudices, but also with a touch of self-deprecating sarcasm, that they referred to the corridor between their classrooms as Anarchists' Alley.

Foubert, a military veteran who had attended Seattle University on the GI Bill, founded the humanities block soon after he was hired as master teacher and chair of the English Department at the new school, which he drove to every morning from his home in Seattle, crossing the floating bridge. With his penchant for reading and thinking, he felt at home in the rains of Seattle, loving nothing more than a book, some big band music, and a tuna on rye sandwich with chips. Elaine Bowe, one of his first students, said he created an atmosphere in which everyone felt "safe to speak up in class." She described him as "funny, calm, patient, sharp – willing to explain and help." Others thought he was more argumentative and demanding than calm and patient. Jim Wichterman, who also was the track coach and assistant football coach, had all of those characteristics as well as a sarcastic touch and a penchant for nicknames. He was not above calling the Dunham girl "Stanley Steamer," referring to the old automobile. In his memoir decades later her son wrote that "Stanley Steamer" was one of the nicknames kids in Texas called his mother when she was a little girl. He probably conflated a few family stories to reach that conclusion. Wichterman said he meant it as a compliment: "The Stanley Steamer was an important thing and I used to tell her she was important." She was also, as he remembered her, "well informed, well read, and a good thinker" who always had an opinion.

Wichterman and Foubert saw it as their mission to infuse a love of learning in their students while at the same time challenging them, opening them up to the beauty, complexity, and tragedy of the larger world, and puncturing myths that surrounded their comfortable middle-class existence. A remembrance forum created in Foubert's honor by former students after he died in 2007 at age eighty-two (he was given a military burial) noted that the classroom methods he and Wichterman employed did not always sit well with the older generation. They were known to provoke "regular parental thunderstorms by teaching their students to challenge norms and question all manner of authority." The protests later came to be called "Mothers Marches," implying some form of large, organized opposition. The reality was that on several occasions two or three parents, usually mothers, came to the school to question the reading assignments. Other parents were fully supportive of the young teachers and even attended informal adult classes at Wichterman's house on Wednesday nights to keep up with their children.

"It was pretty controversial with some of the parents," said John W. Hunt. "They would come up and . . . berate the teacher and complain to the principal that students were reading something they shouldn't be reading or arguing with their parents' political point of view when they shouldn't be doing it." Chip Wall said, "Wichterman and Foubert were instrumental in getting us to think, and anybody who tries to do that, particularly in high school, has trouble. The parents would say, 'Make my kid a thinker but make sure he thinks like I do.'" The syllabus for political philosophy included *The Communist Manifesto,* which perhaps triggered much of the parental concern, especially in the wake of the Stenhouse controversy. But it also included a capitalist manifesto of sorts, Ayn Rand's *Atlas Shrugged,* and the humanities students read many books in between, including *1984, The Hidden Persuaders, The Lonely Crowd,* and *The Organization Man,* along with the writings of Plato and Aristotle and H. L. Mencken. "We soaked it up like sponges," said Susan Botkin Blake. As the rebellious decade of the 1960s approached, Foubert was not an experimental postmodernist or existentialist cynic in any sense; he revered the literary canon. His favorite book was Ernest Hemingway's *For Whom the Bell Tolls,* and his favorite poem was "Fern Hill" by Dylan Thomas ("Now as I was young and easy under the apple boughs . . ."), which reminded him of his carefree youth playing in the orchards of his Wenatchee Valley home. His optimistic hope for humanity was best expressed, he said, in the speech William Faulkner gave in accepting his Nobel Prize in 1950: "I believe that man will not merely endure, he will prevail." In essence it was a more literary variation of what Stan Dunham had said to those Unitarians near Port Angeles: "Why bother."

But in their senior year, taking them out of the 1950s and into 1960, not all of Stanley's classmates shared Faulkner's faith, or Stan Dunham's. "The Doomsday Clock" – the threat of nuclear war – "was as close as it had ever been," recalled Susan Botkin Blake. "And it affected people in our senior class. I remember looking at colleges and there was a sense of malaise that permeated the group. Why bother? The boom is going to happen. It was a topic of conversation. We were aware of it. Stanley was able to laugh it off. She had a sense of hope and not despair." Her sense of hope was not religious – she had announced that she was an atheist – but beneath her sardonic sense of humor was someone who saw the best in other human beings.

Whatever their frame of mind, when it came to moving on from high school most of Stanley's friends ended up applying to the place they were most familiar with, the well-regarded university across the floating bridge in Seattle. John W. Hunt was accepted by Harvard, but it was too expensive, his father said, so he and Chip Wall made plans to enroll at the University of Washington together. So did Susan Botkin Blake and many of the other girls. With her late-November birthday, Stanley was among the youngest members of her class, still seventeen at graduation, and she would be seventeen all through the summer and deep into the next fall. Her plan was to join her friends at "U-Dub," as it was called, but the choice was not hers to make. She had the grades, certainly, graduating with a 3.35 grade point average in a challenging curriculum, including four years of French and advanced chemistry and math. But her father apparently thought she lacked the maturity. He was ready to move on from the Seattle area, she recalled, and told her that she was simply too young to remain there without family nearby.

At eleven-thirty on the morning of June 6, after the final commencement rehearsal, the 140 members of the senior class gathered at the high school's 92nd Street entrance, where the Lakeside Gravel Company poured a fresh sidewalk in which the 1960 graduates could leave their handprints and names. Stanley Dunham left her name behind. As for her future, she wrote in the yearbook that her goal was "to join the Yirka movement" – to have exotic adventures around the world. She would reach that future in ways perhaps not even she could imagine.

Albert Robert Pratt plays much the same role in this chronicle as Frank J. Taylor, the magazine writer whose article on the University of Hawaii caught the attention of Barack Hussein Obama in Nairobi. Bob Pratt did not write, he sold furniture, but if he had not found his way to Honolulu, the path of the Dunham family, and of history, might have been different. Spokane, on the eastern side of Washington across the mountains from Seattle, was Pratt's home territory. Furniture was the family trade; his grandfather owned one of the largest stores in the region. When the Dunhams arrived in Seattle and Stan went to work at Standard-Grunbaum, Bob Pratt and an uncle were running Pratt Furniture in Spokane. The furniture subculture was family-oriented in those days and still small enough that comings and goings could be tracked by word of mouth. Though precisely when and how is not documented, Stan Dunham came to know Bob Pratt and later heard that he had moved to Honolulu and set up shop there after having a dispute with his uncle.

Pratt chose Oahu because he had been to Hawaii during World War II with the U.S. Merchant Marine and was so taken by it that he vowed to return. The split with his uncle pushed him to fulfill that promise and move his wife and two young children with him across the Pacific. They landed in 1958, one year before Hawaii became a state, when the territory's population was starting to boom. Their first residence was a tiny apartment near the Ala Wai Canal. Ten-year-old Cindy and her brother, William, one year older, spent that first Christmas on Waikiki Beach four blocks away, watching old Hawaiians play their ukuleles outside the Moana Hotel. Their father's new business began with a wholesale warehouse that he called Isle Wide Distributors. Within two years he had added a small retail store on South King Street, away from downtown toward the University of Hawaii campus. In the summer of 1960, to help him manage the store, he hired a former competitor from the furniture business in Washington, a garrulous salesman looking for yet another chance, heading even farther west, moving on after lasting better than four years on one job, his longest stretch yet. Here to start life anew in Hawaii at age forty-two came Stan Dunham.

The Pratt family had escaped from their cramped Waikiki apartment by then and rented a house ten miles out of town on Kalanianaole Highway on the way toward the south shore. Development had not unearthed that stretch yet; it was still the land of pig farms and carnation farms and large native Hawaiian families like the Kalihananuis, who lived across the road. The rental was a four-bedroom yellow ranch house, shaped in a sideways T, with a sweeping front yard that broached the two-lane highway and a 450-square-foot storage cottage out back. With no place of his own when he arrived, Stan sublet a part of the house from the Pratts that had its own bedroom, bath, side door, and hallway. Madelyn had to close down the Mercer Island house and finish her work at the escrow department of the bank in Bellevue, so she and her daughter stayed on the mainland for part of the summer before joining Stan in Hawaii. To young Cindy Pratt, these backroom tenants were the oddest people she had ever seen. Stan, she thought, wore big baggy suits that never fit him. His wife seemed withdrawn. And then there was this bookish young woman, a freshman at the University of Hawaii, who lived with them and had such a peculiar first name.

CHAPTER 6

BEAUTIFUL ISLE OF SOMEWHERE

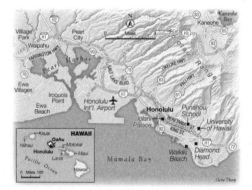

Hawaii was where Barack Hussein Obama had wanted to be since he first read about it in the *Saturday Evening Post*. But now that he was here, where exactly was he? He was on an island 10,731 miles from home, farther from a continental landmass than almost any remote outpost in the world. When a new morning was breaking in Kenya, it was eleven hours earlier on Oahu, the dinner hour of the previous day. He had grown up in the equatorial heat near Lake Victoria, yet the blazing August and September sun in the wash of the Pacific found him griping about the climate. He was in the newest place in America, the fiftieth state of the United States, a designation that became official on August 21, near the time of his arrival. After the chaos and social stratification of Nairobi, and the clamor and ceaseless hubbub of London and New York, two of the cities where he stopped on his way across the world, Honolulu seemed a place apart from all of that, he said, the people "so much more relaxed."

As he surveyed his new landscape in the late summer and early fall of 1959, Obama found some connections to his past. There were hula girls at the airport, at the Waikiki beachfront hotels, and even sometimes on campus, and their graceful swaying reminded him of the *owalo* (sisal skirt) dance in Luoland. The vowel and consonant rhythms of the native Hawaiian language would sound familiar to him. *O-han-a. O-bam-a. Ohana* means "family." One linguistic-geographic connection was more direct; the university campus was thick with kikuyu grass, adaptable and aggressive, imported from Kenya since 1925, named for the tribe. The magazine article that he had read at Betty Mooney's literacy offices in Nairobi appeared accurate so far. He could sense what he called "an inter-racial attitude" quite unlike what he had experienced in colonial Kenya or had read about concerning the mainland United States. Everywhere he looked now he saw a multitude of colors. But most skins were shades of yellow, tan, and brown. If he was in a polyglot paradise, Obama still presented the rare darkest hue.

Popolo, some Hawaiians called him. It was the native term for a blackberry, and a slang word for blacks. It could be considered a slur, but no more so than *haole (HOW-lee)*, slang for whites, even those born in Hawaii. No ethnic group constituted a majority among the native Hawaiians, Caucasians, Japanese, Chinese, Filipinos, Koreans, Portuguese, Samoans, Okinawans, and all of their various combinations, but blacks were a minority among minorities, only 0.8 percent of the population. The 1960 census, conducted within a year of Obama's arrival, found fewer than five thousand blacks in Hawaii out of slightly more than 630,000 residents. Almost all of those were connected to the U.S. military and lived out near Schofield Barracks, Pearl City, and the Marine base at Kaneohe. Only a few hundred black families had long histories in Hawaii, some tracing back to the early nineteenth century, when crew members slipped off merchant ships at Honolulu Harbor to live in a place where having dark skin was less dangerous.

Obama was singular even within the minority among minorities. His manner of speaking evoked an Oxford don, his dialect so precisely British that some fellow Kenyans jokingly called his type Afro-Saxon. Despite the Arabic origins of his given names, no one mistook him for a black Muslim, the first hint being how he introduced himself. As in Kenya, he was *BARE-ick,* with a decidedly British accent, and not the more Arab-sounding *Buh-ROCK.* And at five-eleven and 165 pounds, with black hair and black eyes, he was the *popolo* of *popolo*s, his skin so dark it reminded a new friend of what Nina Simone, the jazz singer, called "deep purple."

In all of these ways Obama was a different ingredient in the Hawaiian stew, so different that both Honolulu newspapers published stories about him during his first weeks on the island. As classes were starting at the University of Hawaii, reporter Shurei Hirozawa of the *Star-Bulletin* drove up to the campus in the Manoa Valley section of the city and interviewed Obama along with two other foreign students from Jordan and Iran. The three represented the first ever from their respective countries to attend the university. Obama told Hirozawa that by working as a clerk in Nairobi for several years he had saved enough money to pay for two semesters at Hawaii – leaving out the financial assistance he had received from Betty Mooney, the Laubach Literacy Institute, and the Tom Mboya–connected African-American Students Foundation.

The article said he was from Kisumu – close enough, and less obscure than the mud-hut villages of Kanyadhiang or Nyang'oma Kogelo. An accompanying photograph showed Obama wearing his trademark eyeglasses, dark-framed and semirimless, arms folded to reveal a silver-plated wristwatch. Here was a portrait of a young man modern in both look and outlook. In his conversation with the reporter, Obama addressed the subject of dislocation, the difficulties young Kenyans of his generation had moving from old to new, from tribal customs they left behind to a Western way of life in which they had no roots. He kept himself out of that equation, using it merely to explain an increase in delinquency in Kenya.

Honolulu's other English-language daily paper, the *Advertiser,* featured Obama in a story that ran during Thanksgiving that semester. This time the

Kenyan student expressed surprise at Hawaii's modernity. Turning Western preconceptions of Africa on their head, he said of his new environment, "When I first came here I expected to find a lot of Hawaiians all dressed in native clothing and I expected native dancing and that sort of thing, but I was surprised." The reporter wondered if Hawaiians quizzed him about his homeland. "Oh, yes," Obama said, laughing. "People are very interested in the Mau Mau rebellion and they ask about race relations in Kenya. I tell them they've improved since the rebellion but are not perfect yet. They also ask if Kenya is ready for self-government. Some others ask me such questions as how many wives each man has back home, what we eat, how I dress at home, how we live, whether we have cars."

He did not answer those questions in the story. Nor, on one matter, was he forthcoming with anyone in this new setting. Neither newspaper readers nor his fellow students knew that he had left a son and pregnant wife behind in Kenya.

Five years out of school, Obama entered the University of Hawaii with an ambitious plan. He announced that he intended to stay three years. That meant he would have to take an extra load of courses nonstop through the summers to amass the required 130 credits and earn his degree in that truncated period of time. Perhaps this was not a typical approach among the seven thousand students on campus, who might rather linger in idyllic surroundings, but Obama had reasons for being in a rush. He was a half decade older than most freshmen and already had the breadth of knowledge and intellectual bearing of a graduate student. He also was intensely focused on the future, his and his country's. A new nation – independent, run by Africans – was coming into view on the horizon, and Obama wanted to be part of it, as did scores of other young Kenyans who scattered to universities across America that fall. The future he saw for himself was in government service, as an expert economist perhaps, filling some position out of reach in the colonial era, and to do that he needed advanced degrees, which would take even more time. His first impressions of Hawaii were all positive, but his gaze was mostly elsewhere and the frame of mind he arrived with could not change: get a degree, move on, get another, go home.

By 1959 the University of Hawaii had grown beyond its housing capacity. Once almost exclusively a commuter campus, it now lured more students from the mainland and foreign countries, who, as well as providing diversity, enriched the school's talent pool. They came for a number of reasons, the gorgeous geography and an expanding curriculum among them, but they were also attracted by a generous tuition system that charged them no more than in-state residents. Finding places for them to live was another matter. The John A. Johnson dormitory, a residence for men, had space for only eighty students in double rooms. Many others were housed elsewhere, Obama among them. With other classmates, he took a room at the Charles Atherton branch of the YMCA on University Avenue at the edge of campus, just "one block *makai*" from the old teachers college building. *Makai* is a local term, one of several directional words on Oahu. As the Hawaii-reared Ron Jacobs wrote in a poem called "Dis Orient," "Mauka are the mountains / Makai is the sea / North, South, East, West / Mean not a thing to me." *Mauka* and *makai* simplified directions on an island with such an irregular amoebic shape, where there were more than four distinct coastlines and the Ko'olau Mountains cut diagonally across the landscape.

The campus was in the midst of a construction boom that began with the university's fiftieth anniversary two years before Obama arrived – the event that sparked Frank J. Taylor's interest in writing his magazine story – but it retained much of the feel of its origins as an agricultural and mechanical college, with grazing dairy cows and chicken coops on property that stretched to Manoa Stream. But as remote as it was and as sleepy as it might seem, the university had intellectual spark, political energy, and a touch of rebellion and freethinking in its subculture. And Obama, even with his three-year plan, was by no means the sort of grind who would spend all of his time pent up in his room at the Y or at Sinclair Library. Student life would not change his essential Luo personality. He loved to be around people and talk, argue, challenge, flirt with women, dance, sing, laugh, and drink, and he quickly fell in with a like-minded band of graduate students and teaching assistants in sociology, anthropology, literature, and biology, many of whom were antiestablishment outsiders. The stereotypes of an apolitical conformist era were as misplaced with this group as they were with Stanley Ann Dunham and her senior cohorts at Mercer Island High across the Pacific. Perhaps the most garrulous of Obama's new friends was Neil Abercrombie, a graduate student in sociology who had arrived for the fall 1959 semester from upstate New York, a place as alien from the Hawaiian environment as Kenya.

Abercrombie, bearded, long-haired, with work boots, colorful vests, and the stout chest of a weightlifter, carried the same bundle of ideas, passions, and maverick instincts with him then that he would take into a political career that saw him become a Honolulu City Council member, a congressman from Hawaii, and eventually, fifty-plus years later, a governor. He first encountered Obama at the Snack Bar, a barracks-style campus hangout off Metcalf Street between the Quadrangle and Hemenway Hall. "You see somebody three times and say, 'Hey, how are you?' – and you sit down and have lunch in the lunchroom. And of course his story was immediately attractive to all of us," Abercrombie explained. The presence of an African student on campus was unusual, but Obama "would have stood out very easily anyway, physically and in terms of his personality and his presence, if you will."

Some of it was his voice, deep, mellow, resounding. "If he said something and the room was not real noisy, everybody stopped and turned around. I mean he just had this wonderful, wonderful voice," said Andrew Zane, another member of the group, who was known as Pake (PAH-kay), slang for "Chinese," which he mostly was. Some of it was his laugh, big and booming. Much of it was his ego. "He was brilliant and opinionated and charismatic and avuncular and *opinionated,*" Abercrombie recalled. People who did not know Obama might be put off by him, he added, "because he never hesitated to tell you what he thought, whether the moment was politic or not, even to the point where he might seem a bit discourteous. But his view was, well, if you're not smart enough to know what you're talking about and you're talking about it, then you don't deserve much in the way of mercy for being ignorant of the subject matter. But he was so obviously himself." In that crowd his attitude was no problem, according to Abercrombie, because "everybody was smarter than everyone else, and everybody let everybody know how smart they were, depending on how much they had to drink."

Obama had taken to smoking a pipe and dressed more neatly than most other students, in blue-gray gabardine slacks and white dress shirts. Dietrich

Varez, who edited *Asterisk,* the school's literary magazine, from a pocket-size office under the staircase in Hemenway Hall, recalled that Obama would stop by now and then on his way from class to pick up a copy of the journal and chat. Author Sally Jacobs, in her vibrant study of Barack Obama Sr., *The Other Barack,* quoted Varez saying that Obama often critiqued poems in his magazine, although in a genial way. During his childhood days in Luoland, Obama often had gone barefoot and lived among barefoot people, yet he seemed shocked when he saw Varez on campus in shorts and no shoes. "You are walking around in the spit of common people," he would say. "Doesn't that bother you?" This reflected Obama's obsession with cleanliness, as well as his sense of superiority, but something larger as well. The notion of a new Africa, moving out of colonialism and into independence and modernity, served as the context for much of what he said and did in these distant surroundings. There would be no bare feet in a new government in Nairobi. "Even then, a lot of our discussions were about what would happen in Africa," Abercrombie recalled.

Events were unfolding swiftly during Obama's first months away from Kenya. Sir Patrick Renison, who had been sworn in as governor in late October, replacing the heart-weary Sir Evelyn Baring, announced a few weeks after taking office that emergency rule would end in early 1960, after eight difficult years. In what Renison grandly called "an act of grace," more than a thousand African natives who had been imprisoned, detained, or restricted would be released, with the first wave of fifty Mau Mau detainees let out from the Aguithi work camp near Nyeri within days. Tom Mboya was in the middle of the action. In late January 1960 he led a delegation to London for a roundtable at Lancaster House with British and colonial authorities to hash out the shape of a new Kenya. The transitional agreement Mboya came away with put black and white Kenyans on the same voting rolls for the first time, expanded the legislature, assured that Africans would have a majority thirty-seven seats out of sixty-five, provided that Africans would run at least seven cabinet departments, and eliminated the practice of reserving lands solely for white settlers. Mboya and his allies made some compromises, especially on the notion of "undiluted democracy" based on one man, one vote; voters had to be literate, or older than forty, or earning more than $210 a year – requirements that disproportionately precluded Africans. Though they did not get everything they wanted, Mboya said, the overall effect was larger than the specifics: "We have exposed once and for all the myth of white supremacy."

Little more than a month later, in early March across the world in Hawaii, Obama saw his Luo mentor on the cover of *Time* magazine, high recognition for a minority legislator from a minority tribe in a faraway country. "Kenya's Tom Mboya" read the caption below a color portrait by Bernard Safran that depicted Mboya in coat and tie, broad nose and dreamy eyes, cylindrical beaded Luo hat fit snugly on his head, a white settler to one side behind him, a native African on the other, and Mount Kenya, symbol of independence, in the background. With Jomo Kenyatta still in prison, Mboya, at age twenty-nine, had become the face of independence. *Time*'s story began with a depiction of his return from London, when the caped Mboya was carried in on the shoulders of supporters at what was called the largest African political rally ever, at a stadium in Nairobi, before a crowd of more than twenty thousand that Mboya silenced with the simple wave of a cow-tail fly switch. "When we left for London, the government was in the hands of the Europeans," he said. "Now it is we who can open or close the door." The crowd began chanting the word of freedom: *uhuru*.

"Whose Kenya is it?" Mboya asked.

"Ours," roared the crowd.

With real power and its many benefits so visible on the horizon, tribal politics in Kenya became more intense and complicated. The outsize publicity that Mboya was receiving in the West did not help him at home. He could draw large crowds and articulate the nationalist position, but the still detained Jomo Kenyatta, "the Burning Spear," as he was known reverentially by his followers, was considered the father-in-waiting of a new country, and his associates became increasingly jealous and suspicious of Mboya, spreading negative stories about him whenever they could. His push for freedom was beyond dispute, but the very compromises he had accepted in the Lancaster House negotiations were now turned against him, and some Kikuyu exiles took to Cairo radio to claim that Mboya was being bribed by the British and manipulated by the American CIA. At the Snack Bar on the Hawaii campus, one of Obama's persistent topics was his fear that creating a unified Kenya would be difficult because of deep-seated tribalism, and that Mboya on a larger stage and people like Obama on a lower level eventually would suffer because of their minority Luo status.

William X. Scheinman, the American most responsible for the wave of Kenyan students coming over, and Mboya's closest friend in the States, shared the larger concern, and was constantly analyzing the political climate and looking for ways that Mboya could survive and thrive. As a circle of Kikuyus displayed more jealousy of Mboya, Scheinman reached the conclusion that the only way Mboya could "smash tribalism" was "by taking a more militant stand [than his antagonists]. It might upset some supporters in the U.S. and Britain, but was the only way," he wrote.

In Honolulu, Obama saw himself as a spokesman and lobbyist for the new Africa. Through his contacts at the Y and his role as the first president of the university's International Students Association, he began visiting churches and political organizations around the island to talk about the changes sweeping his continent. Many of his appearances were promoted in the newspapers as small filler material ("Church to Hear Kenya Student"), but the subject was more volatile, and Obama saw it as his mission to place the debate on an intellectual level and tamp down the raw emotions. In 1960 alone, fourteen new African nations would emerge from colonialism, and in most cases liberation did not come without violence. Stories of rape and murder terrified Westerners, complicating their perspective on the independence movement. On June 4, as Obama was finishing his first two semesters at Hawaii, the *Star-Bulletin* ran an editorial titled "Terror in the Congo," which noted how much damage had been done during a half century of Belgian rule, but was primarily focused on the fears of white settlers there less than a month before independence:

> The Congolese – inflamed with the spirit of independence – want to expel the only culture they possess. What's worse, many apparently intend to do it brutally. Belgian women are stricken with fear. Many of the Belgians are giving up their homes and moving their families to safety. . . . Many predict that after independence day there will be riot and rapine.

The editorial did not escape Obama's notice. After reading it he typed a letter in response that the *Star-Bulletin* published four days later. The letter laid out the strongest arguments against the long and exploitive history of colonialism. Obama conceded that new African nations had made or might make mistakes that he could not defend, but they would learn from those mistakes. "All I am asking for is that we be cool and partial" – one presumes a typo and that he meant impartial – "of what is presented to us by authorities," he concluded. Given the difference between the reality of the Mau Mau rebellion – in which a multitude more Africans than whites were killed by British authorities – and the image of rampaging Africans presented by authorities in the West, this point was well taken in the case of Kenya. But what was most interesting about Obama's letter, considering his own future, was the way he defended Africans against charges of abusing women, in this case the wives of Belgians: "As far as I know there is nothing more respected than a person's wife and if this is so (at least for the African customs I am acquainted with) does it mean that with independence the African is now turning against his cultural heritage?"

If Obama believed he was fighting larger stereotypes here, his words also contradicted the smaller reality of his own family. Hussein Onyango had abandoned wives he was tired of, or driven them off, and had beaten and abused them all, physically and mentally. And as we shall see, Obama leaving a pregnant wife and infant son in Kenya on his way to Hawaii would in retrospect seem the least problematic of his acts of spousal disrespect.

Robert F. Stephens, the U.S. cultural affairs officer in Nairobi, was a whip-smart diplomat, sympathetic to Kenyan nationalism and supportive of the effort to educate future leaders in the United States. But Obama's first year in Hawaii would contradict part of the assessment Stephens gave when not recommending him for the airlift: that he was neither academically qualified nor of the proper temperament for such a rigorous test. To the contrary, Obama proved to be an academic success story in America.

In his first two semesters, he had won a freshman honor from Phi Beta Kappa and become president of the International Students Association. In connection with that role, he was named student chairman of the school-sponsored International Week that summer. A photograph in a school publication showed him smiling broadly, wearing a light suit, white shirt, and bow tie, as he strummed a guitar and sang, surrounded by four young women and two men, all wearing the traditional garb of their various nationalities. His performance in the classroom had impressed university officials enough that they granted him a scholarship starting in the fall, easing his financial worries.

The tuition was eighty-five dollars a semester, plus a ten-dollar registration fee and ten dollars per credit for summer school, which would prove as expensive as the fall and spring semester tuitions for Obama since he intended to carry heavy summer workloads in his three-year plan, taking the maximum number of courses for both the six-week regular summer school and three-week postsession. Betty Mooney, his academic benefactor, had left Nairobi, married Elmer Kirk, a widower, and settled in Tulsa, Oklahoma, where she and her husband had to cover college expenses for two of his children. There was no money left for Obama, but she persuaded the Laubach Literacy Institute to fund the rest of his room and board expenses, which could amount to nearly eight hundred dollars. Obama saved some of that money by moving out of the Atherton Y and taking a cheaper room at 1048-A 10th Avenue, another mile from campus in the Kaimuki district, beginning a pattern of relocating almost every six months. He was also still picking up small support checks from the African-American Students Foundation, which included him in its lists and considered him part of the cohort even though he had not been part of the airlift.

While Obama pursued his ambitious academic plan in the isolation of Hawaii, the debate over the effort led by Mboya and Scheinman to train young Kenyans in American colleges had grown only more intense during its first year of implementation. British and colonial Kenyan officials continued to criticize the enterprise, at times making the contradictory arguments that it was draining Kenyan institutions of their best students or alternatively sending only the rejects and most poorly trained students to America. Mrs. E. D. Hughes, a white member of the Kenya Legislative Council, had returned from a trip to the United States with reports that some students from the 1959 airlift were stuck in little versions of hell, struggling to adapt at second-rate colleges in small towns in rural America without friends, some on the verge of starvation.

This was an exaggeration, as Kenya's minister of education acknowledged after his own inquiry. No one was starving, and many of their complaints were little different from those of any college student in an unfamiliar environment. But some students were running out of funds, others could not adjust academically or socially, and for one reason or another there were many casualties along the way. Among the American colleges attended by the first diaspora of Kenyan students, Hawaii might have been the most remote in terms of location, but socially and academically – in a group that included such obscure schools as Cascade and Diablo Valley, Philander Smith and Warren Wilson, Morris Brown and Jarvis Christian – Obama's choice was above average, and he was thriving. A report by K. D. Luke, who worked for the British embassy in Washington and was assigned to look after the colonial students, detailed the condition of every Kenyan on the airlift, excluding those few like Obama, who came over separately. He noted that twenty-two of the seventy-seven collegians (four of the original eighty-one came for high school) were at historically black institutions in the segregated South, engendering a special set of adjustment problems; that nearly half were at schools with fewer than a thousand students; and that more than half were at colleges with no graduate programs. Obama encountered none of those limitations. Luke found some students facing impossible situations or insurmountable obstacles. Amram Onyundu Okal at Tuskegee Institute in Alabama was "arrested briefly for trying to buy a sandwich at a white counter" and was "looking to transfer to a northern school." Ellingstone K. Mgnolia wanted to transfer from Philander Smith College "because of racial discrimination in Little Rock." And on the opposite end of the racial spectrum, James S. Mgweru landed in Utah as the only African student in a white and predominantly Mormon student body at Brigham Young University, which Luke concluded was "unsuitable" for Africans.

Other students reacted to their new surroundings quite differently. Philip Ochieng, who enrolled at Roosevelt University in Chicago, said later (in an interview, not the Luke report) that it "was not so bad" and that he saw more discrimination against American blacks – "because of economic fear" – than against Africans like himself and the other Kenyan at Roosevelt, John Charles Kang'ethe. The first snowfall in Chicago shocked Ochieng not because of the snow itself, but because it was the first time he had seen "a white person laboring with his hands," shoveling sidewalks. He was also surprised, he said later, to "see white women chumming up to you – that was against the law [in Kenya]." Pamela Odede, one of twenty Kenyan women in the first wave, who was attending Western College, a women's institution in Oxford, Ohio, said she "liked America" but thought it was "too cold." The daughter of Walter Odede, a close associate of Jomo Kenyatta, Pamela was less likely than others to complain after winning a scholarship; she was secretly engaged to Tom Mboya, a romance that symbolized Mboya's unified vision.

In midsummer 1960, as preparations were being finalized for a second and larger wave of students from Kenya and other East African nations to study in America, Mboya found himself maneuvering between political "tribes" – Democrat and Republican – in the United States. He returned to the United States that July on another fund-raising mission, seeking private contributions to pay for four chartered airplanes needed for an expanded second airlift. For the second straight year, State Department officials had declined requests to help with transportation. On July 26 Mboya made his way out to Hyannis Port to meet with John F. Kennedy, the Massachusetts senator who had accepted the Democratic nomination for president only eleven days earlier. Impressed by Mboya and aware of Africa's importance as disputed turf in the cold war with the Soviets, Kennedy decided to support the airlift. At first he promised a modest contribution from the Joseph P. Kennedy Jr. Foundation (named in honor of his older brother, who was killed during World War II), with the idea that other private foundations would match the grant. But when those foundations balked, Kennedy decided that his family's foundation would foot the bill and provide more than $100,000 for the Kenyans. Plans were set for a meeting in Washington on Monday, August 15, to establish an advisory committee for overseeing the Kennedy contribution, a group led by the foundation's president and JFK's brother-in-law, Sargent Shriver, and also including, among others, Gordon Hagberg, the former U.S. Information Service official in Nairobi who, when he lived on Muthaiga Road, had employed none other than Hussein Onyango, father of the Kenyan student in Hawaii, Barack Obama. To keep politics out of it, there would be no public announcement.

No public announcement did not mean no private whispers, however, and Vice President Nixon, JFK's Republican opponent, immediately heard about

Kennedy's decision. The news most likely came to him from an aide who heard it from Jackie Robinson, who was on the board of the African-American Students Foundation but was also a Republican and a Nixon supporter. Robinson had been working his contacts to try to obtain administration support for the airlift, and in fact had met with Nixon to press the cause earlier that summer. In any case, the news energized Nixon, who thought he had developed a strong relationship with Mboya himself a year earlier during their long discussion at the White House, and had been trying, without success, to influence the State Department on the issue – and who, above all, could not abide being outshone by Kennedy on a matter of foreign policy.

Two days before the August 15 meeting that would formalize the Kennedy plan, Nixon set about rearranging things, and he used James R. Shepley, a *Time* magazine journalist on leave to work on his presidential campaign, as his agent. Shepley was a blunt character whose nickname within Time Inc. (where he would rise later to become president and chief operating officer) was "Brass Knuckles Shepley." He spent that weekend and into Monday morning working the telephones, placing many of his calls to Frank Montero, who worked with Bill Scheinman at the African-American Students Foundation. Shepley told Montero that he knew about the $100,000 offer from Kennedy and beseeched them to hold up on agreeing to the foundation money because there was still a chance the State Department would change its mind and fund the project. By noon Monday, Shepley was barking into the phone that it was just a matter of minutes, and soon enough he called Montero with word that the offer was solid. State had agreed to provide up to $100,000 for transportation costs.

When Scheinman and Montero met with Shriver, Hagberg, and the rest of the foundation's advisory panel later that afternoon, Scheinman argued that after more than a year of rejection from State, he did not trust the Eisenhower administration's motives nor the federal government's ability to handle the mission effectively. A decision was made to accept the Kennedy money and tell State to use its funds to bring other East African students to America. This did not go over well with Brass Knuckles Shepley. By Montero's later account, when they talked after the decision was made, Shepley "implied that efforts might be made by his side to suggest in the press that this was a politically motivated act by Senator Kennedy." The political gamesmanship intensified from there. Senator Hugh Scott, a Republican from Pennsylvania and a member of the Nixon campaign's "truth squad," took to the Senate floor the next day to announce with fanfare that the State Department had agreed to finance the airlift, acting as if he had no clue about what had already happened with the Kennedy Foundation. That same day, Jackie Robinson wrote a column to be published the next morning in the *New York Post* that began:

> Good news is all too rare these days, but Monday I received a call from Washington which added up to just that. Jim Shepley, an aide to Vice President Nixon, called to tell me the State Department has decided to pick up the tab for three planeloads of African students which the African-American Students Foundation is bringing over this year to study at American universities.

Robinson went on to tell his readers about his visit with Nixon in Washington earlier that summer and how the call from Shepley was "the happy result." Again, no mention of the fact that the African-American Students Foundation had decided to go with the Kennedy money. Senator Scott then took the floor a second time, now acknowledging the Kennedy Foundation proposal, but stating that it came only after the State Department had agreed to fund the airlift and that "the long arm of the family of the junior senator from Massachusetts has reached out and attempted to pluck this project away from the U.S. government." Turning facts upside down, Scott argued that this amounted to "an apparent misuse of tax-exempt foundation money for blatant political purposes." When presented with an accurate history later that week, Robinson apologized in print; Scott did not.

In the end, early that September, four planes funded by the Kennedy Foundation landed in New York carrying 289 students for training in America. This time the young Africans, all with scholarships, spread out to more than two hundred colleges. Compared to the first airlift in 1959, which involved a single planeload plus a few strays, this larger band of students represented the "crash" program that Mboya felt was needed to train a professional class as the days of an African-led Kenyan nation grew closer.

Frederick Okatcha, one of the students on the second airlift, said that he and his classmates were praised as "the leaders of tomorrow" as they left Nairobi, but the adjustment process for him was as discombobulating as for the pioneers of the year before. Most of the students on his plane had never flown, Okatcha recalled. They left at night, not knowing how long the journey would take, and when they saw lights as they came in for a landing they assumed they were in New York. In fact, it was Khartoum. Seven more stops and another full day to go. After a few days of orientation in Manhattan, Okatcha was put on a Greyhound. He rode the bus through Philadelphia, Harrisburg, Pittsburgh, Columbus, Indianapolis, and St. Louis, where he heard a strange form of English, unfamiliar to him, a deep southern accent, as he transferred to a Trailways bus to Warrensburg, Missouri, home of Central State Missouri College. He arrived on the small campus on a Sunday, and it seemed no one even knew he was coming. Finally, a man came and took him out to dinner and bought him a hot dog, "which I declined to eat, thinking it had to be made from dog's meat." Misperceptions all around. His new classmates asked the oddest questions. "Where did you buy that suit, in England?" one asked. "It must have been in the U.K." And Okatcha, insulted, thought his best response might be, "Yes, and I flew from Nairobi to London naked."

But in Honolulu, acclimated for a year, Obama was in a different place. If he felt any of the same disorientation, it was not apparent to those around him. He seemed to be making friends everywhere, perhaps too many friends of the opposite sex, according to immigration officials, who were monitoring his activities. On Friday afternoons he was among the regulars who drifted over to the apartment of a graduate student, Peter Gilpin, near the corner of Wilder and Poki to eat pizza, read poetry, debate politics, and listen to the recordings of Big Bill Broonzy, the Chicago blues singer. On other nights he could be found drinking beer with local African Americans at the Stardust Cocktail Lounge or George's Inn a few miles farther from campus, or delivering one of his New Africa speeches to the local chapter of the NAACP or church group, or meeting with the Japanese, Filipino, and Korean graduate students to talk about international issues. In need of money, he received permission from immigration officials to take a part-time job and worked for five dollars an hour at a nearby coffee shop and as a temporary summer laborer at the Dole

Corporation. His confidence was only growing, as was his magnetism. As his father, Hussein Onyango, had said, "No place is too far for a bird."

"Beautiful Isle of Somewhere," the Kansas mourners had sung at the funeral for Ruth Armour Dunham thirty-four years earlier at the First Baptist Church in El Dorado, after she had taken her own life in despair on Thanksgiving night 1926 at the auto garage in Topeka. It was an evocation of heavenly peace. Now Ruth's granddaughter was living on a real-world beautiful isle of somewhere, but none too thrilled about it. If Stanley Ann Dunham had had her way, she would have remained in Seattle in the fall of 1960 and joined her friends in the freshman class at the University of Washington. Instead she found herself in Honolulu, living in a converted hallway outside her parents' bedroom in their wing of the rental ranch house they shared with the Pratt family on Kalanianaole Highway. Her mother was working at the downtown office of the Bank of Hawaii, known commonly as Bankoh. The job search this time had been easy for Madelyn. At the request of her old bank in Bellevue, she had gone to the Bank of Hawaii to see if they would be interested in helping the mainland institution set up an escrow department on the island. No thanks, but they could use an escrow officer themselves, and Madelyn was hired. Stan was going to work every morning as well; he held the title of store manager at Bob Pratt's furniture store on South King Street, closer to campus.

Their daughter was seventeen years old, across the ocean from her friends, alone in the newest state, in a very different place and culture. She and her Mercer Island pals had survived with a sense of sardonic humor and intellectual curiosity that seemed suited to sipping coffee in the foggy mist and attending foreign films in dark theaters. And now here she was in this dazzling Pacific sunshine, yet stuck in confined quarters with a father who upset her with his bull and bluster and a mother who was pragmatic but not outwardly warm or expressive; stuck with no obvious way out, without even her own car or a license to drive one. Still, island life had its privileges. Back on the mainland, her friend Susan Botkin was "suffering" to get her weight down in preparation for going through first-year rush at the U-Dub sororities. Botkie had been dieting all summer, anxious about her prospects of making the cut in a Greek system where sorority mothers still pinched girls to see if they were wearing girdles. Then came a postcard from Honolulu with Stanley saying she was wearing shorts and muumuu everywhere.

The first day of freshman orientation at Hawaii was September 19, and classes began a week later, on September 26. These were not ordinary dates in the United States or the world. On the nineteenth Nikita Khrushchev arrived in New York for an extended stay during which the Soviet premier met Cuba's Fidel Castro for the first time (at a hotel in Harlem) and took off his shoes in the General Assembly of the United Nations, pounded his fist, and denounced the West. On the twenty-sixth, in Chicago, Vice President Nixon and Senator Kennedy met in the first televised debate of their presidential race, a fateful hour that helped propel JFK into the White House as voters and pundits focused more on small-screen images than words: Nixon appearing sweaty and needing a shave, Kennedy fresh and vibrant. These were major events that helped shape the fabric of postwar history, yet a small thread from each would reach all the way down into the stories of two unknown students from opposite ends of the world who were both present that fall on the campus of the University of Hawaii.

Russian was a hot language in American academe as the new decade began. Only three years earlier – before the Soviets launched the *Sputnik I* satellite in October 1957, and in so doing seemed to set off an education race as intense as the arms race – only ten high schools and 173 colleges and universities in the United States taught Russian. By 1960 those numbers had soared to 450 high schools and 593 colleges and universities, Hawaii among them. For undergraduates, who were required to earn at least two years of foreign-language credits, Russian had become the third most popular language course at Hawaii that fall, behind only Spanish and French.

Here is when, where, and how the two unlikely family stories of this chronicle weave into the same cloth. On the first day of instruction in Elementary Russian 101, the day of the first Nixon-Kennedy debate, more than two dozen students took seats in Ella L. Wiswell's classroom inside Hawaii Hall, facing Varney Circle, across the street from the Snack Bar. One was the granddaughter of Ruth Armour Dunham. Another was the son of Hussein Onyango.

It is not clear why either Barack Obama or Stanley Ann Dunham enrolled in Russian, but logic leads in a few directions. Obama was already fluent in

Dholuo, Swahili, and English, had taken Latin at CMS Maseno, and had a linguistic facility that allowed him to pick up a smattering of other languages, according to friends. But as he and his peers looked toward a postcolonial Africa that was open to assistance from both East and West, it made sense that learning the language of the other superpower would be of value upon his return. Jomo Kenyatta, expected to be the first leader of an independent Kenya, had learned Russian himself in 1932, when he was recruited to attend Moscow's revolutionary institute for training cadres in the colonial world, the University of the Toilers of the East. That institution was defunct by 1960, but a similar school had opened in Moscow earlier that year, the People's Friendship University (soon to be renamed the Patrice Lumumba Peoples' Friendship University, after the left-leaning leader of the Congo, who was assassinated with the tacit support of the American CIA in 1961). And given the complexity of Kenya's tribal politics, there was another factor that might have influenced Obama. He was a Tom Mboya man, yet in his personal politics he was closer to another significant Luo politician, Mboya's chief rival to the left, Jaramogi Oginga Odinga, an alumnus of Maseno who was more closely aligned with the Soviets. Over the coming years, Odinga would sponsor many talented young Kenyans, including his own son, Raila, for academic training in Eastern Bloc universities in East Germany and Czechoslovakia as well as the Soviet Union. A facility with Russian might serve Obama well in both government and politics.

For Stanley Ann Dunham, signing up for Russian was simply in character. She had already taken four years of French at Mercer Island High, and with her curious mind was on the search for something new and exotic, but also relevant, all of which described Russian.

Of all the chapters in the lives of these two human beings, the time they were together is historically the most important and personally the most obscure, a brief point of confluence with few witnesses or supporting documents. Many of the differences are known. They were from separate continents, of different races. She was still a minor; he was twenty-six. She was a virgin; he was sexually active, a married man, though not acknowledging that fact in his new surroundings, with two children back in Kenya. (Kezia, who had been pregnant when he left Kenya, had given birth to their second child,

Rita, later known as Auma, earlier in 1960.) He had been in Hawaii for a year and knew scores of fellow students on campus. She had just arrived and knew no one. He had his own apartment near the university; she lived with her parents miles away. In many ways, to borrow a term from his family's history in southern Nyanza, she was the *jadak,* the stranger, the alien, not he, even though he stood out physically and she could blend in more easily among their classmates.

Sometime during Susan Botkin's first quarter at the University of Washington, another letter arrived from Hawaii. In this one, her friend Stanley announced that she was dating an African student she had met in Russian class. What stood out to Botkie about her friend's message was not so much the African as the Russian. "I was really impressed that she had opted for Russian," she said. That she was even told about Obama was unusual. One of the many curious things about the relationship was that so few people seemed aware of it. His friends on campus were almost unanimous in saying decades later that they had no memories of Obama hanging out with Stanley Ann Dunham. If they had remembered her, which they did not, they might have known her as Anna, which is what Obama called her. Anna marked a transition in her persona from Stannie Ann to Stanley Ann to Stanley to Anna and finally to Ann. Only one friend said he did recall Anna, or Ann: Neil Abercrombie, the graduate student in sociology and future governor. "And then of course Ann made her appearance," he said, beginning a new line of thought in a long, discursive interview. He was talking about the Friday-afternoon gatherings at Peter Gilpin's apartment at the corner of Poki and Wilder. Gilpin himself did not remember her, nor did Pake Zane, nor even Abercrombie's brother, Hal, who arrived on campus that fall. Another band of Obama friends and acquaintances, all of whom coalesced around the newly established East-West Center on campus, also drew a blank when it came to Ann Dunham, though a different explanation is in order for them, to be considered later. In any event, of the first group, only Neil Abercrombie could bring back her memory, in his own way:

These gatherings, they weren't necessarily formal, but we would see each other and all that. She made her appearance, but she was a girl. And what I mean by that is she was only eighteen [still seventeen, in fact, until November 29]. She had just got out of high school the year before, she was a freshman, and he met her and he brought her at different times. . . . She mostly observed because she was a kid, among other things. Everybody there was pretty high-powered grad student types, and the women were older. She never participated much in the discussions, but she was obviously interested and obviously interested in Barack. He always saw himself in charge of everything. And don't forget he was also very much a man of his time. We're talking the nineteen-fifties culture and we are just beginning to talk about patriarchy, just beginning to try to figure out what feminism is all about, just beginning. In the Beat era women were still seen as servicing men. They hadn't gotten past that, or even in remotely under-standing that dynamic. The whole Kerouac era when you read it now is almost misogynistic. As Thoreau said, you drag your cultural baggage through life with you. In any event, Barack, I expect he dominated the relationship is what I'm trying to say.

The only other account comes from Ann Dunham herself, recalled decades later but filtered through the writing of her son, who had his own narrative imperatives around which to frame her words. Looking back on her from his own young adulthood, he thought she was naïve, guileless, innocent. In his memoir, this is how she describes her first date with the African in her Russian class:

> He asked me to meet him in front of the university library [Sinclair Library] at one. When I got there he hadn't arrived, but I figured I'd give him a few min-utes. It was a nice day, so I laid out on one of the benches, and before I knew it I had fallen asleep. An hour later – an hour! – he shows up with a couple of friends. I woke up and three of them were standing over me and I heard your father saying, serious as can be, "You see, gentlemen, I told you that she was a fine girl, and that she would wait for me."

The enchantment had begun. Within weeks of the first day of Russian class, calculating from what happened later, they were having sex, most likely at his apartment on 10th Avenue in Kaimuki. There is no record of what attracted them to each other. Her son later concluded that some of it could be explained by the images his "mother had carried with her to Hawaii . . . a reflection of the simple fantasies that had been forbidden to a white middle-class girl from Kansas, the promise of another life: warm, sensual, exotic, different." Other women – previous girlfriends, later girlfriends and wives – would say that Obama had an intense sexual magnetism that seemed irresistible. They described him as a seductive talker and flatterer who could take on many different personalities. When he wanted to charm he was very smooth, able to talk his way past resistance. Even during his teenage days at CMS Maseno, his stepmother once said, "he could always talk very sweetly to girls and promise them all that they dreamed." Neil Abercrombie, looking at it from the outside, came to this conclusion: "You're dealing with an extraordinarily charismatic and compelling figure, and from what I understand she probably thought she was in charge of her life and all of a sudden this force of nature comes into her life, right?" Other factors are known and obvious: she was lonesome in a strange place; she was frustrated by her father in particular and was anxious to get out of the house, beyond his reach; she was an intelligent person who would be attracted to Obama's brilliance; she had not had many boys and men express interest in her before; and she was a freethinking young woman who disdained the social conformity and racial biases of her era and would have no qualms about striking up a relationship with an older man from a different country whose skin was black.

Conception occurred in early November. Sometime after Thanksgiving and before Christmas, she realized that she was pregnant. Her Christmas card to Susan Botkin revealed that she was in love and thinking about getting married. Her parents reacted unfavorably to the news. This difficult response was to be expected, perhaps, but on the other hand the situation was not unfamiliar to them considering the family history. Ruth Armour had secretly married Ralph Waldo Emerson Dunham when she was fifteen, against her parents' wishes. Madelyn Payne had run off and secretly married Stan Dunham when she was still in high school, and her parents had not liked anything about the slick-talking older fellow from El Dorado, including the tint of his skin, which had led R. C. Payne to label him a "wop." In her high school graduation supplement in 1940, the editors had predicted that twenty years into the future Madelyn would be writing a column in Minneapolis providing advice to the lovelorn. The twenty years were up, and here she was in the Pacific, far from frozen Minnesota, working at a bank, not a newspaper, but advice to the lovelorn was a most relevant topic. What should her daughter do? Distraught, anxious, but pragmatic, Madelyn advised: Have the baby. Marry the father. "They probably couldn't have stopped us anyway," Ann later said of her parents.

From both sides of the family, the Dunhams and the Obamas, the lore holds that the person most upset about this Hawaiian romance was Hussein Onyango. The Dunhams' account is that Obama's father wrote angry letters to both Barack and Stan Dunham saying that he did not want the family blood sullied by a white woman. The Kenya family story, as later recalled by Obama's stepmother, Sarah, differed in tone, saying that Hussein Onyango's concern was that Barack already had responsibilities back home with Kezia and that in any case one could not be sure that a white woman would be willing to return to Kenya and live as a Luo wife. Either version is plausible, but questionable without evidence of the letters themselves.

The centuries-long history of the Luo going back to their migration from southern Sudan was one of exogamy, taking wives from other tribes by various means. Philip Ochieng, the Luo friend of Obama's who came to the United States on the 1959 airlift, also met an American woman (at Roosevelt University in Chicago) and had a child with her during his stay. He later became a columnist, political theorist, grammarian, and historian in Kenya, and said that the relationships that he and Obama had during their university days overseas could be explained by the larger perspective: "The Kenya Luo are so influenced by other communities they are a mind-boggling heterogeneity of blood, culture, language. One reason is they adopted exogamy early in their southward-ho. They shared with the ancient Hellenes the habit of waylaying foreign women and literally pulling them into bed as wives. So for [Obama] to grab wives from as far away as Hawaii . . . was no big deal." Hussein Onyango himself took a wife from Zanzibar, outside the Luo tribe, and in his own complicated marital history had seized Barack's mother, Akumu, by force, and had left other women with no compunction about his responsibilities to them.

While not refuting the family stories concerning Hussein Onyango's reaction to his son's romance, all of these facts stand in contradiction to them.

Based on college transcripts (only parts of which became available later), November must have been a mess for young Ann Dunham. She was able to finish two courses, Russian and philosophy, and attain full credits for them, but those were the only eight credits she earned that semester, when her grade point average was 1.35. The last day for withdrawing from courses without being penalized was October 17, before she knew she was pregnant. But the first semester extended well beyond the fifteen-day Christmas break, until the end of January. Considering the grading system of 4 points for an A, none for an F, it appears that she aced the two classes she kept up with and dropped three other courses too late to avoid failing grades. During that same period, Obama continued with his advanced class schedule, with no similar troubles, and none of his acquaintances, including Neil Abercrombie, had a clue that he was dealing with a pregnant girlfriend. Nor did any of them know that he was already married and had a family in Kenya. What Ann knew is less clear. She would say later that Obama confided at some point after learning of her pregnancy that he had a relationship back in Kenya but was not married. She knew nothing at that point about the Luo tradition of polygamy.

The discussions between the two students and between Ann and her parents about when and whether there should be a marriage extended into the Christmas break. If Obama did write his father, it likely would have been sometime during that break, from December 21 to January 5. If he sent it by airmail, the letter would have gone via U.S. mail back to the mainland and then through Europe on its way to Kenya, a process that usually took two weeks. By surface mail, meaning by ship, which was cheaper and more commonly used by native Kenyans, it might have taken a month or more. In either case, once the letter arrived in Kenya, it would have taken many more days to reach Hussein Onyango, who was not in Nairobi that fall and winter but working as a cook in a smaller town between the capital and Kisumu. Foreign mail was sorted in Nairobi and carried by special train, the Mail Express, which ran on Tuesdays and Thursdays, to five designated towns east and west: Mombasa, Nakuru, Kisumu, Eldoret, and Kitale. To find him, the letter might have gone from Nairobi to Kisumu to Nyang'oma Kogelo, where there was no post office and infrequent mail delivery; most people came into town once a week to a church or school to see if any mail had been delivered for them there. Could these letters have made it back and forth in a month? If they did, would Hussein Onyango's letter to Stan Dunham not have mentioned that Barack was already married? This would have been news to the Dunhams, and likely would have altered their attitudes and plans.

The first semester ended on January 30. Three days later, on February 2, during the semester break, Stanley Ann Dunham and Barack H. Obama flew from Honolulu to the airport at Kahului on Maui, found their way to the county courthouse in the city of Wailuku, the county seat and a popular tourist destination in that era, and were "lawfully married."

In Hawaii, the beautiful isle of somewhere, this was not so out of the ordinary. According to statistics from the Hawaii State Department of Health, 45.9 percent of all marriages involving black men in Hawaii from 1960 through 1969 were interracial. In fact, during that decade more than a third of all marriages in Hawaii were interracial in some fashion. Other parts of America would not have been so accepting. The Dunham-Obama marriage in Maui that February day in 1961 would have been illegal, breaking state miscegenation laws in Alabama, Arizona, Arkansas, Delaware, Florida, Georgia, Kentucky, Louisiana, Maryland, Mississippi, Missouri, Nebraska, North Carolina, Oklahoma, South Carolina, Tennessee, Texas, Utah, Virginia, West Virginia, and Wyoming. Not only was Hawaii an uncommon state, but Ann Dunham was an uncommon person. As Neil Abercrombie put it, "She was an adventuresome woman. Jesus, she married an African person in nineteen sixty-one, for Christ's sake. That's a big step for any girl to take."

It was also a step that drew the attention of officials at the University of Hawaii, and at the Honolulu office of the Immigration and Naturalization Service. Obama's race was not their concern, but rather his personal behavior. In a Memo to File, a local INS official noted, "Mrs. McCabe, University of Hawaii, Foreign Student advisor, called . . . and reported that Barack H. Obama, a student at the University since 1959 was married on February 2, 1961 to Stanley Ann Dunham, a United States citizen from Seattle, Washington in Maui, Hawaii. The problem is that when he arrived in the U.S. the subject had a wife in Kenya." According to the memo, McCabe also said that Obama had received permission to work up to twenty-five hours a week and was very intelligent, but was acting in a troubling manner. There was a fine line between how Obama acted and the racial attitudes and expectations of those who were watching him, the unanswerable but valid question being whether the official concern was heightened because he was a black man interacting with white women. "Mrs. McCabe further states that Subject has been running around with several girls since he first arrived here and last summer she cautioned him about his playboy ways. Subject replied that he would 'try' to stay away from girls." As for having a wife in Kenya, Obama told his student advisor that "all that is necessary to be divorced is to tell the wife that she is divorced and that constitutes a legal divorce" – which is precisely what he claimed he did with Kezia. The INS decided that it did not have grounds to deport him, but that he warranted a close watch and should be "closely questioned" before being granted another visa extension.

CHAPTER 7

HAPA

Lili'uokalani was the last native queen of Hawaii. In the brutish and upside-down history of how Americans took control of the islands, she was forced from the throne in 1894, held under house arrest in 'Iolani Palace on suspicion of treason, and sentenced to five years hard labor by a military tribunal. Her opponents, bolstered by the U.S. Navy, said they were doing the work of freedom, pushing out a monarchy, ushering in a republic. Just as certainly they ended up serving the purposes of big business and colonial rule, freeing the way for churchmen and sugar and pineapple plantation owners (sometimes one and the same) to run paradise as they saw fit. In his seminal book on Hawaiian history, *Shoal of Time,* Gavan Daws recounts how the Reverend Sereno Bishop took it as his mission to disparage Lili'uokalani so that she would find no sympathy on the mainland. A correspondent as well as a minister, Bishop wrote several columns for the Washington *Evening Star* alleging that the native queen encouraged the dancing of the "lascivious hula" and made sacrifices to the volcano goddess, Pele. Worst of all, Bishop harrumphed, "her blackness was physical as well as moral." She had frizzy black hair and dark skin that proved she and a brother were "the illegitimate children of a mulatto shoemaker."

In Hawaiian lore, the volcano goddess, Pele, is said to reside inside Kīlauea, one of the most active volcanoes in the world, located on the southeastern side of the Big Island. When Kīlauea erupts, according to local oral tradition, Pele is telling them something. For seven days in July 1961, Pele erupted, and again for three days that September. Between those two eruptions, at 7:24 on the evening of August 4 at Kapiʻolani Maternity and Gynecological Hospital in Honolulu, Stanley Ann Dunham Obama gave birth to a baby boy. Pele seemed to have a lot to say during that period, with Kīlauea erupting over thirty-six days in 1960 alone and at least once almost every year thereafter. The stronger connection to Liliʻuokalani might have been the mixed-race complexion of Ann Obama's baby, who was not illegitimate, if any baby could be called such, his parents having married six months before his birth. Barack Hussein Obama II, like the nineteenth-century Hawaiian queen, was *hapa*. As the Certificate of Live Birth read, "Mother's race: Caucasian; father's race: African." In Hawaiian, *hapa* is the name for someone who is half one race and half another. The newest state was full of *hapa* people.

There was nothing particularly exotic about the last name Obama in that place and time. It seemed to fit unobtrusively into the ethnic cacophony of surnames of babies born in Honolulu that week: Arakawa, Caberto, Clifford, Kamealoha, Walker, Chun, Wong, Nakane, Murai, Uyeda, Kanoa, Abele, Torres, Camara, Kobayashi, Ikeda, Kawazoe, and Simpson. The full name, Barack Hussein Obama II, would have looked most out of place exactly where it might be presumed to be least unusual: back in Luoland in Kenya. Giving a son the name of his father, let alone attaching a roman numeral to the end, was outside the Kenyan tradition. "It was not African to do so," noted Charles Oluoch, an Obama relative. "He aped the white people." But not exactly. Although it is a matter of choice, not legality, the use of roman numerals in this case was not following Anglo tradition either. Normally a son with the name of his father is Jr., and II is used when a son is given the name of a grandfather or other older relative but the father has a different given name. But II it was. The father must have liked the ring of it. Or perhaps it was the mother's call even though the world assumed it was the father's – the same as it was eighteen years earlier when Stanley Ann got her name.

In any case, no one called him by that formal name. From the beginning, he was Barry, or Bar, pronounced *Bear*.

Soon after young Obama's birth, likely the next day, Dr. Rodney T. West, a revered obstetrician-gynecologist in Honolulu, was having lunch with Barbara Czurles, then a journalist at the *Star-Bulletin*. Czurles had been a classmate and close friend of Rod West's daughter, Jo-Anne, at Northwestern University. She had visited Hawaii to be in Jo-Anne's wedding in 1959, become entranced by the tropical lifestyle and weather, such a relief from the snow and darkness of her hometown of Kenmore, New York, near Buffalo, and decided to stay, even living with the West family for a time after Jo-Anne had married and moved to California. On that August day in 1961, she and Dr. West met for lunch at the Outrigger Canoe Club on Kalakaua Avenue, a private beach-front gathering place for Honolulu's elite class, with a dining room that looked out *makai* to the ocean between Waikiki and Diamond Head. As she and the doctor took their seats near the lunch buffet, Czurles posed an open-ended question: "Well, Dr. West, tell me something interesting that happened to you this week."

His response, as she later recalled it, was "Stanley had a baby! Now that's something to write home about."

He went on to explain that Stanley in this instance was a young woman, of course, no miracle birth. Stanley was white. The baby was black. The father was an African with an interesting name too. The story seemed so odd that Barbara Czurles did in fact write home about it, sending a letter to her father, who worked at the state university in Buffalo. Mr. Czurles became part of the joke "Stanley had a baby" because he too was named Stanley.

Dr. West met patients at the Straub Clinic, but delivered babies at nearby Kapi'olani, where Stanley Ann Dunham Obama gave birth. West did not deliver Stanley's baby; that task was performed by a colleague, David A. Sinclair. But he could have heard the story from any number of sources – another doctor, a resident working the maternity ward's weekend shift, one of his nurses. "Stanley had a baby" is the sort of anecdote that flits brightly around nursing stations and down hospital cafeteria waiting lines.

When the birth notice appeared in the *Star-Bulletin* a week and a half later, along with other births recorded at local hospitals from August 2 to 6, the parents were identified as Mr. and Mrs. Barack H. Obama and their home address was listed as 6085 Kalanianaole Highway. That was Ann's home address, where she had a makeshift room outside her parents' bedroom. But she and Obama and the infant never lived there. Even if they had wanted to, there was no space. The Pratt family was still there, taking up the rest of the house. Cindy Pratt, the daughter, said that she had no memory of the Dunhams' daughter bringing an infant home. Only a few days after the boy was born, the father had to fill out immigration papers to extend his student visa. The residence he listed on those papers was 1704 Punahou Street, apartment 15.

On August 4, 1961, the day Barry Obama was born, *Life* magazine's cover featured a portrait of President Kennedy and a quote from his recent speech on the Berlin Crisis: "Any dangerous spot is tenable if brave men will make it so."

Before dawn that morning, four American citizens arrived at the Continental Trailways bus depot on Fannin Street in Shreveport, Louisiana, holding tickets for the 5:45 to Jackson, Mississippi. They were two men and two women: Reverend Harold Lee Bethune, Levert Taylor, and the teenage sisters Delores and Marie McGinnie. All four were black. They had been driven to the station by Reverend Harry Blake and David Dennis, the local leader of the Congress of Racial Equality, who had borrowed his grandmother's old green Pontiac for the mission. By any standard, this was a dangerous spot. Assembled inside the depot, awaiting them, stood a squadron of twenty Shreveport policemen and an equal number of Caddo Parish deputy sheriffs who had been tipped off the night before that the early-morning bus riders intended to break local and state laws by stepping foot inside a waiting room reserved for whites.

As the foursome approached, they were intercepted by Patrolman D. N. Meacham. Bethune said he and his compatriots wanted to check the departure time of their bus. Meacham told the reverend and his traveling party to retreat to the colored waiting room and warned that they would be arrested if they disobeyed. Bethune and the others stepped around the officer and entered the whites-only area, where they were met by Harvey D. Teasley, the police chief. Teasley instructed them to leave, saying they were violating the law. Bethune cited federal court decisions that he said gave them the right to use any room open to the public. Leave, the chief ordered again.

The four held fast. They were arrested and sent to the Caddo Parish Jail, where they were charged with disturbing the peace. A half hour later, a squad of deputies found Dennis and Blake sitting in the Pontiac on nearby Travis Street and arrested them for aiding and encouraging the others. It was one episode out of the multitude in America's civil rights movement, a struggle that would make dangerous spots tenable for millions of people in generations to follow, including the *hapa* named Obama born that day thousands of miles away in Honolulu.

For all of its racial diversity, with two-thirds of the population non-Caucasian, Hawaii was not free from segregation of its own. James A. Michener, the writer whose sweeping historical novel *Hawaii,* published in 1959, had popularized the islands and their history for his vast mainland readership, fled Honolulu not long before Obama's birth. He explained later that he left because of the discrimination he encountered in Hawaii with his wife, a Japanese American. They wanted to buy a home in Kahala, a wealthy neighborhood beyond Diamond Head on the way to Oahu's south shore, but were unable to because of discrimination against Japanese. A later investigation found that prospective home buyers in one development in Kahala were taken to a special office and required to display a photograph of their spouse if he or she was not present. There were also three country clubs on the island that would not admit Asian members, Michener said. As a rule, where Asians were unwelcome, blacks in Hawaii were also unwelcome. There was no Jim Crow segregation as overt as in the states of the old Confederacy, but racism was there just below the surface.

That summer of 1961 Honolulu was in the process of a physical transformation that would forever change its image. The tallest high-rise, Foster Towers, was going up twenty-five stories on Kalakaua Avenue, joining a sky-blocking Waikiki beachfront lineup that already included Tropic Seas, Diamond Head Ambassador Apartments, Coral Strand, Center Apartments, and the Tahitienne, with dozens more on the way. Arthur Godfrey, the ukulele-playing radio and television star, who had been traveling to Honolulu for many years by then, familiarizing it to the rest of America over the airwaves in much the same way Michener had on the printed page, reacted with alarm to what he saw when he arrived that year. "Look at what they've done to this place," he remarked to a reporter from the *Star-Bulletin,* as he pointed to the skyscrapers from the lanai of his room at the Royal Hawaiian Hotel. "Simply no excuse for them. . . . If you really want to get sick, go out about five miles on a catamaran and just take a look. Why, this place looks just like Pittsburgh."

As is often the case when famous people rue the loss of paradise, Godfrey, through his broadcasts, was among those unwittingly responsible for what was happening to Waikiki. Hawaii had opened up increasingly to middle-class tourists, his listening base, with the inauguration of jet service in 1959, when Pan Am began ferrying vacationers across from the West Coast on Boeing 707s. From then to around the time of Obama's birth, the passenger traffic at Honolulu International Airport increased by more than a third, and with the swelling crowds came massive hotel development. One boosterish story in a local paper noted that peak-season tourism was up nearly 20 percent from a year earlier. American travelers, it said, seemed to be "shying away from Europe because of the Berlin Crisis, from Africa because of the violent uprisings there, from the Caribbean because of Castro's antics, and from some parts of Asia because of the fighting in Laos and Vietnam. [But] the central Pacific remains undisturbed."

In Kenya, the uprisings of Mau Mau and the emergency were over, and another major step toward the future was being taken. On the same day that Barry Obama's birth was announced in the Honolulu newspapers, Jomo Kenyatta was given his freedom after being detained and imprisoned for eight years, eight months, and twenty-seven days. A vast crowd of Kikuyu supporters lined the wire fence surrounding his compound at Gatundu and chanted as Kenyatta emerged from his house and danced toward them to the beat of tribal drums. Suddenly Tom Mboya and all other figures seemed dwarfed by the old man. "Inside Kenya it has been fully established that Kenya without Jomo Kenyatta is like Hamlet without the Prince of Denmark," declared the Voice of Africa. "There is little doubt that Kenyatta will be the first prime minister of an independent Kenya."

Obama followed the political events back home intently, but he also had more personal concerns in Kenya. During the spring and early summer of 1961, vast swaths of the Lake Victoria basin in Luoland, from the Kano plains to the Yala swamps, had been devastated by the worst floods of the century. The rainfall was so heavy that the great lake rose by 1.25 meters. When Obama heard about the floods, he wrote a letter to one of his Luo acquaintances, Leo Odera Omolo, and asked him to report on the safety and welfare of his first wife, Kezia, who was staying at the compound of her mother and father near Gendia with their two young children, Bobby and Rita. He also wanted Omolo to check on other Obama relatives in Kanyadhiang and around the bay in Nyang'oma Kogelo. Omolo was an inveterate fixer and journalist from western Kenya; he also happened to be a musician who had played guitar with the Kendu Bay band that performed at the dance hall during Christmas 1956, when Obama first met Kezia. Now, according to Omolo and one of Obama's cousins, Andrew Ochung, Obama's concerns about Kezia involved more than the floods. He had received a letter from a friend who worked at the Nyanza nightclub in Kisumu, suggesting that Kezia had been seen in the presence of male visitors at her parents' compound. Word had spread that one of Kezia's brothers had beaten her because of it. "He was trying to inquire to see if I had seen Kezia with another man," Omolo recalled of Obama. "He had information from home. He had heard about it." The contradiction went unstated. Obama had married another woman in Hawaii and had a baby with her, yet he was distraught at the rumor that the wife he left behind might have a male friend. Omolo found everyone safe from the floods, but decided not to get involved in Obama's private affairs.

The Luo are fiercely patriarchal, even when it comes to lineage. With the Luo, the mother is inconsequential. Any child of a Luo man is a Luo and nothing else.

The genealogists who have studied the bloodlines of the baby born to Stanley Ann Dunham Obama and Barack H. Obama in August 1961 have broken it down this way: 50 percent Luo, 37.4 percent English, 4.4 percent German, 3.125 percent Irish, 3.125 percent Scottish, 1.56 percent Welsh, 0.195 percent Swiss, and 0.097 percent French. The Luo break it down like this: 100 percent Luo. It leads to a riddle of sorts. This person, they will say, is not Kenyan; he was born to an American mother on U.S. soil and never lived in Kenya. Yet he is all Luo. He was born a Luo and will always be a Luo and nothing but a Luo, and when his days are done they expect that he will be put to rest in the Luo burial plot in Nyang'oma Kogelo with his Luo relatives.

All this despite the fact that Barry Obama's Luo father was never part of his life. The son would later write that he was separated from his father when he was two, but that is received myth, not the truth. For these Obamas – Ann, Barack, and Barry – the Hawaiian word for family, *ohana*, did not apply. The disparate threads of the Dunhams and the Obamas, Kansas and Kenya, had woven together randomly starting on the day of the first Kennedy-Nixon debate when two students enrolled in the same elementary Russian class in Hawaii Hall. The baby they produced would connect them forever, all the way back into the past, beyond Christopher Columbus Clark, who fought the bushwhackers during the Civil War, and beyond old man Obong'o, who took the Obamas to Kendu Bay in search of fertile land and situated them in a place where missionaries eventually would teach them English. In terms of history, the connection carried meaning outside their imagining. Yet in a practical sense, in the real world of day-to-day living, there never was a unified family, not much of a cloth to unravel.

In the college life of Barack Obama in 1961 and 1962, as recounted by his friends and acquaintances in Honolulu, there was no Ann; there was no baby. In Neil Abercrombie's crowd, the antiestablishment group that carried on a movable conversation from the Snack Bar on campus to George's Inn and Peter Gilpin's apartment, only Abercrombie himself could dredge up memories of Ann Dunham in 1960. By the following year, the year he was married and had a *hapa* son, Obama had developed another large network of friends and acquaintances on campus, this time revolving around the newest academic concept at the university, the East-West Center.

With its opening on campus in January 1961, the East-West Center began bringing scholars from twenty-seven Asian nations, undergrads and grad students, to Hawaii to further their studies in specific fields while also inculcating in them Western traditions of government, politics, history, and culture. An equal number of students and advanced scholars from American colleges were to attend the center to focus on Asian studies. East meets West and vice versa.

There was a second travel component to the program, as the Asian students eventually headed farther east to the mainland and the Americans dispersed west to various Asian countries. As the cold war turned ever hotter in much of Asia, the U.S. government, which supplied more than half the money, saw the East-West Center as a useful resource in the struggle for hearts and minds. Obama the African was not part of the center, but he quickly latched onto it and its students, many of whom were in his economics classes.

The first nine Asian students arrived from Japan, India, Ceylon, Indonesia, Laos, and Cambodia. They took rooms at the Atherton Y, just as Obama had done when he got to Honolulu two years earlier. Naranhkiri (Kiri) Tith, the Cambodian, had studied in Paris and came from a prominent political family; his father, Khim Tith, was a former prime minister. He was already twenty-six, the same age as Obama, and from the moment they met in Harry Oshima's economic development seminar, they were an interesting match – two well-read intellectuals with strong views and magnetic personalities. It was in Oshima's seminar that Tith and Obama developed what became a debating road show on communism. Tith would talk about Red China and its meaning in Asia, and Obama would talk about the Soviet Union and Africa. Tith argued from the liberal middle, Obama from the left, positions that Tith ascribed to their differing experiences. As a student in Paris, Tith had spent countless hours talking with friends about the Soviet repression of the Hungarian Revolution and the French role in Algeria. He was wary of slogans from right or left, and suspicious of the promises of communism in Asia. "I never was a rightist person, but I definitely did not believe in any kind of too-strong propaganda, so that saved me from the communist movement," Tith said.

On the other hand, *BARE-ick*, as he called Obama, seemed taken by the anticolonialist stance of the Soviet Bloc and "saw it as a liberating force." Cambodia had been free of colonialism for more than half a decade by then, while Kenya was still in the last throes of British colonial rule. Obama's position did not surprise or alarm Tith, given the situation in Kenya, but he strongly disagreed with him in their debates, which they took beyond the economics seminar to various religious and social meeting halls around town during the evenings. Tith would talk for fifteen minutes, then Obama for fifteen, and the discussion would continue from there. "He was a very convincing speaker, a very articulate guy," Tith said. "We were respectful of each other. I don't think he ever belonged to the Communist Party, but he definitely had a hopeful view of communism. . . . And we shouldn't forget that he was a minority Luo in Kenya, so he felt a double fight, also with the Kikuyu. It was double jeopardy for him. In any case he felt oppressed twice over. I didn't. We already got our independence in 1953 so I didn't feel that kind of pressing issue he still felt. So therefore he viewed communism as a savior. Whereas my view of communism was totally the opposite of what his was."

Tith estimated that he and Obama debated in public ten or twelve times during the year he was in Hawaii, through the early winter of 1961, and that they also were with each other at many parties and other social events. By chance, he happened to know of Ann Dunham because he occasionally played tennis at the university with a mutual friend. But he had no idea that Ann knew Obama, let alone got *hapai* (pregnant) by him, married him, and had a son with him. "I didn't know," he said. "All that time I didn't know about the existence of that relationship. Although I thought I knew him very well. He never brought her to any parties. I never met her at a party. . . . Only retrospectively I knew [about their relationship], but at that time, no."

Robert Ruenitz was also in Oshima's economics class, where he befriended both Tith and Obama. Ruenitz, one of the Americans at the East-West Center, with an interest in China studies, arrived in Hawaii in September 1961 after finishing graduate courses in international affairs at the Fletcher School at Tufts University. His political take on Obama differed from Tith's to a degree. By his account, the gregarious Kenyan was polemical and a powerful advocate, but seemed more interested in the logic of an argument than the ideology behind it. Obama's sensibility seemed to be "Let us exercise our intellect," Ruenitz recalled. "He could argue either point quite convincingly." The fact that Tith and Ruenitz and many of their cohorts had far more schooling than Obama seemed immaterial; his mastery of economics, both the mathematics and the policy, was as impressive as his verbal skills, they said.

Like Tith, Ruenitz spent time with Obama outside the classroom. They attended many of the same parties and went to various bars to drink beer and eat *pu-pu*, but what stood out most in Ruenitz's memory were the two visits he made to Obama's apartment, or "hut," as he called it, in St. Louis Heights overlooking the campus, 1482 Alencastre Street. This was after Barack and Ann had married, after Barry was born. They were missing. "I could see no sign of other inhabitants," Ruenitz said. "It was monastic at best. A study table and a bed and a light. It was not a dorm. It was private. I think he had a landlord who had built a small attachment to their house. It was small, and I think he had a hot plate for coffee; not very well appointed. It was not close [to campus], but I think each day he would walk to school." The walk took about forty minutes, down to Dole Street then back *mauka* past Kanewai park at the back entrance to the university near the baseball diamond.

The image is fixed in the memory of Bob Craft, another American in the group: Obama is at the end of that long walk to campus. He is standing under a large tree just outside Sinclair Library in a huddle of East-West scholars, chatting. Many of them are wearing flowered Hawaiian aloha shirts and shorts. Obama wears shoes, dark trousers, white shirt. Here comes his voice, with "middle and high tones sitting on top of a deep rumble." And accompanying the voice, the workings of an impressive mind, the smartest person Craft has ever met, his conversations taking the listener "to ways of thinking I had never imagined before." These scholars – Tith, Ruenitz, Craft, their pal David Finkelstein, Ann Niamoto from Japan, and several others – often gathered at the house of Arnie Nachmanoff, a naval staff officer assigned to the CINCPAC fleet at Pearl Harbor. Arnie and his wife, Sue, had attended one of the joint Tith-Obama lectures at a Jewish temple. After the event they talked with Tith, discovered that he shared a love of tennis, and struck up a friendship. Soon they were not only part of the East-West circle, but often hosts of their parties. Obama was a fixture at the parties. But he came alone. Like the others, Arnie Nachmanoff "had no idea that [Obama] was married or had a child." He remembered mostly how cool the African seemed, how he never lost his temper or shouted "but could argue forcefully and articulately."

In the years to follow, drinking would become a defining characteristic of Barack Obama's life. Most of his friends in Hawaii recalled seeing him with beer and liquor, at bars and parties, but only Kiri Tith, who was abstemious himself, had memories that foreshadowed the difficulties to come. Tith said Obama drank "heavy stuff, scotch and things like that," and became a changed person after imbibing too much, getting "even louder, with more gyrations," until "he would pass out – on the floor." But even at his tipsiest, Obama would not spill out private details of his life. "There is something that I noticed about him – although he seemed to be friendly, open, loquacious, there was something unreachable. You didn't know his family at all. He would never talk about it. Never anything personal. . . . So that is kind of mysterious. At that time it was a question mark we all had."

The mystery, in the end, did not involve *where* so much as *why*. Obama's friends at the East-West Center knew nothing about his family because his wife and son were far away. That monastic room up the hill in St. Louis Heights reflected the reality of a man who was married in name only. Within a month of the day Barry came home from the hospital, he and his mother were long gone from Honolulu, back on the mainland, returned to the more familiar turf of Mercer Island and Seattle and the campus of the University of Washington. The question of why they left is what lingers, unresolved. This period, Washington State revisited, is missing from the memoir the son would write decades later. In his account, the family breach would not occur until 1963, when his father left the island. That version of events is inaccurate in two ways. The date: his father was gone from Hawaii by June 1962, less than a year after Barry was born, not 1963. And the order: it was his mother who left Hawaii first, a year earlier than his father.

What provoked her? The strongest line of circumstantial evidence leads back to Obama's own history. He was already a married man when he married Ann. This was legal in Kenya and common among Luo, but neither common nor legal in the United States. Ann broached the subject once, as quoted by her son in the memoir he wrote decades later, explaining to him, "There was the problem with your father's first wife. . . . He had told me they were separated, but it was a village wedding, so there was no legal document that could show a divorce." That explanation was an understandable fudge, considering the circumstances. A mother was talking to her son about a sensitive subject, her relationship with his father around the time he was born, and in doing so she was trying to make the son feel better about a father he never knew. But the situation itself was a lie. She was married to a bigamist, and the probability is that around the time of Barry's birth the lie burdened the relationship so much that she had to flee from under its weight.

There is one other possible provocation, an uglier one: spousal abuse. There is no direct evidence that Obama hit Ann. She never talked about it to her son or family, and in retrospect always tried to give their brief relationship the rosiest interpretation. But as we shall see, Obama physically abused his next wife, another American with similar characteristics. This does not mean that he abused Ann, but it leads to that possibility. In either case, her mother encouraged her escape, and apparently abetted it. She called a friend on Mercer Island to arrange temporary shelter for her daughter and grandson before they found a place of their own, and also provided them with enough money to survive. Once again, the undemonstrative Madelyn was the rock of the family.

Barry was not yet a month old when they left Honolulu in late August 1961. His mom was still only eighteen. She had left Mercer Island a year earlier as Stanley Dunham, brainy and independent, college bound. Of all the ways she could return, this was beyond the imagining of her high school friends: Mrs. Ann D. Obama, also known as Anna, teenage mother. This unlikely transformation did not seem to embarrass her. She called Maxine Hanson and invited her to come over to the family friend's house, and they sat in the sunshine and talked for an hour, mostly about the baby, her *hapa* boy. And she made her way over to Susan Botkin's mother's house with the baby and spent an afternoon there. It was all a bit discombobulating for Botkin. She thought back to those days not long before, when the sharp and sarcastic young woman she knew as Stanley had no idea even how to babysit and seemed out of her element watching Susan deal with two little brothers. Now it was Botkin who felt distant from such obligations. The notion of being married and having a baby – it seemed like such a heavy "anchor to the world." But there they sat in the living room, drinking iced tea and eating sugar cookies, as Ann cradled baby Barry. She looked neither frightened nor intimidated, but rather "so confident and self-assured and relaxed. She nursed him and was burping him, and oh, he pooped, and she handed him to me – 'Here, Botkie.'"

But as open and relaxed as Ann seemed, she was keeping something back. She talked about her husband, how intelligent and interesting he was, and about what life had in store for her, and them, and little Barry. She made it sound as though she were just passing through town, on her way to bigger and better things. Not a hint that she was now, essentially, a single mother, alone and adrift.

After her one tumultuous semester at the University of Hawaii, from which she emerged with credits in only two courses and a grade point average that placed her on probation, for the first time in her life Ann faced academic obstacles. Her return to the Seattle area was not only an escape from personal trauma but also the beginning of her long, slow resurrection as a scholar, an important part of her self-identity. For the fall quarter at Washington, which began on September 19, she enrolled in two night extension courses: Political Science 201: Modern Government, and Anthropology 100: Introduction to the Study of Man. She had moved from Mercer Island to Seattle by then, taking apartment 2 at the Villa Ria Apartments at 516 13th Avenue East in the Capitol Hill neighborhood, two miles from campus. Her apartment was on the first floor, to the right as one entered the building, above the garage, about five hundred square feet. The cheap month-to-month rents at Villa Ria attracted many temporary residents – stewardesses, students, people looking for work. The Polk Directory listed her as Anna Obama, Apt. 2, phone EA3-3348. Marvel Humphrey, Velda Little, and the Toutonghis were listed as neighbors in the building. Joseph Toutonghi, in No. 10, was the superintendent. Mary Toutonghi often babysat Barry, and later remembered him as being "very large and very curious and very alert," not at all the fussy type.

With mere scraps of data documenting her days in Seattle, the grind of her daily life can only be imagined. She was light-years away culturally from the sophomore scene on campus – sorority dinners, football games, drinking parties – and just as far from the nascent counterculture atmosphere she enjoyed as a high schooler from the suburbs hanging out on the fringes of the college coffeehouse milieu. Her waking days were devoted to baby and studies. The transcript of Stanley Ann Dunham Obama at the University of Washington showed that she received a B in Modern Government and an A in Intro to Man – a return to the superior marks she had become accustomed to at Mercer Island High. For the next quarter, starting two days after Christmas 1961, she signed up for two more night extension courses, Philosophy

120: Introduction to Logic and History 478: History of Africa (South), and earned an A in both. For those four courses, each providing five credits, she had maintained a 3.75 grade point average, allowing her to enroll as a regular student for the 1962 spring quarter. Now she signed up for three courses – Chinese Civilization, History of Modern Philosophy, and English Political and Social History – but decided in the end to audit the last for no grade or credit. In the other two, she received B's, five credits each. It was early summer 1962 by then. Her grades had been restored, her life clarified. Time to get back to Hawaii.

As the spring semester at the University of Hawaii neared an end, Barack Obama was consumed with getting into graduate school. Once again, he enlisted the help of his old friend and sponsor, Betty Mooney (now Elizabeth Mooney Kirk). On May 8 Mooney wrote a letter to Tom Mboya asking if there was any way he could find some more financial assistance for Obama. The Laubach Literacy Institute would have continued funding Obama's education if he intended to pursue graduate studies in journalism, but they could not justify subsidizing graduate studies in economics, so far afield from their mission. Mboya's response was swift but not encouraging. "As regards the matter of Barack, I am getting in touch with a few people, but I am not very hopeful, as it has come rather late."

Mooney widened her search, sending out a new curriculum vitae for her former assistant that she had prepared with the help of her husband, Elmer. The first category was *Personal:* "Luo from Kenya. Speaks Luo, Swahili, English." (He had not followed through in Russian enough to become fluent.) "Wife and 2 children in Kenya." (No mention of Ann Obama and Barack H. Obama II.) "Present address – 1482 Alencastre St., Honolulu, Hawaii." (The monastic single room.)

The second category was *Objectives:* "PhD in Economics from Harvard or University of California at Berkeley. Needs financial assistance for graduate study." (This objective is especially interesting for what was left out. In the family story, as Ann later told her son and he recounted in his memoir, the choice was between the New School in New York and Harvard. In that account, the New School had offered him a full scholarship that would have allowed his wife and son to go with him, but he turned it down, in so doing breaking up the family. In reality, the family was already torn apart, and the New School possibility was so incidental to his thinking that Obama did not include it with Harvard and Berkeley. In another section of the CV, he noted that his applications were accepted at Harvard, Yale, Michigan, and California. Again no mention of the New School. Finally, when he listed financial help that had been offered to him by graduate schools, Harvard was the only one mentioned – an alternateship for $1,500.) "Plans for Kenya government work in economic development for East Africa." (He was anxious to get back. Independence was coming. Kenyatta was out of prison. Tom Mboya, his Luo mentor, had married Pamela Odede, one of the original 1959 airlift members, the daughter of a Kenyatta ally. Both Kenyatta and Patrick Renison, the colonial governor, were at the wedding. Mboya's best man was a Kikuyu, representing his hopes for a posttribal culture.)

On May 29 in his room on Alencastre, Obama typed out his own belated letter to Mboya in Nairobi. "Dear Tom," he wrote, "I am sorry that I have not written for such a long time, but I figured you were pretty busy, so I did not bother. Further, I have been busy myself and did not have time. I, however, thought that this was the time when I feel I should thank you for the help which you gave me when I was coming here."

Obama then recounted his many achievements in America, accomplishments that were extraordinary by any measure. He said he finished with a 3.6 grade point average, completed more than four years of work in three years (taking huge credit loads every semester, from sixteen to eighteen hours), participated in graduate-level seminars on economics, and earned honors from Phi Beta Kappa, Kappa Phi, and Omicron Delta Kappa. "These are the highest honours that anyone can get in the U.S.A. for high academic attainments," he boasted. What went unstated was that he had been able to do all that while also enjoying the company of several divergent circles of friends, delivering speeches off campus at churches, the Rotary, Kiwanis, and the Elks Club, and, on the side, fathering a child and getting married.

By the time Obama wrote the letter, he had settled on Harvard, where, he said, he had been offered a fellowship to work on a doctorate. His financial situation was much better since he had also won a grant from the Rockefeller

Foundation. "I intend to take at least two years working on my Ph.D. and at most three years," he said. "Then I will be coming home. I am going to write my dissertation and thesis for the Ph.D. on the Economics of the Underdeveloped areas. Actually I intend it to be in Economic Development and the effect of International Trade on the countries which produce Primary products like Kenya and on the policies that would be necessary to offset the adverse effects that the underdeveloped areas have been facing."

In the next paragraph Obama discussed the Kenyan political situation as though he were Mboya's equal, as if he knew as much about the internal dynamics of the country from afar as someone in the middle of the struggle. His line of thought was astute and arrogant, fitting his persona. Beginning with praise, he offered a subtle criticism, an elbow from the left, concerning Mboya's negotiations with the British over a new constitution. "Thanks for all the good work that you have done to Kenya during all this period, with patience, even when the tide was too strong," Obama wrote. "You have had to contend with spivs and ogpus alike" – *spiv* was British slang for a petty crook; *ogpu* was slang for a Soviet agent – ". . . I think that even though you people made a compromise in order to keep Kenya from becoming another Congo . . . it will be to the worst of Kenya if the . . . government envisaged in the constitution continues. Nevertheless, it may be best that we get Kenya free first before we worry about those problems. As for the outcome, things look quite oblique: It seems as if unless the so called leaders can think in terms of Kenya and not be power hungry, we will not have a stable country."

As the letter neared its end, Obama turned to a personal matter. "I have enjoyed my stay here, but I will be accelerating my coming home as much as I can. You know my wife is in Nairobi there and I would really appreciate any help you may give her. She is staying with her brother Mr. Wilson Odiawo." He was checking once again on Kezia, who had moved with her two young children from Luoland back to the capital after the horrific 1961 floods. He called her his wife, not his former wife. And he made no mention of his other wife, the young American. After reading the letter, Mboya scribbled a handwritten notation to an aide: "Ask Odiawo to see me."

Just as they had when he arrived, both Honolulu newspapers took note of his leaving. John Griffin of the *Advertiser* interviewed Obama for an article that appeared on June 22, the day the Kenyan was to depart for the mainland. "First UH African Graduate Gives View on E-W Center" was the headline. It was typical of Obama that he would have strong feelings about a program of which he was not even a member, and also typical that his views would be smart and well stated. The center was making a mistake by placing its students in a single dormitory, or "herd[ing] them together," as he put it. "They may get to know the other students that way, but they won't get to know the community, the way people live here. . . . Furthermore, the fact that they know this is a conscious policy, will make them resent having to socialize. They should concentrate on the training. That's what people come here for. . . . Let the cultural things be a by-product." No social engineering for the politically socialist Obama.

His perspective on Hawaii as a racial melting pot, a notion that had attracted him to the university in the first place after reading Frank J. Taylor's piece in the *Saturday Evening Post,* had become more nuanced after living there for three years. "Hawaii is not really a melting pot," he said, although the races dealt with one another better on the islands than on the mainland or in Africa. And he found it "rather strange . . . even rather amusing, to see Caucasians discriminated against here." Turning his attention to his own future, he found one lesson in Hawaii that he hoped would apply to Kenya. "There is, however, one thing other nations can learn from Hawaii," he said. "Here in the government and elsewhere, all races work together toward the development of Hawaii. At home in Kenya, the Caucasians do not want to work as equals."

The *Star-Bulletin* article was more of a notice: Obama, an "outstanding student," a "straight A student here for the past three years," had been awarded a graduate faculty fellowship in economics at Harvard and was about to leave. He would take a tour of mainland universities before entering Harvard in the fall. Again, neither article mentioned the wife he had met in Hawaii, nor the baby he had sired there.

Decades later the son would quote his mother's description of why the family broke up. It was because of Harvard, and Old Man Hussein Onyango, and Madelyn, and the young couple themselves, so many things, as she explained it: "We agreed that the three of us would return to Kenya after he finished his studies. But your grandfather Hussein was still writing to your father, threatening to have his student visa revoked. By this time Tut" – pronounced *Toot,* the nickname for Madelyn: *tutu* is "grandmother" in native Hawaiian – "had become hysterical – she had read about the Mau Mau rebellion in Kenya a few years earlier, which the Western press really played up – and she was sure that I would have my head chopped off and you would be taken away. Even then it might have worked out." Ann then described to her son the scholarship to the New School and how it would have paid for everything. "But Barack was such a stubborn bastard he had to go to Harvard. 'How can I refuse the best education?' he told me. That's all he could think about, proving that he was the best. We were so young, you know." Shards of truth in all of it, but obscuring a very different reality.

Obama's first stop on the mainland was San Francisco, where he spent time with other Kenyans who had come over on the first and second airlifts and also found time to have dinner with Hal Abercrombie, the younger of the Abercrombie brothers, who had moved there after two years in Hawaii. Hal and his wife, Shirley, met Obama at the Blue Fox restaurant in the financial district. It was a night Abercrombie would not forget, with Obama revealing a combination of anger and arrogance that frightened him. Shirley was a blonde with a bouffant hairdo, and when she arrived at the side of Hal and Barack, the maître d' took them to the most obscure table in the restaurant. Obama interpreted this as a racial slight, and when the waiter arrived, he laced into him, shouting that he was an important person on his way to Harvard and would not tolerate such treatment. "He took it out on the waiter, not the maître d'. He was berating the guy and condescending every time the waiter came to our table. There was a superiority and an arrogance about it that I didn't like."

Did Obama make his way up to see Ann and little Barry, who were still in Seattle and would not return to Honolulu until later that year? That is not known. Susan Botkin had a memory of Ann talking about following her husband to Harvard, something she may have known about in spring 1962, but there is no record one way or another as to whether he stopped there on his way across the country. She did not follow him in any case. There certainly was enough time, nearly three months, for many side trips. He did stop in Denver, where the Rockefeller Foundation arranged for him to spend a few days at the International Center at the University of Denver. There he met up with an old mate from the Maseno school, Y. F. O. Masakhalia, a Luhya from western Kenya who had arrived in 1960 on an International Institute of Education scholarship. As Masakhalia later recalled, they spent the weekend together, reliving old school days, talking about the future. "We talked about his performance at the University of Hawaii. We were all eyeing to get into Yale, Columbia, Stanford, Harvard. So he said, 'I am admitted to Harvard.' He told me he scored a straight A average at Hawaii. And I said, 'Ah, just like you, Barack. You are always bright.' We had a very cheerful, memorable weekend, and then he went toward Harvard." Masakhalia vaguely remembered Obama saying that he had a wife and family. Whether it was the family in America or the one in Kenya was not clear.

A few weeks later Obama was deep in the heartland, finding his way to Tulsa, where he would stay with his benefactor, Betty Mooney Kirk, the devout Christian missionary and literacy teacher who as much as anyone had made his American adventure possible. Inside their home at 3813 South Rockford Street, the Kirks kept a guestbook listing the wide world of visitors who walked through their doors. Frank Laubach's name was there, and George Wanyee's from Kenya, and friends from Tallahassee and Liberia and Ghana and Mexico and Waco had all signed. In the middle of the listings, in neat, gentle handwriting: "27-7-62 Barack H. Obama, P.O. Box 10818, Nairobi, Kenya, with the love that never dies, I was received."

———◆———

CHAPTER 8

ORBITS

Leroy Gordon Cooper spoke with the flat Oklahoma accent of his childhood, but at one in the afternoon on May 18, 1963, when Gordo bounded off the twin-jet Sikorsky helicopter that had flown him from the deck of the USS *Kearsarge* to Hickam Air Force Base in Honolulu, he was hailed as the first *kama'aina* astronaut. To the rest of the world, he was the least known and most enigmatic of the illustrious Mercury Seven. To Hawaiians, he had all the right stuff. To be embraced as a *kama'aina* meant he was considered a hometown boy with roots on the islands. He had lived right there among them when he had attended the University of Hawaii. It was on the Manoa campus that he met his wife, Trudy, a drum majorette and amateur pilot, and at the Hickam AFB chapel that Gordo and Trudy got married in 1946. Now, at age thirty-six, the fighter pilot turned U.S. astronaut was returning to Hawaii for an exuberant "Hero's Aloha" parade celebrating the splashdown of his historic spaceflight aboard *Faith 7*, the last of the Mercury missions. Gemini would be next, then Apollo: steps one, two, and three in the decade that President Kennedy vowed would end with Americans landing on the moon.

Honolulu police estimated that more than 150,000 people lined the parade route for what was described as the warmest greeting in Hawaiian history, the crowds larger and more buoyant than those that had cheered President Eisenhower in 1953 and General Douglas MacArthur's return from Japan in 1951. The thirty-mile victory loop took Cooper's cream-colored convertible along Nimitz Highway, gliding past the Pratt Furniture warehouse, jogging up to King Street and down to Ala Moana and all the way through Waikiki on Kalakaua, then back on South King to a sea of welcomers outside the 'Iolani Palace. Stan Dunham stood somewhere in that Saturday-afternoon throng, hoisting his chubby little grandson high on his shoulders. Barry Obama, back from Seattle with his mother, was not yet two years old. This might have been the precocious toddler's first memory, or perhaps he just remembered being told about it. Astronauts would come to Hawaii again, looking so cool in their aviator glasses, and Gramps and Barry would go out to see them, but the parade for the *kama'aina* Gordo was the first, and to Hawaiians the most special. "I am doubly grateful that I returned today even if I took the long way around to get here," Cooper said after arriving in Honolulu. Then, to raucous cheers, the lei-draped astronaut added that if he had delayed the landing only four minutes and eight seconds he could have put his spacecraft down in the waters right off Diamond Head (instead of closer to Midway Island).

With his capsule traveling at 17,157 miles per hour, Cooper spent more time in space than any American astronaut before him, orbiting Earth 22.9 times in less than two days. He was not the gabbiest spaceman, but the NASA command set it up so that he could talk occasionally not only to fellow astronauts and officials marking his progress but also to his wife at their home outside Houston and various people stationed around the world. During one orbit he spoke to black African leaders who had gathered in Addis Ababa for a conference, a polite one-way conversation that no doubt had cold war motivations beyond Gordo's political awareness. Tom Mboya and Jomo Kenyatta of Kenya were among those listening. "Hello, Africa. This is Gordon Cooper speaking from Faith 7. I am right now over one hundred miles above Africa just passing Zanzibar. Just a few minutes ago, I passed Addis Ababa. I want to wish you success to your leaders there. Good luck to all of you in Africa." The mission was going smoothly then, and continued smoothly until orbit 19, when the first of a series of malfunctions occurred, culminating with the realization that the automatic system that was to line up the capsule and fire the retro-rockets for reentry into the atmosphere had gone out and Cooper would have to steer the craft in himself, with guidance down below from the Mercury Seven's senior astronaut, John Glenn. Cooper handled the crisis with skill and ease, finally landing the capsule at the intended spot, "right on the old bazoo." In doing so, in showing once again the value of man over machine, he made the cover of the national weekly magazines and, as *Time* put it, "made man's future in space brighter than ever."

The future for the Dunham family also looked a bit brighter. Ann and her boy were back on the island. Her husband-in-name-only was gone. Stan was holding steady at Pratt Furniture, and Madelyn was moving up in the financial world; the only woman escrow officer in Hawaii, she had been promoted to the position of assistant cashier by Bank of Hawaii. The foursome was together again, soon moving from a cramped apartment to a more comfortable house at 2234 University Avenue, a rental with four bedrooms and a spacious lawn, closer to campus and within walking distance of Noelani Elementary School. Barry was not ready for school, though his grandmother thought he could have handled it. "Before he could walk, Madelyn told me he was a genius," her brother Charles Payne recalled. Boasting was not a normal part of Madelyn's undemonstrative personality; that was usually left to her husband. "But with her own family [especially grandchildren] she was more like Stan," Payne said. "I was always struck by the fact that she was convinced they had a genius before he was old enough to do anything."

Her grade point average resuscitated in Seattle, Ann was back in school at the University of Hawaii, coming in with thirty credits and good standing as a sophomore. Her academic progress would be slow and steady from then on, with a few diversions but no traumatic disruptions of the magnitude of her brief tumultuous relationship with Obama. She tried to arrange her courses when someone could look after Barry, either a babysitter or family member. On at least a few emergency occasions, she took him down to the Pratt Furniture warehouse on Nimitz Highway and left him for an hour or two with her dad. Cindy Pratt, by then a teenager, worked at the store part-time. She thought Ann was "stand-offish," but remembered Barry as a good-natured boy: "I remember . . . Barry being down there, and he was so cute. And [a friend] and I would walk with him through the store and he would jump on the beds and whatever else he could do. So cute, so full of life, a twinkle in the eye, giggling all the time."

When freedom came to his homeland, Barack Obama was in Cambridge, Massachusetts, living at 170 Magazine Street near the Harvard campus, sharing rooms with several fellow Africans, including a younger half brother, Omar Okek, who had joined him in the United States to finish high school. He heard the news in the early hours of December 12, 1963, the day of *uhuru* and *jamhuri,* freedom and independence, when Kenya became the thirty-fourth African nation to rid itself of European rule. In a four-hour ceremony in Nairobi, Jomo Kenyatta was sworn in as the first president of the Republic of Kenya. The Burning Spear ignored his prepared speech in English, choosing instead to speak only in Swahili, a move that exhilarated the audience, and he was inaugurated with African symbols of his new office: a shield, a spear, and a three-legged stool. The day held out the promise of a future free from tribalism. Kenyatta was Kikuyu; his vice president, Oginga Odinga, was Luo, and so was his secretary of labor, Tom Mboya, who would also take the role of James Madison in the new nation, orchestrating the writing of a new constitution. Odinga was to the left of Kenyatta and his support was mostly among Luo. Mboya, though Luo, entered the cabinet as a Kenyatta loyalist, believing the only way for Kenya to succeed was by transcending tribal animosity. For this day, Kenyatta agreed. "All through the colonial days, for the purpose of divide and rule, we were constantly reminded that we were Kikuyu or Wakamba or Giriama or Kipsigis or Masai or English or Hindu or Somali," the new president declared. "But now the republic has embodied those features of equality and respect which cut through differences of race or tribe."

Thousands of miles away, at campuses across the United States, scores of bright young Kenyans, Obama among them, heard the call. Since the first large wave of students had arrived in 1959, their numbers had increased year by year, and now they were several hundred strong, all studying and preparing for this day and those to follow, when they could help steer the future of a new nation. For several years their rallying cry had been "Free Kenyatta." On weekends, whenever possible, Obama and other Kenyan students on the East Coast would commute to New York City and gather at the International House on Riverside Drive or at the West End bar near Columbia University at Broadway and 113th. Inevitably their conversations would come around to the days of the emergency, the imprisonment of Kenyatta, his release from prison, and the end of colonialism. Those were issues they all could agree on, whatever their tribal affiliation. Now that Kenyatta was running the country, could his stated ideal of a future beyond tribalism be realized?

As a member of a minority tribe, and as a disciple of Mboya, that was Obama's hope. When he was hanging out with his Kenyan brothers at the West End bar late on a Saturday night, it was an idea that seemed possible. Luo, Luhya, Kikuyu – they all were Kenyans there, drinking the same Budweiser, flirting with the same girls, feeling the same tension between their old lives and the new world, stirred by the same ambitions. They would look around and see the same counterculture poets and Beats at nearby tables, and chuckle about the men in crew cuts and trench coats who seemed so friendly, were always trying to get to know them, and had to be from the CIA. The Kenyans bonded in that setting, just as they did during meetings at the International House, yet there was one small but ominous sign that the divisions of the past could not so easily be overcome. During elections for leadership of Kenyan students overseas, the unity seemed to collapse and tribal sides were taken again, most often Kikuyu versus Luo. Obama, according to others, showed no interest in student politics, or in tribal politics, and though his politics were leftist, that seemed less important to him than sober analysis of the economics of an underdeveloped country, the focus of his studies at Harvard.

Freedom of a different and more personal sort came to Obama a few months after the historic events in Nairobi. On January 30, 1964, an affidavit reached his apartment on Magazine Street by registered mail, requiring his signature upon receipt, which he provided. It was a document stating that Stanley Ann D. Obama was filing for divorce in the First Judicial Circuit, State of Hawaii, Division of Domestic Relations. The grounds were grievous mental suffering. No big deal to Obama; he was long gone anyway, and he still had a wife in Kenya and girlfriends in Boston. The final order came from Judge Samuel P. King on March 5. The bonds of matrimony were dissolved: "It is further ordered that the libellant . . . is hereby granted the care, custody and control of Barack Hussein Obama II, the minor child of the parties hereto, with the right of reasonable visitation in the Libellee, and further that the question of child support is specifically reserved until raised hereafter." Obama was off the money hook, in other words. His interpretation of "reasonable visitation" would come to mean never, or virtually never.

The main man in Barry's life then was his grandfather. For all his idiosyncrasies and failings, for all his eruptions after his daughter announced she was pregnant, Stan was devoted to the little boy. It was Stan who took him to see Gordo Cooper, Stan who carried him down the hot sands of Waikiki Beach, Stan who bought him his first shave ice. Who was this little kid at his side or on his shoulders with a darker shade of skin? Stan had his own line that he used on strangers wherever they went: "This boy is the great-great-grandson of Hawaii's first king, Kamehameha the Great," he would boast, urging tourists to take out their cameras. "I'm sure your picture's in a thousand scrapbooks, Bar," his grandson remembered being told by him later.

The *hapa* boy was too young to know that he was half white, half black, or to understand that in most of American society, because of his genetic combination, he would be called black, or Negro, and that it was not his choice, despite the fact that the only blood relatives he knew were white. He could not yet realize that his very existence in 1960s America was a shock to many people, an attitude described by Cindy Pratt, daughter of Stan's boss at the furniture store. "It was a scandal and a half," she said of Ann's having a black son. "Mostly in those days anything interracial was frowned upon. I remember we were all shocked. Today it wouldn't be anything. In those days it was kind of kept quiet or whatever. . . . My parents were shocked and a little . . . I hate to say we were racially prejudiced, we weren't, but it was not something that was supposed to happen in those days, and it wasn't talked about." For Stan to imply that the little boy was native Hawaiian was mostly an inside joke, but also a way to protect him and the family, even in Hawaii, where there were more interracial marriages than in any other state.

The Dunhams celebrated Barry's third birthday at the house on University

Avenue on August 4, 1964. That very date marked one of the seminal tragic moments in civil rights history, a reminder of the grave dangers faced by those committed to forcing racial equality in America. It was on Barry's birthday that FBI agents in Mississippi, at the end of a two-month search, discovered the bodies of Michael Schwerner, Andrew Goodman, and James Chaney after bulldozing a partly constructed earthen dam in the woods outside the town of Philadelphia. Goodman and Schwerner were white, Chaney black. All three had been voting rights organizers during what was called Freedom Summer. They were murdered by members of the Ku Klux Klan with the implicit acquiescence of local authorities. Coincidence, of course, but in many years Barry Obama's birthday seemed to have a civil rights resonance: the freedom rider arrests in Shreveport on the day he was born, the finding of the young martyrs in Mississippi when he turned three, and then the next year, on his fourth birthday, a pivotal moment in the struggle. On August 4, 1965, the U.S. Senate gave final approval to the conference report for the National Voting Rights Act. "We've lost the South for a generation," President Lyndon Johnson said to Bill Moyers, his aide, when he signed the bill. Perhaps so, but without the changes wrought by that historic act, the future of the boy turning four in Honolulu might well have been vastly different.

It is difficult to say what was running through Ann Dunham's mind when she fell so hard so fast for Barack H. Obama after they met in that Russian class at the University of Hawaii. There is no documented record of their love affair beyond the few snippets provided by her son in his memoir decades later, anecdotes that reveal more about him and the way he interpreted family events than about his mother. But some deeper clues might be gleaned from the story of the woman who fell for Obama next, during his Harvard days. It might be more precise to say *one* of the women who fell for Obama next, since there were others, but she was the one who took the relationship to ends similar to Ann's. Her name was Ruth Baker. She grew up in Newton, a suburb of Boston, attended Simmons College, and was living in a flat with two other women on Park Drive on the Brookline–Boston line during the spring of 1964 when her life intersected with Obama's. On the surface, she had little in common with Ann Dunham. Ruth was twenty-seven then, not seventeen.

She was an Easterner, a college graduate, from the upper middle class, and Jewish. But like Ann she was lonely and looking for adventure. Reflecting on her similarities with Ann decades later, Ruth said, "I think she had a big social conscience. I have one. She loved learning and knowing different people. I loved learning and knowing different people."

Ruth Baker was adrift that spring, teaching ten-year-olds at an elementary school. "I wasn't going anywhere. I was bored, not finding any direction." One afternoon, exhausted as she rode a streetcar home from her job, she struck up a conversation with an African man behind her. He was a student from Nigeria, as open and friendly as she was, and before the ride was over he had invited her to a party at his apartment across the street from hers. They became familiar at the party, and dated for one week, seeing each other every day. Then abruptly and without warning, he disappeared. In talking to his friends, Ruth discovered that he was married and had gone back to Nigeria. They apologized for his behavior, then invited her to another party the following Sunday.

She went. "And there was Obama," and that was that, she recalled. As soon as she saw him, she fell. As soon as he saw her, he made his approach. She was tall, thin, shapely, more of a sexual being than the teenage Ann Dunham. Before the night was out, her address was on a slip of paper in his pocket, and a few days later there he was, knocking on the door of her apartment. A professor accompanied him, a man who appeared to be his friend, and also might have been his ride from Cambridge. It was clear to Ruth that Obama was brainy and commanded respect, but that seemed only part of his personal magic. "He had a charming voice, a deep, captivating voice. And he had a lot of sex appeal. What you call sex appeal. It's when you meet a man and you feel drawn to that man and you feel he is very attractive. There is chemistry, and that's what he had a lot of. A *lot* of." Obama insisted that Ruth visit him at his apartment on Magazine Street, where he and his friends were hosting another weekend party. "Okay, I'll come," she said. That was the opening to an intense relationship. "I was seeing him every day [from then on]. I was living for him, okay – that's what happened. I was taken by him in the sense of being captivated by him. And sometimes I would see him flirting with another girl and I would get very upset. . . . But it was very intense, because I fell in love with him, okay? And as much as he could love someone, he loved me."

Almost every day for two months, she was with Obama in his apartment. She found him charming and invigorating, "never a dull moment." Then he announced that he was returning to Kenya. He did not simply vanish, like the Nigerian, but the news from *BARE-ick* (she pronounced it that way too) caught Ruth by surprise. He had not completed his PhD, but felt that it was time to leave Cambridge, he said. He was tired of America, and homesick. The new nation was up and running, and he wanted to be part of the action. He could finish his doctoral thesis on "an econometric model of staple theory of development" from Nairobi, he told her. She should come to Kenya too, and if she liked it, they could get married.

So many possibilities and problems flowed from that one sentence. She was white and Jewish; he was black and Luo. Kenya was not only distant, it was unimaginable to her. Five years out of college she still had not ventured far from Boston, never flown on an airplane. She knew only a few shards of his personal history: that he was the father of two young children in Kenya and had once had a relationship with a woman named Kezia. Whether he was ever married to her, or divorced, was unclear. No mention of marriage and divorce from another white woman in Hawaii, though he did carry a snapshot in his wallet of a little brown boy on a tricycle who shared his name. In Ruth's state of mind, none of that mattered one way or another. "You come to Kenya, and if you like it we'll get married," he said, and the promise took over. "I was very innocent. I had no idea of any dynamics," she explained later. "I said, 'I will do that.' And I did."

Her parents responded in horror to the news, much as Stanley and Madelyn Dunham had a few years earlier. Ruth's father, without a high school diploma, had risen to the upper middle class through tireless effort building a retail delivery business, selling irons and sofas and other household goods on the installment plan. Her mother was intelligent but repressed by Old World parents who had survived pogroms in Russia and Lithuania and did not allow her to continue her education past high school. Ruth was an only child. Her parents had invested their hopes in her, and now she was telling them that she intended to run off to Africa. One can see patterns here that fit Ann Dunham's story: the vulnerability of the young women, their overwhelming attraction to Obama, his magical effect on them, their disregard for the surrounding circumstances, the family trauma that resulted.

Ruth's mother "almost had a nervous breakdown" when she heard the news. Family friends and neighbors in Newton thought Ruth had gone mad. Her mother sat her down in the back garden of their splendid old suburban home and tried to talk sense into her. Her father hired a private detective to investigate Obama, and he came back with troubling reports. As Ruth recalled later, he told her that Obama "had been going with some women around Cambridge. Somebody accused him of making her pregnant. He had a bad reputation." As it turned out, these reports were coming from Harvard and from the Boston office of the Immigration and Naturalization Service. The INS had been investigating the case of a young Kenyan woman who had come to the United States to study at a high school in Sudbury, Massachusetts, under the sponsorship of the Unitarian-Universalist Committee. When she suddenly left for London without receiving permission, immigration officials looked into the matter and determined that "the young woman had been associating with a male Kenyan student at Harvard, one Barack Obama." They suspected that the young woman had left for London to get an abortion.

In addition, Obama had lied to Ruth about why he was returning to Kenya. It was not his choice at all, but a forced move. The INS, acting in conjunction with officials at Harvard, had denied his visa extension and had ordered him to leave the country no later than July 8. Obama had passed his general exams by then and needed only to write his dissertation to earn a doctorate in economics. But he had caused so much trouble with his personal behavior that neither the university nor the government wanted him around any longer. An INS document recorded on June 8 recounted a conversation with Harvard officials about Obama: "They weren't very impressed with him and asked for us to hold up action on his application until they decided what action they could take in order to get rid of him. They were apparently having difficulty with his financial arrangements and couldn't seem to figure out how many wives he had." Obama tried to fight the visa denial, telephoning immigration officials, pleading with Harvard, but was told the decision was final.

Ruth knew none of this, and all efforts to dissuade her from running off with Obama were ineffective. "He had a bad reputation, but I wasn't listening," she recalled. "I loved my parents very much and they loved me very much. They meant the best, and maybe they were right. But I was going ahead. And they had the neighbors and everybody around trying to persuade this white Jewish girl not to go to black Africa and marry a black man, you know? And I said, 'No way, I'm going!'" A friend drove her to the airport. Ruth was in such a fog that she barely thought about what clothes she should pack. She had no idea how long it would take to get to Nairobi, nor did she have a plan about what to do once she got there. Again, these details were immaterial. From this compulsive behavior, one might catch a glimpse of what drove Ann Dunham in her relationship with Obama. For both women, the overwhelming impulse was to be with him, no matter what.

What brought Obama into these relationships is less clear. Ann Dunham had a sharp mind and an open spirit. Ruth Baker was also smart, but she was more alluring and had another attribute that Ann lacked: money. Obama told many of his friends in Kenya, including Leo Odera Omolo, that he had met an American woman who "had a lot of money and could finance their socializing."

Ruth arrived in Nairobi in August 1964, just after the third birthday of the little boy on the tricycle. Obama was already there, starting a job as an economist at BP Shell. She had written him to say that she was coming, but left before hearing back. He was not there to greet her plane when it landed at Embakasi Airport. "And I was looking for Barack. Where's Barack? No Barack." She found a woman who looked friendly, Mary Radier, an officer at the airport. "I said, 'Hi, uh' – I stood out like a sore thumb, a white woman – 'I'm looking for Barack Obama.' She said, 'Oh, I know Barack. He's a good friend of mine. You come to my house and we'll get him.' So that's what happened. And I can remember where the place was, even, behind the university [of Nairobi], near the United Kenya Club [the gathering place for black and white academics and government officials]. Then she called someone who knew Barack and said, 'Look, Barack's girlfriend from America is here. Tell him to come over.' And he came. It took maybe an hour or two." There were no bad vibes at first. She wanted to be with him and it appeared that he wanted to be with her. He took her home to his house in Rosslyn Estate. One story, tile roof, stone porch, French doors, three bedrooms, sitting room, large kitchen, gorgeous hedges and green all around, coffee fields nearby; all solid and clean, in an upper-class neighborhood that was predominantly white. A promising start.

There was a practical reason why Stanley Ann D. Obama had filed for divorce from Barack H. Obama in 1964. By then she was in a relationship with another man in Honolulu and there was a possibility they would marry. Obama's Luo culture in Kenya allowed bigamy, but Ann could not wed again in Hawaii before obtaining a divorce. Her new boyfriend, like Obama, was older and foreign. His name was Soetoro Martodihardjo, an Indonesian who was born in 1935, making him about the same age as Obama and seven years older than Ann. Since childhood his nickname had been Lolo, and when he came to the United States he gave his name as Lolo Soetoro. Names in Indonesia are an individual art form with no hard and fast rules, so it was not unusual that he dropped Martodihardjo. What was most notable about his name, once he arrived in Hawaii, was something he could not have anticipated. In native Hawaiian, *lolo* is the word for "crazy."

Soetoro passed through immigration at Honolulu Airport on September 18, 1962. He arrived with a J visa, his twenty-one-month visit approved by the State Department's International Educational Exchange Service so that he could attend the University of Hawaii's East-West Center. Holding a degree from Gadjah Mada University in Yogyakarta, his family's ancestral city on the populous island of Java, he was a trained geographer with "a special background in mapping and map interpretation" who had traveled throughout the vast archipelago of Indonesian islands. When he was chosen for an East-West grant, Soetoro was living in Jakarta with relatives and working at Dinas Topografi as a civilian employee for the Indonesian army, the equivalent of a lieutenant, a post to which he was expected to return after his visa expired. He was the first member of his family to visit America, leaving behind a girlfriend who was the daughter of one of his bosses at the mapping agency, and taking with him a newfound talent in ballroom dancing, which he had persuaded one of his uncles to teach him before he left. One year into his American experience, after two semesters on the Manoa campus and a summer on the mainland at Northwestern and the University of Wisconsin, he encountered Ann, an undergraduate interested in anthropology. He was strong but short, shorter than she was, with black hair, bronze skin, and a bright, open smile, and though he was almost twenty-nine he had a boyish countenance, looking more like a teenager. He was also an excellent tennis player, proficient enough to be an instructor, and that is how they met. Lolo was the teacher, Ann the student, on the university courts.

This romance proceeded at a slower pace than the relationship with Obama. Ann was more experienced now, sexually and emotionally, and did not get pregnant again. They played tennis together, attended international events at the East-West Center, and spent much time at the Dunham house on University Avenue, where Lolo met Ann's little boy along with Stan and Madelyn. Barry was two and a half when Lolo entered the scene. In his memoir he recalled how Lolo "endured endless hours of chess with Gramps and wrestling with me," and how Lolo seemed "so full of life, so eager with his plans." The memoir then went on to describe Lolo sitting up late at night and telling Ann about his family's history in Indonesia. As retold secondhand in the memoir it was a tale of heroic struggle against the colonial Dutch, untimely death, and tragic loss of family fortune. This history was mostly false.

Not long into the relationship, Soetoro faced a crisis. On June 20, 1964, his J visa would expire. He had completed his studies at East-West; after entering as a nondegree student, he ended with a master's in geography. The Indonesian army wanted him back, and university officials had no desire for him to linger. To maintain smooth relations with Asian nations participating in the program, they believed it was essential that students return home as promised. According to Sylvia Krausse, another Indonesian at the East-West Center then (she married a German student, Gerald Krausse), the paperwork for Indonesian students included a sworn affidavit in which they agreed to return to their home country. Not wanting to leave, Soetoro figured out how to circumvent the agreement and extend his visa. He took a job at Park Associates, a Honolulu surveying outfit, and persuaded school officials and immigration officers to allow him to remain an extra year so that he could get "practical training . . . in the fields of surveying, mapping, and plotting." The job paid two dollars an hour, but it served its purpose. Halfway through that extra year, in January 1965, he was laid off by Park Associates, which had no more work for him, but quickly landed a similar job with Hawaii Pacific Engineers and Surveyors.

By then he and Ann were talking about getting married. It is difficult to discern with any certainty what role his vulnerability to being yanked back to

Indonesia played in the marriage discussions, but immigration documents reveal that he constantly cited his relationship with Ann in his effort to remain in Hawaii. Her son seemed to circle around the question in the memoir he wrote decades later, when he related the scene where his mother revealed that her relationship with Lolo had taken a life-changing turn: "When my mother sat me down one day to tell me that Lolo had proposed and wanted us to move with him to a faraway place, I wasn't surprised and expressed no objections. I did ask her if she loved him – I had been around long enough to know such things were important. My mother's chin trembled as it still does when she's fighting back tears and she pulled me into a long hug that made me feel brave, although I wasn't sure why."

Did Ann love Lolo? An essential question, no doubt. But if Barry had in fact "been around long enough" to realize its importance, he was an extraordinarily experienced child with perceptive powers and conversational skills far beyond his years. At the time his mother married Lolo, Barry was three and a half.

Just as she had with Barack Obama, Ann escaped from Honolulu for her second marriage, and again took a pass on a wedding celebration, going it alone with her husband-to-be. She and Lolo were married on March 15, 1965, by a justice of the peace on the little island of Molokai, which was part of Maui County. When they returned to Honolulu, they lived in a small unit at 3326 Oahu Avenue where the rent was sixty-five dollars a month plus five dollars for utilities. Lolo was bringing in the same paltry two bucks an hour from Hawaii Pacific, while Ann was attending classes at the university, finding babysitters for Barry when she could.

Lolo's family back in Indonesia was "shocked when Mas Lolo decided to marry Mbak Ann," according to a younger relative, Bambang Utomo. *Mas* and *mbak* are honorifics that translate to "older brother" and "older sister." Bambang's father, who had worked with Lolo at the mapping agency for the military, was called in to explain what had happened in Hawaii. Marriage to an American was not part of the plan when they sent him to the East-West Center. The government threatened to strip Lolo of his lieutenant's rank if he did not return to Indonesia soon. In Hawaii, Lolo and Ann were equally preoccupied, trying to figure out how best to deal with Lolo's visa situation. On

May 24, two months after the marriage and less than a month before Lolo's yearlong extension was to end, he visited the local immigration office to make his case for staying in Hawaii indefinitely, seeking a waiver to the requirement that visitors at the end of their J visas leave for two years before reentering the United States.

His reasons were personal, financial, and political. Leaving would be a hardship for his wife, he said. If forced to return to Indonesia, he would not have enough money to pay for her to accompany him. It would cost six hundred dollars for her travel alone, he claimed, an amount he did not have. They had outstanding bills, including an eighty-one-dollar dental bill for him, and he had been told that he might need some teeth extracted, an additional cost. They were behind in paying their telephone bill. He owed money to an uncle in Indonesia who had given him a 1963 Chevrolet Corvair, to whom he sent small payments whenever someone he knew in Hawaii traveled to Jakarta. They had only three hundred dollars in a savings account, and the value of the Indonesian rupiah was on a dizzying plummet, from about 4,000 to a dollar to 30,000 to a dollar. If he went to Indonesia without Ann, he said, his financial situation would be so tight that he would be unable to send money back to his wife and her son. And if Ann somehow could go with him, she would face undue suffering, cutting short her college education to live in a place where she did not speak the language.

Soetoro bolstered his account of personal hardship with the argument that the political situation in Indonesia made him especially vulnerable. Sukarno, the leader of Indonesia since the nation declared its independence from the Dutch in 1945, had been leaning increasingly to the left. In his annual Independence Day speech in 1964, he had declared "Tahun Vivere Pericoloso" (a phrase he had borrowed from Mussolini), the Year of Living Dangerously. To Soetoro, this seemed perilous. He was anything but a radical, his perspective vastly different from Barack Obama's views about change in Kenya. He was moderate and cautious, looking to conserve what his family had attained, fearing change. Anti-American feeling "has reached a fever pitch in Indonesia in the direction of the Indonesian communist party," he told immigration officials. Family and friends had advised him that "returning would be a dangerous endeavor. . . . With his strong connection to the United States, he would encounter prejudice." Also, corruption in Indonesia was rampant. Land belonging to his family, he claimed, had been confiscated by the governor as part of a land reform plan. Friends had warned him that "any small amount of property he took back to Indonesia would be confiscated at the port by the communist trade unions," returnable only by paying heavy bribes.

On top of all this, the Indonesian army, the military to which Soetoro still had civilian obligations, was involved in a bloody skirmish in Malaysia against the British. "My wife is extremely anxious about the impending separation as I myself am," he wrote in the immigration documents, fearing that the Indonesian situation would only get bloodier. "It is probable that warfare in Indonesia cannot be avoided much longer. I am a trained geographer with a special background in mapping and map interpretation. I have traveled throughout the Indonesian islands and have detailed knowledge of each of the areas and their resources. Due to my former association with the Indonesian army while still there it is quite probable that I would be placed on the front lines doing reconnaissance work in Indonesia's current campaign against Malaysia and the British forces."

This possibility was particularly upsetting to his wife, he said. Was Ann supporting the British position? Did she know the nuances of the East Asian situation? More likely, Soetoro was using her to make his case, a tactic she was more than willing to endorse to keep her new family together. Thus his final argument: "It is from both my wife's and my distaste for this campaign that my wife is distraught for my safety. No reassurances that I have been able to offer her have alleviated her . . . upset condition. I have been advised that a prolonged separation under these circumstances could endanger my wife's health and mental outlook."

Soetoro followed up the interview with a letter from a Honolulu doctor, Toru Nishigaya. It listed no specific ailments, but offered the medical opinion that Ann's separation from her husband "would cause undue hardship and emotional strain." In a conversation with Robert Wooster, an official at the East-West Center, Soetoro claimed that Ann had become ill shortly after their marriage. He said that she was "still suffering from a stomach ailment" and that her doctor had said it might require surgery. But when pressed further about the doctor and his diagnosis, Soetoro "could not remember exactly,"

Wooster added, leaving him with the impression that Soetoro "intends to make every attempt to remain indefinitely with or without E-W Center."

Two weeks before his visa was to expire, Honolulu INS officials granted Soetoro another one-year extension (through June 1966). East-West officials were informed about the decision only after the fact, and were not happy. Soetoro's personal concerns were immaterial to them; they were feeling larger pressures. Robert Zumwinkle, Wooster's boss at the center, wrote a note to John F. O'Shea, the lead INS official on the case, reminding him, "As you know, we have a cable from the embassy of Indonesia requesting by official order that Lolo Soetoro, civilian employee of the Indonesian army, [have his visa] immediately terminated and return to Djakarta, Indonesia."

By the fall of 1965, Sukarno's Year of Living Dangerously was over, but life in Indonesia had become exponentially more dangerous. For months there had been rumors that a coup was coming, that Sukarno would be toppled by his own military, with support from the Western powers. On September 30, in what at first appeared to be a movement to bolster Sukarno, six generals were killed at the command of a group of officers from the air force and the presidential guard. It turned out to be a complicated subterfuge. Communists were blamed for it all, and out of the turmoil came another general, Suharto, who took the opportunity to seize power and slowly ease Sukarno out of the way. What followed was the slaughter of communists, leftists, and anyone considered a danger to the new regime, including Chinese nationals – a bloodbath engineered by Suharto's men with some behind-the-scenes assistance from the American CIA. Estimates of the number of Indonesians killed during the purge ranged from a half million to a million.

While Sukarno was still in power, Lolo Soetoro worried that he would be dealt with harshly by leftists if he returned to Indonesia because he had studied in the United States and married an American. With the rise of Suharto, the circumstances were turned upside down, but Lolo's predicament was no less difficult. The regime seemed distrustful of Indonesian students who had gone overseas. It was during the transition from Sukarno to Suharto, according to Sylvia Krausse, that she and Lolo and the other Indonesian students at the University of Hawaii were ordered to meet with Indonesian government agents who had come to Honolulu to interrogate them. "We had to come. It was rather traumatic," Krausse recalled. "[The feeling was] if I don't come they might do something to my family. We had to fill out forms. 'Who was your neighbor [back home]?' I assume they were trying to find out what affiliations we had. And all of a sudden the regime fell. They came to the university. It was on a weekend. We were in a classroom. Three of them came in. They did not explain why. They just said they were from the government and they had to get more information about us."

Soetoro knew that his time was running out. Shortly after the visit from Indonesian agents, an official at the East-West Center wrote a letter to the Indonesian consulate in San Francisco stating, "Mr. Soetoro . . . assures me that he fully intends to return to Indonesia in June 1966 when his current visa expires and that he has communicated this intention to the military attaché at the embassy of Indonesia in Washington, D.C. He said that his wife intends to return to Indonesia with him." By then Ann had obtained a passport, and she and Lolo had changed strategies. Their plan now was to live in Indonesia for two or more years while he went through the formal immigration process to return legally to the United States with his American wife and her son. Ann sent another affidavit to immigration officials that reversed their previous position and stated that Soetoro's departure would not cause her undue mental hardship.

Five months after she arrived in Nairobi, Ruth Baker became Ruth Obama. They were married at the district commissioner's office on Christmas Eve 1964, with two friends there to witness the event, Joe Kariuki and his American wife. Ruth was still under *BARE-ick*'s spell. At their house in Rosslyn Estate, she had a Luo cook and a maid to assist them. The house was a reflection of Obama's ambition, Ruth thought. After struggling with a job at the *Nation* newspaper, she found more suitable employment at Nestlé in the industrial area of Nairobi, working as personal secretary to the chief executive officer. With her boss's help, she was able to buy a new Peugeot 204 and learned how to drive on the left side of the road. After work she often joined her husband at the Starlight Club, a hangout in Integrity Center that had become the whirling vortex of Nairobi's fun-loving nightlife. "Oh, it was a rocking place. We had a great time," she said later. "With all the prostitutes, and everyone else too.

Including [Tom] Mboya. Everybody went there. MPs went there. [Cabinet] ministers went there. Very many prostitutes, all over the place. But they had great music. They had Congolese music. Everybody was jumping and rocking. Beautiful. What a great time, for people who like to drink and dance. I got tired at three in the morning, but Barack would be able to stay until four or five and then we'd go home."

In the patriarchal Luo society, the man controlled family decisions, and Obama decided that he wanted the two young children he had with Kezia to be under his charge when he returned from America. Kezia herself was in Luoland, but Bobby and Rita, as they were called then (Rita later used only her African name, Auma, and Bobby went by Roy and then Malik), were brought to Nairobi to be near their father. Kezia did not object; she thought Obama was rich and could take better care of them; he had a fancy new car and a big house. Bobby was nearly seven and lived at the house. Rita, only four, was soon boarded at the Maryhill Catholic school in Thika, a dislocation that increased the trauma of being yanked away from her mother. Ruth treated them cordially, but she was unable to give them motherly love, and they were never close. Decades later Auma would describe those days to the half brother who carried her father's name: "This woman, Ruth, was the first white person I'd ever been near, and suddenly she was supposed to be my mother!" The old man, as Auma called her father in retrospect, never spoke to her or her brother "except to scold us," but she remembered that he was constantly bringing friends home – Luo friends, Kikuyu friends, associates from the new government, former Maseno classmates, Americans he had met overseas.

Among the foreign visitors were many who had connections to Elizabeth Mooney Kirk, the former literacy teacher who had been Obama's boss and academic benefactor. In January 1965, not long after Obama and Ruth were married, Betty's stepson, John Kirk, then eighteen, came to Nairobi with a group of young women who were Peace Corps volunteers. They caught a flight from Monrovia, Liberia, and Obama picked them up at the airport and brought them to stay at his house with Ruth for a few days. In a letter recounting what John told her about his trip, Betty Kirk wrote that Obama "had done a lot to make their trip pleasant. They all liked Barack and Ruth very much." Among other things, Obama, casually but sharply dressed in white slacks and short-sleeve white shirt, took them to a nearby game preserve to see the giraffes and warthogs, zebras and lions. Then he and a friend named George, another Luo from the Kendu Bay area, drove John and two of the visitors out to Kericho, to see the vast tea plantations, and farther west into Luoland and the shores of Lake Victoria, where, at George's urging, one of the young women joined in a tribal Luo dance. The Westerners went on to Uganda from there, while Obama and George dashed across the gulf to Kendu Bay, where they partied and drank Tusker beer at the New Nyanza Club.

Later that year Frank Laubach, founder of the literacy foundation that launched Betty Mooney on her fateful mission to Kenya, came through Nairobi on what he called a "literacy safari." On his third day in the capital, after observing literacy classes at schools and churches around the city, he delivered a speech at the United Kenya Club. Obama was there, and invited him to dinner at his home that night. It was the Laubach Foundation's money, after all, that underwrote much of Obama's education. In a diary he kept of his African trip, Laubach wrote of that visit to Obama's house, "He has an American wife. Three highly educated Kenyans dropped in for tea at their home. Here we saw television for the first time since I came to Kenya. The same news was given in Swahili and in English." A few days later Laubach spoke to the Rotary and proposed that the service organization provide $450 a month to pay for a four-page literacy insert in the *Nation* newspaper. In his diary that night, he jotted down the names of some possible editors for the insert and noted, "Barack Obama would be splendid."

Obama had much higher ambitions. He rarely passed up an opportunity to let strangers and colleagues alike know that he had climbed to the highest peak of American education by studying economics at Harvard, and that he soon expected to take a leadership role in the economic development of the new nation. Although he had been booted out of the United States, and Harvard, before finishing his dissertation, he referred to himself professionally as Dr. Obama. The dissertation was nearly completed and merely needed polishing, he would say. But one night during that first year back in Nairobi, robbers entered the house in Rosslyn Estate and made off with the television set and, apparently, his manuscript. "I don't know how or why, but that's what happened," Ruth recalled. "And he never resumed his doctorate." Asked why robbers would steal a dissertation, she said, "Well, sometimes you take brief-cases, sometimes you take different stuff when you are robbing. I don't know why." Did she really believe that story? "Yeah, I sort of do. But I don't think he would have resumed anyway. He didn't have the discipline anymore. I think he probably wrote a lot of it, but he wouldn't have finished it."

Lack of urgency may have played a larger role than lack of discipline. One paper Obama did finish, of far more consequence politically, was a critique of a new economic blueprint of Kenya issued by Tom Mboya's Ministry of Finance and Planning. Mboya, who had taken over the key ministry after completing work on a new constitution, did not personally write the blue-print *African Socialism and Its Application to Planning in Kenya,* known also as *Sessional Paper No. 10.* But the document clearly reflected his nuanced economic and political philosophy. A team of economists drafted it, led by an American advisor, Edgar Edwards, along with Mwai Kibaki, the assistant minister (and future president); Philip Ndegwa, the senior economist; and several brilliant young American-trained economists, among them Harris Mule, Y. F. O. Masakhalia, and Barack Obama. "We were asked – all of us, professionals – to contribute papers on what we understand, what we know about African socialism," recalled Masakhalia. "We all made contributions."

When he unveiled the paper, Mboya called it "one of the . . . pillars on which Kenya is founded." President Kenyatta hailed it as "Kenya's economic bible." Although the blueprint encouraged a form of socialism and indeed used the word *socialism* in its title, it was viewed in cold war terms as a rejec-tion of Soviet or Chinese statism. William Attwood, the American ambas-sador, noted that it "encouraged private investment and explicitly rejected Marxism" as irrelevant to the African situation. Attwood called it "a flexible, pragmatic document that reflected Tom Mboya's practical thinking." Looking back on it decades later, Harris Mule called *Sessional Paper No. 10* "a master-piece of ideological architecture" that featured "flexible guidelines in charting the economic future and spared the country the economic turbulence of so many other African countries." In a 1960s world riven by "isms," Mule said, Mboya astutely pushed for "a variant of African socialism" that advocated a mixed economy.

But Barack Obama, bright and disputatious, always up for an argument, thought the paper was flawed, and he was willing to say so publicly, even though he was one of the economists who was asked for advice beforehand, and even though it was sponsored by his Luo mentor, Tom Mboya. Obama made his case in the July 1965 issue of the *East Africa Journal* in an essay titled "Problems Facing Our Socialism: Another Critique of *Sessional Paper No. 10.*" Obama went through the paper point by point, agreeing here, disagreeing there, praising those responsible for it for at least taking the issues seriously and for attempting to lay out a blueprint with goals and benchmarks. But he challenged the paper's vagueness in defining African socialism. He also thought the drafters were naïve in not realizing that Africans, after decades of colonialism, had the same class distinctions of haves and have-nots as the Europeans, and he attacked the paper for its reluctance to embrace nationalization of businesses and industries, particularly those owned by Europeans and Asians. Sometimes, he wrote, it was the duty of government when considering the "good of society" to "force people to do things they would not otherwise do." The nationalization question was not just a matter of economics, he added:

> One need not be a Kenyan to note that nearly all commercial enterprises from small shops in River Road to big shops in Government Road are mostly owned by Asians and Europeans. One need not be a Kenyan to note that most hotels and entertainment places are owned by Asians and Europeans. One need not be a Kenyan to note that when one goes to a good restaurant he mostly finds Asians and Europeans, nor has he to be a Kenyan to see that the majority of cars running in Kenya are run by Asians and Europeans. . . . We have to give the African his place in his own country and we have to give him his economic power if he is going to develop. The paper talks of fear of retarding growth if nationalization or purchases of these enterprises are made for Africans. But for whom do we want to grow? Is it the African who owns this country? If he does, then why should he not control the economic means of growth in this country?

These were variations of the arguments Obama had often made during his debates with Kiri Tith back at the churches and service clubs in Honolulu. But now the stakes were real.

For all his talk about class and race, Obama lived in a white neighborhood, in a big house, with an American wife, after grabbing his African children away from their African mother. He was, in every way, a man of contradictions. And while he struggled with the future of his nation, his wife struggled as a stranger in a strange land. Her mother had fallen into a deep depression after the escape to Africa. Now Ruth herself was growing increasingly distraught. After living with Obama in Nairobi for several months, she came to know him below his intelligence and surface charm, and to glimpse the depths of his anger and dysfunction.

The accepted family story, retold later by his children and other relatives, would attribute his steady personal decline in Kenya to a string of interconnected professional and political setbacks. There is truth to that version of events, but it greatly downplays how abusive he was, to himself and to women, from the start. He was drinking heavily from the time Ruth came to live with him in Nairobi. Some of his friends at the University of Hawaii – Kiri Tith most prominently – had witnessed his occasional overdrinking earlier, but he was able to keep it from many people. Now it was unavoidable. Ruth described him as an alcoholic: "The truth is he was drinking heavily every night. . . . He wouldn't get to work on time. He wouldn't do his work on time. And you can see a man that's drunk. If he's not steady, and his breath's smelly, and his eyes are red." He drank everywhere and anything, she said, and then would drive home drunk. "So I was petrified. He had some accidents. He had a lot of accidents."

His first serious accident – one of two in his lifetime that resulted in a fatality – occurred during that first year in Nairobi. The person killed in this first accident was a passenger. The horrible twist was that Obama should not have been driving. The car, a new model Fiat, belonged to the passenger, his longtime friend Laban Adede Abiero. Adede, as he was called, came from a village not far from Kanyadhiang in Luoland. Only twenty-five, he held an important job in Nairobi as director of East African Posts and Telecommunications. As his younger brother, Kevin Oriko Abiero, would later tell the story, Adede and Obama had been out late drinking at a bar owned by Adede's father, Justo Abiero. The bar was called Dala, which is Luo for "home." It was located in Kariokor, a sector about a kilometer from downtown. When they were leaving for home, Obama said that he wanted to drive Adede's new car, just off the showroom floor. He had heard that the Fiat had performed well in the most recent safari road rally. Adede cautioned that it was a fast car and that he himself should drive it, but Obama insisted. Obama was older, and bigger, and drunk – and he prevailed. Adede was so cautious that he decided to ride in the backseat. They had traveled less than a kilometer when Obama rammed into a slow-moving trailer as they were negotiating the Ngara roundabout at the entrance to the central business district. Adede was killed on the spot. Obama made it home with only minor injuries.

It turned out that Ruth was pregnant by then, a condition she had not expected or wanted. She felt increasingly fearful of her husband, and thought about having an abortion, but was not able to follow through on a decision. "I was very unhappy. . . . I was very lonely. And I was on my own. I had nobody. I was crying lots of nights . . . and I didn't want a baby. I didn't know anything about babies. . . . I wasn't one of those people who thought about that, and then it happened. In fact I was one of those who thought I would never have a baby." Mark was born late that fall, on November 28. His Luo name was Okoth, which means "born when it is raining."

The baby transformed Ruth; his presence made her feel euphoric. Whatever else was happening in her world, she had him. But her relationship with her husband became only more volatile. Obama could be alternately charming and abusive. He had no time for his infant son and would leave the house for long stretches, telling friends that he would come back when Okoth was done crying. "Men like that . . . can love a woman one day and be a horror to them the next day, and the women are on a seesaw," Ruth would recall decades later during an interview in Nairobi in January 2010. "And that's the way it was. One day he could be fantastic to me and the next day he could be horrible to me."

His father, Hussein Onyango, was a man who hit women, and it turned out that Obama was no different. "Beat, beat, beat," Ruth recalled. "And made me terrified. I thought he would kill me. And he would come home at two or three in the morning and he would say, 'I have to have food!' That's an African thing. And I wouldn't dare resist him. One time someone said, 'Oh, you should fight back.' One time I tried to fight back, and God, we had a fight and I was really hurt. He beat me. He hit me. With his hands . . . mostly on the body, not my face so much. But the body – boom, boom, boom."

The physical abuse was largely hidden from outsiders. The mental abuse was more public, a manifestation of his intellectual arrogance, which was apparent to all but directed most caustically at Ruth, who suffered from low self-esteem. "He always made you aware of his intellect. He was one of those people who would say, 'Hey, I'm so clever!' And he would argue with you and make you feel . . . he enjoyed making me feel inferior. He made me feel inferior by insulting me in front of other people, saying 'Isn't she stupid?' or 'Can't she do this?' or ordering me around, making me feel bad. But the funny thing is I got a lot of friends because of that. A lot of people bonded with me. They felt sorry." Philip Ochieng, a prominent Nairobi journalist and fellow Luo who had been part of the 1959 airlift, said he heard frequent reports that Barack and Ruth had been fighting every night – and then saw it for himself. "I witnessed one fight. Somehow we ended up at his house for a nightcap, and somehow as the drinking was going on a fight started. We had to separate them."

Not long after the thieves took Barack's television and, purportedly, his doctoral thesis, the Obamas moved from Rosslyn Estate to a smaller and less expensive City Council house (a form of middle-class public housing) on Hurlingham Road (to be renamed a few years later Argwings Kodhek Road, honoring a cabinet minister who died in a mysterious crash). The move did not help the marriage. In the early summer of 1966, a family friend stopped by the house when Obama was gone. He too was Luo, with a white girlfriend and a job in the government. Although he knew Obama better than Ruth, he sympathized with her. There was more to it than Obama's drinking, the man told her. Obama was also running around with other women. "He told me he just got fed up with the way Barack was acting, because he was with every woman who came in his sight. . . . He just told me, 'You know, Barack's all over the place with all these women. What are you taking this rubbish for? Why don't you go back to America?'"

Ruth was heartbroken. She had contracted some mild sexually transmitted diseases during her time with Obama, but still had not suspected that he was a serial womanizer. "Innocent as I was, I never thought Barack was that bad, and I still loved him," she said during our interview. But this news overwhelmed her. How could she escape? The friend said he had already developed a plan.

He would take Obama out to Luoland that weekend, and they would hang out at the Nyanza Club in Kisumu, while Ruth left with little Mark for the United States. She bought the plane tickets, told her boss at Nestlé that she had "a bad situation" to deal with, and left.

She knew of only one place to go, Boston, and a few days later she arrived at the front stoop of her parents' house in Newton with Mark, her year-old mixed-race toddler, her *hapa,* in tow. "They were mixed [in their reaction] of course," she said. "A white woman with a black baby. So they found me a house in Cambridge. I didn't have any preconceived ideas. I just knew that I loved them and they loved me and they would help me anyway. So they did."

Ruth and her son were in Cambridge for three weeks when, as she put it, "things happened again." What happened was that Obama appeared. He had pursued her all the way to Boston and knocked on doors and called around until he found her. She did not want him to come over to her place, but he persuaded her to meet him at a neutral location, a hotel lobby. She agreed.

"I'll be different," he said. "I'm sorry. I want you back. I'll be better."

Despite the drinking, the beatings, the womanizing, she still loved him. "He was like this Svengali. The mesmerist. He had this power over me." They went to the apartment of one of his Harvard friends, where Ruth called her parents. She explained to them that she was going back to Africa, that they should not worry, that everything would be okay.

"You make your bed, you have to lie in it," her father said.

At the time that Ruth returned to Nairobi with Obama, Ann D. Soetoro was alone again with her son, Barry, in Honolulu. Lolo had left at the start of summer 1966, having run out of extensions on his visa. Not long thereafter, Ann gave an account of their separated lives to immigration officials who were still deliberating his request to make a legal return to the States.

"My husband left June 20 1966 and went back to Djakarta and is working for the Indonesian government conducting a topographical survey," she wrote.

He is living in a house that belongs to a relative. . . . My husband makes the equivalent of 10 dollars a month American money and relies on relatives for support. To supplement his income, he must rely on selling personal items he bought while in the U.S. I am working at the ASUH [Associated Students of the University of Hawaii] as a Senate secretary. In addition, I have part-time employment grading papers at night and sometimes tutor U of H students. I make $325 from U of H and about $100 per month [in other work] all before taxes. I give my parents $50 per month [for rent and food]. I buy personal things for my five year old boy. I also pay $50 a month for babysitters from 2:30 to 5 p.m. I am trying to save enough money so I can go to visit my husband. We figure on going and staying until my husband's time is done and then come back together.

Ann and her son were still in Honolulu when the next school year began, and she enrolled him in Miss Kazuko Sakai's kindergarten class at Noelani Elementary School. Aimee Shirota, a student teacher that fall, remembered that Barry was accompanied to the class orientation by three adults, presumably his mother and grandparents. The students, a heterogeneous group of Caucasian, Japanese, Filipino, and *hapa* variations, were drawn from a mostly affluent area of Manoa Valley and included the sons and daughters of doctors, writers, and other professionals. To start the morning, they sat cross-legged on the floor in three rows. Barry, taller and heftier than most classmates, was placed in the last row on the left-hand side. He seemed calm and observant, if a bit shy, according to Shirota. When there was a commotion of some sort across the room, he would "crane his neck and smile, but he wouldn't get involved." At the end of her student teaching stint, Miss Shirota left Hawaii to take graduate courses at Kansas State Teachers College in Emporia, up the road from El Dorado, the same school that Ralph Dunham, Barry's granduncle, and Doris Armour, his grandaunt, had once attended. For the first time she experienced snowflakes, blooming tulips, and laundry freezing on the line.

When would Ann and Barry leave Hawaii to join Lolo in Indonesia? By December 1966, three months into Barry's kindergarten, Ann was telling INS officials that she was to receive her BA in anthropology in two months, February 1967. She was trying to land a job with the U.S. embassy in Indonesia, she said, but had not yet received a letter back. Then another hitch: February came and went with no degree because of "a last-minute finding" that she was "short a few credits."

Ann's graduation day came, finally, in August, at the close of summer school. It had been seven years since she landed in Hawaii, age seventeen, living with her parents out on Kalanianaole Highway. In the years since, she had married a man from Kenya, had a son, moved to Seattle and back, and married a man from Indonesia. She had accomplished, in her own unlikely way, what she had set out to do on that long-ago day when she had attended freshman orientation at the University of Hawaii, the day that Kennedy first debated Nixon. Now JFK was dead, Nixon wanted to make another run at the presidency, the summer of love was blooming in San Francisco, college campuses were aroar against the war in Southeast Asia – and Ann and her *hapa* boy were leaving it all. In search of his own *el dorado*, Stan Dunham had taken his family on an incessant westward migration away from the landlocked heartland, from Kansas to the Upper Northwest to Hawaii, and now his daughter was going farther still, following the Pacific from Honolulu another 6,709 miles west, all the way to Jakarta on the faraway island of Java.

CHAPTER 9

"SUCH A WORLD"

Life is a dream, something
Played behind a screen, and I,
Now dreamer, now dancer, am pulled
In and out of existence.

AMIR HAMZAH, "BECAUSE OF YOU"

No member of the Martodihardjo family had married a *bule* before Lolo
Soetoro left home to study in Hawaii. In the national language, Bahasa
Indonesia, *bule* means "stranger," but of a particular type, with white skin.
Ann Dunham Soetoro, Lolo's new wife, had very white skin. *Bule* is a linguistic cousin of *jadak,* the Luo word for "alien" in western Kenya, and *haole,* the
native word for someone (usually a white Anglo) not of Polynesian descent in
Hawaii, but it was not necessarily meant as an insult, more as a matter-of-fact
description. Whatever the intent, *bule* could not be applied to the little boy
Ann brought along. His skin was darker than Lolo's, and his black hair was
curly. What was he? People who encountered him when he arrived in Jakarta
were uncertain how to categorize this six-year-old introduced as Ann's son.
Perhaps he came from Ambon, many thought. Ambon was one of the thousands of islands composing Indonesia, an archipelago dotting an expanse
nearly as wide as the North American continent. It was in the South Moluccas,
nearly fifteen hundred miles east of Jakarta, and the people there were known

for having darker skin, though not as dark as those even farther east in Papua.

Ann and Barry arrived in Jakarta in October 1967. They landed at Kemayoran International Airport after a three-day stopover in Japan on the way west from Honolulu. Decades later the son could summon gleaming shards of memory from that trip: extra peanuts and puzzles and metal pilot's wings provided by the Pan Am stewardesses; his gray clip-on tie and long-sleeve white shirt; bronze Buddhas and green tea ice cream; "bone-chilling rains" and high mountain lakes in Japan; his mother studying Bahasa Indonesia flash cards at night; and then Jakarta at last, and stepping out into daylight, "the tarmac rippling with heat, the sun bright as a furnace." Along with these evocative details, he could also recall the "little guardian" sensibility he took with him at the start of their overseas adventure. He was barely six; his mother was a month shy of twenty-five; yet when they stepped off the airplane he "clutched her hand determined to protect her from whatever might come." The innocent and naïve mother shielded from danger by a world-wise little son – here is a recurring theme in myth and memoir and children's literature. In the story of Ann and Barry, as retold by the son, the premise first surfaced in Hawaii when at age three he asked his mother knowingly whether she truly loved Lolo. But it was in Indonesia that the theme fully took hold. It was an accurate reflection of his perspective, though it unavoidably undervalued how much of an adult's complicated life is outside the comprehension of a child.

Lolo was at the airport to pick them up, with a borrowed car. He had no car of his own then, only a Japanese motorbike. To Barry he looked different from the man who playfully wrestled with him at Gramps and Tut's house on University Avenue. It had been sixteen months since they were last together in Honolulu. Lolo seemed fatter now, and had a mustache. The eyes of a boy notice such things first.

During his long reign, Sukarno had gloried in the grand and modern look. He had built wide boulevards and a shiny new sports stadium for the 1962 Asian Games and oversize monuments everywhere, including one on the main boulevard into town that depicted a young boy and girl extending their arms to welcome visitors. What caught Barry's attention as they drove along the streets of the city of four and a half million people, maneuvering through the traffic of three-wheeled motorbikes along with Fiats, Chevrolets, Fords, and Australian Holdens, was something more exotic. He noticed the statue of Hanuman rising ten stories high, the monkey god with an ape's head on a man's body. The monkey god would outlast all mortals. Sukarno's reign was over; Suharto was in full control now, after a long and bloody transition, and just as Ann and Barry were arriving he had formed the first cabinet of his New Order. The worst of the murderous political purges were over, but there were still spasms of violence. Only days earlier there had been a riot outside the Red Chinese embassy, with bottles and bullets flying.

Their first house was in South Jakarta, at 16 Haji Ramli Street, named for the man who had owned much of the nearby property. He was Betawinese, this Ramli, from the native population of the island of Java, and as a Muslim had undertaken the hajj, or pilgrimage, to Mecca three times, reflected in the Haji in the street's name. It was not much of a street, just unpaved dirt, barely wide enough for cars to pass in opposite directions as it zigzagged at ninety-degree angles through the neighborhood. There were no sewers or gutters, and in the rainy season it was all mud, impassable. Local kids sloshed around with plastic bags on their feet instead of shoes. At night the street was illuminated by twelve electric lampposts, recently installed at the behest of the block leader, Coenraad Satjakoesoemah, who worked at Garuda Indonesia Airlines, but darkness closed hard on the labyrinth of dirt alleyways weaving through neighborhood backyards, the passages often no wider than a man with arms outstretched. The evening air was pungent with *nasi goreng* and *rendang*, fried rice and spicy beef, wafting from bungalow kitchens and street vendors who announced their presence with the hollow knocking of a bamboo stick, *dock-dock-dock-click.*

Far from the wealthier streets of the capital city, this sector, known as Menteng Dalam, was a working-class *kampung* framed by swamps to the left and right of Dr. Supomo Street, the main artery leading to Haji Ramli. Lolo had come from the professional class, but this was all he could afford at the time; it was down the street from the house of one of his brothers, Soegio, a police officer. Many of the residents had been relocated from an area surrounding the massive new stadium, Gelora Bung Karno. Among the closely packed one-story structures, the Soetoro house was much like the others: whitewashed façade, no air-conditioning, primitive toilet, four rooms, orange-red *genteng* tile roof, mango and pine trees in front, white iron fence near the street. Soon enough neighbors would become accustomed to seeing Barry standing behind that fence, jumping up on his tiptoes to peek over the top, sticking his tongue out at passersby. Inside, his room was to the left front, barely larger than a closet, with a wooden cupboard to store his clothes.

The backyard was a sight to behold, Lolo's personal Indonesian zoo: chickens, cockatoos, snakes, turtles, two biawaks (reptiles that resemble miniature crocodiles) in a pond, and a small ape named Tata that he brought back from a mapping assignment with the army in Papua. As his neighbor Coenraad put it, "Lolo was a weird adventurer who loved weird things." Not only did Lolo collect exotic animals, but he also enjoyed eating them, according to a nephew, Haryo Soetendro, known as Pongky. "He ate everything. One of his interests was eating a small lizard [*cecak*]," Pongky recalled. "I accompanied him to hunt for the lizards. He brought the jar and I was helping him catch them. After he got plenty, he would fry them and eat them."

On their first morning in Jakarta, Ann, with her long, black hair and ivory skin, walked up Haji Ramli wearing a sarong. She encountered a neighbor woman, Jacomine Mathilda Madewa, known as Ibu Ita. (*Ibu* translates to "mother," but is used commonly to connote "madam," and there is an even shorter version, *Bu*.) They exchanged hellos. Ibu Ita had worked for the World Council of Churches and knew English. "Then I asked her, 'Who are you?' 'My name is Ann,' she answered. Then came a boy, his skin is dark, about six years old. I ask her, 'Who is this child?' 'Oh, this is my son from a marriage with a Kenyan guy.' Not long after, then came a Javanese. I asked her again, 'Who is he?' 'This is my husband,' she said. So that was all of them? I wondered. That was the Soetoro family. Lolo was a lieutenant working for Dinas Topografi." Ibu Ita invited them in for breakfast and served them bread with chocolate sprinkles and jam. It was the first of many meals Barry would eat at her house. A pretty daughter, Dara, was his age.

"He ate a lot at my house, that naughty boy! My house is big, and he loved to hide under Dara's bed or suddenly disappear at my house when we told him to go home. Even my maids scolded him too, 'Come on, go home. Go home!'" In Javanese, Ibu Ita said, they called that behavior *mbeling*. "You know how a boy is. Barry loved to play at the nearby cemetery named Kober.

He played with his kite, climbed trees with the other kids. If he came back from the cemetery his shirt was so dirty, stained, his hands and legs, too. And he always washed his dirty hands and legs at my house before going home. He played very well with the kids in *kampung* Menteng Dalam. You could see him sit in front of the neighbors' house eating tempeh. His mom allowed him to play with kids and eat anything without worrying that her son got diarrhea." Ibu Ita once brought home a slice of cake from the best bakery in town, Maison Benny, and left it on the dinner table for her family. Barry came in and "ate the whole thing" before anyone else saw it. "My maid came and scolded him big-time," she recalled. "Me, I was just laughing. How could I get mad at him? Besides, the cake was gone anyway."

Among her other duties, Ibu Ita was chairman of the parent-student association for the new neighborhood school, SD Katolik Santo Fransiskus Asisi, which was up and running with 203 students, though the long and narrow army barracks–style structure was still under construction. It was three blocks from Barry's house, closer to Prof. Dr. Supomo Street and the entrance into the *kampung*. As one can deduce from the Bahasa Indonesia name, this was a Catholic school named for St. Francis of Assisi. From the week they arrived in October, Ann had been homeschooling her six-year-old son early each morning, but she was looking for a local school to help with his socialization and followed Ibu Ita's recommendation to enroll him at SD Asisi. He entered first grade in January 1968.

Everything about Barry seemed different to his classmates and teacher, Israela Pareira. He came in wearing shoes and socks, with long pants, a black belt, and a white shirt neatly tucked in. The other boys wore short pants above the knee, and they often left their flip-flops or sandals outside the classroom and studied in bare feet, *nyeker,* a term conveying "chicken feet." Barry was the only one who could not speak Bahasa Indonesia that first year. Mrs. Pareira, known familiarly as Bu Is, was the only one who understood his English. He was a fast learner, but in the meantime some boys communicated with him in a sign language they jokingly called "Bahasa tarzan." They thought he was funny because he was left-handed. When Ann accompanied him to school the first day, Mrs. Pareira was confused. He looked Ambonese. In itself, this was no big deal; the classroom was heterogeneous, with Javanese, Betawanese, Bataknese, Padangnese, Ambonese, Christians and Muslims, Hindus and Buddhists. But he did not look like his mother. "She introduced herself as a foreigner, coming from Hawaii, and she pointed at Barry – 'This is my son.' We – me and the students who saw them for the first time – only asked ourselves, 'How come his mother's skin is bright while her son's is way darker?' It was a big question for us. But watching her drop him off at school [day after day] we became used to the idea that Barry is her son." To the other students, Barry's young mother was even more exotic than he was, with her pale skin, long hair, and pretty dresses.

The school bell rang at seven, the signal for thirty boys and girls to assemble in a straight line on the playground outside the door to Kelas I. They had a short day in store, only two and a half hours, out by nine-thirty. After Bu Is inspected their fingernails for cleanliness, she led them into the room, which was unfinished, with no ceiling and a dirt floor. They recited the Lord's Prayer in unison to start and end class, and twice in between, Barry following along even though he knew neither the words nor the language, until an ending that was familiar to him, "Amen." As a Catholic school, SD Asisi required all students, whatever their religion, to study Christianity. Barry had been registered as a Muslim, but that was merely a formal designation that followed the practice of listing the religion of the father, or in this case stepfather. Lolo was Muslim, though not religious. Ann was an atheist, with a spiritual and humanist bent. Barry was too young to be much of anything, though his mother pounded into him her "disdain for ignorance and arrogance."

Bu Is taught her first-graders simple stories about Jesus from the Holy Bible. "Barry gave his full attention to what I said in Bahasa even though he didn't really understand the meaning. I was wondering what he was thinking while watching me speak in Bahasa!" As it turns out, there is an answer to that question in the memoir he wrote later: "I would pretend to close my eyes, then peek around the room. Nothing happened. No angels descended. Just a parched old nun and thirty brown children, muttering words." The depiction resonates, yet it should be noted that while this was a Catholic school, Mrs. Pareira was decidedly not a nun and only twenty-four, and the teachers who followed her were also young and married.

By the end of first grade, Barry was acculturated. He could sing national songs like "Halo-halo Bandung" and various children's tunes written by A. T. Mahmud, and he knew what many of the words meant. His grades were best in arithmetic, with its universal language, but he was in the top fifth of the class in everything except Bahasa Indonesia, at which the teacher said he was steadily improving. He even started leading the students into formation before class, snapping out orders: *Siaap, grak . . . Lencang depan, grak.* Attention! Fall in . . . Straighten up . . . Adjust to the front . . . Ready. Mrs. Pareira was impressed by his manner: "Seems like his mother was fully taking care of him, and filling his soul only with good things."

In second grade Barry was in Class A, the first of four sections. He was the biggest boy in the room, nearly as tall as his teacher, Cecilia Sugini, who sat him in the back row. "Ibu, boleh saya bantu hapus?" he said to her one morning. May I help you erase, ma'am? He was offering to help her clean the blackboard, which he often did from then on. Mrs. Sugini did not know English, so on rare occasions when she was having a difficult time getting through to Barry, she called in Bu Is from the first-grade class to help.

In the tradition of her father, Mrs. Sugini was a storyteller who used fables to impart moral lessons. Barry and his classmates learned from her the legend of Joko Tarub. Seven female angels descend to Earth to swim in a lake. Joko spies on them and steals the wings of one, Nawang Wulan, so that she is unable to fly back to her palace in heaven. She eventually marries Joko, and has a baby with him, then one day she discovers the stolen wings he had hidden under a rice mill. Disillusioned, her wings restored, she soars up to her palace with their baby and leaves Joko behind, alone with remorse. Who could know that earthly variations of that fable mirrored the life of Barry's mother, past and future.

At SD Asisi Barry developed a reputation as an eager beaver. He was always moving into position, flailing his hands in the air to give an answer, even jumping out of his chair in the back row and moving toward the front. He was such a bold student, bolder than many of the Indonesians, who were shy, thought his third-grade teacher, Mrs. Fermina Katarina Sinaga, known as Bu Fer. She and the others became familiar with his cry, "Saya bu, saya!" Pick me, ma'am. Pick me! How much is twelve times twelve? Answer quickly. How many minutes in an hour? "Saya bu, saya!" Bu Fer did not mind his eagerness, but thought such a big boy need not be so assertive as to step forward from his seat to be recognized. Do it again, she finally warned him, and she would never call on him again. "He obeyed me and walked back to his chair in the back row."

Bu Fer was in her first year as a teacher then, only twenty-one and newly settled in a boardinghouse in the Menteng Dalam neighborhood. She sensed that Barry was not afraid of being wrong; he just wanted to participate, to speak out. The national songs, ingrained in the subconscious of the other students, were wholly alien to him, yet he would barge right in, she recalled. "I remember he was singing a national song, 'Dari Sabang Sampai Merauke,' then he got stuck because he forgot the lyrics but he was cool with that." Sabang is in the westernmost, Aceh province of Indonesia, Merauke in Papua the farthest east, some 3,253 miles from each other; the lyrics are the Indonesian equivalent of "from California to the New York island." In re-creating the scene, she started mimicking the long-ago Barry: "Dari Sabang . . . sampai . . . kemana ya?" – *kemana* means "Where to?" – "and he looked at his friends looking for the answer. It made me laugh out loud."

With all of the political bloodshed that Indonesia had just endured, violence triggered by raw power, fear, and political and ethnic hatred, the classroom of Bu Fer was a place removed. She spoke idealistically of the notion of tolerance in Indonesia. *Tenggang rasa* and *tepa selira*. Live peacefully. *Bhinneka Tunggal Ika*. Unity in Diversity. "I explained to them that they are part of the Indonesian people, who lived from Sabang to Merauke, hundreds of languages and tribes, with different beliefs. Some are wide-eyed, slant-eyed, tanned, dark skin, and so on. When I mentioned about the dark skin, Barry's friends took him as the sample. He was just smiling and didn't take offense to it."

It was in Bu Fer's class that Barry wrote a paper whose message would resurface decades later as a supposed foretelling of lifelong ambition:

Nama saya Barry Soetoro. Saya kelas III Strada Asisia. My name is Barry Soetoro. I am a third-grade student at SD Asisi.

219

Ibu saya adalah idola saya. My mom is my idol.

Ibu guru saya, Ibu Fer. Saya punya teman banyak. My teacher is Ibu Fer. I have a lot of friends.

Rumah saya dekat sekolah. Kalau ke sekolah saya jalan kaki diantar Mama, pulangnya sendiri. I live near the school. I usually walk to the school with my mom, then go home by myself.

Cita-cita saya adalah ingin jadi presiden. Saya suka jalan-jalan keliling Indonesia. Someday I want to be president. I love to visit all the places in Indonesia.

Sudah Selesaaaaaaaaaai. Done. The eeeeeeeeend.

The paper no longer exists, though Bu Fer's memory is precise and there is no reason not to trust it. Yet it would be misleading to draw a straight line from that simple declaration in 1969 to President Obama forty years later. The rest of his adolescence offered none of the signs of oversize yearning that were so readily apparent in some other boys who grew up to be president, most notably Billy Clinton. It was also in grade school that Billy (who, much like Barry, grew up without his natural father) sang a song to his teacher in Hot Springs, Arkansas, about how he was going to grow up to be president. That was no more telling than Barry's paper in Jakarta. But Billy, propelled by his mother and his own desire, kept at that theme year after year from then on, and ran for student elections whenever he could, always wanting the top job, while Barry, as we shall see, followed a decidedly different route, receding from politics for a long time after writing that one predictive line remembered by Bu Fer.

For the most part at SD Asisi, Barry was considered a standup boy, a leader, not just as the teacher's pet who would clean the blackboard and order the others into formation before class, but also as a generous teammate on the playing field. The most popular sport in school was *kasti,* based on rounders, a loose cousin of baseball, with tennis balls, a wooden stick, and bases, five or more depending on the number of players. As his teachers and classmates remembered the scene, as a fielder Barry would scramble after the ball wherever it was hit, but often gave the ball to a smaller teammate to throw at the runner, which was how an out was made. "He was big and tall and could run faster than others, and usually succeeded in beating the opposing team," said Bu Fer, who put Barry in charge of preparing the equipment before recess. "But he never did it for himself or by himself. . . . He didn't control the ball to show how good he was."

In the back row of the third-grade classroom, on wooden chairs behind a long wooden desk, the boy seated next to Barry was Mardanus Hasmoro, known to friends as Mardi, who had returned to Indonesia after four years with his family in Australia, where his father had served as an air force attaché. He was fluent in English but could recall only a few words of Bahasa Indonesia. One day Barry brought in one of the English-language correspondence workbooks from Calvert School in Baltimore that his mother had used with him during their predawn sessions at home. "When I saw it, I said, 'Hey, this is the one I used to learn from in Australia!' And I had already finished it," Mardi recalled. " 'This answer is this, this one is this,' blah, blah . . . and we became fast friends. We speak in English while to the others I used Bahasa tarzan. . . . I cannot speak Bahasa, so Barry was helping me. He explained what Ibu Fer said, almost every word." Mardi struggled especially when it came time for tests, and would have been clueless if not for Barry, who helped him "in silence, out of Ibu Fer's eyes."

For all of Barry's singular characteristics – his darker skin, his large body, his American mother, his intelligence, his desire to answer every question, his leadership skills – he was in essence still just another naughty boy among the other boys on Haji Ramli Street. They teased him by calling him "black berry Black Barry." Johny Askiar and his brother Yunaldi, known as Yul, whose father operated a ceramics factory, lived a block and a half away, and recalled how Barry would race down the street after school and stand at the corner twenty paces from the Askiar house, in shorts and shirtless, his arms folded, his head held high, as though he were saying, *Here I am, come play with me. Who wants to wrestle me?* Often he carried a toy bow and arrow that Lolo had brought back from Papua. They would say that Barry was too noisy, and once they pranked him by throwing him into the nearby swamp, some holding his legs, others his hands and head, as they tossed him into the murky waters near Tebet Mas. Word went out: "There goes Barry into the swamps." But instead of getting angry, the boy whose first years had been spent on the beaches of Oahu only shouted out confidently, "I can swim. I can swim. It's not a problem." The Askiar brothers' older sister, Etti, once pranked Barry by giving him red pepper candy (*permen cabai*) that he liked so much he kept asking for more, until she slipped him a real red pepper. "*Hah, huh, hah, huh* . . . he got all flustered because it was so spicy."

Barry could prank back. Once he told Yul to come close so that he could show him something, and stuck "a turtle right in front of my face." Yul, who was much shorter, jumped up and hit him on the head, but Barry did not get angry. The other kids noted that he had an unusually hard head, so hard that it made your hand hurt when you hit him. Yul said it was like *batu kali,* as hard as a river stone. Vickers Sulistyo, who was called Ikes, one of the neighborhood boys at SD Asisi, described the stone-headed Barry as *jahilnya nggak ketulungan,* such a teaser and prankster. More than forty years later, Ikes still carried a physical reminder of that characteristic, an inability to touch his shoulder with his left hand. Here is how it happened:

> As kids we used to play in small rivers, run around. One time at noon, we played with a bike. Barry kind of wants to drive but I didn't allow him. So I drove the bike and he sat on the back saddle. About fifty meters from my home, where there was a rather sloppy part of the road, he started tickling my ears. I said, "Please don't do that, Barry, please don't," but he kept continuing so we both fell and my left arm broke. The bone was coming out of my skin; my hand was full of blood. I remember he said, "Wah kayaknya tangan lu patah nih" – Oh no, I guess your arm broke.

As Ikes remembered it, Barry backed away slowly, then ran home, embarrassed. Ikes's parents took him to a shaman on Cirebon Street who was believed to be able to fix broken bones. No hard feelings about Barry; they were just kids, Ikes said.

The mischievous boy often lingered at the house of Lolo's brother, wanting to play with the daughters, his stepcousins, Noeke and Endang. "Barry loved to peek at us when bathing," Noeke recalled. "There was a small window at my bathroom and he climbed to the window, then teased me and my sister. . . .

So I splashed the water at him just to make him go away, and he would wait for us in front of the door only to show us that his shirt was wet." The girls got back at him by fooling him with food. He was so hungry and curious it was always easy. They gave him *cabe rawit,* a small hot cayenne pepper, after telling him it was supersweet.

Four decades later, chatting on the patio of the house he had lived in since Barry was one of the neighborhood boys, Coenraad Satjakoesoemah was overcome with emotion thinking about what those few years meant in the life of a future American president. This little *kampung,* with its mix of middle-class and working-class Indonesians, Muslim and Catholic, of all shades of skin, representatives of the different islands and ethnicities of the vast island nation, offered an early lesson in diversity. "That is really what he feels," the street's respected elder said, a hand cupped toward his heart. "Barry is the kid from Menteng Dalam." True enough, Barry's experiences on Haji Ramli Street deepened the characteristics of adaptability and cultural awareness that would thread through the rest of his life, yet what a vibrant and frightful dreamscape all of this was for the young boy! The language, the streets, the games, the food – all so different from anything he had known. Running through the alleyways of Menteng Dalam, he had become so fluent in the manners and language of his new home that his friends mistook him for one of them. Yet he was also always apart and alone, trying to process what he saw, smelled, touched, and ate. Dog meat, snake meat, crunchy crickets, hot green peppers, fried rice, meatballs, swamps, kites, biawaks, puppet shows, mosques and minarets, calls to prayer, bamboo switches. "I would faithfully record [much of this] in letters to my grandparents – confident that more civilizing packages of chocolate and peanut butter would surely follow," he noted later. "But not everything made it into the letters. Some things were too difficult to explain." A man without a nose. A baby who died from evil spirits. Barefoot farmers in barren fields. Life, he was learning, "was unpredictable and often cruel." Tut and Gramps, he thought, "knew nothing about such a world."

He was an adult when he wrote that, planting thoughts back into the mind of a boy. But what could he know about what his grandparents endured beyond the family stories that he was told, stories that often were intended to soothe his anxieties? The touchstones of their lives so easily led to stereotyped assumptions of provincial innocence. They were from Kansas, in the geographic and cultural middle of the American heartland, the territory of Dorothy and the Wizard of Oz. But Kansas, of course, had its own history of violence and oddness, as did the lives of Barry's white forebears. What could be more unpredictable or cruel than the circumstances of Ruth Armour Dunham's suicide on Thanksgiving night 1926 in a dank and dreary auto garage in Topeka? What could be more violently repellent than the scene Charles Payne encountered when his army unit entered Ohrdruf concentration camp in March 1945 and came upon the bodies of Jews stacked like cordwood? What did the barefoot farmers in barren fields in central Java endure that was not known to the grandparents of Madelyn Payne as they dug potatoes from their field in tiny Peru, Kansas, by the dark of the moon? Life had never been as simple or easy or innocent on that side of the family as Madelyn's grandson might have thought.

Madelyn Dunham's last threads to Kansas were now cut. She had gone back one last time, after Ann and Barry had left for Indonesia, for the funeral of her mother, Lee Payne, who went into the hospital in January 1968 and never came out, her body riddled with cancer at age seventy. After R.C.'s retirement, he and Lee had moved from Augusta to Winfield, a midsize Kansas town down by the Oklahoma line, and that is where Madelyn went to pay her final respects. On her way back to Honolulu, she stopped in Kansas City to visit her little sister, Margaret Francine, and also called on her best friend from childhood, Francine Pummill, now Francine Gruver, who lived in Overland Park.

"Francine?" she said on the phone. "Francine, this is Maahhd-lun Dunham." They had been out of touch for several years. Somehow her old friend had acquired an entirely new accent, Francine thought. Gone were the flat A's of their childhood, replaced by something more sophisticated. They went to Francine's country club and had a few glasses of wine, and an hour or so later Madelyn sounded more like Kansas, less affected. Something else about her: she smoked incessantly now, and used a long cigarette holder. Maybe she was channeling Bette Davis.

A few months later, R.C. visited the Dunhams in Hawaii. He had never thought much of Stan, none of the Paynes had, but they got along civilly when together and the visit to the island went smoothly. Old Payne at seventy-six seemed happy and healthy when they put him on a flight home. The morning after he got back to Winfield, he dropped dead of a heart attack.

Lolo's father, Soewarno Martodihardjo, had been a geologist, a prominent profession in an archipelago rich with minerals, natural gas, and oil. He had worked for a Dutch oil company, Bataafsche Petroleum Maatschappij, and finally as the principal of a technical high school, Sekolah Teknik Menengah. His expertise in mining was so extensive that he had written a book about it, in Dutch. He and his wife, Djoeminah, who spoke Dutch, Acehnese, and Javanese, but very little Bahasa Indonesia, had ten children, six boys and four girls. The girls were Warsinah, Soewarti, Soewardinah, and Ratna. The boys were Soepoyo, Soepomo, Soegio, Soegito, Soemitro, and Soetoro (known as Lolo). Even though they all came from the same parents, the children none-theless seemed to reflect the exotic variety and vastness of Indonesia. During his career searching for oil and gas resources, Martodihardjo and his wife moved frequently, and the children were born in different cities and provinces, from west to east across thousands of miles. The oldest sons, Soepoyo and Soepomo, were born in Aceh, farthest west. The oldest daughter, Warsinah, was born farthest east, in Papua, and had dark skin and curly hair, much like the Papuanese. "I believe sometimes your physical appearance is affected by the place where you are born," said Heru Budiono, the son of Soepomo. "Look at my aunties [Soewarti and Soewardinah] and my uncles [Soemitro and Soetoro] born in Bandung. They have the brighter color, tend to get a bit pale."

Bandung is the capital of West Java, the second most populous city on an is-land with the densest population in the world (100 million people on 132,000 square miles). Heavily influenced by Dutch colonialism and surrounded by mountains, Bandung then had the look of a nineteenth-century European city, with a mix of Javanese, Dutch, and Chinese culture and architecture and a temperate climate that averaged seventy-five degrees. Its Dutch nickname was *Parijs van Java,* the beauty of Java. When Lolo was a boy, the family moved once more, from Bandung to Yogyakarta, a historic city that served as the cul-tural center of the island. Lolo attended Dutch-run junior high and high schools

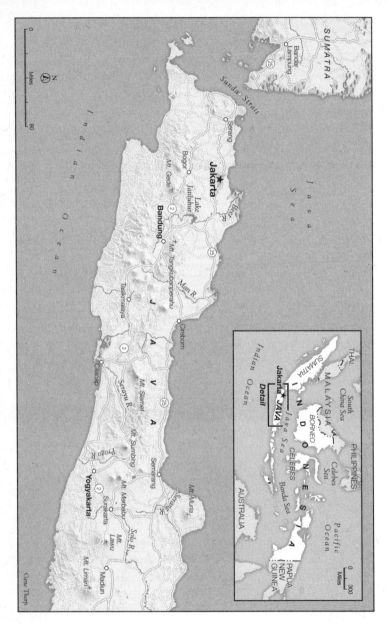

in Yogya and graduated from the prestigious Gadjah Mada University there; his mother still lived there when Ann and Barry arrived in Indonesia. It was her house at 14 Jayeng Prawiran Street – 276 miles from Jakarta, but over the mountains, an all-day train ride – that they visited on several vacations, starting with Christmas 1967. She was a diminutive widow who burned incense and spit betel juice into a little silver spittoon. Barry knew her as Eyang, the Bahasa Indonesia word for "grandmother." Other grandchildren called her Eyang Putri.

Her husband, Martodihardjo, had died on July 28, 1951. Later accounts of the family history, including those in *Dreams from My Father* and various profiles and biographies of the future American president, would state as accepted fact that Martodihardjo was killed while fighting Dutch troops during the final struggle for independence, known in Indonesia as the Dutch Aggression, that took place in the late 1940s. In the memoir and other accounts, his tragic death was said to be compounded by more drama, with the Dutch burning down the family home, forcing the mother and children to scurry to safety and scavenge to survive.

The story is wrong, a concocted myth in almost all respects. Not only did Martodihardjo die two years after the struggle had ended, but he died a most domestic death, far from any battlefield. He fell off a chair at his home while trying to hang drapes, presumably suffering a heart attack. A small notice of his death appeared on page 4 of the *Kedaulatan Rakyat* newspaper a few days later, and while it did not list the cause of death, the wording belies the claim that he died in battle. "It's a Very Sad Thing" was the headline. "For the sudden demise . . . of our respected senior, the Head of Mining Jogjakarta Branch, M. Soewarno Martodihardjo, after more or less of forty years of body and soul devotion to ensure the growth of mining industry in Indonesia. . . . His contribution-devotion will remain and become the reflection for all of us of the new generation he left behind. Division of Mining, Lor 22, Jogja."

It is probable that the Martodihardjo family, like other residents of Yogyakarta, faced some trauma during the late 1940s. Yogya, an ancient royal city under the protection of a sultan, Sri Sultan Hamengkubuwono IX, served as the political center of the independence movement when the Dutch tried to reclaim their colonial authority after World War II. Sukarno and other independence leaders operated out of the Gedung Agung, a palace less than two miles from the Martodihardjo house on Jayeng Prawiran Street. In December 1948, when the Dutch army entered Yogya in what became known as Agresi Militer II, houses were burned, freedom fighters were rounded up, and Sukarno and other leaders were arrested and sent off to detention on faraway Sumatra. The Dutch controlled the city during the day. At night nationalist fighters would filter in, often slipping surreptitiously down a small river called Kali Code that ran only a few hundred meters behind the Martodihardjo house on Jayeng Prawiran Street. Among the several guerrilla armies fighting the Dutch, the most popular was the Tentara Pelajar, the students' army. Lolo, thirteen at the time, was not a member; it is unclear whether any of his older brothers were. The oft-told fable about Martodihardjo dying in the fight against the Dutch also included the notion that Lolo's oldest brother, Soepoyo, suffered a martyr's death as well. That is another fiction. He died of cancer in 1955.

It is also false that the house on Jayeng Prawiran was burned to the ground. No houses on Jayeng Prawiran were torched. (House No. 14, made of cement and bamboo matting known as *gedhek* or *gedheg*, no longer stands, but it was razed decades later.) But it was a fearful time. Curfew sirens wailed at noon and six every evening, forcing people off the streets. All young men were suspect. If they could, families abandoned the city for safer environs. One woman who still lived in the neighborhood six decades later remembered that as a girl she hid behind a large flowerpot when Dutch soldiers conducted a house-by-house search along the short, narrow street. Finally, on March 1, 1949, came a powerful counterattack that helped push the Dutch out for good, an event memorialized as Enam Jam di Yogya, Six Hours in Yogya. This was more than two years before Martodihardjo fell while hanging drapes.

A distinct pattern is evident here in the threads of the Obama story that weave through Kenya and Indonesia. Both countries came out of colonialism into freedom after a difficult struggle against white European nations. And in both instances, the family mythology, or at least the story as passed down to the American grandson (or step-grandson) and subsequently passed along by him, was of a grandfather standing up against the colonialists and facing the consequences of his bravery: Hussein Onyango detained and tortured by the

British; Martodihardjo killed by the Dutch. While a lack of records establishing the truth one way or another makes it slightly less certain that the Hussein Onyango story was false, neither the Kenyan account nor the Indonesian one holds up well under scrutiny.

Throughout his school years in Yogyakarta, Lolo ran with a group of friends that included Siti Fatimah, Khadari, Trinil, Bustami, and Titik Soeharti, his first girlfriend, who lived nearby. With Titik on his back saddle, they rode bikes through the city and out to Parangtritis Beach. She remembered him as easygoing and gentle, with a natural ability to win a woman's heart. From an early age, Lolo was a flatterer, so much so that women adapted a local saying to him: *Lolo ini piye, kambing dibedakin pun pasti dibilang cantik* – If a goat put on makeup, Lolo would compliment the goat too. It would later be said that he looked much like a slightly rounder version of the handsome Indonesian singer Andre Hehanusa, who sang a duet of "To All the Girls I've Loved Before" with Julio Iglesias. When Lolo first lived in Jakarta, after obtaining his geography degree at Gadjah Mada in Yogyakarta, he was considered a "naughty boy," so his older brothers put him under the watchful eye of a strict older relative named Probotjono, the son-in-law of Martodihardjo's brother.

Probotjono was a top assistant at Dinas Topografi, the mapping agency on Gunung Sahari Street that performed surveying services for the Indonesian army. Lolo was able to land a job there too. According to Probotjono's son, Bambang Utomo, Lolo stayed at their house in South Jakarta during that period, was dating the daughter of one of the agency's bosses, and held the civilian rank of *letnan satu,* or first lieutenant, when he was chosen for further studies at the East-West Center in Honolulu. In preparation for his American sojourn, he spent several months essentially quarantined to study English. During his time overseas, he sent many gifts back to Probotjono's family, including a traditional Hawaiian lei for Bambang. But Lolo also caused a family headache when word came back that he had married a *bule* named Ann. "My father was forced to come to his superior's house at night just to explain the situation," Bambang recalled. "The decision had been made. The rank of lieutenant had to be stripped off if he wanted to continue his studies." Lolo was willing to face the consequences and fought to remain in Honolulu until he finally ran out of visa options in June 1966.

By the time Ann and Barry arrived in Jakarta sixteen months later, Lolo was back from survey missions in Papua and working at the Dinas Topografi office, a long commute across town by motorbike from their little house on Haji Ramli Street. Although Lolo and Ann had been husband and wife in Honolulu for a year before his return to Indonesia, it was only when the family was far away from Gramps and Tut that Lolo assumed any pretense of being the little boy's male mentor. Like his mother, Barry took the Soetoro name. He called Ann *mamah* and Lolo *papah* and did not flinch when Lolo introduced him to relatives as his son. "He never pressed things or pretended our relationship was more than it was," Barry would write about his stepfather decades later. "I appreciated the distance; it implied manly trust." To the boy, Lolo "didn't talk much, but he was easy to be with," and had a worldly knowledge that seemed "inexhaustible": how to wring a chicken's neck, how to box to defend oneself, how to change a tire, how to handle beggars, how to deal with women.

Lolo told Barry that his mother had a soft heart. She was too nice to beggars and others beneath her station, he said. Men could not be soft. He showed Barry scars on his ankles and shins that he said were leech marks from his time in Papua. The leeches had attached themselves to his legs while he trudged through remote swamps mapping for the army. They hurt, he told Barry, but they did not stop him from doing what he had to do. The boy asked him if he had ever seen a man killed. Yes, said Lolo. Men are killed when they are weak. And men lose women because they are weak. *If the weak man's woman is pretty, the strong man will take her.*

Within his Indonesian extended family, Lolo had a reputation for being funny and easygoing. He "showed his happy face," as one relative put it. In Javanese culture, they call this characteristic *sumeh*. But on Haji Ramli Street with his American wife, he revealed a different personality. Once they had settled, he became remote from Ann, rarely talking. He started drinking more. "It was as though he had pulled into some dark hidden place out of reach, taking with him the brightest part of himself," his stepson observed later. His transformation was not simply a withdrawal, nor was it entirely hidden from friends and neighbors along Haji Ramli Street. At night, said Coenraad Satja-koesoemah, they could hear screams coming from the Soetoro house. There were constant rumors about Lolo. His views about strong men and weak women seemed more than theoretical. "He never got along with the neigh-bors, while Bu Ann was the opposite," one neighbor said. "He often brought women to his house. The neighbors knew about it and regret what he did to Ann since Ann was a foreigner. They thought it somehow affected the image of Indonesia. 'How come Lolo do such things while his wife isn't home?'" Another neighbor, Ibu Ita, said Ann started confiding in her regarding her troubles with Lolo.

The unraveling coincided with a series of events that outwardly seemed positive. With the help of a wealthy brother-in-law, Trisulo Djoko Purnomo, who was married to his older sister, Soewardinah, Lolo was able to rise from a relatively modest job at Dinas Topografi to a midlevel executive position with Union Oil's subsidiary in Jakarta. A few months later, in January 1970, he moved the family from Haji Ramli Street to a larger house in a more comfort-able neighborhood, on Taman Amir Hamzah Street in the Menteng district of central Jakarta. Soon thereafter, Ann would become pregnant; by the middle of August, she would give Barry a little sister, Maya Kassandra Soetoro.

It seems appropriate here to consider Ann's situation at the start of the 1970s, the extraordinary life of this woman who was not yet twenty-eight. The 1960s would be defined as a tumultuous era, and her life during those ten years certainly accentuated that notion, yet in her own peculiar fashion. If this was a period of experimentation and rebellion, her experiments and rebellions were outside the norm of her generational cohort even as her ideals were in sync with the times. She supported movements of social change – civil rights, peace, liberation – yet played them out in intensely personal and challenging ways. Ten years. From Stanley to Anna to Ann. From Dunham to Obama to Soetoro. From suburban Seattle to Honolulu to Jakarta. A son by a Kenyan. A daughter by an Indonesian. One marriage undone, another marriage troubled. Remember the young woman at Mercer Island High who was searingly smart and independent, sardonic yet optimistic? She had gone through so much since then, so much trauma and adventure, that one could forget what she was before it all. Yet the essence of her character remained unchanged from the seventeen-year-old at the end of her high school years. Now, as then, she was unlucky in love, open to whatever might come her way, fascinated by others yet apart from the crowd, and, no matter her family burden, decidedly her own person.

In the memoir Barry wrote later, he made much of his mother's naïveté during their Indonesia years. This began with the idea that she did not know why Lolo had been called home "suddenly and unexpectedly" in 1966 and was stunned when a relative explained the political realities to her. *Dreams from My Father* portrayed this vividly, describing Ann in a daze, taking a long walk home through the Jakarta heat, "sun high, air full of dust," after being told matter-of-factly that Lolo, like all overseas students from Indonesia, was yanked back from Hawaii because of the bloody rise of Suharto, and that he was conscripted into the army and sent to Papua so swiftly and secretly that his family could not greet his arrival. At best, this was only partly true. There was nothing sudden or unexpected about Lolo's return to Indonesia. Ever since Ann became his girlfriend at the University of Hawaii, Lolo had been fighting to extend his visa, which was only good for nineteen months. The incessant back-and-forth with U.S. immigration officials, East-West Center administrators, and the Indonesian consulate had been the overwhelming issue in their relationship. It was not something that took Ann by surprise; she was thoroughly engaged in the problem. And once Lolo lost that struggle and returned to Indonesia in June 1966, his experience was not entirely mysterious or ominous. He spent much of that period working again at Dinas Topografi and living with relatives in Jakarta.

On the other hand, Lolo did spend time in Papua with the swamps and leeches, which could not have been pleasant. And as for Ann, the extent of the political bloodshed in Indonesia during the purge and the brute power and force of the emerging Suharto regime certainly must have stunned and demoralized her once she settled in Indonesia. Her first neighborhood in Jakarta, Menteng Dalam, had seen its share of political trauma. At the height of the purge, an Indonesian army unit, the Siliwangi division from West Java, set up camp in Jakarta just to the south of Menteng Dalam. The leader of the Siliwangi was in a coterie of military brass whose goal was to abolish all political parties. Coenraad Satjakoesoemah, the airlines official whose house on Haji

Ramli was just being finished during that period, recalled that at least four leftists who lived in the *kampung* "disappeared" soon after the Siliwangi division arrived, and their houses were destroyed. It was a horrible time, he said, when "no one knew who was a friend and who was an enemy." The worst had passed, but Ann could still feel the reverberations. She told Coenraad's wife, Djoemiati, that she was "afraid living in Jakarta with all the uncertainties." That statement to a neighbor underscored another recollection from her son: her admitting to him later that she never would have made the trip to Indonesia had she fully grasped the personal and political circumstances beforehand.

But Ann made the most of it. She woke before dawn every morning to teach Barry from the Calvert School workbooks, then walked through the labyrinth of Haji Ramli Street, wearing flip-flops and carrying her high heels, until she reached Prof. Dr. Supomo Street, there catching a jitney bus to work downtown, where she taught Indonesian government employees and businessmen English as part of a program, Lembaga Pendidikan Pembinaan Manajemen, sponsored by the U.S. embassy. In the Dutch colony, English had not been part of the educational heritage. She would tell her son later that her students were not particularly interested in perfecting English; some were more intent on making passes at her. A bother, but nothing to discourage her. Since that first morning when she had walked down the street dressed in a sarong, introducing herself to neighbors, Ann strove to be accepted by the people of her new land, relatives and strangers alike, and tried to take them on their own terms. She was an intuitive anthropologist, interested in the nuances of culture, the arts and crafts and stories that defined families and tribes and regions. During that first week in Jakarta she joined an *arisan,* a gathering of twenty local women who met in Djoemiati Satjakoesoemah's living room, and offered to teach English to Djoemiati and anyone else who was interested. She also joined a quite different group of women, Westerners who had married Indonesian men, but soon dropped out, she told friends, because "all they did was sit around and complain about their Indonesian husbands and adjusting to what they would be like."

This was typical Ann. She had dealt with such men in her English classes, and at home. Lolo might be a problem. He clearly changed once she married him and especially once he got back to Indonesia. And he might even fit some of the stereotypes that the other women were complaining about. But even so she could not tolerate the limitations and implications of negative stereotypes. She found satisfaction exploring and appreciating culture rather than denigrating it. No surprise that she became active in the Ganesha Society when it was formed in 1970. A museum-affiliated organization whose aim was to preserve indigenous art, the Ganesha Society was named in honor of a zoomorphic deity, an elephantlike being, often balanced atop a mouse. Ganesha is the Hindu god of wisdom, education, and success and the destroyer of evils and obstacles. His honored place in Javanese culture underscores Indonesia's ancestral connection to India and demonstrates how a creatively fluid culture merged so many traditions despite the predominant Muslim religion. For an American woman who was spiritual but not a churchgoer, and who had more than her share of obstacles to overcome, an interest in Ganesha seemed particularly apt.

Whatever flaws Lolo displayed, Ann worked that much harder to become part of his larger family. His nieces and nephews accepted her immediately, calling her Tante Ann, and she was so friendly that even Lolo's mother, who was initially upset that he had married a *bule,* grew deeply fond of her. "The old-fashioned Javanese woman who cannot speak English met an American lady who could barely speak Bahasa, but they could communicate considerably well," recalled Heri Purnomo, one of Eyang Djoeminah's grandsons, the son of her oldest son, Soepoyo. "There was a funny moment once, at the beginning, Tante Ann loves to touch Eyang's head until we tell her that it is forbidden – *pamali* – to touch someone's head who is older than you, especially if it's your parent-in-law. Ann apologized but then explained that in America it showed love and affection."

Barry entered a new school in February 1970, in the middle of third grade. A few weeks earlier, his family had moved from Haji Ramli Street to the pavilion house at 22 Taman Amir Hamzah, closer to the center of town. Amir Hamzah was a national hero, a revered Indonesian poet who had fought for independence and been killed by extremists in 1946 at the early age of thirty-six. "I am a puppet, you are a puppet / To please the puppeteer running out of rhymes," he wrote. Barry's school now was SD Besuki, named for the street on which it sat. It had been around since the Dutch colonial era, going back to 1934, and was regarded as a prestigious institution in a high-class neighborhood. To get there from the Soetoro house, you went down Pangeran Diponegoro Street, past an imposing row of wealthy homes, including one where the first vice president of Indonesia lived, and along Suropati Park, near the U.S. ambassador's residence, and finally to Taman Kodok, or Frog Park, across from the school. Barry's new classmates included the sons and daughters of lawyers, bankers, doctors, members of Parliament, and government officials. The Soetoros were not in that income bracket, but Lolo did have a corporate job now, and belonged to a club.

Their new house was called a pavilion because of its subordinate position as the smaller of two houses on a large plot of land owned by a doctor named Soerono, who was known for his malaria research. The Soeronos lived in the main house, handsome and whitewashed, with three bedrooms, a family room, a living room, and four more adjacent rooms separated by small gardens and ponds. The pavilion house where Lolo, Ann, and Barry stayed was to the right of the main house as you approached from the street, and separated from it by a five-foot cement wall. It was narrow and cool, pale yellow with wooden doors and white interior walls. Ann learned of its availability from a relative of the owners who had visited Lolo's mother in Yogyakarta. The setting was green and commodious and upper middle class, a sharp contrast from the dense alleyways of Menteng Dalam. All along the block, graceful houses were set back from the street. Less than a half block away was Taman Amir Hamzah (*taman* means "park"), a blocklong oval of grass and walnut trees. Behind the living room, separated by a half wall, was a family room where Ann kept her books and typewriter, and which also had a window air conditioner and television set. To the side were Ann and Lolo's bedroom, then a bathroom, Barry's bedroom, a servant's room, and storage area. In the house at various times of the day and night were the parents, the son, servants named Saman and Turdi, two turtles, a parrot whose cage hung from the kitchen ceiling, a dog named Djanggo, who slept near the door, and soon enough a baby sister and babysitter. (In all of that exotica, Turdi might have been the most exotic, a delicate young man who loved to dress in women's clothing and who decades later changed his name to Evi and became a transsexual.)

A boy named Slamet was also around often; he was Barry's friend, and lived with his family in one of the back rooms behind the owner's big house. His dad was Dr. Soerono's driver. Slamet and his brother Yuniadi, like so many Indonesian kids before them, did not know quite what to make of Barry because of his skin color and his *bule* mother – until he opened his mouth and said "*Saya* Barry," I am Barry, and continued speaking in the familiar *lu-gue* (you-me) terms. After two years in Jakarta, he could make his way comfortably in Bahasa Indonesia. They played Monopoly in the living room, Ping-Pong on a table outside Barry's pavilion, and badminton with large tennis rackets. At the end of the block in the opposite direction from the park, they raced up and down a narrow alleyway crammed with small houses and street carts with intoxicating aromas where vendors and their families lived, a path parallel-ing a small river. Barry was accustomed to street foods and ate them like any neighborhood boy. As Slamet recalled, Barry "liked the green beans porridge so much so he made unintentional sounds while chewing . . . it sounded like *cap, cap, cap*. . . . We laughed at him loudly." It was also Slamet, a few years older, who tried to teach Barry the facts of life after Maya was born. "When Bu Ann gave birth to Maya, I asked him, 'Do you know where Maya came through?' 'From what I know, she came through the anus,' he said. 'You are wrong, Barry, she came through the vagina,' I responded. But he didn't believe me. He didn't believe me. I challenged him, 'Why don't you ask your mom?' 'Ah, *ogah*,'" he said. *Ogah* is slang for "no way," showing how fluent in street talk Barry had become.

Lolo knew that Slamet was more experienced than Barry and was con-cerned about what they might do together. "Slamet, come here!" he said one day. "If you ask Barry to play, play and teach him the good things, all right? Don't get any idea of doing any mischief!" But Bu Ann, Slamet said, was the one to whom Barry listened. "She was so elegant, simple. Very strong charac-ter," he recalled. "Also she often got angry at Barry for playing too much with us, but she never showed it to us. Never scolded us. She only said, 'Just go home. Barry needs to do his homework.' That's it, even though she was scold-ing Barry in English minutes back. So I felt respect for her and was rather hesitant in asking Barry to play with us. So if my brother and I want to play with Barry, we watch over the pavilion first, whether he is doing his homework or no. If we see him doing nothing, then we have the courage to call him, 'Barry, Barry.'"

There were at least two competing mythologies surrounding the life of this boy named Barry who grew up to be President Obama. One myth was passed along to him and then repeated by him with various levels of skepticism in his memoir, and a more malignant myth was created by his political doubters when he became a national figure in the United States. In the second myth, intended to portray him as an alien, a *jadak*, someone outside the norm of American life, Islam played a central role. The myth went like this: His Kenyan grandfather was Muslim. His Kenyan father was reared a Muslim. His Indonesian stepfather was Muslim. He learned Muslim doctrine at a Muslim school in Jakarta. The truth is this: Hussein Onyango converted to Islam, but did not follow all of its precepts. His life was more directly shaped by Christian missionaries, and he had no qualms sending his own son, Barack Obama, to Christian schools. Moreover, Barry never met Hussein Onyango, but spent most of his childhood with his white grandfather, Stan Dunham, who was raised a Baptist and became a Methodist in Vernon, Texas. Barack Obama, the father of the future president, was not a Muslim but an atheist. Lolo Soetoro was born and reared Muslim but was even less religious than Hussein Onyango. In any case, he had little or no influence on the boy's spiritual and ethical grounding, which was strongly shaped by his mother. The first time the family visited Lolo's relatives in Yogyakarta, they went to church on Christmas Eve, and when they got home, Ann gave Barry a pile of gifts. One of the Martodihardjo grandsons, Haryo Winarso, remembered the occasion and also his jealousy. "Why did he get a lot of gifts while I don't?" Haryo asked his mother.

And now we come to the final falsehood of the second myth, the school that Barry attended in 1970 and 1971, SD Besuki, a place that in some accounts was described as a Muslim madrassa. SD Besuki was a public elementary school in Jakarta, considered among the academic elite, along with Santa Theresia and Perguruan Cikini (where the children of the first president, Sukarno, studied). One of his classmates was the grandson of Agus Musin Dasaad, among the richest Javanese of that era and a close friend of Sukarno; another was the granddaughter of the minister of labor. Some students were chauffeured to school in luxury sedans or arrived by pedicab. Some were

Muslim, some Christian. Indonesia held the largest Muslim population in the world, 90 percent of the population having converted to Islam since Arab traders brought the religion to the islands in the fifteenth century. But there were still very few exclusively Islamic schools in Jakarta in the late 1960s. As was the case at the Catholic school, SD Asisi, Barry was registered as a Muslim when he enrolled at SD Besuki because his stepfather was Muslim. With other boys in his class, he attended *Jumat* prayer sessions on Fridays in an open-air room on the side of the building. Pak Khudori taught them how to pray and how to read the Koran. His classmates recalled that Barry wore a sarong, and that it was constantly falling from his hips, making them laugh. By his own account, the religion teacher once caught him making faces during prayer and sent a note home to his mother. "My mother wasn't overly concerned. 'Be respectful,' she said." The school also celebrated Christmas and Easter and other Christian holidays. "We didn't know about the Muslim-Christian dichotomy," said one classmate, Dewi Asmara. "We mingled without knowing or asking, 'Hey, what are your beliefs?'"

Religion was taught in the classroom once a week for two hours by a separate instructor. It was one of seven subjects for third-graders, along with Bahasa Indonesia, math, geography, history, art, and sports. The teacher for those courses was a bright young man named Effendi, who remembered that Barry's facility with Bahasa Indonesia was "very good, with a hint of Western accent, something like American cowboy." More than language or skin color, Effendi said, what differentiated Barry was the ease with which he dealt with elders:

This is very different than most Indonesian students. They even flee when they see the principal. We used to have benches in front of the class. The kids usually sat there after recess. Sometimes I just sat there and watched them, in case they fell and got hurt. We had coral stones in the school yard. When I was sitting there, no kids were courageous enough to sit next to me. Barry was the exception. He came and said hi to me. I was a bit surprised. Who is this kid? Why is he so courageous? When I looked at him, I was thinking, "Oh, it's the African." "What is it, Barry?" I used to ask him back. "Where do you live?" he asked me. Then I tell him I live in Setiabudi. "How do you go to school?" he asked. "Sometimes by foot, sometimes bicycle." "Where did you go to school, sir? Was it here as well?" "No, I went to the school for teachers." Those were the kinds of questions Barry asked me. He never asked me about school lessons.

Barry sat in the back row, near another new student, a girl named Cut Citra Dewi. There were two Citras in class, so to distinguish her she was called Citra Baru. *Baru* means "new." But Barry had a difficult time articulating the Bahasa Indonesia *r;* his pronunciation made it sound like *bau.* Citra *Bau,* he called her, not realizing that he was insulting her. *Bau* means "smelly." Because Barry often sweated during recess, Citra returned the insult. She had another spontaneous nickname for him: *si Komo. Komo* is short for "komodo," the reptile from Komodo island in Indonesia, and was also the name of a well-known cartoon character who was big, tall, and dark. Like many others, Citra Baru had a difficult time slotting Barry racially and assumed he was Ambonese. "He didn't look African, his skin was not too dark, but rather light brown," she recalled. "But his hair was funny. Soft, small, curly, and attached to his scalp. His mother used to shave his head so they grow tiny. We mingled with everybody. There were Chinese, Aceh . . . there was no, 'Oh, you are Chinese?' Our childhoods reflected Pancasila so much. We didn't even care about religious differences. It didn't matter."

Pancasila is the doctrinal text of modern Indonesia, and is a key to understanding how misguided is any notion that SD Besuki imposed Muslim indoctrination. Derived from the Sanskrit words *panca* (five) and *sila* (principles), it was created by Sukarno and revised by Suharto as a means of defining the unified philosophy of the nation and its people. The five principles, noble in thought if often horribly contradicted by the actions of a powerful state, were social justice for all; democracy guided by inner wisdom; the unity of all the islands, peoples, and cultures of the archipelago; just and civilized humanity; and a belief in a one and only God. This last principle, often placed first in order, was criticized by some for explicitly rejecting the polytheistic practices of minority tribes in Indonesia. The other major critics were radical Muslims who believed that the Pancasila in its totality was too secular and that the specific principle about one God was too vague and accepting of any monotheism, Christian or Muslim or other, and errant in not using the Muslim term *Allah* for God rather than *Tuhan*, a word more acceptable to Hindus.

At SD Besuki, recital of the Pancasila was far more central to the pedagogy than the weekly Muslim prayer meetings. Cut Citra Dewi and another classmate, Sonni Gondokusumo, one of Barry's best friends at the school, both recalled that he memorized the verses of the Pancasila and could recite them during Boy Scout meetings after school and in front of the entire class during the history hour, even though he was a foreigner. "He was very fond of history, for example the history of the Borobudur temple. He loved that kind of thing," said Cut Citra Dewi. Borobudur, the largest Buddhist temple in the world, was one of Ann's favorite places, located about twenty miles from Yogyakarta in central Java. "He was also very good in explaining about Garuda," the symbol of modern Indonesia, a golden eagle taken from Hindu and Buddhist mythology. "How many feathers on each wing, how many on the neck, chest and tail, he can explain about them all the meaning of each." This always impressed her, she said, though personally she preferred math.

The school day at SD Besuki started early, at seven, and was done at noon. Barry followed a routine, according to Saman, the family servant. Ann would wake up first to walk Djanggo around the park oval, then rouse Barry to teach him from the American correspondence materials. That meant that Saman and Turdi, the other servant, who did most of the cooking, had to rise early too. By six, Barry had taken a shower. "The water came from a big well in front of the servants' rooms," Turdi recalled. "At that time we used a Sanyo pump." For breakfast, Barry liked to eat a pastry sold from one of the street carts out near the park, but Turdi usually cooked hot cereal. "Even when the baker has not passed by yet, I asked him, 'Bar, do you want me to make the oatmeal?' He usually drank a glass of milk." Barry could get to school one of three ways, on the back of Lolo's Honda motorbike, in Ann's office car, or on the back of Saman's bicycle. "Sometimes I feel the bike is leaning toward the back because Barry is big and tall," he recalled. Ann came home at noon, after picking Barry up at school. "Often Barry was still playing with us," said Widianto Hendro, another classmate. "His mother waited patiently for him. By that time, he wasn't a neat and tidy kid anymore. His shirt had been pulled out of his pants. His collar was stained by sweat. His mom was only shaking her head looking at all that." After lunch, she headed back to the office for the rest of the day, and Barry was on his own, playing with Slamet and Sonni and other friends. For dinner, Turdi's specialty was oxtail soup and *nasi goreng*. "Sometimes I made it with canned meat [corned beef] or meatballs. I gave two pieces of red chili with garlic and sweet soy sauce, so it was not the typical red and spicy *nasi goreng*." His mother had Barry take vitamins after dinner that Tut had sent from Honolulu.

In the evening, according to Saman, "if Barry didn't get his home assignments done, Bu Ann would call him to her bedroom, lock him there, and he got punished. Sometimes we heard him cry, but there was nothing we could do except remind him to do his assignments." One of Saman's strongest memories was the posture Barry assumed when reading. He "always was on his back with his feet half folded up in the air. One foot was on top of the other one. Bu Ann loved to do the same thing." Saman said Ann worked harder than anyone he had ever met, at it from before dawn, when she walked the dog and homeschooled Barry, often until after midnight, when he could hear her typing. "For me, who came from a village, it felt a bit strange that there was this person like her who worked from morning to night. And if she went to sleep early she would sometimes wake up at four in the morning and start typing. I knew because sometimes I woke up listening to the noise of her old typewriter." Ann would type out work plans for her English classes, letters to friends, and notes about Indonesian art and archaeology. She also filled her days and nights with hobbies, playing tennis at the courts near SD Besuki, and began what would become a lifelong obsession with Indonesian batiks. Once she tried to do batik herself, Saman said, but failed.

Barry in Indonesia was not just an early coming-of-age story, but also the start of his coming to grips with race. It was more than being teased as *black berry Black Barry* or being thought of as Ambonese, more than having the kids at SD Asisi and SD Besuki rub his taut and curly hair. In his memoir he would tell the story of the time he was sitting in the library at the U.S. embassy at Medan Merdeka Selatan No. 3 in central Jakarta, waiting for his mother to finish work at her nearby office, and stumbled across an article in *Life* about a black man who had tried to lighten the color of his skin with a chemical treatment. Seeing that article, he said, "was violent for me, an ambush attack." He went home that night and "stood in front of the mirror with all my senses and limbs intact, looking as I had always looked, and wondered if something was wrong with me." His memory probably tricked him when he tried to re-create the scene decades later. There was no such article in *Life;* it must have been some other magazine. But that is not the point. The story conveyed what was going on in his mind during those final years in Indonesia, when he became attuned to color in a way he never had before. He even noticed that no one in the Sears Roebuck Christmas catalogue looked like him.

All of his mother's efforts to teach him about his heritage – playing Mahalia Jackson records, reading him books about Martin Luther King Jr., telling him that Harry Belafonte was the "best-looking man on the planet" – now seemed well intentioned but soft and romanticized to him. Here was another variation on the theme: the wise son and the good-hearted but naïve mother. He mocked her "needlepoint virtues." To him, in retrospect, they seemed far from the "day-to-day realities" of the world.

When he looked back on his Indonesia days, he bathed his mother in loneliness. "She wasn't prepared for the loneliness," he explained. "It was a constant, like a shortness of breath." It is possible that Ann later told him precisely that. It might also be that he was projecting his own loneliness on her. Throughout his life, before and after that moment in the library at the U.S. embassy, he exhibited a sensibility of outsiderness and searching for home. This existential condition, the dominant theme of his memoir, grew from many circumstantial roots: his *hapa* status, his missing father, his busy mother. But cut away all the psychology and often it could be reduced to simple physical loneliness. Ann's loneliness had less to do with being in Indonesia than being stuck in a troubled marriage. She loved Indonesia, as would become increasingly clear as her life progressed. There was a popular song during that period by the group Koes Plus called "Back to Jakarta": "To Jakarta, I'll be back, no matter what happens, I have experienced my own life . . . long I've waited, search I must do, or I won't be known again." It was a song of nationalist nostalgia and hope, and seemed to apply more to Ann than to Lolo.

An odd aspect of her relationship with Lolo, in fact, was that she became more Indonesia-centric as he grew more Westernized. He wanted her to go to the company club and socialize with Texas oilmen, and she wanted nothing to do with them. Her thirst for knowledge and culture now competed with his thirst for money and status. The servants, Saman and Turdi, quietly observed the disintegrating relationship. Each of them remembered separate incidents when Lolo, who often appeared to be a docile character, punched a man who was a friend of Ann's. Saman said he saw Lolo and Ann fighting quite often, and believed that once Lolo struck her: "Even there was a time when Bu Ann's nose was bleeding, hit by Pak Lolo. Then they made up again. What happened, happened, it seemed so. It was not every day [that they fought] but rather often. I didn't know what caused the fight." From Saman's observations, though, Lolo "loved to play with women. There was one time . . . when he brought a woman to the house while Bu Ann was out of town to do evaluation." This period was "a bitter memory," said her friend Ibu Ita, who said she felt sorry for Ann, "in a strange country far far away from home."

For several weeks in the summer of 1970, when Ann was pregnant, she sent Barry to Honolulu to live with his grandparents at the big house on University Avenue. He turned nine there, and would remember it as an idyll in paradise – "the ice cream, the cartoons, the days at the beach." When it was time for him to return, after Maya's birth on August 15, his grandmother accompanied him back to Jakarta. As Saman remembered it, Madelyn was limping, her leg bandaged during her stay, which meant she could not be of much help with Maya: "She stayed for a few days. She often told me to get her Coca-Cola and Ooso," an orange-flavored soft drink. "I bought it from Tambak Street, not far from the house. Sometimes I went to buy it with Barry. That old lady seemed to be very friendly and kind. Her relationship with Lolo was . . . cool."

It was Madelyn's only visit to Indonesia. She purchased several Javanese paintings and brought them back rolled up, but never had them framed. Her husband, whose relationship with their daughter was often strained, never made the trip. Stan Dunham was no longer working at Pratt Furniture. He had left the furniture business altogether, after more than twenty years in the trade, to take a job as a John Hancock insurance salesman at the Honolulu agency run by John S. Williamson. The office was near the harbor in the oldest part of town, on the fourth floor of the James Campbell Building on Fort Street. Another variation on the life of a salesman. Now screwdriver sets were more

important than living-room sets. Stan would round up lists of insurance prospects and send the names and addresses to the home office in Boston, which
would then mail postcards to prospects saying they could receive a shiny set
of screwdrivers in a red plastic pouch if they would meet with a John Hancock
agent. "I can just drop them off," Stan would say over the phone.

The work hours gave him some freedom, which Stan needed. He wore
the business outfit, which in Honolulu meant khaki pants and a reverse-print
aloha shirt, purposely made inside out so it was more muted than the tourist
variety, and spent time with his pals on Smith Street in Chinatown, eating and
drinking at Bob's Soul Food and the Family Inn. Selling insurance was not a
job he loved, but as it turned out, walking into the John Hancock agency was
one of the most important actions he ever took. His boss had money and prestige, and something else: he was a prominent alumnus of Punahou School, the
most elite prep academy on the island. Knowing John S. Williamson would
prove useful when it was decided that Stan and Madelyn's grandson should
leave Indonesia and its troubles and return to Hawaii, there to advance his
education.

Barry was too young then to appreciate the effect his years in Indonesia would
have on him, but he would never forget a few overwhelming sensations. One
was of "the vastness of things" on the other side of the world. So many people, so many daily struggles, an ineffable weight of masses overwhelming the
individual. The other was of the gulf between rich and poor, a condition stark
and constant, unavoidable even in the life of a little boy. During his years in Jakarta, in that sense, Barry lived closer to his father in spirit than he ever would
again. He was also closer physically, only the breadth of one ocean away. A
vessel embarking from the coast of Kenya and traveling east could sail across
the Indian Ocean some 4,800 miles and not see land again until approaching
the Indonesian archipelago. It was virtually a straight line from Nairobi to Jakarta, both less than one degree south of the equator. Honolulu, by contrast,
was far to the north of both cities, up near the twenty-first parallel, and more
than twice as far from Nairobi. But if father and son were one ocean and four
time zones apart, it was a vast and empty distance.

CHAPTER 10

MARKED MAN

We weep not for the present pain
nor even for our own distress,
but for the future, being less
in promise than our hope had been.

MARJORIE OLUDHE MACGOYE, "FOR TOM"

arack Obama had added another son to his disparate family just before
Barry and Ann left for Indonesia. In Nairobi on September 11, 1967,
Ruth gave birth to her second child, David Opiyo Obama. "You make your
bed, you lie in it," her father had told her, and Ruth was trying to adjust, again.

"I just loved him and I forgave him a lot and it was very hard for me to break from him. It was just one of those things. He had this power over me," she said of her husband. When Obama yanked her back from her escape attempt in Boston, they had to find new housing in Nairobi upon their return. He had lost a job at BP Shell, largely because of his drinking, and also had lost their house, so they stayed in a small flat at a hotel on Waiyaki Way for a few months before he righted himself. When he landed an important job as senior planning officer at the Kenya Tourism Development Corporation (KTDC) during the same month that David was born, they moved to a new place in Woodley Estate; they had some money again and servants to cook and clean and care for the children. Ruth even took back her old job at Nestlé.

But what Obama's professional ability provided him – another chance – his personal weaknesses threatened. There was always tension between discipline and disrepair. He was an academic who could grasp the most sophisticated ideas – complex macroeconomic models, the philosophy of Schopenhauer, the novels of Camus and Dostoyevsky – yet could not process how his behavior endangered himself and others.

On the morning of Friday, November 3, only two months after he started his new job, he was in a Nairobi traffic magistrate's court trying to avoid a prison sentence. "A drunken driver in charge of a motor vehicle is like a man with a loaded gun," the prosecutor told the court. In Obama's case, according to the medical report, the loaded gun was the equivalent of twelve whiskeys he had downed at a cocktail party before driving home at four in the morning and slamming into the handcart of a milk salesman on Ngong Road. After entering a guilty plea, his lawyer noted that Obama held a graduate degree from Harvard and a high position in the Kenyan government. That swayed the magistrate, who said he would have thrown the defendant in jail but for those mitigating factors. "The services of the accused to the nation will be more valuable outside prison," F. E. Abdullah declared. He fined Obama fifty pounds and took away his driving privileges for a year.

This was at least the third serious crash Obama had survived (the first one killed his friend Adede), and it was taking a toll on his body, especially his legs. A previous accident had left him in traction in the hospital for months. He had developed a limp, and his legs seemed frailer. But the accidents did not compel him to address his drinking problem, and the edict from the traffic magistrate failed to keep him off the roads. He kept driving and never stopped drinking. On one level, the problem was simple: he was an alcoholic. But the forces that shaped his behavior were more complex. He was, in his own way, a big man, and suffering for it. His intelligence and arrogance could not protect him from pressures to succeed financially and lift his extended family, whose members to varying degrees looked to him as their salvation. The fact that he had gone to America and trained at Harvard, its finest institution, magnified the pressure rather than lessened it. His Luo associate, the journalist Leo Odera Omolo, said some Kenyans like Obama who had competed against the smartest overseas came back feeling invulnerable, "like small gods."

When Obama was hired for the tourism development post, the number two job in the agency, he was placed on probation and told explicitly by his boss that "the trial was necessary because of some adverse reports from his former employers." Those concerns did not involve his talent, but drinking and freelancing. Obama eventually passed the probationary period, but not without engendering some reservations. During his early months on the new job, according to minutes of a June 18, 1968, KTDC board meeting, "a few things had been noted such as smelling of alcohol in the morning. It was also noted that Mr. Obama was engaged in some other work outside office hours for which he got payment," a reference to his appearances as a panelist on the state television network without securing permission from his superiors.

Cautions about Obama's behavior did nothing to change him or to diminish his self-regard. By August he was demanding a raise so that his salary would equal that of the senior development officer in the Ministry of Economic Planning and Development. It was an audacious request, and the board considering his situation treated it as such, noting that Obama had only recently passed probation and that in any case the two posts "could not compare." The ministry was exponentially larger than the tourism corporation, and significantly more vital, arguably the most important in the Kenyan cabinet. At the time, it was under the stewardship of Tom Mboya, who could protect his fellow Luo and errant disciple to some extent (at least once keeping Obama from being sacked), but could not dictate his salary at a lesser agency, even in the improbable event that he were so inclined.

That is not to say that Obama was bad at his job, nor that his assignment was unimportant. Tourism played a pivotal role in the economic progress of the young nation, and Obama, who arrived at the agency two years after it had been established, was instrumental in making it a professional operation. "He knew his economics, mathematics, statistics," recalled Nyaringo Obure, who worked as a planner under Obama. As a trained economist, Obama stressed the need for a statistical baseline, which was not available when he arrived. He and Obure implemented a survey to quantify the tourist experience. "We developed a sample at the airport. We picked every tenth person – where they came from, how much money they were spending, what they did," Obure said later. "At that time we had hardly any statistical aspects. It was important to our mission. We were pretty much starting from scratch."

The geography of Kenya made it a potential tourist paradise: the sun-splashed white sands and arabesque architecture along the Indian Ocean coast, the cool clear greenery of the highlands and Mount Kenya, the breath-taking sweep of the Rift Valley, and most of all the vast savannah reserves where safari-going Westerners could encounter Africa's exotic animals – lions, cheetahs, giraffes, zebras, rhinos, hippos, elephants, warthogs, giant cranes, baboons, eland, gazelles, topi, ostriches, wildebeests, water buffalo, hyenas. But in 1964, one year after independence, only 56,419 tourists visited Kenya. The low numbers were partly due to the political uncertainty at the end of colonialism, but mostly they were because of the country's inadequate infra-structure: poor roads and a lack of first-rate hotels, lodges, and restaurants. Obama and Obure spent much of their time touring the country collecting information about what was available and determining when and where more could be developed. The KTDC's function was not only to encourage devel-opment but to take an active financial role in projects so that private investors, mostly foreigners, would not face risk alone. The Kenyan government's stake was often 5 or 10 percent in developments ranging from the new Hilton and Inter-Continental hotels in Nairobi to big safari lodges in Mombasa, Masai Mara, and Tsavo National Park. Tourism was rocketing year by year, on its way to a fivefold increase by the end of the 1960s.

If Obama was seeking to effect systemic change here, it would be a long, slow process. Think back to the critique of *Sessional Paper No. 10* that he wrote in 1965, in which he argued that economic development in Kenya should assist Africans, first and foremost, and not foreign investors. Then consider this: of the ninety-seven hotels, lodges, and restaurants catering to tourists in Kenya during his first year at the tourism development agency, only one was owned by a native African, and of the safari tour operators, only two were native Africans. In an effort to improve the ratios, Obama traveled from Mombasa to Kisumu looking for African-based enterprises that the agency could support and gave loans to six such firms in the first year. He took a special interest in finding projects in western Kenya, which lagged far behind most other sectors of the country in terms of drawing tourists. Even after he lost his driver's license, he made the demanding drive to Luoland, mixing work with a chance to hang out at the Casino Bar and New Nyanza Club, his favorite bars near Lake Victoria. As his colleague Obure recalled, "In several cases he would drive all the way from Nairobi to Kisumu at night, drunk," leaving on a Thursday night and not returning to the office until Tuesday. More than once his wife came to the office in central Nairobi looking for him.

Ruth and the boys joined him for one long trip to Luoland in 1968. Mark was three and David one. They stayed in Nyang'oma Kogelo with his stepmother, Sarah, and Hussein Onyango, and took a side trip down to Kanyadhiang. Obama was the first member of the family to bring a white woman home. His relatives seemed impressed by Ruth. "She was comfortable and could eat anything that was cooked here," said Charles Oluoch, a member of the Obama compound in Kanyadhiang. "Ruth ate *ugali* [a Kenyan porridge] and all kinds of vegetables and even fetched firewood. She would go to the kitchen and cook." They talked to her some in English, but mostly in Luo, with Obama interpreting when he was around. "I learned a bit of Luo," Ruth recalled. "Everybody was friendly. Obama would go into Kisumu to drink every night. I do remember we had to sleep on a very narrow bed. I was extremely uncomfortable and hated that part." The real trauma came once they returned to Nairobi. David had contracted malaria during the visit, and it erupted violently after a brief incubation, sending him to Nairobi Hospital. "I was screaming and yelling," Ruth remembered. "I was breaking down terribly at the hospital because I thought my baby was dying. But he got through it."

As 1968 neared an end, two old friends from America made an appearance in Nairobi. "Hey, BARE-ick," came the telephone call one day. It was Neil Abercrombie with Pake Zane, who had known him in Hawaii, hanging out with him at the Snack Bar and various beer bars and student apartments. In the wake of a dispiriting and bloody political year that had brought the assassinations of Martin Luther King Jr. and Robert F. Kennedy, they were getting away from it all, backpacking their way around the world. They had ventured up the Nile to Uganda and across to the Kenyan capital, and now here they were, camping out in Nairobi's city park, trying to steer clear of dangerous *kanga* gangs. Obama invited them over to his house.

There was no talk about Ann or little Barry. "We didn't bring it up because we knew they had gotten divorced," Abercrombie said. Zane noticed that Obama was "drinking very heavily." Abercrombie sensed that he was "very frustrated . . . his worst fears in his mind were coming true." During their political bull sessions in Honolulu, Obama had often lamented the tribal divisions of his homeland, and five years after independence the historic jealousies and animosities of Kikuyu and Luo in particular had not diminished. Jomo Kenyatta's inaugural promise that the new Kenya would bring them all together seemed hollow. Tribalism was holding him back now, Obama complained, the reason he was stuck dealing with tourism. "He felt he was being underutilized, which was probably true," Abercrombie said. "But everybody's virtue is his vice, and his brilliance and assertiveness were obviously working against him as well."

The Kenyan papers on the morning of July 5, 1969, showed Tom Mboya at Nairobi's Embakasi Airport, arriving the previous day from Addis Ababa after an executive committee meeting of the Economic Commission for Africa. He was toting a briefcase and striding confidently in coat and tie with his top aide, Philip Ndegwa, and brother, Alphonse, at his side. The fifth was a Saturday, and Mboya stopped by his office that morning to catch up on correspondence. He wrote a letter to Bill Scheinman, his American friend, advisor, and benefactor, apprising him of the difficult political scene in Kenya. Jomo Kenyatta was aging and sick, and succession talk was growing more intense. As a Kenyatta loyalist and key member of his cabinet, Mboya was the precarious man in the middle. On one side were the ambitious Kikuyu under Kenyatta, who might work with Mboya out of necessity but wanted to thwart a Luo's rise to the top. On the other side was his main Luo rival, Oginga Odinga, the leader of the opposition party. The Kikuyu had the power; Odinga had more sway over the Luo masses. Mboya had his own brilliance and will, and little else besides sympathy in the West, and even that was complicated. His detractors called him a tool of the Americans. "Ever since my trade union days and the student airlift I have lived with the label of help from America," Mboya wrote Scheinman. Sometimes, he said, he wished that were actually true.

Mboya was not naïve; he was acutely aware of his political and physical vulnerabilities. To maintain some level of privacy, he set up a post office box in Uganda, away from the reach of government snoops. With help from Scheinman, he hired a bodyguard, a Tanzanian sharpshooter. For years he had dealt with rumors that enemies were targeting him. In 1968 Luo elders in Homa Bay near Mboya's ancestral homestead on Rusinga Island confronted Kenyatta with reports that people under the president wanted Mboya killed. "No," said Kenyatta, "T. J. is my favorite son." But the rumors persisted. Later that year, when Mboya was in Siaya district in Luoland, his aides picked up a report that a man released from a mental hospital in Nairobi was tracking him with the intent of cutting off his head with a *panga* knife. As a precaution, several meetings were canceled. When Mboya was in Ethiopia for the pan-African session, a top Luo police official tried, unsuccessfully, to reach him with an alert that there was a new threat on his life.

After spending Saturday morning at his office, Mboya drove over to Government Road with the intent of stopping at Chhani's Pharmacy to buy lotion for dry skin. He and his wife were regular customers and friends of the proprietor, Mrs. Mohini Sehmi. Down the sidewalk from the shop Mboya encountered Barack Obama, who happened to be out walking with the lunchtime crowd of shoppers, accompanying a friend, Mrs. Kinyengi. The greeting was lighthearted. Obama sensed no apprehension on the part of the minister.

"You are parked on a yellow line, you will get a ticket," Obama told Mboya.

"No," Mboya said.

Obama then introduced Kinyengi. The three chatted for about three minutes before Obama and his companion went to a dress shop nearby owned by Mrs. Ogot, and Mboya moved on toward the pharmacy. The door was locked, the shop closed for the afternoon, but Mrs. Sehmi was still there and noticed her friend and let him inside. "He bought some toiletries and stayed with us chatting for about ten minutes, the shop pharmacist and myself were behind the counter talking to him and when he was ready to go I opened the front door again to let him out," Sehmi recalled. "Before he came in I had seen him talking to someone outside, but I hadn't paid much attention at that point. As I opened the door we chatted another minute or so and he started walking outside."

The door to the shop opened at an angle to the street, so Sehmi could not see Mboya after she let him out, but she could hear him, still talking. Then she heard something else. The noise of three shots, or maybe two and an echo.

> I said to him, "What is that, Tom?" And suddenly he leaned aback against the wall. It never occurred to me at that point that he had been hit. Then he slumped against me and we staggered back into the store. I saw blood on his shirt, which was red anyway, and I realized then what had happened. He never uttered a word. He fell into my arms and began to fall to the ground. I now had his blood on my hands and we managed to more or less break his fall and we helped him to the floor. He was now right inside my shop. I closed the door and called the pharmacist and said call the police and ambulance.

The scene out on Government Road was confused, chaotic. People heard shots but could not immediately process what had happened. Several saw a short young man, perhaps five-four, wearing a dark suit and toting a small suitcase, leave hurriedly on foot, before they realized that he might have been the assailant. Obama had moved on by then and did not see the aftermath, or at least was not asked about it during his testimony at the trial. According to Ruth, he made his way home to Woodley Estate soon afterward, dazed and fearful. "[He] said he ran away, afraid he would be shot. He came home and told me," she recalled. "It was such a shock." Ruth had met Mboya once at the minister's big house on Convent Drive. She had seen all the gifts that filled room after room, the china and vases and artifacts from around the world. Mboya was a big man, with "tons of charisma," a man her husband admired. But some people thought he was too powerful, a threat to their own ambitions. "Barack knew what was going on," she said. "But we didn't talk about that. Just that he felt so bad."

Lie low for safety, the poet Macgoye would write, evoking Obama's mood after the trauma. *The highest is gone . . . Burrow if you can, down down / there is no hunter, only the hunted.*

Inside the shop, in the moments after the shooting, Sehmi held Mboya's head in her hands. "I asked him, '[Are] you all right?' But there was no sound from him. His arms went up once and came down slowly and he moved his head once or twice and his eyes opened, but he never spoke. His chest never moved and he was not breathing at all." She looked out the shopwindow and saw a family friend, Dr. M. R. Chaudhry, knocking. After she let him in, the doctor loosened Mboya's shirt buttons and tried mouth-to-mouth resuscitation until the ambulance arrived to speed the dying man to Nairobi Hospital.

News of the assassination shook the new nation as no event before. In life, Mboya was admired if not loved. In death, he became a revered martyr, a powerful symbol of hope crushed by power and corruption. His assassin had not been found yet, but it was widely believed that he was killed by Kikuyus with the complicity of men around Kenyatta. Those who assumed that the Luo divide between Mboya and Odinga would become even wider with Mboya's death, that his loss would not be mourned by Odinga's followers, were grievously mistaken. The opposite happened. In death Mboya transcended politics in a way that he could not in life. Yet his death also touched all Luo the same, as an assault on their existence, and thus sharpened tribal divisions that Mboya had worked so long and tirelessly to overcome.

Vigilant rumour, touched in pride / roamed, bloodhound of the searching thought. First silence, then grief, then ferocious anger rippled in waves across the country. Out in the tea estates near Kericho, hundreds of Luo workers huddled and wept at the news. Farther west, thousands of people were at the annual Kisumu Trade Show when the mayor, Samson Odoyo, received a telephone call at three-thirty with the stunning report from Nairobi. Odoyo collapsed in grief, then was helped into the backseat of a sedan for the long drive back to the capital. "Tom Mboya's been killed" buzzed through the vast throngs, punctuated with sharp wails. Marjorie Oludhe Macgoye, the poet, a Westerner who had married a Luo man and who would later write a lush, lyrical tribute to Mboya that included the lines above, was at the trade show. "I had taken the children to the Kisumu show, and everything stopped," she remembered. "We rushed home, expecting there to be trouble."

The reaction throughout western Kenya "was as if somebody had rung a bell so the Luo could fight Kikuyu," recalled James Mbori, who had attended Maseno School with Obama and was then serving as deputy principal at a school in the Luoland town of Oyugis. "The whole atmosphere became hostile to Kikuyus, and it was terrible. The whole country was in a lot of shock. . . . The Kikuyu in Kendu Bay, Homa Bay, Oyugis, they suddenly disappeared. . . . We called the students together and told them what had been announced on the radio was true and that we had to remain cool and calm without breaking the law of the land."

Closer to the capital, in Central province, which was heavily Kikuyu and the homeland of Kenyatta, the top police official was Dick Opar, a Luo and also a member of the Obama extended family as nephew of Akumu, Barack's mother. Opar had been placed in that job by none other than Tom Mboya. "On that particular day, it just happened that I went to Nairobi and made some orders for uniforms for police officers who were competing in athletic competitions," he said. "I ordered those at noon and said I would come and collect them at two and then come back to Central. Before I came back the word went around that Mboya had been shot. And where he was shot was less than a hundred meters from the sports shop. That was the start of the hell. I had to go back to the province. The reaction was bad. The Luo in Central province reacted very violently . . . beating every Kikuyu in sight. It was a hard time to be in that area." As a Luo, Opar was "sharing the same frustrations" as the rioters, but had a duty to quell the violence. He called in as many Luo policemen as he could to avoid tribal confrontations.

At the hospital in Nairobi hours after the shooting, the corridors were overwhelmed by crowds hoping to catch a last glimpse of Mboya. A reporter for the *East African Standard* was there and recorded the scene: windows and doors broken, fights between mourners and police, people weeping in the hallways, a surge of angry men kicking down doors of the surgical wing, angry mobs outside, stoning cars. When Mboya's body was moved to the City Mortuary, the horde followed, and continued on from the mortuary to his house on Convent Street, where the open coffin lay in state. By Sunday the crowd outside had swelled into the thousands, the property's perimeter guarded by Luo tribesmen. When Vice President Daniel arap Moi, an Mboya rival, arrived to pay his respects, his car was stoned and forced away. Luo priests and witch doctors chanted deep into the night. Across town, at the Kaloleni Social Hall, hundreds more Luo gathered for a community meeting to talk about what should be done in the aftermath of Mboya's murder. Police tried to cancel the meeting, but the crowd would not allow it.

Barack Obama's precise movements during this period are not clear. Ruth said that he disappeared from their Woodley Estate home for several days. Friends said they caught glimpses of him at various events and presumed that he followed the crowds. It is likely that he attended the political meeting in Kaloleni, at some point joined the lines on Convent Street to walk past the open coffin of his benefactor, and took part in subsequent events. One line of thought presented decades later was that he went into hiding after the shooting, feeling especially vulnerable because he had questioned whether Kenyatta henchmen were responsible for killing Mboya. Obama was nothing if not outspoken. But there were dozens of people on the street that day who became material witnesses, and countless more in and out of the government who, like Obama, raised questions about the assassination. He was far from alone in expressing his disillusionment or anger.

In the Kenyan Parliament, J. H. Khaoya accused the Kenyatta administration of trying to manipulate the truth by implying that fellow Luo were somehow responsible for the assassination. Ngala Abok said he was tired of phony condolences and eulogies from the government and wanted action. Another member of Parliament warned that he and others would speak their minds "even if we are rounded up and placed in detention camps." A correspondent for the *Times* of London said the "statement that received the most tumultuous welcome of the afternoon [in Parliament] was to the effect that anyone who thought Kenya could be ruled by one tribe must be dreaming." The journalist Leo Odera Omolo, an operator who knew Obama and did business with both Mboya and Odinga, said he broke the news of Mboya's death to Odinga, the opposition leader. "He started crying right away, with tears coming out," Omolo said. "Their disagreement was political, not personal. But

one was pulling east and one was pulling west and both were getting money"
from their cold war patrons. Odinga told reporters that as Mboya's elder he
was "entitled to point out some of his mistakes," but that did not mean that
they were mortal enemies. Like other Luos, he pointed the finger of blame at
Kikuyus around Kenyatta.

The public outpouring was so emotional and strong that the Kikuyu-
led government could not ignore it. And the sentiment was not just among
Mboya's tribesmen in Kenya, but from people of many other tribes, and from
around the world. "When he was shot the sound rang round the world," said
Harris Mule, another of his American-trained disciples. "Radio stations in the
U.S. broke the news with shock and disbelief. . . . His assassination was front-
page news in the *New York Times, Times* of London, *Le Monde,* and *Times of
India.* The BBC made it the lead item of international news that day." Jackie
Robinson, the baseball immortal and airlift benefactor, called the murder
of his friend "a loss for Africa and the world." American blacks, Robinson
said, had a "tremendous belief" in Mboya and were certain he was destined
for world leadership. President Nixon issued a statement from his vacation
compound in Key Biscayne, Florida, deploring the "senseless violence" and
praising Mboya as "an outstanding African leader." An editorial in the *East
African Standard* noted that Mboya had a rare universal perspective: "Never
did he hate the British, but only the colonialism they stood for. He was the
least color minded of men. He was Luo by birth but got along with Africans of
any tribe, Kikuyu, Masai, Kamba, Giriama, Maragoli . . . to him they were all
one – human beings." Writing in Nairobi's *Nation* newspaper, Philip Ochieng,
a member of the 1959 airlift and friend of Obama's, had perhaps the most sophisticated analysis of Mboya:

> He spoke in sentences so well rounded you felt like giving it up. Being an intel-
> lectual, one of his quietest contributions . . . is that he stimulated the nation
> into *thinking.* And being an intellectual he angered many people with his ar-
> rogant self confidence. Mboya's arrogance has often been the subject of much
> talk against him. It was said he was too impersonal, that he had no feelings for
> anybody, and this is the reason for having so many enemies. If this were so, it
> was a grievous fault, and grievously has he answered for it. But if Tom was a bit

too reserved and inclined to a certain coldness, it was probably a good thing for him. This was probably what raised him above the individual, the tribe, or the race.

At a diminished level, one can see echoes of Obama in that description of his mentor. Though Obama edged closer to the leftist Odinga, he was always an Mboya man.

If Mboya was cool, the reaction to his murder was blinding hot, presenting Kenyatta with a conundrum. He called a cabinet meeting at his country home in Gatundu to discuss whether Mboya could be given a state funeral without risking more violence. Even getting the president from Gatundu back to central Nairobi for the memorial service at Holy Family Basilica was a difficult proposition because of the angry crowds. By some estimates, thirty thousand Luo were outside the basilica when the requiem mass began. They had been gathering since before dawn. When Kenyatta and his security detail arrived, people surged forward and the air was pierced with shouts of "Dume! Dume!" meaning "bull," the symbol of opposition. The presidential sedan was peppered with a volley of shoes. Police responded with tear gas, some of which wafted inside the church, where the archbishop, the Most Reverend J. J. McCarthy, was officiating. Compared with the riotous scene on the street, it was quiet inside, only muffled weeping. Several rows of pews were taken by Mboya's wife and family, then government officials, then disciples and people who had worked for him in the independence movement, during the airlift effort, and after independence. Obama, touched by all three eras, was among that last group. One observer noticed that "shafts of sunlight streamed through the long windows of the cathedral giving the scene melancholy beauty." The archbishop raised a question that echoed across the oceans: "Why should noble men like Tom Mboya, or Martin Luther King, or the Kennedy brothers, be struck down in the flower of life when their ideals and motives are so worthy of praise?"

Early the next morning the coffin was carried down the basilica steps and placed inside a hearse for the long procession from Nairobi all the way west to the family homestead on Rusinga Island. It was a pilgrimage that had been reenacted countless times over the years, the body of a man who worked and died in the teeming capital city being escorted back to Luoland for burial. In the Luo culture, nothing was more important, sacred, or ritualized than a funeral, and Mboya's was the same, only on a vaster scale. A ten-mile convoy of vehicles followed the funeral cortege as it made its way out of Nairobi and up through Central province, Kikuyu territory, and then down the escarpment into the Rift Valley. There was a dense fog all the way down, and red brake lights flashed in the mist as cars plowed into one another. Pamela Mboya, the young widow, was among those slightly injured in the wrecks, but the journey continued onward until they reached the Stag's Head Hotel in the valley, where a local doctor examined her and seven others. Then on around the Mau Forest until the hearse carrying Mboya's coffin developed radiator trouble going up the hills and had to be fixed. Another delay, then on past the tea fields of Kericho. As Luoland neared, the roadsides became more and more crowded, people standing ten and fifteen deep, mile after mile. The cortege reached Kisumu, the capital of Nyanza, at five-thirty. People had been waiting all day, frustrated, angry, lashing out, the crowds so thick the cortege could not pass until police dispensed tear gas. Any sedan that seemed affiliated with the Kenyatta regime was stoned.

With some difficulty, the procession moved through the city and around the gulf, past Kendu Bay and the Obama homestead, and down to Homa Bay, where Mboya's body would rest, again, at a Catholic church until morning. Reporters described Homa Bay as looking like a refugee camp. More than fifty thousand people had gathered there, sleeping in buses, cars, whatever they could find. Early on July 11, the first ferry came from Mbita Point to carry Mboya and the throngs out to Rusinga Island. The shoreline of Lake Victoria offered a vibrant panorama as thousands of Luo tribesmen in ancestral dress, bodies painted, some holding shields and spears, waded into the shallow water, standing there among a navy of canoes and motorboats that had been enlisted to carry mourners out to the island. Here was another reminder of the distance traveled, not only in miles but in cultural transformation, since the first Western missionaries made their way to Luoland at the turn of the century. The tribesmen in the water looked much as they might have seven decades earlier; they stood there in honor of one of their own who could outdress, outtalk, and outsmart almost any of the Brits or other Westerners he encountered in his thirty-eight years of life. This was the dichotomy faced daily by Mboya and disciples like Barack Obama.

It was a brutally hot day, and Rusinga Island offered little shade for the sea of mourners. From Mbita Point, the final journey to the gravesite was another eight miles, the rutted road dipping through fields of sugarcane, sisal, and maize. The Mboya homestead was a compound of two stone bungalows and eight mud huts. They started digging the grave at eleven-thirty and the coffin was lowered at midafternoon as a low wail resounded across the island. Soon came a rain so fierce that the ferry had to stop operations. Oginga Odinga was among thousands who were trapped on the island with no way out. Food and water were in short supply. "The island was so crowded people could not find a place to sleep," recalled Leo Odera Omolo, who had ancestral ties to Rusinga Island himself. "They were walking around all night. It was cold that night." Omolo said he shot a five-ton hippopotamus to help feed people. "It suffered for two hours," he said. "Hippo meat is hard." As Omolo remembered the scene, Barack Obama was "there throughout" and at one point pulled some liquor miniatures from his briefcase.

It was another ten days before government authorities arrested a man they said was the assassin. He was identified as Nahashon Isaac Njenga Njoroge, a Kikuyu, age thirty-two, who had been a member of the Kenya African National Union youth wing in central Nairobi and received training in Bulgaria. KANU was the ruling party, dominated by Kenyatta and the Kikuyus, but it was also Mboya's party.

Everything moved swiftly from that point. His preliminary hearing was held on August 11. The trial followed, at which there were forty-six prosecution witnesses. Barack Hussein Obama was number forty-six. After returning from a business trip to London, he testified on September 8, the day the prosecution rested its case. Under questioning from John Hobbs, the deputy public prosecutor, he recounted their brief meeting, the joke about the parking ticket, introducing his companion, Mrs. Kinyengi. There was nothing unusual about Mboya's demeanor that day, Obama told the court. The crowd on Government Road that lunch hour was also normal.

The defense barely made a case. In fact, after Obama's testimony, the defense attorney, S. N. Waruhiu, told the judge that he had been on holiday and had not worked out with his client how they should proceed. Njenga Njoroge was found guilty two days later, on September 10, and on November 8, at the Kamiti maximum prison, he was hanged. Many Kenyans thought the arrest, trial, and execution were all too fast and easy, covering up a larger conspiracy – a belief that was supported by the words that Njenga Njoroge uttered at some point after his arrest. "Why do you pick on me?" he asked. "Why don't you go after the Big Man?" That phrase would echo through the decades as an implication that Tom Mboya's assassination was the responsibility of powerful people who would never be held accountable – the work of Kenyatta, or more likely the jealous Kikuyu men around the president who could not compete with Mboya and so killed him.

Later in July, not long after Mboya was assassinated, it became clear that Barack Obama was having more problems at the Kenya Tourism Development Corporation. To attribute those difficulties to his despair over Mboya's death, as many relatives later did, was misleading, first, because he had been on notice about questionable behavior from the start, and second, because even the upbraiding he got in July involved the way he was acting earlier that year. In any case, the KTDC general manager, Jeremiah Walter Owuor, submitted a confidential report to the agency's board of directors regarding the "senior development officer, Mr. BH Obama." The questions, again, had to do with drinking and absenteeism. The board instructed Owuor to write a letter to Obama placing him on notice that he had to change.

Tourism was starting to boom around then, and Obama deserved some of the credit. After helping define the agency's role in developing several hotels and lodges, his latest focus was on a project called Bomas of Kenya, a combination museum and heritage park that would re-create the cultures of various tribal villages, or *bomas,* exhibiting their traditional huts, dances, handicrafts, and food. The project fit several of Obama's priorities. It would involve the state and private African ownership and employ scores of African natives. The plan was to build it on land off Ngong Road near the entrance to Nairobi National Park, a wild game preserve that was within a few miles of the Nairobi hotels. Obama got involved in every aspect of the enterprise, from finding the land to determining the specific *bomas* and crafts, analyzing the potential for profits, and coordinating with other city and federal planners.

In the end, his assumption of responsibility was his undoing; his superiors thought he was usurping their power by unilaterally making contract decisions for the project. The first item on the tourism corporation's executive committee agenda at a May 11, 1970, meeting was titled "Arbitrary Action Taken by Executive of KTDC Regarding Boma." Obama, in other words, was in deep trouble. "The chairman [Jan Mohammed, an Asian, not Kikuyu] informed the meeting that it had become apparent that Mr. Obama had no instructions from any authority to award the contract on behalf of the Corporation. This was a serious offence that would remit a severe disciplinary action from the board." Mohammed went on to say that Obama had lied to him, saying that he took the action because his boss, Owuor, had gone to Kisumu at the time, "when in fact the general manager had not gone to Kisumu." Another board member, G. M. Matheka of Mombasa, chimed in and said that before he joined the corporation board, when he was working in the tourism industry on the coast, he had met Obama, who was "posing as deputy general manager," a post that did not exist. Others piled on. M. W. Dunford, proprietor of the Carnivore, a famed restaurant on the edge of Nairobi, noted that the previous board had "passed a resolution that Mr. Obama be dismissed from the corporation and he was only saved by intervention from the ministry" – a reference to protection from Tom Mboya. P. H. Okondo said he was "much more concerned about Mr. Obama's image in public" – his drinking.

All of this pointed to one result: "The committee resolved unanimously . . . that Mr. Obama be asked to resign, and if he did not accept to do so, then the board should dismiss him instantly." Chairman Mohammed was instructed to pass the word along to Obama and sound him out as to whether he would quit or force them to sack him. Obama declined to resign and was fired a month later. His contract with the board did not provide severance pay, but after declaring that "bad feelings should be avoided," the board decided to give him 25 percent of his yearly salary, about six hundred pounds. Without dismissing the dangerous nature of Kenyan political infighting, this did not have the feel of a Kikuyu cabal out to get an outspoken Luo employee. The leaders of the board were Asian and Anglo, and Obama's boss, Owuor, was also Luo. They were not apolitical – no one could be and succeed in Kenya – but they were more business-oriented and less tribal than some other government entities.

Perhaps if Mboya had been alive the outcome would have been different. Another Mboya ally, Y. F. O. Masakhalia, who served as the Treasury Ministry's representative on the tourism corporation board, said he was not at those meetings where the decision to fire Obama was made and added, "If I were there, he would not have gone. He would not have been sacked." In thinking back on Obama and life's turning points, Masakhalia noted that he, a Luhya tribesman from western Kenya, was also distraught and disillusioned after the assassination of Mboya, and thought about leaving the government "in disgust." Instead, he said, he endured. "In the Luhya we have a saying, we say 'An animal which acquires age, also acquires fat.' We like fat animals. So if you want to slaughter a bull, you want it to age. It means you have to devise means of survival . . . you have to acquire some survival tactics, which my brother [Obama] didn't."

The firing accelerated the downward spiral of Obama's life. More drinking, another traffic accident, more time in the hospital with broken legs, more disappearances, more violent confrontations with Ruth. She stayed with him, but his mesmeric hold on her was waning: "I loved him throughout, pretty much, but finally I think I just got tired. Of being lonely. I think I just realized that my life was going nowhere. And then I think I got a candid comment from someone that 'You look so tired.' And I was young. And I thought to myself, 'What am I doing here? Why am I giving up my life like this?'" A cousin from California came through Nairobi on a backpacking trip, just as Neil Abercrombie and Pake Zane had done, and was alarmed by Ruth's domestic agony. "This is not for you," she told Ruth. "You're wasting your life. This guy is no good. You've got to get a divorce." A neighbor in Nairobi, Anna Yadeni, delivered the same message. "And they mobilized me, they mobilized me," Ruth said later. "I just needed a push and I needed some support. And they both gave testimonies to a lawyer and I sued for divorce."

There was another factor that helped her finally make the break. Obama was not around. Using his severance pay and some other money he had talked a rich patron into giving him, he had left Nairobi for a trip across the world. He was without a job, separated from his family, looking for something.

Throughout his troubles, one person had remained interested in him, had written him letters, had kept him up to date on the accomplishments of the son they had together, the boy named Barry.

"My baby bull," Obama would say to friends in Nairobi. "I left a baby bull in America. Someday I will go get him."

CHAPTER 11

WHAT SCHOOL
YOU WENT?

T he days of being called Barry Soetoro ended when the ten-year-old boy returned to Honolulu. Using the surname of his stepfather had been a convenience during his three and a half years in Indonesia; now there was no reason for it. He was Barry Obama again. No need to speak Bahasa Indonesia anymore, either. In the future another exotic tongue would become more useful to him, a creole Hawaiian street slang known as pidgin. *Howzit?* Sound it out and the greeting becomes clear. *Da kine,* an all-purpose word for "something." *Das why hard,* a sardonic explanation for something difficult. *Bra,* brother. And the question whose answer provided the most telling definition of a fellow Hawaiian: *What school you went?*

From the start of fifth grade, Barry Obama's answer placed him among the elite children of Honolulu. Punahou was the school he went. *POO-na-ho,* from the Hawaiian phrase *ka punahou,* which means "new spring." It was the oldest, largest, most prestigious private school in Hawaii, founded in 1841 for the education of the children of missionaries. In its long history, Punahou had evolved into an academic and athletic powerhouse, its status on par with the finest prep schools on the mainland. The seventy-six-acre campus, with twenty-eight buildings and lush green fields rising up a gentle slope at the entrance to Manoa Valley, had the look and feel of an exclusive liberal arts college – and a price tag to match. Tuition for a fifth-grader entering in the fall of 1971 was $1,165, ten times the cost of a semester at the nearby University of Hawaii.

Money did not get Barry in. His mother barely had any, and lived thousands of miles away. He was now staying in a cramped two-bedroom apartment on the tenth floor of the Punahou Circle Apartments, five blocks from school, with his grandfather, who scraped by selling life insurance, and his grandmother, an underpaid bank officer. Athletic potential did not get him there either, not this chubby kid who had been away from any American sport except tennis since he was six. He performed well on the ten-dollar Educational Testing Service entrance exam for fifth-graders, but there was nothing in his record to affirm his grandmother's conviction that he was a genius. Based on his background alone the boy "never would have gotten into Punahou – not in a million years," said Neil Abercrombie, a keen observer of island sociology who had known Barry's father in college. But Barry made the select cut when more than nine out of ten applicants could not. He got in due to several converging factors, including the persistence of his mother, who was tireless at working the system, even from afar; his own winning performance during interviews with the admissions office; a need-based scholarship program that had begun targeting students of his potential and diverse background; and the influence of two wealthy alumni, Stan Dunham's boss, John S. Williamson, at the insurance agency, and Madelyn's boss at the Bank of Hawaii, Frank Manaut, who was on the Punahou board of trustees.

"Welcome to the Punahou family," began the acceptance letter from Roderick F. McPhee, the school's president. *Family* was a loaded term for this boy who never knew his father, whose stepfather was on the way out, and whose mother was across the ocean. By any measure, with its reputation and resources, Punahou's family offered a past, present, and future outside his own family's experience. Looking back on it later, he noted that to his Kansas-rooted grandparents "admission into Punahou heralded the start of something grand, an elevation in the family status that they took great pains to let everyone know." Perhaps Maseno, the private missionary school his father attended, afforded some parallel meaning in the rise of the Obamas in Kenya, but there was nothing comparable on the white side of his heritage. Mercer Island High was a first-rate public school for his mother, but not an institution that by its very name lifted those who went there. As Abercrombie put it, "Going to Punahou makes you different, especially if you are a biracial kid in Hawaii. It gives you an incredible leg up in the possibility of success – material success, life success, or how people commonly measure it."

What school you went? Much of what one needed to know about the social strata of Honolulu could be understood by driving up Mount Tantalus and gazing down at two domed buildings that stood a few miles apart and were connected by Nehoa Street. Below and to the left gleamed Punahou's nineteenth-century landmark, Pauahi Hall, with its distinctive dome of buff (sand) and blue (sea), an emblem of privilege. To the right shone the red and gold dome of President Theodore Roosevelt High, the first English standard public high school in the city, with its native Hawaiian boys who often partook in the annual "Kill Haole Day," when they drove down Nehoa to intimidate rich *buffanblu* white kids. That was changing when Barry came along, with Punahou starting to take in a more diverse student body. A generation earlier, Ron Jacobs, white and Jewish, transferred from Punahou to Roosevelt in ninth grade and was greeted with a push in the face by John (Squeeze) Kamana Jr. Now Kamana's son, John Kamana III, another Squeeze, was himself at Punahou, one year behind Barry. He would become a big man on campus, a star athlete – and on occasion protect *haole* teammates from Roosevelt *mokes,* or local bullies.

Once again, much as in Indonesia, Barry was buffeted by the crosswinds of ethnic assumptions. In Jakarta many local kids looked at all Westerners as members of the wealthy class. In Honolulu many native Hawaiian boys displayed a prove-yourself-or-else hostility toward people with roots on the mainland, known as coast *haole*. Where did this leave a *hapa* boy who lived with white relatives but had just returned from Indonesia and was half African in a place where there were precious few blacks? In Jakarta he was often mistaken for a darker-skinned native of the island of Ambon. In Honolulu there

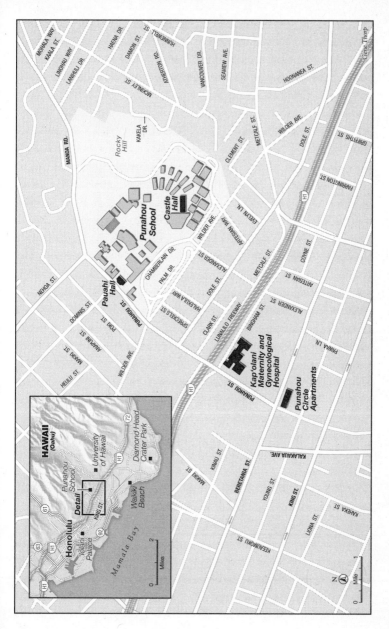

was a variety of options and possibilities. His grandfather had told strangers that the boy was a descendent of *ali'i,* native Hawaiian royalty. In Obama's later memoir, he recalled boasting at Punahou that his father was an African prince. Some classmates remembered it differently, that first he claimed his father was an Indonesian prince.

In retrospect he would say that his name alone separated him, starting with the first day of fifth grade when his teacher introduced him as Barack Hussein Obama. Self-perception is inarguable, one feels what one feels, and new kids in school are likely to feel uncomfortable. But in polyglot Hawaii, even this prep school held more than a collection of Johns and Susans and Binghams and Cookes. In a list of Punahou contemporaries, Barack mingled with the first names Nunu, Kaui, Sigfried, Malia, Lutz, Manu, Linnea, Saichi, Wada, Kalele, and Nini. And for last names, in the O's alone, Obama was there with Oba, Ochoa, Ogata, Ohama, Oishi, Okada, Oshiro, Osuna, and Ota. If he heard "titters break across the room" when Mabel Hefty, the teacher, first enunciated his name, as he later wrote, it was probably because tittering was a chronic characteristic of grade school behavior. Teachers seemed to go to extra lengths to embrace Punahou's diversity. A few years later, Barry's seventh-grade teacher, Miss Kang, posed eight members of her class for a yearbook photo in front of a blackboard that had the white-chalk message MIXED RACES OF AMERICA and a caption that read "Whether you're a Tamura or a Ching or an Obama, we share the same world." Barry, looking pudgy-faced, sporting a paisley shirt and the beginnings of an Afro, flashed the peace sign.

In a society where *hapa* children, representing those mixed races of America, were common if not the norm, surnames could not be a reliable source of identity in any case. One of the boys Barry went through Punahou with was Tom Topolinski. With a name about as Polish as a name can sound, Topolinski had the Chinese features of his mother. Another was John Kolivas. His last name was Greek, but Kolivas looked more like his Korean mother. There were several *hapa* Koreans at Punahou, and they had their own pidgin slang nickname for one another, *yobo,* which means "dear" or "darling" in Korean. People in Honolulu who had not seen Obama in the flesh but only heard his name often assumed he was *hapa* of a different sort, not half black but half Asian. The surname Obama was as common in Japan as in Kenya, perhaps more so, and there were vastly more Japanese on Oahu than Kenyans. In Japanese, *obama* means "little beach."

It was, to be sure, the African part of his heritage that set Obama apart. "Barack is such a beautiful name," Mabel Hefty had said to him on that first day of fifth grade. She knew that his father was from Kenya, a country she was far more familiar with than Barry was. She had spent two years there, from 1966 to 1968, in a Teach Corps program sponsored by the U.S. Agency for International Development. Now, as a good teacher, Hefty was trying to connect with her new student and comfort him. But her pronunciation of *buh-ROCK* must have seemed strange to him. He went by Barry, or Bar, rhyming with *bear*, and the father his mother told him about went by *BARE-ick*. When Hefty asked him what tribe his father was from, a question displaying her knowledge of the country, he heard more tittering from his classmates, as he later recounted the scene, and paused in embarrassment before answering "Luo."

Special agent Stan Dunham had his own cubicle at the John S. Williamson agency, placing him a notch above many colleagues, who sat in the open pen in back. One of those younger salesmen, Rolf Nordahl, an island transplant from Minnesota whose father was Swedish, turned to Dunham for counsel of sorts. There was no one quite like Stan "to waste time with," he said, adding that he also "did want to learn things from him." From the Campbell Building on Fort Street, Stan and Rolf often made their way after work to the bars on Smith Street in Honolulu's Chinatown, a netherworld that embraced gamblers, dopers, gypsy fortune-tellers, tattoo parlors, rhythm and blues joints, hookers, and black soldiers and sailors from the military bases among its clientele, though the draw for the two insurance salesmen was "all very innocent" by Nordahl's account. "The attraction for us was that the bars were open, a place to go and spend an hour . . . and a little to rub elbows with a subelement of a kind. Seeing these other characters. Stan enjoyed that; we both did. One place was called the Alley Cat bar. There were dozens of them in those days. They kind of looked left over from World War Two." Rolf drank Coca-Colas, fifty cents in a short glass, and Stan downed an occasional shot and a beer or two. They were treated with deference; many bartenders and patrons assumed they were undercover cops, or at least that the teetotaler was.

Stan's grandson, Barry, remembered those dark bars, the sodas, blowing bubbles in the Coke glasses. He said later that he was dragged along sometimes, as early as age eleven, soon after he got back from Indonesia. Likely that happened when there was nowhere else for him to go and no one else for him to be with, and Stan was doing his peculiar form of babysitting.

Ever since Barry was old enough to be read to, Ann had tried to educate him in African American history, teaching him about the legacy of black struggle and accomplishment in the United States as best she could. Stan had a different approach, by design or happenstance. During his explorations of Honolulu's underbelly, he came to acquire "a number of black male friends, mostly poker and bridge partners . . . hoarse voices and clothes that smelled of cigars." One of them was a man named Frank Marshall Davis, who was thirteen years older than Stan, already approaching seventy, a black journalist, poet, civil rights activist, political leftist, jazz expert, and self-described "confirmed nonconformist" who wore a gold earring in his pierced right ear and had been under surveillance by the Honolulu bureau of the FBI because of his past associations with the Communist Party. Davis had made his name in black Chicago but had grown up in Kansas, born in the town of Arkansas City, an hour's drive south of El Dorado on old Highway 77. Ralph Dunham, Stan's older brother, remembered meeting Davis when he was in Honolulu on a working vacation for the U.S. Office of Education. They drank together and talked about Wichita and Kansas State and sports and art. As one of the most colorful figures in Honolulu, of any color, Frank – identified only by that first name – became a character in Obama's memoir and a subject of some of his teenage poetry. Because of the themes of the book, and the age (early thirties) at which Obama was writing it, he tended to focus on characters who could accentuate his journey toward blackness. Davis fit that mold. Obama later estimated that he saw Davis "ten to fifteen times." In the book, he wrote that Davis was "pushing eighty" when they met. That is a case of literary license. Davis would not be close to eighty until a decade later, when Barry was in college and paid a visit to his sagging shack near the Ala Wai Canal in an area of Waikiki known as "the Jungle," populated by old hippies who had escaped from the mainland.

Rolf Nordahl, who spent more time with Stan during those forays into the underbelly, never met Frank Marshall Davis and saw young Barry only twice, once at the office, once at home. He and Stan tried to save money during the noon hour by going to the Dunhams' tenth-floor apartment at the corner of Beretania and Punahou for lunch. Madelyn was at work at the downtown bank. Stan seemed a little sheepish about that, Nordahl thought – not that his wife was working, but that she had a more important job than he did, and made more money. Stan prided himself on his sandwiches, toasted just so, stacked high with luncheon meats, sliced diagonally. They would sit on the lanai, look out across the street, and chat between bites. To Nordahl, Stan was "avuncular, he was amusing, and extremely charming," with an unusual voice. If not in the resonant basso profundo range of Barack Obama's, it was sonorous and featured a distinctive accent. "I was kind of used to the midwestern accent [coming from Minnesota], and his was a little different. It was bordering on more proper, almost like a British accent," Nordahl recalled. Something had happened to Stan's diction since his Kansas days, in other words, not unlike what Francine Pummill Gruver discovered to be true of her childhood friend Madelyn when they met in Kansas City that one time decades after high school.

Even more than the accent, what Nordahl found most captivating about Stan were the words that flowed from his mouth. "He had a way of turning words and phrases, and he told jokes. He was a storyteller." Some of those stories remained etched in Nordahl's memory decades later. "One was about how after he came home from the war and was reunited [with Madelyn] someplace in a strange city, waiting for money, and they didn't have any, and they rented a hotel room and were down to two or three dollars. And he said they went out and bought a pack of cigarettes and a comic book and had one of the greatest days of their lives." Stan did not just say they bought a comic book; he told Rolf precisely which one it was and detailed the drama virtually page by page. "I think he said along with the comic book and cigarettes they spent the afternoon having sex. . . . He told that story meaning you didn't have to have a lot of money to have fun."

Another of Stan's favorite stories, one he spun time and again, was how the Kenyan Obama courted and married his daughter. Stan too pronounced his first name *BARE-ick*. "He would start out by saying, 'Have you ever seen

the movie *Guess Who's Coming to Dinner*? Well, I lived it,'" Nordahl remembered. The movie, made in 1967, was still in the public consciousness in the
early 1970s as a period piece on race relations. It was the story of a white
couple (played by Spencer Tracy and Katharine Hepburn), whose daughter
(Katharine Houghton) brought home the man she intended to marry, a doctor who happened to be black (Sidney Poitier). By coincidence, a line in the
movie predicted that the child of this interracial marriage might someday be
president of the United States. But Stan was not so prescient; his version of
the story was more about the various conflicts arising from the relationship
between Ann Dunham and Barack Obama. After spending so much time with
Stan the storyteller, Nordahl listened with interest but a healthy dose of skepticism. "He made it sound like Barack Sr. was some kind of royalty in Kenya
and that was the reason the marriage broke up, because [Obama's] family
would not accept it. Stan made it sound like [Barack] couldn't marry because
of royal blood. Even at the time I thought maybe he was making that part up.
That was like Stan."

Two months into grandson Barry's first semester at Punahou, *Guess Who's
Coming to Dinner* took on a different meaning. Ann had written to her parents
from Jakarta to prepare them, and then a telegram arrived from Nairobi solidifying the plan. Guess who was coming to visit? The old man himself, Barack
Obama Sr., who had not been in Hawaii since he left for Harvard ten years
earlier, in June 1962, and who had not been with his son since Barry's infancy.
Now he was coming to see the baby bull he left behind.

One of the conveniences of where the Dunhams lived, aside from its proximity to Punahou, was that furnished apartments were often available for
short-term visitors. Obama could be close, but not suffocatingly close, down a
few elevator stops from the Dunhams' No. 1008 at the Punahou Circle Apartments on South Beretania. Ann would arrive first from Jakarta; Barack from
Nairobi about ten days later. With both of their latest marriages unraveling,
they would now stay in the same building, though in separate apartments,
for nearly the full month of December and into early January, the longest sus-
tained period of proximity since before their fleeting marriage in 1961.

This turned out to be the only time in the younger Obama's conscious
life that he would see his father in the flesh, but of course he could not know

that then. At age ten, the past was mythology and the future was unimportant. What he knew of his father was only what his mother and grandfather had told him. He did not hear from Madelyn, his Tut, what she would say to the Chicago journalist David Mendell many decades later, that Barack Obama Sr. was "straaaaange." He knew nothing about Ruth, the other white woman who had married his father, or about the nature of his life's struggle since he had returned to Nairobi – his drinking, his womanizing, his abusive temper, his serious car crashes, his job dismissals. Barry could not know that perhaps the luckiest thing that happened to him in his young life was that his father had left, sparing his mother and him years of unpredictability and potential domestic violence.

What he did know was that his father was brilliant. He knew this because his mother kept telling him that his own brains came from Kenya, from his Luo heritage, which was true enough, though there was intelligence on both sides. The rest of what Barry knew about his father fell mostly into the category of *Stan's Book of Tall Tales,* and even at that early age Barry had a notion that his grandfather was not a reliable narrator.

The thirty-seven-year-old man he encountered inevitably seemed different from the boy's imaginings. He was frightfully thin, for one thing, "the bones of his knees cutting the legs of his trousers in sharp angles." And his dress was so unlike what most adults wore in Hawaii or Indonesia, and also different from Western stereotypes of Africans. If anything, he appeared a bit of a dandy, with his ivory-headed cane, "blue blazer and white shirt, and a scarlet ascot, [with] horn-rimmed glasses." He also turned out to be bossy in a way that Gramps and Tut rarely were, the heretofore-missing father suddenly asserting paternal discipline, ordering his son to turn off the television, stop watching *How the Grinch Stole Christmas!,* and instead do more homework. All of this led Barry to conclude that he liked his own conjuring of his father more than the real man. "If my father hadn't exactly disappointed me, he remained something unknown, something volatile and vaguely threatening." He mostly sat around and pontificated, drank beer, and kibitzed, not helping with the dishes, telling not only his son but other members of the family what to do and what they should think. One night he played Luo music he had brought along on old 45 rpm records and instructed Barry to join him in moving to the music. The sounds transported him back to the dance hall at the bend of the oxcart path in Kanyadhiang, where he had first wooed Kezia, and to the Kaloleni Social Hall in Nairobi where the pair had won dance trophies. Now, in Hawaii, he swayed slowly, hypnotically, "bad leg stiff, rump high." *Come, Barry, you will learn from the master.*

There was one small scene from the father's visit, as reported in the memoir, that takes on more poignancy and meaning when considered in the context of the bag of troubles Obama had left behind in Nairobi. At his grand-mother's instruction, Barry ran down to his father's temporary apartment to see if he had any laundry that needed washing. Barry found his father sitting on the bed, shirtless. His mother was there too, her hair pulled back in a pony-tail, ironing his clothes. Tears were streaming down her face. She and Obama had been arguing. Much later she told her son why. Obama had wanted them to reunite, for her to return to Kenya with him and bring Barry (and presum-ably Maya) along. It was a stunningly brazen concept. He was still married to Ruth, and in fact had never divorced Kezia. Ann was still married to Lolo and had a job in Jakarta, and her son was enrolled in a life-altering prep school in Hawaii. It made no sense logistically, practically, emotionally, rationally, legally. Yet it becomes obvious in retrospect how high the stakes were at this mo-ment. As Ruth's experience made clear, Obama had a mesmeric quality that was hard to resist, and he had left Nairobi determined to bring home his baby bull. If it was counterintuitive but nonetheless true that Barry was lucky his father was gone for the first ten years of his life, a second stroke of luck came when, during this holiday reunion in Honolulu, his mother resisted Obama's entreaties to leave with him.

The seminal event during that month-long once-in-a-lifetime coming together involved a visit Obama made to Mabel Hefty's fifth-grade class in Room 307 of Castle Hall at Punahou. Barry was a mess anticipating the visit from the moment his mother told him about the invitation. "I spent that night and all of the next day trying to suppress thoughts of the inevitable: the faces of my classmates when they heard about mud huts, all my lies exposed, the painful jokes afterward. Each time I remembered, my body squirmed as if I had received a jolt to the nerves." His memoir described Hefty as an "ener-getic woman with short gray hair," which was true, if not doing her justice.

Many students who entered Punahou in the lower school counted her as among the best teachers they had at any level. "Mabel Hefty was my all-time favorite teacher," said Troy Egami, who wrote for *Ka Punahou,* the school newspaper, during Obama's era. Hastings (Pal) Eldredge, who taught math and science to fifth-graders next door in Room 308, said he learned more about teaching from Hefty than anyone else: "She was very knowledgeable, well traveled. When she talked about Greek and Roman civilization, she had a firm control of that, and on the Hawaiian civilization, the Hawaiian culture and the events leading up to where we are now, she was very well read." He called it a "stroke of genius" that Duane Yee, then supervisor for grades five and six, placed Barry Obama in Hefty's class, because of her skills and her firsthand knowledge of Kenya.

During her two years in Kenya, Hefty had lived in the town of Murang'a in Central province, north of Nairobi, a region dominated by the Kikuyu tribe. Her job there was to teach elementary school teachers, poorly educated and poorly trained themselves, the fundamental methods of good teaching. She was a practical, worldly woman with a soft heart. In many ways, minus the religious missionary aspect, she was reminiscent of Betty Mooney, the American who had gone to Kenya a decade earlier to teach literacy, happened upon Barack Obama, and had been most responsible for sending him on the path to Hawaii, Ann Dunham, and Barry's conception. Hefty fell in love with the land and its people and treated her Kenyan counterparts as equals in every respect. John Njoroge, the local assistant education officer, at first rebuffed her requests that he call her Mabel instead of Mrs. Hefty. "I've never called a white person by their Christian name," he finally confessed to her, to which she responded, "It's about time you did because we are equals in this business, and the work goes better when friends work together. We are friends, and friends use Christian names."

There is no record that during her Kenyan sojourn Hefty met Tom Mboya, the Luo leader who, along with Betty Mooney, was also responsible for Obama's American trajectory, but it seems likely that she did. Of all the Kenyan leaders, he seemed to make the strongest impression on her. Her son, Scott Hefty, later recalled that she often talked about "a young man with a high position with the Kenyan government. I am sure that his first name was Tom and his last name was something that started with an 'M' and ended with an 'a' . . . that he was very supportive of education and believed that an educated country would be a strong country. That he was being groomed and was a top contender to replace Kenyatta when the time was right. I also remember that she was very sad when he was killed." That could be no one but Tom Mboya. Though her job was in Kikuyuland, she traveled the breadth of Kenya, from Malindi on the Indian Ocean to the shores of Lake Victoria, coming within miles of the Obama homestead. Barry knew none of this, and in any event seemed less and less keen about his teacher's Kenya connection as the day of his father's school visit approached.

News of the African's appearance at Punahou brought a crowd to Room 307. Pal Eldredge, characterized in the memoir as "a big no-nonsense Hawaiian" (he was actually another *hapa*, half Hawaiian, half Anglo), brought his class to see Obama, and Barbara Czurles-Nelson also came, inviting along Dr. Rodney West. Nelson, who now taught at Punahou, had been with Dr. West the week in August 1961 when Barry Obama was born; it was during their lunch at the Outrigger Canoe Club that the doctor had told her, "Stanley had a baby!" So much had happened in that family in ten years, yet now time compressed and here sat the boy Stanley had given birth to, and up front stood his father, talking to Punahou students about the importance of education and telling stories about his homeland, its beauty, the Rift Valley's seminal status as the birthplace of mankind, the lions and elephants and hippos of Kenya, the struggle for freedom – all with what Nelson described as "this lovely, attentive manner." As Eldredge recalled the scene, Barry introduced his father and seemed nervous but proud. Nelson thought Barry "seemed as fascinated as we all were." Barry would say later that he was mostly embarrassed, and relieved when it was over.

His mother had told Barry that his father was brainy, an assessment the old man had no hesitation in emphasizing himself. Before leaving, he praised Barry for being a good student and said that he had that in common with his African siblings. "It's in the blood," he said. Soon enough, he had left, alone. The baby bull stayed behind.

Ruth Obama had gone forward with divorce proceedings in Nairobi while Obama was in Hawaii. When he came back, he pleaded with her to stay with him. Ann had resisted that final time at the Punahou Circle Apartments; now Ruth was being tested, again. "He said 'Don't go through with this,' and I said 'No, I am going through with this.' He came back and said 'Please, don't get this divorce, please don't get this divorce.' But I said, 'No I am going through with this, but we will still live together, and if you can change I will continue to live with you. If you don't, I won't.' That's what I told him, and I lived with him another few months. And of course he didn't change." The final divorce decree came in March 1972. As promised, she had continued to live with him, even after the divorce, until that fall. "At the end of 1972, about November, I had had it. Had it. I got a friend who had a pickup truck and I got a flat in the Westlands, away from him. And I had the legal right so I was strong. So I just moved out with my kids. And then of course he had a shock." Just as when she left him the first time, fleeing to Boston, Obama again tried to find her, but the seduction of the past had now transformed into rage. "And he did find me. And sometimes he would knock on the window to say, 'You are a prostitute! You are a prostitute! I'm going to kill you! I'm going to kidnap the children!' All kinds of stuff."

Ruth had reason to take the threats seriously. Once, when they were still married, he had attacked her on the couch, holding a knife to her throat. This time she had more support, more friends to help her maintain her courage to stay away from him. Soon she met another man, Simeon Ndesandjo, a television executive who had connections to the local police. Don't let this man bother Ruth ever again, Ndesandjo told the police, and Obama never did. Within a year Ruth had married Ndesandjo. She would see Obama only once more, years later, drinking in a hotel bar in Nairobi. "And as soon as I saw him I said, 'Simeon, let's go.' I couldn't stand him. The love I had had turned to such revulsion. I just couldn't stand him then. I hated him. I didn't want to see him, hear him, speak to him. Nothing. So we just left."

Not long after Ruth left Obama for good, Pake Zane, one of his old friends from Honolulu, appeared in Nairobi again. Five years earlier, Zane and Neil Abercrombie had traveled through Kenya as they backpacked around the world, and had been struck even then by their old friend's sour feelings about the state of politics in the nation, his frustrations over not getting a better job than being a planner for the tourism corporation, and his heavy drinking. That was before the assassination of Tom Mboya, and before two more serious car accidents had taken their toll on Obama's frail body. Zane was with his wife, Julie Lauster, this time. On their way up the Nile, they avoided Uganda, where the dictator Idi Amin was raging against foreigners, and came into Kenya through Ethiopia. "This time when I met Barack he was a shell of what he was prior to that, even from what he was in 1968," Zane recalled. "He was using a walking stick and he was very upset. . . . He was drinking very heavily . . . very depressed, and as you might imagine [exhibited] an amount of rage."

Obama had been in yet another traffic accident, and this time, he said, it was a setup; his car had been tampered with, he had been targeted. He said it amounted to a political murder attempt because of his connection to the slain Tom Mboya and his outspokenness in the years since the assassination of the Luo leader. He would have died in his wrecked car, he added, had not a relative come along and found him unconscious at the side of the road and taken him to the hospital. Considered separately, each detail made sense. Obama's being in a traffic accident was commonplace. It was not unheard of that passersby would ignore a wrecked car and an injured person at the side of the road. In the years after Mboya's death, there was a long list of Luo officials who died mysteriously, most of them likely victims of political violence. But there was no evidence of that being the case in this instance, or any other involving Obama, who time and again demonstrated a capacity to harm himself with no help needed from enemies.

Leaving and being left were the repeating themes of Barry Obama's young life. His mother leaving his father. His father leaving the family. Mother and son leaving Honolulu for Seattle. Mother and son leaving Hawaii for Indonesia. Son leaving Indonesia for Hawaii. Son being left with his grandparents in Hawaii. Mother and father rejoining him in Hawaii and leaving him again for Indonesia and Kenya. All in the continuum of the family history. Ruth Armour Dunham leaving life altogether as a young mother. Her boys being left twice in succession, first by her, then by their father. Stan and Madelyn leaving again and again – leaving El Dorado in search of *el dorado;* leaving Kansas for California, leaving Kansas for Oklahoma and Texas, leaving Kansas for Mercer Island, leaving Mercer Island for Hawaii. Obamas also leaving and being left.

Nilotic ancestors leaving the southern Sudan. Obong'o leaving Nyang'oma Kogelo for Kanyadhiang. Hussein Onyango four generations later leaving Kanyadhiang for Nyang'oma Kogelo. Wives and children being left by men. Men leaving towns for cities. Barack Obama leaving Luoland for Nairobi, leaving Nairobi for America, leaving Kezia for Ann, leaving Hawaii for Harvard, being left by Ruth.

The adult that Barry Obama became was shaped by this cycle of leaving and being left. It taught him, inevitably, how to adjust to unsettled circumstances, but at the same time it led him on a long search for order and home. The loneliness and uncertainty of his early years heightened his sensibility as an outsider, an observer, a *jadak,* even as it propelled him toward a future in which he devoted himself to a larger sense of community and participation in the public realm. Having a black African father and a white American mother, dealing with people who regarded him as black, or *hapa,* or Ambonese, or different in one way or another – all the issues of race intensified the outsider aspect of his character. Yet it does not diminish the importance of race to note that the formation of his persona began not with the color of his skin but the circumstances of his family – all of his family, on both sides, not just the absent father, as the title of his memoir suggests. All of his family – leaving and being left.

During his eight years at Punahou, from fifth grade through graduation, Barry found himself adjusting and readjusting to his mother's comings and goings. One might assume from his memoir, in which Ann was barely mentioned during the Punahou years, that she was totally absent, but in fact her absences were intermittent. She was gone, then back for the better part of three years, then gone, mostly but not entirely for another four, with the family reuniting either in Honolulu or Indonesia during summer vacations. Barry's prep school experience was not unlike those of other adolescents separated from parents at private boarding schools, the difference being that he boarded with two much older people, his grandparents. Not long after his father returned to Kenya, his mother left again for Indonesia. In her passport renewal application, approved on January 4, 1972, while she was visiting Honolulu, Stanley Ann Dunham Soetoro wrote *Indonesia* under "Countries to be visited," *return home* under "Purpose of trip," and *indefinite* under "Proposed length of stay." She promised Barry that she and Maya would return as soon as possible. In this case that meant after the better part of a year. Barry was left with his grandparents from midwinter through the end of the school year and into the summer.

After that absence, his mother returned to Honolulu in time to enroll for the fall 1972 semester at the University of Hawaii as a graduate student in anthropology. She and Maya came back without Lolo. Her second marriage would dissolve slowly, without the sudden rupture of her first, but in both cases, despite the misbehavior of her husbands, she would betray no ill feelings about them to her children. Maya heard positive stories about Lolo much as Barry had about Barack, and by their mother's account, the reasons for the missing or oft-missing fathers had more to do with logistics and outside pressures than irreconcilable problems in the relationships. Barack insisted on going to Harvard, and there was no money for the rest of the family to come along; so went the story, just as, in this case, Lolo had to work in Jakarta and Ann had to pursue her studies in Hawaii.

The professor who would become Ann's advisor, and who had served on the committee admitting her to the department, was Alice Dewey, a granddaughter of the famed pragmatist philosopher and progressive educator John Dewey. Alice Dewey herself had spent a year and a half in Indonesia, studying the town markets. As an expert on Javanese culture, she was taken by Ann's fluency in Bahasa Indonesia and her passionate interest in the country's arts and crafts. With Dewey's endorsement, Ann was awarded a full scholarship through the East-West Center and was also given part-time work as a handicraft instructor at the Bishop Museum in Honolulu. She and Barry and little Maya found an apartment at the corner of Poki and Wilder, one block from Punahou and five blocks from Stan and Madelyn. The university was a mile and a half away, easily reachable by foot or bus; this was important because Ann had neither a car nor a driver's license. (In fact, she would never learn to drive in her life.)

As her son later portrayed the scene, the family was scraping by at the poverty line; Ann needed help to keep going as a student and single mother of two children. In his memoir he said the aid came in the form of student grants; later in life he said she also received food stamps, an assertion that could not be documented. By any means their lifestyle was spartan and lacking the comforts of the average Punahou family. Whenever his mother heard Barry or his friends complaining about the lack of food in their fridge, he noted later, "she would pull me aside and let me know that she was a single mother going to school again and raising two kids, so that baking cookies wasn't exactly at the top of her priority list, and while she appreciated the fine education I was receiving at Punahou she wasn't planning on putting up with any snotty attitudes from me or anyone else, was that understood?" A fragment of that sentence, "baking cookies wasn't exactly at the top of her priority list," was a variation of a line that became part of the American political dialogue decades later. "I suppose I could have stayed home and baked cookies," Hillary Clinton, the wife of presidential candidate Bill Clinton, said sarcastically during the 1992 campaign when questioned about her professional career. Ann's son was writing his memoir when Hillary uttered that phrase.

With Poki Street came Maya's first flashes of memory. A filing cabinet (her mother's work). A rocking chair. Bar and she sitting on the rocking chair and rocking back and forth harder and harder until they flipped it over – their intention and their delight. A small television set across the room from the rocker. Little Maya purposely standing in front of it during sporting events, just to irritate her big brother. Her yellow Raggedy Ann blanket stretched out with her toys on it in the hallway on the way to Barry's room, forcing him, annoyed, to step around it. Picnics with Gramps and Tut up Mount Tantalus at little Pu'u 'Ualaka'a State Park. Her big brother lifting her up and swinging her around. Climbing trees together. Kentucky Fried Chicken and Tut's baked beans, homemade coleslaw, and potato salad with the skins on. The Big Sandwich Night ritual, with Gramps and his meats and cheeses and vegetables all laid out with different kinds of breads. His tuna fish sandwiches spiced with dill pickles. Games of Scrabble and checkers. A bowl of nuts with a nutcracker on Tut's coffee table. All glimpses of ordinary family life.

Ann's graduate school interlude in Honolulu paralleled Barry's preadolescence and transition into puberty, a period when boys define and redefine themselves, forming and reforming groups that to varying degrees displace the nuclear family. For Barry, the disruptive circumstances of his life made this process more pronounced and essential. In his search for home, he turned to sports, to home courts. His first court was tennis. His mother played tennis, and so did his stepfather, Lolo. Tennis was in fact how Ann and Lolo met, and it was a sport the family played together in Jakarta, helping to bridge cultural divides. During his first two years at Punahou, Barry spent much of his free time hanging out at the Punahou Tennis Club, six courts interrupted by a covered lanai on the upper rim of the campus. "The tennis court kids spent a lot of time together. We had hours and hours of unsupervised time during which we'd play tennis, do homework, walk down to the playground or another athletic field, play cards, or just hang out and talk," recalled Kristen Caldwell, one of Barry's tennis-playing classmates.

Caldwell remembered that Barry had told her and her sister that he was related to Indonesian royalty, but he seemed normal in every respect, just another of the tennis court kids. He was a bit chubby, as obnoxious as any other boy her age, but also "a very decent tennis player" who wore the proper white tennis shorts and collared shirts and white tennis shoes to meet the dress code. He took lessons after school at a cost of $3.75 per session with a snack thrown in. This was not an inconsiderable sum for a boy whose mother was in school; most likely his grandmother helped pay for it. Several friends who played with him or watched him later said tennis might have been his best game; he was not fast, but he had quick reflexes and sharp instincts, anticipating where the shot would be. His early tennis-playing years became notable, however, not for his skill on the courts but for a single disturbing memory of a racially tinged encounter with Punahou's tennis pro, who, as Obama later described it, "told me during a tournament that I shouldn't touch the schedule of matches pinned up to the bulletin board because my color might rub off."

Kristen Caldwell was there that day and recalled the incident in more detail:

We were standing on the lanai looking at the draw sheets that had just been posted for a tennis tournament, probably the Dillingham Juniors, played at Punahou, though it could have been the Hawaii Junior Sectional Championships, also played there. Everyone does the same thing. You look for your name, then run your finger across the draw to see whom you might play as you advance to later rounds of the tournament. It's a hypothetical; we all know you're not supposed to think beyond the next match, but everybody does it. . . . Barry was doing what we all did, completely normal behavior. But [the pro] came over and told him not to touch the draw sheet because he would get it dirty. He singled him out, and the implication was absolutely clear: Barry's hands weren't grubby, the message was that his darker skin would somehow soil the draw. Those of us standing there were agape, horrified, disbelieving.

As Caldwell remembered it, she and Barry were eleven or twelve, an age when they were not to talk back to elders. Her shock, she said, left her mute, but

Barry handled it beautifully, with just the right amount of cold burn without becoming disrespectful. "What do you mean by that?" he asked firmly. I could see in his eyes that [the pro] had gone too far – his remark was uncalled for; he had crossed a line – and there were witnesses. He fumbled in his response, ultimately claiming that he had only been joking. But we all knew it had been no joke, and it wasn't even remotely funny.

So much for tennis. Basketball soon was Barry's sport. His home court was down on the lower campus in an area that later became a parking lot. Over the years basketball took on more importance as the sport that defined him. In basketball he found a place of comfort, a family, a mode of expression, a connection from his past to his future. It was a basketball, after all, that his father, the apparition from another land, had given him during that Christmas season visitation. Basketball was a city game, a sport that could serve as his way into blackness, his introduction to an African American culture that he hardly knew but was his by birthright as the son of an African and an American. Basketball marked the beginning of his long arc toward feeling at home in black America.

Yet there is another side to this story, another connection that goes back through Barry's white ancestors and their Kansas homeland. Basketball was invented by James Naismith, who came to the University of Kansas to teach and coach the new sport only a few years after writing its rules. Many of the giants of basketball traced their lineage through Naismith and Kansas. Phog Allen, known as the "father of basketball coaching," was a disciple of

Naismith's at KU and went on to coach there from the end of World War I to the Eisenhower era. Adolph Rupp, reared in the town of Halstead, not far from the Dunhams and Paynes, played at Kansas for Allen and Naismith before becoming a coaching legend at Kentucky. Dean Smith, who grew up in Emporia, the town of William Allen White, also played for Allen at Kansas before establishing his reputation at North Carolina. To some degree Barry's basketball gene came out of his Kansas bloodline. His Kenyan father had been an energetic soccer player at Maseno and was often seen kicking the ball around the intramural fields at Harvard during his graduate school days, before he was weakened by the car wrecks, but he did not play basketball. On the other side of the family, there was a hoops tradition, going back to Madelyn's uncle, John McCurry, the long-legged brother of her mother, Lee McCurry Payne, who starred at Peru High in the 1912–1914 period, when the small southern Kansas town had one of the best teams in the region. A love of basketball, if not a talent for it, was passed along to Barry's mother, who as Stanley Ann Dunham was a vociferous fan of the Mercer Island teams in the late 1950s.

How natural, then, for Barry to find a home dribbling a ball on the lower court at Punahou. He was moving into his future while unwittingly connecting to his past. Once he started, he played every day after school: two on two and three on three half-court, five on five full-court. Nice rims with real rope nets, before the onset of industrial twangy chains. Barry as one of a gang of ten and sometimes twenty: Darin Maurer, Greg Orme, Mark Bendix, Tom Topolinski, Dean Ando, Bruce Arinaga, Joe Hanson, Russell Cunningham, Nelson Richardson. Mark Heflin, Marshall Marumoto, Mike Ramos, Greg Ramos. Some regulars with the basketball jones, others just showing up now and then or playing until their parents came to pick them up after work. No parent was picking up Barry. He could scoot home in less than a minute, but rarely had to, and would be out there until the last of his pals left for supper. A few *haole* and a bunch of *hapa* players, these all-American boys, ranging from Arinaga, whose mother was Korean and father Japanese, to the Ramoses, whose father was of Filipino descent (but had Americanized his name from Fidel Ramos to Phil Ramos, changing the pronunciation to *RAY-mus*), to Obama, who was starting to sprout a baby Afro. "When we first headed down to the lower courts, everyone sort of thought that Barry [as an African American] . . . 'I want him on my team,' blah, blah, stereotypical thoughts of kids," Bruce Arinaga recalled. "But it turned out a lot of us were pretty darned good too."

In his lower school years, Barry was the hefty lefty. "He was bigger than a lot of the guys, not only in height but also body mass," remembered Heflin. "I don't know if it was baby fat or what, but he was just stockier back then, and I remember he could definitely use his weight and size to back you in and push you around, which is what you want to do in playground ball, and turn around and take the shot." As they rose up through the Punahou grades, some of the names changed and some boys dropped out as the competition grew fiercer and oriented more toward the official school teams. They would play before classes and during breaks in the day and after school and on weekends. They would play at Punahou and at the public courts at the Washington Middle School on South King Street, visible from the rear window of his grandparents' apartment, and over at the gyms at the university. Year by year, Barry grew taller and slimmer. The one constant was his love of the game and its place in his life.

Late every summer, hedges of night-blooming cereus burst open on the old lava rock walls at Punahou. The delicate white cactus flowers blossomed and faded in one day. Also called moon flowers, they had graced the school perimeter since the middle of the nineteenth century, planted by Mrs. Hiram Bingham, the founding missionary's wife. At about the time that Barry Obama started at Punahou, Robert Earl Hayden, an African American poet from Michigan, wrote of the fleeting flower's "lunar presence, foredoomed, already dying with a plangency older than human cries." Sue Cowing, a poet who lived on Poki Street years before Barry stayed there with his mother and sister, later wrote that she was "vaguely afraid, near your future school / of the night-blooming cereus reaching out from the lava wall." Life's fragility, here and gone – the sensation of leaving and being left.

Not long after the night bloomers brightened Punahou's lava rock walls in August 1975, Barry's mother left again, going back to Indonesia with Maya. After a time in Jakarta, they moved to Yogyakarta on the other side of central Java, closer to the villages where Ann was to conduct anthropological research for her dissertation. Returning to Indonesia was the last thing Barry wanted to do; he chose to hang back with his grandparents at the Punahou Circle Apartments, taking over the bedroom that Stan had laid claim to as his study during the intervening Poki Street years. The floor disappeared once more under a covering of dirty clothes, drawings, books. Barry was bigger now and the apartment seemed smaller. He was entering ninth grade, Punahou's upper academy.

It was around this time that Barry "ceased to advertise" that his mother was white, he said later. He thought mentioning her color was awkward, as though he were trying to "ingratiate" himself with white people. Many of his friends at Punahou never saw Ann and had no idea what she looked like. Some classmates, seeing Stan and Madelyn at school events occasionally, assumed Barry had been adopted by an older white couple. His closer friends, those who made it over to the apartment, knew all about his grandparents, especially Stan. A generation earlier, when Stanley Ann was in high school at Mercer Island, her father's glad-handing ways seemed to bemuse her friends while only embarrassing her. The same held true with Barry and Gramps, who was beloved by his friends. One even went so far as to call Stan cool. "His grandfather was the nicest person I ever met," said Joe Hanson, a classmate who spent many hours at the Dunham apartment watching NBA games on television and hanging out in Barry's room. "I always liked to sit and listen to him. He was older, wise, and could teach you something. He was a nice enough guy to not be overbearing and go 'This is the way it is' – he would listen to you and be more of a friend than an authority." This was a long way from the young Stan Dunham, who during his early years with Madelyn managed to turn off the rest of her family and most of her friends because of what they considered his know-it-all demeanor.

Perhaps some of the braggadocio had drained from him. Stan was fifty-seven now, and in Barry's eyes a defeated figure, "just hanging on." After his westward migration in search of *el dorado,* this was it, this tenth-floor apartment on Beretania five blocks from his grandson's elite private school. There were "no more destinations to hope for." One night, Barry told a close friend years later, when his grandfather had been drinking, Barry grabbed him by the shoulders and asked him, beseechingly, why he was so unhappy. One of the most powerful scenes in *Dreams from My Father,* as devastating as it was lovingly rendered, was the grandson's account of Stan at home inside the Punahou Circle apartment on a Sunday night preparing for the week ahead selling insurance. Here, most vividly, one could see the vast distance between his public bonhomie and his private despair:

> Every Sunday night, I would watch him grow more and more irritable as he gathered his briefcase and set up a TV tray in front of his chair, following the lead of every possible distraction, until finally he would chase us out of the living room and try to schedule appointments with prospective clients over the phone. Sometimes I would tiptoe into the kitchen for a soda, and I could hear the desperation creeping out of his voice, the stretch of silence that followed when the people on the other end explained why Thursday wasn't good and Tuesday not much better, and then Gramps's heavy sigh after he had hung up the phone, his hands fumbling through the files in his lap like those of a card player who's deep in the hole.

The key phrase for every insurance salesman is "call reluctance," explained Rolf Nordahl, his colleague. "It is just really difficult to make appointments with people to talk about insurance." Stan had a tougher time than most. The company paid agents on a salary and commission system, but the salary amounted to an advance against commission sales. In his best year, Stan probably made less than ten thousand dollars, Nordahl estimated. But by one measurement the job at John S. Williamson was worth the agony and the low wage. Those cold calls he was making on Sunday nights, more than anything else, those were for Barry. They helped get him into the Punahou family.

Madelyn, in any case, was the rock of the family, as solid as Stan was soft. Or so it seemed to the outside world. She was practical at work, unsentimental, responsible, clear-eyed, and careful with money. But inside the apartment, her grandson saw the toll her responsibilities were taking. She started drinking more and more. "That's where you started noticing her alcoholism," he said decades later, during an interview at the White House. Tut would come home, he said, "exhausted from work, tightly wound, and go into her room. They [she and Stan] had become more isolated." Looking back on his grandparents during that period, the adult Obama said he came to think of their lives, including the heavy drinking, as generational. In the White House, he said, he often watched the television show *Mad Men,* which explored the lives of advertising executives and their families in New York City in the early 1960s, and despite the geographic and stylistic differences, it reminded him of Stan and Madelyn. "It explains my grandparents, their tastes," he said. One character in the show, Peggy, started as a secretary and rose in the firm. "That's my grandmother, you know, starting out with the low-level secretary job and working her way up. But that whole smokin' and drinkin' . . ."

At Punahou, to further develop a sense of community, students were placed in a homeroom starting as freshmen and stayed with the same group through graduation. Barry Obama was put in the homeroom of Eric Kusunoki, a *sansei* (third-generation) Japanese American who was hired a year earlier to teach typing and accounting and serve as the assistant baseball coach under Pal Eldredge. Kusunoki's grandparents immigrated to Hawaii as contract workers on the pineapple plantations and worked their way up to running a family restaurant called Unique Lunch Room on Waikiki Beach specializing in Hawaiian food. As a boy, Eric had heard his grandfather's stories about Pearl Harbor, how he was preparing for the Sunday church crowd at Unique on the morning of December 7, 1941, when the buzzing started overhead. He saw the Rising Sun symbol on the planes and was so fearful of anti-Japanese reprisals that he swiftly gathered the family's letters and old photographs from Japan and incinerated them in the restaurant stove.

When it came to the composition of his homeroom, Kusunoki was struck by the fact that his ninth-grade class in 1975 was a mix of scholarship students, students from single-parent families, and students who had connections to the school. They ranged from Julie Cooke, whose mother was on the board of trustees, from the Cookes of Castle & Cooke, one of the *kama'aina* Big Five sugar companies that once dominated Hawaii; to Barry Obama, who lived with his grandparents while his mother was a graduate student thousands of miles away; to Whitey Kahoohanohano, whose mother worked in the Punahou office. The dean overseeing the entire freshman class urged homeroom teachers to become "active listeners" and "significant adults" in the lives of their charges, and Kusunoki took the assignment seriously. He opened his classroom no later than seven-thirty each morning and let his students settle in at least a half hour before school started. "Some would come in. Barry would be out shooting hoops, but sometimes he would come in. I had a couple of girls who found a Nerf ball on my desk and made up a game where they tried to throw the Nerf ball through the ceiling fan . . . see if you could get it through the blades. Sometimes it would go flying out the window . . . and Barry would come in and marvel at that and sometimes play with them. But his game was mostly outside."

On most days Barry would stroll into the homeroom in old, domed Pauahi Hall a few minutes before eight with his confident, athletic stride, no different from the gait he displayed decades later. Jill Okihiro, a classmate, could recollect the scene so vividly – Barry entering the room with a basketball in one hand, "never weighted down with a backpack like some; he carried one or two books [in the other hand], and that was it." If there was a rhythm of hipness to the way he walked, he was emulating the professional basketball icons he saw on television, Tiny Archibald and the Iceman, Earl the Pearl and Dr. J. "He was always well behaved, very courteous, very well mannered to everybody, not just me," Kusunoki recalled. "And it wasn't an Eddie Haskell kind of buttering up, just sincere. Always had a big smile, always nice without being obnoxious. He wasn't loud. Without making a grand entrance, he would just walk in the door; 'Good morning, Mr. Kusunoki,' or 'Hello, Mr. Kuz. How you doing?' He was like that every day. I can't recall him having a bad day. I mean he did it in his own subtle way, low key."

Whatever anxieties burned inside Barry, he never revealed them to Kusunoki and rarely showed his vulnerabilities to anyone at Punahou.

For a few years, in ninth and tenth grade, he shared his frustrations with a student two grades ahead of him named Keith Kakugawa. In his memoir, he reinvented Kakugawa as a character called Ray who served a literary function as a symbol of young blackness, a mix of hot anger and cool detachment, the provocateur of hip, vulgar, get-real dialogues. In fact, Kakugawa was another *hapa* student, with a black and Native American mother and a Japanese father. Somewhere between pseudonymous and fictitious, Ray was the first of several distorted or composite characters employed in *Dreams from My Father* for similar purposes. Kakugawa was never in Barry's closest gang of friends, but they did hang out now and then for those two years, and Barry felt freer to let down his guard around him, enjoying "his warmth and brash humor." In the memoir Barry and Ray could be heard complaining about how rich white *haole* girls would never date them. In fact, neither had much trouble in that regard; Kakugawa dated an admiral's daughter from the officers' housing near Pearl Harbor and had the keys to her car, which he often drove around with "the Kid," as he called Barry. In the book, Ray complained about "white folks this or white folks that," a phrase that Barry found "uncomfortable" in his mouth because he unavoidably thought of his mother's smile. But the Kid could grouse about his mother nonetheless. "If anyone heard a word from him when he was upset, I did," Kakugawa recalled. "If I was mad at something he was mad at something. What was upsetting him – that his mother took off again. Seems like she never has time for him anymore – that kind of thing."

In a less visceral and more lighthearted intellectual fashion, Barry also shared some of his inner thoughts with Tony Peterson, a graduating senior during Barry's freshman year. Peterson, who came from a military family at Schofield Barracks, was the only black student in his 1976 class and one of a handful at Punahou, counting the *hapa* students like Kakugawa, Obama, and Rik Smith, whose mother was Indian. (Joella Edwards, who was in Barry's class, left Punahou in ninth grade.) When Peterson first heard that the black Ray in Obama's memoir was Kakugawa, he was surprised. "When I think of the black kids at Punahou, I don't think of Keith because he was half Japanese," he said later. By his real name or any other, Peterson did not make Obama's book, although some characteristics of a composite character in the college section fit him. He first met Barry on the basketball court before school, and soon started a regular session with him and Rik Smith that they jokingly called Ethnic Corner.

One of the oddities of Punahou was a daily schedule arranged so the same class would meet on different days week to week. The school week was the traditional five days, Monday through Friday, but the schedule repeated in six-day blocks, A through F. The first week A would be Monday and E

Friday; the next week would start with a Monday F and go through a D Friday, and so on. This peculiarly complex scheduling was fitting in a school where there were no bells and most classes were seminars where students could eat and drink sodas and do a lot of the talking. There was nothing formal about Ethnic Corner, aside from the ritual of Peterson borrowing money from Obama to buy something at the snack bar, but they had a regular meeting time: every F day at eleven in the morning. They met on the steps outside Cooke Hall, looking across at the Senior Bench, where the jocks and popular people congregated, and talked about classes, girls, and race.

The name Ethnic Corner was tongue-in-cheek:

> Both [Barry] and Rik were biracial. . . . All teenagers are trying to figure out who they are, and for them it was particularly an issue. "Everyone looks at me and sees a black man," Barry would say, "even though I am only half black." He had no personal frame of reference for his blackness. So we gave him that to talk about: How do we explore these things? I was the blackest one, and yet I lived my whole life not with a white parent but with this issue of being academically inclined and people thinking I was white. So we did have issues there. . . . We talked about social issues, a lot about what we were going to be. We talked about stuff like whether we would ever see a black president in our lifetime. None of us talked about whether we might be that person. We talked about racism: Are we treating people fairly without discrimination? We were very aware of the fact that we hadn't leveled the playing field yet, but we were not radical sorts of folks.

What were they going to be? Smith and Peterson said lawyer. Obama had hoop dreams. In Peterson's senior yearbook, his friend wrote:

> Tony, man, I sure am glad I got to know you before you left. All those Ethnic Corner trips to the snack bar and playing ball made the year a lot more enjoyable, even though the snack bar trips cost me a fortune.

Anyway, been great knowing you and I hope we keep in touch. Good luck in everything you do, and get that law degree. Some day when I am an all-pro basketballer, and I want to sue my team for more money, I'll call on you.

Barry

Barry had a sense of humor, but also a flickering hope. A ninth-grade boy could still fool himself into believing he could play. Especially when he lacked a strong desire to do much of anything else.

CHAPTER 12

BARRY OBAMA

A self-selected group of boys at Punahou School who loved basketball and good times called themselves the Choom Gang. *Choom* is a verb, meaning "to smoke marijuana." As a member of the Choom Gang, Barry Obama was known for starting a few pot-smoking trends. The first was called "TA," short for "total absorption." To place this in the physical and political context of another young man who would grow up to be president, TA was the antithesis of Bill Clinton's claim that as a Rhodes Scholar at Oxford he smoked dope but never inhaled. When you were with Barry and his pals, if you exhaled precious *pakalolo* (Hawaiian slang for marijuana, meaning "numbing tobacco") instead of absorbing it fully into your lungs, you were assessed a penalty and your turn was skipped the next time the joint came around. "Wasting good bud smoke was not tolerated," explained one member of the Choom Gang, Tom Topolinski, the Chinese-looking kid with a Polish name who answered to Topo.

Along with TA, Barry popularized the concept of "roof hits": when they were chooming in a car all the windows had to be rolled up so no smoke blew out and went to waste; when the pot was gone, they tilted their heads back and sucked in the last bit of smoke from the ceiling. Barry also had a knack for interceptions. When a joint was making the rounds, he often elbowed his way in, out of turn, shouted "Intercepted!" and took an extra hit. No one seemed to mind. This was a modern variation of the story told decades earlier by Barry's grandfather, of a young Stan Dunham hitching a ride through El Dorado in a black sedan carrying Herbert Hoover, who called out "Butts on that!" when he requested a drag on Stan's cigarette. One difference: Stan's presidential story was apocryphal.

The Choom Gang was a loose confederation of Punahou boys: Mark Bendix, Joe Hanson, Greg Orme, Barry Obama, Kenji Salz, Russell Cunningham, Tom Topolinski, Wayne Weightman, Robby Rask, all from the class of 1979, plus a few others who came in and out, including the Ramos brothers, Mike and Greg, and Tony Peterson's little brother, Keith. Some basketball friends were not choomers, and not all choomers played basketball, but the two tended to go hand in hand. One of the venues of the Choom Gang was the lower basketball court on campus, where by tenth grade they played pickup ball in what they jokingly called the Hack League. These were mostly weekend games during the school year and anytime during the summer, often involving opposing players who were older and bigger. The style was all-out, full of hard fouls, trash talking, twisted ankles, facial cuts, and bruised knees on the asphalt court. To thrive in the Hack League required not only talent and freewheeling elbows but also negotiating skills, since there could be a foul called on almost every play. This is where Barry excelled, according to his buddies. They said he never bullied or became belligerent on the court, even while stating his case and standing his ground. He was not always right, but he almost always won the argument, and he did it without making anyone mad. He exemplified the local pidgin expression "Cool head, main thing."

For teenage boys in pursuit of good times, the island of Oahu was a wonderland. From the basketball courts at Punahou, Choom Gang members often made their way to Aku Ponds at the end of Manoa Stream, where they slipped past the *liliko'i* vines and the KAPU (keep out) signs, waded into waist-high cool mountain water, stood near the rock where water rushed overhead, and held up a slipper (what flip-flops are called in Hawaii) to create an air pocket canopy. It was a natural high, they said, stoned or not. From there they would head *makai* to Sandy Beach (locals call it Sandy's) out past Hanauma Bay on the South Shore, their favorite spot for bodysurfing in the ocean. Barry was not the strongest swimmer, but he was not afraid of the water, not even at Sandy's, one of the most dangerous bodysurfing beaches on the islands. In the other direction, *mauka,* their favorite hangout was a place they called Pumping Stations, a lush hideaway off an unmarked, roughly paved road partway up Mount Tantalus. They parked single file on the grassy edge, turned up their stereos playing Aerosmith, Blue Öyster Cult, and Stevie Wonder, lit up some "sweet-sticky Hawaiian buds," and washed it down with "green bottled beer" (the Choom Gang preferred Heineken, Beck's, and St. Pauli Girl). No shouting, no violence, no fights; they even cleaned up their beer bottles. This was their haven, in the darkness high above the city and the pressures of Punahou.

Whenever the Choom Gang traveled by car, Barry was adept at calling "Shotgun!" and riding up front. One night they held a drag race up Mount Tantalus, Russell Cunningham's little Toyota versus Mark Bendix's Volkswagen bus, also known as the Choomwagon. Barry and Kenji Salz rode with Cunningham; Joe Hanson, Topo, and the others with Bendix. Neither vehicle had much power, especially up a long, constantly winding hill, but off they went, full throttle. The VW pulled in front early. The road was wet. After a few turns, looking back, Hanson and Topo could not see the Toyota's headlights. When they reached the top, they waited ten minutes or more, but still no sign of Kukes, as they called Cunningham. Bendix suggested they head back down the mountain to look. On the way down, they saw a figure who appeared to be staggering up the road. It was Barry Obama. What was going on? As they drew closer, they noticed that he was laughing so hard he could barely stand up. "Where is everyone? Where's Russell?" they asked him.

"Kukes rolled his car. It's upside down in the middle of the road!" Barry said. He told them how he had crawled out a back window as though he were on a SWAT team. They loaded him into the van and headed down to the scene, and there lay the Toyota, wheels up, roof down, like armadillo roadkill belly-up in the middle of the road. No injuries beyond Russell's bloody nose. "You can't drive for shit!" Barry kept saying to him, as everyone laughed. Soon enough reality set in. How were they going to explain an overturned car to the police? They tried to rock it right-side up, but that only broke a window. Plan B was to pile everyone else into the Volkswagen and leave Cunningham there alone to handle it as though it were an innocent mishap. About a half hour after leaving, their curiosity getting the better of them, they drove back and saw the flashing red and blue lights and red flares in the road and Cunningham calmly talking to the police. Had he pointed to them? They rolled on, unsure. But no one followed, and nothing resulted, not even a ticket. "Russ took care of it," Hanson recalled. "He was a trooper."

Later in life, looking back on those days, Obama made it sound as though he were hanging out with a group of misbegotten ne'er-do-wells, what he called "the club of disaffection." In fact, most members of the Choom Gang were decent students and athletes who went on to successful and productive lives as lawyers, writers, and businessmen. One exception was their pot dealer, who was much older, already in his early twenties. He was a long-haired *haole* hippie who worked at the Mama Mia Pizza Parlor not far from Punahou and lived in a dilapidated bus in an abandoned warehouse. Interestingly, the dealer's first name was Ray, the pseudonym Obama later used for the character in his memoir based on Keith Kakugawa. The two Rays were not one and the same. According to Topolinski, Ray the dealer was "freakin' scary." Many years later they learned that he had been killed with a ball-peen hammer by a scorned gay lover. But at the time he was useful because of his ability to "score quality bud." Choices are often shaped by circumstances and opportunity, and in the Honolulu of Barry's teenage years marijuana was flourishing up in the hills, out in the countryside, in covert greenhouses everywhere. It was sold and smoked right there in front of your nose; Maui Wowie, Kauai Electric, Puna Bud, Kona Gold, and other local variations of *pakalolo* were readily available. The war on drugs had not yet started in earnest, and the Hawaii National Guard's Operation Destroy in 1977, when troops went after marijuana crops in the island hills, barely made a dent in the supply. As Ron Jacobs, a legendary island deejay who spun records during that era under the pidgin moniker Whodaguy, once noted, it seemed appropriate that the postal abbreviation for Hawaii was HI.

In the Choom Gang, not counting the older Ray, who was more an accessory, there were no miscreant bullies. There was not even a designated leader. One of the favorite words in their subculture revealed their democratic nature. The word was *veto*. Whenever an idea was broached, someone could hold up his hand in the V sign (a backward peace sign of that era) and indicate that the motion was not approved. They later shortened the process so that you could just shout "V" to get the point across. In the Choom Gang, all V's were created equal. The other members considered Mark Bendix the glue; he was funny, creative, and uninhibited, with a penchant for Marvel Comics. He also had that VW bus and a house with a pool, a bong, and a Nerf basketball, all enticements for them to slip off midday for a few unauthorized hours of recreation – not a difficult thing to do with Punahou's modular schedule.

Without exerting himself in overt ways, Barry Obama held as much respect as anyone within the group. "Never panicked, never fazed, that was Barry," said Topolinski. On the basketball court or anywhere else, he maintained a measure of cool. While others sweated their coursework, Barry never seemed to worry about it and did well anyway. He was not an A student, never in the National Honor Society, and was more interested in history and literature than the sciences. Mari Ota, a *hapa* Japanese Caucasian and the girlfriend of one of his basketball buddies, Darin Maurer, was in chemistry class with him; she remembered that Barry "wasn't that into it" and borrowed her notes. But he impressed his teachers and avoided academic trouble. He never dominated discussions, but always knew what was going on. He was developing the traits of a writer: hang back, look around, absorb, remember, distill, rearrange. Writing came easily to him. "I would spend two or three weeks on a paper and he would do it the night before. He was that intelligent," said Joe Hanson. "And that was no small feat when you were going to Punahou and competing against everyone else. He would not prepare for it but knew what he wanted to talk about and was very good at putting it on paper." The same with tests; he seemed nonchalant, yet performed well. How did he do it? He told his Choom Gang mates that the trick was if you put the textbook under your pillow the night before you would perform better on an exam. "It never worked for me," said Topolinski.

His classroom calm became a matter of pride to his friends, as Jeff Cox learned. Cox arrived at Punahou in his junior year and was never part of the group, though he quickly befriended Russ Cunningham and through him got to know Obama, who stood out immediately. "Barry had the ability to project cool, it seemed to me, that calm, almost a nonchalance. It was all part of the image thing, not just of him but just generally in Hawaii, where in my mind there was some kind of line between sophisticated detachment and just slacker or lazy, and Barry exuded this sophisticated detachment. He had his act together, in a way. He understood how things worked maybe a little better than the rest of us." Cox was in Mrs. Weldon's speech class with Barry, and as the new kid was surprised and heartened when the teacher asked the students to choose debate partners and "Barry walked up and asked if I would be his partner. . . . I don't know why he did it. I've thought about it since and I think maybe he was sympathetic at some level."

Cox was academically competitive and thought he might have an edge over Barry, whom he regarded mostly as a basketball player and leader of a tight-knit gang of friends who were not Big Men on Campus but "more Animal Housey and more fun and in some regards more regular guys." The debate topic for Cox v. Obama was gun control, and Barry, for argument's sake, decided to take the side opposing gun regulation. Years later Cox would become a Republican aide in Washington State and philosophically oppose most gun control, but at the time he had no strong feelings. "I remember thinking, 'Do you know you [Obama] are taking the tougher side?'" In the days leading up to their debate, Barry's friends teased Cox whenever they saw him near their hangout on the benches between Cooke Library and the science center. "Kenji Salz was playing it up in particular. Kenji really adored Barry. 'Barry is going to kill you! He's going to get you!' It was all Kenji would talk about. 'Better watch out, he's got a gun!' Barry was nonchalant about it, but Kenji was playing it up big-time. I got Barry aside and said, 'Look, why don't we just go for B's here.' That way, no big deal. That was my solution. He said okay, whatever."

As soon as the debate began, Cox found himself outfoxed. He went into it in traditional fashion, preparing facts to lay out, one argument after another, gleaned from books and *Time* and *Newsweek*.

And Barry got up there and he just had a few arguments that I hadn't thought of. . . . I was always touching back to this many killed, guns are killing, and he was just bouncing all over the place, but what he did is he went up to that ten-thousand-foot level. I remember him talking about, "How do guns make gun owners feel?" I hadn't thought of that. How am I going to respond? He was very good on his feet, thinking more strategically on what could benefit him. I was sitting there flabbergasted; I remember thinking this is too heavily a philosophical question for me. And the teacher loved it. Barry was very smooth, and I started stumbling around all over the place. I felt he formulated in his own mind while we were doing it a kind of angle or wedge that was different than the angle I had been going. I was literal – one, two, three, four – and he kind of did some audibles. He wasn't pulling out a whole lot of facts, he just seemed to have structured a bunch of little islands that he could jump to.

Barry won. Cox was annoyed. He felt that he had followed debate procedures and Barry had danced around them. The razzing from the Choom Gang continued. In his yearbook, Kenji Salz drew a picture and the caption "Barry . . . You . . . Bang, Bang, Bang." But Obama himself was more conciliatory, writing, "Jeff, I really enjoyed debating with you. You're a nice dude and fun to argue with. Since neither of us took it really seriously."

By the time Cox faced off against him, Barry had already mastered the art of knocking a debate opponent off-balance. He had been practicing almost daily on Gramps, who had tried without much success to assume the role of disciplinarian, laying down what the teenager considered to be "an endless series of petty and arbitrary rules" about use of the car and chores around the apartment. Eventually Barry would regret the way he dealt with his grandfather, but at the time he took advantage of his debating skills: "With a certain talent for rhetoric, as well as an absolute certainty about the merits of my own views, I found that I could generally win these arguments in the narrow sense of leaving my grandfather flustered, angry, and sounding unreasonable."

One of his English teachers at Punahou was Barbara Czurles-Nelson, the former journalist who had followed Barry's journey since the week of his birth, when Dr. Rodney West told her the unusual story of a Stanley giving birth. Barry was not the most talkative student in her class, she recalled. He would sit near the back of the room, relaxed, waiting for his opening in the conversation. One day they were dealing with a philosophical question about what people should most fear. The answers included loneliness, death, hell, and war. Then Barry straightened up. That was the sign that he was ready to participate, Nelson thought, when he was sure to sharpen the class discussion. "Words," he said. "Words are the power to be feared most. . . . Whether directed personally or internationally, words can be weapons of destruction."

When does political ambition first bloom? No one in Bill Clinton's class at Hot Springs High in Arkansas doubted that he wanted to spend his life in politics. His aspirations were obvious. He ran for every student office he could until Johnnie Mae Mackey, the principal, had to tell him he was hogging the spotlight and could not run for class president as a senior but only class secretary, an election he lost. After his junior year he traveled to Washington as a member of Boys Nation and maneuvered his way into position to be the first of his group to shake the hand of President John F. Kennedy in the White House Rose Garden, coming home with a photograph that delighted his mother and symbolized his outsize hopes that he might someday stand there in JFK's spot. There is nothing comparable in the early life of Barry Obama.

It is true that in Bu Fer's third-grade class at SD Asisi in Jakarta, he once wrote "Cita-cita saya adalah ingin jadi presiden" – Someday I want to be president. And his friend Keith Kakugawa claims to have a memory of Barry years later, in Hawaii, standing on the front lawn of Kakugawa's house in Pearl City one night and declaring that he was going to be president of the United States, and if not that, then chief justice of the Supreme Court. Whether that happened or was the sort of memory that took shape only in retrospect, it stands as sole testimony. It is clear that his mother believed he was special and told him he could accomplish anything he put his mind to. But to the vast majority of his Punahou friends and classmates, Barry did not seem destined to make history in politics or anything else. Keith Peterson, a black student one year behind Obama who trailed him like a little brother, said that what stood out about him "was that he didn't stand out." Peterson reflected the prevailing opinion when he said, "There was absolutely nothing that made me think [politics] was the road he would take."

Obama never sought a student leadership position at Punahou. One of the few times his name was connected to politics, it was part of a joke. In the fall of 1978 the students held a mock election for governor of Hawaii. In the straw poll, as counted by the student newspaper, Frank Fasi, the mayor of Honolulu, defeated George Ariyoshi (who won the real election), but also receiving votes were Aerosmith, Donald Duck, My Mom, Richard Nixon, Miss September – and two votes for Barry Obama. Not long thereafter, Neil Abercrombie, then a state senator, visited Punahou and delivered a speech at Dillingham auditorium to juniors and seniors, including Obama. It was not exactly a glowing endorsement of his profession, at least not on the surface. Abercrombie, the old college friend of Barry's father, would spend his career in politics, but nonetheless told the students that politicians were "the lowest form of life." He urged them to "be a lawyer, be a doctor, be an architect. Those are three categories of people who know everything. The Mafia's a distant fourth." Toggling back and forth between quintessential Abercrombie sarcasm and earnestness, he had this advice for those who wanted to go into politics: "I've got the greatest gimmick in the whole world: Be honest, be straightforward. There is a better way in politics. Don't bullshit people. If you don't know, say so. If you think you know, tell why you think you know."

Barry had some of both in him – he could tell the straight truth or say what he thought someone wanted to hear in a manner that would soothe them – long before those traits were put on larger public display. As he said in Ms. Nelson's class, he understood the power and danger of words, and though he did not use them to hurt others, he could deploy them to his advantage.

These characteristics came equally from nature and nurture. His mother was inclined to find the best in every person she met, especially people from different places and cultures. His father had a captivating voice, a mesmerizing presence, a certainty that he was correct, and a love of argument. His grandmother had given up aspirations to be an urban sophisticate like Bette Davis, abandoning all pretensions except the cigarette holder, and year by year had become more practical, steady, and unemotional, with a tendency to say exactly what she felt without being rude. As a professional banker, and a woman, she had matter-of-factly trained many men who would go on to be her bosses. His grandfather was a salesman and storyteller who carried around a copy of Dale Carnegie's *How to Win Friends and Influence People,* though at home he often seemed more like the desperate Willy Loman character in *Death of a Salesman.* Barry was shaped by all of them, whether consciously rejecting one of their traits or unconsciously mimicking another. But his character was also formed by his own particular condition, so unlike that of his parents and grandparents. Growing up *hapa,* living with white relatives but appearing black and being treated as black by society at large, he learned by necessity how to navigate in different worlds and mastered the distinct vocabularies required to connect and thrive in each of them.

In his memoir, he was utterly honest and revealing about what he called his tactics and tricks in dealing with people. There was one notable scene in high school when he was confronted by his mother after a Choom Gang buddy was busted for marijuana possession. This was in the late summer of 1978, when she and Maya were in Honolulu for a few months before heading back for another round of work in Indonesia. The relationship between mother and son was somewhat strained at this point. Ann and Maya stayed mostly at the house of Ann's advisor, Alice Dewey, in Manoa Valley. One day, according to the memoir, Ann marched into his room, wanting to know the details of his friend's troubles with the law. "I had given her a reassuring smile and patted her hand and told her not to worry. I wouldn't do anything stupid. It was usually an effective tactic, another one of the tricks I had learned. People were satisfied so long as you were courteous and smiled and made no sudden moves. . . . They were relieved – such a pleasant surprise to find a well-mannered young black man who didn't seem angry all the time."

His mother was an optimist, sometimes so much so that he considered her naïve, but she was not easily fooled by her son. The soothing voice and calm-down approach did not work with her this time. Her face, he wrote, became "as grim as a hearse" as she questioned his commitment to his studies and his future, and she grew even angrier when he offhandedly said that he might just stick around Honolulu after finishing Punahou. "Damn it, Bar," he quoted her as saying, "you can't just sit around like some good-time Charlie, waiting for luck to see you through!" In the book, Obama concluded this anecdote with a riff on guilt: how his mother's response made him feel guilty and how she explained to him that guilt was actually "a highly underrated emotion" and one of the requisites of civilized society. But looking at the scene anew, there was something else obviously at work. Ann's will – her determination to go forward, to experiment, to be bold, to overcome whatever obstacles were in her way, even those that she put there herself – was always apparent. It was evident when she dated and married and left Barry's father; when she dated and married and left Lolo; when she adapted to Indonesia; when she woke Barry up before dawn to tutor him; when she decided that his best chance in life was to live with her parents and attend Punahou; when she followed her own ambitions as an anthropologist back to Indonesia. Ann had the will to avoid the traps life set for her, and she infused that same will in her son.

Before his ambition found direction, the will was there, even during his Choom Gang days. He was idling, adjusting, assessing the traps. And playing basketball.

It was one thing to play basketball every day on the outdoor courts on campus, quite another to play for Punahou. The athletic model at the school could be compared to Major League Baseball and its farm system. There were three levels of minor teams after ninth-grade intramurals – Junior Varsity A, Junior Varsity AA, and Varsity A – before a player reached the major leagues of Varsity AA. Obama moved his way up the system until finally, in his senior year, he made it to the top. In his book, in one of the scenes with Keith Kakugawa, the character he called Ray, he broached the subject of basketball style, complaining that he did not get the breaks of other players on the team because "they play like white boys do," and that was the style preferred by the coach. Since Kakugawa was two years ahead of him, if this conversation took place Barry would have had to have been a sophomore, a fact that raises two contradictions. First, as a sophomore he was a long way from making Varsity AA, and second, the head coach he was complaining about, Chris McLachlin, was on temporary leave during Obama's sophomore year and did not return until the following season, when Kakugawa was gone.

In his junior year Barry competed for a spot on the top varsity but lost out to Joe Hanson, one of his friends from the Choom Gang. They were about the same height, six-foot-one, and played the same position, small forward. During the previous summer they had gone together to apply for jobs serving ice cream at the nearby Baskin-Robbins on South King, down the block and around the corner from Barry's apartment. Before and after work, Hanson had spent time at the apartment, chatting with Stan Dunham, huddling in Barry's messy room, reading comics, listening to George Benson records, talking basketball. When he made the top varsity and Obama did not, he learned from friends that Barry was bewildered and upset, though he never heard that directly. "He told them, 'I'm a better player than him. I should have made it ahead of him,'" Hanson recalled. "But it didn't strain our relationship at all." The next year Hanson inadvertently smoothed the way for Barry's rise to the top varsity by flunking out of Punahou and creating an open roster spot. But there was slightly more to it than that. For Obama and his pal Greg Orme and two juniors, Alan Lum and Matt Hiu, to make the squad, Coach McLachlin had to cut two seniors who had been on the roster the year before, including the son of the athletic director. "It was so hard to make the team in those days . . . and McLachlin had to cut some veterans to make room for us," recalled Lum, who decades later would be the Punahou basketball coach himself. "So it was amazing just to be on the team. . . . You look back and say that means Barack must have been special. Why would you go through the process of cutting a senior who had already been on the team to keep another senior?"

If Obama was unhappy about his playing time, the truth is he had had to work exceedingly hard just to make the team. He made it because of his intense passion for the game – his will – more than anything else. The notion that he was hampered in his progress because his style was more playground-oriented, that he played "black" and the coach coached "white," distorts the dynamics of his own game, the performance of the other players, and McLachlin's coaching philosophy. The reality was that Barry, as skilled and intelligent a player as he was, could not stand out in this group. He had good court sense and an ability to slash to the basket, but was an unreliable outside shooter and not much of a jumper, contradicting the stereotype of "black" ball. Decades later a story emerged that his nickname was Barry O'Bomber, playing off his last name and a propensity to fire away from long range, but few team members recalled that nickname and said the real gunner was Darin Maurer, who was better than Obama but got barely more playing time. Maurer never started at Punahou but went on to play Division I basketball at Stanford as a walk-on. He was a *haole;* race had nothing to do with playing time.

The subject of Obama and basketball reaches into the complexities of self-perception and race. Since his self-discovery served as the organizing theme of his memoir, it was understandable that he focused the narrative through that racial lens, and that for dramatic effect he sometimes placed more emphasis on certain provocative scenes and topics. The tendency in his self-portrait was to present himself as blacker and more disaffected than he was, if only slightly so. He did this regarding his portrayal of both Frank Marshall Davis, the Frank character in the book, as old and black and cynical, and Keith Kakugawa, the Ray character, as young and black and angry – enhancing their roles in his teenage life at the expense of other people who spent vastly more time with him. And he did the same when it came to basketball. "He loved basketball so much, I think a lot of things have been blown out of proportion," said Alan Lum. "Anybody wants to play. His style of play *was* flashy, but it was okay. McLachlin didn't really put a damper on it. If you did a behind-the-back pass, McLachlin would frown on that, but when it came down to playing time, [Barry] wasn't one of the five best." In fact, Lum and other teammates pointed out, Barry was only occasionally considered one of the top eight, the number of players McLachlin usually used in his rotation, following the substitution pattern of John Wooden, the brilliant coach at UCLA.

These points are not meant to diminish the important role basketball played in Barry's coming-of-age as he began to explore black culture. He saw in it what he saw in jazz, an ineffable artistic expression of what it meant to be black and cool, a brother. A riff on jazz funk is what stuck in Mike Ramos's mind about his first meeting with Barry, at a party where Barry joined a conversation about the saxophonist Grover Washington and said, "You listen to Grover? I listen to Grover!" By his high school days his Afro was becoming more prominent. When he signed the sophomore yearbook of Kelli Furushima, a classmate he often teased and stole pencils from, he drew an arrow down to the bottom of the page where he sketched the top half of a bushy head and wrote, "My afro sticking up over the top again." The first spark of soulful recognition of basketball came not long after he arrived back from Indonesia, when his grandfather took him to see Red Rocha's University of Hawaii Rainbows in 1971, a team fueled by black players who came over from the mainland and played with up-tempo flair. That team (nicknamed the Fab Five long before a Michigan quintet appropriated the name) caught the public's attention by earning a national ranking, winning the Rainbow Classic along with twenty-plus more games, and getting a coveted invitation to the still popular National Invitational Tournament in New York. They also caught the attention of Barry, and when he grew older he often made his way to the UH campus to watch the team or play pickup ball at their gym. "It's almost like he wanted to be more black than he wanted to be a white person," said Joe Hanson, one of his *haole* Choom Gang pals. "He wanted to hang. Like we went to University of Hawaii basketball games, and the guys who were playing, Barry would give them this little nod of the head black-guy type thing. He looked up to the black players more than the white ones." (Eventually, according to Hanson, Barry befriended some of them, went to their parties, and during his senior year dated an older black woman on campus.)

The question of whether Coach McLachlin sufficiently appreciated Barry's style of play diverts attention from the deeper story of the 1978–1979 Punahou team, Obama's role on it, and the impact it had on his life. If the Choom Gang represented his boredom, alienation, and need to find family even in mild rebellion, and if the pickup games on the outdoor courts gave him a place where he could test himself and find himself, the Punahou basketball team in many ways made him a member of a cohesive unit with shared goals for the first time in his life. It also gave him his first taste of what it felt like to win, to be adored, to be a champion. He would acknowledge later to *Sports Illustrated* that McLachlin was "a terrific coach" and that he learned a lot that year "about discipline, about handling disappointments, being more team-oriented, and realizing that not everything is about you." In his rendering, McLachlin came across as a traditionalist coach who stressed fundamentals at the expense of free expression on the court, which is only part of the story. While he did stress fundamentals, McLachlin was a forward thinker whose philosophy at times came closer to New Age than Old School.

A 1964 graduate of Punahou with a master's degree from Stanford who had already led the team to the state championship in 1975 and to the state finals again in 1977 and 1978, McLachlin looked for any edge he could find. He had his players practice meditation, lying down on the court, finding their center, learning breathing techniques to deal with stress. He emphasized repetition and visualization. Shoot one hundred free throws in a row. Visualize making one hundred in a row. Don't leave the gym until you make twenty in a row. Step to the line in a game with that vision in your mind. "We try to teach them to re-create their best day all the time," he said. He gave them self-evaluation sheets and went over the answers with them, and told his players to read Wayne Dyer's books on positive thinking, including *Pulling Your Own Strings* and *Your Erroneous Zones*. ("We looked at each other like, what?" recalled one of his star players, Dan Hale.) He trained his boys to be prepared for anything. *Always have a backup plan* was his daily mantra. If your car broke down on the way to practice, that was not an excuse. You should have prepared for that and had a contingency plan. "He expected you to have Plan B in place," said Tom Topolinski, a backup big man on the 1978–1979 team. "He would say, 'That is part of life.'"

Along with mental agility, McLachlin was obsessed with physical conditioning. His practices lasted an hour and a half, all intensity. "His theory was the best conditioned teams make the least mistakes, so he killed us," said Alan Lum. "A lot of sprints, a lot of defensive sliding and five-man weaves where the ball couldn't touch the ground. If someone forgot and the ball hit the ground we had to start over again." During layup drills before games, he enlisted his wife to keep track of every shot; anyone who missed a layup knew he would be running suicide sprints in practice later. But there were rewards for performing at this level. McLachlin treated his players like adults, members of an elite club, and let them use his on-campus hideaway apartment to hang out and listen to music between classes. He wanted his players to think and act more like a college squad than a high school team, and he drew his inspiration and game strategies from the best college coaches. "It was virtually unacceptable to him for us to play at a high school level," said Topolinski.

Larry Tavares, his starting point guard, said McLachlin confined his criticism to practice and was upbeat during games. It was not just his coaching that made Punahou special. He benefited from a bounty of exceptional talent on the roster Barry made as a senior. They had graduated one star from the team that lost the state finals the year before: Mark Tuinei, who went on to play pro football as an offensive lineman for the Dallas Cowboys for fifteen years before his untimely death in 1999 from an overdose of heroin and ecstasy. The returning players came in with the attitude "We're gonna die on the court before we lose again," said Dan Hale, who replaced Tuinei as a six-foot-six sophomore center, so skilled he made the team as a freshman. Hale was joined on the front line by John Kamana III, the second-generation Squeeze, a sprinter as physical as he was fast, who could outleap players half a foot taller and went on to play fullback at Southern Cal; and Boy Eldredge, Pal's nephew, from Punahou's legendary *hapa* Hawaiian Eldredge clan, an all-around athlete who was considered the team's best defensive player and inspirational leader. Tavares as the point guard (another *hapa* teenager, his father of Portuguese descent, his mother Filipino) was a three-sport letterman and smooth floor-leader, though not much of an outside shooter. (McLachlin established the Tavares Rules, detailing where on the court he could shoot and where he could not.) And the star of the team was Darryl Gabriel, the shooting guard, who went on to play Division I college ball at Loyola Marymount.

Squeeze, Gabes, T, Danny, and Boy. No team in Hawaii, and few on the mainland, featured a more versatile starting five. All five went on to play college sports – baseball, football, or basketball. Topo was the first big man off the bench, and Orme the first small forward – two of Barry's Choom Gang pals. Next in, usually, was the gunner, Darin Maurer, and the reserve point guard, Jason Oshima. Obama was in that mix, and often played well when he went in, but only as the eighth, ninth, or tenth man, depending on the situation.

Troy Egami, who covered the team for the student newspaper, wrote a feature story in which he described Coach McLachlin "giggling boyishly to himself" as he watched "the ritual slam dunk" contest his players enjoyed after practice. "Psychos, all of them," McLachlin muttered under his breath, smiling. Obama, the *hapa* black on the team, might have been one of the psychos, but he was also among the most earthbound; he could not jump high enough to dunk the ball. "Barry's lack of ups was obvious," recalled Topolinski. In fact, McLachlin coined a phrase for the phenomenon: *Barry Obama, famous for his no-jump jump shot!* The coach not only tolerated the high-flying dunk, he made it part of his game plan, especially against Punahou's rival, University High, whose six-foot-ten center could change the intensity of a game with thunderous slams. Dan Hale was instructed to sprint down court whenever the center dunked so Punahou could abruptly switch the momentum with a countering slam at the other end. This was part of McLachlin's larger notion of always having a backup plan. "He even thought that through – the psychology of the dunk," said Hale. "We had to be prepared."

If Obama and Maurer in particular carried a grudge against McLachlin for not giving them more playing time, they did not disrupt the team. "I never saw [Barry] complain or do anything detrimental to the team, to what we were doing," said Hale, the kid center, who played countless hours with Barry in pickup games. "Maurer wanted more playing time. Everybody did. They all worked hard for it." If anything, their inner anger only fueled the team. They channeled their frustrations into practice, pounding away at the starters as leaders of the second string. "We had good, tough practices," Hale noted. "Guys would go at it hard. Taking charges, getting in each other's faces. Maurer was leading the charge for the second team, but also Topo and Barry. They were never going to concede a shot. You got hammered. You never thought you could just take off a practice. You fought every day. Most of the time Barry had [to cover] Squeeze Kamana or Boy Eldredge, and those guys are tough. But we could play with those guys and it was all to better the team. That was the understanding. Your contribution may not be on the court that night at eight o'clock, but what the team reaps is the benefit of your dedication during the week."

After his team finished the preseason schedule, including winning the St. Anthony's Invitational on Maui, McLachlin became increasingly stingy with playing time for Obama and Maurer and most of the other subs. One exception, though not by choice, came in the game against 'Iolani, a smaller private school in Honolulu, on the Friday night of February 2, the first night of the Carnival. In the Punahou social world, nothing compares to the Carnival, a two-day extravaganza of foods (particularly the school's legendary *malasada,* a Portuguese doughnutlike treat), art, auctions, white elephant flea markets, and amusement rides run by the junior class but involving the entire student body, along with faculty and parents. The purpose is to raise money for academic scholarships, such as the one that helped Barry Obama. With the considerable wealth available from the Punahou family, the fund-raising went far beyond the normal school bake sale. For the 1979 Carnival the gross profits were $360,519.01.

But basketball players at Punahou considered Carnival weekend a jinx.

There would be a basketball game on opening night, and usually something would go wrong.

On that Friday afternoon, Barry and the boys were driving back to school after a shoot-around at Neal S. Blaisdell Center, the multiuse arena between Waikiki and downtown Honolulu where they played their league and tournament games. The shoot-arounds were part of the pregame ritual. They returned in a car caravan, with several players jammed into Darin Maurer's van. On the approach to campus, they passed the girls' softball team, and Darryl Gabriel, the star shooting guard, could not resist opening the van's sliding door and yelling out to the girls. Just then, Maurer made a sudden stop and the heavy door slid on its track to close, clobbering Gabriel in the head. "I heard it. THUNK! Whoa! He was down. A big knot on his head," recalled Dan Hale. Alan Lum said, "Gabe had a huge head. His nickname was Pineapple Head." But not even Pineapple Head could withstand the bruising of this playful accident. He was woozy the rest of the night and did not play against 'Iolani, though press reports said he had a swollen ankle. To make matters more problematic, Squeeze Kamana had the flu and could play only sparingly. Their misfortune provided an opening for Obama and Maurer, both of whom played well, though Punahou, in keeping with the Carnival jinx, lost in overtime, 44–42.

In the 'Iolani game and a few others where he saw more playing time, Obama showed a keen court sense. "He could see the pattern and zero in on the opening," said Barbara Czurles-Nelson, who came to all the games and often sat near Barry's grandparents. Stan and Madelyn Dunham were there the night of the 'Iolani game and for almost every game that year. Madelyn sat calmly. It was obvious to Nelson that "she loved that boy." Stan was never quiet, talking and joking his way through the game with anyone who would listen to him. Also sitting nearby were Dan Hale's grandparents, who came to Hawaii from Illinois for the winters. Hale's grandfather, Duke Towner, had been a legendary high school basketball coach in Lexington, Illinois, downstate from Chicago, and he and his wife, Flossie, had grown up in Kansas. The Dunhams and Hales would chat about their midwestern roots while they cheered their grandsons and sang the Punahou alma mater (to the tune of "Maryland, My Maryland") and ended it with the traditional chant: "Strawberry shortcake, Huckleberry Pie, V-I-C-T-O-R-Y."

His name in concrete outside the Punahou cafeteria. The story goes that one of his buddies scratched his name there to get him in trouble.

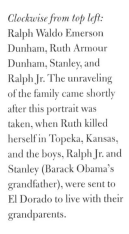

2

Clockwise from top left: Ralph Waldo Emerson Dunham, Ruth Armour Dunham, Stanley, and Ralph Jr. The unraveling of the family came shortly after this portrait was taken, when Ruth killed herself in Topeka, Kansas, and the boys, Ralph Jr. and Stanley (Barack Obama's grandfather), were sent to El Dorado to live with their grandparents.

at Tuesday and Wednesday afternoon.
The Washburn Review, a student

WIFE KILLS SELF

Mrs. Ruth Dunham Ends Life by Taking Poison.

Body Found in Garage on West Sixth Avenue.

Mrs. Ruth Dunham, 25, 703 Buchanan street, ended her life early this morning by taking poison. Dr. H. L. Clark, county coroner, stated it was a case of suicide.

In a letter written before she took the poison, Mrs. Dunham declared the reason for her act was that her husband no longer loved her. She had a disagreement Thursday with her husband, Ralph Dunham, Doctor Clark was told.

The body was found in Dunham's garage, 1137 West Sixth avenue, shortly before 9 o'clock this morning.

In Section 5 of the Sunset Lawns South Cemetery in El Dorado, across the street from an old oil refinery, stands a simple red granite gravestone. It is a lonesome plot surrounded by parched grass, no other markers within fifteen yards. Her relatives are buried elsewhere and her descendants live far away.

5

The gravesite of Barack Obama's great grandfather, Obama Opiyo, in Kenya. The Obamas went back five generations in Kanyadhiang, a village near the upper bay of Lake Victoria, yet were still regarded by some as *jadak*, or alien, because their roots were in Nyang'oma Kogelo, around the bay to the north and west.

Auma Magak (*left*) and Akumu, Obama's Kenyan aunt and grandmother. Akumu, the mother of Barack Obama Sr., fled the family when Barack Sr. was a young boy because of the abuse she received from her husband, Hussein Onyango.

Obama's grandparents not long after Pearl Harbor. Stan Dunham enlisted in the army and went on to serve as a supply sergeant in an ordnance and maintenance company in England and France. Madelyn, meantime, went to work as an inspector on the B-29 assembly line at the huge Boeing factory in Wichita.

8

Stanley Ann with her parents. According to family lore, she was named after her father, who wanted a boy, but in fact there was another inspiration for her unusual name. Madelyn's favorite actress, Bette Davis, played a female character named Stanley in the movie *In This Our Life* in 1942.

When her father, a furniture salesman, moved the family to Vernon, Texas, Stanley Ann (*left, with purse*) attended third and fourth grades at Hawkins Elementary School, where she became part of the Friendly Bluebirds troop. She endured teasing because of her name.

11

Stanley (*top row, fourth from right, without a vest*) belonged to many clubs in high school, including the Mercer Girls social service club, but was always her own person. Growing up amid the gloom of the Cold War, she had "a sense of hope and not despair," one friend said.

Stanley Dunham, Marilyn McMeekin

PETRAM'S TEN CENT STORE

135 Bellevue Square   GI-4-7271

This advertisement for a local drug store appeared in the 1960 yearbook when Stanley was a senior at Mercer Island High near Seattle. In high school, she was an intellectual with a sharp tongue that "could kill."

Barry Obama as a toddler in Honolulu. An American made from the diverse world of color and culture, he was reared by white relatives and grew up mostly in a place, Hawaii, where being *hapa*—half and half—was almost the norm, though the multihued combinations involved mostly Asians and very few blacks.

In Miss Kazuko Sakai's kindergarten class at Noelani Elementary School, Barry (*third row, far left*) was calm and observant, if a bit shy. When there was a commotion across the room, he would "crane his neck and smile, but he wouldn't get involved," said the student teacher.

Despite the mythology of Obama's Muslim roots, evangelical Christian missionaries made the family's rise possible. Barack Obama Sr. (*right*) is shown here with Betty Mooney (*second from left*) who led a Christian-based literacy effort, "Each One Teach One," in Nairobi. She became his mentor, directing him to the University of Hawaii, where he met Stanley Ann Dunham. In the center of the photo is Frank Laubach, the founder of the literacy program.

16

TOURISM OFFICER ON DRINKS CHARGE

By NATION Reporter

A DRUNKEN driver in charge of a motor vehicle is like a man with a loaded gun, a Nairobi traffic magistrate's court was told yesterday when a senior official of the Kenya Tourist Development Corporation was fined £50 and disqualified for a year from driving.

Barack Hussein Obama, pleaded "Guilty" before the Magistrate, Mr. F. E. Abdullah, to a charge of drunken driving.

Insp. Yusuf Malik, prosecuting, said that Obama, while speeding at 4 a.m., collided with a milk handcart on the Ngong Road.

(*left*) Barack Obama Sr. in Kenya with his third wife, Ruth Baker Obama, an American who met him in Boston while he was in graduate school at Harvard, after he and Ann had divorced. Ruth said she was overwhelmed by his sexual magnetism, but finally left him after years of physical abuse fueled by his drinking. (*right*) Obama Sr. was involved in several drunk driving accidents, including this one that made the Nairobi papers. (He eventually was killed in a crash driving home while drunk in November 1982.)

18

After Ann married Lolo Soetoro, an Indonesian she had met at the East-West Center in
Honolulu, she and Barry moved to Jakarta in 1967. Barry's sister, Maya, was born there in
1970. In Indonesia, Barry was overwhelmed by "the vastness of things."

19

During his years in Jakarta, Barry attended local schools, learned the national language,
Bahasa Indonesia, and became immersed in the local culture. His classmates, noting his
darker skin, thought he was from the island of Ambon. Here (*legs crossed*) he visits Lolo's
mother and various relatives in Yogyakarta, the cultural center of Java.

The one and only time father and son met after Barry's parents split during his infancy was when Barack Sr. came to Honolulu for a Christmastime visit in 1971. The old man took an apartment in the Punahou Circle apartments, near Barry's grandparents, and tried to lecture and discipline his ten-year-old son as though he had always been around. Ruth had left him by then, and he tried unsuccessfully to persuade Ann to return to Kenya with him.

Barry (*top row, third from left*) entered Punahou in fifth grade. His first teacher in Room 307 of Castle Hall was Mabel Hefty, an energetic woman beloved by her students, who had traveled the world and spent a year teaching in Kenya. When she learned that Barry's Kenyan father was visiting Honolulu, she invited him to speak to the class.

22

After two failed marriages, two children, and two college degrees, Ann found her vocation as an anthropologist surveying the life and work of villagers on the island of Java, looking for ways to help the peasants and their handicrafts survive in the modern world.

23

Ann was an adventurous woman who fearlessly embraced Javanese culture. She would drink anything and eat whatever was available, whether from a street vendor or in private homes.

Barry Obama (*top row, far right*) made Punahou's varsity basketball team as a senior in 1979, when they won the Hawaii state championship. All five starters went on to play college sports. Obama was the third or fourth man off the bench.

Obama would complain that he did not get enough playing time because he played a "black" style of basketball, but that was debatable. In fact, he was one of the few players on the team who could not jump high enough to dunk the ball. When he did get into games, he proved to be an adept passer who could drive only to his left.

A self-selected group of boys at Punahou School loved basketball and good times and called themselves the Choom Gang. *Choom* was a verb. It meant to smoke marijuana. Barry Obama (*middle right*) was part of the gang, whose lingo included the hand gesture V for *veto*. Also in this photo are his pals Greg Orme (*bottom left*), Tom Topolinski (*bottom center*), and Mark Bendix (*behind and to the right of Obama*).

For their senior homeroom class photo, Eric Kusunoki's students posed at the home of classmate Julie Cooke, a descendant of Hawaii's old *haole* oligarchy. The girls wore flowing dresses and the boys looked like they had just returned from a disco, with Barry Obama (*top row, center*) taking on the role of John Travolta in *Saturday Night Fever*. Kusunoki posed as a butler.

It was not hard for fellow student Lisa Jack, an aspiring Annie Leibovitz, to persuade Occidental College freshman Barry Obama to come down to her off-campus apartment for a photo shoot. He brought along his props—straw hat, bomber jacket, cigarettes—and went through a series of poses. In one roll of film, she said, he "goes from innocent baby to Jimi Hendrix to a Black Panther—from having fun to thoughtful to angst."

Monday June 25ᵗʰ 1984

having been cossetted in Barack's apt. Sat evening,
Sunday, today I arrived back, mentally, in the city.
I got off the subway in Bklyn & smelt good smells
of green things freshly wet. Diana had just got up -
I don't feel as tho it's my house when she's
there - realized I'll feel that more
not going off to work. The eve
lifted by my spirits, as we d
in an extra chapter.
off this morning
trip

After graduating from Columbia, Obama met Genevieve Cook, an Australian who had studied in the United States and shared his love of writing and sense of outsiderness. She, too, had lived in Indonesia as a child. They both kept journals. He wrote mostly about his impressions of city life and his struggle for identity, a subject in her journal as well. "Barack—still intrigues me, but so much going on beneath the surface, out of reach. Guarded, controlled. . . . He is that sort of person—trying hard to be."

It was the election of Mayor Harold Washington that helped lure Obama to Chicago, where he found a sense of home. And it was Washington, later, who led Obama to the conclusion that community organizing could only take him so far. When Washington came down to Roseland to help Obama's Developing Communities Project open a jobs center, Obama realized that the politician's "ability to move people and set an agenda was always going to be superior to anything I could organize at a local level."

31

33

Left: Zirl Smith ran the Chicago Housing Authority during the period that Obama was involved in the effort to rid projects of asbestos. At a meeting at Altgeld Gardens that Obama organized, Smith was shouted down by the crowd and fled to his limousine. *Right:* The Rev. Jeremiah A. Wright Jr., of Trinity United Church of Christ, eventually became Obama's pastor, but another South Side preacher, Rev. Alvin Love (*above*), was more supportive and essential to his rise.

34

No life could have been more the product of randomness than that of Barack Obama. "The only way I could have a sturdy sense of identity of who I was depended on digging beneath the surface differences of people," he told the author in an Oval Office interview. "The only way my life makes sense is if regardless of culture, race, religion, tribe, there is this commonality, these essential human truths and hopes and moral precepts that are universal."

The day after the loss to 'Iolani, the Saturday of the Carnival was forced to a premature close when heavy rains muddied the Punahou grounds and lightning split the skies. Barry Obama did not care. His strong showing gave him more playing time, even against the toughest opponents. When they beat University High in a league tournament game, he came off the bench in the second half and scored six points, winning praise from Honolulu newspaper scribes for his hustle on defense.

We'll die on the court before we lose again was the team's attitude. And soon enough they were in the Hawaii High School Athletic Association championship game for the third straight year. They faced a squad from Moanalua, a public school on a hill out toward Honolulu International Airport that had upset University High in the tournament quarterfinals. On March 10, the day of the final game, McLachlin and his players gathered for a team training meal at Dan Hale's home in Manoa Valley between their school and the University of Hawaii. The Hales frequently opened their doors to Punahou athletes. Dan's older brother, David, in Barry's class, was a competitive swimmer and water polo star. Their father, Dr. Ralph Hale, was a leading figure at the university's medical school. "We always try to have an event like this toward the end of the year," Coach McLachlin explained to Troy Egami, the student reporter who spent the entire day with the team. "When the season gets a little long, we need a little team unity. This is just a good non-gym situation."

It was a sunny day in paradise, and the boys seemed loose as they gathered in the living room before the meal. Some watched a Chaminade game on television; others played the board game Battleship. The twelfth man, Matt Hiu, team prankster and comic, rose and delivered a stirring pep talk that bordered on satirical hyperbole, shouting "GOD ONLY KNOWS! WE WILL NOT BE DENIED! *IMUA OHANA*!" – Go forward with spirit, family! His pal Alan Lum finally shut him up by punching him.

The midafternoon meal was a feast: chili, rice, cold cuts, chop suey, salad, potato and mac salads, cinnamon bars, apple bars, and plates piled high with Super Burgers. The coach's wife, Beth McLachlin, a health food advocate, was the creator of the Super Burger. She had been making them for nine years, starting with her husband's first JV team, a ravenous horde that included Mosi

Tatupu, who went on to star as a running back for the New England Patriots, and the massive Keith Uperesa, who played briefly as an offensive lineman for the Oakland Raiders. The ingredients in the hamburgers included carrots, celery, onions, teriyaki sauce, wheat germ, and what McLachlin described as "a mystery substance that makes them jump higher." The power of the Super Burger was mystical, according to Dan Hale. "It was the power of commitment – we were committed to eating them." This was "the post-hippie era when everything was alfalfa sprouts and soy beans," said Tom Topolinski, yet the Super Burgers tasted so good that he and Barry and their teammates devoured them along with the rest of the food, for better or worse.

"I figure I ain't going to play the first half," said Lum, as Egami watched him attack the training table.

Boy Eldredge walked by with "a heaping plate" of chili and rice. "This is only my second serving," he said. "Coach told me to take it easy on the food today."

"Hawaiian people know how to eat," Topolinski explained decades later. "Boy Eldredge was a freaking pig. I have never met anyone who ate that much food on a regular basis. But he was lean and burned that shit off. But he made us pay for it. He and Matt Hiu were known to be the Gas Bombs. Cleared out the pregame locker room during chalk talk."

After lunch, some players went up to Dan's bedroom, where a Nerf basketball hoop was suctioned to his wall. "Slam dunks," Hale recalled. "Flying slam dunks against the wall. It sounded like the house was crashing down." No-jump Barry could slam-dunk a Nerf ball. Eventually they calmed down, went into meditation mode, visualizing what they would do on the court that night. At five-thirty they left the house – cars, jeeps, and vans backing out of the crowded driveway – and returned to Punahou to get dressed. Darryl Gabriel, a star who acted like one, a cocksure killer, went through his pregame preening, as he described to Egami: "We take showers, blow-dry our hair, brush our teeth, put on cologne like we're going to the theater. Nah, we just like to smell nice for the other team." They dressed in white uniforms, the short shorts of that era, with shimmering blue warm-up suits. Topo was "the biggest Boston freak on the whole campus" and tended to control locker-room music. His theme song of choice, "More Than a Feeling," was blasting away. On the ride to Blaisdell Center, the bus reverberated with the team shrieking "We Will Rock You" and "Poor, Poor Pitiful Me." As they unloaded, someone realized they were wearing the wrong uniforms; Moanalua was to be in white. Greg Ramos, one of Barry's buddies, a junior adjunct member of the Choom Gang, was the team manager; he later acknowledged the mix-up was his fault. No one seemed to care. These hours were supreme for a high school athlete. "The players majestically strode into the arena as their little admirers flooded around them as if they were Blue and Buff Gods," Egami noted. "They willingly signed autographs and received handshakes from parents and well-wishers," including Stan and Madelyn Dunham. Twelve young gods, Barry among them, adored. Topo gazed into the stands as they made their way toward the locker room. "The crowd is UNREAL!" he shouted. Full house, standing room only.

The trainer arrived with the right uniforms, and McLachlin reviewed the game strategy on a chalkboard after they changed. They could hear the roar of the crowd; a lesser game was finishing. The coach started shouting, his players more intense with every word: "We must scramble. . . . We must guard the baseline. . . . We have to run UCLA, Vegas, North Carolina on defense." Then his voice softened. "You know you've come a long way since the Maui tournament. . . . No matter what happens tonight, this year has been a success. . . . I'm proud of every one of you. You're all as good as everyone says you are. You are OUT OF THIS WORLD like all the sports writers say. Listen, we've got the good uniforms, we've got the good bench, and the good basket to start the game. Let's go out there and play thirty-two minutes of clinic basketball. Let's go out there and do it for one more half. LET'S TAKE THIS THING!"

The Buffanblu raced out from the locker room into the arena lights, Boy Eldredge leading the way ("Last half, seniors!" he yelled), followed by his classmates: Gabriel, Tavares, Topolinski, Orme, Oshima, Maurer, and Obama, and underclassmen Kamana, Hale, Lum, and Hiu. Prep school versus public school. Powerhouse versus underdog. Experience versus newcomer. No one expected Moanalua to be there. They were slated to lose long ago to University High. They had two African American brothers, the Johnsons, sparking their rise. "They were on a roll. They were Cinderella," recalled Alan Lum. "I remember stretching before the game, and I remember looking up and it was standing room only and we had a little section of Punahou but the rest was basically Moanalua. And it would have been a great story if they had come in and won, but . . ."

Not a chance. In the opening minutes, Punahou scored fifteen straight points and jumped ahead 18–4. They were pressing, double-teaming, cornering, smothering. Moanalua went eleven minutes and fifty-one seconds during one early stretch without making a field goal, missing fourteen consecutive shots, while Punahou was hitting two of every three shots. Pineapple Head was feeling it, getting feeds on the wing from Tavares and pouring them in. Squeeze was jumping out of the gym. McLachlin, who rarely let up, knew the game was theirs. "I remember him pulling out Squeeze and me in the first quarter, fairly early in the game, and I remember I was confused," Hale recalled. "Why are we going out? Championship game. We gotta go! And he went, 'Danny, look at the score.' And it was something like 35 to 3 [not quite, but almost]. It was such a team of dedication and it all came together at that moment."

Topo was sent in, and Oshima and Obama, and Orme and Maurer. Matt Hiu shouted with excitement, "I might play!" – and he was right. Everyone played. Near the end, Boy Eldredge asked McLachlin if all eight seniors could go in together in the final minute. Barry ended up making the box score, with 2 points, but executed some nifty passes and played stifling defense. Gabriel had 18, Kamana 15, Hale 9, on the way to an overwhelming win, 60–28. At the end, the crowd recognized their brilliance and showered the winners with love and cheers. Little boys rushed the court. Parents and grandparents and teachers and friends came forward after the awards ceremony (Gabes was MVP) and placed lei after lei around the necks of the ecstatic champions.

On the bus ride home, McLachlin choked up speaking to his team. "This particular team in this particular tournament played as good a game as I've ever seen a high school team play. You played a perfect game – and that included everyone who stepped on the court. This is the finest effort by twelve young men that I have ever seen." It was also the last time he coached Punahou basketball. He decided to go out with a perfect game.

Troy Egami was with McLachlin and the players, soaking it in, gathering material for his story, and that night he noticed something for the first time about Barry Obama. Egami was a year younger, but he had known Barry since they played on the same seventh-and-eighth-grade football team coached by Pal Eldredge, when Obama was a chubby lineman who grunted a lot in pads and helmet. Egami watched over the years as Obama thinned out and chilled out. Now Barry wanted to be part of history. He wanted recognition. He wanted to be recorded in this glorious moment. He had seemed so cool and laid-back – *never panicked, never fazed* – but now his burning will was on rare display. "One thing that stuck in my mind was the extent to which Barry . . . was in my face giving me the equivalent of sound bites, giving quotes left and right," Egami recalled decades later. "He made sure he got something he said in the paper. Such good stuff, I couldn't leave it out, though kind of schmaltzy. That night I knew there was a side to him that was scary. This guy is ambitious. He wanted the quote, and he got it": " 'You know,' said Barry Obama in a quiet moment off to the side. 'These are the best bunch of guys. We made so many sacrifices to get here.'"

Virtually none of this part of Barry's basketball history was recorded in *Dreams from My Father*. Nor should that have been expected. Most anecdotes in his memoir flowed through the thematic stream of race. So the reader learned of a few jolting moments of awareness and understandable anger, such as when a JV coach flippantly used the word *niggers* to describe black players in a pickup game, and then lamely tried to differentiate them from people like Obama. The result was powerful storytelling. But what he left out unwittingly made it easier for political critics decades later to portray him as a *jadak,* a stranger in their midst, whose life was outside the American mainstream – a purposefully negative construct derived from distorted history. If there is a representative teenager's life, Barry Obama lived a version of it in Hawaii in the late 1970s. Several things stood out: he went to a prestigious school, he lived with his grandparents, his father was gone, his mother was infrequently present, he was a *hapa* black in a place where most people were a lighter shade of brown. And those traits helped shape his character, but they did not make his life odd or mysterious. He smoked pot with his Choom Gang and goofed around outside the classroom, where he came across as smart and mature if not notably studious. But the central activity of his high school life was basketball. With equally strong roots in the Kansas of his forebears and the playgrounds of black America, basketball connected the disconnected parts of him – and he was good enough to play with "the best bunch of guys" on the best team in Hawaii, one of the best teams in the nation.

The diverse collection at Cooke Library at Punahou, on par with many college libraries, included the canon of black literature. By his senior year, Barry had checked out and read much of it. "I gathered up books from the library – Baldwin, Ellison, Hughes, Wright, Du Bois. At night I would close the door to my room, telling my grandparents I had homework to do, and there I would sit and wrestle with words – locked in suddenly desperate argument, trying to reconcile the world as I found it with the terms of my birth." It was an anguishing process, he said. Each of the great black writers seemed trapped in despair or anger, withdrawing finally to Africa, Europe, and "deeper into the bowels of Harlem, all of them exhausted, bitter men." The story of Malcolm X appealed to him, with "his repeated self-creation," but an assertion in *The Autobiography of Malcolm X* unsettled him, "the wish that the white blood that ran through him, there by an act of violence, might somehow be expunged." There was no violent history in the white blood that ran through Barry Obama. His skin color defined him to much of American society, but his personal history was different, without the same emotional baggage. He had no female ancestors raped by white slave owners. His African father came to America of his own volition, on scholarship, part of a freedom movement in Kenya. Barack Obama II was created by an interracial romance. He grew up comforted by a myth about his missing black father, a fantasy created as an act of love and grace by his white mother. He lived with a white grandfather who perpetuated the myth and a white grandmother who was the bedrock of the family, a woman who did the hard work that supported him without emotion or commotion. "So long as you kids do well, Bar. That's all that really matters," she would say.

In Obama's retelling of his high school life, one of the lasting images is of the day he overheard his grandparents arguing about a strange black man who stood on the corner near the Punahou Circle Apartments where Tut caught the six-thirty bus every morning for the ride downtown to her job at the Bank of Hawaii. In his memoir, he recalled that this black man scared his grandmother with his unpredictable behavior, and that Gramps told her she should not be scared. This made Obama consider his own situation and the assumptions society makes based on skin color. He added that the episode upset him so much that he fled into the night to consult with the mangy old shaman, the black poet Frank (Frank Marshall Davis), at his run-down shack near the Ala Wai Canal, and returned home hours later feeling "for the first time that I was utterly alone." This appeared to be an instance in which Obama slightly rearranged his life's chronology, a literary device that in the memoir's introduction he acknowledged doing here and there. Other documents indicate that the bus stop incident occurred a year later, when he had returned to Honolulu for the summer after his freshman year in college. By then he had seen more of the world and made friends with more black contemporaries, with whom he had probed more deeply into the racial dilemma.

The key phrase in the bus stop account, regardless of chronology, was "utterly alone." Did Barry feel that way in high school, and if so, did that alter his behavior? Writing a bit of self-analysis in the *Punahou Bulletin,* the alumni magazine, twenty years after his graduation, he said that it did: "My budding awareness of life's unfairness made for a more turbulent adolescence than perhaps some of my classmates' experiences. As an African American in a school with few African Americans, I probably questioned my identity a bit harder than most. As a kid from a broken home and family of relatively modest means, I nursed more resentments than my circumstances justified, and didn't always channel those resentments in particularly constructive ways." This might have been offered as an explanation for his Choom Gang escapades, and perhaps as the reason he shunned political leadership roles at school, yet whatever disillusionment he carried inside he kept there. The Punahou family never heard it, barely sensed it. It seeped out once in a while, obliquely, in his writing. He wrote a poem titled "An Old Man" for Punahou's literary magazine laced with loneliness and lost identity.

> I saw an old, forgotten man
> On an old, forgotten road.
> Staggering and numb under the glare of the
> Spotlight. His eyes, so dull and grey,

Slide from right to left, to right,

Looking for his life, misplaced in a

Shallow, muddy gutter long ago.

I am found, instead.

Seeking a hiding place, the night seals us together.

A transient spark lights his face, and in my hour,

He pulls out forgotten dignity from under his flaking coat,

And walks a straight line along the crooked world.

This poem revealed what was churning inside young Barry, who could see more clearly than most of his peers the crookedness of the world. Crooked not in the superficial sense of corruption, but the deeper sense of imperfection. Without dismissing his expressions of angst, it is worth keeping in mind that most teenagers have insecurities and questions of identity. Barry's teachers thought of him as sensible and well adjusted, not as resentful or rebellious. "He was very positive, very warm. I mean he had a serious side too, but . . . he carried himself very well. Or he kept the lid on," recalled Eric Kusunoki, his homeroom teacher from ninth grade to graduation. "He was able to deal with it very well because it never came out in the way he behaved or the way he reacted." The same assessment came from classmates and teammates. Bruce Arinaga, the Korean Japanese *hapa,* thought of Barry as "a happy-go-lucky guy." Alan Lum, an adopted child of Chinese parents, never sensed Barry's discomfort: "He would walk on campus confidently, always smiling. In my mind I thought he was comfortable here." If Obama nursed resentments and was not always constructive, Lum failed to notice, and in fact thought the opposite: "I always looked up to him because what he said was pretty right. He was an honorable person, so I respected him for that. If Maurer said something I would say, 'Come on, Maurer, that's not what we're doing.' If Barry said something, you would think, 'All right.'" Tom Topolinski, the Chinese Polish *hapa,* said that after "many outings, parties, hangouts, games, and trips" with Barry, he picked up no signs of alienation or loneliness: "In Hawaii we are all of mixed races and backgrounds, so it is not a huge topic to converse about our origins." When he was with Barry, Topo added, "there was never any bitterness, identity crisis, or internal strife. . . . I hung out with Barry and the Choom Gang a lot. He never appeared distraught, even after a lot of pot smoking and beer drinking. Barry was stable, and didn't have the mood swings that typically coincide with the teenage years."

Tony Peterson, the older black Punahou student who met regularly with Barry for a year's worth of Ethnic Corner discussions, "didn't doubt all the agony" Obama said he endured, but thought it must have come after their year together because "that was not what I experienced at all. Our little chats were not agonizing. They were just sort of for fun. But we were helping each other find out who we are." Peterson's younger brother, Keith, a year behind Barry and on the fringe of the Choom Gang, had assumed that Obama "was much more comfortable with that [Punahou] environment than I was." Mike Ramos, the Filipino Czech *hapa* a year older than Barry, spent years playing pickup basketball with him. They talked constantly, shared an interest in writing, and tended to look at the world with a similar observer's sensibility. Much like Obama, he later went off in search of his roots, and wrote about the Philippines in a series of short stories he titled *Polvoron,* for a Filipino sugar candy. But during all of their discussions in high school, Ramos "actually had very little clue" that his friend waged such an internal struggle: "Partly I am sure it was because I was so obtuse and into my own introspection." Mike's little brother, Greg, in the class behind Obama, thought of Barry as "the kind of guy who kept people in a good mood. There were always little games you do as kids, teasing each other. He was always in the mix, never on the sidelines." As one of only two Filipinos in his Punahou class, the younger Ramos believed that he was "as much of an outsider as Barry was." Aside from their Filipino background, the Ramos brothers and their sister, Connie, who was in Barry's class, had their own broken home to deal with; their parents divorced during their Punahou years.

The paradox of Hawaii was that it was an ethnic stew where difference was the norm and more accepted than in most places, yet diversity created its own form of tension for everyone. By Dan Hale's account, *haole* had their own racial anxieties even though they had been at the top of the socioeconomic ladder since their arrival on the islands. "I experienced a lot of racism growing up. If you're a *haole* here you're a minority most places," Hale said. "There was a lot of anti-*haole* stuff going on, and I caught a lot of that. . . . I didn't like it. . . . 'Fuck you, *haole.*' Playing basketball helped. [People might say] 'Oh, yeah, you played with my cousin.' I don't think I feared for my life, maybe once or twice." Hale would not forget the day during his Punahou middle school years when he and a friend were "at the Chink Store," and some native Hawaiian boys from William P. Jarrett walked in looking for some Buffanblu to rough up on "Kill Haole Day." "Squeeze," John Kamana III, Hale's basketball buddy, also native Hawaiian, "comes flying out of nowhere" to protect him – "the big hero of the day."

"The Chink Store" – the casual use of that phrase said something else about Honolulu and ethnicity. This was not Dan Hale using a slur. The Chink Store is what everyone in Honolulu called Alexander Grocery, a one-room market near Punahou run by Mrs. Lau that sold the best shave ice in the neighborhood. (Shave ice is the Hawaiian, and local folks would say far superior, version of a snow cone.) Chink Store was applied to Alexander's without a derogatory meaning. People who would not think of calling a Chinese individual a Chink nonetheless had no qualms about saying Chink Store. The faded red wooden Chink Store was part of the landscape of Barry Obama's formative years, a tiny piece of concrete real estate where *haole* and *hapa,* native Hawaiian and African American, Japanese and Korean, Filipino and Portuguese, Chinese and Okinawan, football star and basketball junkie, math nerd and drama kid, blonde girl driving a BMW and dark-haired boy riding the city bus, golden paddler from the Outrigger Canoe Club and bodysurfer from the Choom Gang, found sweet relief.

In a survey of college admissions officers, Punahou was ranked among the ten best secondary schools in the nation. Mrs. Lucille Finlayson was reminded of that status almost every day in her administrative office on the first floor of Alexander Hall, where she arranged the visits of dozens of college recruitment officers and processed a total of 2,440 applications for the seniors, an average of six per student. The college representatives came in November and December, from Brown and Duke in the East, Coe College and Notre Dame in the Midwest, Pomona College and Southern Cal on the West Coast. The recruiter from Occidental, a small liberal arts school on the rim of Los Angeles, appeared at ten o'clock on the morning of November 16. Oxy was one of the more popular possibilities. It was away, on the mainland, but not too far away. Its campus was compact and handsome, its academic reputation first-rate, and both the cultural atmosphere and L.A. weather allowed for the wearing of shorts and slippers year-round. If one could imagine a higher educational branch of Punahou, in other words, Occidental was it. When decisions were made that spring, five Punahou seniors were accepted at Oxy, including two members of the championship basketball team, Jason Oshima and Barry Obama. So much for the idea Barry had tossed at his mother to alarm her – that he was of a mind to stay home for a year and work and go to school part-time. He might still be somewhat of a good-time Charlie, as she called him, but luck was coming his way. He had chosen Occidental, he said, largely because of a pretty girl he had met who was vacationing in Honolulu with her family. She was from Brentwood in L.A., and that was enough for him – along with the fact that he received a scholarship.

The imminent diaspora of Eric Kusunoki's homeroom was fairly typical, with everyone college bound. The students who for four years had begun each school day in Mr. Kuz's classroom would soon be going to Claremont, Colorado, Cornell, Harvard, Hawaii, Michigan, Montana, Occidental, Oregon, Oregon State, Santa Clara, and UC Santa Cruz. Only four were staying in Honolulu, including three slated to attend the university and one – not Barry Obama but Whitey Kahoohanohano – planning to work while attending Kapi'olani Community College. One day in late May, a few weeks before graduation, the homeroom class posed for their yearbook photo. They had recently celebrated with an ice cream social at the president's house, an academic honors assembly (no awards for Obama), a Senior Skip Day, and a Saturday-night potluck dinner at Mr. Kusunoki's home in St. Louis Heights, chomping on chicken and hot dogs and playing with the teacher's eighteen-month-old daughter. By then they had plotted how they wanted to look for posterity. On the scheduled morning of the photo shoot, with their time in homeroom extended for the occasion, they dashed out of Pauahi Hall, clambered into a caravan of cars, and drove to the Manoa Valley estate of classmate Julie Cooke, a descendant of Hawaii's old *haole* oligarchy. They posed in the mansion's living room around an elegant set of couches and tables. The girls wore flowing skirts and dresses, the boys looked like they had just returned from a disco. At the center of the back row stood Barry Obama as John Travolta in *Saturday Night Fever,* wearing a white leisure suit, collar wide, shirt open to the chest, Afro rounded and trim and rising above the throng. "They said, 'Let's dress up, and you can be the butler,'" Kusunoki recalled. "That's why I'm holding a towel in the pose, on my knees."

In another section of the yearbook, students were given a block of space to express thanks and define their high school experience. Barry's display included one photograph of him playing pickup basketball, shirtless, with the caption "We go play hoop," and another that showed him in the white disco suit again, with a more colorful shirt and an even wider collar. Nestled below the photographs was one odd line of gratitude: "Thanks Tut, Gramps, Choom Gang, and Ray for all the good times." Ray was the older guy who hung around the Choom Gang, selling them pot. A hippie drug dealer made his acknowledgments; his own mother did not.

The graduation ceremony was staged at Blaisdell Center the night of June 2. The class assembled at school and rode to the arena in buses. No robes, but matching outfits: the girls in white dresses with long lace sleeves and high lace necks, the boys in seventy-five-dollar blue blazers that bore the Punahou patch, a living stream. They all wore the glossy green-leafy *maile* lei, and the girls also had a delicate *pikake* lei, with its fragrant white flower. Music was at the heart of the graduation ritual; seniors had to sing for their diploma. Since the end of April there had been six weeks of rehearsal for the entire class, mandatory: two unexcused absences and you were out of the ceremony. Classmates had written some of the songs and chosen the others. They sang the school anthem, "Oahu Ahj," and a medley of Hawaiian tunes, old and new, some just for the girls, some the boys, many together. One of the contemporary songs they performed was "This Day Belongs to Me" by Seals & Crofts, from the soundtrack of *One on One,* a Robbie Benson movie about Barry Obama's favorite sport. They sat onstage, in bleachers facing the audience, for the speeches, and then came down row by row to receive their diplomas. David Hale, Danny's older brother, bound for UCLA on a water polo scholarship, was the last boy in the last row. When he reached the stage, he opened his blazer and out flew a dove, winging its way up toward the rafters.

Each student was allotted four ground-floor tickets. Barry's went to Tut and Gramps and his mother and sister. Ann and Maya had flown back from Jakarta only three days earlier. Ann had been going nonstop in Indonesia for three years, moving back and forth between anthropological fieldwork in pursuit of a doctorate and short-term consultancies that helped pay the bills. She was thirty-six now, and she and Maya had just moved from Yogyakarta to Semarang, a busy port city of 1.4 million residents on the north coast of Java, where they lived with a dog named Spot, two rabbits, and, she reported in a letter, "two absolutely hilarious baby goats born on Easter evening." She was still legally married, but her relationship with Lolo was long over and a divorce was coming. She wore a red dress to Barry's graduation, and nine-year-old Maya was in white.

Before Barry left for the postgraduation party at the Pearl Harbor Officers' Club, where Mari Ota's father, a navy captain, guarded the door to make sure no one slipped off to drink or smoke *pakalolo* (futile effort: "A magical night," said Tom Topolinski. "We were all intermingling, passing around joints and Southern Comfort"); and before Barry rode the bus back to Punahou for a middle-of-the-night breakfast that ended in a raucous food fight; and before he took one last walk from the the Dole cafeteria toward the athletic complex, along a pathway where OBAMA had been etched in cement by a friend's mischievous finger, the one lasting reminder of his years there; and before he escaped with his Choom Gang pals out to Makapu'u Beach on the east shore to watch the sunrise – before all that, Barry posed for photographs with Tut and Gramps and Ann and Maya. All smiles, one lei atop another adorning his beloved neck, a family reunited.

CHAPTER 13

RIDING PONIYEM

The young mother and her son, separated by only eighteen years, grew up together, in a sense, but made their way alone and apart. While Barry Obama attended Punahou School in Hawaii, biding his time, playing basketball and hanging out with the Choom Gang, Ann Dunham Soetoro reached a point of clarity in her career. After two failed marriages, two children, and two college degrees, she found her passion as an anthropologist surveying the life and work of villagers on the island of Java, looking for ways to help the peasants and their handicrafts survive in the modern world.

Leaving Barry behind when Ann and her daughter, Maya, returned to Indonesia was partly his choice. No way was he going to drop his buddies and his American existence to live in that strange country again. But perhaps the critical choice was not his. Ann could have chosen to be with him in Honolulu rather than pursue her interests in a distant land during the final years of the 1970s. When she did not, the son struggled to reconcile her contradictions. She exuded goodness and unconditional love, she would do anything for her family – except sublimate her will and sacrifice her career. She had taught her son the importance of empathy, urging him to put himself in others' shoes, and the likelihood is that had he been in her situation, given his will and determination to avoid traps, he would have made the same choices she made. But it would be expecting wisdom beyond the capacity of a teenager for him to absolve his mother then and there. Her absence intensified his feelings of loneliness, he would say, and in moments of anger and self-pity he cursed her selfishness.

For Barry's little sister, their mother's choice produced an entirely different effect. Like her brother, Maya was a *hapa* in Hawaii, but in Indonesia she was Indonesian, and fully at home. She had learned Bahasa Indonesia as a first language, and as the daughter of Soetoro was accepted into the Martodihardjo family. That Ann and Lolo were separated, and soon to be divorced, did not rupture the connection. Ann was still embraced by Lolo's relatives, so much so that she and Maya moved in with Djoeminah, Lolo's mother, Maya's grandmother, or *eyang,* when they arrived in Yogyakarta, the city Ann would use as home base for anthropological excursions into the Javanese countryside.

Maya was under the impression, then and later, that her grandmother had royal blood and was related somehow to Sultan Hamengkubuwono. That blood relationship, Maya believed, explained why her grandmother was able to maintain a home on the grounds of the ruins of the old sultan's pleasure palace. The royalty story appears to be myth, not unlike the myth that Djoeminah's husband, Martodihardjo, was killed while fighting for independence against the Dutch, rather than the prosaic truth that he died falling off a stool while hanging drapes. And not unlike the myths from the Obamas in Kenya that Hussein Onyango was a Luo chief or that he was tortured by the British during the Mau Mau rebellion. Interviews with five Martodihardjo relatives in Yogyakarta and Jakarta turned up none who believed that Djoeminah had royal blood. But the second part of the story is fact. The grandmother did live near the ancient ruins of the sultan's pleasure palace in the Ngasem neighborhood, close to a cacophonous bird market and an alley where women crafted colorful batik prints.

Yogyakarta was independent and soulful, with a magical blend of ancient and modern, and Maya's new home near the historic center was a playland of the senses for an impressionable young girl: birds chirping and cawing, monkeys shrieking, huge turtles lumbering in slow-motion silence; the intense smell of burning wax used in batik printing; open markets everywhere, street sellers hawking wares on five-legged carts known as *kaki lima;* narrow paths winding through the ruins like entrails; badminton matches amid the ruins; walks to the *kraton,* the sultan's new palace; eating snacks and peering through the palace gates to watch elaborate dances and gamelan performances with drums, gongs, and xylophones, and shadow puppet shows that lasted all through the night. Maya's grandmother was part of the exotica, elegant if wrinkled, a diminutive doyenne with her betel juice and silver spittoon who sat there, warmly, incipient Alzheimer's disease confusing her thought patterns. "I couldn't have a conversation with her, but she was just sort of present," Maya recalled. No matter, Maya had an entire neighborhood of "aunties" to look after her when her mother was working.

That happened to be most of the time. Her mother's work never stopped. Alice Dewey, who served as Ann's thesis advisor at the University of Hawaii and shared her interest in Indonesian peasant culture, later remarked, "That woman worked harder than anyone I ever knew." When Barry was a boy in Jakarta, Ann would awake before dawn to tutor him before sending him off to the local schools. She decided with Maya that until age eleven she would avoid the Indonesian schools and teach her exclusively at home. That meant once again waking in the dark to begin lessons, and also, when she could, returning to the task twelve hours later, after a long day of research. And then on to more work after Maya was asleep. Looking back on that period from the distance of decades, Maya could see her mother undergoing a political and personal awakening during that second tour in Indonesia. By trying to understand and empower the subjects of her fieldwork, she came to understand and empower herself. As her daughter put it, "She started feeling competent . . . and I think she really got a voice." She had the tirelessness of someone who loved her work, her long days and nights fueled by an obsession.

Late in the spring of 1977, as Barry finished his sophomore year at Punahou, Ann started the research that would define the rest of her life. She needed help to undertake her fieldwork, and found it in the team of Djaka Waluja and his wife, Sumarni, who served as guides, translators, drivers, and research assistants. Ann recruited them from the Institute of Demography at Gadjah Mada University in Yogyakarta, where Sumarni worked as a research assistant. The trio spent a week filling out forms at the Department of Industrial Matters and other government departments in various locations in the larger District of Yogyakarta, obtaining the permits necessary to conduct research in the handicraft villages. And then their adventures began.

Ann did not drive, and Djaka and Sumarni did not have a car. Their only mode of transportation was a Yamaha Bebek 70cc motorbike with thin wheels, a high, narrow frame, and low horsepower. Either Djaka or Sumarni would drive and the other would stay behind, depending on that day's distance and terrain, until Sumarni accepted another job at the university's medical school and Djaka took over full-time. It was quite a sight – this tall, pale-skinned Western woman with long frizzy hair and a flowing ankle-length batik skirt weighing down the back, riding sidesaddle as the overburdened motorbike chugged along ancient roads wending from Yogya to remote villages fifty to a hundred kilometers away. Most of the roads were made of uneven shards of limestone that could deflate the tires during dry season and proved especially challenging after rains, when molds and mosses turned the surfaces slick. More than once the road became so slippery that Djaka lost control and skidded into a ditch. They were fortunate to suffer nothing more than minor cuts and bruises, he said. Ann, her knee bloodied, broke into laughter after one spill and said to him, "I don't know when I'll be able to experience this kind of thing again, Joko!" (She always pronounced his name Joko, at his suggestion.) After a long and strenuous ride one morning, they took a break near a forest outside Wonosari. "That bike is my hero!" Ann exclaimed. "Can we give the bike a name?" Djaka thought this a fine idea. When Ann asked him what they should call it, he blurted out the first name that crossed his mind. "Poniyem."

A Javanese name as common among villagers as Beth or Sue in the United States, Poniyem had the added value of sounding like it derived from *pony*, a perfect name for the little bike. From then on, whenever they were sputtering uphill in first gear, Ann would hit the side of the saddle and shout, "C'mon, Poniyem! C'mon, Poniyem!"

For most of two years, Ann rode on the back of Poniyem traversing the

Yogyakarta District and farther east and west on Java to study villagers whose livelihoods depended on cottage industries. They spent time in Kampung and Kajar, Pocung and Sumber, Purwosari and Paseseh. They returned again and again to villages that specialized in bamboo basketry and paddy hats, iron and steel blacksmithing, hand-painted batik and heirloom weaving. On a normal day Ann rose at four-thirty, reached the chosen village by seven, conducted interviews and observed people at work all day, returned home by nightfall, then spent several more hours with Djaka translating and transcribing interviews and recording her findings in field notebooks. Working twenty-hour days, slogging through the rain, sweltering in the heat, Ann persisted without complaint. "At most," recalled Djaka, "she would only exhale hard and mutter, 'Well this is nothing, Joko, compared with what we're going to have in hell later.'" For his part, Djaka found the experience so exhausting that he had to drink a supplement called Tonikum Bayer to keep from collapsing.

In her fieldwork, Ann exhibited the curiosity and diligence of an investigative reporter and the exactitude of a scientist. She could stand for hours and watch a blacksmith at work, recording what she saw and waiting for the right moment to pose a question. She would travel to the same village and talk to the same people day after day, week after week, until she was certain she had accumulated enough valid statistical information to support her analysis. She asked detailed questions while constantly leafing through her notebook to cross-check answers with those from previous respondents. If the information conflicted, she would not hesitate to go back to the first source – usually on the same day, according to Djaka – to try to establish the most accurate account. When people said they were unable to answer her questions, Ann would press them harder, often bluntly asking them how they could possibly not know the answer. "She was rather persistent," Djaka said later. Laughing, he added, "It happened often that her respondents got angry at her." By late afternoon, when a day's interviews were done, she would linger and talk to the village elders, asking them to explain the local history or expound on how the encroachment of the modern world had changed their peasant culture. Ann was fluent in Bahasa Indonesia, but most villagers spoke only the native Javanese language, which Djaka would translate for her.

Although Ann had married two unreconstructed sexist men, had spent much of the past decade in male-dominant Indonesia, and had been far from the action when the feminist movement swept across the United States in the early 1970s, she was decidedly a feminist. In her fieldwork, she paid special attention to gender equity issues and the ways, blatant or subtle, that village women were treated unfairly. One of the questions she tried to answer in every setting was this: "When men and women are hired to do the same task, are they paid the same amount?" She never cooked the statistics to make an ideological point. In fact, she found most often that women did receive the same pay as men for the same work, though it was often the case that higher-paying tasks were assigned to men and certain other jobs, with lower pay, were left to women. Often, she noted in her journals, "teasing and derision are the mechanisms used to enforce the sexual division of labor." In a village where clay pottery was made, men did all the stacking and firing, for the most pay, but "a male would face high hilarity if he used the slow wheel, which is perceived to be exclusively female."

In the village of Pocung, one of the historic homes of shadow-puppet craftsmen, Ann learned that the formerly all-male trade had begun to change; forty of the two hundred puppet makers were women. But there was a lingering taboo, she discovered. Women were allowed to make smaller puppets, but could not make the full-size perforated leather figures used in traditional wayang performances. While puppet making survived, many of the other traditional handicrafts had all but died in Pocung, forcing men to improvise livelihoods. By the time Ann did her fieldwork there in 1977, the young men of Pocung had developed their own specialty as long-distance circuit traders. Some would buy oil lamps in the markets of Yogya, take them by train or bus across the island to Jakarta, and "hawk them by shoulder pole around the fringes of the city where there was no electricity." Others would buy birds from the bird market near Maya's grandmother's house and sell them as far away as Singapore and Malaysia.

Among the blacksmiths in the village of Kajar, who enjoyed the highest social and economic status, Ann's field survey recorded six hundred men and only seventeen women. The rest of the women worked in the farm fields from seven to ten each morning and again from two to five each afternoon. In between they performed household chores and cooked for the men working in the blacksmith shops, known as *perapen*. Ann spent several months in Kajar studying the blacksmith trade, looking at the practical side, how it worked economically, and the cultural side, the rituals and ceremonies that shaped the local culture. She noted that each *perapen* was a sacred place with sacred elements within it, including the fire hearth and the nail-shaped anvil, a phallic symbol associated with power. There was a mystical quality to the blacksmiths, she learned: it was thought that they forged human souls. She watched as offerings were given to the fire hearth on the first day of every Javanese week. She observed the annual ceremony known as *Selamatan Empu*, where all of the *empu* (the honored elder blacksmiths) of the village "marched in procession with offerings to the top of a limestone hill behind the village."

Alice Dewey visited Ann in Yogyakarta and accompanied her during a field trip up the winding mountain roads to Kajar. As Ann's thesis advisor, Dewey was struck by how many of her respondents had turned into friends. "We would arrive at the blacksmith village and it was 'Hi, Ann, how are you doing? How is Maya?' She would whip out a notebook and ask, 'How many are you selling?' 'What are the prices?' 'How is business?' 'How is the supply of iron and steel?' She knew the process of forging. She knew the cost of things. She knew all of that." But Dewey came to realize that Ann was just as knowledgeable about the other handicraft subcultures. She could talk weaving with weavers, puppet making with leatherworkers, batiks with batik makers, and ceramics with potters. This was all fascinating, Dewey thought, but unwieldy for the academic purposes of a doctoral thesis. "I said, 'For God's sake, choose one of them!'" Dewey recalled. Not then, but much later, she would settle on the blacksmiths.

Maya also remembered going into the field with her mother now and then; the scenes in the countryside were as evocative as those on the bountiful streets of Yogyakarta. She saw basket weavers and tile makers and once accompanied her mother on a trip to a cigarette factory where they employed girls only a few years older than she to roll clove cigarettes. The girls were chosen for the task because their hands were so small. Ann also took Maya forty miles north of Yogyakarta to see Borobudur, the world's largest Buddhist temple, which was begun as a Hindu shrine in the eighth century, and an equal distance south to the Indian Ocean spot where, according to local lore, the Goddess of the South Seas dwelled. As much as young Maya loved to read from the homeschooling books that arrived from Maryland, these adventures with her mother left a more lasting impression.

Ann was at once respectful of the rural culture in central Java and occasionally alarmed by its injustices. This was one of her defining traits, an ability to understand and empathize with people and look for the beauty and meaning in their lives, without blinding herself to their flaws. That is how she dealt with Barack Hussein Obama, and how she dealt with Lolo Soetoro, and how she viewed the Javanese villagers. Djaka Waluja saw Ann's full range of emotional responses to unfairness as he stood by her side, translating. "There was one time when she saw an old lady carrying heavy stuffs and selling them around, and she was like, 'Where is her son? Why does she still have to work?'" She started crying, which did not surprise Djaka – he knew she was quick to cry – though he thought her tears were misplaced because it was common for elders to work in Indonesia. On another occasion, when she saw an old woman unloading firewood and gasping for breath, he recalled, she became so infuriated that she slammed Djaka hard on the back and said, "Joko, we're heading back!" She walked off toward the blacksmith *perapen,* even though she knew they would not start work there for another hour.

In most ways she fearlessly embraced Javanese culture. She would drink anything and eat whatever was available, whether from a street vendor or in private homes. When they were in Kajar, she and Djaka often ate at the home of Pak Sastro, a wealthy trader and owner of several blacksmith shops. She did not approve of all of his practices – he seemed to have a horizontal monopoly, she thought – but he was a vital source of information, as well as reliable sustenance. When visiting the house of a craftsman in Gunung Kidul one day, Ann was served a "hot thick sweet tea," Djaka recalled. "Without a doubt, Ann downed the whole thing." After a polite chat, she asked to use the restroom, and on the way passed a pond that kept "rather muddy-green-looking water" that she was told was used for cooking and drinking, including the water used for serving her the tea. "Ann somehow lost her urgency to use the restroom," according to Djaka. "She rushed to the side of the house and threw up in silence." From then on, she insisted on carrying her own drink in a tumbler wherever she went.

Ann's family life was always complicated, but particularly so during this period. Lolo, who was working in Jakarta for Union Oil, would come to Yogya periodically to see his mother and daughter and to check on Ann. By then he was living with a younger woman, whom he would marry after he and Ann divorced, but according to relatives he was jealous of Ann and constantly asked about her. "Sometimes Uncle Lolo asked me who is Tante Ann's boyfriend," recalled Heru Budiono, the oldest son of Lolo's brother Soepomo, who also lived in Grandmother Djoeminah's house near the bird market while he studied engineering at Gadjah Mada. "I said I don't know because I never saw them." Heru and Ann shared some living costs: he paid for rice and heating oil, she bought groceries. He thought of her as a "workaholic" who after a long day in the field would stay up through the night typing notes. His lasting image of her is at the typewriter, pecking away, drinking coffee. Black, no sugar. He also remembered her strongest piece of advice: Don't worry about money. The more you worry about it, the more you earn nothing.

Ann rarely discussed personal matters with Djaka during their long days in the field, but some aspects of her private life became apparent to him. He thought she "liked to please and compliment people" and was "easy to fall in love." He never met Lolo, thus was never asked by Lolo about Ann's boyfriends. But he remembered that she had "a close friend" who worked at a museum in Yogya, who was "Javanese, with dark skin and rather muscular." Now and then Djaka would drop Ann off at the friend's house when they came in from the villages. There is some discrepancy about her nightly whereabouts for stretches of time in Yogya. By Maya's account, she and her mother were together at the grandmother's house for all of that period, and Ann tutored her every morning. But Djaka and Sumarni said that Ann often lodged at a boardinghouse in the Pakualaman neighborhood. It remains unclear whether Ann stayed there because it was more convenient for her fieldwork or because of personal considerations. By all accounts, she and Lolo's mother got along well; many members of the Martodihardjo family said they felt a warm bond with her, regardless of her crumbling relationship with Lolo. In any case, the boardinghouse room was small and dark.

Ann's penchant for detail, her patience, her willingness to take all the time necessary for people to trust her, her persistence in search of answers, her empathy, her tirelessness in the heat and rain, her willingness to climb on the backseat of Poniyem day after day and venture into the countryside – all of these characteristics made for a first-rate anthropologist, certainly, but they revealed something more about her. Her friendliness and easygoing nature were accompanied by an uncommon will. In that sense her son was very much like her, perhaps more than he would ever acknowledge. If she was, as he often portrayed her, good-hearted and sometimes naïve, she was also burning to leave her mark. Djaka and Sumarni saw this. She was ambitious, they said. She had dreams and goals, and she talked about them with such confidence that anyone who listened became convinced they would come true. At regular intervals they would see Ann rip a page from her field journal and sketch an outline of her future, where she wanted to go and what she needed to get there. Djaka and Sumarni never met Barry, but they knew about him, largely because of what she wrote on those scraps of paper. Her goals, they noticed, were not just about herself, but also about him. A mother and her only son, making their way alone and apart, yet together.

———◦◦◦———

CHAPTER 14

MAINLAND

He had turned eighteen a few weeks earlier. His face still had peach fuzz and an occasional splotch of acne. The Afro he started at Punahou School had grown a bit fuller but was under control. He was Barry Obama, freshman, from Honolulu. The name, along with those of his two new roommates, was typed on the index card that had been slotted onto the door of Room A104 of Haines Hall Annex in preparation for his arrival. Where he came from might be deduced from visual clues. First there was his little toe. It stuck out from the end of his slippers, or flip-flops as they were called on the mainland. His little toe was straight, rather than cramped and curling inward, a sign that his feet enjoyed a liberated existence, unbound by leather shoes. Then there was the rest of his daily uniform: OP (Ocean Pacific) corduroy shorts or denim jeans, a shell bracelet, polo shirts or tees (including one promoting the Hawaii state senate candidacy of Neil Abercrombie, his father's old Snack Bar friend from college). And finally there was his nonchalance. Maybe his face didn't look Hawaiian at first glance, thought Jeff Yamaguchi, who lived down the hall and whose family was from the islands, but it quickly became apparent that he had the easygoing attitude of a Hawaiian local, "that mannerism and style and personality that is very unique and identifiable from tourists . . . a mentality you develop over time, just 'Whatever.'"

Freshmen from Honolulu were everywhere in Southern California that fall of 1979. From Barry's Punahou class, thirty-two made the flight to the mainland to attend school in the greater Los Angeles area, including the four who joined him at Occidental College, a small liberal arts college fitted like a diamond in Eagle Rock on the Pasadena side of the sprawling metropolis. Oxy seemed like an easy transition for the Hawaiians. The campus was much like Punahou, with gentle slopes, flowering landscapes, graceful tree lines, and handsome buildings. Its academic expectations were equally high, the yearly class size was similar (four hundred to five hundred), and the weather in Southern California offered much of the same sunny balm as Honolulu. Barry's new digs had an even stronger connection to his high school life – a manifestation of disorder within order. The Annex, a narrow addition attached at a ninety-degree angle to the rest of Haines Hall, was a place apart, a loud, messy, diverse, egalitarian redoubt with a plentiful supply of beer and pot and young male bonhomie. In other words, it could pass for a Choom Gang hideaway. All so familiar, but Obama had come to college in search of something more.

In the end, his stay at Occidental would compose only half of his college experience. Just two school years, when he was eighteen and nineteen, from August 1979 to June 1981. A blip in his life, with no sense of completion. But in the development of the person he was to become, Oxy was significant. It was a decompression chamber that helped him surface from the depths of an exotic but unsettled childhood. It was a new racial landscape that brought him into daily contact for the first time with a cohort of African American peers, helping him work through the complexities of his cultural identity in a way that Punahou, despite its *hapa* diversity, could not. It was a school with a subset of intellectual professors and sophisticated students one and two years ahead of him who steered his interests toward politics and writing. It was where he took his first adult steps off a remote island and onto the American mainland, tracing a long arc across the continent from coast to coast and back into the heartland and Chicago in search of home. And it was where, near the end of his Oxy days, in anticipation of that still uncharted journey, he felt the first stirrings of destiny, a sense, he told friends, that he was brought into this world for a purpose.

Obama's personal transformation at Occidental coincided with a larger hinge point in history from the end of one decade to the beginning of the next. He arrived when Jimmy Carter was president and left in the era of Ronald Reagan. During his first year in college, traumatic events cascaded one upon another: November brought the Iran hostage crisis; December saw the Soviet invasion of Afghanistan; in January came word from President Carter that he was reinstituting registration for the military draft because of renewed cold war tensions with the Soviets; by March, Carter was announcing his final decision to boycott the summer Olympics in Moscow; and in April the Democratic president watched helplessly as a hostage rescue mission ended disastrously with a helicopter crash in the desert. Liberalism seemed to be in its death throes, overtaken by a conservative ideology that had its roots in Obama's new California home, as Reagan, the former governor, captured the White House and brought along the supply-side economic theories of Jack Kemp, a graduate of Occidental, and Arthur B. Laffer, a professor at the University of Southern California. The new decade of the 1980s would be characterized later as a time when college students followed the conservative cultural trend, turning away from antiestablishment activism. But at Occidental during Obama's two years there everything was still unsettled and up for debate.

Freshmen entering Oxy that September were welcomed by fire. The San Gabriel Mountains were burning fiercely. Ashes fell like snow on cars in the campus parking lots and the night was lit by an eerie glow from the burning hillsides. Most first-year students were housed at Stewart-Cleland Hall, known familiarly as Stewie, on the south end of campus, but high demand and a shortage of dorm space required some improvising that fall, and Barry Obama was among a small group placed with sophomores and a few upperclassmen in the Annex of Haines Hall, up the hill, where the distant fires were most visible. The Annex was two stories; men on the first floor, women on the second. It would be stretching things to call it coed; women rarely appeared on the first floor unless they were steady girlfriends. It was "the low-rent district," as one resident said, a backdoor kind of place. One way to reach it was from the front, walking past the palms and orange tree, under the three front arches, and all the way through and around Haines and down a flight of stairs to the back ell. But there was another door in the rear of the Annex that opened toward a parking lot, a direct and secluded entryway much preferred by the first-floor guys.

Up nine steps and through the back door, Obama's room was the first on the left past the carpeted stairwell. Obama's roommates were Paul Carpenter, a bushy-blond Southern California boy from Diamond Bar, explosively funny, ironic, with a gap-toothed smile and an up-for-anything attitude, who dressed in beach style and occasionally took his friends surfing (bodysurfing, in Barry's case) near his grandmother's house at Newport Beach; and Imad Husain, an intellectual Pakistani with a droll sense of humor who grew up in Karachi (though his parents now lived in Dubai), finished his secondary education at the Bedford School outside London, spoke with a pronounced British accent, and was partial to peacoats and rugby shirts. Sunny California was Carpenter's comfortable milieu, but it seemed heavenly to Husain, an escape from the drafty dormitory at the British boarding school where he shivered many nights even under five blankets.

Barry and Paul called each other only by their last names. *Hey Carpenter. Hey Obama.* They both addressed Husain by his first name. They were a multihued Three Musketeers, all approximately the same height, in the six-one range, and weight, between 160 and 170 pounds. Imad arrived at the dorm first, Paul and his family hours later, and Barry not until the next day, bringing a suitcase, a box of albums, and a framed picture of his mother and sister. He had spent the day before with Gramps, who had accompanied him to California. Before returning to Hawaii, Stan bought his grandson a present: a beat-up old red Fiat that they found at a Los Angeles used car lot. Carpenter had a gold VW Beetle. Parking spaces were up for grabs outside the Annex. There were coincidences in the histories of Obama and Carpenter that neither of them realized at the time. It turned out that Carpenter's maternal grandfather, Frederick Betts, was from El Dorado, Kansas, the homeland of Obama's maternal grandfather, and was part of the great midwestern migration to California. Imad, though he came from a more moneyed family, shared with Obama an international sensibility, and played an important role in introducing his roommate to other Pakistanis at Oxy who would become lifelong friends.

The subculture of the Annex is best understood in the context of that time and place. Oxy then was an overtly open institution when it came to sex, alcohol, and drugs. One of the myths of twentieth-century American culture is that the 1960s were the heyday of campus freedom, but in fact everything that started then reached far deeper into the fabric of collegiate life over the following decade, even as radical politics and the counterculture sensibility receded. When Bill Clinton, another future president, attended Georgetown University during the heart of the 1960s, the sorts of things accepted later at Occidental as a matter of routine were on the shocking fringe, if not unimaginable. Georgetown was a Catholic institution, which offers a partial explanation, but the example is presented here because Clinton later became a symbol to some, for the most part mistakenly, of the excesses of the 1960s. Even at more historically liberal schools, from Berkeley to Wisconsin to Harvard, one would find a striking difference between the accepted institutional norms in 1967 and 1979.

At the opening of the 1979 school year at Oxy, the house resident and resident advisors in Haines Hall handed out condoms to males, slipping them under the door, compliments of the college. In the yearbook, *La Encina,* the fad that year was for students to pose in beds or bathtubs, ostensibly naked. Although the legal drinking age in California then was twenty-one, alcohol was readily available to everyone on campus with the unspoken consent of the administration. The student association sponsored campuswide parties called Wet Wednesday, Thirsty Thursday, and Fried Friday. The theory was that because students inevitably were going to drink, it was better to have them stay on campus to do so rather than risk their lives and the lives of others driving on the freeways. Drugs, in the form of pot, hashish, cocaine, and amphetamines, were also prevalent, although Oxy was not considered among the country's heaviest party-and-drugs schools. Students said the academics were too demanding for that. Susan Keselenko, then coeditor of the student newspaper, *The Occidental,* offered this assessment: "You could easily get what you needed to get, but it wasn't a big druggie scene. That wasn't what the school was about." Within the realm of Oxy itself, the Haines Hall Annex was actually straighter than a few places on campus. One sophomore who lived next door to Obama moved to the Annex that year specifically to get away from the peer pressure of friends at another dorm who had organized what they called "the Astronomy Quad," a counterculture gathering where heavy drug use was the norm.

Now enter the Annex from the back door for Barry's freshman year. Seventy feet back to front, with six rooms down the left, four down the right. Three students to a room, rectangles that were more deep than wide, but designed for two, and without partitions, making for a barrackslike atmosphere. Beige and blue-gray checkered linoleum floors. Three desks, Smith Corona and IBM Selectric typewriters from home, carbon paper, and Wite-Out; three beds, some rooms with bunks, others with twins. A104 had a bunk and one twin. Carpenter seized the twin on the first day, but the roommates agreed to rotate beds after each term. Open area in the middle, Carpenter's turntable, beanbag chair. A sink in the alcove, near the closets. Across the hall, the rooms had rear windows that looked out on a grassy hillside leading toward other dorms. On the left side, Obama's side, they took in soil and shrubs on a hillock only a few yards away, shaded by a sycamore tree. It was not quite claustrophobic, but sufficiently close quarters to push people out of their rooms, creating what became an Annex hallway society. The hallway, teeming with life, was narrow, only six feet across, "a sort of dim, murky place," as one resident described it, with fluorescent light rods encased in fiberglass lending a faint pinkish glow. A communal bathroom (three toilets, three showers) was not quite halfway down on Obama's side, diagonally across from an indented nook that served as an informal living room, brightened by three floor-to-ceiling French windows and furnished with a potato chip–littered aquamarine carpet and a tattered brown-striped sofa, known as the Barf Couch, along with a fridge and stereo that belonged to Guch, the nickname of Jeff Yamaguchi. He sort of lived out there. The nook was so shallow that when Barry Obama sat on the couch and leaned back and stretched his legs, his feet would protrude into the hallway.

With its camaraderie and incessant horseplay, the first floor of the Annex, like college dormitories everywhere, could attract and repel simultaneously. "It was definitely a guy's hangout," recalled Kelly Lloyd Schafer, one of the few women from the second floor who went down there. "You had to walk through the cloud of smoke. I usually made it through pretty quick." The first floor, she thought, was the diametric opposite of the second floor, which had drawbacks in other ways, especially the pride of snooty upper-class girls who snubbed the first-year girls. No snobbery downstairs. The hallway was a free-for-all forum of sorts, with a permanent conversation on life, philosophy, sex, politics, school. It was also home to the impromptu Annex Olympics: long-jumping onto a pile of mattresses, wrestling in underwear, hacking golf balls down the hallway toward the open back door, boxing while drunk. Then there were the non-Olympic sports of lighting farts and judging them by color, tipping over the Coke machine, breaking the glass fire extinguisher case, putting out cigarettes on the carpet, falling asleep on the carpet, flinging Frisbees at the ceiling-mounted alarm bell, tossing pizza boxes to the floor, and smoking pot from a three-foot crimson opaque bong, a two-man event involving the smoker and an accomplice standing ready to respond to the order "Hey, dude, light the bowl!" The Barf Couch earned its name early in the first trimester when a freshman across the hall from Obama drank himself into a stupor and threw up all over himself and the couch. In the manner of pallbearers hoisting a coffin, a line of Annexers lifted the tainted sofa with the freshman aboard and toted it out the back door and down four steps to the first concrete landing on the way to the parking lot. A day later, the couch remained outside in the sun, resting on its side with cushions off (someone had hosed it clean), and soon it was back in the hallway nook. This was the same couch that Yamaguchi – who worked the overnight shift at the Beverly Hillcrest Hotel, attended classes in the morning, and slept in the afternoon – later claimed as his bed.

Guch, with his Kenwood speakers out in the hall, and Paul Carpenter, with his stereo in the triple he shared with Obama, were considered the music impresarios of the Annex. The edgy Carpenter was known for his extensive album collection and propensity toward high decibel levels, with a preference for new wave, punk, and ska: Germs, Sex Pistols, Ramones, B-52s, Specials, Flying Lizards, Talking Heads, Dead Kennedys, the Clash. Yamaguchi, spinning albums for all to hear, prided himself on his sixth sense as a disc jockey, selecting tunes to reflect the communal mood. "If guys were stressed out and trying to get ready for exams, jazz would be playing. Some kind of instrumental without words so you could focus. If guys were partying, drinking and smoking too much pot, you'd hear R&B or real intense new wave. The tone and mood of that particular area was kind of like being in a club. . . . A lot of times if I didn't have an album out there I'd go in my room and pull it out, or guys would go in their room and get a disc." One of Guch's roommates in A107, Rick Lopez, a second-generation Mexican American with a full beard and earring, could often be heard strumming his guitar and singing Kenny Loggins hits, especially "Whenever I Call You Friend." Stevie Wonder, Bob Marley, Jimi Hendrix, the Police, and John Coltrane were also popular in the Annex, along with local bands who occasionally played on campus, including the Blasters, Los Lobos, and the Naughty Sweeties.

Barry Obama played a lot of Hendrix, Earth, Wind & Fire, and Billie Holiday, but was known in the Annex for his wicked impression of Mick Jagger. He could do the walk, the strut, the face, and act out the dramatic scene of the Rolling Stones onstage at the Altamont Speedway outside Livermore, California, on December 6, 1969, as violence that would lead to murder broke out in the crowd below: "Hey, hey people, sisters and brothers, brothers and sisters, come on now! That means everybody just cool out! They're fightin' a lot. Will you cool out, everybody?"

Like the trio in Room A104, the random collection of Annex men had more ethnic and socioeconomic variety than Oxy as a whole, where the student body was predominantly white and upper middle class. There were seven African Americans, including Ricky Tate, the resident advisor, a senior who had his own single room. They ran the socioeconomic spectrum from a football player who came from the tough streets of Compton to a business major who was trained by Jesuits in Philadelphia and fastidiously ironed his own handmade preppie-style clothes every day. There were American-born Asians and international students from the Asian subcontinent, anglicized Chicanos and waspy Anglos. The Annex was home to budding intellectuals and aspiring writers, party animals and surfer dudes and jocks, including a pitcher, a catcher, a miler, a sprinter, and the star scorer on the basketball team. Barry Obama, with his uncommon family and history, represented a bit of each of them up and down the hallway. He was black and white, preppie and Choom Ganger and sunny surfer, basketball lifer and writer and perceptive observer, wholly American and yet the son of an African and intimately familiar with Asia from his years in Indonesia. His ability to connect across racial and cultural lines, evident at Oxy and thereafter, was not merely a superficial art of survival but more authentically rooted in his life and being.

Much like his pals at Punahou, most of Barry's classmates at Oxy could not see his interiority, how hard he was working to reconcile the contradictions that life threw at him. They thought he was cool, smart without being pedantic, and seemed to have his act together. To Mark Parsons, who came to know him mostly because they both smoked and spent a lot of time together huddling outside the student union, puffing away before going in for dinner, Barry seemed "almost Zen in walking through all the chaos in our dorm." Ken Sulzer, the catcher on Oxy's baseball team, who lived across the hall, thought Barry had a quiet charisma. He was "not a loudmouth," but when he spoke it seemed to snap a rambling discussion into coherence. To Vince Coscino, housed in the room next door, the Annexers were "all just a bunch of college students trying to figure out life. . . . Some were more serious and some less. Some were bigger knuckleheads and some less. I would put myself . . . in a category of bigger knuckleheads, but Barry I would absolutely not put in that category. He was more serious and probably more mature." Briefly, now and then, Obama showed a few people in Haines Hall his vulnerable side. One of those who saw it was Coscino's roommate, Simeon Heninger. A short and sensitive professor's son from Bremerton, Washington, Sim, as he was called, had an obsession with the Kennedy assassination, even bringing a map of Dealey Plaza and the Texas School Book Depository scene with him to school, and was said by the other Annex guys to bear a resemblance to a young Woody Allen, which might explain why his episodes with Obama were framed in existentialist anxiety or absurdity.

A few days into the school year, Sim ran into Barry on the steps of the Art Barn across from the student union. It was a good place to stand if you were looking for someone, or simply hoping to find company. There stood Obama. He seemed striking to Heninger because of his height and his Afro, with a little baby fat still on his face. As they were talking, Obama took out a photograph. "These are my grandparents in Hawaii," he said. It was a picture of Stan and Tut. Heninger was mystified. He resisted the temptation to ask "Why are they both white?" assuming the answer was that Barry was adopted. A small moment, but one that lingered while other memories fade. At the start of their freshman year, everyone was trying to appear hip and independent, released from whatever constrained them in the past, Heninger thought, and here was Obama showing him a picture of his grandparents. Friends had never shown him pictures of their grandparents, before or since. He thought there was "something kind of sad about it." The gesture could have meant many things, universal or particular. It could have been an evocation of homesickness or loneliness, or it could have been a way for Barry to express his own sense of otherness, a young black man with white grandparents, and subtly connect with a new acquaintance who was an outsider himself as a diminutive Jewish kid in a hallway dominated by dudes and jocks. Or it could have been a bit of all those things, along with the more prosaic likelihood that Barry had just opened a letter from Honolulu with that photograph inside when Sim happened along.

The next encounter, of a much different sort, occurred weeks later, on a Friday after a week of midterm exams. People were starting to party in anticipation of a blowout weekend, and Sim already had consumed his share of beer and pot when he met up with Barry, who seemed to be in a similar condition. As they roamed the main corridor of Haines Hall together, they approached a young woman Heninger had met in his freshman year and on whom he still had a crush. They stopped and talked, and the more they talked, the more of a buzz Heninger was feeling, both from his reality-distorting intake beforehand and the pleasure of being in the presence of this good-looking young woman. Then he started to notice that Obama was also enjoying the situation, perhaps too much. Barry launched into a riff on nudity, offering his theory that the human race would be better off if people did not wear clothes. This declaration was made with the urgency of someone ready to strip then and there. What's going on? Heninger wondered. It seemed apparent that Barry was trying to seduce the woman right in front of Sim, who was thinking that getting naked with the girl was okay, but not with Obama in the picture. He wondered what she wanted him to do – get lost? He started to feel embarrassed, then embarrassed about feeling embarrassed. Did his inhibitions bother her more than Barry's free spirit? Did she really prefer "this taller, more exotic, and Afroed freshman"? Sim worried about the predicament Barry had talked himself into and how they would get out of it. The woman saved them. Without seeming alarmed or affronted, appearing sympathetic to the theoretical argument but not ready to put it into practice, she allowed the scene to play out until Barry suddenly stopped. They politely broke off the discussion, and Sim and Barry headed back to the Annex.

As Heninger interpreted this later, once again it was an expression of loneliness or otherness. When Obama was standing there bemoaning the rules about wearing clothes, Sim thought, he was really bridling against all of society's dictates that judged him as an outsider or inferior because of his skin color. His female friend, Sim concluded, shared that view, and turned what could have been an explosive or at least negative situation into something more benign. Human encounters often play out on several levels at once. Heninger could very well have had it perfectly right, while at the same time it could have been true that Obama was just so stoned that he was talking non-sense, and also that he was trying to put the moves on an attractive woman on a Friday night.

By any measure, this incident seemed out of character for Obama, according to other Annex residents. "The ladies liked him, he was very popular, he was a good-looking guy," recalled Mark Roderique, who shared the next-door triple with Heninger and Coscino. "He just played it very cool, very smooth, very laid-back. He was not aggressive or anything like that. He was not really flirtatious. I saw him mostly around guys. . . . There weren't a whole lot of girls hanging around in Haines Annex. There weren't a lot of girls playing basketball. So I mostly knew him around guys." From his perch on the couch, Jeff Yamaguchi saw something similar: "You'd never characterize him as a ladies' man. It wasn't on his radar screen at the time. I can't remember a dorm party where [Obama] would be cavorting with the ladies. Maybe discretion was the better part of valor." He did have many women friends among his classmates, if not a steady girlfriend. Leslie Dudley, who lived on the second floor of Haines, often studied near him late at the library. "Sometimes if I was leaving he would say, 'Leslie, don't go yet. Wait. I'll be ready in five minutes, so I'll walk you back,'" she recalled. He also invited himself along several times when she was going to see movies assigned in her film class. "I remember him telling me that he was coming with me to see the films a couple of times. I remember two of them. In Thorne Hall we saw *Doctor Zhivago*. Afterwards, I was like, 'Omar Sharif is so dreamy.' He was like, 'Julie Christie is the dreamy one.' I said, 'No she wasn't.' We were joking. . . . Then he went with me. . . . I didn't tell him about it or invite him, he said, 'Meet me down here at seven because I'm going to that movie with you.' We saw *8½*. He was like that. If he picked you to be friends, you were just friends. He wasn't shy."

One scene Dudley recalled indicated that Barry carried his mother's conscience around with him and her familiar humanistic advice: *Put yourself in the other person's shoes.* "One time I remember him coming up to me and saying, 'Well, Leslie, I heard you said this to so-and-so' . . . and I said 'Yes' . . . and he said, 'How do you think that made him feel?' My mouth was open. Nobody had made me think about [myself] that way. I probably had said something sarcastic and it came out sounding mean. . . . I'm not sure I'd ever had someone [before then] take an interest in giving me a perspective on how to be empathetic."

Mark Parsons said Obama displayed one small trait that showed he wanted to be a *player:* he wore a lot of "stupid hats." He usually wore them cocked, to look cool. Parsons knew Barry from one angle, as a fellow smoker. They smoked outside the student union together and wherever they could find a hassle-free place. His friends noticed that Barry had a peculiar smoking style, a little affectation. He turned his wrist up and cupped the cigarette between thumb and index finger. He smoked a cigarette the same way he smoked a joint. "I have a sense that he smoked because he was addicted, as I was," Parsons said. That would make genetic sense. On his maternal side, his grandmother was a chain-smoker, unable to quit, and Stan smoked as well, and on his paternal side his father smoked and was addicted to alcohol. But Obama told Parsons there was another reason. "I remember him telling me he would quit after he got married. He didn't want to quit smoking because he said he would gain weight, but after he got married it would be okay to gain weight. I think it was mostly a joke." This was more than a decade before smoking was banned in most public places, but Barry's smoking habit still surprised some people, especially those who played basketball with him.

When Obama arrived at Oxy, basketball was still an essential part of his self-identity. His love of the game had not diminished, and he came with the ambition of possibly making the school team. From his first day on campus, he was among a group of fourteen to sixteen freshmen who were encouraged to play daily games at Rush Gymnasium. It was too early in the school year for the coaches to hold legal practices, but these pickup contests in September and October were viewed as an informal prelude. Although the coaches could not be present, they sent word out as to when the gym would be available. Kent Goss, a six-one guard from La Jolla, spent those two months playing with and against Barry almost every day. His scouting report on the left-hander from Hawaii was familiar: dribble-drive penetrator, liked to go left, not much to the right, smart court sense, not much of an outside shot, average defensively, good teammate, tough competitor, hated to lose, generous with passes, affable, one of the guys, right in there with the give-and-take of trash talk. "We used to give him grief because he went to Punahou . . . which is pretty much an elite school," Goss recalled. "We'd say stuff like, 'You might get away with that at Punahou, but not here.'"

Those informal scrimmages were as close as Obama got to the Occidental team. His days of organized basketball were over. His boyhood dream of making the NBA, the fanciful notion he had lightheartedly immortalized when he signed Tony Peterson's 1976 Punahou yearbook ("Some day when I am an all-pro basketballer, and I want to sue my team for more money . . ."), was over. If he felt undervalued at Punahou, at Oxy it became obvious where his game fit among college players. He was good, but not great. Blake Withers, the hotshot senior guard who lived down where the Annex connected to the main section of Haines, and in whose room the Annexers gathered most nights to watch the Johnny Carson monologue on Withers's rabbit-eared, black-and-white television set, went so far as to call Obama's game "awful." This was far too harsh, but nonetheless reflected a competitive gap even between a powerhouse high school team substitute and a Division III varsity starter. But Obama never stopped playing. At Oxy he became a regular in noon games pitting undergrads against faculty members. He also started jogging regularly, to stay in shape, a brisk twenty-five minutes around the campus. The pickup-game passion would stay with him for the long haul, and he remained thin and steady over the passing years while some more talented players fattened and slowed and their games diminished. Nearly thirty years later, when Obama was running for president and was known as Barack rather than Barry, Darryl Gabriel, the Punahou star, joined him and Danny Hale and Alan Lum and several old classmates in a holiday pickup game at the school gym, and remarked to Hale afterward, "Man, *Barack* is a lot better player than *Barry* ever was!"

Despite its unappealing name, the Barf Couch was at the center of Annex action. It was seedy and comfortably roomy, and when Guch was at work at night, a typical evening might find five or six guys lounging on it and more hanging out on the nearby carpet. The informal salon might start around ten and persist until three in the morning, with people coming and going. One wave would arrive around eleven, when the stacks of the Mary Norton Clapp Library closed, and then a few hours later came another crew of the most earnest students who had been booted from the library's last open refuge, a glass-encased section in the basement known as the Fishbowl. Obama was a Fishbowl devotee, along with some Pakistani friends: his roommate Imad Husain and two older students, Hasan Chandoo and Wahid Hamid, all of whose families came from the upper social strata of Karachi. Besides being open late, the Fishbowl was a place where you could eat and talk. Adam Sherman, whose room was close to the Barf Couch, wrote a story extolling how welcoming the sofa seemed at the end of a long night at the library. After spending three hours at the library "futilely attempting to understand the economic impact of the Brazilian government's trade agreement," Sherman made his way down the Annex hallway through the "outstretched legs of my comrades," cleared a spot on the carpet below the overcrowded couch, and watched as Paul Carpenter muttered the lyrics of a Frank Zappa song and Obama (Sherman called him by his middle name in the story) gripped the bong "in a single hand with practiced coolness" and "let the grayish smoke roll momentarily around his mouth before he gulped down the intoxicating smoke."

John Boyer, a track star from Coronado who lived across the hall with Ken Sulzer, the baseball catcher, and Pete Koester, an all-conference pitcher, recorded various couch activities in his journal. One night he sketched a scene of Barry Obama leaning back on the couch, reading a book and smoking a cigarette. Around him sat Imad Husain, Ricky Johnson, and a few others. The night before, Boyer had joined Barry after an early exit from the library. They stopped by a party, left that to eat at a nearby burger joint named Pete's, where they talked about girls, sex, and drugs, then returned to the Annex and joined a larger bull session on the Barf Couch, the conversation drifting deeper into world politics, including developments in Afghanistan, which the Soviet army had invaded, and Pakistan, where fundamentalist Islam was on the rise and there had been anti-American demonstrations at the U.S. embassy in Islamabad. The Pakistanis at Oxy – wealthy, intellectual, and intensely opinionated, with their worldly presentation of political theories and capitalist panache – brought urgency to these discussions of foreign affairs, while the American students seemed to have less at stake. The potent mix of idealism and self-interest that stirred campus activism during the Vietnam era seemed gone if not quite forgotten. "People would sometimes lament that students seemed apathetic about political issues compared to, say, ten years before, in 1969, which was obviously true," said Ken Sulzer, the catcher across the hall. The number of Vietnam-era vets on campus could be counted on one hand.

For the Annex students, Vietnam was imagined, taken from Michael Herr's 1977 book *Dispatches* and Michael Cimino's 1978 movie *The Deer Hunter*. When Francis Ford Coppola's *Apocalypse Now* opened during their freshman year, Obama and his pals Carpenter and Boyer caught the premiere, riding down to the Cinerama Dome in Hollywood in Boyer's '61 Chevy Impala. "It was ultra-advanced sound and a pretty bitchin' movie, and of course we had political discussions about that, in terms of Vietnam and entanglements," Boyer said. It had been a half dozen years since the United States played out its final scene in Vietnam, with the helicopters hovering over the embassy roof and people desperate to flee as the North Vietnamese army marched triumphantly into Saigon, an evocation of American defeat. Something similar seemed to be happening now, during Obama's first year in college, with the taking of hostages at the embassy in Iran and the cold war aggression of the Soviets invading Afghanistan. Different places, different situations, same sense of American vulnerability. On January 23 of Obama's freshman year, there was even an intimation of Vietnam redux, briefly, when President Carter in his 1980 State of the Union message said he intended to reactivate the Selective Service System in preparation for the possibility of a renewed military draft. (Conscription had been phased out in favor of an all-volunteer force in 1973, and the registration requirement was dropped in 1975.) "I will send legislation and budget proposals to the Congress next month so that we can begin registration and then meet future mobilization needs rapidly if they arise," Carter said.

Obama was among the young men of Haines Hall Annex listening to Carter's address that night. "It was a blow to everyone," Boyer wrote in his journal. "Carter gave his State of the Union address. It looks like we're going to war in a few years. The draft will be reinstated in one month. Everyone is scared. Most are talking of leaving the country." Hours after the speech, the Annex was buzzing. A large crowd congregated around the Barf Couch. Imad Husain found it ironic that if America went to war "Barry and Paul would have to go and I would stay over here [at Occidental] because I was not part of it." In his journal, Boyer took note of the mood, with people shouting "Mexico sounds nice!" and "Let the fucking senators fight their war!" Leaving the country was not something Boyer could contemplate or condone. He came from a conservative military family; his father was a retired navy pilot and his brother was in the air force. His own views had been changing at Oxy, turning more liberal, supportive of Carter's human rights agenda, due in part, he said, to the persuasiveness of his friend Barry across the hall. But "virtually no one was in favor of conscription." The boys of the Annex were anxious, skeptical, looking for immediate escape. "There's a bong going around with gin, grain alcohol, wine, whiskey, and vodka," Boyer wrote. "Food to share. . . . When I got here everyone was stoned or drunk and yelling about Afghanistan or the draft."

Over in A106, first room on the right from the back door, before Boyer and Sulzer's room and across from Obama's, lived a diplomat's son named Phil Boerner, who had arrived at Occidental from Walt Whitman High School in the Maryland suburbs of Washington. Boerner and Obama both liked to write, shared similar political views, and became close friends. Phil's parents, Michael and Dorothy Boerner, had left the capital that year for the father's new posting in London, where he was the economic minister at the U.S. embassy. They were acutely attuned to foreign affairs, and when Phil wrote them a letter about Carter's speech – the possibility of a renewed draft, his opposition to it, and the resurgence of protests on campus (one placard read "Draft Beer, Not People!") – they responded swiftly. They were old-school Democrats who thought Carter was "rather incompetent" but disagreed with their son about the draft. "Re: your comments on draft registration, you can imagine what my own views are," Michael Boerner wrote. "We all registered `. . . in the 1950s without question. It is a little difficult to fathom why the situation should be any different today. . . . It is much more democratic to do it on the basis of a draft which hits all segments of society." The next day a letter arrived from Dorothy Boerner: "I was shocked – but not surprised – at student demonstrations [against the draft]. We really are weak if those in the physically best equipped age group won't bear arms!"

Boerner was one of the more earnest students in the Annex culture, and in Obama he found a kindred spirit. They relished the architecture of conversation, taking a subject and constructing a discussion around it. A mutual friend, Paul Herrmannsfeldt, who was a year ahead of them at Oxy, called their discussions a form of "deep sea diving." "I would say Obama enjoyed deep sea diving and I did too, and I think Phil probably facilitated that," Herrmannsfeldt said. Choose a subject and go deep, with no diversions or tangents. He remembered the three of them hanging out in the Annex and delving into conversations about philosophy, especially "the conflict between the individual desires and what society desires." Boerner recalled a more eclectic set of deep-sea subjects, including "the CIA, El Salvador . . . whatever news was in the *L.A. Times,* Jimi Hendrix, Euro-communism, socialism . . . Marcuse's 'An Essay on Liberation,' Voltaire's *Candide,* how to bring change in the world, the right wing's control of the media, totalitarianism, Alexander Haig, poetry, James Joyce, Kafka, the Enlightenment, enlightened despotism of the eighteenth century . . . Frederick II, Richard C. Allen, the Soviet Union, gigantic traffic jams in L.A., arts of the avant-garde . . . a lot of bullshit, the rise of apathy in America. . . ."

Among the hangouts on campus, the Cooler was at once the least prepossessing and the coolest. It was a nondescript coffee shop, two small rooms on the ground floor of the student center where one could grab a sandwich, sip coffee, smoke, talk, read the paper, and finish crossword puzzles. The Cooler was what one denizen called "a café society bubble," a hangout for journalists from *The Occidental,* the campus newspaper, located in the same building, and the intellectual sets interested in literature and politics. A cartoon in the paper portrayed "the various sections of the Cooler brain." One part of the brain was for *Knowledge of Intense Topics* and another for *Concern for Intense Topics*. Then there were *Posture Nodes, Must Maintain Cool Stance,* and *Special Eyeballs for Checking Out All Who Enter.* The stick figure under the dissected brain was holding a cigarette and drinking "feen" (caffeinated coffee), and her lips were vibrating. This was not the favored place of jocks or frat boys, and only a few of the guys from the Annex made a point of being seen there. Obama was one of those few. A gym rat at first, over time he became more of a Cooler rat. It served much the same purpose that the Snack Bar had for his father at the University of Hawaii two decades earlier. Regulars at the Cooler tended to stake out the same tables every day, and during Barry's freshman year, several intriguing women could be found there, including juniors Caroline Boss, a political activist known for, among other things, her intensity, her refusal to type her own papers, and her espousal of socialism, and Susan Keselenko, an engaging writer who had risen to the position of coeditor of the newspaper and was incessantly smoking Camels and downing black coffee.

Beginning in January 1980, Keselenko shared an off-campus apartment with another junior and former sorority sister, Lisa Jack, an aspiring Annie Leibovitz who went around campus persuading interesting people to let her shoot them with her 35mm Pentax K1000. Susan and Lisa moved from the Alpha Lambda Phi Alpha sorority house to an apartment at 1570½ Hazelwood Avenue, only one block from Oxy's perimeter. Their place was the farthest back of four units in what looked like a truncated roadside motel. Hazelwood was considered a party street for Oxy students. Farther down toward York Boulevard, one house hosted parties month after month, year after year. The Keselenko-Jack apartment was much tamer. They both had cars, and sometimes drove that single block up the street and parked in the lot behind the Cooler, especially if they intended to work past midnight. Boss, Keselenko's close friend, was considered the queen of the Cooler rats. She sat at one of the smaller white Formica tables four back from the front. Her parents were Swiss, and she called her place at the Cooler her *Stammtisch,* a German Swiss designation for a table meant for regulars. Keselenko often joined her, while Jack dropped by now and then to see who was there.

One day while they were having coffee, according to Jack, "Caroline started to tell me about this really good-looking guy. His name is Barry and people are talking about him." Just then, Obama walked in with his friend Hasan Chandoo, who was a junior in the class with Keselenko and Boss. "So in walks Barry Obama being all cute," Jack continued. "He was very gregarious. We just chatted. . . . Caroline said, 'Barry, this is Lisa. Barry, you have to have your picture taken by her.'" To have Lisa Jack shoot profiles of you at Oxy was considered a mark of distinction. She had already taken pictures of Boss and Keselenko and Mark Dery, another writer. Barry gladly accepted the offer, and soon, at about eleven one morning, there he was at the door on Hazelwood, ready and eager for his photo shoot. He was wearing his flip-flops, jeans, and a collared shirt with button-down breast pockets, with a digital watch on his left wrist and a thin Hawaiian band on his right. He brought along a pack of non-filter cigarettes, a wide-brimmed boater hat, and a bomber jacket. Jack did not instruct him on the wardrobe or accessories; they were all his idea – the accoutrements for looking appropriately hip. "He duded up," as Jack later put it.

The apartment living room was her studio, for better and worse, with its green shag carpet and an overturned shopping cart for an end table. She sat him down on the couch, tattered and brown plaid, reminiscent of the Barf Couch in the Annex, but now covered with a sheet so as not to distract from the subject. Barry was "kind of posing at first," not loose enough. Lisa kept talking to him as she shot, getting him to laugh and chat. Obama was more interested in prying information out of other people than revealing much about himself, so Jack let him steer the conversation. She was majoring in psychology but became obsessed with photography after taking a course at Oxy. Now she was in an independent study course with Daniel Fineman. A professor of American literature and theory who was also into photography, Fineman taught her darkroom-based photography and the finer techniques of portraiture and was both helpful and unsparing in his critiques. He understood the allure of portraits for college photographers: models were always available and the ramifications were both artsy and social, since "such quasi-serious events could easily slide into post-portrait coffee or parties." Jack developed her prints for him in the darkroom at Thorne 7C.

After the first round of chitchat with Barry on the couch – here slumped back, there with his right leg crossed nonchalantly over his left knee – he started to experiment, moving around for different poses. It was one of those times when his ambition was unmistakable, much like when he cornered Troy Egami to make certain that he was quoted after Punahou's state high school basketball championship game. He blew smoke like he was on a Bob Dylan album jacket. He put on his hat and cocked it low like he was Jimi Hendrix. He walked toward a heating grate and knelt down like Miles Davis. "These are all his ideas, not mine," Jack recalled. "No one else got up to stand over the [heating] grate with a hat on. Nobody. I think he was into it. He was pleased he had been asked."

For reasons that Jack could not remember later, the Obama photographs were not developed. He never asked for them. Fineman might have criticized them as art. Jack herself might have had some problems with the results. The roll of film remained untouched and forgotten for nearly three decades, until Obama emerged as a candidate for president of the United States and Lisa Jack, a professor of psychology at Augsburg College in Minnesota, remembered that day in her living room at Hazelwood on the rim of Occidental. Digging around in her basement, she found one crinkled print and the entire set of thirty-six negatives. Looking at them again, she was stunned. "In one roll of film, Barry goes from innocent baby to Jimi Hendrix to a Black Panther – from having fun to thoughtful to angst." Out of obscurity, these photographs became rare historical documents, capturing a future president in a moment in time and space. Jack gave them a title: *The Freshman.*

Caroline Boss and Susan Keselenko knew Obama through their Pakistani friend Hasan Chandoo, who loved to talk politics. They also were in a class with Obama during the second trimester of his freshman year. It was Political Science 94, an American foreign policy course team-taught by Larry T. Caldwell and Alan Egan. The lead teacher was Caldwell, a redheaded, freckle-faced expert on the Soviet Union and nuclear arms negotiations who occasionally served as a consultant for the CIA and treated his students almost as though they were junior advisors on the National Security Council. He split them into teams, Group Y and Group A, to write and present papers on some of the most pressing issues of the day. Obama was part of Group Y, as were

Boss and Keselenko and several other high-powered students, including Tim Yeaney, an activist who chaired Oxy's World Hunger Task Force. The topics Caldwell chose for the class were the MX Missile program and the Middle East peace talks. In class Obama was relatively quiet. "I don't remember him talking a lot," said Yeaney. "He wasn't silent, but he certainly wasn't the most talkative." But in the small group, he was "very vocal," especially on the Middle East. The MX Missile question – President Carter's effort to develop an intercontinental ballistic missile that was mobile and protected enough so that it could survive a Soviet attack and provide a counterattack – seemed of less interest to him.

Group Y often met in a classroom at Swan Hall to work on their papers, critiques, and rebuttals. Keselenko, with the sensibility of a journalist, thought the exercise was a bit of role-playing and found it boring. Boss, more of a theorist, took it seriously and thought it was thrilling: "There's nothing quite like feeling on top of your game intellectually and being thrown together with a group whose intellect and energy you have real respect for." Yeaney, who was nearly three years older and one class ahead of Barry, was impressed by how the freshman dealt with a group of upperclassmen. "His intellect was clearly on display. He argued in a way that was very lawyerly. He had a very good knowledge of the world. Better than most people." But there was one characteristic of his group that bothered Yeaney. Boss, Keselenko, and Obama were all heavy smokers, and he was allergic to smoke. It got so thick in the little Swan Hall classroom that smoke seeped out the closed door. He finally fled to a smoke-free environment over at the American Friends Service Committee library in Pasadena, where he worked on a critique of Group A's MX paper.

Obama's main contribution was a critique of Group A's paper on the Camp David Accords. After four days of what Yeaney called "a very healthy and critical debate on what the most appropriate strategy should be," Group Y supported the Middle East peace process but argued that Group A was overly optimistic in thinking that the settlement reached by Menachem Begin, prime minister of Israel, and Anwar el-Sadat, president of Egypt, would have a broader positive effect on other Middle East problems. The critique crafted by Obama and Group Y said that Group A was mistaken in thinking the accords reached in September 1978 and signed in Washington in March 1979 would protect U.S. oil interests, asserted that the Camp David accords were too narrow to resolve the Palestinian question, and argued that Group A's paper placed too much weight on the ability of the United States to be the key player in resolving the dispute. "In conclusion, we feel that the group's paper proceeds from the faulty premise that Egypt and Israel can solve the delicate problem of Palestinians, with the U.S. overseeing and insuring the whole process. This takes a naïve faith in American ability to control the world according to its whims. In actuality, this has not been the case for some time – the U.S. today has limited influence in the Middle East, and must be viewed as a participant, rather than a controller, of the world system." For a lasting peace, the critique noted, the Palestinians themselves had to be included in the process. "Camp David was definitely a step in the right direction, but only by transcending its context and allowing the Palestinians and Arab nations to participate in the settlement can the problem be solved." Caldwell said the critique was "first rate," with the best use of an outline he had seen that year and "a good summary of argument."

Not long into their time at Oxy, Obama's friend Phil Boerner received a challenging letter from his mother, Dorothy, who held a doctoral degree in English. She seemed a tad alarmed by Phil's good-time reports from his Annex hangout. "I'm disappointed Oxy isn't hard!" she wrote. "College is supposed to be an intellectual step up – stretch your mind. Perhaps the teachers/courses you have are not typical – this is something you'll have to be sizing up. It must be awful to have parents that growl when you say you're having a good time! But I don't want to go into debt for that!" Not two months later, Boerner wrote a letter to his grandparents, William and Elizabeth Payne, who lived in the Catskills near Grahamsville, New York, indicating that he had learned his lesson, or that his appraisal had changed, or both. "Occidental is a very hard school and I find I'm spending more time studying than I had planned to when I enrolled in college," he wrote. "Frankly, I don't have much time for anything else."

Obama worked hard in short spurts, as he did in Caldwell's class, but never seemed stressed by the coursework and found plenty of time for other activities. Bill Clinton's classmates at Georgetown and Yale Law School used to tell stories of how he would wait until the final night to cram for an exam, or skip a course for most of the year and then borrow notes from a diligent student who had attended every class and score better on the finals than she did, or sprawl on a couch all night reading a Russian novel that had absolutely nothing to do with the subjects he was studying. Obama had many of these same traits, to a slightly lesser degree. Imad Husain recalled that Barry "didn't take many notes and felt very comfortable . . . his notes were succinct, to the point." Kelly Lloyd Schafer remembered encountering Obama late one night in the hallway of Haines Hall. After spending many hours typing a paper for a class they both were taking, she was finally done and stressed out from the experience, and here came Barry, wearing a button-down short-sleeve Hawaiian shirt, OP shorts and flip-flops, looking like he had not a care in the world, offering his typical, "Hey, Kelly, how's it going?" She asked if he had finished his paper. "Oh, I'm going to get started on that in a little while," he said. Later, he told her he got an A on it. Another friend called him "the man with the magic pen."

In the subjects he preferred, political science and literature, Obama signed up for as many advanced courses as he could take and often was placed in seminars with upperclassmen. Rick Satterlee, a close friend of John Boyer's who had started dating and would later marry one of Obama's Punahou classmates, Mari Ota, was in a small literature seminar with him taught by Anne Howells, and remembered that Howells thought so highly of a paper Obama had written explicating a poem that she read it aloud to the class. "It was obviously the best paper any of us wrote. I recall him rolling his eyes about being called out in class that way. . . . He was clearly at that point a little uneasy about it," Satterlee said. "It was clearly better than anything any of us had written, including those of us that were going to major in the subject." Howells, even if she had embarrassed Obama, became one of his favorite professors and encouraged his writing, though she also had to push him to turn in his papers on time.

Of all the professors at Occidental, Roger Boesche was the one who had the greatest influence on Obama, but it would be overstating the relationship to say that he was a mentor. Decades later the professor of political thought and theory could remember other former students like Caroline Boss and Susan Keselenko vividly but could bring back only a few images of young Barry, perhaps because he was only there for two years. "I do remember Obama, but not in any great detail," Boesche said. "I do remember him in class, in part because he had a different name, Barry Obama. He had a moderate Afro and he was black. That stood out there. He asked some questions and seemed like a smart guy." His other strong memory was encountering Obama in the Cooler one day and handing back a midterm paper for which he had given Barry a B. "I told him he was really smart, but he wasn't working hard enough." Obama, upset, responded that he was working as hard as he could. He later paid a visit to Boesche at his office to talk about it further, and seemed especially upset that Hasan Chandoo had received a better grade. Boesche assumed later that he had struck a nerve; perhaps Obama realized that he was partying too much and not giving full concentration to his classwork.

Boesche (pronounced bo-SHAY) was a prominent figure on the Oxy campus, beloved by students for his illuminating lectures, his openness to debate, his ability to connect theory and philosophy to the political issues of the day, and his willingness to take a role in various causes. He led discussion groups himself (there were no teaching assistants at Oxy) and arranged office hours that would be convenient for his students. He had a way of drawing out the most shy students without embarrassing them, and treated his class like an intellectual community. A product of the 1960s, Boesche was born in the postwar boom year of 1948 and emerged from a conservative childhood in Tulsa, Oklahoma. (There were also Boesches, as it happened, two hundred miles north in the Butler County, Kansas, of Stan and Madelyn's era.) Like many of his generation, he underwent a political transformation, in his case from Goldwater Republican at age sixteen to college antiwar activist at Stanford. By the time he graduated in 1969, "virtually everyone there was against the war, which meant you didn't need to know all the arguments." Boesche was the type who wanted to know all the arguments. He turned down a graduate offer at Harvard, got married, and stayed at Stanford to earn his doctorate, then started teaching at Occidental when he was not quite thirty, in 1977, two years before Obama arrived. His body started failing him in a way that his imposing brain would not. He developed a degenerative condition that left him a hobbitlike figure, his hands severely clenched, his feet requiring special shoes, but the pain could not stop him. When it became too intense to walk, he would back his car up to his office to make it to class.

His introductory course, the first of three Obama took from him, was on American political thought: Jefferson, Thoreau, Lincoln, the Populists, the Progressives, the New Deal. The class ended "with a debate that was popular at that time: Is America run by a power elite or a pluralist democracy?" He also worked his classes through Nietzsche, Tocqueville, Freud, Weber, Sartre, and Marcuse, focusing more on the questions they raised than the answers. He devoted several weeks alone to Friedrich Nietzsche, the nineteenth-century German philosopher, presenting his key works and thoughts along with their various contradictory interpretations, weaving them through Nietzsche's central notion that a thinking person should challenge all doctrines. He also lingered on and probed more deeply into the thought of Alexis de Tocqueville and his conclusion that America would succeed because of its emphasis on community organizations that could perpetuate local democracy.

Boesche's custom in larger classes was to lecture without calling on anybody. But Ken Sulzer, who took one of the courses with Obama, recalled, "If you had something to say and raised your hand, you could say it. . . . Roger was so low-key and so approachable as a teacher that people would just say, 'Can you just go back thirty seconds, because I just missed that.' You wouldn't feel uncomfortable asking that. It was a very comfortable intellectual learning environment with Roger. You would consider Roger probably left of center, [but] there was not a bunch of hostility if you were an Adam Smith or Edmund Burkean conservative. . . . Roger was self-aware. He was not pretending to be dead center. All of us were aware of that, but that didn't really impact a lot of what he was teaching."

Some teachers knew their subject matter but not how to convey it to their students, but Boesche had a notable capacity to explain complicated thoughts in an understandable way without losing the nuances, thought Hasan Chandoo. "We all admired him and learned a lot from him," Chandoo said. "He would come so prepared with his notes, always prepared." Kathy Cooper-Ledesma, who was with Obama in the class that studied Tocqueville, said Barry was one of those who asked the most questions in discussion groups. "The thing that stood out to me, I remember that Barry liked to ask a lot of questions and do a lot of talking. They were always very insightful, but there were a lot of them. A lot." Some of the prolific talkers seemed to be just trying to show off, Cooper-Ledesma said, but Barry was not like that. "He was earnestly trying to get at the heart of what we were talking about. . . . I remember thinking, 'Haven't we talked about that enough? Isn't it time for lunch?' There was nothing wrong with it; he just wasn't done asking questions."

Boesche's students remembered his passion for community, a notion he probed most deeply in his lectures on Tocqueville. He encouraged his students to be part of a wider community and "not only to have individual pursuits," said Cooper-Ledesma, "but to have pursuits that would better humanity and better the common good for all." It was a sensibility that Boesche carried with him from the 1960s. Decades later, when he heard Barack Obama the senator and presidential candidate talk about moving beyond the 1960s, he could not help thinking that the era was perhaps more a part of Obama's learning process than he realized. "As much as he talks about putting the sixties behind us, he was influenced by the sixties," Boesche said decades later. "The college was full of young professors who came out of the antiwar movement or the civil rights movement. So he was influenced by those sixties professors. He may not have thought of it that way, but he was influenced by them."

There was perhaps another, more subtle Occidental influence. Louis Hook, a black student leader, said Oxy had an unstated but unmistakable learning philosophy that was pounded into students in their freshman year and often stayed with them for the rest of their lives. It could be summarized in three words: *listen, analyze, decide*. Obama seemed to work that way anyway, but Oxy certainly reinforced his natural tendency. In any discussion, John Boyer recalled, Obama would listen to everyone else before bringing in his point of view. Jeff Yamaguchi put it this way: "He listens and he listens and he listens, rather than respond immediately to the first thing that's out there. It's like, 'Let's let it percolate for a little. Let's let it simmer.' He reads people really well. He doesn't use the same play for every person. He has different plays in his playbook. He adjusts to the situation."

Among the freshmen at Oxy were two students from Ghana, Kofi Manu and Raphael Badu-Bonsu. Along with two seniors from Uganda, they constituted the African quartet at the school. Manu, the son of a Ghanaian government minister, was interested in diplomacy and history and took several courses with Obama. Because his ear was tuned to the pitch and cadence of British English, he had a difficult time comprehending American English that first year. He needed help with his notes, thinking the professors spoke too fast. A mentor assigned to him by the international student advisor helped him sometimes, and so did his classmate Obama. "In Roger's [Boesche's] political science class Obama would sometimes voluntarily sit next to me and explain the lecture to me or help me write my notes, as well as share notes with me," Manu recalled. They became friends in the classroom and out on the Quad, where they shared a hankering for the "red" cigarettes, Marlboros. Manu said Obama was especially friendly to people who seemed lonely or felt a sense of otherness, like the Africans, and that if they responded well he would continue to seek them out. "If you are alone he will come up next to you and engage you in conversation," Manu recalled. "People would say he was engaging, but I would say it differently. He comes to you. He is drawn to people." Despite what Manu considered to be Obama's "fair" complexion, the name Obama sounded African to him and he was not surprised that Barry's father was from Kenya. At his prep school in Ghana, Manu had studied the independence movement throughout Africa; he was familiar with the Mau Mau and Jomo Kenyatta, and often talked to Obama about what he knew. The Africans called Obama their brother; he told them how much he wanted to go to Africa to see his father and his roots. As the school year was ending, he invited Manu to visit him in Hawaii, but the Ghanaian could not make the trip and visited a cousin in Chicago instead.

When Barry returned to Honolulu for part of the summer of 1980, he staked claim to his old bedroom in Gramps and Tut's Punahou Circle apartment for the last time. His mother and sister were still in Indonesia, living in Semarang, where Ann was a consultant for the U.S. Agency for International Development. At about the time Barry left Oxy for home, a lawyer in Honolulu named William H. Gilardy Jr. filed papers in the Family Court of the First Circuit on behalf of Stanley Ann Soetoro seeking a divorce from Lolo Soetoro. The marriage was "irretrievably broken," Ann said in her affidavit. In fact, they had not lived together in more than six years, since Ann had gone back to Hawaii during her graduate school days and she and her two children had lived on Poki Street, the little family of three housed under the same roof for almost three years, the longest extended period in their lives.

Much as she had with her son and his father, though, Ann had tried to protect her daughter from the pain of a failed relationship. She never spoke harshly of Barack Obama Sr. in front of Barry, and she would not belittle Lolo in Maya's presence. Beyond the men themselves, she exerted great effort in honoring their cultures. In one sense, this was much easier when it came to Maya, since she was born in Indonesia, lived much of her early life there, knew the language, was surrounded by relatives, and even after the marriage breakup saw her father at least once every three months – not often, but exponentially more than Barry saw his father, which was once in his life after Ann and Barack split. But precisely because Maya was tied more closely to her Indonesian roots than Barry was to his father and Kenya, the family rift she experienced was more immediately apparent and traumatic.

Maya would never forget the night at the house in Semarang when she heard her mother arguing with Lolo on the phone. After Ann hung up, she told Maya that she and Lolo were getting a divorce and that Lolo intended to marry someone else. Maya was nine years old. Unlike her brother, she had been with her mother all her life. Hearing the argument on the phone, she was upset by how distraught her mother was, and then another thought seeped into her unconscious. "I was terrified of losing her," Maya recalled decades later. "I had a dream that night that I still remember. Mom standing in the middle of the road, and she was struck by a car, and in the dream she had lost her limbs. Just her torso and her face. And she said, 'Sorry, but you have to go live with your father.' And I was not ready to. Then she got hit by another car. And I remember waking up just sobbing."

The divorce filing in Honolulu stated that sole custody of the child should go to Ann. Just as she had when she divorced Barack Obama, she did not ask for child support, nor did she seek any joint property. Lolo had not contributed support to Ann or Maya since 1974, the affidavit said. She did not need him financially. She and her daughter lived in a four-bedroom house provided by USAID. Ann's work hours coincided with Maya's school hours, so child care was not a problem. She had two full-time live-in domestics, to whom she paid three hundred dollars a month. Her son was in college, supported by scholarships, financial aid, and some assistance from Ann's mother, now a bank vice president and the biggest breadwinner in the family.

When the divorce papers were filed, Barry was in Honolulu for the summer, living with Stan and Tut. It was then that the bus stop incident occurred, a scene involving his grandparents that he later would transform into a parable, first in his memoir, then in a speech about race that he delivered at a critical juncture in his campaign for the presidency in 2008. As noted earlier, *Dreams from My Father* rearranges the chronology and places the scene during his high school years at Punahou. But in Obama's original book proposal, which he wrote several years before the memoir was published, he presented the bus stop episode as the first significant anecdote in the story he wanted to tell, and dated it "between my first and second years in college." With the book not yet formed, there was no reason then for him to manipulate the date. In an interview decades later in the White House, Obama said he could not remember which year the incident took place. The proposal in this case seems a more reliable narrator than the book itself.

Aside from the timing, Obama changed very little of this scene from the proposal, slotting it into his memoir virtually word for word, paragraph for paragraph. He "awoke to the muted sound of an argument in the kitchen." He left his room in time to ask his grandmother what was wrong as she opened the door to her bedroom. "Nothing. Your grandfather just doesn't want to take me to work this morning, that's all," she told him. Barry then entered the kitchen to find his grandfather "muttering under his breath" – and over the next several minutes pried the story out of both of them. Tut had been bothered recently by the presence of a panhandler down at the corner, where she caught the bus to her job at the Bank of Hawaii, and had asked Stan to give her a ride. This angered Stan, who noted that she had dealt with panhandlers before, no problem. "You know why she's so scared this time?" he said to his grandson, whispering. "Before you came in, she told me the fella was black. That's why she's so scared. And I don't think that's right." The words, Obama wrote in the proposal, "felt like a fist to my stomach, but I remember how quickly I recovered." In his "steadiest voice," he told Gramps that his grandmother's fears bothered him too, but it would pass, and in the meantime they should give her a ride. Stan slumped in his chair. He "grew small and old and very sad." They sat in "painful silence" for a time, and then Stan relented and gave his wife a ride to work.

There was one notable change from proposal to book in the scene after Stan and Tut left the apartment. "After they left, I sat on the edge of my bed and thought about my grandparents," he wrote in the memoir. In the proposal, he showed more emotion, writing, "After they left, I sat on the edge of my bed and wept. I wept for my grandmother, who had sacrificed again and again for me, and had poured all of her lingering hopes into my success. She had never given me reason to doubt her love, and yet men who might easily have been my brothers could still inspire her rawest fears. I wept for her, and for myself. A part of me felt utterly alone."

There was no weeping for Tut and Stan in the memoir. One scene in the book had a similar rhythm, and found him weeping, but it came much later, when he wept for his Kenyan father and grandfather. And in the memoir, the "utterly alone" phrase was moved. He did not feel utterly alone on that bed in the apartment in Punahou Circle, but hours later, after he had driven down to see the aging black poet, Frank Marshall Davis, at his shack in "the Jungle" near the Ala Wai Canal, and shared a drink with Davis, and listened as the old man talked about race in America and concluded with something that startled Barry: "What I'm trying to tell you is, your grandma's right to be scared. She's at least as right as Stanley is. She understands that black people have a reason to hate. That's just how it is. For your sake, I wish it were otherwise. But it's not. So you might as well get used to it."

The "earth shook" under his feet, "ready to crack open at any moment," Obama wrote. "I stopped, trying to steady myself, and knew for the first time that I was utterly alone."

There are many ways to deal with existential loneliness. Lisa Jack, the Occidental student and photographer who had shot Barry's stylish pictures a few months earlier, happened to be in Honolulu that summer. Jack was there mostly for work, not play. Her favorite professor at Oxy had encouraged her to study the socioeconomics of Hawaii by taking a job at Palama Settlement, working with troubled adolescents in one of Honolulu's poorest neighborhoods. One night, taking a break from her work, she ended up at a club drinking and partying with some friends. She looked over at another table and there was Barry Obama. "He's got a woman on each leg and one in between, and he's having the time of his life. They were all over him. And he was just hanging out." An exaggeration, perhaps, but Obama was at a table with several women. Jack and Obama caught each other's eyes across the room and he dropped what he was doing to come over to talk. "I'm not a ten, like some of those girls were," Jack recalled. "So I was highly impressed and felt great because he dumped those three girls and we chatted briefly. 'What are you doing here?' 'I'm from Hawaii. What are you doing here?' 'Working at Palama.'" And then he went back to what he was doing, not alone, at least not physically.

When he returned to Oxy, the Annex was out of his life. He had talked to Kofi Manu, the Ghanaian, about finding an apartment with him for their sophomore year, but instead moved into a place with his Pakistani friend Hasan Chandoo, now a senior. It was four miles from campus at the corner of Glenarm and Raymond Avenue in Pasadena, not far from the terminus of the Arroyo Seco Parkway. Vinai Thummalapally, from India, was leaving the apartment for another place, though he would come over often and cook meals there. In most respects this was a different world from the bustling backdoor lair at Haines Hall. No more Barf Couch. Chandoo, whose family was in the international shipping business, wore fine clothes and drove a yellow Fiat 128S that he bought with his own money. It ran better than Obama's red Fiat, which idled often either because it needed repairs or Obama could not scrounge up gas money. Obama often hitched a ride down to Occidental with Chandoo. Although Hasan came from money, his father kept him on a monthly allowance, and he was not living a luxurious life in L.A. or underwriting Obama's existence. Their apartment was unprepossessing: two bedrooms, one bath, and a kitchen. Some Filipino nurses lived on another floor and also, for a time, a large extended family of Mexicans, "eight or nine," as Chandoo remembered it. They could walk to a grocery, but Obama never demanded much in the way of food. His daily staple was a bowl of Total cereal.

They were still college kids, their lives enlivened by parties and women, drugs and beer. Chandoo was a cosmopolite who loved to cooking and music. He was three years older than Obama; they often called each other "brother," and there was a bit of big brother–little brother to their relationship, but in some ways Obama was the more mature of the two. He read more and was a more serious student (one reason he was so upset when Roger Boesche gave Chandoo a better grade on a paper). While Obama would make much of his reckless youth with the Choom Gang at Punahou, he was never in trouble at school. Chandoo was a self-described "awful student" who would rather "play golf, chase girls, get into fights" during his teenage years and had foundered at prep schools in Singapore, one of the centers of the family shipping enterprise, and Karachi, the family home. His grades and test scores at the Karachi American School were barely high enough for him to get into a U.S. college. Occidental accepted him only after he had spent a year at Windham College in Putney, Vermont, an institution with a brief and varied life, opening in 1951 as a school designed to help foreign students improve their language skills and adjust to American academics. It closed in 1977 (at the end of Chandoo's year there), after it had become a safe haven for young American men seeking student deferments to avoid being drafted. For all that, Windham boasted some outstanding faculty members at various points, including John Irving, the novelist, and Peter W. Galbraith, son of the famed economist John Kenneth Galbraith. The younger Galbraith, on his way to a career in foreign policy and diplomacy, supported the reform movement in Pakistan, was a close friend of Benazir Bhutto, the future prime minister, who had gone to grammar school with many of Chandoo's friends, and took it upon himself to serve as Chandoo's mentor, helping get him into Occidental.

At Oxy one of Hasan's nicknames was Can-do Chandoo. This came from a headline in the student paper that described his demeanor as the volunteer head coach of the women's club field hockey team. Field hockey was the national sport of Pakistan, imported by the British, but like many products of Karachi's upper middle class, Chandoo grew up more influenced by American than British culture. The television shows of his youth were *Flipper, Lassie, The Fugitive, The Man from U.N.C.L.E.* His father, Raza Chandoo, loved the music of Nat King Cole, Frank Sinatra, and Johnny Mathis. Hasan became a diehard New York Yankees fan during his time in Vermont, and carried that allegiance to the West Coast, where he rooted for the Los Angeles Lakers during the rise of their Showtime era with Magic Johnson and Kareem Abdul-Jabbar. Obama came around to the Lakers, but had rooted against them, and for the Philadelphia 76ers and his favorite player, Julius Erving, in the 1980 NBA Finals.

Hasan and Barry's place became a regular hangout for the Pakistanis and their friends. Wahid Hamid was a regular, along with his off-campus roommate, Laurent Delanney, a tennis-playing student from France whose father had worked in the United States. Vinai Thummalapally, the Indian, and Asad Jumabhoy, a freshman at Oxy who had grown up in Singapore as a family friend of the Chandoos, were frequent presences at the apartment, along with Imad Husain and Paul Carpenter, who were still sharing a room at Haines Hall. (Asad liked to call Imad and Barry "the two Husseins.") It was in this company that Barry Obama felt most comfortable. "These were my closest friends," he noted decades later, during an interview in the Oval Office. Race was not a factor. Delanney was white, Obama was black, the Pakistanis were various shades, but it was an international sensibility that brought them together, Obama said. "I think there is no doubt . . . they were sort of world citizens, with kind of peripatetic lives. All of them had that sort of shared characteristic of spanning cultures, which I think strengthened our friendships."

Parties were staged at the apartment at least twice a month. Leslie Dudley, who lived in Haines above the Annex during her freshman year and was a friend of Barry's, remembered how he "would always spot me on campus and call me to come over and tell me he was having a gathering and I was coming. I'd roll my head. He'd say, 'No, you're coming.' I was a little hard to pin down and he was together. . . . It was a lot of Hasan's friends and a lot of older people were there. They would play music and have beer. They had a patio, and you'd go out there to smoke. It was a lot of talking. . . . It was a very sociable environment, fun people joking around, a lot of laughing. You'd always meet someone interesting to talk to. It would definitely be more international, more multicultural, multiracial, and you'd get some of the artsy people, people who wrote, who had that creative energy."

This crowd seemed to sense something the Annex guys could not: the fire burning deep inside Barry Obama. Wahid Hamid was Chandoo's age but a year behind him at Occidental. Their family stories were similar: Muslim parents, though from different sects, who left India for Pakistan after the 1947 Partition and rose into the upper middle class there. He was less political than Hasan, with more of a scientific bent, but shared his passion for conversation. He found Obama a like-minded soul who seemed to understand "the nuances of the world" and could comprehend complex patterns. The deeper his discussions with Obama became, the more Wahid could see his ambition. "You would have to get close to him to understand the ambition," he recalled. "If you're friends with somebody who's social, they seem like any other college kid. You'd think he was articulate. But if you get close and really engage around the world and politics, the meaning of life. . . . We used to talk about physics. Obama never took physics, but he could grasp concepts really quickly. You could tell there was a strong ambition there and the need to prove himself. There was a confidence there that, coupled with that ambition, meant he was going to really make a go of it."

Asad Jumabhoy, with an interest in economics, was impressed by the intensity of the political discussions led by Chandoo and Obama. "Some were fiery, some were less fiery," he recalled.

> I was always struck by Barry's mind. One day there was some debate going on . . . and he stepped in and started talking. I was kind of captivated. I listened and listened. I didn't have a car, so Vinai usually drove me back to campus. As I walked out of the [flat] . . . just picture, it's 1980, I'm a Singapore boy fresh off the boat . . . it's a multiracial society with no deep history of conflict between the races. . . . It was a fiery debate and I was impressed by a guy who speaks like that. We're walking to the car and I said, "You know, this guy could be president of the United States. He talks so well." And they started laughing at me. I said, "Why are you laughing?" They said, "Don't you realize he's black?"

During the Christmas break that year, Sohale Siddiqi, a friend of Hasan's and Wahid's who lived in New York, came out to visit. There was a room available at the apartment in Pasadena; Obama had left on a road trip and ended up in San Francisco. On the night of December 31, Hasan and Sohale and some buddies drove up to San Francisco for a New Year's Eve party, and it was there that Siddiqi encountered Chandoo's roommate for the first time. "A lanky, broad-smiling Barry wearing a tattered straw hat endeared himself immediately by greeting me in Urdu slang with 'Kiayaa haal heh, seth?'" (How are you, boss?) Siddiqi asked Obama "how he got any sleep with a snarling wood carved mask hanging over his bed. He laughed in response." The straw hat was the same one he had worn for the photo shoot with Lisa Jack. The wood carving came from Indonesia. The next morning, Obama joined Chandoo and Siddiqi and friends for the long drive back to Los Angeles. Siddiqi stayed for another ten days. "It was nonstop parties, social gatherings, with home-cooked meals by Vinai." There was also an event at Oxy that Chandoo helped with, a visit from the social activist and comedian Dick Gregory, who then espoused "simple living and frugal eating," concepts that Obama in particular seemed to take to heart.

Living off campus that second year, Obama spent even more time at the Cooler, his home away from home. He felt his voice "growing stronger, sturdier, that constant, honest portion of myself." The late-night discussions he participated in now were more intense, more overtly political, more directed at America's role in the world. Chandoo and the other Pakistanis, along with the writers Obama associated with, had a seriousness of purpose and worldly sensibility that cut against the stereotype of Oxy as a haven for spoiled white suburban kids. "I don't think I ever had as intense conversations with anyone as with Hasan," said Caroline Boss. "Always intense, and always with the greatest respect and friendship and kindness. A real keen sense of the importance of it all." Like Boss, the school's leading student socialist, Chandoo was to the left of Obama, who often ridiculed him about the vast distance between his proletarian rhetoric and his comfortable lifestyle. He was dating a junior then, Margot Mifflin, who was not only part of the writing set but also the captain of the field hockey team. Can-do Chandoo. At one party on Glenarm they all danced to "Once in a Lifetime" by Talking Heads – a "sea of people," Obama among them, bodies jerking quirkily, ecstatically to the hypnotic, incessant, poetic rhythm of David Byrne: "Time isn't holding us, time isn't after us, time isn't holding us, time doesn't hold you back . . . letting the days go by, letting the days go by, letting the days go by, once in a lifetime . . ."

Western Kenya remained a territory of the imagination to Barry Obama, the land of a father he barely knew. To one of his friends at Oxy, Eric Moore, it was a real place, its people and geography etched in Moore's mind from the two months he had spent there during the summer. He had been sent to Kenya as a volunteer for Operation Crossroads Africa, a predecessor and smaller version of the Peace Corps, by James H. Robinson, an African American minister. Moore, one year ahead of Barry at Occidental, had signed on with Crossroads along with seven other Oxy students. By chance he ended up within a few kilometers of the Obama homestead in Nyang'oma Kogelo, in the Siaya district of Nyanza province, the heart of Luoland, where he helped construct a new wing – mortar walls, corrugated tin roof – on a rural medical clinic near the village of Ndere. He lived in a mud hut with his hosts and at times slept on the floor of the clinic. There was no electricity or running water. He bathed in the drip of a water tank. No telephones. People walked or were carried for miles to see the lone doctor. Every morning before work, Moore loped off on a long-distance run along the red-dirt roads through the brushy landscape. This did not go unnoticed by a teacher and headmaster he had befriended at the local school, who persuaded him to coach their students for a district track meet in Yala. At the end of his morning run he would stop at the school and lead the children in calisthenics and wind sprints. When the time came for the meet, Moore asked how they were supposed to get there. This seemed like an odd question to the Luo. They walked the ten miles. Then ran.

Obama's friends and acquaintances at Oxy sometimes heard him say that his father was from Kenya. On occasion he would lament that he did not know the old man, that he was gone from the family when Barry was a baby. Once in a rare while the bitterness came out, or expressions of regret. Sometimes that part of the story was left unsaid and the emphasis was placed on his deep and recent family connection to the continent. To have an African father could be seen as a badge of distinction in the jockeying for place among the cohort of blacks at Oxy. But the blood tie was all that Obama had then, along with a few letters from his father (one came to him at Oxy, with the message "Know where you belong"), the memory of that lone visit to Honolulu when Barry was in fifth grade, and the stories he had heard from his mother and grandfather. He had never been to Kenya, never walked the earth around Lake Victoria, and Eric Moore had.

Obama and Moore had much in common. They were tall, athletic, smooth, outwardly confident. Moore, whose mother had been valedictorian at Howard

University in a class with the civil rights legend Andrew Young, had grown up in Boulder, Colorado, attended predominantly white schools, and like Obama had survived and thrived, at least by outward appearances, in an environment where there were few people who looked like him. Moore came to Los Angeles looking for "a more urban African American experience" where he could further sort out his identity. He had no intentions of rejecting his past, or turning away from it, but like Obama was looking for something more. They were among fewer than eighty African Americans out of 1,711 students at Oxy, only 4.4 percent, but still both young men encountered many more black peers there than they had in high school.

They both befriended Kofi Manu, the Ghanaian, and helped him find his way around Los Angeles. "We would get our haircuts together at a place called Magnificent Brothers on Crenshaw," Moore recalled. "We would go to music festivals, cultural festivals." They spent time listening to music, first meeting in the dorm room of a resident advisor at another dorm, where they spent hours dissecting the lyrics to Bob Marley's 1979 album, *Survival.* Marley originally had thought of calling the album *Black Survival,* but did not want to dilute his universal reggae message. *Survival* in any case was among his most overtly political albums – a haunting, tough, pounding, unstoppable expression of the black condition. The jacket featured the flags of forty-seven African nations, with Kenya in the top left corner, Ghana in the upper right. The song titles evoked the struggle of Africa and people in the New World with African blood: "So Much Trouble in the World," "Africa Unite," "One Drop," "Ride Natty Ride," "Ambush in the Night," "Survival" ("Some people got facts and claims / some people got pride and shame / some people got the plots and schemes / some people got no aim it seems"). Obama, Moore, Manu, and a few other friends broke down the songs one by one and debated what they meant, what was going on in Marley's rendition of the world. Manu became so entranced by Marley's music and message that they started to call him Rastaman. Music can be the least appreciated factor among the forces that shape people. It crosses the boundary between universal and personal, and can be as formative as any classroom, friendship, or physical event. Barry Obama could take or leave much of the music that he had heard most often in the Annex, from new wave to punk, enjoying some, tuning out some, but it was the musical language of Bob Marley, and Stevie Wonder, that stirred something deeper inside him. "Obama's consciousness, much like mine, was influenced by music, influenced by a recognition, an understanding of the world through music," Moore said. "Obama's sense of social justice ultimately comes from Bob, or comes from Stevie Wonder. You can't learn all that from a book."

It was through their connection to music and Africa and their friendship with Kofi Manu that Moore started calling Obama the name by which the world would come to know him later. One day, as Moore recalled the scene, he and Obama were

kicking around, sitting around, discussing the world . . . and I said, "Barry Obama? What is that derivative of?" And he told me the story of how his mom had met his father. And I had been to Kenya . . . and he had not been there yet. I was very familiar with where he was from. . . . It was a bit of serendipity in our lives. We were just kind of chatting. I was heckling a bit . . . "Barry Obama, what kind of name is that for a brother?" And he said, "Well, my real name is *Buh-ROCK.* Barack Obama." And I said, "Well, that's a strong name. Rock, *Buh-ROCK.*" And we laughed about it. But for the two years I knew him everyone called him Barry. Barry Obama. And it was cool. He said, "I go by Barry so I don't have to explain myself to the world. You're my bro, I can give you the background on it." But it was basically an accommodation to the Anglo world, Anglo society. You don't want to be singled out, necessarily.

Manu had gone through a similar scene with Obama even earlier. "There are given Christian names and real African names," Manu had told him. "My Christian given name is Samuel, but my real African names are Kofi and Yaw. What's your African name?" In that setting, Obama felt wholly comfortable saying that his name was Barack.

In his memoir Obama would tell a different story about one of the key moments in his gradual transformation from Barry to Barack. He wrote that he was talking to friends named Marcus and Regina. Marcus, portrayed as Afrocentric, had ridiculed him for reading Joseph Conrad's *Heart of Darkness,* and Obama had defended himself by saying that he was reading it to understand "just what it is that makes white people so afraid." After Marcus left, Regina – rendered in the memoir as astute and comfortable in her black identity – asked Obama what Marcus had called him, some African name. *Barack,* he told her. She said she thought his name was Barry. Barack was his given name, he explained. His father's name. His father was Kenyan. *Barack* meant "blessed" in Arabic. His grandfather was Muslim. "It's beautiful," Regina responded, according to the memoir. "Mind if I call you Barack?" Not as long as she pronounced it right, he said.

Eric Moore was not in *Dreams from My Father,* nor could he recognize precisely who Marcus and Regina were. Hasan Chandoo, who was portrayed in the book (and, in a rare instance, was given his real name), was not sure either. He himself was accurately depicted, but to him the other composites, he said good-naturedly, seemed like "mumbo-jumbo." At some places in the memoir, the characters were taken from real life but given pseudonyms. At other times they were composites. Marcus and Regina were composites, inspired in part by two upperclassmen, Earl Chew and Sarah Etta-Harris, but displaying characteristics from many other people as well as from the searching, divided soul of Obama himself. Like Regina in the book, Etta-Harris had studied abroad, winning a Thomas Watson fellowship to spend a year in Andalusia in Spain. But in his memoir Obama gave Regina a family history in Chicago, and that did not fit her. Rather, that aspect of Regina was an early iteration of someone Obama had not met at Oxy and would not know for another ten years, Michelle Robinson, to whom he was married by the time he wrote the memoir in the early 1990s. It was not precisely Michelle's story, but close in many respects, as Obama had Regina telling him about her South Side memories: people so hot in the summer they went out by Lake Michigan to sleep; a vibrant community of taverns, pool halls, churches, kitchen nights with cousins, uncles, grandparents. "A vision," he wrote, "that filled me with longing – a longing for place, and a fixed and definite history." When he told Regina that he envied her, she scoffed. "For what?" she asked. "Memories," he said. That response, Obama wrote, made her laugh and say she wished she had grown up in Hawaii.

This was one of the more telling paragraphs in the book, revealing what Obama thought he had missed out on in his young life and what he so dearly longed for. Though he was writing it in retrospect, long after his Oxy days and after he had finally made his way to Chicago, the early Regina, who existed mostly in his mind, helped trace what would become the arc of his life toward family and home.

Along with Etta-Harris and Michelle Robinson, the Regina character also incorporated a third real-life model. Some of Obama's scenes of Regina reflected incidents that involved Caroline Boss, who was white. The name Regina itself likely came out of Obama's discussions with Boss. Regina was the name of her Swiss grandmother, who came up in their discussions about class, race, and gender. Boss was a formidable figure at Oxy, queen of the Cooler rats, star pupil of the school's noted political science professor, Roger Boesche. As leader of the Democratic Socialist Alliance on campus, she viewed politics from a class-conscious socialist perspective. Boss told Obama that her grandmother Regina spent her life scrubbing floors and doing laundry for the banking community in the small Swiss town of Interlaken. "So when we talked about race and class," Boss said of her discussions with Obama, "I of course took the position that class was a significant feature. . . . The class thing really affects the entire population, regardless of race and gender." Obama incorporated this idea into his memoir. His Regina was black, not white, yet he wrote about "Regina's grandmother somewhere, her back bent, the flesh of her arms shaking as she scrubbed an endless floor. Slowly, the old woman lifted her head to look straight at me, and in her sagging face I saw that what bound us together went beyond anger or despair or pity." He went on to link Regina's grandmother to all women who struggle against the power structure, from the Mexican maids who cleaned up the mess created by the boys at the Haines Hall Annex to his own grandmother, Tut, who rose before dawn every morning to ride the bus to work. "My identity might begin with the fact of my race, but it didn't, couldn't, end there," he wrote.

During his years at Occidental, and as he looked back on that period, Obama struggled in his memoir with the nuances of what it meant to be black. He employed a character named Joyce as the voice of someone of color who did not want to be classified or categorized. Joyce was said to have an African American mother and an Italian father. When Obama asked her if she was going to a meeting of the Black Students Association, she shook her head and said, "I'm not black, I'm multiracial." Assessing this scene, Obama wrote, "The problem with people like Joyce . . . they talked about the richness of their multicultural heritage and it sounded real good, until you noticed they avoided black people. It wasn't a matter of conscious choice necessarily, just a matter of gravitational pull – the way integration always worked, a one-way street." Then Obama turned his critique away from Joyce and toward himself. "I knew I was being too hard on poor Joyce," he wrote. "The truth was that I understood her, her and all the other black kids who felt the way she did. In their mannerisms, their speech, their mixed up hearts, I kept recognizing pieces of myself, and that's exactly what scared me."

It was because of that fear that Obama carefully structured his persona at Oxy to avoid "being mistaken for a sellout." He wanted to be seen with the black activists and foreign students and Chicanos and "the Marxist professors and structural feminists and punk-rock performance poets." He even lumped the Annex rebels into this group, anyone who was alienated and "resisting bourgeois society's stifling constraints." But that was Obama's internal construct; it was not how others viewed him. Among the black students on campus, he was considered closer in spirit to his multicultural character Joyce. At Oxy, for the first time, but not the last, there were blacks who questioned how black Obama really was. Often this was meant not as a critical judgment, but merely as a sociological assessment.

Adam Sherman, a Jewish student from Thomas S. Wootton High in Rockville, Maryland, recalled that his two black roommates at the Annex, Ricky Johnson and Cornelius Moody, viewed Obama's racial history and experience as vastly different from theirs and did not think of him as black. "Ricky was very aware that he had a very different cultural background and a different racial identity. Which was probably one of the things Barry was dealing with at the time. I'm sure Barry aware of that as well. It was an interesting dynamic to watch. Neil and Ricky were my roommates, and I was close friends with Paul [Carpenter], who was Barry's roommate. And Barry, Neil, and Ricky didn't hang out. Neil and Ricky had a different racial identity that didn't include Barry." Another black student in the Annex, Willard Hankins Jr., who came from Compton, called Obama not a friend, but "another black face in the hall." He spent far less time with Obama than with the other African Americans on the floor, Hankins said. "I felt a kinship with the others probably more so because we all hung out together. . . . We were all pretty much from the inner city."

Louis Hook, a senior when Obama was a freshman, was a leader of UJIMA, a black student group on campus, its name taken from a Swahili word that evokes community and responsibility. Hook had grown up in a housing project outside Los Angeles, was the first member of his family to get through college, and categorized the blacks at Oxy into three groups: working-class African Americans with a black cultural bent, middle-class African Americans with a black cultural bent, and middle-class blacks with a multicultural bent. There were only about five blacks on campus who fit that last mold, he said, and one of them was Obama. Some of the African Americans at Oxy, Hook said, "just couldn't tolerate the multicultural style of Obama. They called him an Oreo. . . . We'd get into some discussions about the Oreos." Hook said he understood the black separatists, the multiculturalists, and everyone in between, and tried to act as a bridge to all of them. "Obama was a multicultural mainstream Oxy guy," he said. "He fit right in with anybody. As long as you accepted him, he was good. He felt most comfortable in a multicultural environment. The African Americans he hung with leaned in that direction as well. Eric Moore, some of those folks."

Moore, like Obama, spent a lot of time trying to find his place in the racial mix at Oxy. He took several courses on African history, signed up for the Crossroads Africa program, and went to Clapp Library and checked out recordings of the speeches of Malcolm X and Martin Luther King Jr. just to hear their voices and feel their cadences. But he would not limit himself to the black experience: "I would move freely between a variety of circles, and so would Barack. His roommates were white, Pakistani. We had friends from Africa, Pakistan, and France. Our own rainbow coalition." One of Moore's close friends was Richard Casey, who came out of Compton and eventually rose to become a Harvard-trained doctor. At Oxy, Moore noted, Casey's "inclination was to be in that kind of separate black table, that separate black clique. He said one day, 'Bronson' – that's what he called me, I don't know, after Charles Bronson – he said, 'Bronson, how do you flow so easily between these different groups?' I played football. I was with the late-night smokers. The intellectuals. That was us, a rich tapestry of people. And I know it was the same with Barack." Kofi Manu, with the blackest skin of all, felt closest to Obama and Moore and the multicultural blacks who had been dismissed by some African

Americans as Oreos. There was a bond among all the black students, Manu said, at least to the extent of exchanging hellos and knowing glances when passing on the Quad, but it was the Obama and Moore types who tended to know and care more about Africa, and they were the ones who also took the time to acclimate the Africans to this strange environment, taking them to the store, to the barbershop, to concerts and restaurants.

During the year they shared an apartment in South Pasadena, Chandoo watched Obama deal with these issues. He thought of Obama as black. His roommate's bookshelves were full of works by significant black figures in literature and civil rights. It was Obama's copy of King's "Letter from Birmingham Jail" that Chandoo read. They both had friends of every race and gender and sexual orientation, no big deal as far as Chandoo was concerned. But there was one incident that he would never forget that might have revealed, without words, something about Obama's situation. It involved a two-on-two basketball game at the Oxy gym, Obama and he against two black classmates, both from the inner city, one a black militant, the other a varsity football player. For a Pakistani who grew up playing other sports, Can-do Chandoo was not bad at hoops, but not in the class of the others in this game. He did what he could, but mostly watched in awe as Obama blocked out, rebounded, hustled, did his hesitation move, and shot lights-out, playing with more fire than Chandoo had ever seen before, dominating the game and carrying the roommates to victory. At the end of the game, Chandoo said, "those guys loved him," and there were no questions about Obama's blackness.

His classmates considered Obama "a floater," moving not only from culture to culture but also from political group to political group, dabbling, showing interest, but never staking a home, never grabbing hold of something and making it his. This was a natural part of college experimentation, to be sure, but in Obama's case it reflected a deeper and longer-lasting trend, one that would define his life in and out of politics: his need and ability to avoid traps. The less entrenched he was, the easier it was for him to get out of something and move on. He had enough traps already: the trap of not knowing his father; the trap of growing up in Hawaii, farther from any continental landmass than anywhere in the world except Easter Island; the trap of growing up *hapa*, caught between worlds. Those were the early traps, and he was just now finding his way safely around them. By the middle of his sophomore year, after being steeped in political theory by Roger Boesche, after endless political discussions with Hasan Chandoo, Caroline Boss, with Earl Chew and Sarah Etta-Harris, with Margot Mifflin and Eric Moore, he had become part of Oxy's activist network. Chandoo was constantly writing letters to *The Occidental,* articulating his skepticism about America's intentions in the cold war struggle against the Soviets. He pleaded for American leaders to "spare the Third World in their effort to save them from the communist threat," noting, "There has been enough blood shed in the Third World to know that we do not want this type of benevolent attitude from either the U.S.A. or the U.S.S.R."

There was no Vietnam War to protest against, no single dominant issue providing the combination of idealism and self-interest that could ignite a movement. But they did have one issue to rally around: South Africa and the quest to abolish the racism of apartheid. Since 1977 the Student Coalition against Apartheid had been pushing Occidental's board of trustees to divest all school holdings in corporations that did business in South Africa. The intensity of the divestiture effort ebbed and flowed, depending on its leadership and the normal college distractions and diversions, but it had picked up again just as Obama was getting involved. He and Chandoo participated in a vigil protesting the imprisonment of Nelson Mandela. Chandoo and Boss were behind-the-scenes leaders of the divestiture issue on campus and certainly helped draw Obama into that effort, though in his memoir he offered another perspective on the subtleties of his motivation: "It had started as something of a lark, I suppose, part of the radical pose my friends and I sought to maintain, a subconscious end run around issues closer to home."

However it started, he got into it more every week, and eventually it led him to one of the key moments of his time at Oxy, the first public political speech of his life. It came on a Wednesday afternoon, February 18, 1981, the same day the new president, Ronald Reagan, one month into his presidency, delivered an address to a joint session of Congress outlining his plan for national economic recovery. It was a sun-splashed day in Southern California as Obama stood in the Arthur G. Coons Administrative Center Plaza, looking out on a gathering of a few hundred students. Up on the second floor of Coons, the board of trustees was about to meet, and whenever the door opened to their conference room the clamor outside washed in. Policemen planted themselves outside the locked door. One officer escorted Rary Simmons, a 1953 Oxy grad and trustee from upscale San Marino, down the hallway to the restroom. Black armbands, music, chanting. *Money out, freedom in!* The timeless protest chestnut *The people united will never be defeated!* When Occidental's president, Richard C. Gilman, came into sight on his way to the board meeting, he received a personal greeting: *President Gilman, what's the word? Oxy's not Johannesburg.* Behind Obama stood Caroline Boss, who had fumbled nervously in her introduction of the main speaker, Tim Ngubeni, a South African activist, who had issued the call for Oxy to "invest your money elsewhere" and invited the students to a concert across town that night at UCLA's Royce Hall to raise money for the Steve Biko Fund. Biko was a South African martyr of the freedom movement, a former student leader and promoter of black consciousness who had died three years earlier in police custody in a Pretoria prison. To the side stood Earl Chew and Sarah Etta-Harris, also on the speaking roster, along with Eric Newhall, a comparative literature professor who represented the faculty committee on multicultural education.

Obama had been given a scripted role in the protest drama. What he said was not supposed to be the point of his being up there. It was designed as a bit of guerrilla theater, with students dressed as policemen yanking him from the stage, symbolizing attempts by the establishment, there and in South Africa, to stifle the movement. The microphone was too low for him. He had to hunch over to project his voice, but once he started speaking, he built a cadence: "There's a struggle going on. . . . I say there's a struggle going on. . . . It's happening an ocean away. But it's a struggle that touches each and every one of us, whether we know it or not. A struggle that demands we choose sides. . . . It's a choice between dignity and servitude, between fairness and injustice." And he started to feel that magical surge of energy and power that comes when a speaker has an audience rapt and buying in. In the wings, Eric Moore turned to Tim Yeaney and asked, "Should we go ahead with the plan?" Yeaney said, "Yes!" and they marched up to Obama and dragged him away from the microphone.

Looking back on it later, Yeaney remarked on how even he was struck by Obama's performance, which he thought was an unpolished version of what millions of people would see twenty-five and thirty years later. "It was like eating a really good chocolate cake and someone takes it away from you," Yeaney said. "You want it more. What we intended was someone would say a few phrases, but he really launched into it and the crowd was into it. It was startlingly good. It was much more than we expected. It was genuine. . . . It was very passionate, very heartfelt. It was not dramatic, it was just calm but passionate. . . . Even days afterwards people were just saying how impressed they were with his speech."

There were, in retrospect, two notable and related aspects to this event. The first was that it gave Obama the first intimations of what it was like to move crowds, large or small, with words. *Words,* he had said in Barbara Czurles-Nelson's English class at Punahou years earlier. *Words are the power to be feared most.* But the second revelation was how little the protest meant to him. His favorite professor, Roger Boesche, had spent years involved in the divestiture effort. The first student organizer, who graduated just before Obama reached campus, was a Boesche protégé, Gary Chapman. Another of his disciples, Caroline Boss, had worked vigorously behind the scenes on that and other student protests, and Hasan Chandoo, Obama's roommate, was also involved. His African American cohorts, Chew and Etta-Harris and Moore, all thought that what they were doing was important. But after his own speech was cut off, Obama stopped paying attention to the rest of the rally, by his own account, and that night spoke dismissively of the entire event: "I don't believe we made any difference by what we did today." It was a cutting appraisal, though with some measure of truth. Oxy did not divest for another nine years.

In his class papers at Occidental, he was Barry Obama. The name Barack Obama premiered in public in the inaugural issue of *Feast,* a student literary magazine of poetry and short fiction published during his sophomore year. The editors of *Feast* were Tom Grauman and Alexandra McNear, two fellow sophomores. Grauman would later marry Caroline Boss, but at the time *Feast* was being created he had a serious crush on McNear. He was not alone. Among others in the long line of McNear's suitors, and the one Grauman believed was his main competition, was Obama. Alex McNear, lithe and mysterious, with the face of a young Meryl Streep and a literary bohemian air, came from trust-fund wealth and a sophisticated early life. Robert Erskine McNear, her father, had been president of the Mystery Writers of America and lived in San Francisco, the scion of real estate wealth. Suzanne McNear, her Wisconsin-born mother, was also a writer and a former *Playboy* magazine editor whose grandfather, John Caldwell, had been ambassador to Persia under Woodrow Wilson. Suzanne now lived on the Upper East Side and was a family friend of Jean and David Halberstam, the noted nonfiction writer. It was because of Halberstam, in fact, that Alex ended up at Oxy. He had given a speech there in early 1980 and came back so impressed that even though Alex had never heard of the school until he mentioned it, she decided to transfer there after her freshman year at Hunter College in New York. Tom Grauman must not have realized it at the time, but his decision to place his name above hers on the *Feast* masthead, though he was listed as managing editor and she as editor, did nothing to endear himself to her.

The plan for *Feast*, with the support of Occidental's Department of English, was that it would publish twice a year and limit itself to the written word and abstract illustrations. It was to be serious and rigorous, "not a collection of 'look what undergrads are doing,'" Grauman said. He and McNear wrote a joint letter to *The Occidental* that at once invited submissions and satirically captured their intent:

> 1) Feast upon these words: members of the Occidental community are a group of apathetic quasi-intellectual sports fans, thriving upon criticism of creative minds through contrived rhetoric and bizarre forms of sexual deviance. (Wrong – scratch that.) 2) Feast upon these words: members of the Occidental community are frustrated in the wake of waste land disillusionment – searching for values in a world void of the heart and saturated with the glands. (Right – continue.) 3) Feast is a new journal of campus-related literature. Its purpose is to present writers with fine ideas in a fine atmosphere. Writers should be criticized on the merits of their writing – not on the deficiencies of the pedestal on which they are displayed. . . . We encourage all persons to submit.

The literary set at Oxy was as self-selecting as any other subculture, and they all knew one another. Mark Dery, a senior, was brilliantly fixated on the bizarre and eccentric aspects of modern culture. ("Of all the hapless humans he'd butchered or debauched, not a one had been impressed by his display of predictable psychopathia.") Then there was the hypnotic storytelling of Chuck Jensvold, who would die young, a sort of noir Hemingway of the surf, considered among the most talented writers of a competetive group, winning first prize in the school's Argonaut writing contest. ("I could rely on feel, on feel alone. That thing called feel. That's what it is. Nothing to watch out for. Only water about. Water I knew. Water that carried me, carried me hard: gouging, cutting back in waves, clear black waves. They rolled and broke and tubed, without light, they didn't need it. They had feel.") And there was the close-to-the-bone poetry of Margot Mifflin, who was then dating Chandoo but would later marry Dery. ("Because children play in the street below my room / I hate them / Because no one in their houses died tonight / and because the window between my nose and theirs / is cold and fragile and came down too fast / Because I am ten years old.")

Obama was on the edge of this group, wanting in, starting to think of himself as a writer. It was another way he could break from the mold of the "apathetic quasi-intellectual sports fan."

Obama and Mifflin had been in the same English class in Room 200 of Swan Hall North taught by David James, an assistant professor who served as a faculty advisor for *Feast,* and he submitted for publication in the new journal several works that he had first written for that class, two poems and a piece of short fiction. As the editors and advisors went over them, Grauman recommended that Obama's prose piece be rejected and had the task of delivering that news to him in person. This happened in the Cooler. It did not go well. Obama had written about friends driving somewhere and having a conversation that turned into a deeper conflict, the car stopping and starting, the conflict lurching, unresolved. Grauman thought the story lacked context. It might have been inspired by an incident in Barry's life, but it seemed too spare for readers to fix on.

"I'm sure I was a little prick, but it was the position I had to take," Grauman said later. The rejection infuriated Obama, who said something on the order of "You just don't get it. You're stupid!" – and the argument deteriorated from there, according to Grauman. "We didn't kill each other or anything, though we did have a pretty bad shouting match." There was more to it than the merits of the short story, of course. Beneath that simmered the issue of which one of them deserved the affections of Alex McNear. "We were competing suitors," Grauman said, and that competition "would have contributed to a sense of personal affront" in terms of how Obama received the editorial rejection. She was interested in neither one of them then, as it turned out.

Feast did publish two poems by Barack Obama. One of them, entitled "Pop," had been discussed in David James's class and was well received by his classmates, who thought it was a revealing window into his life. The assumption then, and decades later, when the poem resurfaced and became an artifact for condescending literary criticism of a politician, was that "Pop" was about his grandfather Stan Dunham. There were aspects of the figure depicted in the poem that fit Stan: he smoked, drank, watched television, told jokes, and sometimes seemed small in the eyes of his grandson. But the essence of the work points in another direction, toward Frank Marshall Davis, the old black poet of Honolulu. Obama had visited Davis the previous summer for the first time in several years, after the traumatic bus stop discussion with his grandparents, so Davis's visage was fresh in his mind. He found Davis a colorful figure and liked to write about him, as his memoir later revealed. Also, he called his grandfather Gramps, not Pop, by no means a conclusive hint, but one of many signs. Pop, or Pops, was a nickname more commonly used in the black community for older men. It was a jazz and pool hall nickname. The younger hippies who lived around Davis and acquaintances in the bars on Smith Street often called him Pop or Pops. At the time Obama wrote this, Stan was sixty-two, while Davis was a generation older, seventy-six, more of a Pops. In one stanza Obama listened as Pop told the young man that he was naïve and failed to understand the world because he had not suffered enough. In another Pop "recited an old poem he wrote before his mother died." Stan would say many things to his *hapa* grandson, but not that his life was too easy. He was careless in other ways but always mindful of what Barry, with his darker skin, had to endure. Stan told people he wrote poetry, but he rarely did. He could recite a few limericks, but not his own poetry, and he was only eight when his mother committed suicide. In the scene in *Dreams from My Father* where Obama visited Frank after the bus stop incident, he was wearing reading glasses and drinking whiskey and sitting in an overstuffed chair. "Pop" unfolded like this:

Sitting in his seat, a seat broad and broken

In, sprinkled with ashes,

Pop switches channels, takes another

Shot of Seagrams, neat, and asks

What to do with me, a green young man

Who fails to consider the

Flim and flam of the world, since

Things have been easy for me;

I stare hard at his face, a stare

That deflects off his brow;

I'm sure he's unaware of his

Dark, watery eyes, that

Glance in different directions,

And his slow, unwelcome twitches,

Fail to pass.

I listen, nod,

Listen, open, till I cling to his pale

Beige T-shirt, yelling,

Yelling in his ears, that hang

With heavy lobes, but he's still telling

His joke, so I ask why

He's so unhappy, to which he replies . . .

But I don't care anymore, 'cause

He took too damn long, and from

Under my seat, I pull out the

Mirror I've been saving; I'm laughing,

Laughing loud, the blood rushing from his face

To mine, as he grows small,

A spot in my brain, something

That may be squeezed out, like a

Watermelon seed between

Two fingers.

Pop takes another shot, neat,

Points out the same amber

Stain on his shorts that I've got on mine, and
Makes me smell his smell, coming
From me; he switches channels, recites an old poem
He wrote before his mother died,
Stands, shouts, and asks
For a hug, as I shrink, my
Arms barely reaching around
His thick, oily neck, and his broad back, 'cause
I see my face, framed within
Pop's black-framed glasses
And know he's laughing too.

"Pop" reveals more about the poet than the subject, or composite subjects. Obama the poet, like the memoirist, shows a keen awareness of otherness and life's duality. He looks at Pop and sees something that repels him and attracts him, that he wants to run away from yet knows he must embrace. Pop makes himself small by what he says; Obama shrinks in his physical presence. The same stain on their pants, smelling the same smell, blood rushing from one face to the other. Looking in his own mirror first and then in the reflection of Pop's glasses, he realizes that the old man, who bores him and twitches unhappily in his stuffed chair with his whiskey and his cigarette ashes, nonetheless knows all that he knows. Black or white, black and white, Stan or Frank, Stan and Frank – the same in the end.

Three days after Bob Marley died, in 1981, Phil Boerner was disc-jockeying the noon show on KOXY, the campus radio station. He had prepared a fifty-five-minute tape for the May 14 broadcast, which among other venues was heard over loudspeakers on the Oxy Quad. "The first half was reggae, featuring Sly Dunbar, UB40, and Black Uhuru," Boerner wrote in his diary. "The second half was all Ian Dury and the Blockheads." Jamaica and Great Britain, reggae and new wave, with a nod to Kenya, *uhuru* being the Swahili cry for independence. Before going on the air, Boerner had to deal with Obama's roommate, who had other plans. He had to "fight off" Hasan Chandoo, he noted, who "wanted to take over the show and play Bob Marley, in honor of his death."

In Obama's set at Oxy, there was a pervasive sense of something ending that spring. Marley was dead, liberalism was out of favor in Washington, the adrenaline rush of the apartheid protest had worn off, and most of Obama's closest friends were graduating and leaving California, moving east. Chandoo was heading for London, part of the Pakistani diaspora. Wahid Hamid was taking advantage of Occidental's three-and-two relationship with Cal Tech and planning to finish there. Other friends were going to Spain and Switzerland or Harvard and other Ivy League locales. After only two years at Occidental, Obama was ready to go as well. In late March he and Boerner and Kofi Manu, acting independently but aware of each other's decisions, had filled out applications to transfer to Columbia in New York. As the son of a diplomat, Boerner was accustomed to moving every few years and was feeling restless after two years in Eagle Rock. "I've had enough of Oxy, although I will miss many good friends I made there," he wrote in his journal. "But the school was too small, the city too inaccessible (no car), and life too easy and the students too apathetic because of this. I feel that being in New York, and at Columbia, will alter all of these 'toos' – Columbia is larger, New York is accessible and has good public transportation, and life will be a little harder because both school and private life will be more competitive." Manu found Los Angeles a difficult place for a foreign student without a car or much pocket money, and the Oxy culture could seem so strange; he remembered a party where students dressed up in tuxedos and pretended they were at a casino. The college also suffered from a dearth of black professors and mentors, he said. The academics were excellent, but like many Africans, including Obama's own father, he found magic in the Ivy League name.

Obama's reasoning included all of that and more. Two years at Oxy (during which his cumulative grades were "a B-plus," he later said) seemed like an extension of Punahou School, everything so bright and blue, clean and soft and mellow. It had taken him onto the mainland at last, but it still felt removed, possibly another trap. "Time to get the fuck out of L.A.," Chandoo said, and Obama agreed. He wanted to go deeper into the American experience, and the black experience. "I figured that if there weren't any more black students at Columbia than there were at Oxy, I'd at least be in the heart of it," he said. New York, New York. A dense city, dark and swirling, an urban university, with Harlem nearby. His favorite teachers were neither surprised nor alarmed. Anne Howells, who encouraged his writing, wrote a recommendation for him. Roger Boesche, who helped inspire his interest in politics, understood why some students considered Oxy claustrophobic. "I can easily see him wanting bigger spaces," Boesche said later. The campus then was like an island, with little connection to the big city nearby, as though it would rather be part of Pasadena than Los Angeles. It was not enough for Obama then, Boesche said, looking back from the distance of three decades. "A young Obama now would have a lot more diverse student population with which to interact."

On the quad one day, Eric Moore caught sight of him and asked whether it was true he was planning to leave. With Moore was Rick Casey, a black senior moving on to medical school. "We both tried to discourage him from leaving," Moore recalled. "Rick and I were saying this is a good place to be from. It's small, and all the limitations of the school are understood, but then Rick said, 'Look at me, I just got into Harvard Medical School and no one else did. This is a good springboard for a lot of things.'" Casey remembered the scene distinctly. He was about to leave Los Angeles on a cross-country road trip to Massachusetts with Moore and Ricky Johnson. They had arranged to drive a car for a car service and only had to pay for gas. When Obama announced that he was leaving too, Casey felt "very protective" of his alma mater: "Why would you leave Occidental to go to Columbia?" Obama listened, then said, "I just need a bigger pond to swim in."

Caroline Boss, one of the seniors graduating that spring and bound for Europe, had several conversations with Obama before he left: "It was very clear to me he was transferring for a number of reasons. One was that many, many of his friends were graduating, so there was kind of a sense of, well . . . Another had to do with questions of race. . . . I think he wanted to discover blackness in America. He made it to the continent for starters, and now he would move a little closer to the center of things. He takes this trajectory in his life . . . a personal journey of self-understanding as a black American." But there was another motivation, one that had to do with an emerging ambition and sense of purpose in the world. Oxy lit a pilot light inside him. His will was always there. As he wrote later, his parents had given it to him, each in a particular way: "My fierce ambitions might have been fueled by my father – by the knowledge of his achievements and failures, by my unspoken desire to somehow earn his love, and by my resentments and anger toward him. But it was my mother's fundamental faith – in the goodness of people and in the ultimate value of this brief life we've been given – that channeled those ambitions." His grandmother had thought he was a genius. His mother had believed that he would achieve greatness in a life helping others. And now the two years at Oxy, the classes he took there, the friends he met there, the racial sorting-out he did, the speeches he started to give, the papers he wrote there, the political philosophy he developed there – all of it together helped him start down that path. He still had his Hawaiian *Cool head, main thing* sensibility, but now it would serve him not as a shield from the pain of a young life of leaving and being left, but as the protective armor covering his determination to make a mark in the world.

Many friends and classmates had no sense that his life would lead toward world leadership. He "certainly didn't go around tooting his own horn, even though he was probably getting messages from his professors that he had serious talent," Margot Mifflin wrote later. But Hamid could see his ambition, and to Boss he now spoke of a sense of destiny. "He literally said to me that he felt there was something he was here for. He felt in his heart that greatness was expected of him and he wanted to be prepared for that. He wanted to be prepared."

The acceptance letters came in early June. Obama got in. Manu did not make it. Columbia had already filled its allotment of foreign students, apparently. He ended up staying at Oxy and spending six months of his junior year in Jamaica, land of his beloved reggae singers, and writing a thesis on the impediments to economic advancement on the Caribbean island. Boerner, impatient, had already called and found out he got in. Then he went off to a summer job at Sequoia National Park. On June 13 he received a letter from his pal Paul Carpenter, Obama's old roommate, who sarcastically would put an apostrophe in the last name, making it Irish rather than Luo. Obama and Boerner had discussed sharing an apartment near Columbia, but, Carpenter now wrote Boerner, working it out beforehand with Obama might be difficult: "I'm afraid he may be hard to reach during the summer. He is leaving next Thursday for Indonesia, and continuing westward from there through Pakistan, Paris and London to New York. Knowing O'Bama he will reach the shores of the 'empire state' at the last possible moment, if not later."

CHAPTER 15

END AND BEGINNING

T he insects that feed on dead flesh don't want me, Barack Hussein Obama Sr. would say to explain why he was still alive. It was an African adage, so he said it in Swahili: *Wadudu hawanitaki*.

This was quintessential Obama, with his sharp, defiant sense of humor. But he also believed it, and would say it most often after another acquaintance died, usually on the Kenyan roads. That he had survived so many car crashes surprised even Obama. His body was broken, his legs weakened, but he was aboveground, in the flesh. He had another saying that he delivered in English: "When I die, I will die thoroughly." This addressed both life – he wanted to live thoroughly before death came – and afterlife, something that as an atheist he did not believe in.

The years after his firing from the Kenya Tourism Development Corporation had been very difficult for Obama. Here he was with three wives gone, various children barely seen, three jobs lost, and a series of reckless mishaps behind the wheel; it had been a calamitous downhill slide. But by 1976 he had started to make his way back. His brilliance had never left him, and after a period when he could gain only temporary employment, brought in for a month here or there when the government needed his brainpower, he was hired full-time at the Department of Finance and Planning. In the department directory he was listed far down the bureaucratic ladder, as the number four man in one of twenty-five sections: planning officer in charge of commerce development in the Industry and Infrastructure Section. The fact that he was listed at all – B. H. Obama, extension 849 – was an improvement.

The story he told about who facilitated his comeback contradicted a political conspiracy theory his family later constructed to explain his downfall. They attributed his troubles largely to the fact that he was a disciple of Tom Mboya and had been a witness at the assassin's murder trial, and thus was targeted for misery by Mboya's enemies in the dominant Kikuyu tribe. Obama himself would often say as much, yet his own account of how he was hired seemed to contradict this. As he told the story, he was walking in downtown Nairobi one day when a prominent Kikuyu, Mwai Kibaki, minister of finance and planning in the Kenyatta administration, stopped his car and gave him a ride. Kibaki had studied at the London School of Economics, but the Harvard-trained Obama considered himself the better economist and was not intimidated. Whatever conversation transpired during the car ride, it ended, or so Obama said, with Kibaki offering him a job. Variations of that story were told by Obama's associates. One version had Obama and Kibaki enjoying drinks at the Inter-Continental Hotel, where they were both frequent patrons, and after downing several "double-doubles" between them (Obama's favorite: double the whiskey), Kibaki agreed to hire him. In any case, the hiring happened. "It is true that Kibaki had sent a plea that we take on Obama from the streets. He was out a job. I remember processing his papers," recalled Y. F. O. Masakhalia. There is no doubt that a Kikuyu cabal operated to keep members of the dominant tribe on top, using any means necessary, including violence at times, but if Obama was being blackballed, Kibaki must not have received the message. This was the same Mwai Kibaki who later became president of Kenya and whose tenure was marked by deadly tribal strife when Luo believed he had fixed elections and kept them from power.

Obama's namesake son in America, his baby bull now grown up and advancing from prep school to college, envisioned his father during this time "sitting at his desk in Nairobi, a big man in government, with clerks and secretaries bringing him papers to sign, a minister calling him for advice, a loving wife and children waiting at home, his own father's village only a day's drive away." It was an image that made Barack H. Obama II "vaguely angry" for being abandoned and cut out from all that – but he had no idea.

Up on the third floor of the old colonial-era Ministry of Finance building, the old man shared a secretary but he had no staff, and no family to go home to – or not go home to, as more often had been the case. More than a decade earlier, when he returned to Kenya from his studies in America, he drove around Nairobi in European sports cars, even after his license was revoked. Now, after more than a year on the new job, and without a car for a long stretch, he bought a white pickup truck. He had found quarters in an upscale Nairobi neighborhood not far from the State House (Kenya's White House), sharing a furnished apartment at Dolphin Flats with Sebastian Okoda, a ministry colleague who worked in the fiscal and monetary division on the same floor of Finance and was a Luo from the Siaya district northwest of Kisumu, not far from Nyang'oma Kogelo. When Obama came to him looking for a place to stay, Okoda took him in and gave him one of the three bedrooms. Obama "never contributed towards the rent" for flat No. 5, reserved for government officers, Okoda said, "but he used to help me with food and other household effects." Whenever Okoda's wife visited from their village in Luoland, Obama made a point of showing up for her home-cooked meals. In Okoda's memory, Obama's children, Bobby and Rita (later known as Malik and Auma) rarely came to Dolphin Flats. He remembered a lone occasion when Kezia, Obama's first wife, whom he claimed to have divorced, paid a visit and shared Obama's room.

It was a tentative existence, but then uncertainty was a part of life in Kenya, and an aspect of Obama's life anywhere. Uncertainty about everything except the keen mind that he brought to his work. One might assume from his past speeches and writings – the debates with the Cambodian Kiri Tith in Honolulu, when he would take the anti-Western argument; his 1965 paper offering a leftist critique of the Kenyatta administration's planning – that Obama viewed his government job as an extension of his politics. In fact, he was not a political animal and rarely talked about politics with his peers, except in the most theoretical sense. "Barack hardly spoke politics," said J. B. Omondi, a government colleague, who, like most professional Kenyans in that era, pronounced his name as the British-accented *BARE-ick*, never *Buh-ROCK*, and sometimes called him Barry. "He would just complain about people's lack of knowledge, how they are ignorant." With his reverberant voice and haughty demeanor, Obama often seemed larger than life, or at least larger than his official status. Coming out of the dark years that followed his sacking at the tourism council, he was no more humble, still boastful in front of peers, fearless and at times even condescending toward officials who outranked him. He preferred to be addressed as Dr. Obama, an honor he had not quite earned. Richard Hook, an American economist who was recruited to run the Kenyan rural development project, and who worked on the same floor as Obama for several years, remembered how he would announce himself at meetings – "Good afternoon, I am Dr. Obama from the Ministry of Finance" – with a voice that "was a little this side of Paul Robeson's," referring to the magisterial black singer and actor. Hook and other associates in the ministry knew that Obama had not finished his doctoral thesis, but some, including Obama himself, considered this a mere technicality. "His attitude was he was highly qualified for anything," said Y. F. O. Masakhalia, who eventually rose to the highest position in the Finance Ministry. "He even thought he was qualified to lead the Central Bank. That was his attitude. There were people he had no time for, particularly after he had tested someone's intellectual qualities and found them wanting."

Sebastian Okoda recalled the day he entered Obama's office "and found him busy playing something on a board, just like the way people play chess. I couldn't understand it, so when I inquired from him, he quickly responded, 'You people are only good at writing letters. I am doing mega-planning.'" Joseph Kipsanai, an undersecretary at the ministry, once watched in astonishment as Obama spoke derisively to a boss who had criticized him for being late with an assignment. As Kipsanai recounted the scene, Obama asserted that he knew more about economics than his superior ever would, that he had been trained in the United States, at Harvard, and had once even been the man's teacher for a semester at Makerere University in Kampala. "So," Obama said, "don't ever talk to me like that again." Suffice it to say that attitude did not go over well. Yet there were many times when Obama's performance matched his boasting and his lightning-quick mind completed a task faster and more skillfully than anyone else in the office could. "Barack was very bright," noted J. B. Omondi, who was director of external aid, with duties that involved soliciting help from wealthy European nations. Whenever the opportunity arose, Omondi said, he would bring Obama along for donor meetings with the Europeans, and also recruited him to write papers. "One time the permanent secretary, Nicholas Nganga, wanted an urgent paper on the restructuring of Kenya Airways," Omondi said. "Barack and I were called in at eleven a.m., and I was there because money was required in the restructuring effort. We were told that the paper was required by the PS [permanent secretary] by three. Nganga told Obama to 'knock out the paper.' Within an hour Barack had delivered. We delayed my office secretary to type it over lunch. When the [European] donors assembled, everything was ready. This paper was discussed for a whole week."

By 1979, with Obama's professional resurrection entering its third full year, a generation had passed since the first wave of Kenyans had gone to America to fulfill Tom Mboya's grand plan to train the future leaders of an independent African nation. Mboya himself had been dead for ten years, his assassination serving as bitter testimony to how problematic it was to realize his dream of lifting Kenya out of tribalism. But even with Mboya gone if not forgotten, his remote mausoleum reachable only by a ferry that plied the waters of Lake Victoria to Rusinga Island, the common feeling was that the Africans who had studied in America represented an important part of his legacy. A generation later, veterans of the 1959–1962 airlifts could be found in important posts in virtually every ministry and among Kenya's literary elite. Obama was exceedingly proud of his American period, blocking out the reality of its unhappy ending. Friends and associates were never told the entire story, that authorities denied him a visa extension and forced him out of the country. His mannerisms and accent were British, but his bias was toward America. One associate said, "Obama would hardly speak to [you] if you hadn't gone to America."

But some Kenyan professionals saw a more complicated side of the aftermath for students who were sent out of Africa for higher education, not only those who went to the United States under Mboya's sponsorship but also those who studied in the Soviet Union and Eastern Bloc nations under the sponsorship of Oginga Odinga. J. B. Omondi, who stayed in Africa and studied at Makerere University in Uganda, expressed this sentiment. "You know what, these boys [who studied abroad] were living a life that you wouldn't live with a decent wife," Omondi said. "Most of them were abandoned by their wives. Quite a number of the boys on the airlift . . . came back empty-handed. They were living beyond their means. They looked desperate and kept begging. A lot of these people who went to America and Russia were failures who couldn't advance in Kenya."

Obama certainly advanced during his second chance in government. Promotions might have come slower for him than for some colleagues, but he did rise nonetheless. In 1977 he had moved up from the number four planning position to number three in Industry and Infrastructure, and did the work of the number two man because that position was vacant. The next year the cabinet department had been reorganized and Obama was named one of three planning officers, just below the top level at the Industry, Commerce, Tourism, and Infrastructure Section, responsible for planning in several critical areas: road development, building and construction, the postal service and telecommunications, and harbors and airways. By 1980 the principal economist for the section had left and Obama performed his functions while not holding the title, though he was listed as a Planning Officer I and all other economists in the section were ranked Planning Officer II; the following year both of the top jobs in the section were vacant and Obama essentially ran the office, though again his job title had not changed.

His assignments entailed considerable travel in Africa and Europe. One of his first trips was to Addis Ababa, where he led a Kenyan delegation at a meeting with the United Nations Economic Commission for Africa to discuss regional development in a poverty-riddled swath of territory encompassing the borderlands between Kenya and Ethiopia. The most interesting part of that trip had nothing to do with the plan, but rather with a family connection that closed a generational circle. At the Kenyan embassy in Addis Ababa, and teaming with Obama in the discussions, was Dan Rachuonyo Mboya, the son of Paul Mboya. People named Mboya were critical in the Obama family story over the generations, for better and worse. Paul Mboya, unrelated to Tom Mboya, was the Luo chief in the Kendu Bay area who had called Barack's father a *jadak* – alien, outsider – during a heated confrontation and had forced Hussein Onyango and his family to move from southern Nyanza across the Gulf of Kavirondo and up to the ancestral homestead in Nyang'oma Kogelo. The bad blood between the families was resolved when the sons worked together more than three decades later.

At some economic conferences and technical meetings in Africa and Europe, Obama was the sole representative or lead delegate for Kenya, a sign that his status was above his official title. He represented Kenya in a technical committee meeting to discuss the construction of a Kenya–Sudan Road link and took a principal role in those efforts for years. He also traveled to the African capitals of Kampala and Lusaka and to Paris and Oslo and Brussels. Kenyan cabinet ministers and permanent secretaries in economic planning and foreign affairs sought his counsel on interregional issues, and he routinely prepared memos for them, signing off with his initials, *BHO*. He also frequently sent work letters directly to Kenyan ambassadors overseas, in essence assuming the role of a cabinet minister. While his habit of usurping more power than his job description called for led to his firing years earlier at KTDC, there were few similar complaints in the economic planning ministry, where he was well respected and, in a bureau so understaffed, desperately needed. His friends in the department protected him, according to Masakhalia, who included himself in that category. "But he had people under him to control, and he did it reasonably well," Masakhalia added. "He was at his best when he defended the Kenyan position during international functions."

That is not to say that Obama was now an easy case. He was still giving his bosses headaches because of his drinking and the way he spent money during his travels abroad. When J. B. Omondi accompanied Obama to Zambia for a convention on labor economics, they stayed together at the Inter-Continental Hotel in Lusaka. "I remember after our drinks and when we thought we had retired to our rooms, Barack would slip out and go to the casino," Omondi said. "One day he used all the money he had, about two thousand shillings. The whole of it went, disappeared. He suddenly was broke. To help him, I decided to share with him the little allowance I was left with, so for the entire

time we stayed there, he lived off me." Obama's ministry knew about his tendencies and began assigning someone to look after him overseas, but that did
not always work. Omondi said that for a trip to France for "a very important
meeting," he and Masakhalia asked a deputy to monitor Obama, but "somehow he used all his allowance" and Omondi had to send him more. Joseph
Kipsanai also found himself loaning Obama money on several occasions when
he had lost all his cash. He said that he usually got repaid, "but there was one
five-hundred-shilling loan I did not get back. So when Obama Jr. became
president I was going to write him and say I want the five hundred shillings
back. It was a lot of money at the time."

Obama was known for keeping his own peculiar hours. "I am not a clerk!" he
would say by way of explanation. "I am not bound by time."

The official workday started at eight o'clock. There were days when
Obama would stroll in at eight-thirty or nine. And days when he arrived at
eleven. And days when he was there long before anyone else, settling behind
his desk in the middle of the night, at three or four in the morning, without
ever going home. And days when he had finished an assignment and did not
come in at all. The scheduled lunch break was from 12:45 to 1:45. Obama
often left the office for lunch around 1:30 and would not return until 2:30 or
2:45, if then. Most of his time out of the office was spent at bars. He could go
two days without eating – "I don't want to be an *oyondi*," a Luo word meaning
"of a big tummy," he would say – but he never went long without drinking.

It was in bars that the dichotomy of Obama's existence was most striking.
His drinking life, as one associate described it, was "a tale of two cities." He
frequented bars high and low; bars where he wanted to be known and bars
where he wanted to disappear; bars where he could flex his brain muscles
to impress important people and bars where he could find women for cheap
sex; bars that carried him back to where he had come from and bars where he
could preen about what he had become; bars where the white and black elite
mingled and bars in which a European rarely, if ever, set foot. Wherever he
went, he drank and smoked profusely, preferring the British cigarette brands
State Express 555 and Benson & Hedges, and though some of his suits had
become threadbare, he always made an effort to look cool, with his brown

leather jacket and shades. He had a reputation to uphold as *Atuech Wuod Akumu*, the well-dressed son of Akumu.

At lunch or after work he was a regular at the hotel bars inside the Inter-Continental and Hilton, establishments he had helped get developed during his years at the tourism council. It was at the hotel bars that he mingled with two future presidents, Mwai Kibaki and Daniel arap Moi, and a future prime minister, Raila Odinga, the son of Oginga Odinga, along with high-ranking finance bureaucrats like Masakhalia and Harris Mule. "The Inter-Continental was good because he could meet the elite there," said Peter Castro Oloo Aringo, a longtime member of Parliament who represented a district that included Nyang'oma Kogelo. "He liked to go there and test his mind against them. He would test them, sometimes he would rebuke them, and that could turn into a problem. But the Inter-Continental was a political hotel at the time . . . a center of elites gathering, and so he enjoyed going there." Rank meant little to Obama in those situations; his charisma and confidence carried him through, along with the effects of alcohol. The bars customarily diluted whiskey with water or soda or even hot milk, but Obama wanted none of that. Johnnie Walker Black Label and VAT 69 were his preferred blends, and if a bartender asked him about water, he would harrumph, "How can you waste a drink with water?" More whiskey, not water, he would say. *Double-double.* It became another of his nicknames, Mr. Double-double.

For Obama, associating with the elite was a matter not so much of survival as pride. Sebastian Okoda recalled, "Every time I would ask him about the whereabouts of any person, he would quickly respond in Kiswahili, '*Wewe Okoda unajua watu wadogo wadogo* – You, Okoda, you identify yourself with less important people, small people!' Barry loved to move about and be associated with the big shots. . . . He used to spend a lot of money on such people. One time he told me he was earning a pittance and that most of his money ended up buying whiskey for big people." As he gadded about Nairobi, just as on his trips overseas, Obama often ran out of money and turned to friends for help. When Okoda once told him that he had no money to lend him, Obama responded incredulously, "Where does your money go? You don't drink, don't spend it on *malaya* [prostitutes], you just sip beer!"

Obama did all of the above. After drinking with the elites he often slipped away for the underworld experience of River Road, which was both a street and the designation for an eight-square-block jumble of bars and dimly lit and unmarked after-hours clubs where cheap beer and women were readily available. River Road was a popular hangout for Luo and Luhya tribesmen who worked in Nairobi. At the edge of the high-crime sector was a chaotic staging area for perpetually overcrowded jitney buses, known as *matatus,* that carried passengers from the capital to the far stretches of western Kenya and back. One of the streets delineating the border of the River Road sector was named for Tom Mboya, the slain Luo martyr, and several bars evoked the Luo homeland. Obama was a patron of the Nyanza Club, with its striped blue-and-white markings, on Kamae Road off Luthuli Avenue, and the Nyanza House, a yellowish building on Mfangano Street. In the span of a day he could go from hobnobbing with the elite in a hotel bar to drinking and womanizing with the multitudes of River Road, then head back across town to the Starlight Club, the well-heeled music and disco lounge at Integrity Center, where he would dance and drink and party into the morning. Almost anytime day or night he had "a tremendous capacity for whiskey," as one associate put it. "My wife used to complain, 'His drinking is too much: How do you cope?'" said J. B. Omondi. He dealt with Obama, Omondi told his wife, Ann, by not trying to keep up with him. After a drinking binge, out of money and voraciously hungry, Obama might go with Omondi to his house with the expectation that Ann would cook his favorite meal. "They would come deep in the night and demand that I make them *aliya,*" Ann Omondi recalled. *Aliya* is a traditional Luo dish in which the beef is dried in the sun for days, smoked, and then cooked. "They would demand I sit by the table and listen to their stories. It didn't matter the time of the night it was. Barack was a very bright chap, but he drank an awful lot."

While the son he barely knew was at Occidental College, slouching on the Barf Couch and hanging around the Cooler, writing poetry about Pop and learning about Nietzsche, dancing to Talking Heads and deciphering the lyrics of Bob Marley, delivering a speech denouncing South Africa and debating the politics of Iran and Israel, Afghanistan and Pakistan, Obama Sr., back in Kenya, was dealing with the loss of his father. Hussein Onyango, the tough old patriarch of the Obama clan, died at age eighty-three in 1979, the twentieth anniversary of son Barack's fateful departure for the University of Hawaii. Only recently retired, at Barack's urging, from his long career as a cook for white patrons, Hussein Onyango had lived out his final years at the compound in Nyang'oma Kogelo, dispensing herbs and tilling the hard red soil for the planting of kale and corn. He had witnessed the British colonial period from beginning to end. He had prepared meals for the British, fought for them, and accompanied them to war. He had lived through the rebellions of Piny Owacho and Mau Mau and the rise of the independence movement, and outlived the Burning Spear himself by one year, Jomo Kenyatta having died in 1978 at eighty-four. He had married a collection of wives, Arab and Luo and Luhya, had left some and kept some and physically abused most, and had made legions of enemies and friends around the swath of Lake Victoria from Kendu Bay to Kisumu and beyond. He had watched his smartest son, Barack, the one who disappointed him by leaving Maseno School early, redeem himself in America by training at Harvard, its preeminent university, and come home a lettered man who would replace him as the head of the Obama clan, the one relatives turned to for prestige and money. Before dying, Hussein Onyango had met a grandson who was half white and American – not Barack II, the baby bull thousands of miles away, son of Ann, but Mark, in Nairobi, son of Ruth. Of Barack II he knew only what he was told: a smart boy with an Obama brain.

The funeral followed Muslim rites, his body cleansed and shrouded in a clean white sheet. The burial plot was on the family grounds, not far from the shade of a graceful mango tree. Hussein Onyango's last wife, Sarah, recalled that it was "a big occasion, many people turned up." Five brothers and their extended families arrived from Kanyadhiang, and Barack and other family members and friends made the long drive from Nairobi. There were so many people, Sarah said, "that they had to sleep in the open air because we couldn't afford to take care of them all in the houses available."

The concern his friends had about Obama only increased over the years, even as he made his way back in the government. They thought he was under too much pressure, real or imagined. He was generous with his money, when he had it, but felt that his extended family expected too much of him. He worried incessantly about tribalism in Kenya and how it affected his job. After Kenyatta's death, the presidency was taken by Daniel arap Moi, who was not Kikuyu but Kalenjin, a minority tribe from the Rift Valley. Obama still felt that he was being held back because he was Luo. He did not trust Moi, he told his friend Peter Castro Oloo Aringo, the member of Parliament from Luoland. Aringo, who was often part of a drinking group with Obama, was among a group of friends who thought Obama would be more secure if he took a new wife. "We wanted Obama to settle down," Aringo said. They conducted a search in Nairobi first, talking to some local schoolteachers, "but they couldn't stand him because he looked arrogant." Finally someone identified a tall, gentle, and accommodating young woman named Jael Atieno Onyango, who came from the flatlands of the Nyando district east of Kisumu on the way toward the Rift Valley. Jael was twenty-two; he was twice her age. Obama had already dated Jael, taking her to a party held by a friend in Kisumu who wanted to honor his academic achievements. The friends had to overcome two obstacles in their matchmaking, Aringo said, first, to "convince Barack that he needed a wife," and second, to create a dowry for him. After running off with Kezia, impregnating Ann, and mesmerizing Ruth, this was, in a sense, his first arranged marriage. He and Jael moved into a small house in Mawenzi Gardens not far from Kenyatta National Hospital, where he had been laid up for several months after his first serious car wreck.

This was a busy time at work. In preparation for Kenya's twentieth anniversary of independence, the government intended to issue its Fifth Development Plan, and Obama was named the chief planner for the building and construction sector. He spent time planning and negotiating the construction of major roads that would link Kenya with its neighbors to the north, Ethiopia and Sudan, an effort that required outside financial assistance and took him to London. In Washington one day, a representative from the International Monetary Fund entered the office of a colleague, Kiri Tith, and said that he had been at a meeting in Nairobi with a man named Barack Obama who claimed that he knew Tith from the University of Hawaii and hoped that Tith would call him. "I did give him a ring," Tith recalled, "and we talked about three times after that. The first call was near the end of 1981. He was really happy to hear from me. We were good friends. I was the one he would joke around with in Hawaii. He was relaxed with me. We talked about where we stayed at Harvard" – Tith had studied there too – "about old friends. And he was a little bit upset about corruption in Kenya and political instability."

In their conversations Obama pressed Tith about global economics. Tith's job at the IMF dealt with Africa and Asia, and he also taught courses on the economies of developing countries at the Johns Hopkins School of Advanced International Studies. Obama wanted to know why Africa was struggling more than Asia. "We compared notes. Cameroon. South Africa. Ivory Coast. All places I had dealt with," Tith said. "I gave feedback that the problem in Africa was tribalism, and of course he agreed with me immediately. People were appointed [to jobs] according to tribal relationships and not degree of expertise. I got a sense he was disappointed. He never hesitated about speaking up about that, about being a minority tribe. He felt he had a limit as to how far he could go. He talked about that. He said unless Kenya became more integrated it would not change. That was the conclusion." But unlike some Obama acquaintances, Tith did not accept the idea that his frustrations led him to drinking. Tith had seen enough of that behavior in person long before, in Honolulu, when Obama was a college student, young and free from tribal strife, and more than once drank himself into a stupor.

Tith was not the only person who reconnected with Obama from across the ocean during that period. So too had his own namesake son. One day he received a letter from his baby bull in America, the first letter Barry had written his father in several years. In it, he broached the idea of visiting Kenya for the first time, a notion that prompted a return letter from Nairobi to Los Angeles. It was "a pleasant surprise" to hear from his son after so long, Obama Sr. wrote back, explaining that the reason he had not corresponded more was because of "too much travel" as he was "attending to Government business, negotiating finances etc." He promised to do better, and said that he and all of Barry's brothers and sisters in Kenya were looking forward to seeing him. "When you come we shall together decide on how long you may wish to stay. Barry, even if it is only for a few days, the important thing is that you know your people and also that you know where you belong. Please look after yourself and say hello to mum, Tutu and Stanley. I hope to hear from you soon, Love Dad."

Ann Dunham Soetoro, who kept her second husband's name after their divorce, was hired as a program officer for the Ford Foundation in 1981 and moved from Semarang back to Jakarta. A decade earlier, when her son, Barry, was ten, she had sent him out of Indonesia to attend Punahou School in Honolulu. Now Maya, who was about that same age, stayed with her mother and was enrolled at the Jakarta International School. Proximity to the mother is a major influence in the development of any preadolescent. Why, in parallel situations, had one child left and one stayed? Several reasons. Maya, with an Indonesian father, had far stronger ties to the country, and Ann wanted to keep her within reach of her cultural heritage, something she could not do with Barry and his Kenyan father. The grandparents in Hawaii, Stan and Tut, were approaching retirement age, and asking them to go through another cycle as surrogate parents would have been problematic. Ann also was fully at home in Indonesia by now. She had cultivated a garden of friends, she was freed from the burdens of a second difficult marriage, and with her new job she was earning more money than ever before.

The transition to Jakarta International proved as challenging for Maya in some ways as Punahou had been for Barry. The school was about as large as Punahou and nearly as wealthy and Westernized, serving the sons and daughters of expatriates who worked for the UN, multinational corporations, universities, and nongovernmental organizations like the Ford Foundation. Paradoxically, many of Maya's early adjustment problems came because of her mother's love of Indonesia and determination to ensure that her daughter was not alienated from her roots. At a time when girls there were wearing Jordache jeans, Ann sent Maya to school with what amounted to cultural doll costumes. They were "beautiful bunting dresses with these homemade petticoats underneath them," Maya said, but she hated to wear them in public and was embarrassed when other girls laughed at her. She started surreptitiously packing extra clothes in her bag to change into once she had escaped her mother's sight.

Aside from an art class where students learned basic batik methods, there was little connection in that era between Jakarta International and the Indonesian community. The only Indonesians Maya saw at school all day were janitors. The students sang corny American songs, watched *Pygmalion,* and did everything in English, which was also something new for Maya. "I had spent my childhood running around Indonesian villages, so I was fluent in Indonesian even though I wasn't able to read it or write it very well. Everyday Indonesian is what I have. It is not very sophisticated, but it was what I talked all day, and I found it very confusing to be at a school where they spoke English all day." Like Barry at Punahou, she was one of a kind, in her case the only *hapa* Indonesian in her class. One day she brought photographs to school to show her classmates. They were of white people she had never met, her mother's and grandparents' relatives back in Kansas, a place she had never been. "I'm not sure why I did that," she said later. "Acceptance, I guess."

The bunting dresses Ann wanted her daughter to wear to school fit with her humanistic philosophy, a perspective she had pounded into both Barry and Maya. As a woman of the world, a multiculturalist before that term was popularized and politicized, Ann despised the homogenization of daily life and the condescending attitude some Westerners showed toward different cultures. She had the personality of a collector, attracted to people and artifacts that were singular, interesting, authentic, representative. Her life was a splash of color. Her wardrobe was dominated by batik skirts, dresses, and blouses, and her rooms were decorated with vivid textiles and exotic rice paddy hats she collected in travels across the vast Indonesian archipelago. She also brought home a collection of world dolls for Maya. "There was a black girl named Elizabeth wearing a gingham dress and there was Sacagawea and there was an Inuit and a kind of hippie guy with peace signs and psychedelic colors and long hair, and a Dutch boy and Dutch girl wearing clogs and a Japanese girl in a kimono and a Chinese girl with beautiful up-done braids – you get the picture," Maya recalled later. Looking at these dolls – "a veritable UN" – in retrospect, she thought they evoked her mother's beauty but also her naïveté, a longing for something that did not exist. Maya would come to think of the dolls as "a museumification of culture," stereotypes much like the bunting dresses.

There was something deeper at work here, a sensibility that both Maya and Barry took from their mother, and often struggled mightily against even as they appreciated her motives. Barry was about this same age in Indonesia when he started to feel what Maya was sensing now – that Ann was softening the world around them in a loving but impossible effort to protect her *hapa* children from life's difficult realities on matters of race. She infused them, Maya said, with a sense that

> we are basically all the same and we can get along and we can learn to love one another and we can reach out to one another and appreciate each other's differences and the beauty residing therein. But make sure that laughter was the prevailing form of communication and that nothing ever became acrimonious and that everything was pretty and everything was sacred and everything was properly maintained and respected – all the artifacts and ways of being and living and thinking. We didn't need to make choices. We didn't need to discard anything. We could just have it all. It was this sense of bounty and beauty.

From this perspective, Ann saw mixed-race children as exemplars of the world as it should be. "To her we were fortunate that we straddled the worlds. . . . She didn't want us to suffer with respect to identity. She wanted us to think of it as a gift, this fact that we were multiracial," Maya said. "It meant she was perhaps unprepared when we did struggle with issues of identity. She was not really able to help us grapple with that in any nuanced way. Perhaps she felt that if she did acknowledge the difficulty of it, she would feel guilty, that she hadn't succeeded in protecting us and surrounding us with enough love."

For all of her idealism and supposed naïveté, Ann had an emotional reserve. Like her mother, Madelyn, she was not a hugger. And she never lost the wry, sarcastic touch that had been part of her repertoire since her high school days on Mercer Island. Nothing was sacred as a target of her humor, not even race. Alice Dewey, her mentor in anthropology, remembered that Ann once "claimed she married an African and then an Indonesian so her kids wouldn't have light skin and get sunburned all the time." Ann's own skin was porcelain white, framed by jet-black long hair. She also told Dewey once, not joking this time, that she "always sailed through Customs because she looked like a Kansas schoolteacher and everyone immediately trusted her" – a statement her two children would never be able to make. Along with that trustworthy Middle American aura, there were only a few traces of Kansas left in her, mostly in pronunciation and idiomatic speech. She said *warsh* instead of wash, and the days of the week were *Mundee, Tuesdee, Windsdee.* She would complain that Maya and Barry were "as slow as a herd of turtles in a cloud of peanut butter," or would tell them something that was "just between you and me and the fencepost." Kansan was just one small aspect of her multilingual presentation. She was fluent in Bahasa Indonesia, knew French, Latin, some Hindi and Urdu, and could throw in some native Hawaiian. Maya said it was not uncommon for her mother to move from one language to another in the same sentence.

Lolo Soetoro also lived in Jakarta then, working for Union Oil. Soon after the divorce from Ann he had married a young second wife, Erna Kustina, who quickly gave him a son. Lolo was not a completely absent father, as Obama Sr. had been for Barry, but he was not a predictable part of Maya's life. His young wife was insecure and did not want Maya around. Every few months, Lolo might come around to take Maya to the Petroleum Club, where he was a member, but that was about it. Her strongest memory of her father during that era involved an obsession with bargains. He would drive up into the rural hills and come back to the city with crates of cheaply purchased cabbages and carrots for his relatives, and also habitually bought T-shirts in bulk from his company. "I would have like twenty Union Oil shirts with my name on them," Maya recalled. "On my still growing body – not sure if that was considered highly fashionable!"

The Ford Foundation, a multibillion-dollar grant-making organization, walked a fine line in Indonesia. As in other outposts around the world, it was operating in a country where the political regime was authoritarian but anticommunist and viewed by the U.S. government as a pro-Western bulwark in the cold war. Fifteen years after his bloody rise, President Suharto had solidified power and was slowly opening the economy at the same time that he was suppressing dissent. In a country with few outlets for public discourse, especially for those pushing democratization in all its various forms, the Ford Foundation offices in Jakarta served a vital function, sponsoring a wide range of social development programs and promoting human rights and environmental causes. Ann Dunham Soetoro was in the middle of the action. After her appointment as program officer for women and employment, she spent most of her time "helping people who were pushing the envelope a bit – more than a bit," according to a colleague, David McCauley. "She was unique in the sense that she was American but spoke Indonesian fluently and had been married to one and immersed herself in the culture there and could relate to it and be accepted by it."

Jakarta served as headquarters for the Ford Foundation's Southeast Asia Regional Office. It was based in a white Dutch colonial house at J1 Taman Kebon Sirih near the central business district, adjacent to one of the old Jakarta canals that flooded two or three times a year during the rainy season. Muddy waters seeped into the building, soiling the floors and lower shelves of bookcases. From the main entryway and reception desk, visitors turned left and navigated a busy hallway lined with offices, one of which was Ann's. McCauley, who specialized in natural resources issues, worked in the room next door, and was struck by the constant stream of people who came through to see Bu Ann when she was in town and not traveling to a weekly assignment at the Bogor Agricultural Institute, or farther afield to Sulawesi and other Indonesian islands, or occasionally to India or Pakistan. "The potential grantees would come to Jakarta, and in her case other people who wanted to see her because she knew them as part of the network," McCauley said. "She had a lot more visitors [than anyone else]. People were constantly coming to see her."

There is a certain symmetry in the larger story of Barack Obama and Ann Dunham Soetoro, father and mother of a future president, as they made their way professionally thousands of miles from each other and farther yet from their son. They were in the same general field, both working to bolster the economies of developing countries, but coming at their work from opposite directions, quantitative and qualitative. The father in Kenya was absorbed with impersonal numbers and the big picture, analyzing data and working out theoretical models from the remove of his Nairobi desk. The mother in Indonesia was never happier than when she was on the scene with villagers or hosting groups of women in her Jakarta office, studying their jobs and crafts, trying to help them survive and thrive in a changing economy. They shared a certain magnetism that set them apart from the crowd, but of very different sorts: Barack with his voice, his facility with words, and his irrepressible belief that he was the smartest person in the room; Ann with her sense of adventure, her good humor, and her passionate interest in her work.

Richard Hook had worked for several years on the same floor with Barack at the Finance and Economic Planning Ministry in Nairobi, and by chance later ended up in Jakarta intersecting with Ann. As one of the few people who could connect the dots in their professional lives, he noted their striking differences. "Obama was macro and Ann was micro," he said. In this case the difference involved more than economic approaches. "Barack as I knew him in Kenya, I could visualize how he and Ann would not really be a good long-term bet," Hook said. "Their approaches to life, their feelings about people, were so different. Barack Sr. was manipulative, would use people, jockey people, and position them. Ann was not that way. If you met her she exuded a human warmth and kindness when she was around. You never left a conversation with her feeling worse."

Less than a month into her new job, Ann had traveled to India at the invitation of a Ford Foundation colleague and spent several days studying organizations in the countryside and the cities that were formed to assist women in the workforce. The visit deepened her sense of how powerless women could band together to help themselves and informed her involvement in the emerging field of microfinancing thereafter. Her fascination with small-scale economics went back to her anthropological studies of blacksmiths, potters, batik makers, and other handicrafts workers in the villages outside Yogyakarta, but now she had access to money and the authority to try to assist them. It seemed like a seamless transition, but this was a major step, crossing over from the world of observer and writer to the realm of organizer and funder. She had joined a defined subculture, the development community, and become a player on the political stage, prefiguring the path her son would follow later.

Indonesia had more Muslims than any nation in the world, more than 150 million then, on the way to 200 million. For the most part, they practiced a moderate form of Islam, less fundamentalist than the sects that became more prevalent throughout the archipelago decades later. In Indonesia, Islam was softened by the region's earlier experience with Hinduism and Buddhism, and also to some extent overshadowed by the recent rise of nationalism. In her graduate research, Georgia McCauley, David McCauley's wife, had conducted a study of elderly women on Java, asking them what was more important to them, being Indonesian or being Muslim. "Generally speaking, it was more important for them to be Indonesian," she said. "It meant your family would stay in the country and not leave. That, for grandmothers and mothers, was more important." For political reasons, those priorities were shared by Indonesia's rulers, from Sukarno through Suharto, who said they were nationalists first, Muslims second.

Championing the economic rights of women in a male-dominated society that practiced what Ann once called the "gentle oppression" of women was no easy prospect, but she took to the challenge. She became an expert on labor law and recommended grants supporting the legal rights of women employees in the cigarette-making and textile industries and on tea plantations. She led a worldwide working group within the Ford Foundation on microfinancing for women artisans. In coordination with universities throughout Indonesia, she helped establish programs that encouraged women to become involved in business, and to make their participation more culturally accepted. And she helped found and became the first editor of an Indonesian professional journal, *Women and Work*.

These efforts rarely challenged the Suharto regime directly, but aimed instead to empower women by organizing from the bottom up. Ann was particularly suited for the task, a strong-minded feminist who could use her cultural fluency to navigate around overt political barriers and subtle social ones. "She was very progressive in her views, particularly on women but more generally on the openness of the society, to ensure that all voices are heard," noted David McCauley. "That was not very easy in Indonesia. . . . She very much wanted to ensure that decisions were made in consultative fashion rather than top-down fashion. Indonesia had a tendency to be male-dominated and top-down, so it provided a fertile challenge for her. The political system in Indonesia was pretty much fixed; there was not a lot you could do with overt political parties. That was not the way you got things done, it was controlled and circumscribed by the ruling regime. So you tried to develop alternative groups, social groups, professional associations."

Ann's modest house on a leafy street in the comfortable Kebayoran Baru neighborhood, made available to her by the foundation, provided an informal social group of its own, attracting regular visitors in the same way her office did, in this case not so much grant supplicants as Indonesian intellectuals, anthropologists, historians, editors and writers, colleagues in the development community, and friends and acquaintances from other countries. It was "a mélange of people," said Nancy Peluso, who went on to become a professor of anthropology at the University of California and had met Ann while on an undergraduate research project on Java studying women and markets. "Even though Ann lived in the expat community, she didn't live any kind of regular expat life." She surrounded herself with delightfully iconoclastic and fearless women like Sidney Jones and Julia Suryakusuma, who could cross the cultural divides as easily as she did. Georgia McCauley, who arrived in Jakarta with two girls, three years old and six months, and "a workaholic husband," became like a little sister to Ann and was awed by the passing parade. "There were always friends, people hanging out, having tea, talking. She would say, 'Oh, so-and-so is going to drop by.' Then she would proceed to tell you the wonderful story of this person. It seemed like they were all brilliant, wonderful people hanging around. So I would wonder, 'What could she possibly say about me?' She would have filmmakers. I would think, 'Am I ever lucky or what?' for her to include [me] in fascinating evenings."

Georgia quickly learned that being Ann's friend meant she should not confine her circle to expatriates and separate herself from the local culture. When her girls had birthdays, Ann arranged the entertainment, insisting, "You must have this Indonesian puppet master for the party!" She also encouraged Georgia to learn Bahasa Indonesia and lined up a teacher for her. It took Georgia several weeks to realize that her tutor was the mother of a well-known Indonesian economist, part of Ann's collection of fascinating people. When the young mother became concerned that her cook would not make American food, but only Indonesian food, Ann came to the rescue. "With two little girls, that wasn't working as well as I would have liked, but I didn't want to throw someone overboard. So Ann knew I was having this challenge and she took this person on. And she didn't mind at all that Indonesian was all the cook could make. I never would have gotten rid of her. The cook was a bit of a character. Ann had infinite patience." Her defining trait was not just a willingness but an eagerness to see the world from different angles, how different people did things: how they made art, made music, made families. Not surprisingly, she loved foreign films.

Marty Chen, who met Ann at Ford Foundation conferences around the world, shared her obsession with textiles and other village enterprises, and appreciated the depth and specificity of their conversations. "I could say, 'Tell me about batik,' and she could tell you everything, down to the last detail. It was so vivid, such a passion and love for it . . . her encyclopedic knowledge of it, not just as technique, not just a textile, but a way of being. . . . Baskets, the issues of street vendors, the issues overlapped so much it was fun to talk it through. And her knowledge was fantastic. And there was that passion as well. I am a maven when I get onto my topics, and she was like seeing a glorified better image of myself." To Chen, Ann looked like "a charismatic earth mother," but she took offense at attempts to characterize her as a carefree hippie. Decades later, shortly after Ann's son was elected president of the United States, Chen attended a dinner at Harvard Square that included the former director of the Jakarta office of the Ford Foundation, Tom Kessinger. Kessinger, informal and friendly, always ready to host newcomers, had hired Ann. He had admired her knowledge of Indonesian culture and had encouraged her efforts to promote women, but found her somewhat distant and less efficient in handling the bureaucratic demands of the job. "He was at the far end of the table, [saying] she was just a flower child, a hippie. And he said she wasn't very good at RFPs. Those are the forms you have to prepare for the Ford Foundation, a Request for Proposal." Chen interrupted Kessinger and said, "I'm sorry, I have a slightly different story line. I don't know if she could write an RFP, but she knew rural Java as well as anyone." The different perceptions, Chen thought, represented "the male Ford Foundation versus the female anthropologist. . . . That is so unfair. Like saying she was a single mother and hippie."

Chen, like some other people who knew Ann professionally, said she never heard her talk about her son. Georgia McCauley, whose relationship was deepened by their common experience in Hawaii, recalled that Ann unfailingly talked about Barry whenever they got together. "In Hawaii we have this thing called 'talk story.' It is rude to start with business, so you start with friends and family. Every conversation would start with Barry because he wasn't there. She would tell you, 'Oh, he got into Columbia.' He decided to do this, do that. My children grew up hearing about 'Barry this, Barry that' all the time." Nancy Peluso agreed that "Ann talked about him all the time," but noted that on those few occasions when she saw Barry "he was your average teen, not that interested in hanging out with Mom."

Obama Sr.'s mother, Akumu, was living in the town of Kosele then, a small village about twenty miles from Kanyadhiang and Kendu Bay in western Kenya. This was more than three and a half decades after she had fled the abuse of Hussein Onyango and left her young children, including Barack, in their relocated compound in Nyang'oma Kogelo with their stepmother, Sarah. Barack had maintained a relationship with Akumu during adulthood, visiting her now and then when he made the long trek back to Luoland from Nairobi. When he paid a call on her in the fall of 1982, he was upset to see her living conditions. She had remarried, but appeared lonely and unhappy. Barack urged her to move. Go back to Nyang'oma Kogelo, he told her, or if that was not acceptable, he would buy land elsewhere where she could live in peace. "My mum refused and said she didn't want to go to Kogelo," recalled Auma Magak, Barack Sr.'s younger sister. "She said she wanted to be where she was."

Barack left Akumu with gifts, including several blankets, then drove to Kendu Bay, where he met Auma at the South Nyanza Bar. He complained to Auma that he was having trouble with mothers. He was bothered that Akumu would not move, and he'd already had a run-in with Sarah in Nyang'oma Kogelo. "On that day, he drank so much – more than I had ever seen him do. I also took so much alcohol," Auma said. "He had brought me a blanket. He gave me six thousand shillings . . . and told me to use some of the money to take care of our mother, Akumu. He told me to get Razik for him, that he wanted to talk to him." Razik was Auma's oldest son, Barack's nephew, a few years younger than Barry Obama, his American cousin. "I went back and pulled Razik along that evening and took him to the bar. I used to drink so much. Barack told Razik, 'I want you to study and be like me. I want you to read hard.' On that day, Barack bought beer for all those in the bar. He bought crates of beer."

For all his troubles, Obama was by nature a generous man when he could afford to be. The money and blankets and other gifts he brought to his family during that visit, the round of beers at the bar in Kendu Bay – all were in keeping with his behavior when he went home. Whether he was visiting the old compound in Kanyadhiang or the newer one in Nyang'oma Kogelo, he would make a point of stopping at every home and sharing something, food or clothing. During his bleak period in the early 1970s, it was difficult for him to match expectations, but later, with his steady job as a government economist, he supported not only Jael and eventually an infant son he had with her, George, but also the raft of relatives out by Lake Victoria, even helping some young nephews in Razik's generation with school fees. When Hussein Onyango was alive, he often complained that his son was too loose with money. "How do you go on buying people beer?" he would ask, as Sarah recalled their conversations. "How do your friends come to know that you have the money? Does money itch you?"

The Luo had another saying to describe Obama's generosity: *Thuol oonge o ofudome.* He didn't have snakes in his pocket. Meaning he was not afraid to reach in.

To describe his driving, friends drew not on Luo culture but on British children's literature. "He was like the character in *The Wind in the Willows,* Mr. Toad," explained Philip Ochieng, the political journalist who also wrote columns about books and word usage. "That is Obama. . . . Get behind a wheel and get too excited. It is a state of mind, not whiskey. . . . Obama had that mentality." Mr. Toad was one of the quirky anthropomorphic characters created by Kenneth Grahame in his classic, and some descriptions of him could have been written with Barack Obama in mind. Two responsible characters, Rat and Mole, worried about how they could teach him to be a sensible Toad and not the Terror of the Highway. Mr. Toad had been in the hospital after car wrecks three times already, Mole noted, to which Rat added, "And he's a hopelessly bad driver, and quite regardless of law and order. Killed or ruined – it's got to be one of those two, sooner or later." One difference: Rat and Mole kept pushing Mr. Toad to reform his reckless ways, and eventually he did. No such luck with Obama. According to Ochieng, he was typical of a generation of wild drivers, the first in their families with access to automobiles, who habitually wanted to speed and pass. Tom Mboya was the same way, and got in several accidents before he was assassinated. Ochieng counted Obama as one of the four fastest drivers in Nairobi, the others being the politicians J. M. Kariuki, Martin Shikuku, and President Daniel arap Moi.

After visiting his relatives in Luoland, Obama had taken another business trip to Addis Ababa to work on the joint development projects between Kenya and Ethiopia. Soon after his return, he spent the evening of November 23 drinking at one of the off-license bars on the Kenyatta National Hospital grounds, where men sat on wooden crates and sipped beer and whiskey costing about a third less than the price at regular bars. Late that night – there were reports that it was around eleven, but that is uncertain; it could have been later – Obama started to drive home, following a route that took him along Elgon Road. That stretch of land between the hospital and his house in Mawenzi Gardens was largely undeveloped then. The unlit, two-lane road was bordered by sunflowers, shallow ditches, dense bushes, and an occasional telephone pole. Obama was within two hundred yards of where he would make the final turn toward his neighborhood when he lost control and his car struck a pole.

No one witnessed the accident. That he had been drinking was known; that he was speeding was assumed based on his history and the wreckage. Whether he died instantly or lingered for hours is unclear. William Onyango, a journalist for the *Nairobi Times*, wrote that police did not reach the scene until three the next morning. "The car was extensively damaged and the body had to be wedged out."

As relatives later told the story, the police were not aware of Obama's identity when they took his lifeless body to the Nairobi mortuary. On the morning of November 24, a woman from his home village of Kanyadhiang arrived at the morgue to collect the body of a relative. She saw a body lying on the floor, realized that it was someone she knew, and let out a scream. "The mortuary attendants were surprised that the person lying on the floor was Barack Obama. They asked her, 'You know this person?' The body was dumped there by police," said Charles Oluoch, the Obama relative whose father had been adopted by Hussein Onyango as a young boy.

When she awoke that morning Jael was surprised that Obama had not returned. His fourth wife was accustomed by then to his staying out late drinking, but it was rare for him not to show up by morning. She called his office.

413

No one there knew his whereabouts. She called relatives in Luoland. No information there either, until hours later, when news came of the Kanyadhiang woman who had seen his body at the mortuary.

Obama's third wife, the American Ruth Ndesandjo, read about his death in the Nairobi papers. "I was not surprised, not surprised because he had been heading that way for a long time," she said later. "I didn't make a thing about it, because he wasn't part of my life. . . . If you want to block something out, you block it. And then it isn't a part of you anymore." Ann Dunham Soetoro, his second wife, the one he was with the most briefly, mother of his namesake, did not block him out. When she finally heard the news in Indonesia, she wept.

In Kosele, when Akumu got word of her son's death, she cried out *"Awino Migosi!"* – The royal one is dead! That was her name for her favorite son, *the royal one.* Her daughter Auma said she then collapsed "and never recovered until she died."

In Kanyadhiang, Charles Oluoch and other Obama relatives were devastated by word of his death. "It was a great blow to the Obama family," Oluoch recalled. "Obama was one of our sons and we were very proud of him. So when he died it really shocked us all. . . . We were shattered when he died. We were confused. . . . We were torn apart. . . . And it took us twenty years, for his son to come along, for the Obama name [to rise] again."

In Nyang'oma Kogelo, the news was broken by George Were, a cousin of Obama's who owned a nightclub in Kisumu. Were had received a telephone call from Nairobi; he drove straight to the village and gathered up Sarah, and together they made the long drive southeast past the tea plantations and across the Rift Valley toward the capital.

Sarah and other relatives suspected then, and maintained later, that Obama had been killed for political reasons. "It would appear he was killed and the people behind it faked an accident," she maintained in an interview decades later. "I suspect some of his enemies were hunting him down." The Kanyadhiang relatives had similar suspicions. Elly Yonga, whose father was Hussein Onyango's nephew, was living in Nairobi then, and drove with Charles Oluoch out to the stretch of Elgon Road where the accident occurred. He wondered why it took so long for anyone to find Obama and the wrecked car near the bushes by the side of the road. "There were a lot of suspicions," Yonga said. "But we could not substantiate it." The political situation in Kenya that fall was volatile enough to intensify doubts about the official story. A few months earlier, in August, there had been an unsuccessful military coup against President Moi, and several air force officers had been arrested and sentenced to hang. Moi launched a clampdown on all perceived dissidents. University students and political opponents were arrested; most of them were Luo, including Raila Odinga, charged with sedition, and his father, Oginga Odinga, who was placed under house arrest. But there is no evidence that Obama was targeted during the aftermath, and most of his colleagues and friends concluded that he was the victim of his own reckless driving. The person who killed him, they believed, was himself.

By Luo tradition, the burial could not be in Nairobi, but only in Luoland. Obama was to be interred at his family compound. The question was, which one? His relatives in Kanyadhiang wanted him laid to rest where he had been born, near the grave of his grandfather Obama Opiyo. The Nyang'oma Kogelo relatives, led by Sarah, insisted that he be buried there, next to the grave of his father, Hussein Onyango. The dispute was finally resolved by Oloo Aringo, the politician from Siaya district, who worked it out so the burial would be in Nyang'oma Kogelo but the Kanyadhiang contingent would bring the body back to Luoland and play a role in the service, with many of the arrangements organized by Elly Yonga's father. A meeting was held at Kaloleni Social Hall, the center of activity for Luo in Nairobi, where friends and acquaintances were asked to donate money for the funeral. Colleagues at the Finance Ministry, according to Y. F. O. Masakhalia, covered many expenses for the mortuary, the coffin, and round-trip transportation from Nairobi. They also gave the widow Jael a job as a messenger. When Robert Ouko, the economic planning minister and a prominent Luo, expressed interest in the funeral, the service was pushed back several days so he could attend. Caleb Omogi, one of Obama's oldest friends and drinking partners, was among those accompanying the body in the funeral cortege, along with Obama's stepmother, two of his wives (the first and fourth, Kezia and Jael), and some of his children from four marriages. Many relatives made the trip in a rented bus.

The body rested in an open coffin at the compound in Nyang'oma Kogelo as Caleb Omogi and his traditional *nyatiti* band played through the night, singing laments in praise of Obama. Elly Yonga's father spoke for the Kanya-dhiang clan. Stories were told about Obama's generosity, including a time when he was driving home to Luoland from Nairobi and saw a group of people walking along the highway's edge carrying a dead woman wrapped in a mat. He recognized some of them as villagers from Nyang'oma Kogelo, stopped his car, and asked, "How are you going to carry the body to her home?" They said they would continue walking, carrying her on their backs. Obama, as the story was told, drove home, unloaded his luggage, cleaned out the car, and drove back to find the roadside processional. He loaded the body and as many mourners as his car would hold and drove them to the burial site. Now, at his own funeral, people were comparing him to his father, Hussein Onyango. They had many similar characteristics, it was said, but the son was kinder to strangers.

Masakhalia addressed the funeral gathering. "I am mourning a friend of my childhood," he said, referring to their days together at the Maseno boarding school. He talked about how they got together in America, when Obama was on his way from Hawaii to Harvard and stopped to see him at the University of Denver. Obama, he said, was one of the most intelligent people he had ever known. Oloo Aringo told the crowd that Obama was a victim of tribalism. The system, he said, was "consuming some of its very brightest intellectuals." Robert Ouko, the highest-ranking official there, made the same point, but more cryptically. "He was very bitter, as if he knew something," recalled Charles Oluoch. "He was twisting words. He didn't say it directly, but the way he was twisting his words you knew there was something, as if it was not a normal accident." Perhaps the relatives were the ones twisting Ouko's words, hearing what they wanted to hear, but Ouko's bitterness, if it was there, eerily presaged his own fate. Eight years later he was mysteriously killed, and this time the death had all the markings of an assassination by President Moi's henchmen.

Muslim by birth, atheist by choice, Barack Hussein Obama left the world in a Christian service, covered in a dirt plot next to his father. He was buried not in a clean sheet but in a suit and tie. The Seventh Day Adventists had in-troduced the Obamas to the Western world. Now their thoughts accompanied *the royal one* into the ground.

There, in that shallow grave in the corner of the homestead under the shade of a mango tree, out in the red-dirt scrubland of western Kenya, is where one story ended. It was the story that ran from Obong'o to Opiyo to Obama Opiyo to Hussein Onyango to Barack Obama to his son, that went from Nyang'oma Kogelo to Kanyadhiang and back; that went from Luoland to Nairobi and back; that went from a mud hut to Hawaii and Harvard and back. An African story that wound itself into an American story that began with the suicide of Ruth Armour Dunham in a dank auto garage in Topeka, Kansas, on Thanksgiving night in 1926, and ran through Stanley Dunham and Madelyn Dunham to Stanley Ann Dunham to her son. This second story never circled back, it only zigzagged forward, leaving El Dorado in search of more *el dorados* – leaving Kansas, leaving California, leaving Oklahoma, Texas, Washington State, Hawaii, Indonesia, Los Angeles. These two unlikely stories came out of this world to connect and create a third and different story that now wended toward an even unlikelier place, the White House. The old story was about the world that made the American son, Barack Hussein Obama: nature and nurture, acceptance and rejection, leaving and being left. The new story was about how he remade himself: finding and being found. It would begin as the old one would end, with the first sentence of his memoir, the moment he learned of his father's death:

A few months after my twenty-first birthday, a stranger called to give me the news. I was living in New York at the time, on Ninety-fourth between Second and First.

———◈———

CHAPTER 16

THE MOVIEGOER

I now have an apartment in New York, you'll be happy (I hope) to know. I will be sharing it with Barry Obama, a friend of mine from Occidental College." When Phil Boerner offered that news in a letter to his girlfriend, he had finished his summer job at Sequoia National Park in California and was visiting the home of his grandparents in Grahamsville, New York, in the Catskills, a two-hour drive from Manhattan. This was on August 25, 1981, a week before orientation day at Columbia College. "He just transferred to Columbia, too," Boerner continued, referring to Obama. "He's black and from Hawaii and has the typically Western casual outlook on life. I haven't seen the apartment yet, but I understand we will have separate bedrooms and a living room as well (plus bathroom and kitchen of course). The rent is $180 a month for each of us. I wanted a less-than-$200 place, so this fits the bill."

On the following Saturday morning, Boerner arrived outside the five-story apartment building at 142 West 109th Street between Columbus and Amsterdam with a station wagon stuffed with a box frame, a mattress, a dresser, and many boxes of books that he had stored in Harlem at the home of Dr. Emmett Bassett, an old family friend who drove down from 168th Street to help him unload. Obama was already inside apartment 3E and had left a note at the entryway: "Yell up to me when you get here, the buzzer doesn't work." That might have been an early sign that the place did not exactly fit Boerner's bill, but too late now. The move-in took about ten trips between the street and the third-story walk-up. The college boys struggled together with the box frame while Dr. Bassett effortlessly toted the mattress up alone.

If Obama went to New York in part to connect more deeply with his blackness, the life of this older African American professional was a fascinating place to start. Emmett Bassett evoked much of the history of race in twentieth-century America. Born in 1921 in Virginia, he attended a one-room segregated schoolhouse and went to college at the famed Tuskegee Institute in Alabama, where he was among the last agricultural disciples of George Washington Carver, the noted botanist and inventor. While in graduate school in Massachusetts, he met his future wife, Priscilla, at a protest outside a roadhouse that refused to serve blacks. Priscilla was white, and after they were married, the landlord of their first apartment in Springfield locked the doors and kept them out after he learned that Bassett was black. Their car was sabotaged by someone who poured sugar into the gas tank. Bassett made history as the first black in the nation to earn a doctoral degree in dairy technology, at Ohio State, and later taught microbiology at Columbia and the New Jersey College of Medicine and Dentistry. He and Priscilla remained committed social activists through the decades. They started a fund at the NAACP in 1955 to provide assistance to the mother of Emmett Till, the fourteen-year-old black youth from Chicago who was murdered in Mississippi after being accused of flirting with a white woman, and participated in hundreds of marches and protests over the ensuing decades, including long vigils outside the South African consulate in New York protesting apartheid.

But on the day Obama's roommate was moving in, Dr. Bassett was not so much a living history resource as a very big man who could haul an unwieldy mattress up the stairwell all by himself. A missed opportunity, perhaps, but in many ways it was representative of Obama's experience over the next four years in New York, from late summer 1981 to midsummer 1985, a time in his life seemingly so spare that it later inspired its own mystery-laced

characterization by journalists as "the Dark Years." He went east with every intention of confronting the world, yet ended up more disengaged than engaged.
He arrived determined to escape the sun-splashed ease of Hawaii and Los Angeles and affirm his racial identity near the epicenter of American blackness,
yet ended up living with white and Pakistani roommates, or alone, making no
lasting relationships with African Americans at Columbia or in the city as a
whole, spending more time away from school with old friends than on campus
with new ones, and entering into successive love affairs with two young white
women, Alexandra McNear and Genevieve Cook, the first a former classmate
from Oxy, the second an Australian with connections to Indonesia.

Nothing is so tempting for conspiracy theorists as what appears to be a hole
in a life, a lacuna that can be filled with all sorts of imagined nefarious activity,
but there was no real mystery to Obama's New York days. He was not a mis-
anthrope. He did not disappear into thin air for a year or more. There were
conditions – social, geographic, and personal – that explained how and why
he lived as he did. One perceptive depiction of him during that era was offered
by Boerner, his roommate on 109th, who likened Obama to the main character in Walker Percy's novel *The Moviegoer,* "where you're not participating in
life but you're kind of observing, one step removed."

Although Obama had left Occidental with what seemed like enough ambitious propulsion to carry him into a more active period, he instead receded
into the most existentialist stretch of his life. As he put it himself decades later
during an interview in the Oval Office, "I was leading an ascetic existence,
way too serious for my own good." He was still the outsider, the *jadak,* searching for home. If he did not actually lose himself in the fictions of cinema, as
Percy's protagonist Binx Bolling did, he did experience life as a series of movies. In most outward ways, compared to what came before, his time in New
York was a minimalist existence, without the sprawling cast of characters that
surrounded him at Oxy and Punahou and the exotica of Hawaii and Indonesia. He felt no attachments to Columbia or to the first jobs he landed after
graduation. But it would be a misreading to say that he was tamping down his
ambitions during that period. Just the opposite, in fact. If anything, his sense
of destiny deepened. He was conducting an intense debate with himself over
his past, present, and future, an internal struggle that he shared with only a few

close friends, including his girlfriends, Alex and Genevieve, who kept a lasting record, one in letters, the other in her journal.

It is exponentially easier to look back at a life than to live it, but in retrospect it also becomes apparent that New York was crucial to Obama in another way. If he had not quite found his place yet, he was learning what directions not to take and how to avoid turns that would lead him off the path and into traps from which it would be hard to escape. Even when he was uncertain about much else, Obama seemed hyperalert to avoiding a future he did not want. "Like a tourist," he would later write, "I watched the range of human possibility on display, trying to trace out my future in the lives of the people I saw, looking for some opening through which I could reenter."

Obama arrived in New York a week before Boerner, but when he reached 109th Street he did not have a key to the apartment and could not find anyone to give him one. He spent his first night in the big city outside, curled up in a nearby alleyway, and woke up with a white hen pecking at his face. He remembered that he had the telephone number of Sohale Siddiqi, Hasan Chandoo's Pakistani friend who had stayed with them in Pasadena the previous Christmas holiday. Siddiqi (identified by the pseudonym Sadik in Obama's memoir) was relatively new to the United States, arriving in 1980, and was staying in a cramped studio apartment across town on First Avenue. "I got an unexpected phone call very early in the morning," he recalled. "It was Barack. I told him to come over. He arrived pretty disheveled with all of his belongings in a suitcase. . . . I wouldn't say he was happy, but he was cool. He crashed on my couch [before gaining access to his own apartment]."

When Obama settled in with Boerner at last, he found one oddly familiar aspect to his Columbia routine: the walk to school. Here was a variation of his high school days: five blocks from the front door of his walk-up to the lower boundary of campus, the same distance as from his grandparents' apartment on South Beretania to the old lava rock walls gracing the lower entrance to Punahou School. Then and now the most direct route passed a church and a hospital, but instead of seeing Central Union Church of Honolulu and Kapi'olani Medical Center on his walk up Punahou Street, Obama now went by the majestic Cathedral of St. John the Divine and St. Luke's Hospital

Center as he made his way up Amsterdam. V&T Pizzeria and the Hungarian Pastry Shop were also along the way (no Honolulu equivalents). Once he reached 114th Street, he could turn left at John Jay Hall and head toward Butler Library, continue two blocks farther up Amsterdam to the traditional black iron entrance gate near Hamilton Hall at 116th and turn left into the heart of campus along College Walk, or proceed yet another two blocks north up Amsterdam to the School for International Affairs building, home of the Political Science Department. The final block of that last stretch was on a downward slope, and on a clear day Obama could take in a panoramic view of Harlem to the north.

But aside from the walk to school, there was nothing cozy about his new home. His apartment made the most rudimentary college dormitory seem luxurious by comparison. The south side of 109th was a depressing bulwark of a block, with an uninterrupted wall of five-story apartment buildings shadowing the street from Columbus on the east to Amsterdam on the west. One-forty-two was the fourth door from the corner with Amsterdam, a dirty pale brick exterior with gray fire escapes zigzagging up the front. Up three flights of stairs was Obama and Boerner's place; the apartment across the hall was an empty shell that had been burned out, black smoke stains still visible on the outer walls. The door to apartment 3E opened into the kitchen; as Boerner recalled, it had "five locks, including the bar that goes in after you get inside," though there were no break-ins and nothing inside worth stealing. The bathroom was off to the side, and two bedrooms ran railcar-style back to the left from there, first Obama's then (so much for privacy) Boerner's, leading to a living room with two windows that looked across the street to a Consolidated Edison building that dominated most of the block to the north, an impenetrable, windowless fortress. The new residents of 3E would not learn the full extent of their apartment's disrepair until the nights turned colder; the heating usually did not work, and on those rare occasions when it did the blast was so intense they had to open all the windows. Hot water was also scarce, forcing them to take many of their showers at Columbia's gym.

Such was their welcome to the peculiar world of Columbia in the early 1980s. Pern Beckman, Boerner's cousin, who had entered the college a year earlier, had warned Phil that summer, "If Columbia offers you anything at all, take it. Life is just much easier first semester if you have a place on campus." But even if Obama and Boerner had wanted campus housing, as transfer students none was available to them. Columbia was suffering from an acute housing shortage, with only about 60 percent of its undergraduates able to live on campus. Several old residence halls were undergoing renovations, and one new high-rise dorm opened that fall, adding 645 more rooms, but that wasn't enough to resolve the situation. Obama and Boerner got to Columbia at the worst possible time, just as off-campus housing was becoming more expensive, except in neighborhoods that were far away or nearby but more dangerous. "The policy in the early eighties of not offering housing to transfer students was a painful one," said Roger Lehecka, then dean of students. "Five years earlier it had been no big deal" because of the availability of affordable off-campus housing. But the city was changing in ways that Columbia was not keeping up with, Lehecka recalled, and with the rise in housing prices by 1981 more students wanted to stay in dorms, including upperclassmen who normally would move to apartments.

In the list of problems transfer students faced, the lack of heat and hot water that Obama and Boerner endured was not the worst. Lehecka was more concerned about students who had to look many miles away to find something affordable or who ended up with no permanent place and spent months or semesters floating from friend to friend and couch to couch. As dean of students, he pushed the administration to resolve the housing problem, arguing that inevitably it would diminish the quality of the school as a whole, and though his argument eventually prevailed, it would not be until the end of the decade that Columbia could claim to have sufficient housing for all of its students. Too late for the transfers from Oxy. The first explanation for Obama's shadowy existence during his New York years was that prosaic: a question of housing. Had he lived on campus, scores of people would have known him right from the start. "We didn't have that acculturation like at Oxy, where you stay at a frosh dorm and get to know a lot of your classmates," Boerner said later. Lehecka, recalling his thinking as he pushed for better housing alternatives, put it this way: "How could you expect them to thrive if you didn't provide them a reasonable place to live?"

Beyond the housing situation, disaffection with the college scene – not the classes, but the overall ambience – was commonplace at Columbia. Barak Zimmerman, a Jewish student from California, had no idea another young man was walking around campus with a variation of his uncommon first name, but then again Zimmerman did not know many classmates. At an alumni event decades later, he said something to an old classmate along the lines of "I don't really remember you because I really avoided campus and I avoided the people on campus. I felt like my friends and I were these alienated people surrounded by an army of khaki-wearing conformists." To which came the reply "Hey, we all felt like that." As explained by David Rakoff, a New York writer and satirist who also attended Columbia in the early 1980s, it was "something of a badge of honor not to have to depend upon the campus for your social life." The undergraduate college was still all-male, the last single-sex bastion in the Ivy League, its administrators bickering with sister school Barnard over whether their merger would be equitable or a male-dominated marriage. This was all part of an atmosphere, as one member of the class of 1983 put it, that "ended up attracting . . . people who, by their own self-selection, were not . . . very social or very into a broader set of school activities." Whether they were exceptions to the rule or proof that being a college outsider is not debilitating, the Columbia set overlapping with Obama's time there included waves of successful financiers and lawyers and several future public figures, among them George Stephanopoulos, White House aide to President Clinton and television host; Michael J. Massimino, an engineer and NASA astronaut; Hilton Als, the theater critic; Julius Genachowski, chairman of the Federal Communications Commission; Marcus Brauchli, editor at the *Wall Street Journal* and *Washington Post;* Michael J. Wolf, a broadcasting and technology strategist who ran MTV; the rock journalist Michael Azzerad, a biographer of Kurt Cobain and Nirvana; and Rakoff, the writer and public radio humorist.

When Obama arrived, Columbia, led by Michael I. Sovern, who took over as president in 1980, and New York City, with its emphatic mayor, Edward I. Koch, elected in 1978, were still laboring to recover from turbulent recent pasts. Only six years earlier, the city had been insolvent and desperately seeking federal help, which was not forthcoming, the predicament summarized unforgettably in the *Daily News* headline "Ford to City: Drop Dead." On campus, even though more than a decade had passed, there were still bitter divisions that went back to the radical student protests of the late 1960s, when the issues included not only the Vietnam War but a land invasion of sorts much closer to home: Columbia's effort to expand east and north in Morningside Heights, displacing poor black and Hispanic tenants along the way. By the time Obama signed up as a political science major, there were still distinguished professors in his department so estranged as a result of those old political fights that they would stride past one another in the hallway without so much as making eye contact.

The disarray on the streets and the campus conspired to make the Columbia experience a gritty one. How rough was it? One answer came when the student newspaper felt compelled to run a piece describing how nearby emergency rooms had refined the medical art of removing cockroaches from people's ears. On campus, maintenance had been deferred for years and many of the buildings were badly in need of renovation. Hamilton Hall, the grand old structure named for Alexander Hamilton, a famed alumnus of what was originally King's College, was the building that defined the college's purpose, the usual home to its core curriculum courses, Literature Humanities and Contemporary Civilization. Now Hamilton was streaked with grime and in a general state of disrepair that lingered from the protest occupation days of 1968. One student said it looked "like a New York City school," which was not meant as a compliment. The little that was fresh and new at Columbia when Obama arrived did not generate rave reviews, especially the school's belated expansion east into the area that had proved so contentious earlier. While praising East Campus, a commodious new high-rise dormitory on Morningside Drive between 117th and 118th Streets, Ada Louise Huxtable, the architecture critic for the *New York Times,* noted nonetheless that it had many of the characteristics of a maximum-security prison.

The analogy seemed all too apt. Barak Zimmerman lived at East Campus, with its faux marble sinks and Berlin Wall security procedures, and from the window of his suite at night as he looked north and east he could see orange-red flames flicker in the darkened urban landscape, not votive candles but hollowed-out buildings set afire in Harlem. The neighborhoods south, below 110th Street, and east of Broadway, including the block where Obama and

Boerner lived, were considered sketchy, many streets pockmarked with abandoned and boarded-up buildings infested with rats and roaches. Crime was a familiar topic of conversation, a reality intensified by popular culture and gallows humor. David Rakoff would later write that his mother's purse was stolen on the very day that his parents dropped him off at school, an act of thievery that surely increased their worries about their boy but thrilled him because it "conferred a modicum of street cred with zero injury." He could never match the incident a few years later, when three Columbia freshmen trudged home with a carpet they found and were basking in the good fortune of their curbside bounty until they unfurled the rug and discovered a corpse inside with two bullet wounds through the head. Then there were the gruesome stories Columbia rowers brought back from workouts on the Harlem River, separating Manhattan from the Bronx. Along with dodging slicks of raw sewage, at least twice during the early 1980s the rowers saw what they called "floaters," dead bodies in the river, one being the dockside body of a fully dressed dead postman.

Steve Holtje, a writer in Obama's graduating class, remembered being with a group of people at Plimpton Hall, a Barnard dorm at 121st and Amsterdam, when the security guard called up on the Centrex phone system to announce, "Hey, somebody's trying to break into your car." The guard said he could not try to stop the break-in because he was not allowed to leave his post, so Holtje and friends – three men and a woman – rushed down and confronted the burglar, who escaped and fled into Morningside Park. "When the police finally arrived, they refused to pursue him into the park," Holtje recalled. "They didn't think it was safe to go into Morningside Park after dark." Crime, added Holtje, who was mugged in a subway stairwell, "was sort of like expected. You couldn't read the *Daily News* without seeing the constant parade of crimes that they were trumpeting." Colin Redhead, a black freshman in 1981 from Trinidad, was robbed at gunpoint by two young men as he walked a woman friend, a waitress at the café inside the Papyrus bookstore, to her apartment building on 112th between Broadway and Amsterdam early one morning during his first semester. "At first I said I had no money because I was a dumb freshman," he recalled. That did not work; the robbers took his wallet (with enough cash for a People's Express ticket to Florida the following day), his watch, and money from the café that the waitress had forgotten to deposit in a nearby bank.

Whenever Steven Waldman, editor of the *Columbia Daily Spectator,* returned late at night from the library to his room at River Hall over by Riverside Drive, he found it safest to walk in the middle of 114th Street "to minimize the odds of getting mugged." Michael Ackerman, who played drums in the Columbia marching band and took a political science class with Obama, remembered that at orientation upperclassmen passed down to new students the safest ways to negotiate the subway system. They were told to transfer in Midtown to the 1 or 9 line, a move that ensured they could get off just outside Columbia's main gate at 116th and Broadway, rather than stay on the 2 or 3 line, which stopped at 116th, several blocks to the east, and required a dangerous walk back through Morningside Park. A variation of that predicament was soon made famous in John Sayles's 1984 movie *The Brother from Another Planet,* in which a cardsharp riding the subway said, "I have another magic trick for you. Wanna see me make all the white people disappear?" Moments later the subway public address announcer barked, "59th Street and Columbus Circle, 125th Street next!"

If Obama heard that warning at his orientation on August 31 it would have meant little to him. Unlike many of his classmates, he came to Columbia in part because of, not despite, its proximity to Harlem. He had no qualms about walking from 109th Street north into Harlem, exploratory forays into a culture he felt kinship with but knew mostly through books, a black community, he would note later, that "I had so lovingly imagined and within which I had hoped to find refuge." He had read the literature of James Baldwin and studied the history of Adam Clayton Powell Jr., the famous Harlem congressman; now he could walk the same streets and enter the same churches. But it was not what he had hoped. Almost everything but a gospel choir seemed drearier, less welcoming, more fractured.

Obama's introduction to New York was conflated in *Dreams from My Father.* Phil Boerner, his white roommate, was omitted entirely, just as Paul Carpenter had been from the Occidental days. The apartment on 109th was mentioned only so Obama could relate the story of his being locked out that first night in New York. In Boerner's stead, Obama focused his memoir on the character he called Sadik, modeled on Sohale Siddiqi, who would become his roommate the following year at an apartment on the other side of Central Park. Columbia itself barely rated a mention in the memoir, serving mostly as a plot device to get Obama to New York. He felt no need to describe his courses or professors, but he did write about the graffiti on the lavatory walls as reflections of racial discord. In one scene in the memoir, he quoted himself telling Sadik upon arriving in New York that he had spent the previous summer "brooding over a misspent youth." It was "time to make amends," he said. Now he was determined to get his act together and be of some use to society. He would read more deeply, eat more healthily, start running more frequently to keep in shape, and lay off marijuana, if not quit smoking. Sadik responded by calling Obama a bore.

In reality the transition was not so sudden and dramatic. He had started changing earlier, and he was never that much of a deadbeat in the first place. He began reading in earnest at Punahou, a habit he maintained throughout his Choom Gang days, and he started running regularly during his freshman year at Occidental. All through his two years at Oxy, even when he was participating in the Barf Couch subculture, he was engaged intellectually. In fact, he seemed to have as many of those intense "deep-sea diving" conversations about literature and philosophy at Occidental as he did at Columbia. He was regarded as serious, if not ambitious, during his two years in California, and though he and Hasan Chandoo were known for their parties, his pot smoking by then was diminishing. By the time they reached Columbia, Boerner said, "we were both fairly disciplined."

The summer that Obama said he spent brooding about his past was also full of travel and adventure for him. He had not gone home to Hawaii to stay with his grandparents at Punahou Circle; instead, leaving Los Angeles on June 18, he had flown to Jakarta to visit his mother and sister at their house in the Menteng neighborhood. Ann came up with the money for the trip from the Ford Foundation's special travel fund for the education of dependent children. He bought an around-the-world Pan Am ticket that allowed sixteen stops. While in Jakarta, of all places, Obama had secured his first New York lodging, the 109th Street apartment, which he learned he could sublet from the boyfriend and future husband of Nancy Peluso, Ann's young anthropologist friend in Indonesia's expat community. At the time, though Obama admired his mother's tireless efforts on behalf of poor working women, he was skeptical of the role of U.S.-based institutions in the Third World, not only multinational corporations but development organizations like the Ford Foundation. His perspective had been shaped in part by the opinions of the international friends he made at Occidental, including Hasan Chandoo, who had often criticized the notion of American benevolence, arguing that, in supporting military dictatorships, it had done as much harm as good in the developing world.

It was to Chandoo's home turf in Karachi that Obama traveled next on his summer Asian tour. After graduating, Chandoo had returned to Pakistan for a few months before heading off to London, where he would work at an uncle's office in the family shipping business, writing telexes and taking letters of credit. Their Oxy classmate and friend Wahid Hamid was also in Karachi, and Obama had arranged to split time between their two homes, spending a week and a half at Chandoo's, then a week and a half at Hamid's. In traditional Pakistani style, Chandoo and Hamid both went to pick him up at the airport with a greeting party of seven cousins and friends in two cars. While waiting in the bustling lobby, Chandoo took note of the Red Caps, who were mostly black Pakistanis of African origin. He wondered what they would think when they saw him and his pals pick up their dark-skinned American brother. Chandoo lived in an upper-middle-class enclave known as the Pakistan Employees Cooperative Housing Society, not far from Dirgh Road. His family home was elegant but not ostentatious, a modern bungalow set back from 42nd Street, with beautiful gardens and several servants, including driver, cook, gardener, and cleaning person. He and Barry shared his old bedroom.

Pakistan then was under martial law, ruled by General Muhammad Zia ul-Haq, who had seized power in a military coup, deposing Prime Minister Zulfikar Ali Bhutto in 1977 and executing him a year later. At first Zia had taken the role of chief martial law administrator, saying he would not abrogate the Pakistani Constitution and that national elections would be forthcoming. Now, four years into his reign, he was calling himself president, but martial law was still in place and opposition parties were banned. Much as in Indonesia, foreign policy considerations brought the United States into an alliance with a military regime in the cold war struggle against Soviet communism. Zia was an anticommunist, and along with the United States was instrumental in supplying arms to the mujahedeen in neighboring Afghanistan after the Soviet invasion in 1980.

During his three weeks in Pakistan, Obama was nowhere near the Afghan action. He spent most of his time in Karachi, a sprawling city built amid the desert and wetlands on the coast of the Arabian Sea. Every morning during the first week and a half, he went for a run in Chandoo's neighborhood, alone, but stayed safe and managed to find his way back. They also played basketball, went to the seashore to swim and lounge around at the Sandspit and Hawke's Bay beaches, and roamed the streets of the largest and most cosmopolitan city in Pakistan. Chandoo, still in his leftist period and thinking that he would someday go into Pakistani politics, made a point of taking Obama through the poorest sections of Karachi, driving them around in a comfortable sedan.

As Chandoo delivered his lectures on the inequities of rich and poor in his country, he was greeted with the same sharp retorts that Obama had sent his way during their late-night conversations at the apartment in Pasadena. "Here you are driving around in this fancy car talking about how you are going to help these people!" Obama said. Chandoo would try to defend himself; he noted that he refused to use the air-conditioning at his father's home until the servants also had air-conditioning. Along the way, Obama learned more about the religious and cultural nuances of that part of the world and the sharp distinctions in wealth, class, and power. Every evening at dinner, often at the homes of various relatives of Chandoo's or Hamid's, he listened to intense discussions about politics and religion. Chandoo was Shia, Hamid was Sunni (the majority sect among Sindhi), but both were heavily Westernized and not dogmatic. The Chandoo clan was "religious, but liberal," according to Chandoo. "Everyone was allowed to speak their mind."

When he switched to Hamid's house in a sector called the Defense Housing Society he again was in the embrace of a large family, with Hamid's sister and her two young children living next door. Near the end of the trip, the Oxy trio and assorted Pakistani friends ventured east toward Hyderabad (in Pakistan, not India), following the Indus River valley through the history-rich

Sindh province. It was not a hardship tour; they rode in two air-conditioned sedans. Although the trip was not simply for Obama, but something Chandoo and Hamid had wanted to undertake even before they knew their pal was coming, it served nonetheless as another opportunity for Chandoo to show Obama the economic and social inequities of his country. They stayed at the feudal estate of the well-established Palpur family, whose son was Hamid's old Karachi Grammar School friend.

It was not a glamorous setting – the land was barren and mosquito-ridden – but the family they were visiting essentially owned the entire village and enjoyed the benefits of their territorial power. "When we walked the land Barack would see the poor peasants, the plight of the Pakistani farmer, the equivalent of black sharecroppers," Chandoo noted later. Among the feudal workers at the farm were a few men of African descent. Obama met one of them, Hamid recalled, but "he couldn't speak the language and that guy couldn't speak English. I think we sat across from each other and they kind of nodded to each other. They had a similar heritage. The Arabs brought people from Africa many, many years ago." The African worker Obama met was "an old man who had been on those lands for many years. . . . We weren't sitting at a table; it would be out in a courtyard and that individual would be sitting on a *charpai*. It's a rudimentary kind of bed made of wood and ropes; that's where he slept. Obama and the man would have felt some familiarity by physical appearance. Maybe he hadn't seen somebody like this come and visit his boss." That night, the young Pakistanis played bridge.

At age twenty Obama was a man of the world. He had never been to south-central Kansas or western Kenya, the homelands of his ancestors, yet his divided heritage from Africa and the American heartland had defined him from the beginning. He could not be of one place, rooted and provincial. From his years living in Indonesia, where he was fully immersed in Javanese schools and culture; from his adolescence in Hawaii, where he was in the polyglot sea of *hapa* and *haole*, Asians and islanders; from his mother's long-term commitment to development work overseas; from his friendship with the Oxy Pakistanis and his extended visit to their country – from all of this he had experienced far more global diversity than the average college junior. He knew about shave ice and *malasada*, the fried pastry coated in sugar of Honolulu, and about *permen cabai,* the red pepper candy of Jakarta; now he picked up a simple Sindhi chicken curry recipe from the Pakistanis that became a staple of his home cooking during the New York years: caramelize some onions; toast a spice mix of turmeric, coriander, garlic, and cumin for a minute or two; throw in six chicken thighs and a bit of water; cook until the skin falls from the thighs. He knew the ways of different cultures better than he knew himself.

Phil Boerner started taking banjo lessons that fall. On the list of irritations at 109th Street, his plucking was far down the list, below the lack of privacy, lack of hot water, and lack of heat. When the nights turned colder, the roommates took to sleeping bags for warmth and spent as little waking time in apartment 3E as possible, holing up in the stacks of Butler Library up on 114th, parts of which were open all night. Some mornings, eager to flee their unaccommodating quarters, they walked to the corner of Broadway and 112th to eat at Tom's Restaurant, the place immortalized later as the fictional Monk's, a familiar meeting place for the characters in the television show *Seinfeld.* A full breakfast went for a buck ninety-nine; half a chicken with soup and two vegetables, four dollars. Not that all Columbia students were poor, far from it, but there was something about the far Upper West Side milieu that encouraged them to choose among modest booth-and-counter restaurants the way Princeton students would divide into selective eating clubs. "There were three diners in the neighborhood. You had your allegiance to one," recalled Peter Lunenfeld, a rower on the heavyweight crew whose time at Columbia overlapped with Obama's. Students tended to pick a favorite from among Tom's, the Mill Luncheonette, and the College Inn and stick with it for the duration. Lunenfeld was a regular at the Mill, which was run by two Holocaust survivors and their Puerto Rican chef. Across Broadway and up the street from Tom's, the Mill was also where the overnight crew from the *Columbia Spectator* usually straggled in for breakfast, served all day for a dollar forty-nine.

During fall afternoons, Obama could be seen now and then in fatigues and a black T-shirt, perched on the wide front steps of Low Library, taking in the passing scene between classes. Three or four times a week, when there were open hours on the court late in the day, he would walk up to the Dodge Physical Fitness Center for pickup basketball games. Ron Sunshine, a freshman during Obama's junior year, remembered asking him one day, "How did you get so good?" As ever, Obama had a propensity to drive only to his left, but Sunshine thought he was a "natural leader" with uncanny court sense. "Well, I played high school ball," Obama responded. It was hard to resist Sunshine's evocative surname, translated by ancestors from Zonneschein, the Russian version of a German name, but Obama gave it a syncopated twist. "RON Sunshine," he called out when the freshman canned a jump shot. Obama also took Spanish with Sunshine, fulfilling one of Columbia's requirements. After class one day, standing on the sidewalk at 116th and Broadway, he pulled out a pack of cigarettes that caught the younger student's attention: so cool and exotic, black and thin and sweet smelling. They were Djarums, a brand of *kreteks,* the most popular cigarettes in Indonesia, made with an intoxicating blend of tobacco and cloves.

One of Obama's hangouts on free nights was the West End on Broadway near 114th, dark and smoky, where he dragged on Djarums or Marlboros, drank beer, and occasionally sat in the live jazz room to the left of the front door, taking in the nightly performances of old alumni of Count Basie's band like the drummer Papa Jo Jones. The rich history of the West End was well-known, from the Beats to the Rads, from Jack Kerouac to Mark Rudd, but what Obama did not know was that he likely sat a few times at the very table where his father once held court during his expeditions from Cambridge in the early 1960s to hang out with fellow Kenyan students. Imagine if a time-lapse camera had captured the two Barack Hussein Obamas two decades apart at the same corner table: the first answering to *BARE-ick,* the second to *Buh-ROCK;* the first wearing glasses; both downing beers, but the first one far more; both smoking and chatting in their deep voices; the first older and more outwardly boastful, but both searching far from home, wondering about their place in the world.

Among the waitresses at the West End during the younger Obama's time was a Barnard student named Alison McParlin Davis, the daughter of Howard McParlin Davis, an art historian who was one of Columbia's most beloved professors. Alison, whose nickname was "Guitar Woman" because she studied jazz guitar at school, worked the night shift from seven to two in the morning. She likely waited on Obama, but that is not what makes her story worth considering for a moment alongside his. In terms of race, family, and identity, the very issues Obama was still struggling with, they were opposite sides of the same coin. Davis, like Obama, was the product of a mixed marriage, but in her case her mother, Grace Taylor Davis, was black and her father was white. She was the lone child of the relationship, just as Barry was for Ann and Barack Sr., though the Davis marriage in New York endured while the one in Hawaii did not. The black side of her family traced back from Brooklyn to Alabama, where her grandfather once played cornet in a jazz band with W. C. Handy. Like Obama, she was relatively unaware of racial issues until she got to prep school, in her case the Westover School for girls in Connecticut.

Black and white, white and black, half and half, *hapa* – one difference between Obama and Davis had to do with the shade of their skin. Unlike Barack Hussein Obama Sr., Grace Taylor Davis was extremely light-skinned; she could "pass" for a white person. Her daughter was even paler, with freckles and green eyes. One of the early experiences that alerted Barry Obama to his skin color was when the tennis pro at Punahou School told him not to touch a tournament schedule pinned to the bulletin board because his "color might rub off." Alison Davis suffered a similar shock, but from the opposite perspective, when one of the black girls at Westover told her she could not accompany them to a gathering of African Americans at eastern boarding schools but instead should "go back to your own kind." Davis said she had grown up color-blind, or as oblivious to color as humanly possible, and was confused by the rejection. What was her kind? She thought of the Sunday dinners she had enjoyed with her mother's family in Brooklyn, and the summer gatherings of black professionals and their families up at their cottage on Greenwood Lake. It was only then, Davis said, that "it dawned on me that I was biracial." At about the age that Barry Obama decided to stop announcing to the world that his mother was white, Alison Davis started carrying a photograph of her mother in her wallet to convince people that her mother was black.

Most of the doubters were white, she said. Unlike that one girl at boarding school, the vast majority of blacks were not fazed by her pale appearance. "I think this was because so many African Americans, including myself, have slave backgrounds and thus have white ancestors from master-slave relationships," Davis said. "It's easier for blacks to understand how I could look the way I do." During her later college years, which coincided with Obama's time at Columbia, she became intensely interested in African American literature and started collecting African memorabilia, inspired in part by her uncle, Council S. Taylor, a noted black anthropologist. Like Obama, she had friends of all colors and backgrounds, but she was less curious about her blackness than Obama was during those years. Even though much of society at first glance assumed she was white, she had experienced everyday interactions with black members of her family since her childhood, something that Obama missed entirely.

The bands playing at the West End during Obama's first year included a group called So What, a name inspired by the first cut of the Miles Davis album *Kind of Blue*. It was a jazz fusion group led by Steve Bargonetti, a guitar player and recent Columbia graduate who, like Obama and Davis, was of mixed race; his father was Italian and his mother, Ada Askew Bargonetti, was black. During his Columbia years, Bargonetti "got hassled from both sides" a bit – blacks at first questioning his ethnicity because of his name, whites unsure because of his skin color. But he overcame those suspicions largely through music. "There were racial inferences from both sides which were completely disavowed once we started bringing people together via music," he said. So What was popular among blacks and whites. The central gathering place for blacks on the Columbia (and Barnard) campus was the Black Students Organization (BSO). Bargonetti, with his name and light skin, felt rejected when he attended a meet-and-greet there, sensing that "there seemed to be those that knew each other and wanted to keep it that way." But when his music was accepted, so was he. The same people who seemed standoffish before "would come to my shows and love my music. So more power to good music."

The BSO gathered on the first floor of Hartley Hall, in the Malcolm X Lounge, where the walls were lined with pictures of famous black leaders. Greg Smith, a premed student from Lexington, Massachusetts, who arrived the same year as Obama, called the lounge "a little oasis, a getaway, like 'I don't have to explain myself, I don't have to prove anything.' You learn as an African American in an Ivy League school, you learn to speak two languages. This probably relates to Obama his whole life. You learn to be bilingual

435

when you're in there and you're talking about the philosophy of Aristotle or Kierkegaard and you want to make erudite explanations of symbolism in the world . . . and then you want to let your hair down and say, 'Yo, wassup? I'm still in New York. Be chill. Where you gonna be hanging? Let me tell you what these crazy people did to me today.'" Derek Hawkins, a varsity basketball player from South Jamaica, Queens, sometimes served as the deejay at parties there, spinning "club music, R&B, Evelyn 'Champagne' King, early rap, Run DMC, LL Cool J, Grandmaster Flash and the Furious Five, Kurtis Blow."

Wayne P. Weddington III, who came to Columbia College from Central High in Philadelphia, remembered seeing Obama at meetings and parties in the Malcolm X Lounge. He described Obama's personality then as "very island mentality . . . always smiling, nice guy," but also thought of him as "a mature, engaged, cerebral, responsible guy." He recalled that Obama would stay late at BSO meetings to talk about life and politics; Weddington would flee early. Weddington was more social, less serious, and not above making fun of Obama's name. At parties, he would shout *buh-ROCK OBAMA* like the bray of a horn. At the time, Weddington recalled, Obama was pursuing a black woman from Barnard ("she had green eyes; she was pretty") who was one of the leaders of the BSO. "It was kind of hard to carry on those things without people knowing," he said. But Obama never took a lead role with the group, and did not make much of a mark beyond Weddington's memory.

It is hard to imagine a young Bill Clinton participating in any organization without exchanging stories with every person in the room, flirting with every girl, and leaving a lasting impression, for better or worse. By contrast, some of the most active members of the Black Students Organization could not remember Obama at their meetings or parties. Again, he was more the observer – here admiring, there critiquing, always learning, but from a distance. Danny Armstrong, who attended most of the events, was director of political affairs for the organization for part of that period and has the sort of mind that holds on to names, faces, and dates. He did not know Obama from the BSO, nor from the Columbia gym, where he also spent much of his time. "I don't recall him ever being involved," Armstrong said. "I've not talked to anyone who knew him." It was only decades later, when Obama emerged as a national figure, that one image came back to Armstrong. "I didn't know him, but I remember seeing him walking across campus. I can literally visualize it": Obama with a backpack, on the walkway to Ferris Booth Hall (the student center, known as FBH, that was to be replaced a decade later), not far from Furnald Hall and the Journalism building. "He looked much as he looks now, walking across campus with his books by himself. I picture him in that pilot-type jacket and maybe some dark slacks on. He had a purposeful walk, moving, going about his business."

The pilot-type jacket could have been the same bomber jacket he wore for some of those photographs taken by Lisa Jack during his freshman year at Occidental. The Obama stride was distinctive, memorable. What was going on inside his head – that was the mystery. Like many contemporaries who came across Obama at Punahou, Occidental, and Columbia, Wayne Weddington could not see that the laid-back Hawaiian was churning inside, trying to sort out his own identity and the complexities of race in America. It was about his New York years that Obama in his memoir offered his most pessimistic take on the state of race and class and the urban condition. Something about the density or scale of New York, he wrote, made him finally "grasp the almost mathematical precision with which America's race and class problems joined; the depth, the ferocity, of resulting tribal wars; the bile that flowed freely not just out on the streets but in the stalls of Columbia's bathrooms as well, where, no matter how many times the administration tried to paint them over, the walls remained scratched with blunt correspondence between niggers and kikes."

The last reference, implying there were ineradicable tensions between black students and Jewish students at Columbia, mirroring larger tensions in the city, was a bit of a stretch. Bathroom walls were the Internet comment boards of an earlier era, where anonymous ugly screeds were commonplace. African Americans and Jews were certainly two of the stronger "tribes" in New York, and the ups and downs of their relationship were well chronicled. Columbia, by the nature of its location and history, had a larger Jewish representation in its student body than other Ivy League schools. Blacks, however, constituted about 5 percent of the total in 1981. The class that entered in 1979, which was the class Obama joined as a junior, represented a two-decade low point in minority recruitment, down from a high of about 10 percent in

1972 and 1973, a statistic that greatly troubled the dean of students and set him on a mission to change the demographics. In surveying minority students on campus, Roger Lehecka found that they liked the city but felt the administration was unfriendly. That was probably unintentional, he determined, but it had to change.

But for the most part, when others described the atmosphere at Columbia during the early 1980s, they did not portray it in starkly divided racial terms, though there were certainly racial incidents. Greg Smith, who served as a jazz deejay on the college radio station, remembered attending a fraternity party one night that was advertised as a "bacchanal," where students were told to arrive with two dollars and a piece of fruit. Smith walked in carrying an orange and was met at the front door by a frat boy who said, "Oh, I don't think we take watermelons." And Smith had another story: "Some black students were going towards East Campus. There was a group of white students, males, who saw them laughing and talking as they were going toward them. The whites stopped and said, 'Hey where are you going?' [My friends said] 'We're going to East Campus.' They said, 'Hey, can we see some IDs?' Some of the blacks said, 'Well, can we see your IDs?' As I recall no one really showed anything. It was more talk, like 'You're not belonging.' There was a security guard who came in. It might have been a thing where he recognized them. . . . They were just kind of being jerks, like 'Hey, we know what goes on, these guys who come here from the neighborhood and try to do something.'" This sort of incident, Smith added, "wasn't very common. It didn't happen daily. I got the sense that most of the people had their eyes open and knew this was a diverse campus and people did come from different backgrounds." On the whole, he said, he "always felt pretty at home" at Columbia.

Timothy Guilfoyle played basketball at Columbia during the late 1970s, was a graduate student and resident dorm director there during the Obama years, and went on to become a professor of American urban and social history at Loyola University of Chicago. "I never felt like there were racial tensions on campus, but I am white. I might have been oblivious to it," Guilfoyle recalled. As a basketball player, both on the varsity team and in intramural leagues as a graduate student, Guilfoyle constantly interacted with blacks on campus. His assessment was not meant as a critique of Obama's perspective.

He had read *Dreams from My Father* and considered teaching it in his courses, he said, because it dealt so deeply with the process of choosing a racial identity and also raised "a lot of profound questions . . . about how we think about race and how African Americans think about race, debates they go through among themselves that most Americans are largely oblivious to."

Much like the distinction at Occidental delineated by Louis Hook, a leader of the black student group there, Wayne Weddington noticed "a palpable difference" within Columbia's black community between "those who came from the middle class and those who did not." His three freshman roommates at Carman Hall were black and represented this bifurcation. One was a star cricket player and brilliant engineer from British Guyana; the other two were football players from urban high schools. The twenty-five or so blacks in his class, Weddington said, ranged from "very unpolished all the way up to very polished." Weddington, whose father was a doctor, counted himself among the middle-class blacks more open to relationships across racial lines. He dated a foreign student at Barnard who came from Poland. He felt the derision of working-class blacks "for being soft or proper or a wannabe." His closest friends at Columbia were two Haitians, Eddy Anglade, a library grind in pre-med, and Jacques Augustin, the son of a domestic, a multilingual social whirl-wind who could talk his way into the hottest nightclubs, including Studio 54 in its heyday, and knew everyone on campus, including Obama, with whom he shared an international sensibility. (Augustin became a successful international entrepreneur in the export-import trade, and was killed in a plane crash in Taiwan in 1998.)

One unavoidable subject for Weddington and other blacks at Columbia involved affirmative action. "Almost every year there were white friends of mine who would talk about that, [saying] blacks didn't belong here, they were taking spaces away from capable people who didn't get in, they knew a guy who was number one at his school and didn't get in, so how did this black guy get in? I pursued friendships in all quarters and beliefs. I'd rather know what you think of as a difference of opinion than avoid you because of a difference of opinion. So if a lot of people think one way, there's probably some merit to it, even if I don't agree." Weddington would say to them that as long as there were white students who performed less well – "and I had 1280 and 1320 on the SATs" – no one could tell him he didn't belong. "You couldn't say I took his place. Get over it. It was sensitive. I think we all heard that at different points." If Obama did not hear complaints from white classmates then, he did thirty years later, when political opponents questioned how he was admitted to Occidental and Columbia (and later Harvard Law School), demanding to see his test scores and grades.

The sensitivity of the affirmative action issue, at least in retrospect, was in the eyes of the beholder. Michael Ackerman said the question of who belonged at Columbia was not an issue for him or his white friends during the early 1980s. Ackerman could think of only "one guy in the entire student body while I was at Columbia that anybody might have said that about," a tall basketball player who left school prematurely. "I never heard people say, 'What the hell is that guy doing here?' to anyone with the exception of him. Nobody would have said that about Obama. He pulled his weight. He did more than that. Columbia is a place where everybody's smart and everybody's got things going on. It's hard to shine in that environment because everybody's equal. If you stand as an equal that speaks volumes about how qualified you are, and he certainly did that."

Phil Boerner said he was not aware of race being part of the equation when he interacted with his roommate, and he did not realize how much Obama might have been brooding over the subject until a decade and a half later, when he read the memoir. "One of the things that surprised me when I read his book was what he wrote about the black student world and the rest of it," Boerner said. "I wasn't aware of him looking at things in such racial terms. . . . To me he was a regular guy. I didn't consider him a black regular guy or anything like that. We had different backgrounds, but we both had lived in different countries and knew a little bit about the world." Beyond the African American friends from Occidental who visited when they came to New York, Boerner could not remember other black students coming by the apartment, though that might have been more a reflection of its dumpiness and lack of privacy than anything else. He and Obama did often discuss political issues, including what was happening in South Africa. Decades later, Boerner still had a flyer from an anti-apartheid event he probably attended with Obama on October 21, 1981, at Altschul Hall on the Barnard campus, where the film

The Rising Tide was shown and the speakers included David Ndaba of the African National Congress. The sponsors of the event were Students against Militarism and the Black Students Organization.

The gathering in Altschul Hall offers another opportunity to freeze a moment, compare Obama to a contemporary, see how uneven his path was, and appreciate what a vast and unlikely journey still lay ahead, physically and mentally. Only six months earlier, he had stood in the Arthur G. Coons Administrative Center Plaza at Occidental and delivered the first political speech of his life, a critique of Oxy's investments in firms that did business with South Africa. That day in the California sun had stirred something inside him; he realized that he could move a crowd with his words, and yet he came away from it with mixed feelings, the doubter in him believing that student protests were mostly for show, even if the cause was just. He had arrived in New York with a sense of mission that had overtaken him during his final months at Oxy, yet he was still repressing any inclinations toward traditional political engagement, still looking for an opening through his own cynicism. He was not able to live in the moment; life seemed too scripted, with people playing their parts. He was still the Moviegoer.

And here in that same audience at Altschul Hall sat Danny Armstrong, the black student who could not remember seeing Obama at BSO meetings but did have the one image of him loping across campus. Armstrong was a sophomore that fall, a year behind Obama. He had entered Columbia in 1980, arriving from Compton, California, recruited to play basketball. His public identity up to that point had been on the court, as a small forward or shooting guard, yet he was already interested in politics. One of the first things Armstrong did when he arrived in New York was volunteer at the 1980 Democratic National Convention held at Madison Square Garden. At his freshman dorm he was known to burst into spontaneous renditions of Dr. King's "I Have a Dream" speech, which he seemed to have memorized. But it was that night at Altschul Hall, watching a movie on apartheid and listening to Ndaba, the South African speaker, that changed him forever, showing him what he would later call "a path of light." After the movie he volunteered to pass out fliers for a rally at the law school; soon after that he got the BSO involved in the anti-apartheid movement, and within a few months he was the main speaker at an anti-apartheid rally on campus. As he remembered it, the administration was still shell-shocked from the 1968 protests, and his rally was to be staged on the same day that alumni would be in town. It had to be moved to an obscure location on the back side of Low Library and its glorious steps; it was drizzling, and aside from his cousin who was visiting from L.A. "maybe two or three other people" were there – but that was the start. He spent the next two years building the anti-apartheid movement on campus; his interest took him to Zimbabwe and into politics again as an aide in the presidential campaign of Alan Cranston, the Democratic senator from California, and eventually to Ghana and finally back to the Los Angeles area, where he devoted his life to helping disadvantaged youths through a program he started called Find a Tree.

Obama at Columbia, making those seemingly purposeful strides down the walkway toward FBH, had not yet found his path of light. In retrospect, Armstrong wished they had met during their days together on campus. "I used to think of myself as a hotshot political organizer, and I had the future president right there and I didn't get him involved," he said. A reasonable regret, but in truth it was Obama's choice.

Considering how determined he was to come to New York, Obama did not seem eager to shed past connections and start anew once he got there. He lived with a classmate from Occidental; his first guests at the apartment were from Occidental, including Paul Carpenter and his girlfriend, Beth Kahn; he kept in constant touch with his Pakistani friends; and he returned to Los Angeles at the first opportunity, during Columbia's semester break. A trip back to Southern California was welcome if for no other reason than because it would allow him to warm up. The 109th Street experience had proved so bone-chilling that the roommates decided to flee the cheap but uncomfortable quarters after that first semester, even though they had not arranged a replacement. Long before Thanksgiving, Obama had concocted a desperate plan. Their lease was to expire on December 7, but rather than pick it up themselves (they were subletting), he suggested they let it run out, not pay the last month's rent, and stay until they were evicted or found another place. "All of November we looked for another apartment, but to no avail," Boerner reported later in a letter to his grandmother. When phone service was cut and the heat went off for good, Boerner fled to the house of family friends in Brooklyn Heights and Obama slept on the floor at a friend's place on the Upper East Side until he finished his exams and escaped to Los Angeles. Now they fit the category that so worried Dean Lehecka: housing vagabonds moving from couch to couch.

Boerner thought they might continue looking for an apartment to share, but it never happened, and he eventually moved from the temporary lodging in Brooklyn Heights to a room in a nursing school dormitory way up near 168th Street in Washington Heights. He and Obama maintained their friendship, meeting now and then. They would drink beer and eat bagels, go out for Chinese food at Empire Szechuan or Hunan Garden Chinese, take long walks down the length of Broadway, watch Knicks and Nets games on television, and talk about classes and writing. They both kept journals, a mixture of daily diaries and poetry and short fiction. "We were both into that," Boerner said. He was certain then that his friend wanted to be a writer.

In the Manhattan telephone directory for 1982, Barack Obama's number was 410-2857, his address 339 East 94th Street, apartment 6A. This is where he lived for the better part of a year with Sohale Siddiqi. Like Obama's Oxy friends Chandoo, Hamid, and Husain, Siddiqi was a product of Karachi's upper middle class. His family had lived there and in London, his father at various times running a stone quarry, importing machine tools, and serving as a middleman dealing arms to the Pakistani military. Sohale, born in 1959, had attended Karachi Grammar School, the elite institution that had also educated Benazir Bhutto, who before the decade was out would rise to become Pakistan's prime minister. He considered Benazir "haughty and domineering," but was close friends with her younger sister, Sanam, known as Sunny, who was in his class at KGS. Sunny visited Sohale in New York at least once when Obama was there. On one of the apartment walls, one friend remembered, the roommates had hung a poster of Benazir and Sunny's father, Zulfikar Ali Bhutto, the former Pakistani leader who had been executed a few years earlier. Others said the Bhutto poster had been in Chandoo's apartment in Pasadena. Siddiqi did remember two pieces of art that Obama put up: framed posters of Picasso's *Blue Nude* and Gauguin's Polynesian painting *When Will You Marry?*

The apartment was between First and Second Avenues on the border between East Harlem and Yorkville, in what once had been a largely German neighborhood. Lou Gehrig, the famed Yankee, who also attended Columbia, had been born in a four-story building at 242 East 94th, only a block away, in 1903. By the time Obama got there, the residents were mostly Puerto Rican and the setting, as he described it, was "uninviting . . . treeless, barren" with "soot colored walkups." A small park was nestled nearby on the other side of First Avenue, and beyond that FDR Drive and the East River. The commute to Columbia, seven long blocks west to Central Park, then around the reservoir, across to Broadway, and north another twenty-two blocks, was a long grind by foot, with a steady incline for the first stretch to the park. Obama usually walked, sometimes taking an alternate northern route through Harlem. Only when the weather was difficult would he catch a crosstown bus on 96th Street over to Broadway and ride the subway up two stops from there.

The living conditions were comparable to the place on 109th, or worse: an even steeper trudge up a dimly lit stairwell; floors that slanted uncomfortably, with gaps between the boards and chips revealing several layers of paint; a front door that led into the kitchen, with no space for a table; miserably low water pressure in the shower; and broken controls on radiators that blasted too much heat and steam, forcing the tenants to keep the windows open. The cockroaches were so big, Siddiqi observed one day, that they looked "like dates on legs," a simile that Obama the writer appreciated so much he said he might borrow it for future use. In his memoir he described sitting on the stoop and watching the passing scene. There was no stoop, but there was a fire escape outside his bedroom. His was the larger of two, a benefit he earned by beating Siddiqi in a winner-gets-the-best-room footrace in the Columbia gym. Siddiqi was not a student, but Obama would sneak him into the gym now and then by passing along his Columbia ID. "I fancied myself a good sprinter. I suggested we race for it," recalled Siddiqi, who at five-feet-seven was outpaced by the long-striding Obama. The smaller bedroom he was allotted after losing was "the size of a walk-in closet."

As unpleasant as the place was, housing was so coveted in Manhattan that Siddiqi felt compelled to claim on the lease application that he had a lucrative catering job, fabricating a company and listing friends as references, when in fact he was a waiter at an Upper East Side restaurant. "It was pretty amusing. There were a lot of people who wanted the place – middle-class folk. . . . When we got there a lot of people were filling out the application. I said to Barack, 'There's no way in hell we're gonna get this place.' Because people looked much more clean-cut, cultured, more affluent, like white middle-class young New Yorkers. Barack and I were a bit of an odd couple and . . . we were not looking too savory. I suggested we needed to fudge the application. I was a waiter and he was a student . . . but he refused to fudge his. We got it with the proviso that Barack couldn't be on the lease. I paid the rent and he paid me. They [the landlords] didn't want his name on the lease because he was a student." The rent started at $450 a month.

Obama provided the stereo and most of the records, a collection he had started to build at Occidental: Stevie Wonder, Van Morrison, Bob Dylan, Talking Heads, Bob Marley, and, as Siddiqi remembered, "a lot of albums from the Ohio Players; I had never heard of them before or since." In place of Boerner's banjo, Obama now heard Siddiqi's guitar playing and singing. One of his favorite tunes was "Moonshadow" by Cat Stevens: "Yes I'm being followed by a moonshadow . . . Moonshadow, moonshadow." It was a catchy tune with simple lyrics open to various interpretations, including that it was about living in the moment and finding joy in what you have. Obama, despite his adaptability and easygoing exterior, was certainly not living in the moment. He would write later that he "got too comfortable in his solitude" during that period and "didn't get many visitors."

Boerner and a few other old Oxy acquaintances came by now and then, along with an occasional Pakistani friend of Siddiqi's, but for the most part the roommates felt alone against the world. Their friendship was never deep. They rarely confided in one another, and Obama did not engage Siddiqi in conversations about politics or literature, though he did once take him to an anti-apartheid rally at Columbia and to a Jesse Jackson rally in Harlem. (According to Siddiqi, they both left unimpressed by Jackson.) Obama seemed to have no use for rigid thinking of any sort. "My housemate was fond of saying, 'The truth usually lies somewhere in between,'" Siddiqi said. "I can't recall specific instances that he made that remark, only that he said it often." Obama seemed far more interested in reading than partying and chasing girls, two of Siddiqi's preoccupations. "He made some attempts to make serious conversation with me, but it didn't go very far. I was shallow," Siddiqi recalled, adding, "He used to wake up earlier than me and go to college or the library or whatever. I would rise later. I can't remember doing much together at all except working out in the Columbia gym and later jogging at the Central Park Reservoir. . . . He used to come to the restaurant, Jewel, where I was working, and have a drink, at the most two, and leave fairly early. It seemed to me he always had his nose in his books. . . . He was very hard driven, disciplined and on track. It seemed unnatural to me. I didn't think it was great behavior for someone his age."

Siddiqi had no ambitious track of his own, but he did have one great hope: to become rich. Making money was not a subject that interested Obama, though he did offer Siddiqi two bits of homespun advice he had picked up from his grandmother over the years. As Tut the bank vice president had said, *Find a niche and fill it* and *Build a better mousetrap and the world will beat a path to your door.* Those sorts of aphorisms had once been the domain of Obama's grandfather, the Dale Carnegie–spouting salesman, but Stan was re- tired now and more interested in jokes, corny or bawdy or both, than inspira- tional messages. Siddiqi remembered that Stan once sent Obama a red nylon wrist strap with a secret compartment for hiding money and a note that said, "If it doesn't fit your wrist, you know where to wear it."

Early in the summer of 1982, before Obama's senior year at Columbia, his mother and sister, Maya, came to New York from Indonesia. Ann was only thirty-nine, Maya twelve. Obama, who was just turning twenty-one, of- ficially an adult and thinking himself wiser than his family, as college kids tend to do, acted like an insufferable scold. Taking a page out of his old man's book of haughty behavior, he chided Maya for watching too much television, just as Barack Sr. had done with him during that long-ago Christmas visit to Honolulu when Barry was almost Maya's age. In his memoir, capturing the sensibility he had back at Columbia, he wrote that he felt disconnected from his mother and sister because they seemed so content staying at the Park Avenue apartment of one of Ann's friends and enjoying typical bourgeois tourist activities – "berries and cream at the Plaza, ferry to the Statue of Lib- erty, Cézanne at the Met." He also took digs at his mother for working for an establishment organization, the Ford Foundation, and for dragging him to a movie, *Black Orpheus*, a French-made film that translated the ancient Greek myth of the charming Orpheus trying to recover his wife from the underworld into a tale of poor black Brazilians during Carnival. Obama found it naïve and insulting, but he noticed that his mother loved it. He wanted to bolt from the theater until he was struck by an epiphany about her: "I felt as if I were being given a window into her heart, the unreflective heart of her youth. I suddenly realized that the depiction of childlike blacks I was now seeing on the screen, the reverse images of Conrad's dark savages, was what my mother had carried with her to Hawaii all those years before, a reflection of the simple fantasies that had been forbidden to a white middle-class girl from Kansas, the promise of another life: warm, sensual, exotic, different."

It was a powerful insight with the touch of condescension he occasionally brought to ruminations about his mother. It also read like a riff he had scribbled into his journal at the time. Obama was deeply conflicted about his mother during those years. He was desperately trying to find his own identity and make his own way in the world, and as he later confided to a close friend, he was intent on separating himself from his mother, at least in part "in an effort to extract himself from the role of supporting man in her life."

Near the end of that visit, Obama went to the Park Avenue apartment, where he and Ann apparently discussed his father. In the memoir he established this as the setting where she finally told him her version of how she and Barack Sr. fell in love at the University of Hawaii and why the old man had to leave for Harvard without them – the mythology of the family that never was. This seemed like another instance when *Dreams from My Father* placed events out of chronology for the purposes of smoothly advancing the narrative. Another scene more likely did take place then and there. Ann noticed that Barack had an envelope with him addressed to Obama Sr. in Nairobi. She fished out two stamps for him. With his acute eye for detail, he recalled that the stamps had been stuck together in the summer heat and that she steamed them apart. What was the letter about? He was contemplating a visit to Kenya to visit his father. She thought it was a wonderful idea for the two of them to finally get together, but added, "I hope you don't feel resentful towards him."

Ann and her son could not know that the father and son reunion would never happen.

Not long after Ann and Maya left, Obama heard from Alexandra McNear, the former Oxy classmate who had enchanted him when she was editing the literary magazine *Feast*. Alex had always been fond of Barry, as she called him, and "thought he was interesting in a very particular way. He really worked his way through an idea or question, turned it over, looked at it from all sides, and then he came to a precise and elegant conclusion." She was also physically "attracted to him and thought he had a good sense of humor." Alex was in New York that summer after her junior year, taking a theater course at New York University and working at a book-packaging company in Lower Manhattan. All she had to do was call; Obama was interested. Her mother's apartment at 21 East 90th Street and Madison Avenue was an easy walk from the walk-up he shared with Siddiqi. They met at an Italian restaurant on Lexington Avenue. As she recalled the night, "We sat and talked and ate and drank wine. Or at least I drank wine. I think he drank something stronger. It was one of those dark old Italian restaurants that don't exist in New York anymore. It was the kind of place where they leave you alone. I remember thinking how happy I felt just talking to him, that I could talk to him for hours. We walked slowly back to my apartment on 90th and said goodbye. After that we started spending much more time together" – often spending the night. First it was at his apartment; when her mother left for Nantucket for the summer, they were more often at her place.

For nearly two months, until it was time for her to return to Occidental, they were lovers in Manhattan. Alex remembered that as a summer of walking miles through the city, lingering over meals at restaurants, hanging out at the apartments, visiting art museums, and talking about life. She recalled one intense conversation in particular as they stood outside the Metropolitan Museum of Art. He was obsessed with the concept of choice, she said. Did he have real choices in his life? Did he have free will? How much were his choices circumscribed by his background, his childhood, his socioeconomic situation, the color of his skin, the expectations that others had of him? How did choice influence his present and future? Later, referring back to that discussion, he told Alex that he used the word *choice* "as a convenient shorthand for the way my past resolves itself . . . not just my past, but the past of my ancestors, the planet, the universe."

He felt pressure to go with the flow, he said later. "Was I going to give in to what I felt was the gravitational pull of graduate school, getting a degree in international relations and working in the State Department, in the Foreign Service, or working for an international foundation? That would have been a more obvious path for me given my background." Then there were the expectations of his mother and grandmother, the two most influential people in his life. He thought they would love for him to follow up Columbia with law school, a clerkship, and a law practice, and culminate his career with a seat on the bench. Is that what he wanted? Did he have other choices? His obsession with the concept of choice, he said, "was a deliberate effort on my part to press the pause button, essentially, and try to orient myself and say, 'Okay, which way, where am I going?'"

Back at school that fall, Obama and Phil Boerner took a class together "for the first and only time." It was Modern Fiction 1 in the Comparative Literature Department, taught by Edward Said, the Jerusalem-born Palestinian who had emerged as a major international figure four years earlier with the publication of *Orientalism,* his postcolonial critique of Western historians and writers for what he considered their imperialist misinterpretations of the Middle East. In his literary criticism, Said, then forty-seven, was prodigious and controversial, a postmodernist known for his subtle if critical interpretations of Western writers, starting with Joseph Conrad, the author of *Heart of Darkness* and the subject of his first book. In his memoir, written a decade later, Obama referred critically to Conrad and *Heart of Darkness* several times, but he did not seem to get much out of the class. Boerner said they signed up because they were interested in fiction and wanted to be writers, but did not like Said's approach. "We didn't have a good reaction to the class. Said seemed to be really into literary theory. And I'm more into, and Obama too, into judging works by themselves and not getting caught up in various feminist-leftist-whatever interpretations. And Said seemed to be really into that." Boerner later wrote a master's thesis on Jonathan Swift's *A Tale of a Tub,* a satire of criticism "where the author's intent is so far removed it's almost irrelevant." His assessment of

Said's intellectual construct was superficial, Boerner said, but nonetheless the class reminded him in some ways of Swift's satire.

Said was also a Palestinian activist and a sharp critic of Israeli policies. When Obama entered politics decades later and he and Said appeared at some functions together, an attempt was made by conspiracy theorists to draw their relationship back to some professor-student ideological bonding formed at Columbia. Boerner dismissed the notion that "[Obama] and Said were in cahoots." The class was impersonal, conducted in a large lecture hall, with teaching assistants and little interaction with the professor. Said's Palestinian perspective then, according to Boerner, was something "that I don't think we were even aware of." A few months after they took the class together, Obama brought it up in a letter to Boerner, who had taken off a semester. Said had not issued grades for the first-semester class "until a month into the new term," Obama noted, "and he cancelled his second-term class, so we should feel justified in labeling him a flake."

The long-distance relationship with Alex McNear during that time was conducted mostly through a series of passionate letters sent between his apartment in Manhattan and hers in Eagle Rock. By her account, the passion was as much about ideas and words as about their romance – what she later called "that dance of closeness through language." Alex was interested in postmodern literary criticism, and her arguments brimmed with the deconstructionist ideas of Jacques Derrida, the French philosopher. In one letter, she told Obama that she was writing a paper in her modern poetry class at Occidental about T. S. Eliot's *The Waste Land*. His reply wove its way through literature, politics, and personal philosophy.

"I haven't read The Wasteland for a year, and I never did bother to check all the footnotes," Obama wrote. "But I will hazard these statements – Eliot contains the same ecstatic vision which runs from Munzer to Yeats. However, he retains a grounding in the social reality/order of his time. Facing what he perceives as a choice between ecstatic chaos and lifeless mechanistic order, he accedes to maintaining a separation of asexual purity and brutal sexual reality. And he wears a stoical face before this. Read his essay on Tradition and the Individual Talent, as well as Four Quartets, when he's less concerned with depicting moribund Europe, to catch a sense of what I speak. Remember how

I said there's a certain kind of conservatism which I respect more than bourgeois liberalism – Eliot is of this type. Of course, the dichotomy he maintains is reactionary, but it's due to a deep fatalism, not ignorance. (Counter him with Yeats or Pound, who, arising from the same milieu, opted to support Hitler and Mussolini.) And this fatalism is born out of the relation between fertility and death, which I touched on in my last letter – life feeds on itself. A fatalism I share with the western tradition at times. You seem surprised at Eliot's irreconcilable ambivalence; don't you share this ambivalence yourself, Alex?

"I can't mobilize my thoughts right now, so I paraphrase Nietzsche – something to the effect that perfection, ripeness, does not care for the future, progeny. A perfection, a ripeness, of a moment, or housed in an individual. I leave you to piece together this jumble. Since I began writing this postscript, snow has covered the earth and filled the air, the city disappearing like a dream."

The daily loneliness of Obama's New York existence invariably emerged in his letters. He was trying to find his place in the whirl of humanity while at the same time refining the literary riffs that filled up page after page of his journals – images of a snowbound city and a run around the indoor track and the essence of an Ethiopian waitress. "Moments trip gently along over here," he wrote in a different section of the *Waste Land* letter. "Snow caps the bushes in unexpected ways, birds shoot and spin like balls of sound. My feet hum over the dry walks. A storm smoothes the sky, impounding the city lights, returning to us a dull yellow glow. I run every other day at the small indoor track [at Columbia] which slants slightly upward like a plate; I stretch long and slow, twist and shake, the fatigue, the inertia finding home in different parts of the body. I check the time and growl – AARGH! – and tumble onto the wheel. And bodies crowd and give off heat, some people are in front and you can hear the patter or plod of the steps behind. You look down to watch your feet, neat unified steps, and you throw back your arms and run after people, and run from them and with them, and sometimes someone will shadow your pace, step for step, and you can hear the person puffing, a different puff than yours, and on a good day they'll come up alongside and thank you for the good run, for keeping a good pace, and you nod and keep going on your way, but you're pretty pleased, and your stride gets lighter, the slumber slipping off behind you, into the wake of the past.

"After getting clean, I go to the Greek coffee shop across the road (if I have my rubbers on I clomp through the snow packs, for the sake of that fine crunchy sound) and have the best bran muffin in New York City – dark and fibrous, little bristles sticking out, or left on the plate to be collected later with the fork – and coffee and a glass of water. I light a cigarette, make some talk with the Ethiopian cashier with big murky eyes and the sly smile, and a small tattoo on her right hand in foreign code. Step out into the blades of wind and head for the library, the trucks and cabs rumbling by."

Obama was the central character in his letters, in a self-conscious way, with variations on the theme of his search for purpose and self-identity. In one letter, he told Alex that it seemed all his Pakistani friends were headed toward the business world, and his old high school buddies from Honolulu, the outsiders of the Choom Gang, were "moving toward the mainstream." Where did that leave him? "I must admit large dollops of envy for both groups," he wrote. "Caught without a class, a structure, or tradition to support me, in a sense the choice to take a different path is made for me. . . . The only way to assuage my feelings of isolation are to absorb all the traditions [and all the] classes; make them mine, me theirs."

Here, at age twenty-two, was an idea that would become a key to later understanding Obama the politician and public figure. *Without a class* meant that he was entering his adult life without financial security. *Without a structure* meant he had grown up lacking a solid family foundation, his father gone from the start, his mother often elsewhere, his grandparents doing the best they could, but all leading to his sense of being a rootless outsider. *Without a tradition* was a reference to his lack of religious grounding and his *hapa* status, white and black, feeling completely at home in neither race. Eventually he could make a few essential choices in terms of how he would live out his personal life, moving inexorably toward the black world. But in a larger sense, in terms of his ambitions beyond family, he did not want to be constricted by narrow choices. The different path he saw for himself was to rise above the divisions of culture and society, politics and economics, and embrace something larger – embrace it all. To make a particular choice would be to limit him, he wrote in the letter to Alex, because "taken separately, they are unacceptable and untenable."

Looking back on that period from the distance of the White House, Obama recalled that he was then "deep inside my own head . . . in a way that in retrospect I don't think was real healthy." But the realization that he had to "absorb all the traditions" would become the rationale for all that followed. "There is no doubt that what I retained in my politics is a sense that the only way I could have a sturdy sense of identity of who I was depended on digging beneath the surface differences of people," Obama said during an interview on November 10, 2011. "The only way my life makes sense is if regardless of culture, race, religion, tribe, there is this commonality, these essential human truths and passions and hopes and moral precepts that are universal. And that we can reach out beyond our differences. If that is not the case then it is pretty hard for me to make sense of my life. So that is at the core of who I am."

During his Columbia days, he discussed his struggle for identity not only with Alex but with a few friends from the Pakistani crowd. One of his acquaintances in that group was Mir Mahboob Mahmood, known to his friends by his nickname, Beenu. Mahmood had attended Karachi Grammar School with Siddiqi and Hamid, studied political theory at Princeton under Sheldon S. Wolin, and was now working as a paralegal in a New York law firm and attending Columbia Law School. An intellectual with a black belt in karate, he enjoyed discussing political theory and literature with Obama in a way that Siddiqi could not. Among this set of Pakistanis, he had the closest ties to his country's ruling class, and the sophisticated attitudes to match, what one friend called "a privy council feel" that would have impressed Obama. They were never the closest of friends, not like Obama and Chandoo, yet their conversations seemed to bring out Obama's innermost thoughts and hopes.

Thinking about their New York days together, Mahmood remembered how, "for a period of two or three months" when Obama was living at 94th and First with Siddiqi, Obama "carried and at every opportunity read and reread a fraying copy of Ralph Ellison's *Invisible Man*. It was a period during which Barack was struggling deeply within himself to attain his own racial identity, and *Invisible Man* became a prism for his self-reflection." There was a riff in that book that Mahmood thought struck close to the bone with Obama. The narrator, an intelligent black man whose skills were invisible to white society, wrote, "America is woven of many strands; I would recognize them and let it so remain. It's 'winner take nothing' that is the great truth of our country or of any country. Life is to be lived, not controlled; and humanity is won by continuing to play in the face of certain defeat." His friend Barack, Mahmood thought, "took very, very seriously the lifelong challenge of continuing to play in [the] face of certain defeat."

According to Mahmood, young Barack also took very seriously the channeling of grand ambitions. He mostly kept this side of himself hidden, but revealed it occasionally to the Pakistanis. Wahid Hamid saw it at Occidental, and Mahmood saw it in New York. By his account, they had known each other only a few months when Obama posed this question to him: "Do you think I will be president of the United States?"

What did this mean? "I think it was a very serious question, and clearly, at least in my mind, this was where he was headed," Mahmood recalled. His answer then: "If America is ready for a black president, you can make it."

When Obama, during the White House interview, was asked about Mahmood's account, he said that he could not remember such a conversation, and that people had a natural tendency to apply memories to him retroactively, but added, "If he has a vivid memory of it, I won't deny it." The ambitious path he saw for himself then, Obama said, remained vague. "I don't think I could see a clear path [to the presidency]," he said. "At that age I was much more interested in being a leader outside of politics. If you had asked me during that time what kind of career I'd love to have, more likely I would have said something like a Bob Moses [the civil rights leader], maybe with a slightly higher profile than that. . . . I would not have precluded politics, but during that period I was pretty skeptical of it. There weren't a lot of political figures at that time that I particularly admired. . . . Remember the political context of this time. This was a period where Ronald Reagan had been elected, a lot of excesses of the left, the student movements, the Democratic Party, had been rejected by a big chunk of the country. It wasn't like there was some natural place to land."

In a letter postmarked November 22, 1982, Obama wrote to Alex that he would be coming out to Los Angeles for the semester break. He intended to arrive on December 22 and stay first with Hamid, who was then living in

Pasadena and finishing classes at the California Institute of Technology, where he had transferred as part of a special program that allowed students to study three years at Occidental and two at Caltech. Alex would be in New York when Obama reached L.A., but she planned to return to the West Coast immediately after Christmas and reunite with Obama at her apartment in Eagle Rock. The letter announcing his travel plans also included a reflection on human interaction. Obama had intentionally isolated himself from the Columbia experience, yet intellectually he could see the limitations of his hermetic life.

"Yes with every person one meets, one is presented with a weakening of one's certainty, a shakedown of the habits and grooves of separate existence," he wrote. "A challenge which most people react to by fear or flight. They misunderstand the nature of the challenge. It lies in forging a unity, mixing it up, constructing the truth to be found between the seams of individual lives. All of which requires breaking some sweat. Like a good basketball game. Or a fine dance."

The day after Barack mailed the letter, his father was killed in a car accident in Nairobi: *A few months after my twenty-first birthday, a stranger called to give me the news. I was living in New York at the time, on Ninety-fourth between Second and First.*

"Listen, Barry," said a woman describing herself as an aunt in Nairobi, "your father is dead." A father he had barely known, gone. His grandparents thousands of miles away, and his mother farther away still. It would be hard to overstate the loneliness young Obama felt at that moment, by himself in New York.

At first he kept the news to himself. Siddiqi knew that there had been an overseas call to the apartment; he had taken it, and passed the phone along to Obama. But he was not told the reason for the call and did not figure it out until years later, when he read about it in *Dreams from My Father*. Phil Boerner and other of Obama's New York friends were also not told. In December, when Obama and Alex reunited in Los Angeles, he casually mentioned it. It "was not an emotional telling on his side," she said.

They stayed at her apartment for most of two weeks. Alex wrote in her journal then that Obama "was the closest friend I had, and that I really loved him but didn't know if we could sustain a relationship."

Homer Herodotus Sophocles Plato Aristotle Demosthenes Cicero Vergil. The names of the great Greek and Roman thinkers that are etched across the top of Butler Library have a special meaning at Columbia, where the classics have long been the essence of the college, the shared requirement of every undergraduate. If transfer students were treated as second-class citizens when it came to housing, they nonetheless were expected to satisfy Columbia's distinctive core curriculum requirements with few if any exemptions, completing the demanding regimen in two (or three) years rather than the normal four. For Obama, even though Occidental had put him through a somewhat similar inculcation in the classics, this meant that to earn his degree he was expected to take yearlong seminars in Contemporary Civilization and Literature Humanities (known as Lit-Hum), along with several other core courses. Here was a second prosaic explanation for Obama's relative obscurity during his two years at Columbia: for other students, the core curriculum requirements were usually dispensed with in the first two years, but Obama was taking them as a junior and senior, placing him in classes not with his contemporaries from the class of 1983 but with freshmen and sophomores.

E. Warwick Daw, a freshman in 1982 when Obama was starting his senior year, remembered being in a Contemporary Civilization discussion section with him. There were about twenty in the class, the professor on one end, students around a long rectangular table. Obama sat near the middle, his back to a window on 118th Street, Daw directly across from him. They were to read about five hundred pages of philosophy a week. Plato, Aristotle, Locke, Mill, Descartes, Hume, Kant, Nietzsche, Marx, Camus, Sartre, Marcuse. "I remember he did pretty well in that class," Daw said. "He talked a lot. I remember him being really involved in the discussions. . . . It was fairly serious discussions about philosophy. I seem to recall that he was one of the better students. . . . He was having a good time of it."

Even from a distance, it appeared to others that Obama was deeply into his studies, though not a grind. Amelia Rugland, a Barnard student from northwestern Connecticut, often sat at the same table with him during the lunch hour in the cafeteria of John Jay Hall, and remembered that he routinely ate and read a book at the same time. "You know most people don't study at the table when they eat unless it's finals, but he always had a book and he was always studying as well as eating," Rugland recalled. "We'd say, 'Hi, how you doing, Barry?' He was partially studying and partially eating and partially being in the conversation." He was friendly enough, Rugland said, and "laughed if people were laughing," but to her "it seemed like he felt at the edges." She also often saw him at Butler Library, heading up to a spot on the fourth floor where the chairs were comfortable and the walls were lined with classics.

> When you'd see him walking in the hall he always looked like he was thinking of something. . . . He was interesting. He didn't talk to everybody and know everybody's names. He was not gregarious. It was more that he was obviously very aware of other people and their surroundings. . . . He just seemed really engaged in what he was working on. He didn't seem like a grind, slogging, putting in the hours like you're turning the gears on a machine. I don't mean to romanticize it. I was a little intimidated by him because I thought it was so cool that he was that way. . . . When he was in the hall at the library . . . sometimes it looked like what he was studying was having an exalted effect on him. It was very noticeable.

By Bill Clinton's senior year in college, his fellow students knew him so well they were tired of him. He had run for office every year at Georgetown, shaken every hand on campus, delivered countless speeches, ingratiated himself with the Jesuit administration and most of his professors, and trained himself to get by on four or five hours of sleep a night because a professor had said that was the habit of history's great men. He had also landed a part-time job on Capitol Hill, working in the back room of the Senate Foreign Relations Committee, preparing himself for a life that eventually would take him to the White House, where one of his top aides was George Stephanopoulos, a generation younger, whose time as a student at Columbia overlapped with that of another future president's, Barack Obama. There are different ways to make an impression in college. Clinton was an exaggeration of the typical student politician, larger than life, bringing more of everything. Stephanopoulos was quieter, but had a memorable sharpness to him. After Michael Ackerman, a fellow student at Columbia, met Stephanopoulos, he asked a friend who had introduced them, "Who was that guy? He was so impressive, that guy." He thought Stephanopoulos seemed "bound for glory."

Ackerman did not have that same sense about Obama, who was in one of his political science classes. "Obama didn't strike you in that way. He was a very smart guy and a very good guy. It just wasn't his way. He was laid-back and measured and charming, smart. But it wasn't like he was devastating." Ackerman's strongest memories of Obama came from times they waited in the hallway for the doors to be unlocked for the start of the Strategies in World Politics class in the School for International Affairs building (later known as the School for International and Public Affairs, SIPA). Ackerman would come early because he was interested in a young woman in the class and could dependably find her in the hallway several minutes ahead of time. He did not know why Obama showed up early, but thought the motivation might have been an interest in the same woman, who had "long dark hair and beautiful blue eyes . . . [and] dark olive skin." (Obama was often dependably late for most things, one characteristic he shared with Clinton.) Ackerman ended up talking with Obama more than with the woman. By his recollection, Obama was constantly smoking. "I daresay every time we were waiting he lit up at least one cigarette or he was smoking one when I rolled up," Ackerman recalled. Puffing away, slouched with his backpack, Obama would talk to Ackerman about what was going on in the world and in the class. His comments "were always sharp and insightful."

The number of black professors at Columbia then could be counted on one hand. Nathan Huggins, a prominent historian of the Harlem Renaissance, had just left for Harvard. Elliott Percival Skinner, who had been LBJ's ambassador to Upper Volta, was back as an anthropologist, along with George Bond. Charles V. Hamilton, a political scientist, had won the Mark Van Doren Award for Excellence in Undergraduate Teaching in 1982 and was a revered and approachable figure on campus, known familiarly as Chuck to many of his students. One of his teaching disciples, Wilbur C. Rich, recalled that "the hallway outside his office at the southwest end of the SIPA building was often filled with students discussing city administration, presidential politics, and changes in the black leadership class." Hamilton was both a radical – he had been the coauthor with Stokely Carmichael of the influential book *Black Power: The Politics of Liberation in America* – and a pragmatist. He would argue, according to Rich, that "no matter how sympathetic candidates were to black causes, they could do nothing to help African Americans if they alienated their mostly conservative electoral base and never took office."

Hollis Lynch was the other noted black scholar at Columbia, an expert on African history, who in 1981 became the first professor in residence at the college, a function he maintained throughout Obama's two years there and until 1985. Lynch was a familiar presence in Wallach Hall, devoting hours each week to interacting with students and bringing in guest speakers for weekly sessions, including Charles Rangel, the congressman from Harlem, and Alan Cranston, the senator from California. He also taught a popular course called the Black Urban Condition. For part of the class, he said, "we took a stroll, visiting major landmark sites in Harlem . . . Harlem Hospital, the Schomburg Library, some of the major churches, Sylvia's restaurant, and so on." It sounded precisely like what Obama had gone to New York to do and learn, yet Lynch did not know him. "I don't recall Obama. I would have remembered if he had taken any of my courses. I was pretty prominent and active as the first professor in residence on the campus. My impression is that Obama did not make a splash. He never came to my attention and he never sought me out. I don't know if he sought out other black professors." There are no indications that Obama looked to any of the black professors as mentors.

There were four sections in Columbia's Political Science Department. Professor Hamilton was a leader of the American politics section. The others were theory, comparative politics, and international relations. There were some big names in the international relations section, including Zbigniew Brzezinski, who had been the national security advisor under President Carter, and Roger Hilsman, who had resigned from LBJ's State Department in protest of his Vietnam policy. Obama's concentration in his political science major was international relations, yet neither Brzezinski nor Hilsman could remember him. The one course where he made an impression was a senior seminar on American foreign policy taught by Michael L. Baron. It was not a lecture class, but a discussion seminar that focused on key moments in modern foreign policy decision making, from the Korean War to the Cuban

Missile Crisis to the Strategic Arms Limitation Treaty negotiations of 1969 and 1979. Around the rectangular seminar table, as Baron remembered it, sat eight young men "oriented to do something with their lives," and among them Obama was "one of the best one or two students in the class." He wrote a paper on arms negotiations between the United States and Soviet Union that earned an A. According to others in the class, Obama approached the discussions from an international perspective. He talked about his father being from Kenya so much that at least one student assumed Obama himself was from Kenya. It was obvious that he had read the material and understood it, and could keep the discussion on point.

One day during the second semester of his senior year, Obama entered the side door of Earl Hall, Columbia's religious affairs and social action headquarters, to research a story he was writing for *Sundial,* the college's weekly news magazine. He found the organization he was looking for, Arms Race Alternatives, in the front room on the first floor of the old domed building. Mark Bigelow, a graduate student at nearby Union Theological Seminary, worked as the office administrator, answering the phone and filing correspondence for the director, Don Kent, a graduate student at Columbia's Teachers College. Kent was one of the founders of Arms Race Alternatives, along with many of the chaplains attached to the college. During the 1960s Earl Hall was considered the epicenter of the radical movement, the place where Mark Rudd and his cohorts plotted their protest activities. But by early 1983, in the heart of Reagan's first term as president, the student body was tame if not apathetic. There was some interest in the nuclear freeze campaign, and Danny Armstrong was starting to build the anti-apartheid movement on campus, but few students were intensely involved in either. Arms Race Alternatives was more educational than activist. It sponsored programs in Earl Hall's auditorium that illuminated nuclear arms issues. Brzezinski took part in an ARA debate, and Daniel Ellsberg of Pentagon Papers fame came to speak, along with a leading peace activist from Germany's Green Party.

Kent was accustomed to dealing with Steven Waldman and other editors and reporters from the student newspaper. He usually provided them with information about upcoming events, but was rarely quoted, and the same held true for Bigelow, his assistant. Now in came Obama, taking a seat across from Kent. "I'm pretty sure he called ahead of time and said he wanted to do this article and he would like to stop by, and I said fine and he stopped by. I assume he had a notebook in his hand. I don't think he taped it, but he could have." Questions and answers, for about a half hour. Nothing out of the ordinary. If Obama had been painfully shy or outlandishly hilarious, Kent would have remembered more. But he was just another well-educated, well-spoken, thoughtful kid coming in and asking questions. Kent had always hoped to draw more students to the cause, so he felt grateful that someone at least was showing interest. And when the *Sundial* issue came out, he and Bigelow grabbed up copies. "It was a big deal that we got this article placed. We were happy about . . . it was a cool thing to get ink."

The story ran in the March 10 issue of *Sundial.* "Breaking the War Mentality," by Barack Obama. It focused on two campus groups, not only Arms Race Alternatives but also Students against Militarism, and quoted Don Kent at length, much to his surprise, referring to him casually as Don in the second reference, and also quoted Bigelow, his assistant. Kent talked about how "people my age remember well the air-raid drills in school" and others remember the Cuban Missile Crisis, both of which "left an indelible mark on our souls, so we're more apt to be concerned" about the nuclear arms issue than students who grew up in the 1970s and early 1980s. But he sensed a growing interest. The audience at a convocation the previous fall was large, a few hundred students had joined the ARA mailing list, and there seemed to be noticeable anticipation on campus for a planned June 12 rally in Central Park supporting a nuclear freeze (an event that in fact turned into one of the largest mass rallies in U.S. history, drawing over one million people). "It seems that students here are fairly aware of the nuclear problem, and it makes for an underlying frustration," Bigelow told Obama. "We try to talk to that frustration."

Rob Kahn of Students against Militarism, a smaller but more activist-oriented group at Columbia, said in the article that his organization was trying to increase involvement by finding issues that directly affected students, such as a bill in Congress that would withdraw federal financial aid from students who failed to register with the Selective Service. Kahn had talked to Obama for an hour one day as they sat at a cafeteria table at Ferris Booth Hall. It was a peculiar interview, Kahn recalled later. Obama "probably looked me in the eye more than I'm used to or kind of like," reflecting what he assumed was Obama's seriousness of purpose. "In the corner of my mind," Kahn said, as he answered one earnest question after another, he could not help thinking that Obama was making too much of his group. "I thought, 'This is a group of fifteen people that meets once a week and doesn't do much.'" He had a sense, Kahn said later, that Obama "was like a goody-two-shoes . . . asking in some ways exactly the correct questions and taking us all that seriously when we were just kind of this antiwar group that wanted to hang out and pretend we were cool." But the publicity was worth it, so he kept talking.

While the article gave an account that Don Kent said "in retrospect holds up as pretty accurate," the report more than anything was a means for Obama to express his own worldview at the time. He was a skeptic softened by a touch of optimism, a young man who seemed to wish that he had lived in a more challenging age, or at least was trying to shake off the numbing effects of his generation's comfortable existence.

"Most students at Columbia do not have firsthand knowledge of war," he opened the piece, writing more than a decade after most American troops had come home from Vietnam.

> Military violence has been a vicarious experience, channeled into our minds through television, film, and print. The more sensitive among us struggle to extrapolate experiences of war from our everyday experience, discussing the latest mortality statistics from Guatemala, sensitizing ourselves to our parents' wartime memories, or incorporating into our framework of reality as depicted by a Mailer or Coppola. But the states of war – the sounds and chill, the dead bodies – are remote and far removed. We know that wars have occurred, will occur, are occurring, but bringing such experiences down into our hearts, and taking continual, tangible steps to prevent war, becomes a difficult task.

Later in the article, after quoting Kahn saying that his group had to believe as an article of faith that "people are fundamentally good," Obama wrote, "Perhaps the essential goodness of humanity is an arguable proposition," but after observing a recent meeting of Students against Militarism, "with its solid turnout and enthusiasm, one might be persuaded that the manifestations of our better instincts can at least match the bad ones."

At the time, Obama seemed to be struggling with his own instincts. Maybe he was not as earnest and correct as Rob Kahn had assumed during their interview. In the days between when he finished writing the story and *Sundial* published it, he wrote a letter to Phil Boerner, who had taken the semester off to be closer to his girlfriend in Arkansas. Obama said that he had been sending out "letters of inquiry" to various social service organizations in hopes of finding a job after graduation that June, and would be "making up a resume (no comment) soon. I've also written an article for the *Sundial* purely for calculated reasons of beefing up the thing" – the "thing" in this case being not the magazine but his résumé. "No keeping your hands clean, eh?"

The style of Obama's letter to Boerner – like his letters to Alex – was more indicative of the way he wrote in his journal, and eventually in his memoir, than the constricted syntax and jargon of his piece in *Sundial*. He told Boerner about a trip he had taken back to L.A. to see their old classmates, his second return to Occidental since they had left. It was, he wrote, "the standard fare – good relaxation with the Paki crowd," along with dinners with Alex McNear, lunches with Chuck Jensvold (part of the writing set at *Feast*), and tennis with others. He had kept from Boerner the fact that he and Alex were in a relationship. "The whole process was like a spiral back in time; nothing had changed except my perceptions, it seemed." Back in New York, school mostly bored him, with its "long stretches of numbness punctuated with the occasional insight." (Perhaps the moments of insight explained the expressions of exaltation that his friend Amelia Rugland noticed at the library now and then.) He seemed more taken by a February blizzard "that was fun the first two days, the garbage and disrepair concealed by the fine white powder, cars inching along on the shrunken roads so that it seemed like a small town." "Nothing significant, Philip," he added. He was still searching for meaning, for his place. "Life rolls on, and I feel a growing competence and maturity while simultaneously noting that there isn't much place for such qualities in this mediocre but occasionally lovable society."

Alex was struggling with herself and her relationship with Obama late that winter and spring. Earlier, during the Christmas holiday, she had announced to her mother and sisters that she intended to transfer to Harvard to study under a French feminist. They told her that made no sense, since she had only one semester to go at Oxy. But although she returned to Eagle Rock for that spring semester, she had failed to enroll in classes, dropping out temporarily. She started working for a Pasadena psychiatrist, transcribing tapes of his sessions with patients. "Not your average run-of-the-mill patients," she recalled. Day after day she was paid to eavesdrop on the world of dysfunction. She sensed then that something was changing in her relationship with Obama. "Although I loved him, I wasn't sure we were going to sustain the relationship, primarily because I had all these unresolved conflicts and we were seeing each other so infrequently. . . . In a very subtle way the feeling wasn't as strong as in the summer, fall, and winter," she said later.

She wrote Obama, expressing the fear that he was becoming less interested in her. He wrote back on April 4 that she was mistaken. He was "burning the midnight oil" to finish his studies, he said. And he was, as usual, consumed by the effort to find himself.

"I feel sunk in that long corridor between old values, modes of thought, and those that I seek, that I work towards," he confided. "It's a somewhat dangerous position to be in, since neither future nor past serves to buttress the present; and this ambivalence is acted out in my non-decision as yet about next year. Not that I mind too much. I loosen the reigns and bob along in the gush of the city, touching the unconscious pain of the old woman next to me on the subway, nodding off on the stiff plastic, fingers half gloved and clutching at a misshapen bag while the other passengers stare away. Or ferreting out that sneaky spirit of communion and understanding in the young punk rocker giving up his seat so a black couple and their baby can sit together. Or reading June Jordan speak with strength, turning her vulnerability into trembling, effective anger, an anger that admonishes me to get off my butt. Or listening to intelligent conversation at the next table in the coffee shop. Or any number of things which can make me humble and proud, and less lonely."

In his next letter, Obama informed Alex that after graduating he planned to spend several months in Indonesia and Hawaii. They both were struggling in different ways, he said. He was lonely, searching for connections wherever he could find them: "I don't distinguish between struggling with the world and struggling with myself. . . . I enter a pact with other people, other forces in the world, that their problems are mine and mine theirs, and the contradictions within us are between us and to be found in the movement of the sea, or the tears of a child or the New York Post sports page. The minute others imprint my senses, they become me and I must deal with them or else close part of my-self or make myself and the world smaller, lukewarm. And the helpful part of this is to populate both my nightmares and my visions, and gives me the nec-essary illusion that my struggles are the struggles of the first man, the river is the original river, and that my brief interludes outside the limits of the human construct are still connected to what's going on within."

And he connected himself to Alex through that loneliness. He thought back to the time during his last visit when they were at his friend Wahid Hamid's apartment "in that timeless reddened room, a young black man with his arms behind his head, staring at the ceiling with moist eyes, and a young white woman resting her head on his arm, alone and facing the swirl-ing expanse, outside the room, inside themselves, separate in the eye of the storm." It was the only time in their relationship that he overtly differentiated himself from her by race. Her letters, he added, presented such "a tight and forceful fabric of words" that he sometimes assumed she was as together as her sentences and paragraphs. But "when I discover that beneath this armor you are tangled and lonely, my assurance fades and I feel like forgetting the whole enterprise and taking you with me to Bali or Hawaii."

He did not endear himself to her by adding that, tempting as running off with her might be, it would mean "to live in some sense of compromise and retreat."

Within a month he received his college degree. He had received mostly A's in his coursework during those two years, he said later, and finished with a 3.7 grade point average. Including his two years at Occidental, his college education had cost about fifty thousand dollars for the four years and was a family effort. About half came from scholarships and student loans, a bit from off-the-books part-time summer jobs, and most of the rest from his grandmother Tut, who had devoted part of her salary each year to his education. His degree was from Columbia College, in political science. At Occidental everyone knew him; at Columbia he had been almost an apparition. Greg Smith, a black contemporary who became a doctor, retained only a vague memory of a tall, skinny guy with big ears playing pickup basketball. But there was something else about those Columbia days that stuck in Smith's mind, a scene he wished he could talk about with Obama decades later. There was an old-fashioned black gentleman who would walk through the campus. He was about five-six, with a mustache, bespectacled, salt-and-pepper hair, nattily dressed in jacket and tie no matter the weather. Smith and his friends did not know the man's name, but they loved the hipster lilt in his voice, reminding them of some old reel of Cab Calloway. They would be sitting in the sunshine on the steps of Low Library, taking in the day, and the old man would come by and smile and say, "How are you doing today, sir? How are you doing today, Doctor? You learning something today?" And then there were times, Smith remembered, when the old man would survey the group of them and say proudly, "Right here, we could have a future lawyer, a future doctor, a future president of the United States!"

Obama skipped the graduation ceremonies, finishing his time at Columbia much as he had begun: isolated and apart from the college scene. He had his résumé completed by the time he finished classes. It was a thin document beefed up by his high school experiences and that *Sundial* article. He sent off letters looking for a job in community organizing. He had read about Harold Washington's election as the first black mayor of Chicago and thought it might be rewarding to work out there. Then he left on the familiar wanderings of his young life, boomeranging west to Los Angeles, staying with Alex for a week. The notion that he would take her with him to Bali or Hawaii was not mentioned. She felt bereft when he left, alone, moving on to a three-month journey that would take him to Indonesia and then back to Hawaii.

During that trip, he made a five-day stop in Singapore, where he was greeted by Hasan Chandoo and Asad Jumabhoy. Chandoo had spent much of his prep schooling there and still had family there; Jumabhoy had returned home there from Occidental. He was three years behind Hasan and one year behind Obama in school, so this was the summer before his senior year. He came from a wealthier family than Hasan and Wahid. He was third-generation Singaporean; his relatives had arrived there in 1915 from India, or to be precise, a part of India that later became Pakistan after the Partition of 1947. The Chandoos had experienced a variation on that theme, though they never considered themselves fully Singaporean. Hasan's family had started in Burma and India, but migrated to Karachi after the Partition, then business took them to Singapore. Asad's father knew Hasan's in the upper reaches of Singapore's business world. One family in shipping, the other in trading. "We had no private jet, but it wouldn't be out of reach," Asad recalled. "I would say Hasan and my family come from old prosperous Indian trading families. . . . The point is you could pretty much do what you wanted. When I wanted a car, the only way I got a car was I had to get straight A's. It was not a question of how to put the money together."

It was into that opulent world that Obama stepped during his 1983 summer hiatus. One ostensible reason for the visit, aside from the fact that it was on the way to Indonesia, was to watch Jumabhoy play polo. He was on the national team, which had a match in the Southeast Asia Games. The fancy cars, the exquisitely outfitted people, the snooty airs, it all overwhelmed Obama, and he and Chandoo left the match before it was over. But that night they went to a disco, the Chinoiserie at the Hyatt Hotel, where the jet-set milieu was even more pronounced. "Lots of models hanging around, all the pretty people, the A-list," Jumabhoy recalled. He introduced his friend Barry to the crown prince of Pahang, a state in Malaysia, and to Najib Razak, who would go on to become the prime minister of Malaysia. In that setting, Obama was the quiet American. "He was very quiet. He'd meet people very politely. He wouldn't go into any deep conversation or engage," Jumabhoy said. "You wondered. 'I'm putting you in touch with these kinds of people and you're not engaging.' [But] the moment he stepped out of the disco with Hasan and me, he was fine. He would just withdraw. It's hard to imagine what was playing in the foreground or the background for him."

Not so hard, in truth. The polo and disco scene left Obama feeling dispirited, as much as he liked his friends. For several years he had used sarcasm to needle Chandoo about the apparent hypocrisy of his left-wing politics and luxurious lifestyle, and here, in Singapore, was the most glaring representation of what he had been talking about. "An incongruous place, Singapore, slick and modern and ordered, one vast supermarket surrounded by ocean and forest and the poverty of ages," he reported in a letter to Alex. "Mostly peopled with businessmen from the States, Japan, Hong Kong, as well as various family elites of Southeast Asia. Everything is bought and sold, with unconscious satisfaction. From discothèques to the Finals of the Southeast Asia Games polo match. . . . Asad and his brothers make up half the Singapore team."

When he arrived in Indonesia, Ann was still working at the Ford Foundation and Maya was on summer break from the Jakarta International School. To Obama, this place halfway around the world, once so familiar, now seemed alien as well. He had lived there for four years as a boy and had been visiting dutifully since his Punahou days. But now, as he focused more on his self-identity and his future, Indonesia seemed distant. He was once again the Moviegoer. In a letter to Alex, he confessed that he felt "a little disconnected." The faintly familiar smell of burning wood, the sights he took in from "behind a dashboard or French window" – all appeared separated from his present and his past. "I can't speak the language well anymore. I'm treated with a mixture of puzzlement, deference, and scorn, because I'm an American. My money and my plane ticket back to the U.S. overriding my blackness."

The previous summer, when Ann brought Maya to New York, Obama focused on what he saw as her weak spots. He noted that this woman who prided herself on fighting for the poor and disenfranchised was staying at a friend's posh apartment on Park Avenue. He privately ridiculed her naïveté for her expressed love of a movie, *Black Orpheus,* that he found condescendingly dreamy about the lives of poor black Brazilians. Now, a year later, his sardonic sniping at what he viewed as his mother's inconsistencies continued. In his letter to Alex he reported that his "mother and sister are doing well, the former doing development work focusing on women's industries and labor unions . . . but the struggling seems out of her, and the colonial residue of her lifestyle – the servants, the shopping at the American supermarket, the office politics of the international agencies – throw up continual contradictions to the professed aims of her work."

It was easier for Obama to see what unsettled him about his mother's existence than to chart his own future. A few days after this harsh assessment, he scribbled a postcard to Phil Boerner that read like a brief ode to escapism. "I'm sitting on the porch in my sarong, sipping strong coffee and drawing on a clove cigarette, watching the heavy dusk close over the paddy terraces of Java. Very kick back, so far away from the madness. I'm halfway through vacation, but still feel the tug of that tense existence, though. Right now, my plans are uncertain, most probably I will go back after a month or two in Hawaii."

He wrote another letter to Alex once he reached his grandparents' apartment in Honolulu. She was upset with him now, certain that he was distancing himself. In his own cautious and ambiguous way, he said as much, confiding that he felt a progression from romantic love "to the more quotidian, but perhaps finer bonds of friendship." His immediate plans were "still uncertain," he reported. He wrote this letter with a bleeding pen that created smudges. "Unless a job of some interest pops up soon, I'll be flying back to New York at the end of this month, and will see you on my stop to L.A. (Excuse the shitty condition of these pages; I had been typing up letters to prospective employers for the last two hours with maniacal tidiness.)"

When he returned east in late September, he had no job, no place to live. Wahid Hamid, having finished his program at Caltech and launched into the business world, was living on Long Island, and Obama stayed with him for a week, then spent two weeks with Sohale Siddiqi in Manhattan before finding an apartment to share with two other renters up near Columbia. In a letter he wrote to Alex postmarked November 17, he lamented that the salaries for community organizing were "too low to survive on," so he hoped to work "in some conventional capacity for a year in order to store up enough nuts to pursue those interests the next. I've been slow getting the machinery of the job hunt in motion due to some cash flow problems (one week I can't pay postage to mail a resume and writing sample, the next I have to bounce a check to rent a typewriter etc.)." In the meantime, he took temporary employment where he could find it. He spent one week supervising a group of temp workers who moved the files of the Fire Department of New York from one building to another. It was, he reported, "a fascinating experience affording me a taste of the grinding toil of a low white collar job, as well as the ambivalent relationship" between bosses and workers. Just one week, yet something about that job gave him a boost in his incessant search for self-identity. He had been living in the rarefied environments of Oxy and Columbia, self-absorbed with his choices in life, contemplating it all on an intellectual plane, deep into his own head, and here were people talking about sports and life and family in ways that were not fraught with complicated meanings and symbols. "I felt a greater affinity to the blacks and Latinos there (who predictably comprised about three fourths of the work force . . .) than I had felt in a long time, and it strengthened me in some important way," he told Alex.

He ended his letter to his now former girlfriend as though he were closing another chapter of his life. "So what else? Manhattan streets are broad and bumpy; the cool crisp grey of fall glows on the teeming faces of the midtown rush; the drunk slides back and forth on his subway seat under the gaze of the neat older woman knitting her mauve yarn; the pigeons comb the cobblestones on Riverside, white and grey and plump; the varying sounds reach from many sides, deep and shrill, from far away and nearby, twining through one another. I feel lonely yet surefooted, and hope all goes well for you."

CHAPTER 17

GENEVIEVE AND
THE VEIL

December 1983. A Christmas party in the East Village at 240 East 13th Street. It was BYOB, and Genevieve Cook brought a bottle of Baileys Irish Cream. The host was a young man employed as a typist at Chanticleer Press, a small Manhattan publishing company that specialized in coffee-table books: wildlife, sharp color photographs. Genevieve had worked there a few years earlier as an administrative assistant to the publisher, but had left to attend graduate school at Bank Street College, near Columbia, and was now assistant-teaching second- and third-graders at Brooklyn Friends School. She was between apartments and living temporarily at her mother and stepfather's place on the Upper East Side. When her former workmate had called to invite her, she left it a maybe, not certain about his intentions, but finally decided "Hey, what's to lose?"

The party in the sixth-floor apartment was well under way when Genevieve arrived, lights dim, Ella Fitzgerald playing on the stereo, chattering people, arty types, recent college grads, some in the publishing world, none of whom she knew except the host. She went into the kitchen, to the right of the front entrance corridor, looking for a glass, then decided it would be less fussy to drink straight from the bottle. That was her style. She fancied smoking non-filter Camels and Lucky Strikes. She liked drinking Baileys and Punt e Mes, an Italian vermouth. Standing in the kitchen was a guy named Barack wearing blue jeans, T-shirt, dark leather jacket. They spoke briefly, then moved on. Hours later, after midnight, she was about to leave when Barack approached and asked her to wait. They plopped down on an orange beanbag chair at the end of the hall, and this time the conversation clicked.

He noticed her accent.

Australian, she said.

He knew many Aussies, friends of his mother, because they had lived in Indonesia when he was a boy. So had she, before her parents divorced, and again briefly in high school. As it turned out, their stays in Jakarta had overlapped for a few years starting in 1966. They talked nonstop, moving from one subject to another, sharing an intense and immediate affinity, enthralled by the randomness of their meeting and how much they had in common. They had lived many places but never felt at home. They looked at the world the same way, as outsiders.

At night's end, as Genevieve recalled that first encounter decades later, they exchanged phone numbers on scraps of paper. "I can't remember whether we agreed we'd have dinner during the week before I left [that night], or whether he rang and then we organized it. I'm pretty sure we had dinner maybe the Wednesday after. I think maybe he cooked me dinner. Then we went and talked in his bedroom. And then I spent the night. It all felt very inevitable."

Obama was six months out of Columbia when Genevieve Cook came along and engaged him in the deepest romantic relationship of his young life. There had been other girlfriends before her, but none quite like Genevieve. She called him *BAH-rruck,* with a trill of the *r*'s. She said that is how he pronounced it himself, at least when talking to her. He was living on the Upper West Side then and working in Midtown in a job that paid the rent but did not inspire him. He was still in a cocoon phase, preparing for his larger cause, wondering about his place, keeping mostly to himself, occasionally hanging out with his Pakistani friends, who partied too much and too hard, he thought, but were warm and generous and buoyant intellectual company, always willing to debate philosophy and the political issues of the day. Genevieve offered something more. She was three years older than he, born in 1958. She kept a journal, as he did; thought of herself as an observer, as he did; brooded about her identity, as he did; had an energetic, independent, and at times exasperating mother, as he did (though the two women were otherwise quite different); and burned with an idealism to right the wrongs of the world, as he did. She was studying for her master's degree at Bank Street with the frame of mind that she would "save every black and Hispanic child in New York City."

A few weeks into January 1984 they were seeing each other regularly on Thursday nights and weekends. Thursday nights she would be up in his neighborhood anyway, finishing one of her Bank Street classes at the 112th Street campus, and usually stayed at his place. He was living then as a boarder in a fourth-floor walk-up at 622 West 114th Street, only two blocks to the north. It was a three-bedroom rent-controlled apartment, no. 43, that was leased by Dawn E. Reilly, a dancer who studied movement therapy at Teachers College at Columbia University and drove a Yellow Cab out of Queens for a few months during that period. Dawn called Obama "Barry," never Barack. He must have introduced himself that way, using different names for different people. She was rarely home, in any case, and usually saw him only on Sunday mornings. She remembered that Obama would lounge around, drinking coffee and filling out the *New York Times* crossword puzzle, bare-chested, wearing a blue and white sarong. The building was owned by a Holocaust survivor. Cockroaches were a part of daily life, though the window views were grand and the upkeep was a definite improvement from the places he had shared with Boerner and Siddiqi. It was a railroad-style layout, with Dawn taking the smallest bedroom, a converted walk-in closet essentially, where she had built a bunk bed. Barry's bedroom was closest to the front door, offering a sense of privacy and coziness. Genevieve described it in her journal this way: "I open the door, that Barack keeps closed, to his room, and enter into a warm, private space pervaded by a mixture of smells that so strongly speak of his presence, his liveliness, his habits – running sweat, Brut spray deodorant, smoking, eating raisins, sleeping, breathing."

Genevieve's journal-keeping started in 1975, during her final year at the Emma Willard School, an academically rigorous prep school for young women in Troy, New York, and continued through her undergraduate years at Swarthmore College and on into adulthood. By the time she met Barack she was filling out the third of four treasured notebooks she had bought at a *pasar* (market) when home with her family in Indonesia: thick, narrow-ruled, hand-bound in thread, the pages six by eight, the covers of paper batik patterns with leather strips in green, red, or blue along the spine. She was right-handed and used only fountain pens, black or blue ink, and wrote whenever she felt like it, sometimes once a week, sometimes twice a day. Barack had been keeping a journal of his own for a few years by then, since the summer after Oxy, when he went off to Pakistan with Hasan and Wahid. His notebooks were black, hard-bound, slightly smaller than Genevieve's. He tended to keep his stored in his bedside table drawer, and wrote more systematically than she did, usually at the end of each day. Her journals were introspective, recording her interior life, even her dreams. His reflected his writing discipline, less about emotions, more often richly descriptive scenes of the city and its characters.

As the relationship began, Genevieve was taken by Barack's mind and the vibrancy of their discussions. She noted in her journal "those first few times of talking to him, where intensely I would hear and understand and absorb words he spoke – ideas he spoke, and the energy – a heightened, thrilling sense of connections snapping in my brain – mental exhilaration." It occurred to her, she wrote, "that I have not experienced the kind of intellectual stimulation Barack offers me since I left college."

Day by day, week by week, her perceptions of him became more complicated, her mood rising and falling.

January 10, 1984

Wonder where it will go with Barack. He's not "my man" – but I wonder if I will always know him.

January 12

This really strong feeling that Barack has offered me something — but what's interesting is that I'm not couching it in terms of need or emotional dependence or love (maybe a little bit).

January 22

What a startling person Barack is — so strange to voice intimations of my own perceptions — have them heard, responded to so on the sleeve. A sadness, in a way, that we are both so questioning that original bliss is dissipated — but feels really good not to be faltering behind some façade — to not feel that doubt must be silenced and transmuted into distance. Also really nice to hear from him that a question of trust needn't exist on the level of can we continue being friends despite sexual convolution.

January 26

. . . recognition of how much fear Barack has opened me up to — truth and honesty — how is he so old already, at the age of 22? I have to recognize (despite play of wry and mocking smile on lips) that I find his thereness very threatening. . . . Distance, distance, distance, and wariness. I am wary — very clear — I really wonder where it's all going, all this with Barack.

February 18

Coming back from running, standing in the doorway with his finger ticking back and forth on my arm. Underneath, where neither of us really feel it, I think there is a lot collecting, connecting.

February 19

Despite Barack's having talked of drawing a circle around the tender in him — protecting the ability to feel innocence and springborn — I think he also fights against showing it to others, to me. I really like him more and more — he may worry about posturing and void inside but he is a brimming and integrated character.

Today, for the first time, Barack sat on the edge of the bed — dressed — blue jeans and luscious ladies on his chest [a comfy T-shirt depicting buxom women], the end of the front section of the Sunday Times in his hand, looking out the window, and the quality of light reflected from his eyes, windows of the soul, heart, and mind, was so clear, so unmasked, his eyes narrower than he usually holds them looking out the window, usually too aware of me.

February 20

I really like about Barack that he's obviously kindling something in me — my voice to myself. He encourages it and w/o knowing what it says, leaves room for it. . . . On Sunday I woke up, waiting for Barack to wake, writing a bit more — feeling severed from him through b'fast (lack of physical connection — it means so much more than lust, after all) . . . and then reading Neruda's poetry — excellent translation — powerful words, the truth in existence so much prettier for the poetry — and reading it really transfigured my thoughts, emotions, mood — and I just lay, w/ my head on Barack's lap and my eyes closed, w/ words and words and words lapping, lapping through my tongue and soul and I felt older, wiser, in harmony w/ things; the calm after the storm.

February 22

Barack — sensing his need stronger than I'm ready to believe — being drawn by it.

February 24

My British humour comes through with him — very uncommon. An uncommon, earnest young man. He is very beautiful — more than he thinks himself to be. Oooooo I can't wait to be in Brooklyn with spring coming . . .

February 25

*Trying to change the scene — wishing he and I were walking through NY
those days I had off — wanting to meet in a bar . . . while the routine of
it is already feeling stultified somewhat — it's all too interior, always in
his bedroom without clothes on or reading papers in the living room . . .
the sexual warmth is definitely there — but the rest of it has sharp edges
and I'm finding it all unsettling and finding myself wanting to withdraw
from it all. I have to admit that I am feeling anger at him for some reason,
multi-stranded reasons. His warmth can be deceptive. Tho he speaks sweet
words and can be open and trusting, there is also that coolness — and I
begin to have an inkling of some things about him that could get to me.*

February 27

*Told me I was growing to be a fine strong young woman — I know it
sometimes, but felt good to hear. It's stuck in my mind, his saying you're
sweet to me, that I'm kind — as if he's not accustomed to that, has not
had much of that. The little boy who has his grandmother's eyes. . . . An
image at dinner of being with Barack, 20 years hence, as he falters through
politics and the external/internal struggle lived out — cabbages and kings,
children's nappies and ideals.*

March 5

*. . . wish I could remember what I said and what B. said as I lay crying
— I jumbled a lot of stuff together — a lot of projection — sad aloneness.
I feel too responsible for other people's pain — as if I should prevent it or
fill the gap for them — and suffer fools for fear of hurting their feelings.
Barack said he used to cry a lot when he was 15 — feeling sorry for
himself. Of course he's right about some of it being self-pity. . . . B. is
sweet. He buys me butter and won't let important things go unspoken.
"Speak to me."*

Much later, after the publication of *Dreams from My Father*, and after Barack Obama became famous, curiosity arose about the mystery woman of his New York years.

> *There was a woman in New York that I loved. She was white. She had dark hair, and specks of green in her eyes. Her voice sounded like a wind chime. We saw each other for almost a year. On the weekends, mostly. Sometimes in her apartment, sometimes in mine. You know how you can fall into your own private world? Just two people, hidden and warm. Your own language. Your own customs. That's how it was.*

Obama did not name this old girlfriend even with a pseudonym – she was just "a woman" or "my friend." That she remained publicly unidentified throughout his rise to national prominence became part of the intrigue of his New York period's "Dark Years" narrative. His physical description was imprecise but close. Genevieve was five-seven, lithe and graceful, with auburn-tinged brown hair and flecks of brown, not green, in her hazel eyes. Her voice was confident and soothing. Like many characters in the memoir, he introduced her to advance a theme, another thread of thought in his musings about race. To that end, he distorted her attitudes and some of their experiences, emphasizing his sense that they came from different worlds. Decades later, during an interview in the White House, he acknowledged that while Genevieve was his New York girlfriend, the description in his memoir was a "compression" of girlfriends, including one who followed Genevieve a few years later when he lived in Chicago.

Genevieve Cook came from not one but several distinguished families. Her father, Michael J. Cook, was a prominent Australian diplomat who had served as ambassador to Vietnam, a delegate to the United Nations, and number two man in Indonesia. In the 1980s, at the time Barack met Genevieve, Cook was heading the Office of National Assessments, the Australian equivalent of the intelligence assessment arm of the Central Intelligence Agency. Years later he would become ambassador to the United States. Cook was a cold warrior, a staunch conservative who disliked what he saw as the "soft option" traits of American culture and was allied with Republicans in the United States and

Tories in Great Britain. Among other traits, as a *Sydney Morning Herald* article described him, he was "infamous for his chronic dislike of the Fourth Estate." Genevieve's mother, born Helen Ibbitson, came from a banking family in Melbourne and was an art historian who specialized in the art and architecture of Cambodia and Indonesia. She was a woman of high standards for her children and impeccable taste in architecture, art, and clothes.

Michael and Helen divorced when Genevieve was ten; her younger siblings, Lucinda, Francesca, and Alex, were eight, three, and two. Helen soon remarried into a prominent American family, the Jessups. With homes in Georgetown and on Park Avenue in Manhattan, Philip C. Jessup Jr. served as general counsel for the National Gallery of Art in Washington. For many years before that, when Genevieve was in boarding school and college in the States, her stepfather and mother lived in Indonesia, where he was a top official at the International Nickel Company during a period when it was undertaking extensive mining operations, benefiting from a lucrative, if politically and environmentally controversial, relationship with the Suharto regime. International Nickel's PT Inco subsidiary on the island of Sulawesi ran the largest open-pit mine in Indonesia. Phil Jessup and Helen had vast international connections in the higher circles of politics, business, and art. In the diary that George H. W. Bush kept during the fourteen months he was envoy to China, he noted on May 26, 1975, that he "went to lunch with Phil Jessup Jr. and his Australian wife, both here from Indonesia."

The Jessups were establishment Democrats with deep liberal connections. Phil's father, Philip Caryl Jessup Sr., had been a major figure in American postwar diplomacy. He had served as a technical advisor to the U.S. delegation at the creation of the United Nations, was ambassador-at-large under President Truman, was a close friend of Secretary of State Dean Acheson, and later, by appointment from President Kennedy, was a member of the International Court of Justice in The Hague. In the early 1950s Senator Joseph McCarthy had labeled him "a security risk with unusual affinities . . . for Communist causes." Dwight D. Eisenhower, then president of Columbia before his election to the White House, had defended Jessup, saying his loyalty to American liberty was beyond dispute. During his later years Jessup, who had received his doctorate from Columbia, served on the law school faculty there as a professor of international law. The most prestigious moot court competition in the world was named in his honor, the Philip C. Jessup International Law Moot Court Competition, known familiarly as the Jessup. He had homes in two strongholds of the eastern establishment: Newtown in Bucks County, Pennsylvania, and Norfolk in the Berkshire foothills of northwestern Connecticut, as well as an apartment in Manhattan. By the time Barack met Genevieve, he had been slowed by Parkinson's disease.

The connections are fascinating: Jessup Sr.'s link to Columbia, Barack's alma mater. Phil Jessup's, Helen Ibbitson Jessup's, and Michael Cook's to Indonesia. Both Barack's mother and Genevieve's mother were devotees of Indonesian art and culture. Ann Dunham Soetoro loved Indonesian shadow puppetry, and so did Helen Ibbitson Jessup, who by 1990 would curate and write the catalogue for an exhibit of Indonesian court art that toured the United States, an exhibit that brought Genevieve to tears, showing her that underneath her mother's "impeccableness" lay someone with a remarkably sensitive eye for "the ineffable, for the spiritual, expressed in form." Ann had some of that same essence. Ann and Helen did not know each other, but there was one extraordinary coincidence connecting the families: Genevieve's stepbrother, Tim Jessup, was an anthropologist in Indonesia and knew Ann well; he was often among the expat visitors to her home in Jakarta.

In Genevieve's conversations with Barack, her family was seldom a topic. Now and then she complained about the "domineering" nature of her elegant and upper-class liberal mother, but that was about it. She considered her stepfather and father men of great integrity, with vastly different viewpoints and personalities, but both men were oriented toward politics and power in a way she was not, and her mother was very much a social being in a way she was not.

Barack provided an escape from all that, a sanctuary. She felt that she had far more in common with him than with her relatives. "That wasn't my world," she said of the social circles of her mother and stepfather and father. "I was through and through infused with the sense of being an outsider, like Barack was."

At Swarthmore, where she majored in anthropology, Genevieve had written her senior thesis on the sense of disconnection that she and other children of diplomats and peripatetic expats experienced. For that thesis, which she titled *Dancing through Doorways,* she interviewed sixteen students at the college in that category, what she would call cross-cultural kids. "To dance in doorways is to dance on thresholds, partly in and partly out, suspended neither here nor there, moving in a realm of ambiguity," she wrote. Her findings coincided with what she saw inside herself, the psychological condition of liminality – caught in between, dislocated: "When you belong to more than one culture, it feels like you don't belong anywhere, and that is one of the effects. On a very profound and deep level you feel like you have no identity. If you look too deep, there is nobody there. When you grow up that way, you are painfully conscious of that feeling."

In Barack Obama she had found a kindred soul, dislocated, caught in between, dancing through doorways in the same way. But she could see that this also led to distance and caution, a sensibility in Barack that she described with the metaphor of a veil: "I used to talk to him a lot about the veil. It felt like he had a veil hanging down between himself and the outside world. And nothing got past that veil without double checking, inwards and outwards. Mentally observing character, dispassionate, balancing one thing against the other . . . that was just so essentially him."

March 9, 1984

It's not a question of my wanting to probe ancient pools of emotional trauma . . . but more a sense of you biding your time and drawing others' cards out of their hands for careful inspection – without giving too much of your own away – played with a good poker face. And as you say, it's not a question of intent on your part – or deliberate withholding – you feel accessible, and you are, in disarming ways. But I feel that you carefully filter everything in your mind and heart – legitimate, admirable, really – a strength, a necessity in terms of some kind of integrity. But there's something also there of smoothed veneer, of guardedness . . . but I'm still left with this feeling of . . . a bit of a wall – the veil.

March 20

I'm a little worried about Barack. He seems so young and defenceless these days.

March 22

Barack — still intrigues me, but so much going on beneath the surface, out of reach. Guarded, controlled . . . Have this feeling of wanting to take Barack away . . . he resists tho, I think, my efforts at pulling him away . . . chained and wanting to unravel it all only by himself. He is that sort of person — trying hard to be.

March 25

He feels all these people asking him to undo himself, be something he feels he's not, show things to appease other people's projections, regardless of whether they're in him or not.

April 3

He talked quite a lot about discontent in a quiet sort of way — balancing the tendency to be always the observer, how to effect change, wanting to get past his antipathy to working at B.I.

The initials in that journal entry stood for the place Obama worked. From the lobby of 1 Dag Hammarskjold Plaza on Second Avenue between 47th and 48th, up the elevator to the seventh floor, you entered the business world, or the journalism world, or some combination of the two. Maybe it was less than either, just an information service, updating the same dry reports week after week, year after year. But there were suggestions of derring-do in the early days of the enterprise, intimations of spookdom, always denied, of nondescript men in seemingly bland jobs who had worked around the world for the CIA. Not that the place itself was a front, just that it might have been a convenient cover for a few agency types. It certainly had the name, Business International – B.I., as it was known.

Obama had first visited the office as a job applicant late in the summer of 1983, months after he graduated from Columbia and months before he met Genevieve. His résumé likely was sent to Business International from the placement office at Columbia's School for International Affairs, which had a long-standing relationship with B.I., a firm in constant need of bright young college graduates with some knowledge of the world. Obama had taken the mandatory copyediting test and performed well, and Cathy Lazare, head of reference services, had interviewed him for an entry-level research and editing position, and was impressed. He seemed intelligent and mature, with good writing skills and an international flair, with a father from Kenya and a mother in Indonesia, where he had once lived. Lou Celi, vice president in charge of the global financial services division, conducted the final interview. Obama "did not stand out in any material way. He seemed like a nice gentleman, smart," Celi recalled. From what Celi could determine, Obama was interested in pursuing a career in editing and writing. "Not fiction, he wanted to be in journalism. He fit the profile. He came from the right school and had a background in international relations, he was eager to get into writing and editing, and he didn't require a lot of money. We hired him at entry salary," in the mid-teens, eventually bumped up to $18,000 a year.

Business International had been operating for nearly thirty years by the time Obama went to work there. Established in 1954, its stated goal was "to advance profitable corporate and economic growth in socially desirable ways." What that entailed, for the most part, was compiling and constantly updating newsletters, reports, and reference materials for corporations that did business around the world, detailing how various countries regulated foreign investments and businesses and pinpointing places of opportunity or danger. Multinational corporations were far less sophisticated then, and the World Wide Web was not yet available, so B.I. filled the information void for hundreds of corporations. The yearly fees ranged from about $6,000 to the $120,000 that Chase Manhattan Bank paid to receive every B.I. publication plus a hundred extra hours of specific research.

If there was even a slight veneer of power and influence to B.I., any of the gloss of corporate America to the place, much of it came from the twelfth floor, the redoubt of its executives, led by the chairman, Orville Freeman, the former

Minnesota governor and U.S. secretary of agriculture under Kennedy and
Johnson, whose suite was lined with framed photographs evoking his glory
days with the Democratic presidents in Washington. But the ambience of the
seventh floor, and the reality of the day-to-day work there, was more evocative
of a lowly trade journal and its usual posse of smart and underpaid hacks than
of a slick business operation staffed by men in suits. Which leads to another
minor case of literary license involving Obama's memoir: the few paragraphs
he devoted to his experiences at B.I. and his descriptions of the office atmosphere were seen as distortions and misrepresentations by many of the people
who had worked with him.

In his book Obama described B.I. as a "consulting house" to multinational
corporations. "I had my own office, my own secretary, money in the bank," he
wrote. "Sometimes, coming out of an interview with Japanese financiers or
German bond traders, I would catch my reflection in the elevator doors – see
myself in a suit and tie, a briefcase in my hand – and for a split second, I would
imagine myself as a captain of industry, barking out orders, closing the deal,
before I remembered who it was that I wanted to be and felt pangs of guilt for
my lack of resolve."

It was an exaggeration to define B.I. as a consulting house. One of his former colleagues described it as "a small company that published newsletters on
international business. . . . It was a bit of a sweatshop. . . . Sure we all wished we
were high-priced consultants to internationals." Another called it "high school
with ashtrays." Obama's office was the size of a cubicle, barely large enough to
fit a desk, and faced an interior hallway; he had no secretary, and the dress code
was informal; people in his position rarely if ever wore suits. "He dressed like a
college kid," said Lou Celi, who had an image in his mind's eye of Obama coming to work now and then in white pants. One colleague remembered Obama
wearing the same dark pants, nondescript shirt, and narrow tie day after day,
like a uniform. Japanese financiers and German bond traders were not part of
the equation. Norman Wellen, then the chief executive officer at B.I., said that
though he did not know Obama then, in retrospect he understood the young
man's intentions and did not mind the fact that the book "swayed from the
truth," the author taking "a little liberty in terms of his description of meeting
with bankers and so forth." Obama spent the vast majority of his time trying to

decipher arcane financial data, waiting for long-distance calls, and queuing up for time on one of the Wang word processors in what was called the bullpen across the hall from his desk, under a poster by the hipster cartoonist Lynda Barry that featured a poodle with a Mohawk, not exactly corporate art. As one coworker put it, "We were little writers sitting in front of Wangs." Were the elevator doors shiny enough to catch the reflection of an emerging captain of industry? One former colleague said yes; others scoffed at the idea.

"Obama worked at a very, very low position there," said Ralph Diaz, the vice president of publications. "In my own view he greatly embellished his role. The part about seeing his reflection in the elevator doors? There were no reflections there. . . . He was not in this high, talking-to-Swiss-bankers kind of role. He was in the back rooms checking things on the phone. He might call somebody. He probably called Zurich to check a fact, but wasn't doing heavy-duty interviewing." Diaz said he thought Obama was using the embellishments for dramatic effect, an understandable device in "a book that reads more like a novel." The intention seemed obvious: to set up a Faustian dilemma. "Here he was in an important position in the corporate world, serving the gods of money, a rising star. He looks at his image all decked out in a suit and decides to abandon that future." Another colleague characterized Obama's morality tale this way: "He retells the story as the temptation of Christ . . . the young idealistic would-be community organizer who gets a nice suit and barely escapes moving into the big mansion with the white folks."

A harsh perspective. Genevieve put it in different terms in a poem she wrote to him:

> d'aimer c'est de profiter
> *none of this stock exchange garbage –*
> *just need to make it clear,*
> Monsieur le directeur,
> *Pin-stripe (blue) suit in*
> *foothills on borderlines*

As she deconstructed the poem later, "none of this stock exchange garbage" was "a direct allusion to his job at B.I." and "the jab about Monsieur le

directeur was me scoffing at the possibility that he would get anywhere playing that game in those foothills. He didn't actually wear a suit to work, but in
my opinion, he might as well have, a concept which would have been anath-
ema to both of us."

Everyone on the seventh floor knew of Obama and his job in reference services as an editor for Financing Foreign Operations and occasional writer for
Business International Money Report. The Manhattan-based staff was small
enough, fifty or sixty people, that he could not almost disappear, as he did at
Columbia. If nothing else, they would hear his name over the office paging
system. Jean Reynolds Schmidt, whose time at B.I. overlapped briefly with
Obama's, said his name stuck in her head because she heard the receptionist
page him so often: "Barack Obama, line two." He was only Barack at work,
never Barry. One of his superiors there, Barry Rutizer, a senior editor, had
what he thought was a running joke that utterly failed to provoke Obama. "My
name is Barry and his name is Barry, so I kept calling him Barry," Rutizer said.
"He very patiently corrected me every time I said that. He never laughed. He
never got upset. He just corrected me. Because I'm a jerk, I kept saying that to
see if I could get a different reaction, but I never did."

A few coworkers thought Obama was aloof, with an arrogance that bordered on condescension. Some, when they heard he was a Punahou School
alumnus, assumed that he must be a trust-fund kid. One colleague, a graduate of City College of New York, thought Obama looked down on him from
his Ivy League perch. Most were more positive, finding him calm, polite,
and disciplined. Cathy Lazare, his immediate boss, was perhaps closest to
him, tutoring him like a big sister, and thought he was a quick study, easy to
deal with and self-assured. But he was never one of the gang. There was a
distinct culture among the younger cohort at B.I. – lunches, coffee, the Irish
bars along Second Avenue, cigars and beers in the Wang terminal bullpen
during deadline nights, thirty-two-ounce Buds on the rooftop late on Friday
nights – that he stood apart from, by choice. "He was discreet and kept to
himself," said Michael Williams, who worked with Obama on one project.
Steve Delaney, who edited a money report from a desk across the hall from
Obama, said, "There was a fairly close group of people that were all roughly
the same age, in their first or second jobs out of college, and they would grab

lunch together and do pub crawls together, and I honestly don't remember him going." There was a sense that Obama had a girlfriend, but he did not talk about her at work. Genevieve stopped by once or twice to pick him up there, but did so quietly, without notice. One coworker thought he had much in common with Obama in that they both went to Columbia and lived Uptown and were runners, but when he suggested they jog together in Riverside Park after work, Obama brushed him off, saying, "I don't jog, I run." This attitude gave some coworkers a sense, as one put it, that "we weren't sure if he liked us as much as we liked him."

It was a question that touched on Obama's sensibility during that period. Whether he liked his coworkers was incidental to what he was thinking then. By early 1984 he was absorbed with Genevieve and with figuring out his place in the world. Whatever and wherever that would be, it would certainly not involve Business International or anything like it. He had turned away from the rhetoric of the left, doubting its practicality and turned off by radical remnants of the 1960s, but he was also leery of acceding to the lure of the business world, leaving him without an ideological comfort zone, still searching. Genevieve knew that he harbored faintly articulated notions of future greatness, of gaining power to change things. Once, when they were in Prospect Park, they saw a young boy in costume playing out a superhero role. They started to talk about superheroes, the comics he enjoyed as an adolescent in Honolulu, and intimations of "playing out a superhero life." She considered it "a very strong archetype in his personality," but as soon as she tried to draw him out, he shut down "and didn't want to talk about it further." A more comfortable way for him to express his yearnings was through books and authors. He spoke forcefully of what he saw in Ernest Hemingway: "[T]he integrity of grasping for those times, those visions, that are ones of true magnificence and profundity." Hemingway, he thought, was unapologetic about seeing things in mythic perspective, not naïve but with a raw, human thirst for something meaningful and grand. He and Genevieve "had conversations all the time about that sort of thing," she recalled. She thought of Barack as being "in constant questing to find that avenue of how he was going to do what he wanted to do – act out some vision which I was happy to label 'stars in your eyes.'"

B.I. represented a holding pattern, a place where he could earn some money before moving on to his future, but it was also a convenient setting for his internal story. In what his mother characterized as "a rather mumbled telephone conversation" with him over the long-distance lines between New York and Jakarta, he described his job to her. "He calls it working for the enemy because some of the reports are written for commercial firms that want to invest in [Third World] countries," Ann reported in a letter to her mentor back in Honolulu, Alice Dewey. Later, when he wrote those few paragraphs about B.I. in his memoir, he repeated that idea: "Like a spy behind enemy lines, I arrived every day at my mid-Manhattan office and sat at my computer terminal, checking the Reuters machine that blinked bright emerald messages from across the globe." His mother, ever the optimist when it came to her son, apparently saw more merit to the job than he did. "He seems to be learning a lot about the realities of international finance and politics," she noted in her letter to Dewey, "and I think that information stands him in good stead in the future."

Obama wrote a letter to his former girlfriend, Alex McNear, during that period, the last he would write to her. As in his telephone conversation with his mother, he expressed a distaste for the corporate world. He wrote Alex on Business International stationery, but crossed out the logo on the envelope and scribbled in his own address on West 114th Street. Among other things, he told her about a new girlfriend, praising Genevieve without naming her, for the way she handled his moods: "I've also become quite close to an Australian woman who teaches at a Brooklyn grade school. She doesn't put up with a lot of my guff, and has a good sense of humor without any cynicism, which is a good tonic for my occasional attitude problems."

If he imagined himself a spy behind enemy lines, he played the role carefully. He gave his work the time that was called for, no more and no less. He arrived at nine and left at five, rarely if ever staying late, as many coworkers did, and never coming in late, as some did when they had been drinking too much the night before. He was in no way a slacker; he performed his job efficiently, with more clarity and less fuss than many of his coworkers. As one colleague of a slightly higher rank said, he never "demonstrated any desire to be outstanding and get himself promoted." He smoked incessantly, but so did many people at B.I., so that was not obtrusive. In an office where Lou Celi was screaming out orders like a hard-bitten city editor to an overworked and stressed-out staff, Obama never seemed flustered. He maintained that Hawaiian style, *Cool head, main thing*. But according to Dan Armstrong, who considered Obama a friend, there was one exception. Armstrong remembered seeing Obama get into "a huge argument" with an older colleague named Dan Kobal. The subject was the CIA. "It was heated and brief. The argument was in the hallway," Armstrong said. "It was pretty loud. I don't think it was discreet at all. It touched on some deeply held belief of Barack's. . . . I think it was uncomfortable. It was just the two of them. . . . Barack was attacking it and Dan was defending it." Kobal did not remember the incident and said that it was not his style to yell, but added, "I can't say that Dan Armstrong is wrong." He postulated that he and Obama might have been talking about Africa. Obama, he said, "may well have been" anti-CIA then, which Kobal was not. He believed that the CIA hired "good dedicated people" who did their job of gathering information.

The section in *Dreams from My Father* where Obama wrote about feeling like a spy ended with another thought that wove back to the central theme of his book: race and identity. "As far as I could tell I was the only black man in the company, a source of shame for me but a source of considerable pride for the company's secretarial pool," he wrote. There were two dark-skinned Puerto Ricans, Fred and Sam Cesario, who worked in the mailroom, and Brenda Vinson and another black woman worked in the library. Vinson also covered the switchboard. One black woman was on the professional staff, but not in the New York office. She was Lois Dougan Tretiak, described by Lou Celi as "a brilliant woman who ran our China practice." Obama could not have known that Tretiak had a connection to his late father. She had been at the East-West Center in Honolulu when Barack Sr. was a student at the University of Hawaii, and was part of the East-West cohort including Kiri Tith and Robert Ruenitz that often gathered with Obama and others at parties at the home of Arnie and Sue Nachmanoff.

But Brenda Vinson, the librarian and receptionist, is more relevant to an understanding of Obama and the trajectory of his life. Whatever discomfort he felt about working at Business International, however distant he seemed to much of the staff there, Vinson represented something else. She was fourteen years older than Obama, not quite a mother figure but perhaps more like an aunt. Their friendship was superficial in the sense that it did not extend beyond chitchat in the office, yet deep in showing Obama something that he longed for: warmth, pride, unconditional acceptance, a larger sense of community and family. Vinson had a hard time with his name when she was paging him from the reception desk. "His name was strange for me – anything that's not Jones, Willie, and John. I'm a southern girl, I said 'BRAAAK' with my southern accent," she recalled. But as a young, smart, handsome black man in an office that was overwhelmingly white, he was her pride and joy, and the comfort she and her black library colleague gave him, however transient, was not something he had experienced very often in his life as he struggled with his racial identity. Obama's coworkers noticed that he liked to hang out in the library and that his demeanor changed when he was there. They would see him joking and laughing, enjoying what one called "a special affinity" with Vinson. "He seemed friendlier in that room, more at ease," said Lou Celi.

"He was talkative to us," Vinson recalled. "He talked to us in the library. He just had a lot of respect for us and we were proud of him, because there were not too many Afro-Americans working for the company. . . . I tell everybody that he was an officer and a gentleman. . . . To me it means he was very respectful and he was a really nice person. He never got out of place." There was absolutely nothing out of the ordinary about this bonding, a routine occurrence among people who connect over race, language, or cultural interests in a setting where they find themselves in the minority. But for Obama, whose *hapa* life inherently presented more complicated choices than other people faced, Brenda Vinson and the sense of home in the library at Business International signified another marker on his path toward choosing how he would define himself as a black man.

May 9, 1984

But he is so wary, wary. Has visions of his life, but in a hiatus as to their implementation — wants to fly, and hasn't yet started to take off, so resents extra weight.

May 16

It so delights me that from time to time Barack will talk about the more private, inner aspects of what he sees and feels of our relationship — not out of some need to bring up and solve a problem (which is what I tend to do), but merely to communicate it. It is something I could well learn to do. To trust him, myself, whatever's cooking there in my brain — the good and the cloudy.

May 26

Dreamt last night for what I'm sure was an hour of waiting to meet him at midnight, with a ticket in my hand. Told me the other night of having pushed his mother away over past 2 years in an effort to extract himself from the role of supporting man in her life — she feels rejected and has withdrawn somewhat. Made me see that he may fear his own dependency on me, but also mine on him, whereas I only fear mine on him. . . . He wants to preserve our relationship but either felt or wanted it to be well protected from some sense of immediate involvement.

June 4

I woke up to an image, a feeling of Barack in the ways that he is round and soft and young.

June 10

Barack frets about the continual comfort I am always willing to offer — recognizing it as feeling good, but also chafing against the threat of its impeding a rawer sense of "the struggle" (Mythology of the heroic struggle . . .). . . . It was fun dancing w/ him last night — the right tune, the right flavor — of childlike happiness, release, recognition in movement. . . . I tried to give a lot of it to B. today / has probably made him feel guilty or smothered in some part of him.

Genevieve was out of her mother's Upper East Side apartment by then. Earlier that spring she had moved and was sharing with a fitness trainer the top floor of a brownstone at 640 2nd Street owned by the secretary at the Brooklyn Friends School in Park Slope. She was finishing her assistant teaching at BFS and in the fall would start teaching on her own for the first time, at PS 133 in Brooklyn. The routine with Barack was now back and forth, mostly his place, but sometimes hers.

When she told him that she loved him, his response was not "I love you too" but "Thank you," as though he appreciated that someone loved him. The relationship still existed in its own private world. They spent time cooking. Barack loved to make a ginger beef dish that he had learned from Sohale Siddiqi. He was also big on tuna fish sandwiches made the way his grandfather taught him, with finely chopped dill pickles. For a present, Genevieve bought him an early edition of *The Joy of Cooking*. They read books together and talked about what they had read. For a time they concentrated on black literature, especially the women writers Maya Angelou, Toni Morrison, Toni Cade Bambara, and Ntozake Shange. The authors and topics were a change from a book club that Barack had briefly been part of, before he met Genevieve, that had gathered at the Soho condo of Paul Herrmannsfeldt, an Oxy friend who had taken a publishing job in New York. Phil Boerner had also attended, and other Columbia acquaintances, including George Nashak and Bruce Basara, and they sat around talking about Sartre and Nietzsche and Beckett and Rilke. "It was a brief thing," Boerner recalled, "because what would happen was, you'd pick something, I'd pick Sartre, and you'd rely on your knowledge of it from having read it rather than reading anew. . . . It was an honest attempt to discuss intellectual ideas."

If Barack and Genevieve went to social occasions as a couple, it was almost always with the Pakistanis. "Me and the Paki mob and that was it pretty much," Genevieve said later, recounting Obama's circle. Hasan Chandoo had moved back from London and taken a place in a warehouse at the bottom of Brooklyn Heights. His fiancée, Raazia, an artist and the daughter of a prominent Karachi banking family, was finishing her studies at the Rhode Island School of Design, but would come down for weekends. Wahid Hamid, starting a rise up the corporate ladder that would take him to the top of PepsiCo, lived on Long Island with his wife, Ferial (Filly) Adamjee, who had attended Karachi American School with Hasan and later studied at Syracuse University. Sohale Siddiqi was also part of the crowd, along with Beenu Mahmood, who lived at 93rd and Riverside with his wife, Samia, familiarly known as Cheenan, a world-class cook. It was a moveable feast, sometimes at Siddiqi's place, sometimes at Mahmood's, now and then at Chandoo's, and it was invariably a matter of bounty and excess, friends losing themselves in food and conversation. Obama for the most part declined alcohol or drugs. "He was quite abstemious," Genevieve said. She enjoyed the warmth of the gatherings, but was usually ready to go home before he was. He was pushing away from the Pakistanis too, politely, for a different reason, she thought. He wanted something more.

June 20, 1984

Curious this thing in Barack, where he identifies "skipping out" on e.g. Sohale's dinner, with the taking of different paths. He doesn't just see it as preferring to stay home and start a new story. Somehow splitting himself off from people is necessary to his feeling of following some chosen route? which basically remains undefined. And am I to be left behind also? That he may feel he's striking out? Shedding encumbrances, old images, the known and comfortable . . .

June 27

But the abruptness and the apparent lack of warmth w/ which B. left them was jarring.

Beenu Mahmood saw a shift in Obama that corresponded to Genevieve's perceptions. Among the Pakistani friends, Mahmood was the one to whom Barack had once confided his grand political ambitions in the form of the question of whether he could ever be president of the United States. Now Mahmood could see Obama slowly but carefully distancing himself from the Pakistanis as a necessary step in establishing his political identity. For years, when Obama was around them he seemed to share their attitudes as sophisticated outsiders who looked at politics from an international perspective. He was one of them, in that sense. But that is not what he wanted for his future, and to get to where he wanted to go he had to change – not cut off the Pakistanis as friends, but push away enough to establish a clear and separate identity. As a result, Mahmood recalled, "the first shift I saw him undertaking was to view himself as an American in a much more fundamental way."

In preparing for his future, Obama disciplined himself in two activities: writing and running. When he was on the Upper West Side, he would run in Riverside Park. When he was in Brooklyn, he would run in Prospect Park. He was what Genevieve called "a virtuous daily jogger," and that was one of the differences between them. She would run too, but without his discipline and not as far. "One of the reasons he was maybe such a dedicated jogger was part of him still felt he was the fat boy, which I found hard to see," Genevieve said later. He had indeed been a chubby boy from infancy through seventh grade, when his body started to elongate. Genevieve noticed that despite his thin physique there was still a certain softness to him, which explained the "round and soft" in that earlier journal reference: "There was this still quite raw and close to the surface aspect of himself which had to do with being the fat boy, or chubby boy, that people laughed at, that no one knew quite where to put, and who had a deeply ambivalent notion of being loved or not."

For weeks that summer, Genevieve challenged Barack to a footrace. Not long-distance, but a sprint. If they sprinted, she insisted, she would beat him. He had been through this a year before, when he lived with Siddiqi and they had a runoff for the largest bedroom. No such prize this time, only pride. He kept putting it off. "His response was merry disbelief," Genevieve recalled. "By merry I don't mean he laughed at me, though he was amused. He had this way . . . where he inhabits a mocking space – it's sort of a loving mocking – as if to imply 'Ah, the frailties and tendencies we all have to be delusional, self-deceiving, preposterous even, but you are cute, and I like you better for it.'" Finally he relented. They picked a day, went to the park, and chose a walkway lined by lampposts for the dash. Her diary entry:

> On Sunday Barack and I raced, and I won. I ran so fast my body transformed
> itself onto another plane. We ran, he started off behind me and I just said to

myself stay ahead, stay ahead and my body became a flat thin box w/ my arms and legs coming each precisely from a corner. And I didn't know how long I could keep it up, but I was going to try – my whole sight concentrated on the lamp post when I felt him slow and yell you beat me, at first I thought he was giving up, but then I realized he'd meant the lamp post on the left and I'd really won! The feel of the race was exhilarating, but I didn't feel very victorious. Barack couldn't really believe it and continued to feel a bit unsettled by it all weekend a bit I think. He was more startled to discover that I had expected to win than anything else. Anyway, later in the shower (before leaving to see *The Bostonians*) I told him I didn't feel that good about winning, and he promptly replied probably cos of feelings of guilt about beating a man. In which case, no doubt, he'd already discovered the obverse feelings about being beaten by a woman. Nevertheless, it was a good metaphor for me, despite, as I confessed to Barack, that in some ways it would have appeased some aspect of my self-image to have tried and lost. But I didn't; I won.

Since the death of his father, Kenya had been weighing on his mind. He talked to Genevieve about wanting to visit his family there, and about how his Kenyan relatives thought Barack Sr. had been killed by his enemies, not by his own drunk driving. In her journal Genevieve noted that Barack mentioned his father while also talking about the mass murders that July at a McDonald's in the San Ysidro section of San Diego, a horrific event in which twenty-two people were killed. "He spoke of his reaction of tears the night he watched the news report of the mass murder in McDonalds," she wrote. "Interesting that he was connecting the 2 as examples of how he's wary of feeling prescribed emotions, when in fact the tears he cries are, I'm sure, buried tears over his dad, and the loss over all the years without him."

Not long after that, Barack had a dream about his father. It was a dream of a distant place and the lost figure brought back to life, a vision that later inspired his memoir's title. In this dream, as he recounted it in *Dreams from My Father,* Barack rode a bus across a landscape of "deep fields and grass and hills that bucked against an orange sky" until he reached a jail cell and found "father before me, with only a cloth wrapped around his waist." The father, slender, with hairless arms, saw his son and said, "Look at you, so tall – and so thin, gray hairs, even," and Obama approached him and hugged him and wept as Barack Hussein Obama Sr. said the words Barack Hussein Obama II would never hear in real life: "Barack, I always wanted to tell you how much I loved you."

Genevieve remembered the morning he awoke from that dream: "I remember him being just so overwhelmed, and I so badly wanted to fix him, help him fix that pain. He woke up from that dream and started talking about it. I think he was haunted." She was fascinated by dreams, interpreted their subconscious meaning much more than he did, and wanted him to talk about it further, but "he wouldn't let me get in there as much as I wanted to." She wrote about it later in a stanza of a poem for him:

> *Fear and sorrow of abandonment will go on aching*
> *Being turned away within the jailer's cell*
> *you should have thought to ask him for the key*
> *love will set you free*

More prosaically around that time, at work Obama was updating a Financing Foreign Operations report on Kenya, compiling economic data that his father would have known off the top of his head. Maria Batty, who was his copy editor on the project, remembered that they spent two weeks on the report, that it was about twenty pages, and that Obama was a clear writer whose copy was "very clean."

It was also during that period that he received a long-distance telephone call from a half sister he had heard about but never met. This was Auma, the daughter born to Kezia, the first wife of Obama Sr., not long after he left Kenya for Hawaii. Auma told Barack that she was planning a trip to New York, a prospect that thrilled him. He said she should stay with him, and was eagerly anticipating her long-awaited visit when she called again to say the trip had been canceled due to a tragedy in the family. The roads of Kenya had claimed another victim, a son of Mr. Toad. David Ndesandjo, the younger son of Obama Sr. and Ruth Baker, now Ruth Ndesandjo, half-brother to both Barack and Auma, had been killed in a motorcycle accident. The word from Nairobi was that David, unlike his older brother, Mark, had laid claim to his African heritage and essentially broken away from his white mother and identified himself with the rest of the Obama clan. Now he was dead. If Barack discussed this call with Genevieve, she could not remember it.

They did talk about race quite often, as part of his inner need to find a sense of belonging. She sympathized with and encouraged his search for his identity. If she felt like an outsider, he was a double outsider, racial and cross-cultural. He looked black, but was he? At times he confessed to her that "he felt like an imposter. Because he was so white. There was hardly a black bone in his body." At some point that summer she realized that "in his own quest to resolve his ambivalence about black and white, it became very, very clear to me that he needed to go black. I told him that. I think he felt very encouraged by my absolute conviction that his future lay down the road with a black woman. He doubted there were any black women he would feel truly comfortable with. I would tell him, 'No, she is out there.'"

Beenu Mahmood saw the same thing as Genevieve: Barack's internal struggle with his racial identity. He related it to his memory of Obama carrying around that dog-eared copy of Ellison's *Invisible Man,* and also to his memory of the day Obama wondered whether he could ever be president. Trying to embrace his blackness, Mahmood thought, was

the second and probably the biggest shift I saw [in Obama during the New York years]. To be honest, he had never had many black friends. Not that he had anything against that, just that he was part of that other set, the international set. So for him this was a big thing. And I saw that switch happen most markedly during the period that I was very close to him. Barack was the most deliberate person I ever met in terms of constructing his own identity, and his achievement was really an achievement of identity in the modern world. . . . That was an important period for him, first the shift from not international but American, number one, and then not white, but black.

Early in Barack's relationship with Genevieve, he had told her about "his adolescent image of the perfect ideal woman" and how he had searched for her "at the expense of hooking up with available girls." Who was this ideal woman? In her journals, Genevieve conjured her in her mind, and it was someone other than herself.

First:

> *I can't help thinking that what he would really want, be powerfully drawn to, was a woman, very strong, very upright, a fighter, a laugher, well-experienced — a black woman I keep seeing her as.*

Then:

> *Thing is, I can imagine the kind of woman Barack could really get involved w/, 'fall in love' w/ — she looks like that woman I saw running [in] the park — light skinned black woman, close cut hair, strong small body, very pretty, and she would be challenging and vivacious in company. Possibly artistic.*

Not quite, the future would reveal, but close.

In *Dreams from My Father* Obama chose to emphasize a racial chasm that unavoidably separated him from the woman he described as his New York girlfriend:

One night I took her to see a play by a black playwright. It was a very angry play, but very funny. Typical black American humor. The audience was mostly black, and everybody was laughing and clapping and hollering like they were in church. After the play was over, my friend started talking about why black people were so angry all the time. I said it was a matter of remembering – nobody asks why Jews remember the Holocaust, I think I said – and she said that's different, and I said it wasn't, and she said that anger was just a dead end. We had a big fight, right in front of the theater. When we got back to the car she started crying. She couldn't be black, she said. She would if she could, but she couldn't. She could only be herself, and wasn't that enough.

None of this happened with Genevieve. She remembered going to the theater only once with Barack, and it was not to see a work by a black playwright. They saw the British actress Billie Whitelaw perform monologues from two plays, *Rockaby* and *Footfalls,* written for her by Samuel Beckett. The one time they were in the midst of an entirely black audience there was nothing angry about the scene. They went to the Fulton Street Cinema in downtown Brooklyn to watch Eddie Murphy in *Beverly Hills Cop*. "I was the only white person in the audience," Genevieve recalled. "We were surrounded by this black audience watching a black movie. It was such a wonderful, uplifting, mind-blowing experience . . . one of the most deliciously culturally immersed, free-hearted, group one-mind experiences I have ever been part of. I think we laughed so hard our bellies hurt. We came out of there so high."

There was no fight, no crying in the car (neither of them had a car in New York), and no scene where she questioned why black people were so angry. She identified with African Americans, she said: "My feelings about being white were extremely ambivalent." When asked about this decades later, during a White House interview, Obama acknowledged that the scene did not happen with Genevieve. "It is an incident that happened," he said. But not with her. He would not be more specific, but the likelihood is that it happened later, when he lived in Chicago. "That was not her," he said. "That was an example of compression. . . . I was very sensitive in my book not to write about my girlfriends, partly out of respect for them. So that was a consideration. I thought that [the anecdote involving the reaction of a white girlfriend to the angry black play] was a useful theme to make about sort of the interactions that I had in the relationships with white girlfriends. And so that occupies, what, two paragraphs in the book? My attitude was it would be dishonest for me not to touch on that at all . . . so that was an example of sort of editorially how do I figure that out?"

Obama wrote another scene in his memoir to serve a dual purpose, exposing what he saw as a cultural gap with Genevieve. He described how his New York girlfriend finally persuaded him to come with her to the family's country estate in Norfolk, Connecticut, for a weekend:

> The parents were there, and they were very nice, very gracious. It was autumn, beautiful, with woods all around us, and we paddled a canoe across this round, icy lake full of small gold leaves that collected along the shore. The family knew every inch of the land. They knew how the hills had formed, how the glacial drifts had created the lake, the names of the earliest white settlers – their

ancestors – and before that, the names of the Indians who'd once hunted the land. The house was very old, her grandfather's house. He had inherited it from his grandfather. The library was filled with old books and pictures of the grandfather with famous people he had known – presidents, diplomats, industrialists. There was this tremendous gravity to the room. Standing in that room, I realized that our two worlds, my friend's and mine, were as distant from each other as Kenya is from Germany. And I knew that if we stayed together I'd eventually live in hers. After all, I'd been doing it most of my life. Between the two of us, I was the one who knew how to live as an outsider.

The differences in this case between Barack's portrayal and Genevieve's recollections are understandable matters of perspective. It was her stepfather's place. They rode the Bonanza Bus from New York and got off at the drugstore in Norfolk. It was indeed a beautiful autumn weekend, though colder than expected, and Obama did not bring warm enough clothes, so he had to borrow some from Genevieve, and complained about it. The Jessup property was fourteen acres, with woods, brook, and pond. The summer cottage was a prefab from a Sears Roebuck catalogue, built in the 1920s, with several smaller houses around it, including a chicken shed; an elegant stone building designed by Phil Jessup's mother's brother; a studio where Jessup Sr., the diplomat and law professor, did his writing; and a second prefab house that went up in 1958, where Barack and Genevieve had an evening meal with her parents. The notion that the Jessups had been among the earliest white settlers and that they knew the names of the Indians was what Genevieve called "a gross exaggeration." The library was exactly as he described it, cluttered with photographs and memorabilia of the grandfather's distinguished career. The family mostly watched the evening news in there and played Charades.

From the distance of decades, what struck Genevieve most in the memoir was his description of the gravity of that library, the vast distance between their worlds, and his conviction that he alone was the one who knew how to live as an outsider. She felt as estranged from that milieu as he did, and he knew it, and over the ensuing decades it was Barack, not Genevieve, who would move closer to presidents, diplomats, and industrialists, into the world of an insider.

"The ironic thing," she noted, "is he moved through the corridors of power in a far more comfortable way than I ever would have."

Genevieve had started teaching at PS 133 on Butler Avenue in Park Slope that fall of 1984. She had fretted about it all of the previous summer, and now that she was in the classroom it proved more difficult than she had anticipated. She arrived still hoping that she could save every disenfranchised child in the city, but quickly realized that she had "enormous plans and zero capacity to carry them out one step at a time." She hated the school system and loathed writing lesson plans. She worried about her inadequacy and started drinking more to cope with the anxiety. She thought of quitting her job, and confided to Barack one day that she had mentioned it to a colleague, who told her that if she stayed she would end up with a nice pension. "That was the only time he raised his voice and got really, really upset with me," she recalled. "He went berserk about the trade-offs he saw his grandparents make for some supposed safety net at the expense of something. . . . he meant at the expense of their souls."

That was something Barack, in his own self-assessment, deeply wanted to avoid. He said he would never keep a job just for security. In early December, after one year at B.I., exactly as he had planned, he walked into Lou Celi's office again, this time for an exit interview. The boss had wondered about Obama all along, mostly because they were opposite types. Celi was wired all day, always on edge, sometimes over the edge, according to some of the employees, and he preferred people as energized as he was. To him, Obama seemed too laid back, not engaged. He liked extroverts "that were go-getters, that were hustlers, that got really excited about their jobs." Obama, he thought, lacked those qualities and "seemed a bit of a lone wolf." Celi could not see him as a leader. Not that Obama was difficult; to the contrary, he struck Celi as remarkably even-keeled, with an inner peace and confidence, "very at ease in his own skin." Some employees "would get uptight, some would cry, some would get angry, some would get nervous," but Obama was always cool. And that is how he appeared now, in Celi's office for the last time, explaining why he had decided to leave.

Celi found their conversation confusing at first. He expected that Obama would tell him that he was leaving for another job, or that there would be an offer and a counteroffer, but instead Obama told him calmly that he had no other job lined up. "He just said he wanted to do something else," Celi recalled. "I told him – like I told many young people then – it's important to have a plan. He just seemed not exactly clear of what he wanted to do. I told him he might be making a mistake, leaving a job when he did not have any plans except a vague notion that he maybe would do some public sector work. In my view that was typical Barack. He was like a rolling stone. . . . He had a lot of confidence to just think he could move on and things would work out. . . . He always looked sure of himself. And he always had the same look. There was not great emotion I could see in his expression. It was kind of matter-of-fact."

At around the same time he quit his job, he also left the apartment that he had shared with Dawn the taxi driver on 114th Street and moved in with Genevieve. It was to be a temporary arrangement, until he left for Hawaii over the Christmas holidays. When he returned, he would find a place of his own, he said. Their time living together did not go well.

December 2, 1984

Want to sit and chronicle the small turns and cogwheel teeth of current changes; the past week of teaching, the weekend, more moving [Barack into her apartment] – zones of uncertainty, redefinition and as yet unaccustomed ways of coping with the hiatus Barack's situation puts him in, me in. But it's still revolving and being experienced – still stuff to be reflected over, held in the head, not marked down on paper.

December 10

After a week of Barack and I adjusting to each other's constant presence and his displacement, I expect that this week will make it hard to be alone again when he has gone [to Hawaii for Christmas]. We got very irritated w/ each other Fri. night and Saturday, talked about it.

December 13

Induced a flare-up yesterday between Barack and me over a suddenly felt irritation at doing the breakfast dishes. Then I was less than honest when I broached my irritation w/ Barack in the vein of, I'm going to tell you I'm irritated, but only because I don't want to be, and expected him to just let it roll off his back. . . . Living w/ someone, you inevitably turn your private frustrations out on that person, because that kind of projection is such a basic and pervasively influencing ego defense mechanism. And too, as one is so unaware of the other person's living reality, I had not taken into account Barack's feeling of being displaced and in the way. In the end he said I know it's irritating to have me here, and I wanted to say and mean, no of course it isn't, but I couldn't. That has been the biggest surprise, that rather than enjoying his extended presence like a very long weekend, as I think I thought I would, and reveling in the comfort of reliably having someone to eat dinner with, and talk to and go to sleep with, I've been . . . resentful I suppose — no — as he said, impatient and domineering. . . . How beneath the surface things are after all. So many masks we wear to filter it all — the mask of our job, the mask of surviving, the masks of our desires and what we want to see and believe. The trouble is we don't always recognize them as masks.

Before he left for Hawaii she bought him an expensive Aran wool cable-knit white sweater at Saks Fifth Avenue to replace an old one he had inherited, likely from his grandfather, that had holes in it and that Genevieve liked to wear. He was embarrassed that she had spent so much money on it.

When he returned from his western travels in mid-January, he was still without a place of his own, so he was back in her apartment in Park Slope. He had landed his first organizing job for the New York Public Interest Research Group, a nonprofit public action group founded in 1973, inspired by the national organization created by the citizen activist Ralph Nader. Obama had focused his ambitions on organizing since his last year at Columbia, while acknowledging that he was not entirely certain what it meant. One of the

NYPIRG officers who interviewed him, Chris Meyer, later told the journalist Ben Smith that he remembered Obama had "a presence and assurance you just don't see in your average recent college grad." He was hired at a salary that was barely more than half of what he had earned at B.I., and his job was to organize students on the Harlem campus of City University of New York, focusing on environmental and student aid issues. One winter's day he took a busload of students down to Washington, where they plodded the corridors of the Long-worth and Rayburn Buildings trying to find congressional aides who would listen to their pleas to restore federal student aid cut by the Reagan administration. At the end of a long day, Obama walked west along the Mall, then circled around to Pennsylvania Avenue and passed in front of the White House.

He was succeeding at the job, by most standards, bringing more students into the organization and rejuvenating the chapter. But the issues seemed secondary to him, and he went to work every day with that same sense of remove and distance that he had carried with him at Columbia. Looking back on it decades later, he said that first organizing job "had always felt sort of like a tryout of organizing as opposed to plunging into it in a serious way." When he talked about the job with Genevieve, he mostly just said that it was depressing, which captured his mood much of that winter and early spring of 1985.

In his memoir, explaining his relationship with Genevieve to his Kenyan sister, Auma, he wrote, "I pushed her away. We started to fight. We started thinking about the future, and it pressed in on our warm little world."

Genevieve had a different perspective:

My take on it had always been that I pushed him away, found him not to be "enough," had chafed at his withheld-ness, his lack of spontaneity, which, eventually, I imagined might be assuaged, or certain elements of it might be, by living together. Because it felt so intrinsically to be part of his character, though, this careful consideration of everything he does, I saw it, then, as a sort of wound, one which, ultimately, I decided I was not the person he would "fix" it with. So I pushed for a while, in my frustration, and then gave up, and basically rejected him. Living together in Park Slope was the end, it just so didn't go well. And we began to "fight," as he says. The space there was very not private, which didn't help.

January 25, 1985

*All the disconcertingness of seeing and being w/ Barack again — finding
it so disruptive instead of a sweet re-meeting — I think both of us finding
it hard to pull our energies away from our "private projects" and be
focused on one another. . . . Both of us in that year willing to focus on
our relationship as we wanted, yes, but also in the context of relief from
the external world in which we weren't fully living and occupied with
— he at B.I., me for my own slow growth/non-acceptance reasons. It's
changed, from both our sides — I actually find his interruption of my
focus on school as damaging, disconcerting — but that's ok — he's really into
travelling his path with concentrated determination as well.*

February 4

*Who is this boy/man/person, Barack Obama? We communicate, we
make love, we talk, we laugh. I insulted him the other night — a retaliatory
fuck you for having passed comment on my always wimping out at
dinners with the gang, offended that I place distance between us by saying
you stay, I'm leaving early. Made him yell at me about being insecure
all the time, didn't I know he wouldn't invite me (or some such) if he
wasn't in love with me. . . . But I find now that questions of who he is
reflect back on myself, and back to the middle ground. Both of us feeling
dissatisfied, wanting something more — but he from himself, and me from
the pair of us — what we are together — a sense that we were idling away
time, successfully killing the hour with small talk and mocking frivolities.
. . . I don't really know or understand how he feels, privately, about me,
us — But then I expect I am merely making complicated what to him is
simple, apparent, without need of explanation. . . .*

*Some sense of the veiled withholding that I still feel flutters between us —
constantly respun from both our ends.*

Six weeks later, Genevieve moved from 2nd Street to an apartment on
Warren Street in Brooklyn. Barack helped her move, then found a place to

sublease on Eighth Avenue in Hell's Kitchen. He and Genevieve continued their earlier routine of seeing each other on weekends, but things had changed.

April 1, 1985

My bedroom smells sweetly of hyacinths, which I bought at Key Foods, and I have zipped home from my only excursion today — eating dinner w/ Barack at Cuisine of . . . Felt jaggly at 1st, B. too cos he picked up someone else's keys. Zipped home on my bike from the subway — the bicycle and its quickness is wonderful. Good weekend. An uneventful end/ beginning to Barack's move from living w/ me to living [elsewhere]. The ease came back: an interlude to the day to day, like we're used to.

April 28

Annoyed B. intensely this a.m. by whining about it all — tho he laughed and talked me out of it as we walked into Brooklyn Heights. He has returned this p.m., sobered by whatever thoughts he's been playing football w/ this afternoon, and acting a tad hostile. When he talks of enjoying being alone, I wonder that he so regularly attends this weekend pattern of ours.

May 6

Spent a restless hour tossing things in my mind before I fell asleep last night. Barack succumbed yesterday to the weight of inertia and did what is more characteristic of me: questioned and doubted that there was anything between us except bozeling [lazing around in bed], and towards that his tone was somewhat scathing. Haven't really felt like making love with him recently — not sure why. . . . I was silent and somewhat withdrawn on Saturday afternoon and annoyed w/ B. who had no key and kept asking me if I'd be home by 2.30. I was, and waited till 5.00 until I heard from him. Didn't feel bad, just quiet, and didn't feel like going to dinner and being sociable, but went anyway. . . . Went to bed cold

*and distant. Got out of bed before B. woke up, no longer annoyed, but
quiet and uncommunicative. I thought B. was merely responding to me
— but he had his own thing going. He sat around until 6 pm in his kain
[sarong] reading the paper and watching B.B. [basketball]. . . . As he
was leaving B. said he felt strained — and I must say I was, I felt at the
time, dishonest in not voicing the thought that I had introduced a mood
and he was responding. But on the other hand, how someone responds and
interprets the situation is their own doing, and the ensuing conversation
was enlightening to both of us I think.*

A week later Genevieve wrote in her diary that during a lunch conversation
with a colleague at school she had called Barack "a prick." By the following
week, their relationship was mostly over.

May 23

*Barack leaving my life — at least as far as being lovers goes. In the same
way that the relationship was founded on calculated boundaries and
carefully, rationally considered developments, it seems to be ending along
coolly considered lines. I read back over the past year in my journals, and
see and feel several themes in it all . . . how from the beginning what I
have been most concerned with has been my sense of Barack's withholding
the kind of emotional involvement I was seeking. I guess I hoped time
would change things and he'd let go and "fall in love" with me. Now, at
this point, I'm left wondering if Barack's reserve, etc. is not just the time
in his life, but, after all, emotional scarring that will make it difficult
for him to get involved even after he's sorted his life through with age and
experience. Hard to say, as obviously I was not the person that brought
infatuation. (That lithe, bubbly, strong black lady is waiting somewhere!)*

Obama had been thinking about Chicago since April 28, 1983, when Harold
Washington made history, sworn in as the city's first black mayor. His hope
initially had been that he could land a job in the Washington administration
after he graduated, which only showed how unschooled and naïve he was. Not

until a decade later, when he was fully immersed in the give-and-take world of Illinois politics, would he learn how crucial it was to have a patron, or "Chinaman," as it was called in that inimitable legislative milieu. In the spring of 1985, from the remove of New York City, having visited Chicago only once in his life, on a summer tour of the mainland with his family when he was twelve years old, Obama had no Chinaman, but he did have something. He had a telephone call from Jerry Kellman.

The connection began when Obama was at the New York Public Library and came across the latest copy of *Community Jobs,* a publication of six to eight pages that listed employment opportunities in the social justice and social services fields. One listing was for a group called the Developing Communities Project that needed a community organizer to work in the Roseland neighborhood on the South Side of Chicago. Right city. Right line of work. Obama sent in his résumé and cover letter, something he had done many times before with no luck. Two matters left unstated in the ad were that Kellman, who oversaw the project, specifically wanted an African American for the job, and that he was getting desperate. Along with the listing in *Community Jobs,* he had placed ads in the *Chicago Tribune* and *Detroit Free Press.* From those and personal referrals, he had worked through a list of about thirty candidates, but none felt right. "I wasn't even contemplating filling the position until I found someone I felt could do it," he said later.

Obama's application was intriguing, though it gave no indication of his race. The résumé noted his Hawaiian childhood. The surname sounded Japanese. Kellman's wife was Japanese. He knew that Obama could be a Japanese name and that Japanese Americans were common in Hawaii. It would take a conversation to find out more, so he reached Obama in New York and they talked on the phone for about an hour. At some point, without asking directly, Kellman came to the realization that Obama was black. It was even more apparent to him that this applicant was smart and engaging and interested in social issues. Definitely worth a deeper look. Kellman told Obama that he would be in Manhattan the week after next to visit his father, a theatrical copyright attorney who lived near 92nd and Broadway, and suggested they get together then. The meeting took place in Midtown, at a coffee shop on Lexington Avenue.

In the handbook of community organizing as Kellman learned it, a key tool was the one-on-one. It was what it sounded like: a conversation involving only two people, the organizer and someone else, a person the organizer was trying to understand. It could be a housing tenant, a neighborhood leader, a pastor, a possible ally, or an organizer-in-training. There were two competing lines of thought among organizers about how to approach one-on-ones. Saul Alinsky, regarded as the father of community organizing, taught his disciples that the centerpiece of any discussion was to learn what was in the self-interest of the person being interviewed. Kellman and others, who to various degrees broke away from the Alinsky method, believed that everything revolved around narrative. Until you listened to and valued someone's story, in all of its particularities, beyond self-interest, you could not move him or her to action. But using either philosophy, many aspects of the one-on-one were similar. "An organizing interview is all about motivation. And the question is 'Why?' And you approach it biblically," Kellman later said. By "biblically" he meant throwing obstacles in the way, challenging, agitating. "When God wants someone to do something, in scripture, they always refuse him, like the scene in Exodus where Moses comes up with one excuse after another about not going back to Egypt."

It was in that sprit that Kellman challenged Obama, throwing questions in his path as obstacles, one after another. Why did he want this line of work, with its low pay, long hours, and endless frustration? How did he feel about living and working in the black community for the first time in his life? "I asked him, 'Why do you want to do this? Why do you want to organize? You graduated from Columbia. You are an African American when corporations are looking for people like you. Why don't you do something else?' But first, Why? Where does this come from? What place and how deep does it come from? And what I got from him was that the people in the civil rights movement were his heroes. And I also got from him that his mom was a social activist, an academic social activist, but a social activist."

Not all organizers were alike, Kellman realized, but they usually had to have at least two attributes in common. One was a feeling of outsiderness. Kellman himself had grown up in New Rochelle, New York, the quintessential upper-middle-class suburb, the comfortable world epitomized in *The Dick Van Dyke Show*. The sitcom's creator, Carl Reiner, and his son Rob, the future

Meathead, lived only a few blocks away. Yet Kellman felt apart from society. His parents went through a difficult divorce when he was a freshman in high school. He was Jewish, yet eventually would convert to Roman Catholicism. He was shaped by the issues of the 1960s and started organizing against the war in Vietnam and for racial equality when he was fifteen. At New Rochelle High he helped elect the first black president of the student body, Arthur Lloyd. All of that went into his feeling of being an outsider and drove him as an organizer. In a one-on-one, the interviewer reveals personal things like this to get the other person to open up. Obama, ten years younger than Kellman, offered his own outsider credentials: growing up without a father; living apart from his mother for several years; being from Hawaii, where there were few other blacks; negotiating different worlds as a *hapa,* half black, half white, in a society that regarded him as black; surviving as a young black man but without the shared history of his black peers. All of that gave Obama an outsider's sensibility. People like that, Kellman reasoned, either felt a strong need to conform as adults and fit in with everyone else or identified fully with other outsiders, a necessary attribute for work with poor people whose lives were filled with difficulties and disappointments.

So he asked the follow-up questions: *Are you angry? What makes you angry? If stuff doesn't make you angry, you don't stay with this work.* Yes, Obama said, he was angry. He listed the social conditions that upset him and that he wanted to work to change. *Have you ever failed?* Obama's academic pedigree, from Punahou through Occidental to Columbia, suggested that he was accustomed to success. In the world of community organizing, Kellman knew, that could be troublesome. "My concern was that he would just burn out very quickly. People who came out of a privileged education and had met with a lot of success hit the streets as organizers and suddenly encounter a level of frustration and failure they had never encountered before. . . . And so I wanted to know if he had failed at something, because they are all going to fail at organizing. No one ever succeeds at organizing in the beginning." Only a year earlier, Kellman's group had hired "this wonderful young woman who had succeeded in everything she had ever done." On the streets, trying to organize and failing at it, she had a nervous breakdown. Obama said no problem, he had failed, he knew failure, he could handle failure.

Kellman was taken by the answers. "I was satisfied that his motivation was identity – pursuing a path that his heroes had pursued in some fashion, that he wanted to figure out who he was, especially in terms of the African American piece, and that he wanted to learn. He seemed really curious."

As the conversation progressed, Obama turned the tables and started interviewing Kellman. He wanted to make sure that Developing Communities Project was legitimate and serious. This wasn't some far-left enterprise, was it? He had moved beyond that, he said. Later, when presenting the scene in his memoir, he would describe Kellman (the pseudonym he used for Kellman was Marty Kaufman) as "a white man of medium height wearing a rumpled suit over a pudgy frame," his "face heavy with two-day-old whiskers, behind a pair of thick wire-rimmed glasses, his eyes set in a perpetual squint." It was an appearance, Obama noted, that "didn't inspire much confidence," yet Kellman seemed smart and committed, if "a little too sure of himself." Obama turned his questioning to Chicago and what this disheveled white man could teach him. Kellman wondered what Obama knew about Chicago. Not much. "Hog butcher to the world," Obama said, reciting the famous Carl Sandburg line. Not anymore, the stockyards had closed, Kellman responded. Obama mentioned the Cubs, perennial losers, and Harold Washington, the town's new winner.

He pressed Kellman for more observations about the city and the South Side neighborhoods, what was happening with the steel mills, the decline of factory work, the fraying of families and communities. As they talked, it became obvious to Kellman that Obama was his man. He mentioned a "preposterous" salary: ten thousand a year. Obama asked for a car allowance. Kellman said okay. But to seal the deal, he had to do the exact opposite of what recruiters usually do. The more he talked about how bad things were, the more Obama wanted the job. Another young person who was going to save the world. But organizing will beat that out of him, Kellman said to himself. Chicago will beat that out of him.

There was something else going on here that Kellman could not see. Obama had talked to his friend Beenu Mahmood about his decision in a broader context, one that transcended his desire to become a community organizer. That job was part of a larger mission, as Mahmood interpreted his friend's actions, a matter of Obama taking the necessary step of credentialing himself in the black world as he made his way to a political future.

Before leaving New York, Obama spent two thousand dollars on a blue Honda Civic that he would drive into the heartland to start his new life. He also took along the white cable-knit sweater that Genevieve had given him for Christmas. It would comfort him in the cold Chicago winter.

CHAPTER 18

———◦◉◦———

FINDING AND
BEING FOUND

. . . and one
day I get a certain feeling and I'm
in chicago and I know I lost it say,
400 years ago in africa,
but on this particular day, I just know
I'm going to find it in chicago
it doesn't matter what it is.
no, it really doesn't matter what it is,
or where I lost it either.
what matters is the feeling of finding
(there is a law of finding),
what matters is finding on lost days,
and I'm finding that some days
what matters as much is being found.
                    CAROLYN M. RODGERS, "PRODIGAL OBJECTS"

C hicago, not New York, was the place to make it in the mid-1980s. In extraordinary sequence in 1984 and 1985, not long after Harold Washington broke the race barrier as the city's first black mayor, three young African Americans began new jobs in town. The first to arrive was a television personality who came from Baltimore to host *AM Chicago*. Within two years she had her own eponymous show, and soon Oprah Winfrey would be one of the richest and most famous people in the world. Next came a basketball player from North Carolina, the first-round draft choice of the NBA's Chicago Bulls. Four months into his rookie season, a soaring Michael Jordan graced the cover of *Sports Illustrated* with the headline "A Star Is Born," and soon enough he also would become one of the most recognizable names and faces on the planet. And last, via New York, came Barack Obama, essentially anonymous and unknown in Chicago except to the fellow who hired him as a community organizer and to a granduncle, Madelyn Dunham's younger brother Charles Payne, who lived in Hyde Park and worked as a librarian at the University of Chicago.

"The most segregated city in America" was the notorious label pinned on Chicago in 1959 by the U.S. Civil Rights Commission, and the statement retained a measure of truth a quarter century later, especially when it came to housing patterns, even as the balance of power was changing. Yet that negative distinction obscured the city's rich racial history. Chicago was at once divided and empowering. Its sprawling South Side housed more black citizens than any other urban sector in America, including Harlem and Bedford-Stuyvesant in New York. Chicago had long been a polestar for African Americans, drawing the masses and the elite. From the days before World War I through the 1960s, in the many iterations of what became known as the Great Migration, more than a half million blacks made their way north to Chicago, many lured by factory jobs, all fleeing the overt Jim Crow racism of Mississippi and Alabama and other southern states. Over the course of those decades, Chicago also had attracted black luminaries in sports, music, and literature, from Jack Johnson to Joe Louis to Muhammad Ali; from Joe "King" Oliver to Louis Armstrong to Mahalia Jackson; from Langston Hughes to Richard Wright to Gwendolyn Brooks. National empires had been built in black Chicago, including the religious empire of Elijah Muhammad and the Nation of Islam, the black empowerment empire of Jesse Jackson and his Operation PUSH, and the media empire of John H. Johnson and his *Ebony* and *Jet* magazines, purveyors of middle-class African American tastes. In so many ways old and new, Barack Obama's adopted hometown was the beating heart of black America, with the promise now, with Washington's rise, of transcending race. As Obama told Zeke Gonzalez, a local interviewer, years later, "Chicago was the most exciting thing going on at the time." He knew of no other city that seemed so energized and hopeful.

When Obama arrived in Chicago in July 1985, he was trying to find a few lost objects, in the words of the poet. One was a home; another was a clearer sense of moral purpose. At various times during his young life, he had scorned what he viewed as his mother's naïve romanticism, criticized her professional choices, such as working for the Ford Foundation, however well-intentioned, and expressed low-level anger about her frequent absences from his life. Yet he would never shed a sensibility that she, more than anyone, had nourished in him – that he was expected to do good. Even from thousands of miles away, even during the years in New York when he was pushing her away and shutting her out, her voice was the conscience of his inner life. The stinging admonition she had delivered during his Choom Gang days – "Damn it, Bar, you can't just sit around like some good-time Charlie" – reverberated in his mind. Now it took on a meaning beyond getting serious about school (mission accomplished) to the broader notion of getting serious about helping humanity. Chicago, he said later, offered "the promise of redemption."

Obama often lamented that he was born too late to participate in the civil rights struggle, with its unambiguous righteousness and moral clarity. Perhaps young people of most generations longed for some earlier time when life seemed more dynamic and motivations purer. Bill Clinton, fifteen years older than Obama and on the opposite end of the baby boom era, frequently said that he wished he had come of age during World War II, when the call to duty was for a "good war" with a noble cause, rather than when America was engaged in a war in Vietnam that he opposed and did not want to fight in. Obama was confronted by no war, good or bad, and no overriding single cause. Even as he headed toward an activist future, a fair dose of ambivalence, if not cynicism, had built up in him. It was evident a few years earlier in the way he reacted to his first foray into politics, the anti-apartheid speech he gave at Oxy: dismissing the entire event, saying he did not think it made a whit of difference. And it was there in the letter he wrote to Phil Boerner during his senior year at Columbia, wondering whether his growing sense of

competence and maturity would be worth much "in this mediocre but occasionally lovable society." But that apparent cynicism was only a protective
shield for his innate romanticism. He was more like his mother than he cared
to admit. It was just that he had not found himself yet – and the world was
not as he wanted it to be.

Alone in his blue Honda Civic, Obama took the familiar route from New
York, following the turnpikes of New Jersey and Pennsylvania, through the
mountain tunnels, around Pittsburgh, below Cleveland, hooking up to I-90
across Ohio and northern Indiana toward Chicago. He got off to a late start
and stopped the first night in a motel in Pennsylvania, where he recorded in
his journal the sense of exhilaration and fear he hauled with him to this new
life. He had only been to Chicago during one cross-country trip with his
mother, Tut, and Maya during the summer of 1973. Was he doing the right
thing now? He recalled the words of a security guard at Business International
who had told him he was out of his mind to turn away from a lucrative job.
He remembered the arguments he had with his mother over whether it was
more effective to work inside or outside the system, and how she had told him,
"Building institutions is a very tough business and [you] may turn out to do
more good by working within the institutional structure." He thought to himself that night, "I've got no idea how this is going to turn out." The geography
of the Midwest was so foreign to him that on the second day, as he drove along
the Indiana Toll Road and looked off to his right at the massive steelworks
of Gary, he assumed that he was already in Chicago. As he kept going, finally
reaching the city, and driving up through Jackson Park and into Hyde Park, he
thought, "This is nicer than I expected."

He had made the move with his life's belongings in the car, without bother-
ing to secure housing beforehand, and spent the first three nights crashing at
the apartment of his Pakistani friend Beenu Mahmood, who was interning the
first half of that summer at the Chicago headquarters of Sidley & Austin, one
of Chicago's elite law firms. Mahmood had an unfurnished apartment in the
Flamingo Apartments in Hyde Park, with a view overlooking Lake Michigan.
Obama slept on the floor in the living room until he found a place of his own
nearby. His first address was 1440 East 52nd Street, apartment 221. It was

"a comfortable studio" on the second floor of a four-story redbrick building with twin peaks near the corner with Blackstone. Fifty-second was one-way, running away from the lake, which was about a quarter mile to the east beyond South Shore Drive and Burnham Park. The short fourteen-hundred block was lined with squat apartment buildings, but a block south on East 53rd were several inexpensive restaurants that served as his dorm cafeteria of sorts, Mellow Yellow and Valois in one direction and Harold's Chicken Shack in the other, along with his barbershop, the Hyde Park Hair Salon, one of the oldest black-owned businesses in the neighborhood.

It was fitting in many ways that Obama settled in Hyde Park, the historic community hugging Lake Michigan, six miles southeast of the Loop. Not only did Harold Washington, the mayor whose election started Obama thinking about Chicago in the first place, live two blocks away, but Hyde Park was among the most integrated neighborhoods in Chicago, with a population that, like Obama himself, straddled two worlds, almost equally black and white. For better and worse, this characteristic was largely attributable to the University of Chicago, the dominant institution in the community. In an urban redevelopment effort that began long before Obama arrived and amounted to deliberate social engineering, the university had expanded acre by acre over many years, dislocating almost thirty thousand people, most of them black, who could no longer afford the housing prices. Opponents called this process "Negro clearance." The long-range effect was to keep the area integrated, while other neighborhoods on Chicago's South Side turned overwhelmingly black. That diversity, though created by a dubious process, made Hyde Park one of the most vibrant and accepting communities in the city.

In intimate conversations with Genevieve Cook before he left New York, Obama had confided that he felt some measure of trepidation over the prospect of immersing himself in Chicago's black world. In that sense, Hyde Park was a halfway base camp for him. His daily work was eleven miles away on the far South Side, in neighborhoods where, as he wrote in a letter to Phil Boerner, "you go ten miles in any direction and will not see a single white face." It took him twenty minutes to drive from 52nd Street to the organizing office at Holy Rosary Parish on 113th, taking the Dan Ryan Expressway most of the way. During his first week in town, he explored the vast expanses of Chicago in his rattling little car. One bright early-summer day as "the sun sparkled through the deep green trees," he drove the length of the black neighborhoods of the South Side, navigating King Drive from 25th to Palmer Park at 115th and then back up on Cottage Grove Avenue to Hyde Park. On another day he and Jerry Kellman, his nominal boss, explored the industrial quarters of Wisconsin Steel, which had closed abruptly in 1980, one of many steel mills that had shut down or severely reduced its labor force in recent years, demolishing the economics and self-identity of working-class white, black, and Hispanic neighborhoods. Between 1979 and when Obama arrived, about sixteen thousand steelworkers had lost their jobs in the industrial crescent from Gary through Calumet to the South Side, a region that had been the largest producer of steel in the world.

Obama also ventured north to Rogers Park and spent three hours with Kellman one weekend afternoon strolling the lakeshore paths of Montrose Harbor, where "the boats were out of their moorings." The purpose of that walk, Kellman said later, was "to get to know him and to figure out what the issues would be for him" as he began his new job. Based on their first conversation at the coffee shop in New York, Kellman had pegged Obama as a writer, an identity that could cut both ways for an organizer. Kellman assumed a hard-edged personality during those years, covering his insecurities with a streetwise machismo. He admired writing, but said that fiction writing in particular, Obama's main interest, might be the one profession more difficult to make a living at than organizing. And it was one step removed from an activist life anyway, he told Obama. "You can either change stuff or you can write about it." On the other hand, Kellman thought the skills of a writer were helpful in organizing work. Both writing and organizing, he said, centered on the notion of story. He stressed the importance of narrative, believing that narrative was how you changed the world. Before you could get people to act, first you had to listen to their story, get their story, understand their story. This came from the one-on-ones, from the technique of listening and agitating that Kellman had used during that first meeting with Obama in New York, and now used again as they walked in Montrose Harbor, and that he and his colleague Mike Kruglik would turn to in subsequent days during walks in Palmer Park across from Holy Rosary. Listening – foraging in the community for people's stories, then summarizing them in typed reports – was the first assignment Obama took on as a community organizer.

What was a community organizer? Charles Payne, Obama's granduncle, who lived only six blocks away from Barack in a house at 58th and Blackstone, had no idea. "It was always a mystery to me what he was doing," Payne said later. "Community organizing didn't mean a thing to me. And yet Hyde Park seemed to be full of them."

More than that, Hyde Park was the cradle of the movement, home turf of Saul Alinsky, a University of Chicago sociologist who died of a heart attack at age sixty-three in 1972, thirteen years before Obama came to town. Alinsky was an American authentic, radical and pragmatic, who had established the modern activist principles of community organizing and inspired thousands of disciples. He got his start in the 1930s organizing Back of the Yards, a white working-class neighborhood behind the massive Union Stockyards, where he had been researching the causes of the area's high juvenile delinquency rate, and later founded the Industrial Areas Foundation (IAF), which served as the hub of a network of community organizations around the country that followed his techniques. Alinsky's worldview revolved around the concepts of power and self-interest. Ordinary people, as individuals and in concert as a community, were not automatically given power; they had to agitate for it for themselves. Not power for its own sake, but power to shape their lives and their economic and social environments. Since power filled any vacuum, to be powerless was to invite manipulation and oppression by outside forces – wealthy interests and large institutions. To get people to act in concert, an organizer had to pinpoint mutual points of self-interest, find the areas of commonality in a disparate group. The Alinsky method demanded ideological flexibility and an aversion to charismatic leadership. No permanent friends and no permanent enemies. People had to build their own frameworks and institutions that would last, not affix their hopes to leaders who would come and go. The process, the idea, the tangible accomplishment – all were more important than personality. Yet it was not a bloodless, faceless notion. It was essential to understand the interests, hopes, and backgrounds of those on the other side, those you were negotiating with – politicians, corporations, government agencies, schools, other organizations – to again search for points of mutual self-interest. But, as Ernesto Cortes, one of Alinsky's noted disciples in Texas, put it, in the end there must be "a bias toward action, a willingness to do combat, to agitate, to draw a line at some point."

By the time Obama reached town, IAF had moved far beyond Chicago, focusing much of its attention on New York, Texas, Maryland, and California, leaving organizing in Chicago for the most part to groups whose leaders had been trained by Alinsky but had broken away from him in one way or another. Kellman and his colleague Mike Kruglik were part of that splintering, aligning with Greg Galluzzo, a former Jesuit who was forming an alternative to IAF called the Gamaliel Foundation. They had all been trained in the Alinsky method but differed with certain parts of it. Like many intramural disputes, the reasons for the breach could seem contradictory or inconsequential to an outsider. Galluzzo and his followers argued that pure Alinsky was too rigid and confrontational. IAF directors made a similar assessment of the Galluzzo style. But although their details differed, their larger motivations were similar: pushing for more jobs, better educational opportunities, safer streets, fewer home foreclosures.

On one level, at least, religion was essential to the organizing movement. The IAF was connected to the liberal social action wing of the Catholic Church, whose parishes served as sponsoring members of local organizations. The parishes provided community leadership from the ranks of laypeople, nuns, and priests and paid dues to keep the organizing apparatus going. There also were yearly grants from the Catholic Campaign for Human Development, run by the U.S. Conference of Catholic Bishops. In many areas, the ecumenical breadth eventually widened to include other denominations, but there remained a Catholic underpinning to the movement, even while some of the key organizers were Jewish or nonreligious. All of this context was in play when Obama came to Chicago. The group that hired him, the Calumet Community Religious Conference, was sponsored by Catholic priests in the steel mill belt below Chicago, where whole parishes were reeling from the loss of industrial jobs. When they decided to organize in the neighboring black sections of the South Side, a separate organization was formed, Developing Communities Project, with the idea that it would need a different model of leadership and church affiliations to make inroads, meaning preferably an African American organizer who could move beyond the Catholic parishes and recruit assistance from Protestant black preachers. That is why Obama was hired.

Although Kellman offered Obama the job during their meeting in New York, he did not have the formal authority to do so. Organizers were expected to stay in the background while laypeople made key decisions for themselves. In this case, Developing Communities Project (DCP) had a board of directors, composed mostly of black citizens from the community along with a few priests, who had been dissatisfied with two people who briefly had tried out for the job, including Kellman's compatriot Kruglik. The fact that Kruglik was white did not help, placing an earnest, well-meaning man in a difficult position. Loretta Augustine-Herron, one of the board members, said that race was only one factor. "Mike just didn't seem to understand what our needs were," she said later:

> Have you ever talked to somebody and you explained what your needs were and they misinterpreted it? He repeated it back to us and it was what *he* wanted it to be. It wasn't a good fit. Jerry [Kellman] was angry and he made this broad statement that he didn't care what we did, he was going to hire Mike. We said basically, and we were all in agreement, "You can hire him if you want to, but you're not going to hire him for us." And then one of the priests, John Calicott, pointed his finger at Jerry and he said emphatically, "I don't know where you've been looking. You've got to go back and look again and find an organizer out there that understands our needs and looks like us."

Soon enough, in came young Barack Obama for an interview with the DCP board in a downstairs conference room at St. Helena of the Cross Church. There sat Yvonne Lloyd, Loretta Augustine-Herron, and Deacon Dan Lee, three community members on the board, along with a handful of priests. Obama arrived neat and fresh, wearing slacks, a sport coat, and shirt and tie. "He came in and he had a seat and he seemed to be very comfortable with himself," Augustine-Herron recalled:

> He's six months older than my oldest child. I looked at him and I said, "He's not going to make it. He is not going to make it." That was my first opinion.

But as we got into the interview, he was so interesting. His comfort level. He was just very at ease. . . . Not laid back, just comfortable. It allowed for a really good interview, a good exchange. The other thing is he was honest, and you can't buy honesty. Honesty isn't something you can put on for an interview. You either portray that sense of honesty or you don't. If we asked him about difficult things – and we were very clear that he was not from Chicago – we'd say, "What do you do in this case or that case?" He was honest about his knowledge of the area, his knowledge about the situations. He would give us examples of things he could do, things he wouldn't do. He would say, "I'm not familiar with that, but things like that are things we will learn together." He didn't give us a snow job, like put your blinders on because he is going to dazzle you with b.s. . . . He didn't promise the moon, and we weren't looking for that.

Augustine-Herron's concerns had dissolved by the end of the interview. "He could have been purple for all we cared. We wanted somebody who was sensitive to our needs, which he was." He satisfied them in a way that Mike Kruglik could not, yet over the next few years Obama would grow close to Kruglik and rely on him often as a friend and mentor, in the end more than he relied on Kellman.

The black women in the room that day, Augustine-Herron and Lloyd, along with their friend Margaret Bagby, quickly ushered Obama into their world. "Rett," as they called Augustine-Herron, had five children and a husband she would later divorce. Lloyd was a nonstop talker with eleven children. Bagby was heavyset and constantly complaining about the discomfort of squeezing into the backseat of Obama's compact car. In Obama's memoir they were given different names: Loretta was Angela, Yvonne was Shirley, and Margaret was Mona. By whatever names, the three women were a generation or more older and treated Obama with protective concern as they would a favorite nephew, but were disarmed by his quiet confidence and generally followed his lead. They told him stories, instructed him on the cultural mores and idiosyncrasies of the South Side, accompanied him to endless meetings, warned him about which neighborhoods to steer clear of at night, pointed him toward other people who could be part of the network, and worried about his "health and welfare," his dilapidated car, and his abstemious eating habits. (Loretta:

"We'd take him to lunch and we'd have sandwiches and burgers and he'd have a spinach salad. We'd say, '*Spinach* salad? What's that?'" Yvonne: "You didn't want to say, 'Oh, God!' I'd look at Loretta and she'd look at me. We knew what to expect when he said he was going to have lunch.") Even though they could be nervous and he was preternaturally calm, their presence comforted him – no need for trepidation. Augustine-Herron and Lloyd had moved into homes on the same block of the Golden Gate subdivision down by 130th Street on the same day twenty years earlier, the day before Mother's Day, and had been best friends ever since. Their children attended the same schools and their families worshipped at the same church, Our Lady of the Gardens, in nearby Altgeld Gardens, the southernmost project of the Chicago Housing Authority. Bagby was their Golden Gate neighbor.

Obama saw them almost exclusively for work and did not spend much time at their homes. What dinners they shared together were in the social halls of various churches. He maintained some of his characteristic reserve, ever the anthropologist, the participant observer, yet they drew him in nonetheless with the sheer warmth and noise and immediacy of their lives. Here was the day-to-day world of urban black America, a place that for all of his travels he had never really experienced before. He had driven through the streets of south-central Los Angeles and walked up and down Lenox Avenue in Harlem, but this was different. In Chicago, Obama was finding – and being found.

The office at Holy Rosary was no place for a community organizer to find much of anything. It was a cramped space, the Developing Communities Project headquarters consisting of two small rooms for four people, with two clunky computers and nowhere to conduct large meetings. It was difficult to hold a private conversation. When Kellman and Obama wanted to talk they would take a walk in Palmer Park or slip over to the McDonald's a few blocks away. The office certainly was not the best place to take calls from a former girlfriend. During the first month Genevieve Cook telephoned Obama a few times. She didn't have his home number on East 52nd Street, but knew where he worked. Kellman recalled that Obama would get in one of the rooms alone and close the door when a call from New York came. For her part, Cook remembered making the calls: "I think I might have rung him twice, and might have been drunk, feeling sorry for myself." Her former lover, she said, made it clear in his own gentle but cool way that he was not so eager to hear her voice. "Then he did this thing he does, this cutting off thing he does," she said. He did not call her back, nor let her know later when he was visiting New York.

Much of his office time was spent typing up one-on-one reports from his forays into the nearby Roseland community. A one-on-one served four purposes for an organizer. First, it helped determine the subject's self-interest and establish points of commonality. Second, the mere process of listening helped build a relationship. Third, it was a means of gathering information about the neighborhood, church, politics, traffic, crime, and other aspects of community life. And fourth, the process of talking out loud tended to bring clarity to thoughts and concerns. The reports Obama wrote after each one-on-one followed a specific format out of the organizer's handbook. The names of the persons interviewed. Their jobs or positions in the community. What issues they raised with Obama that they might be willing to work on further. Their leadership potential in a community organization. And then, in greater detail, their personal stories. Obama the writer took special interest in the personal narratives. "Barack's reports were different than everybody else's," Kellman recalled. At first they seemed too academic, more like surveys, but after some prodding they became longer, more detailed, more evocatively written, grist for his own short stories and journal writing. He had heard stories, Obama later wrote, that were "full of terror and wonder, studded with events that still haunted or inspired them. Sacred stories."

"Welcome to God's Friendly Church. We enter to worship. We depart to serve." The words were on the front marquee of Lilydale First Baptist Church, a well-kept building of tan brick at the corner of Union and 113th, one mile west of Holy Rosary. On a sunny afternoon, when there were no students outside Christian Fenger High, the troubled public school up the street, the setting appeared deceptively serene. East-west traffic was sparse on 113th, and the cross streets were lined with shade trees and comfortably spaced brick homes. To the west one block was South Lowe, a north-south avenue that, like so many in Chicago, threaded for miles through the socioeconomic strata of the city. On that same avenue, seventy-eight blocks to the north, in the heart of an ethnic Irish neighborhood called Bridgeport, stood a one-story bungalow that had been home to Richard J. Daley, the iconic mayor who had run Chicago for two decades, spanning nearly six terms, until his death in 1976. Obama's new hometown, as he wrote in a letter to Phil Boerner, was "a city of neighborhoods, and to a much greater degree than NY, the various tribes remain discrete, within their own turf."

By the summer of 1985 the Reverend Alvin Love had served as Lilydale First Baptist's pastor for about a year. The church itself had relocated to 113th in the Roseland community only twelve years earlier, moving southwest in search of more space from a smaller building at 95th and Michigan Avenue in the old Lilydale neighborhood that gave the church its name. Love was still suffering from the effects of that move. His congregation was drawn primarily from the old neighborhood and was dominated by elderly members who would come to worship on Sunday and then leave. "So I was really struggling with getting my congregation engaged in the community and becoming a part of the community," he recalled. There were break-ins at the church. They could not keep a PA system; as soon as a new one came in someone would steal it. The unemployment rate in the neighborhood was high and worsening, with all the accompanying sociological effects: domestic violence, drug abuse, despair. How could he change all that? How could he get people engaged in the church and the community? Those were the questions he was asking himself, sitting in his second-floor office one summer afternoon, when he looked out the window and saw a young man stroll down the sidewalk from the west, turn up the entryway, and ring the doorbell.

This happened now and then. Usually it was someone down on his luck who needed money or food. Love was alone in the church, without his normal security, but decided to answer the door. The young man said he was learning about the neighborhood and hoped he could steal fifteen minutes of the pastor's time. Love let him in, ushered him into his cozy office, the venetian blinds partially drawn, the bookshelf behind his desk lined with biblical histories. The visitor sat in a straight chair with gray cloth backing; he wore khakis, a short-sleeve shirt, and comfortable walking shoes. The pastor was skeptical, thinking a pinch was coming sooner or later, a request for five dollars or a sandwich. "And he came right in and kind of disarmed you with that spiel about his name," Love recalled. "My name is Barack Obama and I'm going through the community trying to meet the leadership and the pastors, and I just want to talk about some of the things happening in the neighborhood to see what can be done. . . . You're probably wondering about that name and my accent. I've got this funny accent because my mother's from Kansas and my dad's from Kenya."

Obama was there for a classic one-on-one, except the standard procedure was to set up an appointment, not walk in off the street with a cold call. He had done several one-on-ones already, but most had been with members of Catholic parishes. Reverend Love was his first Baptist minister. They ended up talking for an hour and a half, and the pinch never came. Obama provided his narrative first, how he was born in Hawaii and lived in Indonesia and how his young life was shaped by the instability of constant movement. Love then told his story, also one of uprooting. He talked about how his family had moved from Chicago back to DeKalb, a small town in Mississippi, in 1960, where he attended segregated schools and where he and other black children were "forced to stay on our farms or face the threat of being lynched" after Dr. King and his civil rights supporters marched across the Edmund Pettus Bridge in Selma, Alabama, in 1965. Not long after that, he told Obama, they moved back to Chicago, settling on a godforsaken half-block street on the West Side near 13th and Western; 1313 Heath Street was his address, "a bad omen all around," a double dead-end with a barrel factory on one end and railroad tracks on the other. He was living there, fourteen years old, when King was assassinated and the black populace rioted in fury; Mayor Daley ordered his police force to "shoot to kill," tanks rolled up to the end of the block, and Love watched as the clothing store where his mother was buying a suit for him on layaway burned to the ground. When he went south, Love said, he was "a city boy in the country." And when he came back to Chicago he was "the country boy in the city."

It was through their personal stories that Love and Obama found their commonality as people who endured childhoods where they never felt at home. The conversation turned to the neighborhood and its many needs and problems. Obama repeated that he was there to help, and looking for leaders and allies in the Roseland community. He peppered the preacher with questions. *Who are the members of your church? How involved are they in the community? What do you want to change? What is the world as you see it and the world as you want it to be?* That last was quintessential Alinsky. In every training session of community organizers, it was the first exercise. Write down the world as it is, the world you confront every day, with all of its frustrations and imperfections, and then write down the world as you want it to be. The gap between the two was always vast. Alinsky's point was that you could never reach the world as you want it to be, but the only way to get close was to first have a firm grasp of the world as it is, without illusions. As Obama asked his questions, Love realized they had more in common than their sense of early dislocation. Obama was addressing the same issue Love had been brooding about since he arrived at Lilydale: How could he engage his church in the community, building his congregation and improving the neighborhood at the same time? "I thought it was a godsend. Everything I was asking about and wondering about, and here's this guy who just walks in off the street and says 'Here's how we can get it done,'" Love recalled. "Which is exactly what I was interested in. And it worked. The next couple of years I would daresay half or better than half my members [came from the immediate neighborhood and] walked to church."

The meeting with Reverend Love marked Obama's tentative first step into the subculture of South Side preachers. One by one, he visited other nearby churches, seeking to form a coalition of pastors to support Developing Communities Project and give it the bona fides it desperately needed in the black neighborhoods. It was a slow, difficult task, but Obama realized that it was essential. Without the preachers, he would be lost.

Years later, in the first proposal he wrote to publishers about the book that would become *Dreams from My Father,* first titled *Journeys in Black and White,* Obama would use two episodes from his early experiences to establish "some of the territory" through which his book would travel. The proposal began with the scene where his grandmother in Honolulu expressed her fears about waiting down at the bus stop where a strange black man was loitering. That anecdote was juxtaposed with the first meeting he had with a group of black preachers on the South Side during his community organizing days.

In the proposal, as in the eventual memoir, the role that Reverend Love played in setting up the meeting and supporting Obama was lost in the novelistic haze of conflated chronology and pseudonyms. The story in both forms was presented the same, virtually word for word, with one exception. *Dreams from My Father* used a pseudonym for Obama's chief antagonist among the ministers, while the proposal actually identified him, Reverend Sampson. That was Al Sampson, the pastor at Fernwood United Methodist Church at South Wallace and 101st. Sampson, who had been in the Fernwood pulpit since 1975, was a confidant of Mayor Washington's and had his own illustrious if underappreciated civil rights history. He had participated in early sit-ins in Raleigh as a student at Shaw University and served in both the NAACP and the Southern Christian Leadership Conference in Atlanta before being ordained by Dr. King himself. Sampson was a big man on the South Side, literally and figuratively, but Barack Obama did not know him, and he did not know young Obama.

"A tall man walked into the room. He wore an expensive double-breasted suit and his hair was straightened and swept back in a thick pompadour. Against his scarlet tie hung a large gold cross." That is how Obama depicted the opening of their first encounter. A colleague informed Brother Sampson that he had just missed an excellent presentation from "this young man, Brother Obama," about planning a meeting with the local alderman. Sampson poured himself some coffee and then asked, "What's the name of your organization?" – and it deteriorated from there.

"Developing Communities Project," Obama replied.

"Developing Communities . . ." His brow knit. "I think I remember some white man coming around talking about some Developing something or other. Funny-looking guy. Jewish name. You connected to the Catholics?"

Obama acknowledged his organization's connections. Sampson continued on his roll, which Obama later depicted like this: "Listen . . . what's your name? Obama? Listen Obama, you may mean well. I'm sure you do. But the last thing we need is to join with a bunch of white money and Catholic churches and Jewish organizers to solve our problems. They're not interested in us. Shoot, the Archdiocese in this city is run by stone cold racists. Always has been. White folks come in thinking they know what's best for us, hiring a bunch of high-talkin' college-educated black folks like yourself who don't know no better, and all they want to do is take over."

That was not precisely the way Love remembered the confrontation unfolding, but close enough. The pastor went on the attack, Love said, "but didn't point to Barack or call him out by name. But he did say, 'We don't need people from outside coming in telling us how to handle our business.' Or 'We don't need people who don't know what's going on in Chicago' – everyone in the room knew he was talking about Barack." Decades later, Love either could not recall that the "Judas" (his word) was Sampson or was reluctant to identify him. Kellman had no such qualms, declaring, "Sampson was the guy who baited Barack about Jews and Catholics – he was an early Bobby Rush." (A later Obama nemesis, Rush was a former Black Panther who became a Chicago congressman and would be challenged by Obama in the Democratic primary in 2000 for a seat in the U.S. House of Representatives. Rush prevailed in that campaign by blatantly defining Obama as an outsider – there it was again, another form of Kenya's *jadak* – not an authentic black Chicagoan with credentials in the community.)

What Love did remember clearly was how "surreal" it was to see the meeting of pastors turned around like that. "I was just amazed. Totally stunned [by the attack on Obama], he said. He had assumed that the pastors were in agreement, all in it together, with the only motivation being to improve safety in the neighborhood. But he and Barack had failed to take into full account the politics of the situation and the laws of self-interest. What if this particular pastor was a close ally of the alderman they were planning to confront, perhaps even on his payroll? The meeting fell apart, but Love counted it as "a failure and a victory at the same time. Because what we intended to do didn't happen, but it taught us an awful lot about making sure you know who's in the room and who's with you. When you go to battle, make sure you know who the soldiers are. That was a great, great lesson." He was also struck by how Obama handled the confrontation. "To Barack's credit, he didn't get up from the back of the room and come to defend himself. He left it there and let the guy say what he needed to say, what he was going to say, and trusted the rest of us to stay on point. We failed, but tried. Barack absorbed it. But then, as soon as it was over, he waited until the guy left, and said, 'Now, what just happened? Let's make sure we understand what just went on so we can go from here and not make this kind of mistake again.'"

In trying to bring the Roseland pastors into the fold, Obama began his archaeological discovery of the layers of history and politics embedded in the South Side. There were historic reasons for black resistance to the Catholic Church – its ethnically separated schools and neighborhoods – even as some of the fiercest advocates for social change came out of its liberal wing. And on his new turf there were political minefields everywhere, egos to soothe and relationships to work out on almost a block-by-block basis. Obama's basic territory, he was learning, enfolded two separate wards, the thirty-fourth and the ninth. During that initial session, they happened to be meeting in the ninth ward but discussing mostly thirty-fourth ward issues, which created some tension that became apparent only after the fact. There was also a simple matter of age at work here. Obama was only twenty-four, and looked even younger, and Reverend Love was thirty-one, a baby by South Side preacher standards. The thinking was "Why do we need you to come tell us what to do?" Love recalled. "Particularly at his age. They had been here forever. I was the youngest preacher. My place was to sit down and be quiet and be told what to do. The other pastors were sixty and beyond." Many pastors would stay in their positions for thirty or forty years, allowing for turnover only every generation or so. Love was in the first wave of young preachers who would take to South Side pulpits in the mid-1980s.

Obama the writer, the Moviegoer, the participant observer. Three variations of the same characteristic. Wherever he went in Chicago, he had a pen and notebook with him. He constantly jotted notes or doodled. Since his lower school days at Punahou, when he got into superhero comics, he had shown a penchant for sketching figures and faces. "He was always doodling, drawing, writing. He could draw," Loretta Augustine-Herron recalled. "He would draw when we were in meetings, things like that. He usually had a legal pad." As the months went by, his self-identity as a writer intensified, even as he became more absorbed with his community organizing work. On November 20 he reported on his new life in a letter to Phil Boerner: "Since I often work at night, I usually reserve the mornings to myself for running, reading and writing." In New York his routine was to run the length of Riverside Park along the Hudson; now Lake Michigan was at his side, "as big and mutable as an ocean."

Chicago was "a handsome town, wide streets, lush parks, broad, lovingly crafted buildings," he observed, but although it was "a big city with big city problems" it seemed markedly different from New York, the urban geography so much more spread out and the people "not as quick on the pickup." The weather was changing, and although Obama had experienced four northern winters in New York, his body was still attuned to the sunshine of his youth in Hawaii and Indonesia, and his new home promised something more ominous than anything yet. "I live in mortal fear of Chicago winters," he confessed.

The letter was three pages on legal-size paper. It was handwritten, like his journals, neat and notably upright and legible in his left-handed, modified-cursive penmanship. Enclosed in the envelope was "the first draft" of a short story he had written. "If you have the patience, jot some criticism on it, let George mark it up, and send it back to me as soon as possible, along with some of the things you guys have written." George was George Nashak, a Columbia graduate who was a friend of Phil's and had been part of the book club that met at Paul Herrmannsfeldt's apartment in Soho. In an addendum at the bottom of the letter, Obama explained the story's motivation: "P.P.S. I work w/ churches a lot in the black community, which may explain context of story."

A quarter century later, Boerner did not have a copy of the short story – he must have sent it back, with his critique – nor could he remember much about it. Obama was unknown then, of course, and there was no reason for any of his friends or colleagues to think he would be a best-selling author someday, let alone president. Nor did Obama have reason to keep his writing close. He eagerly sought out amateur editors and critics, including Kruglik and Kellman among his organizing colleagues. Kellman likely read the short story Obama sent to Boerner.

The story I remember most is about a storefront church, really a basic, struggling church. Calamity in the church and how people struggled to survive. In a storefront church, there is a small group of people who just have this incredible intimacy with each other and are totally in some ways unperturbed by the fact that they are so fringe from anything institutional. They are struggling to pay the rent while other churches are sitting on millions of dollars. So I remember him writing a story about a storefront church and the personalities. . . . The

flavor, though not nearly as good, was James Baldwin. Which, I am sure, he
read. . . . When I was reading it, I was interested, but thought he better stick to
organizing.

In response to Obama's letter, Boerner eventually sent a short story of
his own to Chicago for critique. The story was inspired by the office where
Boerner was working, and Obama assessed it with the acuity of a writing
coach. While there was nothing imaginative in his response, it was solid advice
and revealed how seriously he took the craft. "Enjoyed reading your story.
You've got a good sense of how to put dialogue together and describe scenes
with a few quick strokes," Obama wrote.

A couple of suggestions: 1) careful about too many adverbs, particularly describing how people speak (Paul asked disbelievingly, etc.) It can get cumber-
some and a bit intrusive on the reader; 2) resist the temptation of easy satire
(the laziest S.A. Acnt . . . the newest Asst A Exec). Good satire has to be a little
muted. Should spill out from under a seemingly somber situation; 3) Try to
get the basic stats on the characters out of the way early {Paul was 24} so that
you can spend the rest of the story revealing character; 4) Think about the
key moment(s) in the story, and build tension leading to those key moments.
Basically, it's a good start, hope you've had time to do more. (One last suggestion might be to write outside your own experience – write a story about your
Grandmother in Armenia, or your sister in college: I find that this works the
fictive imagination harder).

You can either change stuff or you can write about it, Kellman had said.
Obama was still trying to do both, but the question was whether he had the
temperament for both. There were certain aspects of organizing at which he
excelled. While Loretta Augustine-Herron and Yvonne Lloyd were wary of
some streets, even in familiar neighborhoods, and warned Obama away, he
had no qualms about walking down any block or entering any house, no matter how threatening or odd. His life's history was at work here. When you
spend several formative years starting at age six immersed in an unfamiliar culture on the other side of the world, walking the exotic alleyways and pathways

of the Menteng Dalam neighborhood of Jakarta, and figure out how to survive and thrive there, learning the language, seeming so at home that Indonesians come to think of you as one of them, nothing after that can seem too intimidating. But Lloyd was shocked one day when Obama reported that he had eaten at the house of a woman who was known for being a packrat, with old newspapers and detritus stacked high everywhere. "I said, 'Did you go over and eat in that house? It's not exactly the safest place in the world.' . . . He'd say, 'Yeah, it was interesting.' We'd say, 'You need to stay away. Don't walk through there.' He'd laugh. It didn't bother him. He was on that level with all of those people. I don't know how he managed it because they were leery [of anyone walking up to their doors]. It was the way he approached them. That has a lot to do with why they would let him in. It's like he belonged. Now he didn't, and we know he didn't, but he gave them kind of that feeling."

Over time Obama proved to be a first-rate student, and then teacher, of one-on-ones. In this realm again he drew on the adaptability and universal sensibility he had acquired from his life experiences and from his mother, the academic anthropologist who could relate to her subjects on a warmly human level. As a teacher, he was the sympathetic participant observer. David Kindler, who joined the Chicago organizing effort about a year after Obama, observed his teaching methods at the training workshops the Gamaliel Foundation sponsored at the Divine Word Seminary at Techny, near Northfield, about nineteen miles north of the city. In that setting the one-on-ones would be conducted in front of an entire room of forty or so people. The method was for the trainer to share something of his own vulnerability in order to draw similar revelations from the subject. Obama would "get somebody up in front of the room. He'd listen to them. He'd encourage them. He'd share something about himself [usually about the father he never knew], not because he was a manipulator," Kindler said. "He was great at it because he actually cared about people and he was unafraid to share about himself. It's creating a safe environment for somebody else to share. . . . There were a handful of people who had that ability, but he was by far the youngest who could do it."

Similarly, the lay leaders of Developing Communities Project, including the three women and Deacon Dan Lee, though much older than Obama and wiser in the ways of the South Side, were also his disciples, learning from him how to stay calm and focused, a later iteration of *Cool head, main thing.* At community meetings, he would stand in the back, rarely interfering, as they took the lead along with other people from the neighborhood, approaching them only if he thought they were getting too feisty or carefree. "He tried to be stern with us," Lloyd said. She remembered the night that a speaker they had invited to a community meeting was straying all over the place, not making a coherent presentation, and she said something to Loretta and they both started laughing. Barack "looked over and then he came and sat between us and I leaned back [to talk to Loretta again] because it was something else I thought was funny and Loretta started laughing again. He looked at us and just laughed, and he smiled and walked away." He wanted them to follow his mantra, Augustine-Herron said: *Take the high road. Take the high road.*

This leads to the characteristic that was most problematic for Obama as an organizer, a tendency that would crop up again and again later in his career: his caution. In that first interview at the New York coffee shop, Kellman had been satisfied that this biracial young man who never knew his father carried enough anger inside him, enough outsiderness, to be effective in a job that demanded a sense of outrage. He also realized that Obama's makeup made him a master of diversity. "Put him with all kinds of people, and he is king of the room. He has seen so many different kinds of people, been so many different kinds of places." In those early months in Chicago, Kellman also saw that Obama had sharp instincts about how to frame an issue. But it was also becoming apparent how cautious Obama was and how much he wanted to avoid confrontation.

The trait that Genevieve Cook took note of on a personal level during their relationship in New York was manifesting itself on a larger professional stage in Chicago. Obama, Kellman came to believe,

> was one of the most cautious people I've ever met in my life. He was not unwilling to take risks, but was just this strange combination of someone who would have to weigh everything to death, and then take a dramatic risk at the end. He was reluctant to do confrontation, to push the other side because it might blow up – and it might. But one thing Alinsky did understand was that within reason, once something blows up, to a certain degree it doesn't hurt, it helps. You are

supposed to be cautious about taking on issues you can't win, but Obama was more cautious than you need to be. But just saying cautious doesn't tell the whole story. Once it had all been put out, once he had considered all the options, he was willing to take a very significant risk. But his instinct was always toward caution. Sometimes people attribute that to him being African American, but I think it was intrinsic to his nature. It wasn't the angry black man in this case [the argument that it would be hard for an angry black man to prevail in a white-dominated society] because everyone around him [on the South Side] was black.

For better or worse, Kellman was Obama's opposite, frequently proposing "an aggressive kind of action." Obama, he said, "would resist that, storming City Hall, that kind of thing. . . . When I would suggest these things he would be resistant." In organizing parlance, a confrontation with a public official was called an "action." When people who lived in West Pullman, the old neighborhood between Roseland and Altgeld Gardens, proposed an action at the office of their state senator to push for help erecting stop signs and fixing potholes, Kellman's notion was to employ aggressive tactics, showing up unannounced and making noise and forcing a response. Obama "wanted to be more conciliatory." He set up an office-hours appointment with the senator and asked him for assistance rather than demanding it. "Civility, being respectful, was always very important to him," Kellman recalled. "He did not want to burn bridges."

Understanding the context of this Obama trait is essential – both its roots in his past and its meaning to his future. The obvious psychological point, made by Obama himself several times in his memoir, is that he had grown up mastering the art of pleasing people. He understood that being polite and nonthreatening could help him get what he needed. But as Kellman pointed out, on the South Side this had nothing to do with behaving a certain way as a black man in a white society, since he was dealing overwhelmingly with African Americans. It had more to do with growing up biracial, with his white mother and white grandparents, and figuring out how best to make his way through many different worlds. And there was something else at work here: his innate assessment of how to avoid traps. Perhaps his behavior was not so much passive as strategic. The state senator that Obama was reluctant to confront in West Pullman was Emil Jones. A decade later Obama would join Jones in the Illinois state senate, and Jones would serve as his political bene-factor from then on. For many reasons, the case could be made that Obama's later rise to the U.S. Senate and the White House would have been impossible without the powerful state senator's help. Emil Jones was to become Barack Obama's "Chinaman" – and that might not have happened had Obama be-haved more confrontationally the first time they crossed paths.

Community organizing was a hard slog, Obama confided from his Hyde Park apartment. "Lots of driving, lots of hours on the phone trying to break through lethargy, lots of dull meetings. Lots of frustration when you see a 43% drop out rate in the public schools and don't know where to begin denting that figure." At first he said he felt frustrated 95 percent of the time. If it got better for him eventually, the improvement was marginal, by his calculations, cutting the frustration quotient to about 80 to 90 percent. Most problems seemed of a magnitude beyond possible fixing at the community level, but an essential aspect of the job was to focus on the world as it is to find what was practical and physical and changeable. The asbestos problem at Altgeld Gar-dens fit that description.

In the Chicago chapters of *Dreams from My Father*, Obama devoted several pages to the Altgeld Gardens asbestos case, and when he ran for president in 2007 and 2008, journalists began researching the story to assess his cred-ibility. Some reports asserted that Obama claimed more credit for resolving the problem than he deserved. Others questioned his efficacy, noting that the asbestos was not removed from Altgeld Gardens until after he left the job. At the least, Obama in his memoir did not tell the complete story.

There were two separate narrative threads here that wove together midway through the action. One thread came from another housing project run by the Chicago Housing Authority, the Ida B. Wells Homes in Bronzeville, a histori-cally black neighborhood north of Hyde Park. Linda Randle, a social services activist based there, was arriving at work one morning when she noticed a yellow tarp hanging from the side of a building and an odd-looking machine outside. Nearby stood workmen in protective masks. Curious, she knocked on the face shield of one worker to get his attention and asked what was going on.

Removing asbestos, he said. That seemed odd; she had been dealing with tenants the night before and no one mentioned that asbestos was being removed from the apartments. There was a reason for that, she was told. They were removing asbestos only from the first-floor offices of the CHA's tenant services department.

The notion that "they were removing asbestos for employees who were there eight hours but not for tenants who were there twenty-four hours" infuriated Randle. She contacted Martha Allen, a journalist friend then writing for the *Chicago Reporter*, a small monthly magazine on race and poverty. By coincidence, Allen herself had been curious about asbestos in Chicago's housing projects. She had grown up in Ida B. Wells, and her parents had been among the first tenants in the extension, which went up in 1955. They had lived in apartment 105, on the same floor now being cleared of asbestos. As part of a Medill graduate program in journalism, she had covered the education beat in Washington and could not forget photographs she had seen while reporting on a federal government decision to provide funding to schools for asbestos abatement. "Wow, that looks familiar to me!" she said to herself. The asbestos looked exactly like the white stuff that came off the insulation on pipes beneath the radiators that she and other kids had played around every day in the projects. "You could see the white powder falling out of it, and it just triggered a memory of my childhood," she said. Her father had died of lung cancer at age seventy-one, and she was now wondering whether his death was linked to asbestos, a known cancer-causing agent. She was having haunting dreams, night after night, of her father sitting in his easy chair in that apartment, watching the news. "It was a very eerie feeling in that apartment," she said of the place in her dreams. "It wasn't like home to me. It was very scary." Now she thought she had a psychological explanation for those dreams. With Randle's assistance, she started investigating, taking samples from fifteen apartments in Ida B. Wells and sending them out for analysis.

At about the same time, and perhaps even before Randle encountered the men in masks, Obama was making his rounds at Altgeld Gardens and came across an unusual notice in the newspaper: the CHA was advertising for the removal of asbestos from the manager's office. This struck him the same way it did Randle at Ida B. Wells. If there was asbestos in the manager's office,

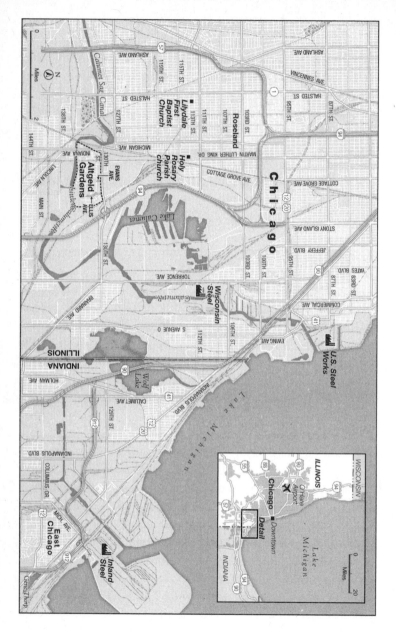

there must also be asbestos in the apartments. Why should the city officers get preferential treatment? He started asking tenants about it and saw that it could become a significant issue that might inspire Altgeld Gardens tenants to become more involved in fighting for better living conditions. His first decision, Jerry Kellman concluded later, underscored Obama's sharp instincts. He did not frame it solely as an environmental issue; in a setting where citizens had to worry about daily survival, the paucity of jobs, the proliferation of guns and drugs, that might be a hard sell. Instead he made it a question of basic fairness. The powers that be were taking care of their own, leaving the little people behind. Put that way, the asbestos cause resonated, and more Altgeld residents wanted to get involved.

Obama and Randle worked in the same field and encountered each other at regular meetings of the Community Renewal Society, a century-old Chicago social services organization that published the *Chicago Reporter.* Sponsored by the United Church of Christ, the society's stated mission was idealistic – to eliminate race and class barriers in the community – but its methods were practical and hard-nosed in the fashion of the Industrial Areas Foundation and the Gamaliel Foundation. It was at a CRS meeting that Randle told her colleagues in the organizing world about the asbestos problem at Ida B. Wells and how she and Martha Allen had launched their own investigation. As Randle was talking, Obama slid into the seat next to her and whispered that he had encountered a similar situation at Altgeld Gardens. They decided to join forces to pressure city officials.

Their first joint action was staged on May 28, 1986. Randle led a group from Ida B. Wells and Obama recruited a small band of residents from Altgeld Gardens: Hazel Johnson, mother of seven and grandmother of four; Cleonia Graham, mother of five, including a baby; Evangeline Irving, mother of four; a few children, an elderly illiterate man, and Barack's usual aunt-buddy trio of Augustine-Herron, Lloyd, and Bagby. They were all headed to the CHA offices downtown to demand a response from the city's housing director, Zirl Smith. Obama had been in Chicago slightly less than a year. In *Dreams from My Father,* he wrote that this moment, taking his ragtag group downtown on a yellow bus, changed him in a "fundamental way," the sort of change "that's important not because it alters your concrete circumstances in some way (wealth, security, fame) but because it hints at what might be possible and therefore spurs you on, beyond the immediate exhilaration, beyond any subsequent disappointments, to retrieve that thing that you once, ever so briefly, held in your hand." Quite a statement, considering what happened.

They waited in the hallway at CHA headquarters for nearly an hour, then were let into an anteroom. Zirl Smith's secretary kept saying that he was not available and that his assistant was not available. Randle, an excitable person, a self-described "rabble-rouser," was in a mood to agitate. "Barack, they're playing with us!" she fumed. Obama tried to soothe her. He had enough trouble trying to keep his people in line, let alone worry about a colleague. "Linda, you need to calm down," he told her. "You know the only thing you're doing is raising your blood pressure." She noticed that Obama "never said 'I'm frustrated' about anything." But there was one telltale sign: "We were standing there and I noted that he had smoked one cigarette and then he lit another. I said, 'Oh, he's having one of those Two Cigarette Moments!'" Two Marlboros in a row, sometimes the second going before the first was put out, was a sure sign of Obama's anxiety.

Then the elevators started dinging open and the lobby filled with reporters and cameramen who had been tipped off about the action – and immediately the posture of the housing officials changed dramatically. Not long after Obama put one of his Altgeld residents up for an impromptu press conference, he and his group were ushered into a meeting room where they were able to elicit a promise that CHA would conduct tests of asbestos at the project and that Zirl Smith himself would attend a community meeting at Our Lady of the Gardens at six-thirty on the evening of June 9. Before they all went home, at Randle's suggestion, Obama bought some famous Garrett popcorn for everybody to enjoy on the bus ride back to the far South Side.

The story was a sudden sensation. Walter Jacobson, a major figure in Chicago television news, whose acerbic investigative commentaries on government corruption for WBBM were influential, heard about the confrontation at the CHA offices from a producer who was on the scene. He called Martha Allen that afternoon, remembering that she had visited the station several weeks earlier and mentioned that she was doing a story for the *Chicago Reporter* on asbestos in CHA projects. "Where is that story?" Jacobson now asked her. "It's at the publisher," Allen responded. "It may be out in about five days." He asked her to slip him an early copy and he would get it on the air that night. "I went to my editors and they were absolutely giddy," she recalled. "That's what the *Chicago Reporter* lives for. Walter did the story. He was sitting behind a desk doing a commentary." In introducing Jacobson's piece, the WBBM anchor took note of the day's confrontation at CHA headquarters, and said that the Altgeld Gardens residents had wrung a promise out of housing officials that they would test for asbestos at the project.

Then: "More on the asbestos in public housing in 'Walter's Perspective.'"

There is evidence tonight of a lot more asbestos in public housing. And, in fact, the people who are concerned about it have good reason to be concerned. There is a tough little newspaper in Chicago called the *Chicago Reporter* which is at the printer tonight with a story [titled] . . . "Asbestos in CHA Apartments Poses Possible Health Hazards" . . . the result of making visits to 15 apartments selected at random in the Ida B. Wells Project at 36th and Vincennes.

The 15 apartments in 7 buildings – in every one of them, says the *Reporter,* there are pipes insulated with asbestos. And the newspaper has pictures of children living among those pipes. The asbestos inside the apartments is exposed and it's been found along the bottom of radiators, in the living rooms, bedrooms, kitchens, storage rooms and hallways.

Day by day the story grew from there. Jacobson did another commentary the next night, detailing his own efforts to get answers from the housing authority. The director of public affairs was "out to lunch" whenever he called and never phoned back, he reported. Mayor Washington's former press secretary, who had returned to private public relations and had secured a city contract to do publicity for the housing authority, also never called back. "It's the handling of a crisis, Chicago-style," Jacobson told his viewers. "The mayor's former press secretary is getting his $23,000; the public affairs director of the CHA is getting her lunch, while the people who live in the CHA continue getting poisoned by asbestos." Politicians could not ignore the story. Bobby Rush, then an alderman whose ward took in Ida B. Wells, called for council hearings on the issue. Emil Jones, whose state senate district included Altgeld

Gardens, urged the housing authority not to wait for more studies but to start removing the asbestos immediately. Bobby Rush and Emil Jones, both on-stage in an early scene, long before anyone knew what Barack Obama would become, two men who would emerge as the antipodes of his later political life, the former his electoral nemesis, the latter his essential patron. In the media, Jacobson's WBBM colleague, the investigative reporter Jim Avila, was on the story by then. At a council hearing held at Madden Field House, Zirl Smith saw Avila approaching with cameras, turned on his heels, and scooted away down the hallway, disappearing behind the first available door, which had a large picture of Mickey Mouse on it and happened to be the boys' restroom. Avila patiently waited outside until the housing director emerged. Smith refused to be interviewed, but later agreed to talk to WBBM if they would not show him escaping behind Mickey Mouse. "It seems to me they're panicking," Avila said. "And when they panic, you know they can't argue with the facts."

Martha Allen's full investigative report came out in the *Chicago Reporter* later that week. It raised the stakes. Along with the findings of asbestos in the fifteen apartments tested, it quoted Dr. Alan Leff, director of Pulmonary Medicine Services at the University of Chicago, saying, "Mesothelioma would be my major concern. Although it's a rare cancer, mesothelioma is not related to the amount of asbestos inhaled. You don't need long exposure and it's [almost always] fatal." There were more calls for action from politicians, intensifying the pressure on Mayor Washington and his housing director, who was reeling from charges of favoritism and neglect. Among the calls Martha Allen received after her story was published was one from someone expressing anger that she focused on Ida B. Wells instead of Altgeld Gardens. "At Altgeld they were upset because they were the pioneers. The CHA was focusing on fixing up the problem where the cameras were, and there weren't any cameras at Altgeld. They called me and blessed me out because I had one sentence or two on Altgeld in my story. I said, 'You know what? My editors decided to focus on Ida B. Wells. I actually wrote about the problems in Altgeld, but by the time the editors were done with it, it was one sentence.'" One reason, she explained, was that the asbestos at Altgeld was not as visible as at Ida B. Wells. "If I could have found more widespread, really visible signs of asbestos they would have been in my story more."

Who from Altgeld Gardens called to complain? It might well have been Barack Obama, she thought, but decades later could not say for certain. "I don't know who called up to complain. It was someone from Altgeld who was upset. I can't remember if it was Obama or not." At the time, Allen recalled, she didn't pay a lot of attention to him. "I'm embarrassed to say this handsome young man just didn't grab me. I was singularly focused on the story. He was much younger than I was anyhow. . . . He did [at some point] give me his telephone number to contact him. I looked in one of my old telephone books and there was his number. He knew I was working on the story. I was getting information from him, he was getting information from me on the progress of my story. For me, he was a news source."

The dramatic climax, if not the resolution, came at the June 9 community meeting at Our Lady of the Gardens. Whatever concerns Obama had about getting his people involved seemed needless now. Everyone was there, packed into the plain brick church near the back of the Altgeld Gardens grounds. Linda Randle and Martha Allen were there. Reverend Love, Loretta, Yvonne, and Margaret were there. Jerry Kellman was there, the lone white face in the crowd. Hazel Johnson was there, and Cleonia Graham and Evangeline Irving and several hundred more residents of the Gardens. Local television crews were there, along with reporters Cheryl Devall from the *Chicago Tribune* and Marilynn Marchione from the *Chicago Sun-Times*. Marchione estimated the audience at five hundred, Devall at seven hundred; by any count, it was massive, overflowing. Obama stood in back, but his organization was out front. To the side of a bank of microphones at a desk was a long banner that read "Developing Communities Project." Everyone was there, it seemed, except the figure they had all come to confront: CHA director Zirl Smith.

Obama had had a difficult time persuading some residents of Altgeld Gardens to take leading roles at the meeting. They were intimidated by the large crowd and the cameras. Kellman listened behind the scenes as Obama – *Cool head, main thing* – bolstered their confidence and soothed them: "You are the most qualified person. I have every confidence. All you have to do is get up and tell the truth. You're going to do a fantastic job and all of us are going to be right there behind you. Nothing to be afraid of." "He was able to convince some of the ladies by being very patient and constantly supporting them,"

Kellman recalled, "and projecting onto them the quality and strength he saw in them." Then, as fifteen minutes went by, then a half hour, then forty-five minutes, what were they to do?

Linda Randle took the microphone at one point and started talking about her findings at Ida B. Wells. A disastrous move. The Altgeld audience began chanting, "We were first! We were first! We were first!"

All the disappointments and resentments of life at Altgeld Gardens started spilling out. Even within the troubled projects of the Chicago Housing Authority, the Gardens in some ways represented a lower circle of hell, not as violent as some, but as neglected and hopeless as any, partly because of geography. It was a neighborhood on the edge, literally and figuratively, isolated on the far southern edge of the city at the end of what was known in the South Side as the Hundreds. As the name implied, the Hundreds were the blocks on the grid south from 100th Street to the end of town. Altgeld Gardens, entered at 130th Street from the cross street Ellis Avenue or Evans Avenue, was a place apart, an island cut off even from the rest of the Hundreds, separated by railroad tracks, industrial wastelands, and polluted marshlands, with no full-scale groceries or stores, only one bus line, and one elementary school; the older children had to ride the bus five miles north up I-94 and off at 113th to Christian Fenger, the high school down the block from Reverend Love's church in Roseland. John Peter Altgeld, the man for whom the housing project was named, was a nineteenth-century Illinois governor. Here was his namesake legacy: one desolate block after another of low-lying buildings, dark brown brick, two stories. The federal government had opened the development in 1945 with the specific noble cause of providing solid housing for a few thousand black workers employed in the steel mills and factories as part of the war effort. The factories were long gone, the mills closing, nothing but emptiness for miles around. And now, even when it came to asbestos, the residents of Altgeld Gardens felt overlooked. All the publicity and attention was going to Ida B. Wells. "So they began to shout over me as I was talking, 'We were first!'" Randle recalled. "It started to go down at that point. It started to go down."

Kellman was in the thick of the crowd, trying to keep a low profile. "Not [low] enough, from Obama's point of view," he said later. "He was already being called a tool of the Jews and Catholics. . . . I was the only white person there and he didn't want it to look like he was taking orders from us, which he wasn't. I was there because I wanted to see it, and also I could maybe be a help to him. He did not say, 'Jerry, don't come.'" By Kellman's reckoning, he proved to be a help and a hindrance. He thought he offered sound advice by suggesting to Obama that he get his resident leaders together to caucus at the side of the room to decide how they wanted to keep the evening going, and he also felt positive about encouraging the crowd to start chanting at various points. "The stupid thing," he acknowledged in retrospect, "was trying to lead the chanting. That's what he got mad about. He didn't need that. The chant was something about asbestos. I get overenthusiastic. Impulsiveness to some degree is my style."

Finally, after the rustling audience had waited for an hour and fifteen minutes, Zirl Smith entered the room. The CHA director could not help but grasp that Our Lady of the Gardens was no sanctuary. He was greeted with boos as he settled into a seat behind a long table. Soon enough a resident moderating the evening was standing above him and blaring into the microphone, "Do you have a plan? Do you have a plan?" Smith said he could not say until his office had finished analyzing samples taken from various apartments. Cries of "No! No!" rocked the room. When Smith tried to reach for the microphone again, the moderator pulled it away, starting a tug-of-war of sorts as people chanted, "Take it away! Take it away!" Obama, in the back of the room, cringed as the meeting deteriorated further. Smith, unable to make his case, got up and strode to the door, heading into the darkness in search of his waiting car. The crowd followed fast behind, now chanting, "No more rent! No more rent!" Reporters covering the event heard Smith complain that outsiders who "do not live in Altgeld" were the organizers and agitators of the meeting.

Linda Randle looked over at Obama and noticed that he was having another Two Cigarette Moment. Other than that, he remained outwardly cool, and when everyone else had left, after Smith's Ford LTD sedan had lurched slowly and then screeched away into the early-summer night, after Obama had walked past an impromptu huddle where some local politico was complaining that the whole issue had been cooked up by Mayor Washington's enemies as some kind of white plot, the young community organizer called his resident leadership group together to review what had happened. In an immediate sense, the evening had been chaotic, unresolved, disastrous. But in the long run it would serve its purpose. Hundreds of people had been roused from the lethargy of their daily lives. The most powerful housing official in Chicago had learned viscerally that he was dealing with an unhappy constituency. Altgeld Gardens was not first, never first, nothing came first to that isolated southern outpost, but after Ida B. Wells and Stateway and a few other projects, the CHA got funding from the federal government and the asbestos was removed, not just for the manager's office, but for the residents.

"From my story, the CHA removed the asbestos from the buildings I focused on first," Martha Allen recalled. "It took a whole lot of work for Altgeld to get some of that attention." Obama, she said, was at the center of that work.

Ann and Maya were stationed back in Hawaii. The verb *stationed* was often most appropriate for Ann because she seemed always on the move, like a foreign service officer, with houses but no permanent home. She was constantly finding something; a life of searching was her natural habitat. When she left the Ford Foundation in the spring of 1984, she also gave up the house the foundation had provided for her in the Kebayoran Baru district, the wealthy neighborhood in South Jakarta not far from the diplomatic row and SD Besuki, the school that her son had attended a decade and a half earlier. A young professional expat named Rick Monteverde had heard that the house would be available and stopped by to see it just as Ann was packing. As he remembered it, she was distracted and not too helpful, treating him like an inconvenience, waving her hand: "Oh, just look around." But she did happen to tell him that she was returning to Hawaii to finish her doctoral thesis. "And she started going off about how she had been this child bride. "I just thought, 'Who is this woman telling me she was a child bride?'"

Along with dissertation work at the University of Hawaii, Ann had another reason to return to Honolulu. Maya had been accepted at Punahou School for her freshman year starting in the fall of 1984, following the path blazed by her older brother, who had graduated from the elite prep school five years earlier. "She was a little concerned at that point," Maya said later of her mother. "She wanted me to have an American education because she felt that I should go to college in the U.S." After leaving Indonesia, where Maya had spent most of her first fourteen years, they settled into apartment 402, a small corner two-bedroom on the top floor at 1512 Spreckels Street, just below Wilder Avenue, near the Punahou campus, not far from the lava rock wall with its night-blooming cereus. During Maya's first week at school, as she was walking across the grounds toward the Dole cafeteria, she saw something etched in the pathway that startled her. That night she called her older brother with the news: "Your name is in the concrete!"

Finding and being found; leaving and being left. Ann did not intend to have her daughter spend her high school years separated from her, as Barry had. Not that Ann was home all the time. For the next few years she roamed in and out of Hawaii, visiting Indonesia and taking on temporary assignments in Pakistan as a consultant for the Asian Development Bank and the UN International Fund for Agricultural Development. Sometimes, when school was out, Maya went with her; at other times Maya stayed back and was looked after by her grandparents and family friends. But Maya's relationship with Tut and Gramps was different from Barry's. "Barack was with them when they were both working and vigorous. They raised him, in a way. They had a big hand in it. They took care of him and they were very proud of him in a way one would be of a son. I spent a lot of time with them but I was never as close. . . . My mom really raised me. It wasn't fifty-fifty. It was ninety-five to five. She was my primary parent."

By the time Barack reached Chicago, when Maya was in tenth grade, their grandfather had retired after twenty years in the furniture business and another twenty selling insurance. The glib salesman had ended his life's work, which he never liked and never did well. He was a smart man who had not come close to fulfilling his potential. During the years Barry lived with him, the grandson alternated between taking pleasure in outsmarting the old guy and feeling some combination of sadness and anger witnessing the despair of someone who was unfulfilled. In telling Genevieve Cook about the time he grabbed Stan by the shoulders and shook him and asked him why he was so unhappy, his point was to emphasize that he never wanted to be in that position himself. It was not just the dreams from his father that pushed Barack Obama, spurring him toward some still undefined life of accomplishment, not just the outsize confidence that his mother had in him, but also a reaction to the way Gramps had lived, a life that he thought was too small. But Stan in retirement was released in a way. Now he could play golf and bridge, take cruises, cook, and talk, the things he enjoyed.

Stan even traveled back to Kansas in June 1985, around the time Barack was heading for Chicago. It was for the fiftieth reunion of El Dorado High's class of 1935. Stan had always played it both ways when it came to his school days. He identified alternately with the class of '35, which included most of his friends and should have been his graduating year, and the class of '36, with which he graduated after being held back a year for his misbehavior. This time the dinner was held at the Moose Lodge and drew seventy-nine members of the class, along with guests from other classes, including Stan's older brother, Ralph, from the class of 1934, who came out to Kansas from his home in Alexandria, Virginia. He and Stan took a room together in Wichita in an empty apartment at a retirement community where their aunt Doris lived. Doris – the former Miss El Dorado, the beautiful younger sister of their mother, Ruth, of whom they carried only shards of memory nearly sixty years after she had killed herself with strychnine in that Topeka auto garage – was the last living blood relative in the generation before theirs, in her eighties now. "She was very close to both of us," Ralph recalled. "We took our meals with her." It was Stan's last fine time in Kansas.

In retirement in Honolulu, he was the same as ever, without the accompanying work-related angst. While his grandson focused on the narrow parameters of Stan's life, his granddaughter saw something else, an exaggerated response to those frustrations. "He was not sensible," Maya recalled of Stan, "in pretty much every way. . . . He would throw lavish parties, make a big deal out of holidays, cook in excess. Always too much food. Too much everything. There was something excessive about him."

In contrast, there was nothing publicly excessive about their grandmother Tut, who then and always would be a significant and underappreciated influence on Barack in particular, in terms of his personality and the possibilities of his life. The coolness in Obama's behavior came not just from the laid-back Hawaiian attitudes of his teenage years, but from the deeper well of his grandmother's reserve. *If it's not broken, don't fix it* was one of her maxims. She kept the same furniture in their Punahou apartment for decades. When you called her on the phone, she would say what she needed to say and no more. Stan could blab on the phone for hours, deep into the night, and so could his daughter, Ann, who in some respects was more like her father than she would care to admit, footloose and garrulous. Tut could not tolerate gossiping or cloying behavior. She kept her own troubles, her struggle with alcoholism, private. As Maya put it, Tut "wasn't particularly warm and fuzzy, but neither was she cold and unapproachable. It was more she would approach you very sensibly, 'Now let's take a look at X, Y, Z.' It wasn't aloofness, it was just that she didn't think much of gushing." Obama was never a gusher either, and had his grandmother's physical spareness in other ways during those early years of adulthood. He traveled light, his clothes and living accoutrements neat, unadorned, modest, nothing extra. Even through all those years of struggling to find himself, and his home, his tendency was to get to the point, whatever it was.

During Maya's Punahou years, she occasionally visited Tut at the Bank of Hawaii office at 111 South King Street in downtown Honolulu, where she was a vice president. "She was sensible in her stride, in her demeanor," Maya thought. "Rather 'no nonsense.' Clearly well respected and well-known at work. I would go down to work with her sometimes and she would walk very confidently down the hallway. . . . She was always dressed immaculately, very pressed. She always wore high heels. There was a time when she wore wigs a lot because her hair was skimpy. . . . Some wigs were updos, but usually sensible, modest, never past the shoulder." Madelyn had been a significant figure in her banking world, a regular presence at conferences and conventions, often flying to the West Coast to take part, active in the American Institute of Banking, the Mortgage Bankers Association, and the National Association of Banking Women, and legendary among the scores of Bank of Hawaii officers who had risen under her tutelage, which one eventual vice chairman of the institution, Alton Kuioka, likened to that of "a drill sergeant." She was admired if not fawned over. It was during Maya's high school years, while Ann was also in Honolulu, that Madelyn also retired. They attended the party held for Madelyn at the bank. "I remember quite vividly that there was a good bit of fun and a sense that things would not be quite the same around there," Maya said later. "I also got the sense that in addition to respect people had granted her they had developed a bit of affection for her as well. . . . She seemed to inspire affection because people could rely on her, trust in her to take care of things. . . . She was sad to be retiring but also in a sense relieved. She had very high standards for herself."

In Chicago her grandson had just celebrated his twenty-fifth birthday and had made a move, but within the neighborhood. He left one Hyde Park apartment for another, ending up at 5429 South Harper, apartment 1-N, another solid dark-brick building a few blocks south of his first place and even closer to the restaurants on the 53rd Street strip. The social problems ("25% unemployment . . . infant mortality on par with Haiti") he encountered every time he drove farther south into the territory of his organizing job remained "daunting," he noted in a letter to Phil Boerner, "and I often feel impotent to initiate anything with major impact." Nevertheless he intended to stick with it at least for another year, until the end of 1987, he reported. "After that, I'll have to make a judgment as to whether I've got the patience and determination necessary for this line of work."

His responsibilities had increased after the first year. Kellman had left Chicago and ventured farther around the industrial rim of Lake Michigan to start a new organizing effort in Gary, Indiana, which in many respects was more troubled and forlorn than the South Side, lacking any remnant of a middle-class black base. Now Obama shared an office with his assistant, Johnnie Owens, a streetwise product of the South Side who had majored in urban geography at Chicago State and risen to a professional job downtown at Friends of the Parks, a nonprofit agency whose self-apparent mission was to support the city's park system. Obama had visited the Friends of the Parks office on the eighth floor of the historic Monadnock Building one day to find out what sorts of grassroots pressure could be applied to the Chicago Parks District to get more recreation resources to the far South Side. He was in his familiar uniform: khakis, dark brown bomber jacket, white shirt with the sleeves rolled up. Owens was surprised by the fact that Obama took off his watch and set it down in front of him as though he were keeping time. And as they drank coffee and chatted, Owens was also struck by the line of questioning. After they had talked about the parks, the politics of the city, and urban issues, Obama smoothly steered the conversation toward Owens's life – what his parents were like, the environment in which he grew up, the quality of his public education. It was a classic one-on-one, the possible purpose of which would not become clear until later. It was much like the first meeting with Reverend Love. They ended up talking for two hours.

Obama methodically drew Owens deeper into his world. They exchanged phone numbers at the end of that first encounter, and not long afterward joined forces for reconnaissance missions of city parks in Roseland and surrounding neighborhoods, checking on upkeep, safety, and the condition of playgrounds. One day they were walking through a park, commiserating about the bleak environment offered neighborhood children, with broken glass everywhere. "And all of a sudden these gunshots go off," Owens remembered. They ducked. "We didn't know where it was coming from. We looked at each other. *We're at a playground where children play and hear gunshots going off. This just isn't right.* That underscored the need for change. That taught us things need to happen for the better quickly. No time to waste." Owens and Obama talked on the phone, had lunch now and then, attended community meetings and Parks District hearings. Over all that time Obama was making a sales pitch for Owens to join him as a community organizer. *How effective do you think you can be helping people build power working from downtown? Why not come out and do some real work in the neighborhoods?*

At first Owens did not want to leave a comfortable job that he had worked so hard to attain. "I was kicking and screaming from the time he made the offer, because I liked working downtown," Owens recalled. "He understood the psychology. It's prettier down there. It's clean. It's more exciting." To close the deal, Obama appealed to Owens to live up to his values, then matched the salary at Friends of the Parks and offered the further inducement of an advance for a car, precisely what Kellman had done to lure Obama from New York. It worked – with one twist. Obama assumed Owens would buy a cheap clunker like his beat-up old blue Honda, but instead he used the advance to buy a spanking-new Nissan Sentra. "He was a little bit angry," Owens recalled of Obama. "He understood the logic of it" – fewer repair costs – "but every time he used the car he framed it as 'the car *I* bought.' We always had a little tension about it. . . . It showed me a side of him that annoyed me a little bit. He said it was the car *he* bought. It was half joking, but there was some serious-ness behind it."

There was an unspoken tension here, nothing significant, but revealing. It had to do with backgrounds and choices. Obama was in Chicago by choice, working as a community activist by choice, living an ascetic life by choice. Owens was from Chicago and of the South Side. His range of possibilities was not as wide as Obama's; this was his life, not a stop along the way to some-where else. During their first months working together, Obama did not tell Owens what he had acknowledged to Phil Boerner – that he might leave com-munity organizing altogether after another year – but Owens could sense that Obama had other options. There was something studied about his existence that became apparent when Owens visited his apartment on South Harper. "What was fascinating was that someone so intelligent and clearly sophisti-cated was living as barebones as he was. I could tell it was a conscious effort to do that. I thought, 'Maybe he has larger ambitions down the line and now he's trying to focus on getting a certain experience and understanding of what it means to live a certain way.' The more we talked, the more I could tell that he had larger ambitions in mind. You'd go by his house and his bookshelf . . . clearly the books he had, they weren't just there for display." *The Power Broker* by Robert Caro. A treatise on black intellectuals. *Reveille for Radicals* by Saul Alinsky. "Stuff like that. He had classical as well as jazz music in his record library, lots of Miles Davis, some Coltrane. I remember Thelonious Monk. It was a small little sound system, decent enough to hear the music well. It was sort of like a student. . . . In retrospect it was clear he was hoping to gain some organizing experience and he was willing to take a low pay grade to get it."

During his first months in town in 1985, Obama had lived such a "monk-like" existence that Jerry Kellman worried he would burn out with all work, no play. But he started dating soon enough and was in a serious relationship with a graduate student at the University of Chicago not long after Owens came on board at DCP more than a year later. There were a few familiar aspects to this relationship. First, his new girlfriend was studying anthropol-ogy. Perhaps her field of study was a coincidence, but it followed a pattern. Genevieve had majored in anthropology at Swarthmore; Barack's mother was getting her doctorate in anthropology at Hawaii. The essential characteristics of anthropologists are to be keen observers, excellent listeners, sympathetic outsiders with a capacity to embrace and understand different cultures, languages, religions, social mores. Stanley Ann Dunham had those traits even before she chose her life's work in foreign lands and inculcated them into her only son, and now he was finding those same qualities in the young women of his life. Second, this Chicago anthropologist was, again, not African American, a fact that made Obama's later rendering of his breakup with Genevieve (or the composite New York girlfriend that included his version of Genevieve) in *Dreams from My Father* all the more curious.

I realized that our two worlds, my friend's and mine, were as distant from each other as Kenya is from Germany. And I knew that if we stayed together I'd eventually live in hers. After all, I'd been doing it most of my life. If, as Obama wrote in his memoir, that was the reason he pushed away from Genevieve, because inevitably she would draw him into the white world, he was there again with this new relationship – even though he had moved to Chicago in part to draw the arc of his life deeper into the black world, where he was starting to find a home. There is no lesson here beyond the obvious point that a lonely heart goes where it goes, whatever the larger plan. The Chicago girlfriend went not only unnamed but essentially unmentioned in the memoir. There was one glancing reference to her, in a scene where Obama was disturbed by the boom box racket coming from some young men on the street outside his apartment one night and left a stay-over friend upstairs as he went down to confront the rabble-rousers. But the relationship with the Chicago anthropologist was serious, much like the one with Genevieve in New York, and lasted about the same length of time. It is likely that the scene that Obama's memoir placed in New York, involving the angry black play and his girlfriend lamenting that she could do everything but be black herself, in fact was something that happened with his Chicago girlfriend. This relationship ended much like the one with Genevieve, when Obama was ready to make his next career move. "Everything didn't revolve around race," said Jerry Kellman, who saw Obama and the girlfriend now and then when they visited his family – Jerry and his Japanese American wife, April, and their son, Adam – at their home in nearby Beverly. "They were both very independent people."

Even as he was insinuating himself into the South Side culture and finding comfort in the black world there, Obama remained the participant observer, never able to fully lose himself in that new world. The argument that gained popularity decades later among some detractors that he harbored a deep-seated animosity toward white people was a preposterous misreading of his nature. His perspective was universal, removed, not racial. He had reservations about people of every race when it came to tribal thinking. In private conversations with Johnnie Owens, he did not hesitate to point out what he saw as hypocritical aspects of prevalent black attitudes. "He was very clear about the unreasonable aspects of how blacks saw things in the community," Owens said. "For example, when African Americans would complain about 'They always show us when somebody kills somebody . . . they show a picture of a black person on TV.' People would say, 'They always do that!' Barack would say [privately to Owens], 'We *do* do that!' Or oftentimes folks would be angry about the school system. He would say, 'Well some folks didn't prepare their kids well for school!' He believed there was a lot more accountability that needed to take place in the African American community. He sounded like an outsider." Owens understood that perspective, but was more sympathetic to the visceral point of view of victims of racism. "I had known very few [blacks] who had expressed those opinions so deeply [as Obama]. I don't think he expressed them to other African Americans. He said those things to me. He didn't say them openly or publicly. I probably wouldn't have said them back in those days. . . . While they may be true, in the depth of my feeling about racism I understand sometimes where the anger and frustration comes from . . . to complain about things that white America does while at the same time not being as fully accountable, I understand some of the pain that comes out of."

Obama's search for home in the black community was not something he talked about regularly with his newfound friends and associates, but Reverend Love at Lilydale Baptist could feel it every time they were together. When they first met, Obama had almost apologized for the Kansas roots in his way of speaking, but to Love he sounded enough like a brother. "Even though you knew he was educated, he had some nuances in the way he spoke. He didn't say 'you all,' he said 'y'all.' Some of the words with 'nt,' you never heard the 't.' Those kinds of things. And I don't know if that was intentional on his part or if he picked it up and that was simply who he was. But he didn't sound different until he started talking strategy and policy and things like that – then he became more an intellectual. . . . Usually he had a certain amount of slang that I think validated him when he spoke." One talent Obama decidedly did not have during that period was the smooth public speaking style of a South Side preacher. "He had a very choppy speaking style when he started organizing," Love later said. "The few times he was in front of a meeting and had something to say, he would break his ideas up, his style was not fluid." But Obama spent many Sundays sitting in the back pews at various black churches listening to one master orator after another spin magical allegorical stories of faith and survival. He would come back and tell "Rev" how "impressed he was that a Baptist preacher could get up and go to talking. He learned quite a bit from simply watching some of those people. . . . [When he started], he was clear on paper, but when he said it, it was choppy."

Pragmatism brought Obama into the churches in the first place. To organize people in Roseland and nearby neighborhoods, he had to elicit the support of the black pastors. That goes back to the reason he was hired. Once he started attending, he came to appreciate the churches as the equivalent of a graduate school education, offering many subjects: elocution, rhetoric, political science, sociology, black history, anthropology. Then, slowly, came the final piece, the religion itself. Most of his conversations with Reverend Love were about community organizing, but gradually they began to talk about religion. "He is trying to make sense out of it, and the more successful he becomes the more pressure there is on him to find a church," Love said. "Because suddenly, he is the executive director of a church-based organizing group, and he is not in a church. He asked me if I thought that it was a conflict, and I said, 'Yeah, it is kind of a conflict.' But I suggested to him that he should not join a church just simply to fulfill a requirement, that he had to get his relationship with God settled first, and then join the church he was comfortable with." Love watched that relationship evolve. "The more he worked with churches, the more he began to experience that there was a theological framework even for the civil rights movement. And all of that was built on personal relationships, so he started investigating his own faith commitment and what he really believed. That probably took him a couple of years to go through that."

There was much for Obama to overcome. He was an inveterate doubter, an intellectual skeptic. How could that coincide with religious faith? His mother was a spiritual humanist; she honored all faiths but believed in none. He remembered how she dragged him to church on Christmas, just as she took him as a young boy in Indonesia to the magnificent Borobudur Buddhist temple outside Yogyakarta, and to a Japanese Shinto shrine and a Hawaiian burial site. Ann was essentially an atheist who disapproved of what she considered the narrow-mindedness and self-righteousness of so much of organized religion. As usual, it was his mother, far more than the father about whom he titled his memoir, who figured most heavily in his thinking. His experiences in Chicago, he later wrote,

> forced me to confront a dilemma that my mother never fully resolved in her own life: the fact that I had no community or shared traditions in which to ground my deeply held beliefs. The Christians with whom I worked recognized themselves in me; they saw that I knew their Book and shared their values and sang their songs. But they sensed that a part of me remained removed, detached, an observer among them. I came to realize that without a vessel for my beliefs, without an unequivocal commitment to a particular community of faith, I would be consigned at some level to always remain apart, free in a way that my mother was free, but also alone in the same ways she was ultimately alone.

Finding and being found – it would take a church. Here again, questions of politics and pragmatism emerged. If he chose a church within the boundaries of the Developing Communities Project, he ran the risk of alienating all the other pastors. Love, whose political instincts were sharpening along with Obama's, suggested that he "go meet with a pastor who was outside of our district, our geographical boundaries." That was L. K. Curry, Lacy Curry, the pastor at Emmanuel Baptist at 83rd and Damen, who had built his corner church from ten members in 1973 to thousands-strong by the mid-1980s. Obama went to see Curry, who took note of the young organizer's zeal for social justice and sent him along to a colleague who was more active in that realm, Reverend Jeremiah Alvesta Wright Jr. at the Trinity United Church of Christ. Trinity was also outside Obama's organizing district, though barely. "Our boundaries were 95th Street on the north, and Trinity sat on the north side of 95th Street," Love noted. "I used to tease Barack, 'You joined a church as close to the boundaries as you could get.'" It would take time for Obama to join and become fully engaged in Wright's church, a place where he would be baptized and married; that would not happen until later, during his second time around in Chicago, but the process started then, in October 1987.

Wright, Philadelphia-bred, son of a preacher, former Marine corpsman, with his vibrant, athletic nature, his silvery goatee, his fierce rhetoric, and his blunt intelligence, was a phenomenon on the South Side by the time Obama met him. No reticence here; he had a sizable ego and the personality of an agitator, hot to Obama's cool. He had grown his church to more than four thousand members, and done it in an encompassing way, maintaining a strong working-class base while attracting more and more members of the black professional class from the next generation. There was enough diversity within the congregation for almost any South Sider to feel at home. Jerry Kellman thought of Obama's arc toward organized religion – first committing himself to church, then to that specific church – as part of the larger choice "that he wanted to live his life in the black community. . . . Trinity was also part of that long search for home. He wasn't a member of the church during those first three years, but he was drawn to it, he was drawn to Jeremiah. Trinity wasn't elitist, though it was the place to be for bright young African Americans."

In practical terms, when it came to connecting his organizing work to the community, Reverend Love turned out to be more valuable than Reverend Wright. Trinity had the money and the social programs, but not the readiness to be part of a network. When it came to coalitions, Wright preferred to think nationally, not locally. He was a member of the Samuel Dewitt Proctor Conference, an alliance of big-name preachers around the country who saw it as their responsibility to set the agenda for the black community. Whereas Wright was twenty years older than Obama and presented himself as a wise man, Love was closer to Obama's age and saw that they could rise together, interconnected. They talked often about change and how to effect it, and how difficult it was to turn institutions around when you were down at the bottom. As Obama delved deeper into religion, Love grew more interested in organizing. He worked with Obama and the DCP directors to bring a worker training center to Roseland. He sent ten members of his church to Techny for weeklong Gamaliel Foundation training sessions, some of which were run by Obama himself. Those one-on-one sessions, Love said decades later, counted among the most lasting positive effects of Obama's years in community organizing: "He did those training sessions for my core people here at Lilydale and that has paid off in spades for me for the last twenty-five years." Love considered Obama the most effective trainer he encountered in Chicago – patient, calm, excellent at drawing people out and inspiring them. Yet he too could see that Obama was not perfectly suited for all aspects of the Alinsky or Galluzzo method. "His temperament and personality didn't seem to fit with the agitation component," Love said. "They were completely different. Barack did not agitate. No fist pounding. No raising of the voice. He had that calm, rational, let's think this through demeanor, let's find a common ground. He's had that all along and that's helped shape him. Sometimes I wish he would pound his fist on the table."

How long would Obama last in the organizing world with that temperament? It was a question that Ernie Cortes, a legendary Texas organizer and national leader of the Industrial Areas Foundation, had already considered. Cortes had met Obama the previous summer at a ten-day IAF training session held at the Mount St. Mary's College campus in Los Angeles. Johnnie Owens had also come along, he and Obama both sponsored by grants from Chicago's nonprofit Woods Foundation. During the day they spent hours role-playing, studying the meaning of power through examples in history, from the classical age to modern Nicaragua. Cortes, with his long hair, bulky chest, and confident demeanor, dressed in a sport coat without a tie, served as the moderator, a sort of Greek God who could impose his thoughts and will on the trainees as he wished, always with a point in mind. His lessons were clear: *Don't be passive. Don't get stuck in ideology. Don't rely on the kindness of others. Don't be self-delusional. Look at the world clearly. Don't give your power away.* His favorite role-playing scene involved the Melian dialogue from Thucydides' *History of the Peloponnesian War.* Melos was a Greek island in the Peloponnese that in the years 416–415 B.C. faced an invasion threat from the powerful Athenians. The dialogue was an intricate philosophical and practical debate between the Athenians and Melians on the wisdom or foolishness of an impending invasion. "The dialogue is a back-and-forth between Melians and

Athenians on whether to surrender or be destroyed," Cortes said. He wanted his organizers to end with a firm conviction to not be Melians.

Obama seemed impatient with the role playing, according to Cortes. "He thought by virtue of his intellect and personality he could bring people together. He never had an edge, what we call a bias toward action, a willingness to combat, to draw a line at some point." But Cortes could see that this was "a talented, bright guy" who was eager to learn – so bright, in fact, that they tried to hire him away from the Chicago group. He just needed the right mentor, Cortes thought, someone who could teach him the proper balance, the delicate tension between power and love and how they were not opposites "but conjugal, self-interest and self-sacrifice, they go together." During those days in California, Cortes often sat next to Obama on the bus as the group traveled through Los Angeles to various sites and actions. "He was trying to figure out who he was, whether he wanted to do this work or not," Cortes recalled. "We talked mostly about his father, the fact that he did not know him. So I said to him, 'Why don't you go to Kenya?'"

The thought had weighed on Obama for years: He would go to Africa. He knew nothing at first about what he would find there, beyond what his mother had told him and what he had gleaned from those few letters Barack Sr. had sent from Nairobi. Now the old man was five years gone, and the constructed story of his life was disintegrating, year by year.

"P.S. I will be in Wash. D.C. from Dec. 20–24 to visit a brother who moved there. If you're in D.C. then to visit your folks, then we can get together. My brother's name is Roy Obama, his ph. (202) 546-3397."

Obama wrote that in November 1985, in a letter to Phil Boerner. In his memoir, the trip to see this brother came later, after he had learned much about his father and his Kenyan family from a visit to Chicago by his sister Auma. In a family of many half siblings, Roy and Auma had the same mother and father, Barack Sr. and Kezia. They both had endured the trauma of that breakup and years of violence and separation when their father was married to the American, Ruth. Roy was called Bobby back then, and later would go by Malik, but in the 1980s he was simply Roy. He had married an American himself, a former Peace Corps volunteer, and had moved with her to Washington, but the marriage was collapsing by the time he and his half brother made contact. Barack's holiday visit proved mostly unsatisfying. He could not stay with Roy because of the imminent divorce, and ended up in a dreary hotel. Roy was a big man, over two hundred pounds, with a deep voice and jovial outward personality. Inside that round face Barack saw the face of their father, and at dinner Roy told Barack that he was haunted by the old man. Nothing Roy ever did was good enough for Barack Sr., he said. And now he worried that his father's demons had become his own. As they navigated the streets of the nation's capital, Barack became alarmed by his brother's driving. Roy treated the roadway "like bumper cars." Their father had died in a traffic accident. Here was a reincarnation of Mr. Toad. Roy was distracted; this was not the time for brotherly bonding. After one day, Barack cut short the visit and returned to Chicago.

In the narrative of *Dreams from My Father,* before Obama made that truncated trip to Washington, but well into his organizing days in Chicago, he was paid a visit by Auma. There was one apparent discrepancy in his account. Obama described his anxiety as he waited for Auma's arrival in Chicago – how he raced from the parking lot to the airport terminal as fast as he could, "panting for breath," holding an old photograph of his never-seen sister in his hand, his eyes "scanning the crowds of Indians, Germans, Poles, Thais, and Czechs gathering their luggage." Decades later Auma would tell a different story, first reported by Roger Cohen, a columnist at the *New York Times.* By her account, she was afraid the visit might not go as planned, so to protect herself made arrangements first to visit a friend named Elsie at Southern Illinois University. She arrived in Chicago not on a transatlantic flight but at the end of a seven-hour ramble through the Illinois cornfields by bus. They would have met at the downtown Greyhound station, not at O'Hare.

Whether he heard it first from Roy or Auma, and however Auma made her way to Chicago, in the end the transformative moment was the same. What Barack learned was devastating, disillusioning. The mythology carefully constructed by his mother was shattered. His missing father was far from what had been portrayed – not the moral man, not the freedom fighter, not the polished professional. Brilliant, yes, but brilliance splintered by drinking, despair, dissolution, and disappointment. The revelations, Obama wrote later, disoriented him "as though I had woken up to find a blue sun in a yellow sky." That seems overly dramatic, considering how dubious he was about his father for so long. But in the end this revised history was both alarming and strangely liberating. Where once he felt an obligation to live up to his father's standards, he would thereafter carry a different burden, not necessarily lighter but less debilitating and more energizing. Now he would achieve not to please his late father, but to redeem him.

Two and a half years into his Chicago life, Obama had developed an attachment to the city, less exhausting than New York, more intense and variegated than Los Angeles. He had served his apprenticeship on the South Side in an endlessly frustrating job that nonetheless meant at least as much to his development as it had to the people he was trying to help. As Mike Kruglik later reflected in a revealing documentary, *Becoming Barack:* "When Obama came to Chicago he was already good looking. He was already beautifully spoken. He was already quite polished but politically he was a baby. And he found these concepts, principles, disciplines, techniques of community organizing were mother's milk to the baby. And that's how deeply he drank of them and how powerfully they nurtured his thought and development." But now he was about done with it. He had picked up the most valuable lessons: he had learned how to listen and how to relate to people, and he had come to understand the concepts of power. Community organizing could take him only so far without becoming another of life's traps. It represented something noble but inevitably limiting – in that sense much like his mother's life and career – that shaped him but that he wanted to move beyond.

There was no single transformative moment, but two specific incidents had struck him as clear examples of the limits of this work. One involved the fight to keep a steel mill open. They had the people, the workers, the churches, everything on their side, but in the end that meant nothing, he realized, compared to the dollars-and-cents decision that would be "made in some boardroom." The local community "might have input, but only at the margins." Another lesson came when Mayor Washington traveled to Roseland to appear at an event with Obama and his DCP leaders. Obama had prepared his organizers for the event, going over what they should say to the mayor to press for more attention for their neglected neighborhood. "I got together all my leaders and told them to make sure to pin him down, this, that, and the other," Obama said later, expounding on his organizing days during an interview in the White House. "And he comes out and they were all looking at him starry-eyed, and he was making jokes and flirting with the women and . . . you just had this sense that his ability to move people and set an agenda was always going to be superior to anything I could organize at a local level."

Here was the charisma of power. Power that was larger, more encompassing, and that could come only from politics and established institutions, power that demanded a more granular understanding of how the world worked. He decided to apply to law school and sent applications to Harvard, Stanford, and Yale.

The past was falling away. At midmorning on November 25, 1987, Harold Washington was talking to an aide at his desk at City Hall when he collapsed of a massive heart attack. Within hours, the first black mayor in Chicago history was dead. In a sense, the idea of Harold Washington had brought Obama to Chicago, but his experience in the city had done precisely what Jerry Kellman thought it would: it had made him a realist, without the blinders of false optimism, able to look at the world as it is. He had watched Washington struggle for legitimacy against the old-line white city political structure in what became known as the Council Wars, fights that in their blind tribal ferocity and racial implications only demoralized the confrontation-averse Obama. He had watched many bureaucrats from the mayor's administration – the housing administrators involved in the asbestos issue were only one example – turn away from suffering constituencies. And he had studied the ways Washington had succeeded and failed. "He liked Harold," said Kellman. "Everyone did." But it was nothing close to hero worship. If Obama ever considered Washington a role model, those thoughts were gone before the man was. By the time Washington died, Obama was looking at him through rational eyes. His focus was "on how effective Harold was in getting things done, or not," said Kellman. "It was detached analysis of what worked and what didn't."

Kellman knew Obama would be moving on soon. Earlier that fall, they had attended a conference together at Harvard Divinity School and shared a room for a few days at the Copley Square Hotel in Boston. Obama retired early; Kellman was a night owl. The theme of the conference was politics and the black church. There was much reminiscing about the good old days of the civil rights movement, but among many notable speakers, the presentation that stood out was by William Julius Wilson, the University of Chicago sociologist. In graph after graph, Wilson showed how a community disintegrated when jobs disappeared: the correlation between unemployment and domestic violence, unemployment and alcoholism, unemployment and divorce, unemployment and mental health. One day as they were taking a stroll across the Harvard Quad between sessions, Obama told Kellman, "There's something I need to tell you." His tone was deferential and warm. He said he was planning to leave his job and go to law school. He had sent in applications and would hear back in a few months. There were two reasons for the decision, he said. First, he did not want to end up like his father. Law school would send him on the way toward economic security, something his father never had. And second, he had concluded that community organizers did not have enough power. Their work was important on the street level, where small victories were hard earned, but to change the conditions that Professor Wilson laid out so clearly would require a power that was wider and stronger. Law school would arm him with more skills, more power to effect social change. It would allow him to engage in a more public life. Kellman thought this meant Obama might try to follow Harold Washington and run for mayor of Chicago. He had never heard what Obama's Pakistani friend Beenu Mahmood had – that question from Barack about whether he could be president.

The acceptance letter from Harvard arrived in the mail in February. Obama had kept his future plans closely held, sharing them with only a few close friends. Johnnie Owens was told one day when he stopped by the apartment in Hyde Park. "The way he said it was, 'John, are you ready to lead?' I said, 'Yeah, of course I am,'" Owens recalled. "I didn't understand why he was asking. He said, 'Well, you know the time is closer than you think.' He said, 'I'm leaving.' I thought, 'Why, you son of a gun! You're just gonna leave!' I left my job and now you're telling me you're leaving?' He continued to say, 'I'm going to Harvard and I'd like you to take on the directorship and I'll work with you on the political side to make it happen.'"

The news came in two beats, as Owens remembered it. First Obama said he was leaving. Then a pause. Then he was going to Harvard. He asked

Owens how he felt about it. Well, of course, Harvard was a great opportunity, Owens replied. Anyone could understand why he would want that to happen. But something was eating at Owens, a suspicion that this was in the works from the beginning, from the day Obama had first interrogated him in that one-on-one at the Friends of the Parks office downtown, the first step in luring him into community organizing. "He was probably looking for somebody to replace him when he met me, that's almost a certainty," Owens said decades later. The thought annoyed him a bit, but in the long run, whatever the intentions, if he was recruited "in good faith or not in good faith," the results were the same, and overwhelmingly positive. Leaving the comforts of downtown, getting back into the community, being tested, expanding his horizons, taking a leadership role, having a solid base – it was all for the better, Owens concluded, and all because of Obama.

A few months later, with his life in relative order, Harvard awaiting, Chicago firmly established as home, notions of a political future still amorphous but taking shape, Barack Hussein Obama II at last set out in search of his African roots. He spent a few weeks in Europe on the way over. In his memoir, he wrote about that leg of the trip with a sense of disengagement, or estrangement, much as he had done when describing the world of Genevieve Cook's family. He was the Moviegoer again, or the Invisible Man, one step removed, the disconnected observer. He recorded the passing scene in his journal, describing "children chasing each other through the chestnut groves of Luxembourg Garden" in Paris and night falling over the Palatine in Rome as he waited "for the first stars to appear, listening to the wind and its whispers of mortality." But through it all he was edgy and defensive. Stopping in Europe had been a mistake. It was beautiful, he conceded. "It just wasn't mine. I felt as if I were living out someone else's romance, the incompleteness of my own history stood between me and the sites I saw like a hard pane of glass."

All of that changed the moment he landed in Nairobi. For the first time in his life, he wrote, he enjoyed "the comfort, the firmness of identity." The sensation washed over him when a woman who worked at British Airways recognized his last name. In truth, that was not the big deal he thought it was. The same thing had happened when Ruth Baker, white and Jewish, had arrived at the same airport twenty years earlier. A friendly airport employee then had also recognized the name Obama, happened to know the Barack Obama she was looking for, and had even offered her a place to stay until she found him. But life is all in the context, and young Obama took his greeting as a sign of family comfort. As in Chicago, he was finding and being found.

In Nairobi he stayed with his newfound African sister, sleeping on her living-room couch. Auma, with an intellect at least the equal of her father and American brother, had spent much of the decade studying at the University of Heidelberg in Germany and was now teaching at the University of Nairobi. When she was busy, he would walk around town, taking many of his meals at a small teahouse near the campus. When she was free, they would drive around the city in her baby-blue Volkswagen Beetle. She spoke German and was partial to German things, but the VW was ten years old and barely functional. It broke down once on the road across from Uhuru Park, and Auma and Barack had to push it to the curb until some young men came to fix it. Barack was surrounded by curious relatives in Nairobi – aunts and uncles, cousins of various sorts, sisters and brothers also of various sorts, some, like Auma and Roy, clearly the offspring of his father, others possibly not. Everyone embraced the newcomer, pounding him with affection, and it took him some time to realize the ruptures in the clan. Barack Sr., with his American education and his professional job, had been the big man in the family, and they all had a claim to his legacy, genealogical and financial. There was Akumu, Barack Sr.'s biological mother, and his two sisters, Auma and Sarah. There was Kezia, the first wife, and Jael, the last. And there was the other Sarah, now known as Granny or Mama Sarah, who had been Hussein Onyango's last wife and laid claim as Barack Sr.'s mother figure and matriarch to the generation of the younger Auma and Barack. They were all still contesting the old man's will. He did not die a wealthy man, but he had more money than the rest of them. The internecine dispute was not something Barack expected to encounter or wanted to unravel, so he relied largely on Auma to sort things out for him.

Obama had come to Kenya hoping to put all the pieces of his shattered genealogy back together again. His young life had been a struggle to integrate the disparate parts of his history in a way that would make him feel whole. Instead his trip offered only more contradictions that were hard to reconcile. He found a sense of warmth among his Kenyan relatives that he had never felt before, but beneath that he also gleaned the divisions that defined African life, if not all of humanity. Day after day he learned more about the unresolved tribalism separating Luo and Kikuyu and African and Asian. One morning when he and Auma went to a travel agency to book tickets, Auma complained about the "arrogant" Indians who ran the shop. Another racial stereotype, and one that for Barack hit too close to home. It made him think about Hasan Chandoo, Wahid Hamid, Imad Husain, Sohale Siddiqi, Vinai Thummalapally, Asad Jumabhoy, Beenu Mahmood, all his Pakistani and Indian friends, "friends who lent me money when I was tight and had taken me into their homes when I'd had no place to stay." He thought Auma was being closed-minded; she thought he was being naïve.

Everything he saw and heard in Kenya was material for his journals. He wrote in them every day, usually devoting at least two hours to them each morning or night. Part III of his memoir, titled "Kenya," came almost directly from what he wrote in those journals, and for that reason was "by far the easiest to write," he said later. "I almost transcribed my journal into the book." Easy for him, perhaps, but a little less so for Henry Ferris, who edited most of the first edition of *Dreams from My Father* for Times Books. Ferris found Obama quick and easy to work with, but he spent much of his time paring down the manuscript, which was "bloated" in places. Ferris also recalled that the Kenya section had not been written when he first received the manuscript and that Obama in fact traveled to Kenya a second time for further research before turning in the last part of the book. Asked about that second trip decades later, during an interview in the Oval Office, Obama said, "I did take a second trip to Africa, but all the stuff that I learned about the family, that was all in the first trip. The second trip was essentially me doing more background on things like Kenyan history. That was as close as I came to fact-checking, was that second trip. But that initial narrative, that I did not compress, that all happened on the first trip."

There were two memorable episodes during Obama's first journey to Kenya. One was in Nairobi, when Auma took him to see their father's third wife, the second American, the one after Ann Dunham, Ruth Ndesandjo. The visit as he described it in *Dreams from My Father* was disorienting and uncomfortable, a culture clash. He started by portraying Ruth's neighborhood, the Westlands, as "an enclave of expensive homes set off by wide lawns and well-tended hedges." This was rendered in contrast to the cramped apartments where the city dwellers among the Obama relatives lived. He also compared it to the commodious suburban homes of wealthy Punahou classmates in Honolulu, and recalled "the envy I felt toward those classmates whenever they invited me over to play in their big backyards or swim in their swimming pools." It was not just envy that he recalled, but also "the sense of quiet desperation those big, pretty houses seemed to contain." With that prelude, little sympathy could flow toward Ruth. The only reason he and Auma went to see her, he wrote, was because she had invited them, and had done so impersonally, by sending a messenger with a note requesting their presence at her house. There is much about Obama's description of this encounter in his memoir that Ruth would later dispute. By her recollection, Barack and Auma showed up unannounced, discombobulating her. Auma "was the catalyst, she brought him to my house, that's what I remember," Ruth said later. "I have a sitting room. I was sitting on the couch. My husband was in his chair. I thought Mark was in the other chair." Mark was her first son by Obama Sr. He had taken the name Ndesandjo and was home on break from his physics studies at Stanford University. "And then Auma came in. She hadn't alerted me, as I remember. I like to be alerted. This was pretty traumatic. She said, 'This is Barack.' Or 'This is Dad's son from Hawaii.' Now this was a time when I couldn't face something like that, okay? And everyone wanted to know about Obama Sr., and as I remember it, I closed up. I had nothing to say."

The tension of that moment is understandable on all sides. There was no reason Auma would have had fond feelings for Ruth. Auma had endured a traumatic childhood, being yanked from her mother to stay with an alcoholic father, a cruel if matter-of-fact reality in the rigidly paternalistic Luo society. And Ruth, by her own admission, offered Auma no motherly comfort, saving that for her own sons. When Auma and Barack appeared at Ruth's house, it was nearly two decades after she had left Barack Sr. and six years after his death, yet her experiences with him remained so searing that she could not easily accommodate the presence of this American son. "I gave him a very cold reception," she acknowledged later of that meeting, "but I didn't have the capacity to talk with him or exchange with him because he was a reflection of a man I hated. So I didn't want anything to do with him." In the memoir, Obama wrote that the cold reception included her asking him snippily why he kept the surname Obama and, upon hearing that he was accepted at Harvard Law School, surmising that his academic success must have been because he didn't grow up with his father. Ruth later said she did not remember making either of those comments. She knew that Barack Sr. had been brilliant, so she never would have doubted the intelligence of his offspring and was ostenta-tiously proud of the intellect of her son Mark, who was also the old man's son. But she also believed that anyone who did not have to live with Barack Sr. was lucky.

The other episode occurred out in Luoland, when Barack and Auma and her mother, Kezia, and a few other relatives took the overnight train from Nairobi to Kisumu and at daybreak clambered onto a crowded *matatu* (the Kenyan jitney bus) for the ride up to Nyang'oma Kogelo to see Mama Sarah. Many of his Luo relatives vividly remembered this trip to the Lake Victoria region. Part of the time, the American was with sister Auma, they recalled, and part of the time with brother Roy, who had returned from Washington and was reinventing himself in his homeland. With the extended family divided between central and southern Nyanza, Barack divided his time as well, visiting the competing locales of the Obama story, the Kanyadhiang homestead near Kendu Bay where Barack Sr. was born and the Nyang'oma Kogelo homestead where Hussein Onyango and Barack Sr. were buried. Nyang'oma Kogelo was where Mama Sarah lived, and because of family friction was also the preferred place of Auma, who called it "Home Squared." She went with him there, but not to Kendu Bay.

The relatives at the Kanyadhiang compound then and later would con-sider themselves the lost people of the Obama story. Most were not named in *Dreams from My Father* or were given pseudonyms. Barack stayed in Kanyadhiang for two days. He slept on the hard mud floor of a thatched-roof hut belonging to Elly Yonga's mother. This was just up the oxcart path from the dance hall where Barack Obama Sr. had met his first wife, Kezia. Elly's father was the son of Opiyo Obama, the brother of Barack Sr.'s father, Hus-sein Onyango. He was nine years older than Barack Jr. and lived in Nairobi then, but came out when he heard that the American relative was visiting. Also at the compound was Charles Oluoch, whose father, Peter, had been taken in by Hussein Onyango before Barack Sr. was born, and who was considered Barack Sr.'s older brother. Barack Sr. had lived with Peter and his family in Mombasa on the Kenyan coast after he left Maseno. Charles was seven years older than Barack Jr. The strongest memory he and Elly Yonga had of Barack Jr.'s visit was that he recoiled at the fish they served with bones and eyes still in it. He did eat the rice and *ugali*. They kept photographs of the visit, young Barack wearing denim jeans, a short-sleeve white shirt, and tennis shoes. There was also a younger cousin, Razik Magak, who had some experience with Westerners working as a beachboy at a resort on Lake Victoria. His mother was the older Auma, Barack Sr.'s younger sister, who ran a charcoal shop on the side of the road and was an alcoholic, as her older brother had been. "My mom told us, 'He's your brother. He's the son of my brother Barack,'" Razik Magak said later, recalling Barack's visit. "So I said 'Oh, okay. . . . Everyone was curious about him. We had all heard the stories. . . . We knew there was a son over there." Razik and Barack hung out together for a day, fishing for Nile perch in Lake Victoria, drinking *chang'aa*, the homemade whiskey, and smoking weed. "Barack was experimenting with too many things during the visit, his first time in Africa. It was *Test this. Test this*. He said, 'I eat so much, so many things.' There was a time he complained of stomach upset."

Most of the side trip was spent in Nyang'oma Kogelo, Home Squared. Among the sensations Obama experienced there, one day stood out, at least as he described it in *Dreams from My Father*. Nothing special happened that day: he followed Mama Sarah to the market, enjoyed the "nutty-sweet taste" of sugarcane, mended a hole in the property fence, and watched the old woman grab a rooster and slit its neck. Nothing special, yet its everyday ordinariness made Barack feel that "everything I was doing, every touch and breath and word, carried the full weight of my life; that a full circle was beginning to close, so that I might finally recognize myself as I was, here, now, in one place." The mood was broken only once, he recalled, when he found himself alone with Granny and the conversation stopped abruptly after they had exhausted their knowledge of the other's language. She had said "Halo," he had said

"*Musawa*," and that was that, at least in the book. The scene, as Mama Sarah recalled it later, had a more provocative twist.

In Luo, a grandson is known as "a little husband." When her American grandson, or step-grandson, walked down the road carrying potatoes for her, some other grandsons started to tease her. "Now she has got a young white husband," they joked. "Now that she has found a white man, so it seems she has already left us."

"Yes," she said, "I have a brand-new husband. You always left my things outside to be rained on. Now I have a man who can take care of that."

Obama laughed along with everyone else. He had no idea what they were talking about.

In his memoir, Obama presented a twenty-page section as one long narration from Mama Sarah on the complicated family history, from Obong'o to Opiyo to Opiyo Obama to Hussein Onyango to Barack Obama. She did not speak English, and he did not know Luo, so the unbroken discourse was said to have come through Auma's translation while he took notes in his journal. Some of the story was true, some of it family mythology, none of it easy or comfortable – a story of grueling journeys, splintered relations, cruel husbands, suffering women, tribal superstitions, racist colonialists, great expectations lost in alcohol. After the story was finished, and after Barack had been shown some of the tangible remnants of the lives of his forebears, the registration book that his grandfather had to carry as a native servant, a letter that Betty Mooney had written trying to get his father admitted to an American college, he stepped out of Mama Sarah's hut and into the yard, walked to the corner by the mango tree, fell to his knees between the graves of Hussein Onyango and Barack Hussein Obama, and wept.

When Obama returned to Chicago from his African sojourn, he brought gifts for Loretta, Yvonne, Margaret, Deacon Dan, and Johnnie, and also for Adam Kellman, Jerry's son, and Henry Kruglik, Mike's son. The women of Developing Communities organized a party for him at Chuck Cavallini's in suburban Midlothian. He seemed to relax, Loretta remembered, with tie off, collar open, shirtsleeves rolled up. A life of leaving and being left had come full circle. He would be leaving soon, but never again in the same way. "I made these enormous attachments, much deeper attachments than I would have expected," he said later of that time. This made leaving difficult in one sense, but easier in another. "I knew that I would come back. . . . I had relationships there, people who cared deeply about me and that I cared deeply about." In Chicago he had found the place to which he could always return.

The old blue Honda Civic was gone; he had sold it before departing for Europe and Africa. Now he had another car, a used yellow Datsun that cost five hundred dollars. A hole would grow in the floorboard, but the engine was good enough to get him where he had to go. No life could have been more the product of randomness than his. From the heritage of Hussein Onyango, the *jadak,* and Ruth Armour Dunham, the young suicide victim; from a chance meeting of students in Russian class in Honolulu; from the chaos of peripatetic ancestors; from a childhood in distant Hawaii and more distant Indonesia; from the rootless feelings of a double outsider as a biracial and cross-cultural kid; and after nine years, starting from the moment he reached Occidental and the mainland, of intense introspection, trying to figure things out, to make sense of his life – from all that he had found not only a home but a path, and was driving hard now, toward Harvard Law, a stop on the way to his family's unimaginable destination, his own *el dorado.*

CODA

Barack Obama was twenty-seven when he reached Harvard Law School. An unpredictable jumble of happenstance, skill, propitious timing, uncommon will, and sheer luck would carry him forward from there, but the basic design had been set for his future. He knew, at last, who he was, and had a sense of what he wanted to be.

1989 At the end of his first year at Harvard, Obama returns to Chicago to work as a summer associate at Sidley & Austin, the elite firm where his friend Beenu Mahmood had interned. His mentor there is Michelle Robinson, who proves to be the strong black woman Genevieve Cook had predicted would come into his life.

1991 Obama is elected president of the *Harvard Law Review,* the first African American leader in its history.

1992 In February, Stanley Armour Dunham dies of cancer in Honolulu at seventy-three. In October, Barack and Michelle are married in Chicago.

1995 *Dreams from My Father* is published in July, to little public notice. Four months later, on November 7, Stanley Ann Dunham, Barack's mother, dies of uterine cancer, three weeks before her fifty-third birthday.

1996 Obama is elected to the Illinois state senate, serving in the Democratic minority in Springfield.

1998 Malia Ann Obama is born in Chicago.

2000 Obama runs for the U.S. House of Representatives in Chicago's First Congressional District in a primary challenge against incumbent Bobby Rush. He loses.

2001 Natasha (Sasha) Obama is born in Chicago.

2002 Democrats gain control of the Illinois state senate after redistricting, placing Obama in the majority for the first time.

2004 Obama wins the Democratic primary election for the U.S. Senate, delivers the keynote address at the Democratic National Convention in Boston in August, and becomes an overnight sensation. *Dreams from My Father* jumps from the remainder bin to bestsellerdom. That November he easily wins the Senate seat.

2007 On February 10, Obama announces his candidacy for president.

2008 On August 28, twenty years after he left Chicago for Harvard Law, Obama accepts the Democratic presidential nomination in Denver on the forty-fifth anniversary of Martin Luther King Jr.'s "I Have a Dream" speech. On November 2, Madelyn Payne Dunham, his grandmother, dies in Honolulu at eighty-six. Two days later, on November 4, Obama defeats Republican senator John McCain of Arizona in the presidential election.

2009 On January 20, Barack Hussein Obama is sworn in as the forty-fourth president of the United States, the first African American president in history.

ACKNOWLEDGMENTS

For the final year of researching this book, I was lucky enough to have Gabrielle Banks, an extraordinary journalist, working with me from across the continent in Los Angeles. This marked the first time in ten books that I had a full-time assistant, although that description does not do her justice. From late January 2011 through Thanksgiving, when the manuscript was completed, Gabrielle was tireless and skillful in finding people and gathering information from interview subjects and documents, unfailingly enthusiastic in our shared mission to figure out Barack Obama and his family, and invariably precise in her editing and fact-checking. My gratitude in this case extends also to David Shribman, for whom Gaby had earlier worked at Pittsburgh's *Post-Gazette*. His e-mail recommending her came out of the blue, as though he were reading my mind.

Julie Tate, a world-class researcher at the *Washington Post,* somehow found extra hours in her week to help as well in all of those same ways. As many of my *Post* colleagues would attest, Julie is a force of nature, with an uncanny ability to find anything and anybody, and there is no one better to have on your side.

The process of writing a book is a long and winding journey. This one, for me, was especially so, in the best sense possible. The research took me around the world, to many places I might never have gone to otherwise, and the exhilaration of the adventure was heightened by the many wonderful people who helped along the way.

My wife and I had an unforgettable time tracing Obama's roots in Kenya and were lucky to be in the company of what we called the O Team as we explored the territory from Nairobi out to Lake Victoria. The O Team consisted of Kennethy Opala, Beatrice Okelo, and Gideon Okusi. In their vivid presence, we became Odavid and Olinda. Ken, one of Nairobi's top young journalists, was expert at finding documents and dealing with the many people and strands of the Kenya side of the story. I found Beatrice during a summer in Madison when I needed someone to translate several documents from the Dholuo language and she turned out to be the one Luo student at the University of Wisconsin. As it happened, Beatrice grew up in a village only a few miles from where the Obamas lived, and was returning home on holiday during the weeks of our trip, so she also served as our interpreter in western Kenya. Gideon came to us through his work as a driver for Stephanie McCrummen at the *Post*'s Nairobi bureau, and he proved to be so much more than a driver. We never would have found our way around Kenya without his skill and fearlessness. Thanks also to Zoe Alsop, who got me started in Kenya; Lisa Lawley Nesbitt, who helped the team greatly in Nairobi and Mombasa; and Peter Slen, Opeter the Hippo Man, who became part of a backseat comedy duo with my wife during our harrowing drives across the country.

To reach Indonesia, I booked what was called the longest nonstop flight in the world, leaving Newark at eleven at night and landing in Singapore nineteen hours later, then taking the last little hop down to Jakarta. The flight, and the entire trip, would have been daunting if not for an old friend who tagged along – the adventurous Mark London, who, when not practicing law in Washington, D.C., likes to hang out in remote stretches of the Amazon. Mark served as my videographer and photographer, and with his good humor kept things rollicking wherever we went. The peerless Fenty Effendy, another great young journalist, served as our guide and interpreter in Indonesia. Although Fenty had been helping me from afar for more than a year, it was not until I reached Jakarta that I fully realized how revered she was by her colleagues in Indonesia, and how blessed I was to have her on the team. She had an uncanny knack for getting the story and, while doing everything else, including producing a national television interview show, showed us a marvelous time with her many lively friends. Mark and I began and ended our trip in their midst at Decanter, which is now my favorite wine bar in the world.

The Hawaii part of the story connected me to Ron Jacobs, a character unlike any I have met in forty years in journalism. How to describe RJ? Rumbling baritone, relentless pain in the butt, expert on native Hawaiian music, island historian, poet, author, punster, Rams fanatic, creative talent, able guide, researcher, and photographer. My trips to Hawaii were brightened considerably not only by friendly strangers and gorgeous weather and scenery but also by several conversations with Maya Soetoro-Ng, Obama's warm and insightful little sister. For an April trip to Kansas, we stayed first with the life-affirming Von Drehle clan in Kansas City before heading south and west, down the Flint Hills toward El Dorado, a drive made memorable by the moonscape vista of earth recently burned to black to enrich the soil for grazing cattle. I had known of Kansas roots in my family, but it was not until we explored Butler County that I realized the dot on the map where my grandmother was born – Leon, Kansas – was situated between El Dorado and Augusta, the towns of Stanley Armour Dunham and Madelyn Payne Dunham, Obama's maternal grandparents. Our perceptive guides in Kansas were Lisa Cooley at the Butler County History Center, Belinda Larson at the *Augusta Gazette,* and Sonja Sommers Milbourn at Butler Community College.

I owe special debts of gratitude to Bonnie Crarey Ryan at Syracuse University Library, David Easterbrook at Northwestern's Melville J. Herskovits Library of African Studies, and Robert Stout, a retired army engineer who became a master of Internet research. Also helping dig out archival documents or find people scattered around the country were Tim Frank in Washington, Sterling Greenwood in Texas, Philip Lipson in Seattle, Kalie Kissoon and Dean Schaffer at Stanford University, and my great friend Neil Henry in Seattle and Berkeley. Neil, who had lived in Nairobi while working at the *Post,* was also helpful in reading the Africa chapters. Other early readers of the manuscript were Paul Hendrickson, magical writer, and Pat Toomay, magical thinker. Jim Warren, who has done close readings of all my manuscripts, performed that task again, this time bringing along his knowledge of Chicago. Jim and his far better half, Cornelia Grumman, not only offered wisdom on Barack Obama but also provided places for me to stay in Chicago and New York. Don Graham, the most prolific reader at the newspaper company he runs, was also generous with his reading time, as was Maralee Schwartz. Bob Woodward was there when I needed him for wise counsel. I can always count on my close pals Michael Weisskopf, Rick Atkinson, and Anne Hull. Thanks also to Rebekah Weisskopf; Jane Atkinson; Elsa Walsh; Michael and Beth Norman; Jim Wooten and Patience O'Connor; Chip Brown and Kate Betts; Blaine Harden and Jessica Kowal; Bob Kaiser; Leonard Downie; Glenn Frankel; R. B. Brenner; John Feinstein; Trip and Heddy Reid; Mike Kail; Del Wilber; Kim Vergeront and Andy Cohn; and the Lombardi theater family – Eric Simonson, Tommy Kail, Judith Light, Dan Lauria, Bill Dawes, Keith Nobbs, Rob Riley, Chris Sullivan, Tony Ponturo, and Fran Kirmser. My former *Post* colleague Bill Drozdiak helped me in the most unexpected and deeply appreciated way.

From Clinton to Obama, with eight books in between, I've relied on the same people to guide my way. My agent through it all has been Rafe Sagalyn, a font of sound advice when he is not slouching down the Bethesda fairways lowering his golf handicap (or perhaps even when he is). And my one and only editor has been the incomparable Alice Mayhew, who always seems to know exactly what I need to do to keep going. Thanks also to Lauren Clark and Shannon O'Neill at the Sagalyn Literary Agency, who keep Rafe in line, and to the devoted and talented crew at Simon & Schuster: Jonathan Karp, Julia Prosser, Rachelle Andujar, Jackie Seow, Ruth Lee-Mui, Karyn Marcus, Rachel Bergmann, Jonathan Evans, and copy editor Judith Hoover.

In spending so much time studying the generations of another family, I was constantly reminded of how fortunate I've been with my own family: my brother, Jim, and sister-in-law Gigi; my sister, Jean Alexander, and brother-in-law Michael; my sister-in-law Carol Garner and her husband, Ty; my brother-in-law Dick Porter and his wife, Mary Ann; and my father-in-law, Ritchey T. Porter, along with a talented passel of cousins, nephews, and nieces.

Andrew, in Tennessee with his wife, Alison, and the delightful Eliza, the little goose; and Sarah, in New Jersey with her husband, Tom, and the joyous redheads, Heidi and Ava, fill my life to overflowing. Once again and as always, there would be no meaning to any of this without Linda, the quirky saint who has been at my side for forty-two years – making lifelong friends wherever we travel; snuggling close on long airplane flights; taking pictures and videos of all we see; cleaning toothpaste off my tie, food off my cheek, hair off my sport coat; singing alternate verses to Robert Earl Keen's "Then Came Lo Mein" on a five-hundred-mile drive back to Washington; driving me crazy and crazy in love; reading every word, first and last, pushing me to make it clear and true – a wondrously good partner for the story of our lives.

NOTES

ONE: IN SEARCH OF EL DORADO

Key archives for primary documents related to Kansas in chapters 2, 4, 5, 9, and 18 include Kansas State Historical Society in Topeka; Topeka Room, Topeka and Shawnee County Public Library; Butler County Historical Society; *Augusta Daily Gazette* archives; Wichita Public Library; Virginia Ewalt private collection, Augusta.

1   *On Thanksgiving morning in 1926:* Narrative account of Ruth Armour Dunham suicide in Topeka and events immediately following drawn from *Topeka State Journal*, Nov. 25–27, 1926; *Topeka Daily Capital*, Nov. 26–27, 1926; *El Dorado Times*, Nov. 26–Dec. 1, 1926; *Wichita Eagle*, Nov. 26, 1926; *Topeka Classified Business Directory*, 1924–26; *Polk County Directory* 1923; *Wichita Beacon*, Oct. 12, 1915; *El Dorado Times*, Oct. 28, 1926; Sedgwick County, Kansas, Marriage Records; Thirteenth Census of the United States: 1910, Sedgwick County; Fourteenth Census of the United States: 1920 – Population, Sedgwick County; Fifteenth Census of the United States: Population Schedule, Butler County; author observations at sites in Topeka, El Dorado, and Wichita; interviews with Ralph Dunham Jr.

7   El dorado *is Spanish for:* Description of El Dorado history and oil boom drawn from *Paradise Lost*, book II ("and yet unspoiled / Guiana, whose great city Geryon's sons / Call El Dorado"); Castaneda, *The Journey of Coronado*; White, *Kansas* (214, 268–69); Green, *Midian* (184–85); Clymer, *The Kingdom of Butler County*; Theresa Welty, "El Dorado Oil," Butler County Historical Society paper; Clymer, *Farewells*; Shortridge, *WPA Guide to 1930's Kansas* (1939); interviews with Lisa Cooley, Lola

May Barnes. The universality of the notion of El Dorado extended its reach even to Kenya, the other homeland in the Obama story. In Elspeth Huxley's 1959 (1962) book, *The Flame Trees of Thika*, she wrote about her family's oxcart trip from Nairobi to their new home in the country: "If you went on long enough you would come to mountains and forests no one had mapped and tribes whose languages no one could understand. We were not going as far as that, only two days journey in the ox-cart to a bit of El Dorado my father had been fortunate enough to buy in the bar of the Norfolk Hotel from a man wearing an old Etonian tie."

10 *Harry Ellington Armour and Gabriella Clark Armour had been among the search-ers:* Interview, Ralph Dunham Jr.; Fifteenth Census of the United States: 1930 – Population Schedule, El Dorado Township; Sheriff's Deed, District Court of Butler County, Kansas, February 12, 1938: Default of loan taken out in 1926; Registration card, Local Board No. 1, Wichita, Kansas, 1918, Henry E. Armour; Magnolia Petro-leum corporate records.

11 *The boys were motherless, but lived in a home with two women:* El Dorado *Times*, Oct. 26, 1926; Clymer, *Kingdom of Butler County*; Fifteenth Census of the United States: 1930 – Population Schedule, El Dorado Township; Zachary Lamb, "El Dorado's Kafir Korn Carnival," Butler County Historical Society paper; *Kafir Corn Carnival*, compiled by Renea Albert, Butler County Historical Society; Bobbie Athon, "Kansas Flip for Kafir Corn," Kansas State Historical Society paper; "Butler County's Nine Kafir Corn Carnivals," in *Butler County's Eighty Years* (96–98); inter-views with Lisa Cooley, Ralph Dunham Jr.

13 *Around the time the Dunham sons landed in El Dorado:* El Dorado *Times*, Nov. 25, 1926.

13 *There was no Jim Crow segregation in El Dorado:* Clymer, *Farewells*, Law obituary, Apr. 26, 1920.

14 *It came against the 1920s backdrop of a resurgent Ku Klux Klan:* Charles William Sloan Jr., "Kansas Battles the Invisible Empire," *Kansas Historical Quarterly* 40, no. 3 (1974); Roxie Olmstead, "The Klan in Butler County," Butler County Historical Society; *Time*, Oct. 6, 1924; *The Autobiography of William Allen White*.

16 *After fixing the car:* Interviews with Ralph Dunham Jr.

16 *The question of whether Kansas would be free:* Carl L. Becker, "What Kansas Means to Me" ("The Kansas struggle is for Kansas what the American Revolution is for New England; and while there is as yet no 'Society of the Daughters of the Kansas Struggle,' there doubtless will be some day. For the Kansas struggle is regarded as the crucial point in the achievement of human liberty."); William Allen White, *Kansas: A Puritan Survival*; Eric Foner, *Free Soil, Free Labor, Free Men*; William W. Freehling, *The Road to Disunion*; David M. Potter, *The Impending Crisis*.

18   *The family had moved to the outskirts:* Interviews with Ralph Dunham Jr.; *El Dorado Times*, obituary of Christopher Columbus Clark, Jan. 12, 1937; Clymer, *Farewells*, Jimmy Dodwell obituary, 1935, C. B. Dillenbeck obituary, 1925; author observations in El Dorado.

22   *On at least one occasion she reined him in:* El Dorado Times, Nov. 5, 6, 7, 1935. The first story called for a banner headline, "Five Persons Die in Fire," with the subhead, "Huge Gasoline Transport and Automobile Crash on Highway East of El Dorado," and a second subhead, "Victims Are Trapped in Blazing Machines When Driver of Car Swerves in Front of Carrier to Avoid Hitting a Cow; Bodies Burned beyond Recognition, Are Not Identified for Several Hours." Interview, Ralph Dunham Jr.

23   *Late in the winter of 1935:* Interviews with Ralph Dunham Jr.; *Wichita Beacon*, Feb. 18, 1935. The headline noted, "[Hoover] Declines to Comment on National Affairs," and the article proved the point, quoting the former president: "There is absolutely no political significance to my trip. My route home is by way of El Paso and it was just as easy to come through Wichita as not to. But then, I wanted to visit with friends. Yesterday I had lunch with my very good friend, William Allen White, and today I have the pleasure of being with my good friend, Senator Allen."

24   *Stanley graduated one year late:* Interviews with Ralph Dunham Jr., Clarence H. Kerns; *The Gusher '36.* The oil motif was featured throughout the yearbook, including an essay by classmate Maryalyce King called "The Refinery": "Now we are to set forth on a journey into the world. We have been well prepared, and the gasoline, our acquired knowledge, which is one of the most refined products of our processing, shall furnish the motive power for our future efficiency."

25   *Only days after Stanley Dunham left high school:* Journal Entry of Judgment, Butler County District Court, June 26, 1936.

25   *Augusta, Kansas, in 1936:* Narrative description of life for the Payne family and friends in Augusta based on interviews with Charles Payne, Rae Janette Marshall, Francine Pummill Buchanan, Earl Mercer, Sidney Devere Brown, Francine Kennedy, Virginia Ewalt, Nina June Parry; Allison, *Augusta, Kansas*; Clymer, *Kingdom of Butler County*; Augusta City Directory; author observations at sites in Augusta.

30   *Anyone driving the last section:* Shortridge, *WPA Guide to 1930s Kansas*; interviews with Francine Pummill Buchanan, Nina June Parry, Charles Payne.

32   *Along came Stanley Dunham:* Interviews with Charles Payne, Ralph Dunham Jr., Francine Pummill Buchanan, Frances Kennedy, Virginia Ewalt, Nina June Parry.

33   *Near the end of the school year:* Augusta High School Supplement, Class of 1940, *Augusta Daily Gazette*, May 24, 1940; interview, Sidney Devere Brown.

TWO: LUOLAND

Key archives for primary documents related to Kenya material in chapters 2, 4, 10, and 15 and parts of 6, 7, 8, and 18 include Kenya National Archives, Nairobi; Kenya National Archives (microfilm), Syracuse University Library; U.S. Immigration and Naturalization Service; Melville J. Herskovits Library of African Studies, Northwestern University; Gendia Mission Museum, Kendu Bay; Frank C. Laubach Collection, Syracuse University Library; Hoover Institution Library and Archives, Stanford University; Tom Mboya Papers and William X. Scheinman Papers, Special Collection, Michigan State University Library; Frank J. Taylor Papers, Stanford University Library; Mooney family private collection.

36 *Some Luo in Kanyadhiang had a different name for him:* Narrative description of Hussein Onyango in Kanyadhiang based on interviews with Nicholas Owino Rajula, Charles Oluoch, Elly Yonga, Auma Magak, Andrew Ochung; author observations near Lake Victoria; South Nyanza documents, annual reports 1920–51, Kenya National Archives, Syracuse University Library.

40 *Paul Mboya had been ordained as a pastor:* South Nyanza documents, Kenya National Archives, Syracuse University; interviews with Daniel Ochient Abuya, Benson Nyang'ive, Charles Oluoch, Andrew Ochung, John Aguk, James Mbori; Carscallen Papers, Gendia Mission Museum.

41 *The leader of Piny Owacho: Standard* (Kenya), Feb. 13, 2010 ("Grave Vandals Rekindle Ojijo's Memory 67 Years Later"); interview, Leo Odera Omolo; "Jaluo," in *Karachuonyo Constituency Political and Economic History.*

41 *The relationship . . . became increasingly strained:* Interviews with Charles Oluoch, Elly Yonga, Daniel Ochient Abuya, Benson Nyang'ive, John Ndalo Aguk, Leo Odera Omolo, Andrew Ochung, Dick Oluoch Opar.

43 *By then the Luo had experienced six decades of interaction with Europeans:* Kavirondo Province Annual Reports, history sections, 1894–1926, 1951; Kenya National Archives, Syracuse University; Churchill, *My African Journey*; Odhiambo and Cohen, *The Luo of Western Kenya*, chapter 21; Brendon, *The Decline and Fall of the British Empire*; interviews with Gilbert Ogutu, Philip Ochieng.

46 *The evangelism began in late November 1906:* Gendia Mission Museum. From Carscallen's account there: "In the autumn of 1906 our British Union Conference decided to open work in British East Africa and asked me to go out to that country to commence the work. Peter Nyambo, a negro student from South Africa, and I sailed from Hamburg, Germany, on October 1, 1906. After an exceedingly hot trip through the Red Sea, we arrived in Mombasa nearly three weeks later."

47 *The grip white men held on western Kenya:* Gilbert Ogutu, Centenary Lecture, Maseno School; South Kavirondo Province Annual Report, 1911, 1920–26,

Nyanza Province Annual Report, 1951, Kenya National Archives, Syracuse University Library; Churchill, *My African Journey*.

49 *Onyango missed that melee:* Interviews with John Ndalo Aguk, Charles Oluoch, Elly Yonga, Sarah Ogwel, Joseph Nyabande Opar, Dick Opar, Andrew Ochung, Auma Magak.

52 *For all the family melodrama:* Interviews with Paula Hagberg Schramm, Philip Ochieng, John Ndalo Aguk; author observations of Kaloleni and Westlands neighborhoods in Nairobi; Kennethy Opala report on Kaloleni.

54 *Sarah Ogwel, would relate a story:* Interviews with Sarah Ogwel, John Ndalo Aguk, Dick Opar, Zablon Okatch, Charles Oluoch, Auma Magak.

56 *When he was fourteen, young Obama was among three boys:* Account of Barack Obama at CMS Maseno drawn from interviews with James Mbori, Y. F. O. Masakhalia, Gilbert Ogutu, Auma Magak, Charles Oluoch, Philip Ochieng; Ogot, *My Footprints in the Sands of Time*, Maseno chapter; CMS Maseno documents, Kenya National Archives, Nairobi.

66 *Rather than return home:* Interviews with Charles Oluoch, Dick Opar; Obama, *Dreams from My Father*, 416–20.

THREE: IN THIS OUR LIFE

67 *But the quote took on a new meaning five years later:* Account of birth of Stanley Ann Dunham and choice of name drawn from Augusta High yearbook 1938; *El Dorado Times*, Dec. 1, 1942; *In This Our Life*, Turner Classic Movies, IMDb; interview, Charles Payne.

69 *Madelyn was back in Augusta:* Interviews with Charles Payne, Francine Pummill Buchanan, Virginia Ewalt, Hazel Grady Gruver.

70 *Before he left, Charles experienced a revelation concerning his brother-in-law:* Interview, Charles Payne.

70 *Madelyn's role in the workforce:* Narrative account of Madelyn Dunham's work on the B-29 assembly line at Boeing plant in Wichita drawn from Boeing documents, Local History Archive, Wichita Public Library; Peter Fearon, "Ploughshares into Airplanes," *Kansas History*, Winter (1999), 298–314; *Wichita Eagle*, Mar. 8, 1942; Davis, "Wichita: Boom Town," *Current History*, January 1941; *Boeing Plane Talk*, 1943–45; interviews with Hazel Grady Gruver, Charles Payne, Virginia Ewalt, Nina June Parry, Frances Kennedy.

76 *Charles Payne enlisted the same month:* Interview, Charles Payne.

76 *Stanley Dunham . . . was in many ways a natural for army life:* Account of Stanley Armour Dunham's military service drawn from Enlistment Records, Sedgwick County, Kansas; 1802nd Ordnance Supply and Maintenance and 1830th Ordnance Supply and Maintenance reports, Mar. 17, 1943–Feb. 7, 1945, Frederick

W. Maloof, Capt. Ord. Dept., Commanding, Air Force History Index, reel 359, National Archives at College Park; also a comprehensive Associated Press report by Nancy Benac, Betsy Taylor, and researcher Randy Herschaft, May 30, 2009.

78 *Charles Payne was also in France by then:* 89th Infantry Division of World War II website; Liberation Day: Eyewitness Accounts of the Liberation of Concentration Camps, Center for Holocaust Studies Documentation and Research, 1981; World War II Operations Reports 1940–48, 89th Infantry Division, box 10973, entry 427, National Archives at College Park.

81 *Back in Butler County:* Clymer, *Farewells.*

82 *Charles Payne, with his icy toes and fingers:* Interview, Charles Payne.

82 *Two of the largest POW camps . . . were in Salina and Concordia: Newsletter of the Butler County Historical Society* 10, no. 3 (2003); interview, Lisa Cooley.

83 *The Dunhams found an apartment in a makeshift complex:* Interviews with Ralph Dunham Jr., Charles Payne; University of California transcript.

86 *The job he landed was . . . in Ponca City:* Interviews with Bob Casey, Charles Payne, Ralph Dunham Jr., Hugh Dickens, Francine Pummill Buchanan. Casey said of their boss, Jay Paris, "Mr. Paris was a self-made man. He grew up in Guthrie, Oklahoma, and moved to Ponca City and worked at the flour mill to start, then ended up getting into the furniture business and was very successful at it. It was the largest furniture store originally, but a brother who worked for him and whom he taught the business went on his own and was a terrific competitor."

89 *Stannie Ann became Stanley Ann in Vernon:* Narrative account of Stanley Ann and her family in Vernon based on interviews with Carole Ann McDonald Perry, Frances Shepherd Lowe, Larry Lambert, Bill Ivins, Betty Phillips McAphee, Janice Folmar Smith, Sunny Rutledge Hawkins, Janice Kays Richie, Karen McGee, Sharon McNabb Bennett, Betty Parr Jones, Tim Reeves, Kelly Couch; "I Remember," Hawkins Elementary School yearbook, 1951–52; Vernon Independent School Health Record for Stanley Ann Dunham, 2227 Roberts, phone 2375-W.

89 *The public swimming pool was whites-only:* Interviews with Tom Oliver, Thessalonia "Tess" Favors Willie.

92 *Stanley's grandson understood the old man's penchant:* Obama, *Dreams from My Father,* 18–19; interview, Charles Payne.

FOUR: NAIROBI DAYS

95 *In his résumé, Obama:* Barack H. Obama résumé, prepared by Elmer and Elizabeth Kirk, presumably for financial aid applications, 1962; *Barack H. Obama: Through the Eyes and Heart of Elizabeth Mooney Kirk.*

95 *Back in Kendu Bay:* Interview, Leo Odera Omolo.

95 *For several years . . . he worked for the Hagberg family:* Interview, Paula Hagberg Schramm; Hagberg family papers.

96 *The father's connections . . . to Tom Mboya:* Interviews with John Ndalo Aguk, Philip Ochieng, Leo Odera Omolo; author observations in Kaloleni.

97 *His final journey home in . . . 1956:* Interviews with Sarah Ogwel, Auma Magak, Charles Oluoch, Elly Yonga, Leo Odera Omolo, Dick Opar; Joseph Nyabande Opar, Peter Castro Oloo Aringo, Andrew Ochung: Elizabeth Anderson, *London Mail*, Jan. 6, 2008.

100 *This was an American named Sara Elizabeth Mooney:* Interviews with Marian Kirk, Joyce Kirk Coleman, Michael Kirk; *The Key, Kenya Adult Literacy News*, 1958–59, Laubach collection, box 237, Syracuse University Library; *Barack H. Obama: Through the Eyes and Heart of Elizabeth Mooney Kirk*; *Koinonia Magazine*, July 1960; Barack H. Obama, *Otieno Jarieko, Kitabu mar ariyo – Yore mabeyo mag puro puothe*, East African Literature Bureau.

107 *Americans began to take deeper notice of Kenya:* Thurman, *Isak Dinesen*.

108 *another Kenyan was touring the country:* Account of Tom Mboya's 1959 visit to the United States drawn from Papers of Melville J. Herskovits, Northwestern University Library; *New York Times*, Apr. 9, 13, 14, 16, May 1, 7, 1959; *Washington Post*, May 9, 1959; Reuters, May 17, 1959; Tom Mboya Papers, Hoover Institution Archives.

113 *The generational progression of every family:* Account of Frank J. Taylor and the article that brought the University of Hawaii to Obama's attention drawn from Frank J. Taylor Papers, Department of Special Collections, Stanford University Libraries, box 19, letters and documents related to *Saturday Evening Post*, 1957.

116 *The United States had become the place to go:* Interviews with Philip Ochieng, Robert F. Stephens, Mansfield Irving Smith; Mansfield Irving Smith, *The East African Airlifts of 1959, 1960, and 1961*, PhD diss., Syracuse University, 1966; African-American Students Foundation Papers, Hoover Institution Archives; Tom Mboya Papers, Hoover Institution Archives; Jackie Robinson, *New York Post*, Sept. 11, 1959.

118 *The late summer of 1959:* *Times* (London), Sept. 7–9, 1959; Department of Justice, U.S. Immigration and Naturalization Service, documents regarding Barack H. Obama, including date of entry.

FIVE: AFRAID OF SMALLNESS

121 *Stanley Ann once told her uncle:* Interview, Ralph Dunham Jr.

122 *Mercer Island sits in the middle of Lake Washington:* Gellatly, *Mercer Island Heritage*; author observations.

123 *Stan had taken Madelyn to the El Dorado Country Club:* Polk's El Dorado City Directory 1955; " 'Do You Remember': Theme Prevails at Events of Reunion of the

High School Class of 1935," *El Dorado Times*, June 27, 1955. During their hiatus in El Dorado, the Dunhams lived at 1435 Olive Street. While Stan worked at Farm n' Home, Madelyn took courses at El Dorado Junior College.

123 *The island culture was caught between old and new:* Interviews with Susan Botkin Blake, Maxine Hanson Box, Chip Wall, John W. Hunt; Gellatly, *Mercer Island Heritage*; *Mercer Island Reporter*, Jan. 5, 1958.

125 *"In the back of his mind":* Obama, *Dreams from My Father*, 17.

125 *". . . it was when he felt he wasn't being given his due as master of the house":* Interview, Charles Payne.

126 *Stanley's friends mostly enjoyed being around her father:* Interviews with Susan Botkin Blake, Maxine Hanson Box, John W. Hunt.

127 *If anyone was ready for change:* Interview, Maya Soetoro-Ng; scene of road trip from Scott, *A Singular Woman*.

128 *In a high school culture celebrating brawn and beauty:* Mercer Island High yearbook (*Isla*), 1958, 1959, 1960. In the 1958 yearbook, there is a photograph of fans in the stands of a varsity basketball game, and Stanley can be seen cheering in the third row. There was reason to cheer that year: the team, led by center Bill Hanson, her friend Maxine's brother, went to the state tournament.

129 *As an only child:* Interviews with Susan Botkin Blake, Maxine Hanson Box, John W. Hunt, Chip Wall.

131 *around to the story of John Stenhouse:* "Out of a Man's Past," *Time*, Apr. 11, 1955.

132 *The school quickly established a faculty:* 50th anniversary remembrances, Mercer Island High School, Class of 1960 (1960–2010); interviews with Susan Botkin Blake, Maxine Hanson Box, Chip Wall, John W. Hunt; Gellatly, *Mercer Island Heritage*; *Mercer Island Reporter*, 1958–61.

134 *not all of Stanley's classmates shared Faulkner's faith:* Interviews with Susan Botkin Blake, Chip Wall, John W. Hunt.

135 *At eleven-thirty on the morning of June 6:* *Mercer Island Reporter*, June 1960.

135 *Albert Robert Pratt plays much the same role:* Honolulu City Directory 1961; interview, Cindy Pratt Holtz.

SIX: BEAUTIFUL ISLE OF SOMEWHERE

140 *Obama was a different ingredient in the Hawaiian stew:* "Young Men from Kenya, Jordan and Iran Here to Study at U.H.," *Honolulu Star Bulletin*, Sept. 18, 1959; "Isle Inter-Racial Attitude Impresses Kenya Student," *Honolulu Advertiser*, Nov. 28, 1959.

142 *By 1959 the University of Hawaii had grown:* "University of Hawaii Proudly Celebrates 50 Years," *Sunday Advertiser* supplement, Mar. 24, 1957; general catalogues and other University of Hawaii documents, Hawaii State Library.

142 *He loved to be around people and talk, argue, challenge, flirt with women:* Interviews with Neil Abercrombie, Andrew (Pake) Zane, Peter Gilpin; Dietrich Varez, *Obama-land*, Ron Jacobs interview oral history.

144 *Events were unfolding swiftly . . . [in] Kenya: Times* (London), Oct. 25–Nov. 1959; Mar. 1960; *Daily Nation*, Oct.–Dec. 1959; *East African Standard*, Oct.–Nov. 1959; *Time*, Mar. 7, 1960.

146 *William X. Scheinman, the American:* Scheinman letter to Hon. Tom Mboya, P.O. Box 10818, Nairobi, Kenya, Dec. 20, 1960. Scheinman considered himself a master political strategist. He ended his letter, "As you have said many times before I fully appreciate the need for national unity, and this of course is why you have always cooperated with those who are now trying to destroy you. But it must be equally apparent that there will never be unity among [the present political leadership] and related elements. It must come out of your leadership in the country and among the people. I would go on to say that once you have secured dominance – and it is quite clear to everyone – at that point you might well consider using the carrot instead of the stick to give some of these fellows a graceful way out."

146 *Through his contacts at the Y: Honolulu Star-Bulletin,* Feb. 13, 1960, Jan. 8, 1962. The little notices in the paper rarely got the facts right about Obama. The January notice carried the headline "NAACP Will Hear Ghanaian Student" and began, "Barack Obama, University of Hawaii student from Ghana"; the February notice said Obama happened to be in town for the Afro-Asian student seminar.

146 *the* Star-Bulletin *ran an editorial: Star-Bulletin*, June 4, 1960; letter to editor, *Star-Bulletin*, June 8, 1960. At the end of Obama's letter, the newspaper attached an editor's note: "The Star-Bulletin did not predict that misrule would come. The editorial said that there are many predictions of riot and rapine. As to the writer's general criticism of the Star-Bulletin editorial, that editorial specifically pointed out that [in] back of all the Congolese difficulties is the stark fact that for too long the Congolese were treated as menial subjects."

148 *While Obama pursued his ambitious academic plan:* Narrative account of the second year of the Kenyan airlift and the political machinations involving Senator Kennedy and Vice President Nixon drawn from interview, Robert F. Stephens; Papers of Betty Mooney; African-American Student Foundation file, Hoover Institution Library and Archives; Charles Diggs Papers, Howard University Archives; K. D. Luke, advisor to colonial students in North America, "Report on the '81' Kenya Students Who Arrived in North America by 'Airlift Africa' in September 1959," British Embassy, June 1960. Point 8 of his ten-point introduction read, "What must be prevented if at all possible is a continuation of the flow to North America, and in particular to the United States, of underfinanced students, who are sometimes poorly qualified. In my view their presence in this country can do much harm. For

if he is unsuccessful the underfinanced student will tend to speak bitterly of all those who have been concerned in his education, including his institution and this country."

154 *If Stanley Ann Dunham had had her way:* Interviews with Susan Botkin Blake, John W. Hunt, Cindy Pratt Holtz.

155 *The first day of freshman orientation:* University of Hawaii bulletin, 1960–61; *New York Times, Washington Post,* Sept. 20, Sept. 27, 1960.

155 *Russian was a hot language:* J. T. Shaw, "The Teaching of Russian in the United States," *Modern Language Journal* 45, no. 8 (1961).

155 *the two unlikely family stories . . . weave into the same cloth:* Account of Stanley Ann Dunham meeting Barack H. Obama drawn from interviews with Maya Soetoro Ng, Susan Botkin Blake, Charles Payne, Neil Abercrombie, Andrew (Pake) Zane, Peter Gilpin, Rolf Nordahl; University of Hawaii general catalogue, 1960–61; Obama, *Dreams from My Father,* 8–10, 126–27.

160 *The centuries-long history of the Luo:* Interview, Philip Ochieng.

161 *Based on college transcripts:* University of Washington transcripts, Stanley Ann Dunham (with grades transferred from University of Hawaii); University of Hawaii general catalogue, 1960–61.

161 *Foreign mail was sorted in Nairobi:* Kennethy Opala, African Investigative News Service, Nairobi, report on mail service to western Kenya in 1960s.

162 *Three days later, on February 2:* Marriage facts recorded in divorce records, Mar. 5, 1964, First Judicial Circuit State of Hawaii Division of Domestic Relations.

162 *It was also a step that drew the attention of officials:* Memo for File, Lyle H. Dahlin, U.S. Department of Justice, Immigration and Naturalization Service, Honolulu, Apr. 11, 1961.

SEVEN: *HAPA*

164 *Lili'uokalani was the last native queen of Hawaii:* Daws, *Shoal of Time.*

165 *at 7:24 on the evening of August 4:* State of Hawaii Certificate of Live Birth, Barack Hussein Obama II.

165 *There was nothing particularly exotic about the last name: Sunday Advertiser,* Aug. 13, 1961.

166 *Soon after young Obama's birth:* Interview, Barbara Czurles-Nelson.

167 *Only a few days after the boy was born:* U.S. Department of Justice, Immigration and Naturalization Service, Honolulu, Application to Extend Time of Temporary Stay. His student visa was due to expire August 9. In the same form, Obama was given permission to work twenty-five hours a week.

167 *On August 4, 1961: Life,* Aug. 4, 1961.

167 *Before dawn that morning:* Interview, David Dennis; Ed Freeman, "Negroes Jailed Here in Integration Try," *Shreveport Journal*, Aug. 4, 1961; "Four 'Riders' Are Held in Parish Jail," *Shreveport Times*, Aug. 5, 1961.

168 *For all of its racial diversity:* Rich Budnick, *Hawaii's Forgotten History.*

168 *Honolulu was in the process of a physical transformation:* Honolulu Star-Bulletin, Aug. 4–12, 1961.

169 *In Kenya, the uprisings . . . were over:* Daily Nation, Aug. 14, 1961.

169 *Obama . . . had more personal concerns:* Interviews with Leo Odera Omolo, Andrew Ochung.

170 *The genealogists who have studied the bloodlines:* William Addams Reitwiesner, *Ancestry of Barack Obama.*

171 *In the college life of Barack Obama:* Interviews with Naranhkiri Tith, Robert Ruenitz, Arnie Nachmanoff, David Finkelstein.

175 *The mystery . . . did not involve where so much as why:* Obama, *Dreams from My Father*, 125–26; interview, Ruth Ndesandjo.

176 *Barry was not yet a month old when they left Honolulu:* Interviews with Maya Soetoro-Ng, John W. Hunt, Maxine Hanson Box, Susan Botkin Blake; Seattle City Directory, 1961–62; University of Washington transcripts, Stanley Ann Dunham; Philip Lipson and Charlotte LeFevre report on Ann Dunham in Seattle and interview with Mary Toutonghi.

178 *Once again, he enlisted the help of . . . Betty Mooney:* Kirk Family Collection; *Barack H. Obama: Through the Eyes and Heart of Elizabeth Mooney Kirk*, letters and documents of Betty Mooney.

EIGHT: ORBITS

184 *Leroy Gordon Cooper spoke:* Honolulu Star-Bulletin, May 16, 17, 18, 1963; Sunday Star-Bulletin & Advertiser, May 19, 1963; Time, May 24, 1963; Life, May 24, 1963; Newsweek, May 27, 1963; interviews with Ralph Dunham Jr., Neil Abercrombie; Obama, *Dreams from My Father*, 22.

186 *The future for the Dunham family also looked a bit brighter:* Interviews with Charles Payne, Cindy Pratt Holtz.

187 *When freedom came to his homeland:* Interviews with Frederick Okatcha, Philip Ochieng, Leo Odera Omolo, James Mbori; Times (London), Aug. 13, 1963; Mboya, *Freedom and After*; Daily Nation, Dec. 13, 14, 1963.

188 *an affidavit reached his apartment on Magazine Street:* Stanley Ann D. Obama, libellant v. Barack H. Obama, libelee, Grievous Mental Suffering, Libel for Divorce, Motion and Order, First Judicial Circuit, State of Hawaii, Division of Domestic Relations.

189 *For all his idiosyncrasies and failings: Dreams from My Father*, 25; interview, Cindy Pratt Holtz.

190 *Her name was Ruth Baker:* Account of Barack Obama Sr.'s relationship with Ruth Baker based on interviews in Nairobi with Ruth Ndesandjo, conducted in Nairobi Jan. 19 and 22, 2010, on the back lawn at Madari Kindergarten, where she has been the headmistress since its inception in 1980. She started by saying, "I know him best. I loved him very much. He had a great brain but ruined himself because of drinking." One of her sons, Mark Ndesandjo, sat in on the interviews but did not participate.

195 *By then [Ann] was in a relationship with another man:* Account of Ann's relationship with Lolo Soetoro and their dealings with the United States based on interviews with Alice Dewey, Maya Soetero-Ng, Charles Payne, Sylvia Krausse; U.S. Department of Justice, Immigration and Naturalization Service, involving memos to and from Travel Control Unit; University of Hawaii Office of the Vice-Chancellor; U.S. Department of State, International Educational Exchange Service; Office of the Executive Director, Institute for Student Interchange, East-West Center, University of Hawaii.

201 *Five months after she arrived in Nairobi:* Interview, Ruth Ndesandjo.

202 *Among the foreign visitors:* Frank Laubach, "The Literacy Safari to Kenya – Summer 1965," Laubach Collection, box 236, Africa-Kenya, Syracuse University; *Barack H. Obama: Through the Eyes and Heart of Elizabeth Mooney Kirk*; interviews with Marian G. Kirk, Joyce Kirk Coleman, John W. Kirk.

203 *The dissertation was nearly completed:* Interview, Ruth Ndesandjo.

204 *One paper Obama did finish:* Barack H. Obama, "Problems Facing Socialism: Another Critique of Sessional Paper No. 10," *East Africa Journal*, July 1965; *African Socialism and Its Application to Planning in Kenya*, Republic of Kenya; *Teach Yourself Citizenship*, No. 28, Melville J. Herskovits Library of African Studies, Northwestern University.

206 *The accepted family story:* Account of Obama's drinking and driving based on interviews with Naranhkiri Tith, Kevin Oriko Abiero, Charles Oluoch, Elly Yonga, Rispah Gili Agua.

207 *The baby transformed Ruth:* Interview, Ruth Ndesandjo.

209 *Ann D. Soetoro was alone again:* Account of Ann in Honolulu and Barry at kindergarten drawn from interviews with Alice Dewey, Maya Soetero-Ng, Aimee Shirota; U.S. Immigration and Naturalization Service, Soetoro file; Obama, *Dreams from My Father*, 30–31.

NINE: "SUCH A WORLD"

212 "Life is a dream . . .": Amir Hamzah, "Because of You." Hamzah was born in Sumatra in 1911 and died in 1936; the Indonesian Council on World Affairs and the traditional community of the Sultanate of Langkat declared 2011 "The Year of Amir Hamzah" to celebrate his life and works.

212 *Perhaps he came from Ambon, many thought:* Interviews with Jacomine Mathilda Madewa Pattiradjawane, Israela Pareira, Dewi Asmara, Mardanus Hasmoro, Yunaldi Askiar.

213 *Ann and Barry arrived in Jakarta:* Obama, *Dreams from My Father*, 31–32.

214 *Their first house was in South Jakarta:* Author observations of neighborhood; Fenty Effendy observations; interviews with Jacomine Mathilda Madewa Pattiradjawane, Coenraad Satjakoesoemah, Yunaldi and Johny Askiar.

215 *The backyard was a sight to behold:* Interview, Haryo Soetendro.

215 *On their first morning in Jakarta:* Interview, Jacomine Mathilda Madewa Pattiradjawane.

216 *Everything about Barry seemed different to his classmates:* Description of Barry at SD Asisi drawn from interviews with Israela Pareira, Mardanus Hasmoro, Yunaldi Askiar, Johny Askiar, Fermina Katarina Sinaga, Satria Kartika; author observations of school.

222 *Barry could prank back:* Interviews with Yunaldi Askiar, Vickers (Ikes) Sulistyo.

222 *The mischievous boy often lingered:* Interview, Noeke Dwinalistiany.

223 *Four decades later:* Interview, Coenraad Satjakoesoemah; Barry's exotic view of life in Jakarta evoked in Obama, *Dreams from My Father*, 33–52.

224 *Madelyn Dunham's last threads to Kansas were now cut:* Interviews with Charles Payne, Francine Pummill Buchanan.

225 *Lolo's father . . . had been a geologist:* Interviews with Heru Budiono, Bambang Utomo, Heri Purnomo, Sonny W. Trisulo.

227 *The story is wrong, a concocted myth:* "It Is a Very Sad Thing," *Kedaulan Rakyat* (newspaper), July 31, 1951. Heru Budiono, the oldest of the fourteen sons of Soepomo, Lolo's second-oldest brother, said in an interview, "Martodihardjo fell when he was trying to fix the curtain at his house in Jayeng Prawiran . . . and died at the house [of an aunt] after he received medical treatment in a hospital."

228 *It is also false that the house . . . was burned to the ground:* Interviews with Heru Budiono, Titik Soeharti Suhardjono.

229 *Throughout his school years . . . Lolo ran with a group:* Interview, Titik Soeharti Suhardjono in Yogyakarta.

229 *When Lolo first lived in Jakarta:* Interview, Bambang Utomo.

230 *By the time Ann and Barry arrived in Jakarta:* Depiction of life on Haji Ramli Street and Lolo's jobs drawn from interviews with Coenraad Satjakoesoemah,

Jacomine Mathilda Madewa Pattiradjawane, Noeke Dwinalistiany, Trisulo Kjoko Purnomo; Obama, *Dreams from My Father*, 33–52.

232 *Menteng Dalam, had seen its share of political trauma:* Interview, Coenraad Satjakoesoemah. "Everyone didn't know who was a friend and who was the enemy during that period," Satjakoesoemah recalled.

234 *"I am a puppet, you are a puppet":* Amir Hamzah, "Because of You."

235 *To get there from the Soetoro house:* Descriptions of route to school and of the house on Amir Hamzah based on author observations in company of Mark London and Fenty Effendy, the North Star of Jakarta journalists; interviews with Saman and Turdi, the household servants. Turdi later changed his name to Evi and announced that he was transgender.

236 *A boy named Slamet was also around:* Interview, Slamet Dadi. Slamet, whose father was the driver for Dr. Soerono, became a driver himself as an adult for the Indonesian Ministry of Religion.

237 *The first time the family visited Lolo's relatives:* Interview, Haryo Winarso.

237 *And now we come to the final falsehood of the second myth:* Account of academics, Pancasila, and religious teachings at SD Besuki drawn from interviews with Effendi, Dewi Asmara, Cut Citra Dewi, Sonni Gondokusumo.

241 *the start of his coming to grips with race:* Obama, *Dreams from My Father*, 29–30.

243 *The servants . . . quietly observed the disintegrating relationship:* Interviews with Saman and Turdi, the household servants. Saman came from Yogyakarta to work in Jakarta. Turdi came from Salatiga in Central Java.

243 *He had left the furniture business altogether:* Interviews with Rolf Nordahl, Maya Soetoro-Ng.

244 *Barry was too young then to appreciate:* Interview, Barack Obama, White House, Nov. 10, 2011.

TEN: MARKED MAN

245 "We weep not for the present pain . . . ": Marjorie O. Macgoye, "For Tom," in *Make It Sing and Other Poems*.

245 *and Ruth was trying to adjust, again:* Interview, Ruth Ndesandjo.

246 *On the morning of Friday, November 3: Daily Nation*, Nov. 4, 1967.

247 *When Obama was hired for the tourism development post:* KTDC board meeting minutes, Sept. 8, 1967: "The executive committee confirmed that Mr. Barack Obama be appointed to the post . . . on trial period of six months and probation of a year."

247 *Cautions about Obama's behavior did nothing to change him:* KTDC board meeting minutes, Aug. 1968.

248 *That is not to say that Obama was bad at his job:* Interviews with Nyaringo Obure, Jasper Okelo, Y. F. O. Masakhalia.

249 *In an effort to improve the ratios:* "80 per cent of Tourist Trade in Foreign Hands," *East African Standard*, Feb. 2, 1969; interview, Nyaringo Obure.

249 *Ruth and the boys joined him for one long trip:* Interviews with Ruth Ndesandjo, Sarah Ogwel, Charles Oluoch.

249 *As 1968 neared an end:* Interviews with Neil Abercrombie, Andrew (Pake) Zane.

250 *The Kenyan papers on the morning of July 5, 1969: Daily Nation,* July 5, 1969; *East African Standard,* July 5, 1969; Tom Mboya Papers, Hoover Institution Library and Archives, Stanford University.

251 *After spending Saturday morning at his office: East African Standard,* Sept. 9, 1969, report on Obama's testimony at Mboya murder trial:

The trial entered its second week yesterday with evidence from Mr. Barack Hussein Obama, a senior development officer with the Kenya Tourist Development Corporation who flew to Kenya at the weekend after a visit to Britain. Replying to a question from the Deputy Public Prosecutor Mr. John Hobbs, he said that Mr. Mboya had been a personal friend. He recalled that on Saturday, July 5, he went to Government St., Nairobi, with a companion, Mrs. Micahel Kinyengi. . . .

Mr. Hobbs: "You yourself spoke to Mr. Mboya after he got out of the car?"

Mr. Obama: "Yes."

"Was there anyone with him?"

"He was alone."

"Can you give us some idea of how long you talked to him?"

"About three minutes."

"Did he say anything to you to indicate he was frightened of anything?"

"No, he did not give me this idea. In fact I recall how the discussion went. It was merely joking. I told him, 'You are parked on a yellow line, you will get a ticket.' He said, 'No.'"

252 *The noise of three shots, or maybe two and an echo:* Narrative account of Mboya's assassination, the reaction, and funeral drawn from *East African Standard,* July 6–12, 1969; *Daily Nation,* July 6–16, 1969; *Times* (London), July 7–10, 1969; interviews with Philip Ochieng, J. B. Omondi, Ruth Ndesandjo, Leo Odera Omolo, James Mbori, Andrew Ochung, Marjorie O. Macgoye, Dick Opar, Charles Oluoch, Elly Yonga, Y. F. O. Masakhalia, Peter Castro Oloo Aringo.

260 *it became clear that Barack Obama was having more problems:* Account of Obama's sacking from KTDC drawn from KTDC board meeting minutes May 11, 28, 1970; June 2, 15, 1970; interviews with Y. F. O. Masakhalia, Nyaringo Obure, Ruth Ndesandjo.

ELEVEN: WHAT SCHOOL YOU WENT?

265   *Tuition for a fifth-grader:* Punahou files of Kelli Furushima, Barry Obama's classmate.

265   *Money did not get Barry in:* Interviews with Neil Abercrombie, Rolf Nordahl, Ron Jacobs; Dr. Richard Kelley's Weekly Briefing, November 2008 (Kelley, chairman of Outrigger Hotels/Resorts, served on the Punahou board with Manaut).

266   *What school you went?:* Interview, Ron Jacobs; author observations in Honolulu from Mount Tantalus and between Punahou and Roosevelt.

266   *Barry was buffeted by the crosswinds of ethnic assumptions:* Obama, *Dreams from My Father*, 25; correspondence with Kristen B. Caldwell, March 28, 2009.

268   *he would say that his name alone separated him:* Punahou lower school yearbooks, 1972, 1973, 1974, Kelli Furushima personal files; interviews with Tom Topolinski, John Kolivas.

269   *"Barack is such a beautiful name":* Obama, *Dreams from My Father*, 59; interview, Scott Hefty (Mabel Hefty's son).

269   *Special agent Stan Dunham:* Interview, Rolf Nordahl; Obama, *Dreams from My Father*, 76–78; Davis, *Livin' the Blues.*

272   Guess Who's Coming to Dinner *took on a different meaning:* Interviews with Ruth Ndesandjo, Charles Payne, Ralph Dunham Jr.; Obama, *Dreams from My Father*, 66–69.

274   *The seminal event during that month-long once-in-a-lifetime coming together:* Narrative of Obama Sr.'s visit to Punahou School drawn from interviews with Scott Hefty, Pal Eldredge, Barbara Czurles-Nelson; unpublished memoir of Mabel Hefty; Obama, *Dreams from My Father*, 69–70.

276   *Ruth Obama had gone forward:* Interview, Ruth Ndesandjo.

277   *Not long after Ruth left Obama for good:* Interview, Andrew (Pake) Zane.

279   *In her passport renewal application:* U.S. Department of State passport file, Stanley Ann Dunham Soetoro. The passport photo attached to the application showed Ann wearing a headband in her long hair. Her height was listed at 5'5½", with brown hair and brown eyes. She listed her occupation as teacher.

280   *She and Maya came back without Lolo:* Narrative of Poki Street days drawn from interviews with Alice Dewey and Maya Soetoro Ng. Maya was interviewed four times in Honolulu in 2008 and 2009. Obama, *Dreams from My Father*, 75.

282   *His first court was tennis:* Correspondence with Kristen B. Caldwell, March 28, 2009.

283   *Basketball soon was Barry's sport:* Interviews with Rae Janette Marshall, Bruce Arinaga, Tom Topolinski, Mike Ramos, Greg Ramos, Joe Hanson, Mark Heflin.

285   *hedges of night-blooming cereus burst open:* Robert Earl Hayden, *The Night-Blooming Cereus*, 1972; Sue Cowling, "Hope from Poki," 2008. Cowling's poem was

published in *Obamaland*, the delightful color program-book put together by famed Honolulu disc jockey and music historian Ron Jacobs.

286 *His closer friends . . . knew all about his grandparents:* Interviews with Barack Obama (White House, Nov. 10, 2011), Greg Ramos, Mike Ramos, Joe Hanson.

286 *Perhaps some of the braggadocio had drained from him:* Obama, *Dreams from My Father*, 55; interview, Rolf Nordahl.

288 *At Punahou, to further develop a sense of community:* Interview, Eric Kusunoki.

289 *he shared his frustrations with a student two grades ahead of him:* Interview, Keith Kakugawa.

290 *In a less visceral and more lighthearted intellectual fashion:* Interview, Tony Peterson. Recalling those days and how they were described in *Dreams from My Father*, Peterson said later, "I was very disappointed when I read the book to not see my name in there. But what was interesting to me was how he characterized his Punahou experience, because that year that I knew him is not included at all. He is reporting accurately from his own perspective, but the tension he began to feel was after that year. . . . I don't doubt at all the agony he began to feel later, but it was not what I experienced at all."

TWELVE: BARRY OBAMA

293 *A self-selected group:* Narrative of Barry and the Choom Gang drawn from interviews and correspondence with Tom Topolinski and Joe Hanson, two members of the group, and interviews with Greg Ramos and Keith Peterson. In *Dreams from My Father*, Obama acknowledged his teenage experimentation with drugs. He included a modified version of the overturned car story, using pseudonyms. In a Dec. 30, 2004, interview with *Rolling Stone*, he said, "I did all my drinking in high school and college. I was a wild man. I did drugs and drank and partied. But I got all my ya-yas out."

297 *His classroom calm became a matter of pride:* Interviews with Jeff Cox, Joe Hanson, Mark Heflin, Kelli Furushima, Bruce Arinaga, John Kolivas, Barbara Czurles-Nelson. In her English class, Barbara Czurles-Nelson taught a poem on how heroes are formed:

> *The laurels go not to the ones who earn*
> *The victory with strength but to the one*
> *Who stepped into the pattern from the side*
> *And was the alchemy that turned the tide.*

She said that reminded her of Barry Obama.

300 *When does political ambition first bloom?:* Maraniss, *First in His Class*; interviews

with Fermina Katarina Sinaga, Keith Kakugawa, Keith Peterson; "Abercrombie Preaches Views," *Ka Punahou* (newspaper), Dec. 15, 1978; *Ka Punahou*, Oct. 6, 1978.

302 *he was utterly honest and revealing about . . . his tactics and tricks:* Obama, *Dreams from My Father*, 95.

303 *Barry competed for a spot on the top varsity:* Interviews with Joe Hanson, Mike Ramos, Tom Topolinski.

304 *For Obama . . . to make the squad, Coach McLachlin had to cut:* Narrative account of Barry Obama's senior year with the Punahou varsity basketball team based on interviews with Alan Lum, Larry Tavares, Tom Topolinski, Dan Hale, Clyde Mizumoto, Mike Ramos, Greg Ramos, Joe Hanson, Troy Egami; *Honolulu Advertiser*, Mar. 6–11, 1979; Troy Egami, "Basketball Coach Mclachlin," *Ka Punahou*, Mar. 9, 1979; Troy Egami, "Basketball Triumphs after 3 Year Drought," *Ka Punahou*.

316 *"I gathered up books from the library":* Obama, *Dreams from My Father*, 85.

316 *In Obama's retelling of his high school life:* Obama, *Dreams from My Father*, 87–91; contrasted with *Journeys in Black and White: A Book Proposal*, by Barack Obama (original proposal for book that morphed into *Dreams from My Father*). In the proposal, Obama made the case for his book: "The texture and spirit of the writing will derive from the tradition of the autobiographical narrative, typified by such works as Maya Angelou's *I Know Why the Caged Bird Sings*, Maxine Hong Kingston's *The Woman Warrior*, John Edgar Wideman's *Brothers and Keepers*, Wole Soyinka's *Ake*, Mark Mathabane's *Kaffir Boy*, and Russell Baker's *Growing Up*, as well as such travelogues as William Least Heat Moon's *Blue Highways* and V. S. Naipaul's *Finding the Center*. Such works take on the narrative force of fiction, and invite the reader to share in the hopes, dreams, disappointments and triumphs of individual characters, thereby soliciting a sense of empathy and universality that is absent in too many works on race in America."

318 *This poem revealed what was churning inside young Barry:* Interviews with Pal Eldredge, Eric Kusunoki, Bruce Arinaga, Alan Lum, Tom Topolinski, Tony Peterson, Mike Ramos, Greg Ramos.

319 *The paradox of Hawaii:* Interview, Dan Hale; Jacobs, *Obamaland*, 42.

320 *In a survey of college admissions officers: Los Angeles Times*, July 17, 1977; Kelli Furushima Punahou files.

321 *On the scheduled morning of the photo shoot:* Interview, Eric Kusunoki.

322 *In another section of the yearbook: Oahuan*, the Punahou yearbook, 1979.

322 *The graduation ceremony was staged at Blaisdell: Oahuan* yearbook 1979; *Honolulu Advertiser and Star-Bulletin*, June 4, 1979; *Ka Punahou*, Apr. 16, 1979; interviews with John Kolivas, Tom Topolinski, Kelli Furushima, Barbara Czurles-Nelson, Maya Soetoro-Ng, Mari Satterlee.

THIRTEEN: RIDING PONIYEM

325 *For Barry's little sister:* Interview, Maya Soetoro-Ng. Obama's sister, a high school humanities teacher, was interviewed four times in Honolulu in 2008 and 2009.

325 *Maya was under the impression . . . that her grandmother had royal blood:* Interviews with Maya Soetoro-Ng, Trisulo Djoko Purnomo, Heru Budiono, Sonny Trisulo, Bambang Utomo, Heri Purnomo. Heri Purnomo: "As far as I know, Eyang Djoemi-nah didn't have any royal blood. I've never heard that information. . . . If she had royal blood, my father and his siblings would have been bearing the royal title as well." Trisulo Djoko Purnomo: "She was just an ordinary people."

325 *Yogyakarta was independent and soulful:* Interview, Maya Soetoro-Ng; author observations of the *kraton* area of Yogyakarta in the company of Fenty Effendy.

326 *Her mother's work never stopped:* Interview, Alice Dewey.

326 *Ann started the research that would define the rest of her life:* Narrative account of Ann's anthropological research in central Java drawn from interviews with Alice Dewey, Maya Soetoro-Ng, Djaka and Sumarni Waluja; *Peasant Blacksmithing in Indonesia*, original version, 1992. Ann dedicated her dissertation "to Madelyn and Alice, who each gave me support in her own way, and to Barack and Maya, who seldom complained when their mother was in the fields"; unpublished manuscript, Djaka and Sumarni Waluja, "Working with Obama's Mother"; Ann Dunham Sutoro, professional biography, compiled by David McCauley; *A Singular Woman* by Janny Scott offers great detail on Ann's anthropology research; also author observations in Yogyakarta. Among Maya Soetoro-Ng's memories of those years with her mother: "Most of her work was within a day's range of Yogya. We spent time at the ocean, where supposedly the Goddess of the South Seas dwells. And the largest Buddhist temple in the world (Borobudur). Yogya was a center of the arts. All the temples were Hindu-Buddhist, so the stories I grew up with were those. I knew all the puppets. Those were the stories that animated my early life."

FOURTEEN: MAINLAND

334 *His face still had peach fuzz:* Photos of Lisa Jack; interviews with Jeff Yamaguchi, Paul Carpenter, Sim Heninger, Ken Sulzer.

336 *Freshmen entering Oxy that September were welcomed by fire:* Interview, Paul Carpenter.

338 *The subculture of the Annex:* Narrative account of Obama, his roommates, and the atmosphere in the Annex and the Barf Couch drawn from interviews with Jeff Yamaguchi, John Boyer, Ken Sulzer, Sim Heninger, Blake Withers, Paul Carpenter, Vince Coscino, Mark Roderique, Leslie Dudley, Kelly Lloyd Schafer, Phil Boerner, Paul Herrmannsfeldt, Mark Parsons, Willard Hankins Jr., Adam Sherman; journal of John Boyer; "Back to the Annex," short story by Adam Sherman.

350 *Among the hangouts on campus, the Cooler:* Interviews with Susan Keselenko, Caroline Boss, Tom Grauman, Lisa Jack, Alexandra McNear; photos of Lisa Jack.

353 *It was Political Science 94:* Account of Occidental academics drawn from interviews with Caroline Boss, Tim Yeaney, Susan Keselenko, Roger Boesche, Hasan Chandoo, Ken Sulzer, Kathy Cooper-Ledesma, Louis Hook, Leslie Dudley; copies of four papers in Pol. Sci. 94 with Dr. Caldwell and Dr. Eagan: "The MX Missile: Superiority Not Worth the Price, a Rebuttal by Group Y," Caroline Boss, Timothy Yeaney, Susan Keselenko, Larry Wilks, Barry Obama, Michael Tayar, Chris Weitz, Ra'uf Glasgow, Chris Brown; "Critique of the MX Missile by Group A," "Critique of Group A by Group Y," "The MX Missile: Bigger Is Not Better," by Group Y.

359 *Among the freshmen at Oxy:* Interview, Kofi Manu.

360 *When Barry returned to Honolulu:* Divorce papers for Stanley Ann Dunham from Lolo Soetoro, Family Court of the First Circuit, Honolulu; interview, Maya Soetoro-Ng; *Journeys in Black and White, A Book Proposal*, by Barack Obama; Obama, *Dreams from My Father*, 87–91.

364 *When he returned to Oxy:* Interviews with Barack Obama (White House, Nov. 10, 2011), Hasan Chandoo, Wahid Hamid, Asad Jumabhoy, Sohale Siddiqi, Paul Carpenter, Leslie Dudley, Roger Boesche, Caroline Boss, Susan Keselenko, Alexandra McNear.

368 *Western Kenya remained a territory of the imagination:* Account of Obama's interaction with black students at Occidental drawn from interviews with Eric Moore, Kofi Manu, Louis Hook, Adam Sherman, Willard Hankins Jr., Richard Casey, Caroline Boss, Hasan Chandoo; Obama, *Dreams from My Father*, 108–12, 115–17.

377 *But they did have one issue to rally around:* Account of anti-apartheid movement and rally at Occidental drawn from interviews with Caroline Boss, Hasan Chandoo, Eric Moore, Tim Yeaney, Susan Keselenko, Mari Satterlee, Bob Bovinette, Roger Boesche, Ken Sulzer, Sim Heninger, Kent Goss, Kathy Cooper-Ledesma, Rick Satterlee, Phil Boerner, Rary Simmons, Richard C. Gilman; Obama, *Dreams from My Father*, 105–8; "Students Demand Divestment," *Occidental*, Feb. 20, 1981.

379 *in the inaugural issue of Feast:* Account of the literary journal *Feast* and Obama's writings for it drawn from interviews with Tom Grauman, Caroline Boss, Alexandra McNear, Lisa Jack, Susan Keselenko; "Pop," *Feast*, Spring 1981.

384 *Three days after Bob Marley died:* Account of final days of spring semester 1981 at Occidental and Obama's decision to transfer drawn from interviews with Hasan Chandoo, Phil Boerner, Wahid Hamid, Caroline Boss, Eric Moore, Richard Casey, Kofi Manu, Roger Boesche, Paul Carpenter.

FIFTEEN: END AND BEGINNING

389 *The insects that feed on dead flesh:* Interview, Sebastian Okoda: "He was involved in so many accidents, and when I inquired he would tell me in Kiswahili, 'Mr. Okoda, *wadudu hawanitaki,* that's why I'm still alive.' He would say this especially if a friend of his died. He was very comical."

390 *The story he told:* Interviews with Joseph Kipsanai, J. B. Omondi, Y. F. O. Masakhalia, Charles Oluoch, Elly Yonga, Sarah Ogwel.

391 *Up on the third floor:* Interviews with Sebastian Okoda, J. B. Omondi, Y. F. O. Masakhalia.

394 *His assignments entailed considerable travel:* Ministry of Finance documents, 1976–82, Kenya National Archives, Nairobi. Many of the documents concerning various conferences and meetings in Africa and Europe were written by Obama, who was regarded as one of the most coherent writers in the ministry. As early as 1976 he was the author of "Report of Kenya-Sudan Link Joint Technical Committee Meeting Held in Khartoum from 1st November to 5th November 1976." As the note-taker as well as writer, he was notably precise: "The state of roads on the Sudan side from Khartoum to Juba to the Kenya border was summarized by Mr. Ibrahim who informed the meeting that from Khartoum to Juba, a distance of over 1,200 Km., there were two means of transport, i.e. steam on the river Nile or by rail to Wau and from Wau to Juba by an all-weather road. From Juba to Kenya one could file Nimule to Gulu or toward the proposed road via Torit, Kapoeta to the Kenya border. With regard to the proposed road there is 135 Km. of engineered, all-weather, narrow road to Tirit."

395 *His friends in the department protected him:* Interviews with Y. F. O. Masakhalia, J. B. Omondi, Joseph Kipsanai.

396 *Obama was known for keeping his own peculiar hours:* Interviews with Sebastian Okoka, Peter Castro Oloo Aringo, Joseph Kipsanai, J. B. Omondi, Leo Odera Omolo, Ann Omondi, Joseph Nyabande Opar, Andrew Ochung.

398 *Hussein Onyango, the tough old patriarch:* Interviews with Sarah Ogwel, Peter Castro Oloo Aringo, Joseph Nyabande Opar.

400 *This was a busy time at work:* Interview, Naranhkiri Tith; Obama, *Dreams from My Father,* 114.

402 *Now Maya . . . stayed with her mother:* Interview, Maya Soetoro-Ng.

404 *Ann had an emotional reserve:* Interviews with Alice Dewey, Maya Soetoro-Ng.

405 *The Ford Foundation . . . walked a fine line:* Account of Ann's work at the Ford Foundation drawn from interviews with Alice Dewey, Maya Soetoro-Ng, David McCauley, Georgia McCauley, Richard Hook, Nancy Peluso, Marty Chen.

411 *Barack had maintained a relationship with Akumu:* Interview, Auma Magak.

412 *To describe his driving:* Interviews with Philip Ochieng, Charles Oluoch, Elly Yonga, J. B. Omondi, Ann Omondi, Sarah Ogwel, Peter Castro Oloo Aringo, Joseph Nyabande Opar, Dick Opar.

413 *No one witnessed the accident:* Narrative account of Obama Sr.'s death and aftermath drawn from "Economic Planning Man Dies in Crash," *Nairobi Times*, Nov. 30, 1982; interviews with Auma Magak, Charles Oluoch, Elly Yonga, Sarah Ogwel, Joseph Nyabande Opar, Dick Opar, J. B. Omondi, Y. F. O. Masakhalia, Andrew Ochung, Leo Odera Omolo, Peter Castro Oloo Aringo; Obama, *Dreams from My Father*, 3.

SIXTEEN: THE MOVIEGOER

418 *"I now have an apartment in New York":* Phil Boerner letter, Aug. 25, 1981; interview, Phil Boerner.

421 *"Like a tourist," he would later write:* Obama, *Dreams from My Father*, 122.

421 *Here was a variation of his high school days:* Author observations on Upper West Side and in Honolulu; interview, Barack Obama (White House, Nov. 10, 2011).

422 *The south side of 109th:* Interview, Phil Boerner; author observations.

422 *Such was their welcome to the peculiar world of Columbia:* Narrative account of housing situation at Columbia and safety issues in neighborhood drawn from interviews with Barack Obama (White House, Nov. 10, 2011), Roger Lehecka, Tim Guilfoyle, Phil Boerner, Barak Zimmerman, Michael Ackerman, David Rakoff, Michael J. Wolf, Peter Lunenfeld, Wayne P. Weddington, Wayne Allen Root, Steve Holtje, Colin Redhead, Steven Waldman, Greg Smith.

427 *Obama's introduction to New York was conflated:* Obama, *Dreams from My Father*, 3–5, 113–15; interviews with Phil Boerner, Mir Mahboob Mahmood; communications with Sohale Siddiqi.

429 *It was to Chandoo's home turf:* Interviews with Hasan Chandoo, Wahid Hamid.

432 *Phil Boerner started taking banjo lessons:* Interview, Phil Boerner.

433 *"How did you get so good?":* Interview, Ron Sunshine.

433 *One of Obama's hangouts:* Interviews with Alison McParlin Davis, Steve Bargonetti, Phil Boerner.

435 *The BSO gathered on the first floor:* Account of Black Students Organization and African American experience at Columbia 1981–83 drawn from interviews with Barack Obama (White House, Nov. 10, 2011), Daniel Armstrong, Wayne P. Weddington III, Greg Smith, Lisa McParlin Davis, Wanda Phipps, Harvey Plante, Colin Redhead, Eddy Anglade, Derek Hawkins, Willie Dennis, Timothy Guilfoyle, Roger Lehecka, Michael Ackerman.

442 *Considering how determined he was:* Interviews with Barack Obama (White House, Nov. 10, 2011), Paul Carpenter, Alexandra McNear, Phil Boerner.

443 *This is where he lived . . . with Sohale Siddiqi:* Interviews with Mir Mahboob Mahmood, Phil Boerner, Alexandra McNear, Andrew Roth, Sohale Siddiqi, Wahid Hamid; Obama, *Dreams from My Father*, 113–15; author observations of neighborhood.

446 *Early in the summer of 1982:* Obama, *Dreams from My Father*, 122–27; interview, Maya Soetoro-Ng.

448 *Obama heard from Alexandra McNear:* Interviews and correspondence with Alexandra McNear; also interview with Barack Obama (White House, Nov. 10, 2011).

449 *Back at school that fall:* Interview, Phil Boerner.

450 *The long-distance relationship:* Interview, Alexandra McNear; Obama letters dated Sept. 26, 1982, Nov. 22, 1982, Feb. 14, 1983, Apr. 4, 1983, May 3, 1983.

453 *During his Columbia days:* Interview, Mir Mahboob Mahmood.

454 *Obama wrote to Alex that he would be coming out to Los Angeles:* Letter to Alexandra McNear, Nov. 22, 1982; Obama, *Dreams from My Father*, 3–5.

456 *The names of the great Greek and Roman thinkers:* Account of curriculum at Columbia and Obama's classes drawn from interviews with E. Warwick Daw, Amelia Ponomarev, Michael Ackerman, Michael J. Wolf, Hollis Lynch, Timothy Guilfoyle.

460 *One day during the second semester:* Account of Obama's article in *Sundial* drawn from interviews with Mark Bigelow, Don Kent, Robert Kahn; *Sundial*, Mar. 10, 1983; letter to Phil Boerner, Mar. 3, 1983.

464 *"I feel sunk in that long corridor":* Obama letter to Alexandra McNear, Apr. 4, 1983.

465 *"a young black man with his arms behind his head":* Obama letter to Alexandra McNear, May 3, 1983.

466 *There was an old-fashioned black gentleman:* Interviews with Greg Smith, Barack Obama (White House, Nov. 10, 2011).

466 *he made a five-day stop in Singapore:* Interviews with Hasan Chandoo, Asad Jumabhoy; Obama letter to Alexandra McNear, June 27, 1983.

468 *When he arrived in Indonesia:* Obama letter to Alexandra McNear, June 27, 1983; postcard to Phil Boerner, July 1983.

469 *When he returned east in late September:* Interviews with Barack Obama (White House, Nov. 10, 2011), Wahid Hamid, Alexandra McNear; Obama letter to Alexandra McNear, Nov. 15, 1983.

SEVENTEEN: GENEVIEVE AND THE VEIL

471 *December 1983. A Christmas party:* Narrative on Genevieve Cook and her relationship with Barack Obama from December 1983 to June 1985 based on several long interviews with her. She also provided numerous written documents, including the journal she kept during that period. She now has a different surname but prefers to keep it private. Some of Obama's friends in New York knew of Genevieve but did not know her last name. A few friends spent more time with Barack and Genevieve as a couple but were careful about protecting her privacy when interviewed for this book. She was contacted without their assistance and made her own decision about talking and providing documents.

478 There was a woman in New York: Obama, *Dreams from My Father*, 210–11; interview, Barack Obama (White House, Nov. 10, 2011).

478 *Genevieve Cook came from not one but several distinguished families:* Philip C. Jessup obituaries, *New York Times*, Feb. 1, 1986, and *Philadelphia Inquirer*, Feb. 2, 1986; "Ambassador on the Warpath," *Sydney Morning Herald*, Mar. 11, 1993; "Dr. Helen Ibbitson Jessup, an eminent scholar of South-East Asian arts," *Sydney Morning Herald*, Dec. 23, 2002; Helen Ibbitson Jessup, "Court Arts of Indonesia," Nov. 1990; Paul Richard, "Under Java's Spell," *Washington Post*, June 8, 1991; "International Nickel Company's $850 Million Indonesian Industrial Complex," *New York Times*, Apr. 14, 1978; interview, Genevieve Cook.

484 *In his book Obama described B.I. as a "consulting house":* Obama, *Dreams from My Father*, 135.

484 *It was an exaggeration to define B.I.:* Interviews with Lou Celi, Norman Wellen, Ralph Diaz, Dan Armstrong.

486 *Everyone on the seventh floor:* Interviews with Jean Reynolds Schmidt, Barry Rutizer, Michael Williams, Gary Seidman, Dan Armstrong, Peter Kennedy, Brent Feigenbaum.

487 *B.I. represented a holding pattern:* Interview, Alice Dewey; letters of Alice Dewey given to author; Obama, *Dreams from My Father*, 135.

488 *If he imagined himself a spy:* Interviews with Dan Armstrong, Dan Kobal.

489 *The section . . . where Obama wrote about feeling like a spy:* Interviews with Brenda Vinson, Lou Celi.

492 *a book club that Barack had briefly been part of:* Interviews with Phil Boerner, Paul Herrmannsfeldt.

492 *"Me and the Paki mob":* Interviews with Genevieve Cook, Hasan Chandoo, Wahid Hamid; letter from Mir Mahboob Mahmood.

495 *Not long after that, Barack had a dream:* Obama, *Dreams from My Father*, 128.

496 *More prosaically around that time:* Interview, Maria Batty.

496 *This was Auma:* Obama, *Dreams from My Father*, 136–37.

498 *One night I took her to see a play:* Obama, *Dreams from My Father*, 211. During an interview at the White House on November 10, 2011, President Obama acknowledged that this account was "a compression" of events that occurred at different times with different girlfriends.

499 *The parents were there:* Obama, *Dreams from My Father*, 210.

503 *One of the NYPIRG officers:* Ben Smith, "Frighteningly Coherent in New York," *Politico*, Jan. 30, 2007.

508 *Obama's application was intriguing:* Narrative depiction of Kellman recruiting Obama based on interviews with Jerry Kellman and Barack Obama; Obama, *Dreams from My Father*, 140–41.

EIGHTEEN: FINDING AND BEING FOUND

513 *and one / day I get a certain feeling:* Carolyn M. Rodgers, "Prodigal Objects," in *We're Only Human* chapbook, 1996.

516 *Alone in his blue Honda Civic:* Account of Obama's drive and arrival in Chicago drawn from interviews with Barack Obama (White House, Nov. 10, 2011), Mir Mahboob Mahmood, John Owens, Jerry Kellman; letter to Phil Boerner, Nov. 20, 1985.

517 *In intimate conversations with Genevieve Cook:* Author interviews and correspondence with Genevieve Cook.

517 *His daily work was eleven miles away:* Author observations on Chicago's South Side; letter to Phil Boerner, Nov. 20, 1985; interview, Jerry Kellman.

519 *What was a community organizer?:* Interviews with Charles Payne, Jerry Kellman, Ernie Cortes; Alinsky, *Reveille for Radicals*.

521 *Although Kellman offered Obama the job:* Interviews with Loretta Augustine-Herron, Yvonne Lloyd, Jerry Kellman.

522 *The black women in the room that day:* Interviews with Loretta Augustine-Herron, Yvonne Lloyd.

523 *The office at Holy Rosary was no place . . . to find much of anything:* Interviews with Jerry Kellman, Genevieve Cook.

524 *"Welcome to God's Friendly Church":* Narrative account of Obama's dealings with Reverend Alvin Love and the black preachers drawn from interviews with Rev. Alvin Love, Jerry Kellman; *Journeys in Black and White: A Book Proposal*, by Barack Obama; Obama, *Dreams from My Father*, 160–62.

530 *Wherever he went in Chicago, he had a pen and notebook with him:* Interviews with Loretta Augustine-Herron, Jerry Kellman; letter to Phil Boerner, Nov. 20, 1985.

532 *There were certain aspects of organizing at which he excelled:* Interviews with Loretta Augustine-Herron, Yvonne Lloyd, David Kindler, Jerry Kellman.

536 *Community organizing was a hard slog:* Letter to Phil Boerner, Nov. 20, 1985.

536 *The asbestos problem at Altgeld Gardens fit that description:* Narrative account of asbestos issue at Altgeld Gardens and Ida B. Wells Homes drawn from interviews with Linda Randle, Martha Allen, Jerry Kellman, Jim Avila, Loretta Augustine-Herron, Yvonne Lloyd; "Walter Jacobson Perspective," WBBM-TV, May 28, 29, 1986, June 5, 1986; *Chicago Reporter* 15, No. 6 (1986); Marilynn Marchione, "Asbestos Peril Reported in Ida B. Wells Homes," *Chicago Sun-Times*, May 29, 1986; "CHA's Chief Flushed Out: Reporter Stalks Smith in Restroom Retreat," *Chicago Sun-Times*, June 6, 1986; Cheryl Devall, "CHA Director Booed from Talks on Asbestos," *Chicago Tribune*, June 10, 1986; Obama, *Dreams from My Father*, 235–48.

546 *Ann and Maya were stationed back in Hawaii:* Interviews with Maya Soetoro-Ng, Rick Monteverde.

548 *Stan even traveled back to Kansas:* Interview, Ralph Dunham Jr.; *El Dorado Times*, July 1, 1985.

548 *there was nothing publicly excessive about their grandmother:* Interview, Maya Soetoro-Ng.

550 *He left one Hyde Park apartment for another:* Letter to Phil Boerner, Oct. 21, 1986.

550 *Now Obama shared an office with his assistant, Johnnie Owens:* Interview, John Owens.

552 *But he started dating soon enough:* Interviews with Barack Obama (White House, Nov. 10, 2011), Jerry Kellman, John Owens, Loretta Augustine-Herron.

553 *Even as he was insinuating himself into the South Side culture:* Interview, John Owens.

554 *Obama's search for home in the black community:* Interviews with Alvin Love, Jerry Kellman; Obama, *Dreams from My Father*, 280; Obama, *The Audacity of Hope*, 205–7.

558 *How long would Obama last:* Interviews with Ernesto Cortes, John Owens.

559 *"I will be in Wash. D.C. . . . to visit a brother who moved there":* Letter to Phil Boerner, Nov. 20, 1985; Obama, *Dreams from My Father*, 262–67.

560 *In the narrative . . . he was paid a visit by Auma:* Obama, *Dreams from My Father*, 207–22.

562 *The past was falling away: Chicago Tribune*, Nov. 26–28, 1987.

562 *Kellman knew Obama would be moving on soon:* Interviews with Jerry Kellman, John Owens.

564 *But through it all he was edgy and defensive:* Obama, *Dreams from My Father*, 301: "I began to think that my European stop was just one more means of delay, one more attempt to avoid coming to terms with the Old Man."

564 *All of that changed the moment he landed in Nairobi:* Narrative account of Barack Obama's journey to Kenya drawn from interviews with Barack Obama (White House, Nov. 10, 2011), Ruth Ndesandjo, Sarah Ogwel, Charles Oluoch, Elly Yonga,

Peter Castro Oloo Aringo, Henry Ferris, Auma Magak, Razik Magak; Obama, *Dreams from My Father*, 304–430; *Journeys in Black and White: A Book Proposal*, by Barack Obama.

570 *A life of leaving and being left:* Account of Obama leaving Chicago drawn from interviews with Barack Obama (White House, Nov. 10, 2011), Jerry Kellman, Loretta Augustine-Herron.

BIBLIOGRAPHY

Of the many books on Barack Obama and his family, the two that I found most deeply reported were Janny Scott's *A Singular Woman*, about his mother, and Sally Jacobs's *The Other Barack*, about his father. Scott and Jacobs, both first-rate journalists, were contemporaneously exploring parts of the same ground I was, so I ran across their tracks now and then, and admire their tenacity. Because my book involved a wider scope, I knew from the beginning that their works would be published before mine and would include information that I might have wished to have had to myself. I was, for instance, the first to interview Barack Sr.'s second American wife, Ruth, who later granted interviews to Jacobs. But no information is sacred, and when it comes to a world figure like Obama it is foolish to think in those terms. In another book, *The Bridge*, David Remnick displayed once again his keen intellect and profound sensibility on issues of race. Over the next century, hundreds of books likely will be written about the first black president in American history, adding new information and layers of understanding along the way. Here is a list of books I turned to during the course of my research.

Algren, Nelson *Chicago: City on the Make*, University of Chicago Press 1951.

Alinsky, Saul *Reveille for Radicals*, Vintage 1989.

Allison, Burl Jr. *Augusta, Kansas*, Allison 1993.

Anderson, Benedict *Imagined Communities* Verso 1983.

Anderson, David *Histories of the Hanged* Norton, 2005.

Attwood, William *The Reds and the Blacks* Harper & Row, 1967.

Barnett, Donald L. and Karari Njama, *Mau Mau from Within* Modern Reader, 1966.

Biles, Roger *Politics, Race and the Governing of Chicago* Northern Illinois University Press, 1995.

Brendon, Piers *The Decline and Fall of the British Empire* Knopf, 2008.

Budnick, Rich *Hasaii's Forgotten History*, Aloha, 2005.

Burrows, John *Kenya: Into the Second Decade* World Bank, 1975.

Castañeda, Pedro de *The Journey of Coronado* Fulcrum, 1990.

Churchill, Winston *My African Journey* Heron Books, 1962.

Clymer, R. A. *Farewells* Butler County Historical Society, 1986.

——., *The Kingdom of Butler County* Butler County Historical Society, 1986.

Cohen, David William, and E. S. Atieno Odhiambo *The Risks of Knowledge* Ohio University Press, 2004.

——., *Siaya* Ohio University Press, 1989.

Davis, Frank Marshall *Black Moods* University of Illinois Press, 2002.

——., *Livin' the Blues* University of Wisconsin Press, 1992.

Davis, Shelby Collum "Wichita – Boom Town," *Current History* January 10, 1941.

Daws, Gava *Shoal of Time* University of Hawaii Press, 1968.

Dewey, Alice *Peasant Marketing in Java* Free Press, 1962.

Dowden, Richard *Africa: Altered States, Ordinary Miracles* Public Affairs, 2009.

Drake, St. Clair, and Horace R. Cayton *Black Metropolis*, University of Chicago Press, 1945, 1962.

Dunham, S. Ann *Women's Work in Village Industries on Java* University of Hawaii, 1982.

Elkins, Caroline *Imperial Reckoning* Henry Holt, 2005.

Fath, A. E. *Geology of the El Dorado Oil and Gas Field* State of Kansas, 1921.

Firstbrook, Peter *The Obamas* Preface Publishing, 2010.

Fremon, David K. *Chicago Politics Ward by Ward* Indiana University Press, 1988.

Gellatly, Judy *Mercer Island Heritage* Mercer Island Historical Society, 1977.

Glauberman, Stu, and Jerry Burns *The Dream Begins* Watermark, 2008.

Goldsworthy, David *Tom Mboya* Heinemann, 1982.

Green, William Allen *Midian* Copycat Service Co., 1964.

Grimshaw, William J. *Bitter Fruit: Black Politics and the Chicago Machine* University of Chicago Press, 1995.

Grossman, James R. *The Encyclopedia of Chicago* University of Chicago Press, 2004.

Guzman, Richard R. *Black Writing from Chicago* Southern Illinois University Press, 2006.

Harper, James C. *Western-Educated Elites in Kenya, 1900–1963* Routledge, 2006.

Hayden, Robert Earl *The Night-Blooming Cereus* Paul Breman Ltd., 1972.

Huxley, Elspeth *The Flame Trees of Thika* Penguin, 1962.

Jacobs, Ron *Backdoor Waikiki* Niniko, 1987.

——., *Obamaland* Trade Publishing, 2008.

Jacobs, Sally *The Other Barack* Public Affairs, 2011.

Kenyatta, Jomo *Facing Mount Kenya* Secker and Warburg, 1953.

Kirk, Elizabeth Mooney *Barack H. Obama: Through the Eyes of Elizabeth Mooney Kirk* Self-published, 2010.

Klintworth, Lawrence P. *Oil Hill* Butler County Historical Society, 1977.

Koch, Christopher J. *The Year of Living Dangerously* Penguin, 1983.

Macgoye, Marjorie O. *Make It Sing* East African Educational Publishers, 1998.

Mboya, Tom *The Challenge of Nationhood* Praeger, 1970.

——., *Freedom and After* Little, Brown, 1963.

Mendell, David *Obama* Amistad, 2007.

Meredith, Martin *The Fate of Africa* Public Affairs, 2005.

Nordyke, Eleanor C. *The Peopling of Hawaii* University of Hawaii Press, 1989.

Obama, Barack *The Audacity of Hope* Three Rivers Press, 2006.

——., *Dreams from My Father* Times Books, 1995.

Ogot, Bethwell *My Footprints in the Sands of Time* Anyange Press, 2003.

——., *Decolonization and Independence in Kenya* James Currey, 1995.

Ogot, Grace *The Other Woman* East African Educational Publishers, 1992.

Pacyga, Dominic A. *Chicago: A Biography* University of Chicago Press, 2009.

Price, Jay M. *El Dorado* Arcadia, 2005.

Remnick, David *The Bridge* Knopf, 2010.

Rister, Carl Coke *Oil: Titan of the Southwest* University of Oklahoma Press, 1949.

Robinson, Marguerite S. *The Microfinance Revolution* World Bank, 2001.

Schwartz, Adam *A Nation in Waiting* Westview Press, 2000.

Scott, Janny *A Singular Woman* Riverhead, 2011.

Shachtman, Tom *Airlift to America* St. Martin's Press, 2009.

Shortridge, James R. *The WPA Guide to 1930s Kansas* University of Kansas Press, 1939.

Stephens, Dorothy, *Kwa Heri Means Goodbye*, iUniverse, 2006.

Stratford, Jessie Perry *Butler County's Eighty Years* Butler County News, 1934.

Thurman, Judith *Isak Dinesen* St. Martin's Press, 1982.

Tidrick, Kathryn *Empire and the English Character* Tauris Parke, 2009.

Vickers, Adrian *A History of Modern Indonesia* Cambridge University Press, 2005.

Walker, Clarence E., and Gregory D. Smithers *The Preacher and the Politician* University of Virginia Press, 2009.

West, Cornel *Restoring Hope* Beacon Press, 1997.

White, William Allen *The Autobiography of William Allen White* Macmillan, 1946.

Wilson, Gordon *Luo Customary Law* Colony and Protectorate of Kenya, 1961.

Wright, Jeremiah A. *From One Brother to Another* Judson Press, 2003.

——., *Good News* Judson Press, 1995.

Wrong, Michela *It's Our Turn to Eat* Fourth Estate, 2009.

PHOTO CREDITS

INDEX

Index

Punahou Tennis Club, 282
Purnomo, Heri, 234
Purnomo, Soewardinah, 231
Purnomo, Trisulo Djoko, 231

Rachuonyo Social Hall, 99
racism, 13–14, 29, 69, 130, 168, 514
    in Vernon, Tex., 89–90, 91–92
Radier, Mary, 194
Railroad Building Loan and Savings Association, 10, 25
railroads, 16–17
Rainbows, 305–6
Rakoff, David, 424, 426
Ramos, Greg, 284, 294, 313, 319
Ramos, Mike, 284, 294, 305, 319
Rand, Ayn, 134
Randle, Linda, 536–37, 539, 540, 543, 544, 545
Randolph, A. Philip, 108
Rangel, Charles, 459
Rask, Robby, 294
Ratner, Payne, 72
Ray (drug dealer), 296, 322
Razak, Najib, 467
Reagan, Ronald, 336, 377, 454
Redford, Robert, 107
Redhead, Colin, 426–27
Reed, Herman, Jr., 30, 92
Reeves, Mrs. Roy, 4
Reeves, Tim, 89, 91
refineries, 9, 119
Regina (char.), 371–73
Reilly, Dawn E., 473
Reiner, Carl, 509–10
Reiner, Rob, 509–10
religion, 520
Renison, Patrick, 179
Request for Proposal, 410
Reveille for Radicals (Alinsky), 552
"Rhapsody in Blue" (Gershwin), 30
Rich, Wilbur C., 458–59
Richardson, Nelson, 284
Rift Valley, 248

Rising Tide, The, 441
River Road, 398
Roarke, Raleigh, 131
Roberts, Helen, 104, 106, 115
Robeson, Paul, 392
Robinson, Jackie, 108, 111, 117, 151, 152, 256
Robinson, James H., 369
Rockefeller Foundation, 179–80, 182
Rockwell, Norman, 114
Roderique, Mark, 344
Rodgers, Carolyn M., 513
Rolling Stones, 341
Roosevelt, Eleanor, 108
Roosevelt, Franklin D., 28
Roosevelt Democrats, 28
Roosevelt University, 149–50
Rosie the Riveter, 73
Rosslyn Estate, 194, 201
Royal Air Force, 76
Royal Hawaiian Hotel, 169
Royal Technical College, 117
Rudd, Mark, 460
Ruenitz, Robert, 173–74, 489
Rugland, Amelia, 456–57, 463
Rupp, Adolph, 284
Rush, Bobby, 529, 541, 542
Rusinga Island, 257–58, 259
Russian language, 155
Rutizer, Barry, 486
Rutledge, Sunny, 91

Sadat, Anwar el-, 354
Sadik (char.), 428
Safran, Bernard, 145
Said, Edward, 449
Saigon, 348
Saint-Dizier, 78, 81
St. Francis Hospital, 67
St. Mary's school, 58
Sakai, Kazuko, 210
Salina, Kans., 82
Salz, Kenji, 294, 295, 298, 299
Saman (servant), 235, 240, 241, 243

ABOUT THE AUTHOR

David Maraniss, an associate editor at *The Washington Post* and fellow of the Society of American Historians, is the author of critically acclaimed bestselling books on Bill Clinton, Vince Lombardi, Vietnam and the sixties, Roberto Clemente, and the 1960 Rome Olympics. He won the 1993 Pulitzer Prize for his coverage of Clinton, was part of the *Post* team that won the 2007 Pulitzer for coverage of the Virginia Tech tragedy, and has been a Pulitzer finalist three other times. He lives in Washington, D.C., and Madison, Wisconsin, with his wife, Linda.